ESSENTIAL ELEMENTS for Band

COMPREHENSIVE BAND METHOD

TIM LAUTZENHEISER • JOHN HIGGINS • CHARLES MENGHINI
PAUL LAVENDER • TOM C. RHODES • DON BIERSCHENK

Percussion consultant and editor
WILL RAPP

Dear Music Educator,

Along with my fellow authors, I am proud to introduce you to *Essential Elements*.

This exciting band method is based on a sequential-learning curriculum certain to bring success to you and your students. *Essential Elements* features the time-tested cornerstones of its predecessor, the popular *Essential Elements for Band*, plus an abundance of new material, all designed to develop a foundation for the positive growth of your band program.

Each student book includes online access to play-along audio tracks, giving your students the experience of playing with professional musicians from day one of their musical career. Music theory, history, conducting, and improvisation are also integrated throughout the book in support of the National Standards for Arts Education.

Ongoing research continues to show the importance of music as it relates to learning. Scientific data now confirms what music educators have intuitively known for years: students who study music attain a higher level of achievement in every facet of life.

Therefore, YOU play a vital role in the development of every child who chooses to be a member of the band; YOU MAKE A DIFFERENCE!

Thank you for selecting *Essential Elements*. Best wishes for a joyful and memorable year of music-making.

Sincerely,

Tim Lautzenheiser

MUSIC, an essential element of life.

To create an account, visit:
www.essentialelementsinteractive.com
Student Activation Code
EEBD-1774-0261-9580

ISBN 979-835012055-4

TABLE OF CONTENTS

SEQUENCE OF

Director Page	13-15	16-25	16-25	26-31	32-38	39-42	43-47	48-53	54-61	62-67	68-77	78-83
Student Page	**1**	**2**	**3**	**4**	**5**	**6**	**7**	**8**	**9**	**10**	**11**	**12**
Rhythms				Long Tone	4/4				Perc. only:		2/4	
Theory					Note Names Time Signature		Key Signature: Concert B♭	Harmony				
History	Individual Instrument							Mozart		Rossini		
Terms		Embouchure	Music Staff Ledger Lines Measures Bar Lines	Beat Notes and Rests	Double Bar Repeat Sign Clef Sharp Flat Natural	Breath Mark		Fermata Perc.: Rudiments	Pick-Up Notes Dynamics *f*, *mf*, *p*		Tempo Allegro Moderato Andante	Round
Special Features		Tone Production Instrument Care Mouthpiece and Reed Workouts	Instrument Assembly and Playing Position				Duet: *Split Decision*	Duet: *London Bridge*			Pages 11C and 11D - Additional Special Horn and Oboe pages	Perf. Spotlight Band Arr.: *Aura Lee* *Frère Jacques*
Quiz Assessments					Note Names, Repeat Sign	Notate pitches and Rhythms on a staff, Repeat Sign	Time Signature, Key Signature, Counting Mixed Rhythms	Understanding Music Symbols, Note Names		Pick-Up *mf*, *f*	Conducting	
Note Sequence												
Flute				F ♭E D	C ♭B	(Review)						
Oboe				F ♭E D	C ♭B	(Review)						
Alt. Oboe				▲ Regular and Forked C ♭B A	G F	(Review)					Oboes only: Pages 11C, 11D Forked Forked and Regular	
B♭ Clarinet B♭ Bass Clar.				G F E	D C	(Review)						
E♭ Alto Clar.				D C B	A G	(Review)						
E♭ Alto Sax. E♭ Bar. Sax.				D C B	A G	(Review)						
B♭ T. Sax.				G F E	D C	(Review)						
B♭ Trumpet Bar. T.C.				G F E	D C	(Review)					Tpt. only	
F Horn				C ♭B A C ♭B A	G F G F	(Review)						
Alt. F Horn				G F E	D C	(Review)					Horns only: Pages 11C, 11D	
Trombone Bar. B.C. Bassoon E. Bass				F ♭E D	C ♭B	(Review)					E. Bass only	
Tuba				F ♭E D	C ♭B	(Review)						
Kybd. Perc.				F ♭E D	C ♭B	(Review)						
Percussion Techniques		Matched Grip Traditional Grip					Multiple Bounce	Flam	R L R L R L R L Paradiddles	Multiple Bounce Eighth Notes	R R L L Flam Taps	Let Ring
New Perc. Instruments				Snare Drum	Bass Drum			Triangle		Sus. Cym. Wood Block Crash Cym.	Tambourine (Sus. Cym. Roll)	
Correlating Band Arr. Levels											▲ Explorer Level	

ESSENTIAL ELEMENTS

Director Page	84-90	91-97	98-102	103-109	110-119	120-127	128-134	135-142	143-150	151-156	157-159	160-167
Student Page	**13**	**14**	**15**	**16**	**17**	**18**	**19**	**20**	**21**	**22**	**23**	**24**
Rhythms		𝅗𝅥.	$\frac{3}{4}$		Perc. only: ♬♬	Perc. only: ♪♬				♩. ♪ ♪ ♩.		
Theory				Accidental Key Signature: Concert E♭		Theme and Variations		Phrase Key Signature: Concert F				Intervals
History			Grieg Latin American Music	Japanese Folk Music			African-American Spirituals Ragtime	J. S. Bach	Schubert Blues		Dvorák	
Terms	Measure Number	Tie	Accent	1st & 2nd Endings		D.C. al Fine	Natural ♮ Slur Tbn.: Glissando	Multiple Measure Rest Perc.: Simile			Largo	
Special Features	Perf. Spotlight Band Arr.: *When The Saints* *Old MacDonald* *Ode To Joy* *Hard Rock Blues*		Conducting Essential Creativity: Composition	Band Arr.: *Sakura, Sakura*	Duet: *Jolly Old St. Nick* Essential Creativity: Improvisation	Daily Warm-Ups		Duet: *Minuet* Essential Creativity: Phrasing	Duet: *Bottom Bass Boogie*		Perf. Spotlight Solo with Piano Accomp.	Brass: Lip Slurs Clarinets: Upper Register
Quiz Assessments		Pick-Up Tie 𝅗𝅥.			Key Signature Accent $\frac{3}{4}$ Dynamics		Slur D.C. al Fine Counting			♩. ♪ ♪ ♩. Slur Pick-up		Intervals
Note Sequence												
 **Flute**												
Oboe		▲ Forked and Regular							Alt.			
B♭ Clarinet **B♭ Bass Clar.**												
E♭ Alto Clar.												
E♭ Alto Sax. **E♭ Bar. Sax.**												
B♭ T. Sax.												
B♭ Trumpet **Bar. T.C.**												
F Horn				Opt.	Opt.			Opt.				
Trombone **Bar. B.C.** **Bassoon** **E. Bass**												Tbn. Alt.
Tuba												
Kybd. Perc.												
Percussion Techniques			R L R L R R L R L R L L Double Paradiddle LR L R RL R L Flam Accent Rim Shot						One Measure Repeat	Closed Roll		
New Perc. Instruments			Maracas Claves	Snare Drum – Snares off	Sleigh Bells							
Correlating Band Arr. Levels												▲ Performer Level

SEQUENCE OF

Director Page	168-175	176-181	182-191	192-196	197-204	205-209	210-214	215-221	222-227	228-233	234-241	242-249
Student Page	**25**	**26**	**27**	**28**	**29**	**30**	**31**	**32**	**33**	**34**	**35**	**36**
Rhythms							♪, 𝄾					
Theory				Scale Chord Arpeggio					Enharmonics Chromatic Notes			Intervals
History				Haydn		*"Hatikvah"*		Sousa *"O Canada"*		Saint-Saëns Beethoven	Tchaikovsky	
Terms	Trio	Common Time 𝄴 Repeat Signs			Soli			Maestoso	Chromatic Scale			
Special Features	Trio: *Kum Bah Yah* *When The Saints* Clarinets: Crossing the Break	Conducting Essential Creativity: Composition			Perf. Spotlight Band Arr.: *School Spirit* *Carnival of Venice*	Daily Warm-Ups				Duet: *Theme From Symphony No. 7*		Perf. Spotlight Band Arr.: *America The Beautiful* *La Cucaracha*
Quiz Assessments				Note Names Repeats with 1st and 2nd Endings, ♩. ♪, ♪ ♩.			♪, 𝄾, Dynamics	Meter Changes, Conducting, ♪ 𝄾, ♪ ♩.			Scale Counting Mixed Rhythms	
Note Sequence												
Flute												
Oboe												
B♭ Clarinet B♭ Bass Clar.									Alt.	Alt.		
E♭ Alto Clar.									Alt. Alt.	Alt.		
E♭ Alto Sax. E♭ Bar. Sax.			Alt.						Alt.			
B♭ T. Sax.			Alt.						Alt.			
B♭ Trumpet Bar. T.C.												
F Horn												
Trombone Bar. B.C. Bassoon E. Bass												
Tuba												
Kybd. Perc.												
Percussion Techniques	Closed Roll		Two Measure Repeat	Extended Roll							L R L R L L R Flamacue	
New Perc. Instruments							Cowbell		Timpani	(Tamb. Shake)		(Timpani Roll)
Correlating Band Arr. Levels										▲ Artist Level		

ESSENTIAL ELEMENTS

Director Page / Student Page	250-256 **37**	257-263 **38**	264-271 **39**	272-283 **40**	284-295 **41**	296 **42**	297 **43**	298-302 **44**	303 **45**	304-341 **46**	304-341 **47**	342-343 **48**
Rhythms												
Theory								Composition Improvisation				
History		Brahms or Mozart										
Terms												
Special Features	Perf. Spotlight Band Arr.: *Theme From 1812 Overture*	Perf. Spotlight Indiv. Instr. Solo with Piano Accomp. Perc. Ensemble	Duets: *Swing Low, Sweet Chariot, La Bamba*	Rubank® Scale And Arpeggio Studies	Rubank® Scale And Arpeggio Studies	Rhythm Studies	Rhythm Studies	Creating Music	Essential Elements Star Achiever chart	Fingering chart Perc.: Rudiment chart	Fingering chart Perc.: Rudiment chart	Reference Index
Note Sequence Kybd. Perc.												
Percussion Techniques			Rim Knock									

COMPLETE LISTING OF MATERIALS

BOOK 1

STUDENT BOOKS (with Essential Elements Interactive)

00870243	Flute
00870244	Oboe
00870245	Bassoon
00870246	B♭ Clarinet
00870247	E♭ Alto Clarinet
00870248	B♭ Bass Clarinet
00870249	E♭ Alto Saxophone
00870250	B♭ Tenor Saxophone
00870251	E♭ Baritone Saxophone
00870252	B♭ Trumpet
00870253	F Horn
00870254	Trombone
00870255	Baritone (B.C.)
00870256	Baritone (T.C.)
00870257	Tuba
00870258	Electric Bass
00870259	Percussion (incl. Keyboard)

ADDITIONAL STUDENT RESOURCES

www.essentialelementsinteractive.com

TEACHER MATERIALS

00870242 **CONDUCTOR BOOK**
Includes full score, all student text, teaching aids, access to online videos and Bonus Songs, plus much more.

00862586 **TEACHER RESOURCE GUIDE**
Includes Book 1 Lesson Plans, reproducible student activity pages, plus much more, all on CD-ROM

00870496 **PIANO ACCOMPANIMENT**

USING ESSENTIAL ELEMENTS

ESSENTIAL ELEMENTS is a comprehensive method for beginning band musicians, and can be used with full band, like-instrument classes or individuals. It is designed with fail-safe options for teachers to customize the learning program to meet their changing needs.

The Conductor book includes all the music and text from the student books, plus time-saving **EE Teaching Tips** throughout the score. As in the student books, the introduction of a new concept is always highlighted by a color box.

STARTING SYSTEM

Use the unmeasured **Long Tones** to establish good tone production from the very beginning, and use the **Quarter Note** exercises to teach pulse and rhythm. These two different types of exercises are alternated during the introduction of the first five notes. In this way, students can concentrate fully on tone production with each new note, and still make rapid progress toward performing their first **real melody**.

Beginning with exercise 27, each new note is introduced with a long tone at the left margin of the student page. Emphasizing long tone practice will help develop solid tone production.

RHYTHM RAPS

After establishing the quarter note pulse, all new rhythms are presented as clapping exercises in the innovative **Rhythm Rap** format. After each Rhythm Rap, the identical rhythms are played on simple pitches in the next exercise. Finally, they appear in an appropriate melodic setting in the subsequent (3rd) exercise.

PLAY-ALONG TRACKS

Play-along tracks are available for all exercises in the book. The first 130 exercices have the melody for each instrument. From the very beginning, students can model tone production and technique by listening to a professional soloist playing ***their specific instrument!***

There is a one measure count-off before each track. These tracks are performed on real instruments...not synthesized by a computer. Real instruments support the phrasing and dynamics, teaching musicality from the start. And they explore a rich variety of musical styles and cultures, with classical, rock, jazz, country and world music.

F HORN AND OBOE

The unique considerations for Horns and Oboes are addressed with the **optional starting system** on pages 4A through 11A in their books. These **Left-side** pages (Horns only/Oboes only) are written down a perfect 4th from the unison band, placing them on ideal starting notes for these instruments. The facing **Right-side** pages, 4B through 11B, are in unison with the full band and offer octave options for the Horns where appropriate.

For students using the Left-side (Horns only/Oboes only) starting system, there are 2 additional pages: 11C and 11D. These unique **"Range Builder"** pages introduce the 4 new notes needed to combine these students with the full band (for page 12 to the end).

With each Horn and Oboe book, students receive **two play-along options**, featuring a professional soloist and accompaniments for **either** starting system. If you chose the Left-side (Horns only/Oboes only) pages, simply have the students practice with the appropriate tracks. Play-along tracks for pages 11C and 11D are also available online.

PERCUSSION

The 128-page Percussion book takes a **complete percussion** approach. Each regular student page is expanded to a 2-page spread which includes the **optional auxiliary percussion** parts and clear playing instructions for all instruments.

The last 48 pages are the complete **Keyboard Percussion** parts. The included Play-along tracks feature all the percussion...including drums, auxiliaries and keyboards.

On pages 344-359 of the Conductor book, look for the special **EE Percussion Tips** which relate solely to Percussion.

PRE-PLANNED FIRST CONCERT

Because research shows that students are more likely to succeed if they perform a concert for their parents during the first 8 weeks, ESSENTIAL ELEMENTS includes a complete pre-planned concert program on student pages 12-13. At this point, students have learned just 7 notes. The material is flexible in design...featuring a warm-up, a duet (or 2-part band arrangement), a round, a piece to feature the woodwind, brass and percussion sections, an encore-style piece, etc.

The concert for parents could also include highlights of the music learned earlier in the year, as well as demonstrations of the instrument families.

The music on these 2 pages can also be used as a culmination activity to test or review all previously learned skills.

PERFORMANCE SPOTLIGHTS

In addition to the pre-planned first concert, there are 6 more **full band arrangements** throughout the book. Plus, the **duets** and **trio** can be used as ensembles or played by the full band. Performances for relatives, community organizations, or for the school itself are highly encouraged.

There are 2 **solos with written piano accompaniments** for each instrument. The first solo experience is Dvorak's *Theme From "New World Symphony"* on student page 23. On student page 38, upper woodwinds perform Mozart's *Eine Kleine Nachtmusik*, while brass and lower woodwinds play Brahms' *Theme From Symphony No. 1.*

A special solo for snare drum, *Hungarian Dance No. 5*, is found on student page 23. Offenbach's *Can Can*, arranged for percussion ensemble (4-6 players) is found on page 38 of the Percussion (and Keyboard Percussion) books.

DAILY WARM-UPS

You can establish good practice habits with this systematic approach for developing tone and technique. Use the Daily Warm-Ups on student page 18, replacing them with the second set of warm-ups when the class reaches page 30. In addition to tone and technique exercises, each includes a Bach chorale with simple harmony.

RUBANK® SCALE & ARPEGGIO STUDIES

Developed from classic Rubank etudes, these supplemental exercises on student pages 40-41 provide many different teaching opportunities. They are excellent for expanding individual technical skills, and may be introduced as extra challenges when appropriate for individual players or sections.

If the entire band has reached these pages sequentially, they can also be used as full band **warm-ups** and **technique builders**. Additional performance skills can be reinforced by varying the tempo, dynamics, etc.

EE RHYTHM STUDIES

These supplementary rhythm exercises appear on student pages 42-43. Notated on a single-line staff with 4 measures per line, they are very easy for students to read. The rhythms advance sequentially, and can be used in any length of measure groupings. Simply choose the beginning and ending measure, plus any repetition desired.

Start by using a single pitch throughout the measure(s) selected. Then change pitch only at the beginning of measures. By specifying how often to change pitch, the rhythms can become very challenging.

The use of these supplementary exercises should be started in the early stages of a student's development.

MUSIC THEORY, HISTORY, AND CROSS-CURRICULAR ACTIVITIES

All the necessary materials are woven into the learning program—right in the student books. With teaching time in such short supply, it would normally be impractical to take class time to relate music to history, world cultures or to other subjects in the curriculum. But ESSENTIAL ELEMENTS correlates these activities to the concepts and music throughout the program. These Theory and History features are highlighted by **color** boxes and appear at 36 locations in Book 1.

As a result, teachers can efficiently meet and exceed the **National Standards for Arts Education**, while still having the time to focus on music performance skills.

CREATIVITY

Essential Creativity exercises appear in several places throughout Book 1. These are preliminary activities de-signed to stimulate imaginations, and to foster a creative attitude toward music. At any time after students complete exercise 137, you can direct them to the Creating Music activities on their page 44. This page can be used as a complete lesson on Composition and Improvisation. By completing the activities, students are guided through basic concepts about how melodies are created.

ASSESSMENT

On student page 45, there is a complete list of 28 **Star Achiever** exercises. These include the Essential Elements Quiz and Creativity exercises, the Performance Spotlights and additional lines which encompass all the notes and skills used in Book 1. On the students' page, they can fill in a star for each item which they pass.

Teachers can use this basic checklist to keep track of student performance assessments. In addition, there is a detailed list of items to evaluate **(EE QUIZ ASSESSMENTS)** above each quiz in the Conductor score. Each of these indicate all the new material and skills taught since the previous quiz.

ADDITIONAL RESOURCES AVAILABLE

TEACHER RESOURCE GUIDE

This valuable resource integrates various subject areas of the school curriculum into the band program, including assessment and enrichment materials and a convenient ready-to go set of lesson plans. A CD is included with editable word processing files.

PIANO ACCOMPANIMENT BOOK

Easy piano accompaniments for all the exercises in Book 1.

CORRELATED MATERIALS

The ESSENTIAL ELEMENTS BAND SERIES includes original and popular music, arranged for beginning band. Each publication is correlated to one of five specific "levels" within Books 1 and 2 (see the Sequence Of Essential Elements chart in the Conductor book for details). Contact your music dealer or the publisher for information on the latest releases in this series.

Director A brief instrument history appears on page 1 of the corresponding student book.

Flute

Flutes were known to exist in ancient civilizations. Over the years, they have been made of wood or metal. Early flutes, such as recorders, are played pointing forward. The other type of flute, called a transverse flute until the mid-1800s, is played to the side.

In 1847, Theobald Boehm designed the modern flute. This flute is capable of playing with more volume than older flutes. The keys Mr. Boehm added also allow the instrument to play a full chromatic scale, and help it to play better in tune.

The flute family includes the C Flute (the most common), C Piccolo, Alto and Bass Flutes. As the highest pitched members of the concert band, marching band and orchestra, flutes play melodies, harmonies and solos, and are important members of the woodwind family.

J. S. Bach, Claude Debussy and Ralph Vaughan Williams are important composers who have written music for the flute. Some famous flute performers are Louis Moyse, James Galway, Claire Chase, Jasmine Choi, and Bobbi Humphrey.

Oboe

Origins of the oboe can be traced to late 13th century shawms. This family of double reed instruments was prominently featured in music of the Middle Ages (500-1430).

Frenchman Jean Hotterre is credited with inventing the oboe in 1660. The name "oboe" is actually a mispronunciation of *hautbois*, the original French word for a "high wood" shawm instrument. In the 19th century, instrument makers created an oboe fingering system modeled after the flute designed by Boehm. Today, most oboes are made with the Boehm system.

The oboe family includes the Oboe in C (the most common), Oboe d'Amore in A and the English Horn in F. In concert band and orchestra, the oboe plays solos and blends with other woodwind instruments. It is the highest pitched double reed instrument.

C.P.E. Bach, Beethoven, Mahler, R. Strauss and Vaughan Williams are important composers who have included the oboe in their writing. Famous oboe performers include Heinz Holliger, John DeLancie, Toyin Spellman, Katherine Needleman, and Titus Underwood.

Bassoon

The earliest ancestor of the bassoon was called the dulcian. This one piece double reed instrument provided the important bass line in early 16th century music.

Multi-sectioned bassoons first appeared in France in the 17th century. Carl Almenräder (1786-1843) is the most significant contributor to the design of the modern bassoon. He improved the sound and note capabilities of the instrument, and published a paper about his innovations. In 1831, he and A. J. Heckel founded a factory which manufactured the modern German system bassoon.

Originally, there were five members of the bassoon family. The two surviving instruments today are the Bassoon and the Contrabassoon. In concert band and orchestra, these versatile instruments add to the bass line, play solos and blend well with other instruments.

Vivaldi, Mozart, Mahler, Villa-Lobos, Saint-Saëns and Stravinsky are important composers who have included the bassoon in their writing. Famous bassoonists include Bernard Garfield, Sherman Walt, Judith LeClair, Gustavo Núñez, and Daniel Matsukawa.

Clarinet, Alto Clarinet, Bass Clarinet

In 1690, the German instrument maker Johann Denner invented the clarinet by transforming the double reed "chalumeau" *(shall-you-mo)* into a single reed instrument. Since the chalumeau could only play notes in a low range, he added a "register key" to allow his new instrument to play higher notes. The word clarinet comes from the Italian word *clarino*, used for an older type of high-pitched trumpet. Today the low range of the clarinet is still called the "chalumeau register," because of the low notes of the original chalumeau.

By the 1840's, two French instrument makers named Klosé and Buffet had created a clarinet fingering system modeled after the flute key system designed by Boehm. Nearly all clarinets today are made with the Boehm system.

The clarinet family includes the B♭ Clarinet, the A Clarinet (used in some orchestra music), the B♭ Bass Clarinet, the E♭ Soprano and Alto Clarinets, the E♭ Contrabass Clarinet and B♭ Contrabass Clarinet. Fingerings are virtually the same for all clarinets, making it possible for a clarinetist to play any of the instruments. As one of the primary instruments in the sound of a concert band, clarinets play melodies, harmonies and solos.

Mozart, Brahms, Weber, Bartok and Hindemith are among the important composers who have featured clarinets in their writing. Some famous clarinetists include Richard Stoltzman, Benny Goodman, Eddie Daniels, Stanley Drucker, John Bruce Yeh, Sabine Meyer, Anthony McGill and Doreen Ketchens.

Alto Saxophone, Tenor Saxophone, Baritone Saxophone

In the 1840s, Adolphe Sax invented the saxophone family. In today's concert band, saxophones play harmonies and blend with other band instruments. Saxophones are also very popular jazz and solo instruments.

The saxophone family includes the B♭ Soprano, E♭ Alto (the most common), B♭ Tenor, E♭ Baritone and B♭ Bass Saxophone. Fingerings are virtually the same on all saxophones, making it possible to play any saxophone.

John Philip Sousa wrote for saxophones in his band compositions. Bizet, Ravel, Debussy and Prokofiev included saxophones in their orchestral writing. Duke Ellington's jazz arrangements greatly defined the unique sound of the instruments, both in solo and ensemble playing.

Some famous alto saxophone performers are Eugene Rousseau, Sigurd Rascher, David Sanborn, Charlie Parker, Cannonball Adderley and Baptiste Herbin.

Some famous tenor saxophone performers are Eugene Rousseau, Sigurd Rascher, Branford Marsalis, John Coltrane, Michael Brecker and Chris Potter.

Some famous baritone saxophone performers are Eugene Rousseau, Sigurd Rascher, Gerry Mulligan, Pepper Adams and Denis DiBlasio.

Trumpet

The origins of the trumpet can be traced to ancient Egypt, Africa and Greece. These "natural" valveless trumpets were made of wood, bronze or silver. In the Middle Ages (500-1430), these instruments played only lower notes. During the Renaissance era (1430-1600), they performed at many ceremonial functions. Gradually, players began to develop their higher range, especially in the Baroque era (1600-1750).

Heinrich Stölzel introduced a valve trumpet in Berlin in 1814. By 1830, the B♭ Cornet was introduced in Europe. Valves made it possible to play all the notes of a chromatic scale on these two closely-related instruments.

Cornets and trumpets are the highest pitched members of the brass family. As one of the primary instruments in the sound of concert bands and jazz ensembles, they play melodies, harmonies and solos. A trumpet is longer than the more conically shaped cornet. In this book, we refer to the B♭ Trumpet, but the instructions apply to both instruments.

Virtually all important composers have written music for the trumpet, including J.S. Bach and W.A. Mozart. Some famous performers are Maurice André, Adolph Herseth, Doc Severinsen, Wynton Marsalis, Alison Balsom and Philip Smith.

F Horn

The modern horn evolved from 16th century hunting horns. These instruments did not have valves, and changed notes by using various "crooks" or tuning slides. Most horn players had to perform with several crooks that allowed them to play the correct notes.

In 1660, the *trompe* was introduced in France. This instrument's tubing had 2 1/2 coils, and retained the nickname "French" horn. However, German instrument makers actually perfected today's horn. Stölzel and Bluhmel added valves to the horn in 1818, which eliminated the need for crooks. Rotary valves, introduced in 1853, are commonly found on today's horns. "Single" horns in F have 3 valves, while "double" horns in F/B♭ have 3 valves and a thumb key.

Horns provide an important, full middle voice in the concert band. They blend well with all instruments, and play solos, melodies and harmonies.

Mozart, Beethoven, Mahler, R. Strauss and Wagner are all composers who have featured horns in their writing. Some famous horn performers are Barry Tuckwell, Philip Farkas, Dennis Brain, Max Potag, Gail Williams and Sarah Willis.

Trombone

Trombones were known to exist in the 15th century. Unlike other instruments, the shape of today's instrument remains close to the original. In the 16th century, trombones were a common town and court band instrument. There are several kinds of trombones, and the tenor is the most common. Valve trombones were developed in the 1800s. In 1839, the bass trombone was invented. An extension allows this instrument to play lower notes.

The trombone's slide gives the instrument unique playing features. An extremely important member of the concert band as well as a popular jazz instrument, trombones play solos, melodies and harmonies.

G. Gabrieli, Beethoven, Mahler and Stravinsky are important composers who have included trombones in their writing. Some famous trombone performers are Glenn Miller, Urbie Green, Bill Watrous, Kai Winding, Wycliffe Gordon and Trombone Shorty.

Baritone

Origins of the baritone can be traced to ancient Rome, where bronze and brass instruments called "tubas" often played at military and ceremonial functions. The baritone horn, also known as a tenor tuba, first appeared in Germany in the 1830s. It is the final version of Adolphe Sax's "saxhorn baryton."

The euphonium, closely related to the baritone, was also invented in the 1830s. The tubing of the euphonium is wider (more conical-ly shaped) than the cylindrial tubing of the baritone. Both instruments have 3 or 4 valves and play the same pitches.

Baritones and euphoniums can be played using either bass clef (B.C.) or treble clef (T.C.) fingerings. They are important tenor or bass voiced instruments of the concert band. Baritones play solos and harmonies, and they blend well with other instruments.

John Philip Sousa, Percy Grainger and Alfred Reed are important composers who have included baritones in their concert band writing. Some famous baritone performers are Leonard Falcone, Brian Bowman and Rich Matteson.

Tuba

Ancient Roman instruments used during military and ceremonial occasions were called "tubas." Actually, these bronze or brass instruments were ancestors to the trumpet.

For centuries, several attempts were made to invent a bass instrument for the brass family. These instruments included the serpent and the ophicleide. The modern tuba, featuring 3-5 valves, was developed in the 1820s. Tuba bells either point straight up or curve forward (a recording bass). In 1898, John Philip Sousa developed the sousaphone for marching bands.

The tuba family includes the BB♭ Tuba (the most common), EE♭ and E♭ Tubas, F and C Tubas. Tubas are the important bass foundation instrument of the concert band. They play bass lines, blend with other instruments and play solos.

Wagner, Mahler, R. Strauss, Vaughan Williams and Hindemith are composers who have included tubas in their writing. Some famous tuba performers are William J. Bell, Harvey Phillips, Roger Bobo, Arnold Jacobs, Charles Daellenbach and Øystein Baadsvik.

Electric Bass

The invention of the Electric Bass (1950) is credited to one man, Leo Fender, a California guitar maker who wanted to create an amplified version of the double (string) bass. In its early years, the Electric Bass, also known as the Fender Bass or Bass Guitar, was used primarily for popular dance bands and early rock 'n roll groups.

Today, the Electric Bass has become one of the most popular instruments and is found in many types of music groups - jazz and rock bands, pit orchestras, sacred music, and even marching bands. Its distinct, amplified sound is considered to be the one of the most significant influences on musical style in the last 40 years.

Most Electric Basses have four strings, tuned to the same pitches as a double bass. Recently, five and six string basses have become common with players who want to expand the range and versatility of the instrument.

Many players have become well known because of their innovative, distinctive bass lines with the Electric Bass: Paul McCartney (The Beatles), James Jamerson (Motown), Jaco Pastorius (Jazz/Fusion), Victor Wooten (Contemporary/Funk), Marcus Miller (Funk/R&B), Geddy Lee (Progressive Rock), Hadrian Feraud (Jazz/Fusion) and Thundercat (Various).

Percussion

Percussion instruments were invented by prehistoric cultures. However, most percussion history is connected with military groups. Drums were used in the 700 A.D. Moorish invasion of Africa. These instruments were ancestors of the snare drum and timpani. Both the Scots and Swiss developed the snare drum around 1300.

Around 1450, Turkish military bands featured triangles, cymbals and several sizes of drums. The instruments used in these "Janizary Bands" communicated signals to large numbers of fighting troops.

J. S. Bach, Mozart, Beethoven, Berlioz, Debussy, Sousa and Stravinsky are all important composers who have included percussion in their writing.

Common percussion instruments are the snare drum, bass drum, crash cymbals, triangle and timpani. Famous percussionists include Vic Firth, Peter Erskine, Buddy Rich and Al Payson.

Keyboard Percussion

Keyboard percussion instruments were known to exist around 3500 B.C. in the Orient. The xylophone is probably the oldest keyboard percussion instrument, while the vibraphone is a 20th century American invention.

The initial purpose of the glockenspiel, or orchestra bells, was to aid 13th century Dutch bell masters in tuning their tower carillons. The similar bell lyra was used by German armies after 1870. Today, keyboard percussion instruments are used in marching bands, concert bands and orchestras.

Saint-Saëns, Mahler, Tchaikovsky and Hovhaness are all important composers who have included keyboard percussion instruments in their writing.

Common keyboard percussion instruments include orchestra bells, xylophone, marimba, vibraphone and chimes. Clair Musser, Milt Jackson, Gary Burton and Lionel Hampton are famous keyboard percussionists.

Director Pages 2 and 3 in the student books contain the basics for getting started. Guidelines for posture, breathing & airstream, and detailed descriptions on producing the essential tone are reproduced here as they appear in each student book. In addition, your own suggestions and techniques will help provide a thorough foundation for each beginning instrumentalist.

Specific step-by-step instructions for instrument assembly are shown on page 3. Review the principal parts of the instrument and point out the need to handle musical instruments carefully. Spend time with your beginning instrumentalists to insure that they are using proper posture and correct playing position for their specific instrument.

The percussion book includes pages for both "Matched Grip" and "Traditional Grip." Be certain percussionists are looking at the correct pages to reflect the percussion starting system you wish them to use. A list of basic percussion instruments appear on page 4-A of the student percussion book (Director page 25). Identify all percussion instruments and mallets for your students and instruct them on your preference for the set-up of the percussion section.

At the bottom of page 3 in each student book, there are some basic elements for reading music. Your students should understand these music symbols before moving on to the first playing exercise on student book page 4.

Supplemental instructional videos have been recorded by experienced teachers, corresponding to various concepts and techniques for different instruments. This icon ▶ indicates that a video has been recorded for this instrument. These videos can helpful for both the student and the teacher. See page 1 for instructions on accessing these videos online.

Flute

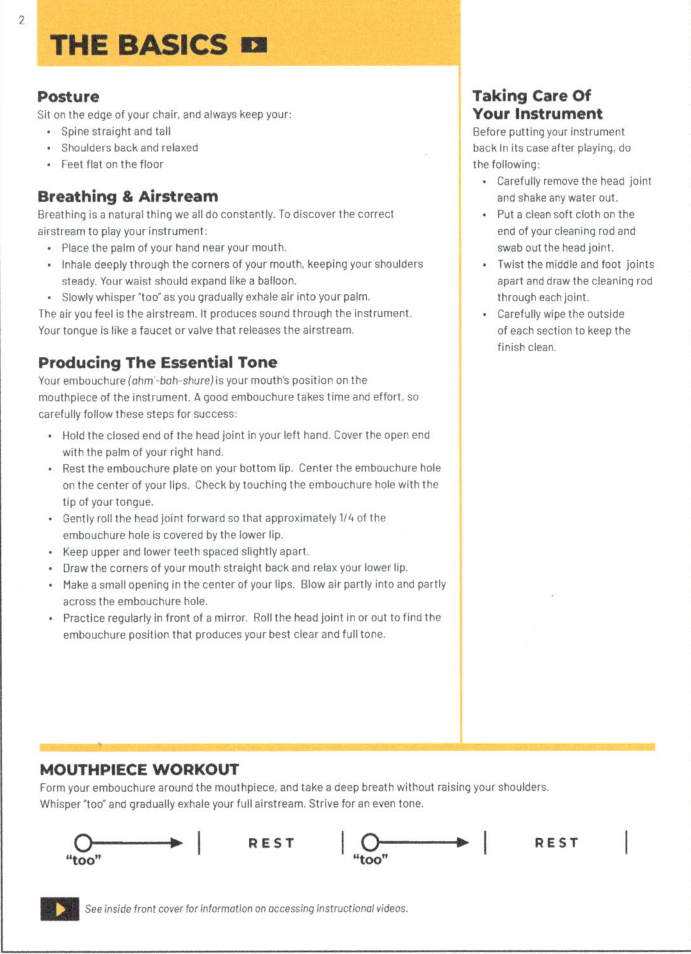

2

THE BASICS ▶

Posture
Sit on the edge of your chair, and always keep your:
- Spine straight and tall
- Shoulders back and relaxed
- Feet flat on the floor

Breathing & Airstream
Breathing is a natural thing we all do constantly. To discover the correct airstream to play your instrument:
- Place the palm of your hand near your mouth.
- Inhale deeply through the corners of your mouth, keeping your shoulders steady. Your waist should expand like a balloon.
- Slowly whisper "too" as you gradually exhale air into your palm.

The air you feel is the airstream. It produces sound through the instrument. Your tongue is like a faucet or valve that releases the airstream.

Producing The Essential Tone
Your embouchure (*ahm'-bah-shure*) is your mouth's position on the mouthpiece of the instrument. A good embouchure takes time and effort, so carefully follow these steps for success:
- Hold the closed end of the head joint in your left hand. Cover the open end with the palm of your right hand.
- Rest the embouchure plate on your bottom lip. Center the embouchure hole on the center of your lips. Check by touching the embouchure hole with the tip of your tongue.
- Gently roll the head joint forward so that approximately 1/4 of the embouchure hole is covered by the lower lip.
- Keep upper and lower teeth spaced slightly apart.
- Draw the corners of your mouth straight back and relax your lower lip.
- Make a small opening in the center of your lips. Blow air partly into and partly across the embouchure hole.
- Practice regularly in front of a mirror. Roll the head joint in or out to find the embouchure position that produces your best clear and full tone.

Taking Care Of Your Instrument
Before putting your instrument back in its case after playing, do the following:
- Carefully remove the head joint and shake any water out.
- Put a clean soft cloth on the end of your cleaning rod and swab out the head joint.
- Twist the middle and foot joints apart and draw the cleaning rod through each joint.
- Carefully wipe the outside of each section to keep the finish clean.

MOUTHPIECE WORKOUT
Form your embouchure around the mouthpiece, and take a deep breath without raising your shoulders. Whisper "too" and gradually exhale your full airstream. Strive for an even tone.

▶ *See inside front cover for information on accessing instructional videos.*

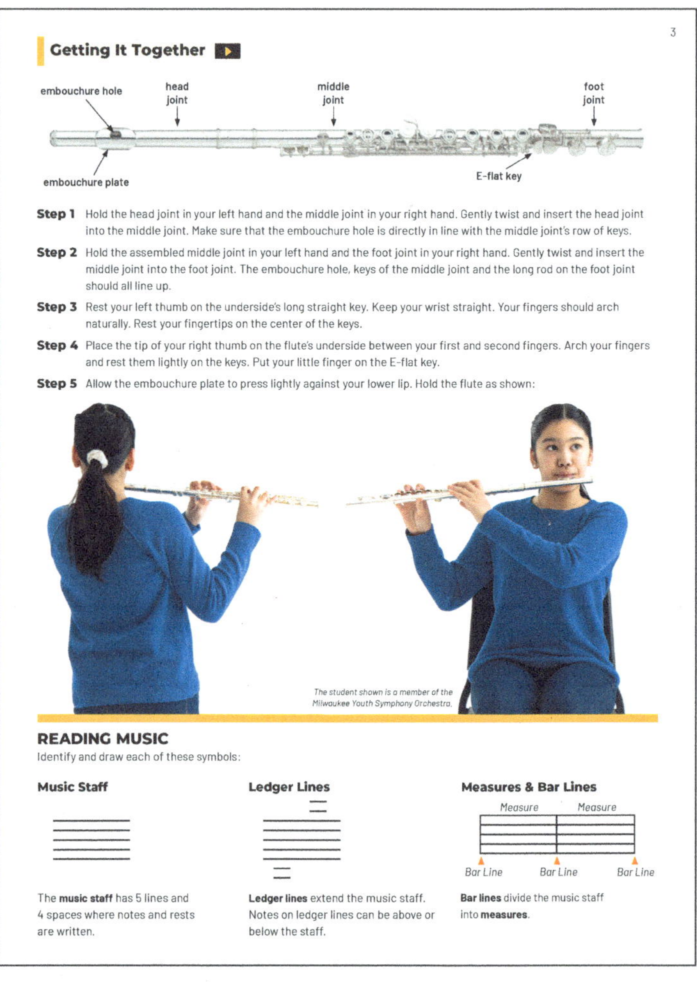

3

Getting It Together ▶

Step 1 Hold the head joint in your left hand and the middle joint in your right hand. Gently twist and insert the head joint into the middle joint. Make sure that the embouchure hole is directly in line with the middle joint's row of keys.

Step 2 Hold the assembled middle joint in your left hand and the foot joint in your right hand. Gently twist and insert the middle joint into the foot joint. The embouchure hole, keys of the middle joint and the long rod on the foot joint should all line up.

Step 3 Rest your left thumb on the underside's long straight key. Keep your wrist straight. Your fingers should arch naturally. Rest your fingertips on the center of the keys.

Step 4 Place the tip of your right thumb on the flute's underside between your first and second fingers. Arch your fingers and rest them lightly on the keys. Put your little finger on the E-flat key.

Step 5 Allow the embouchure plate to press lightly against your lower lip. Hold the flute as shown:

The student shown is a member of the Milwaukee Youth Symphony Orchestra.

READING MUSIC
Identify and draw each of these symbols:

Music Staff
The **music staff** has 5 lines and 4 spaces where notes and rests are written.

Ledger Lines
Ledger lines extend the music staff. Notes on ledger lines can be above or below the staff.

Measures & Bar Lines

Bar lines divide the music staff into **measures**.

Oboe

2

THE BASICS

Posture

Sit on the edge of your chair, and always keep your:

- Spine straight and tall
- Shoulders back and relaxed
- Feet flat on the floor

Breathing & Airstream

Breathing is a natural thing we all do constantly. To discover the correct airstream to play your instrument:

- Place the palm of your hand near your mouth.
- Inhale deeply through the corners of your mouth, keeping your shoulders steady. Your waist should expand like a balloon.
- Slowly whisper "too" as you gradually exhale air into your palm.

The air you feel is the airstream. It produces sound through the instrument. Your tongue is like a faucet or valve that releases the airstream.

Producing The Essential Tone

Your embouchure *(ahm'-bah-shure)* is your mouth's position on the reed. A good embouchure takes time and effort, so carefully follow these steps for success:

- Soak the blades only of your reed in a small plastic cup (1-2 oz.) for 3-4 minutes.
- Open your mouth so your teeth are slightly apart.
- Roll your lower lip over your bottom teeth. Remove the reed from the water. Gently place the tip of the reed on the center of your lower lip.
- Cover your upper teeth with your upper lip, and firmly close your lips around the reed. Your lips support the reed. Be sure your teeth do not touch it.
- Adjust the position of the reed so the tip barely touches your tongue.

Taking Care Of Your Instrument

Before putting your instrument back in its case after playing, do the following:

- Carefully remove the reed and blow air through it. Return to reed case.
- Gently twist apart the upper and lower sections. Drop a weighted swab through the lower section and pull it out the bell. Return the lower section and the bell to the case.
- Swab out the upper section or clean it with an oboe feather and return it to the case.

REED WORKOUT

Form your embouchure with the reed in place and take a deep breath without raising your shoulders. Whisper "too" and gradually exhale your full airstream. Strive for an even tone.

REST

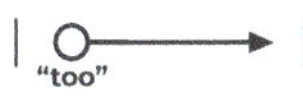

REST

See inside front cover for information on accessing instructional videos.

3

Getting It Together

Step 1 Soak your reed (see page 2). Rub a small amount of cork grease on all corks, if needed. Clean hands.

Step 2 Hold the upper section near the top with your left hand. Grasp the lower section with your right hand, holding it near the bottom. Gently twist the upper and lower sections together. The upper section's bridge key(s) must be directly over the lower section's bridge key(s).

Step 3 Hold the instrument near the top of the upper section with your left hand. Grasp the bell with your right hand. Press down on the round bell key, raising it. Twist the bell onto the cork of the lower section. The bell bridge key must be directly over the bottom bridge key.

Step 4 Put the reed in your mouth (see page 2). Form your embouchure and blow forcefully through the reed to remove excess water. Carefully insert the cork of the reed all the way into the reed well on the upper section.

Step 5
Put your right thumb under the thumb rest. Place your left thumb just below the octave key. Your fingers should curve naturally. Hold the oboe as shown.

The student shown is a member of the Milwaukee Youth Symphony Orchestra.

READING MUSIC

Identify and draw each of these symbols:

Music Staff

The **music staff** has 5 lines and 4 spaces where notes and rests are written.

Ledger Lines

Ledger lines extend the music staff. Notes on ledger lines can be above or below the staff.

Measures & Bar Lines

Measure Measure

Bar Line Bar Line Bar Line

Bar lines divide the music staff into **measures**.

Bassoon

2

THE BASICS

Posture

Sit on the edge of your chair, and always keep your:

- Spine straight and tall
- Shoulders back and relaxed
- Feet flat on the floor

Breathing & Airstream

Breathing is a natural thing we all do constantly. To discover the correct airstream to play your instrument:

- Place the palm of your hand near your mouth.
- Inhale deeply through the corners of your mouth, keeping your shoulders steady. Your waist should expand like a balloon.
- Slowly whisper "too" as you gradually exhale air into your palm.

The air you feel is the airstream. It produces sound through the instrument. Your tongue is like a faucet or valve that releases the airstream.

Producing The Essential Tone

Your embouchure *(ahm'-bah-shure)* is your mouth's position on the reed. A good embouchure takes time and effort, so carefully follow these steps for success:

- Soak the entire reed in a small plastic cup (1-2 oz.) for 3-4 minutes.
- Open your mouth so your teeth are slightly apart.
- Pull your jaw back. Keep your jaw in this position when playing bassoon.
- Roll your lower lip over your bottom teeth. Remove the reed from the water, and gently put it on the center of your bottom lip.
- Cover your top teeth with your upper lip, and firmly close your lips around the reed. Adjust the reed so your top lip nearly touches the first wire.
- Keep your jaw back. Your lips support the reed. Be sure your teeth do not touch it.

Taking Care Of Your Instrument

Before putting your instrument back in its case after playing, do the following:

- Carefully remove the reed and blow air through it. Return to reed case.
- Remove the bocal and blow air through the larger end to remove excess moisture.
- Take the instrument apart in the reverse order of assembly. Swab out each section with a cloth swab or cleaning rod. Drop the weight of the swab through each section and pull it through. Return each section to the correct spot in the case.

REED WORKOUT

Form your embouchure with the reed in place and take a deep breath without raising your shoulders. Whisper "too" and gradually exhale your full airstream. Strive for an even tone.

REST

REST

See inside front cover for information on accessing instructional videos.

3

Getting It Together

Step 1 Soak your reed (see page 2). Rub a small amount of cork grease* on all corks, if needed. Place the seat strap across your chair, or put the neckstrap on. Clean hands.

Step 2 Hold the wing (tenor) joint in your right hand, insert into the small hole of the boot joint, with small twists. The curve of the joint should face inward and align with the other hole on the boot joint.

Step 3 Hold the long joint in your left hand. Grasp the boot joint in your right hand. Gently push the smaller end of the long joint into the boot joint. Adjust until the locking mechanism engages.

Step 4 Grasp the bell with your right hand, and use your thumb to press on the key to lift the connection lever. Gently twist the bell on the long joint's cork. Align the connecting bars.

Step 5 Put the boot joint end of the instrument into the cup of the seat strap (or hook the neck strap to the ring) and adjust. If using a handrest, insert into the foot joint.

Step 6
Hold the bocal at the curve in your right hand. Gently push the cork on the bocal into the small opening of the wing joint. Align the vent and the whisper key pad. Put the reed on the end of the bocal. Hold the bassoon as shown.

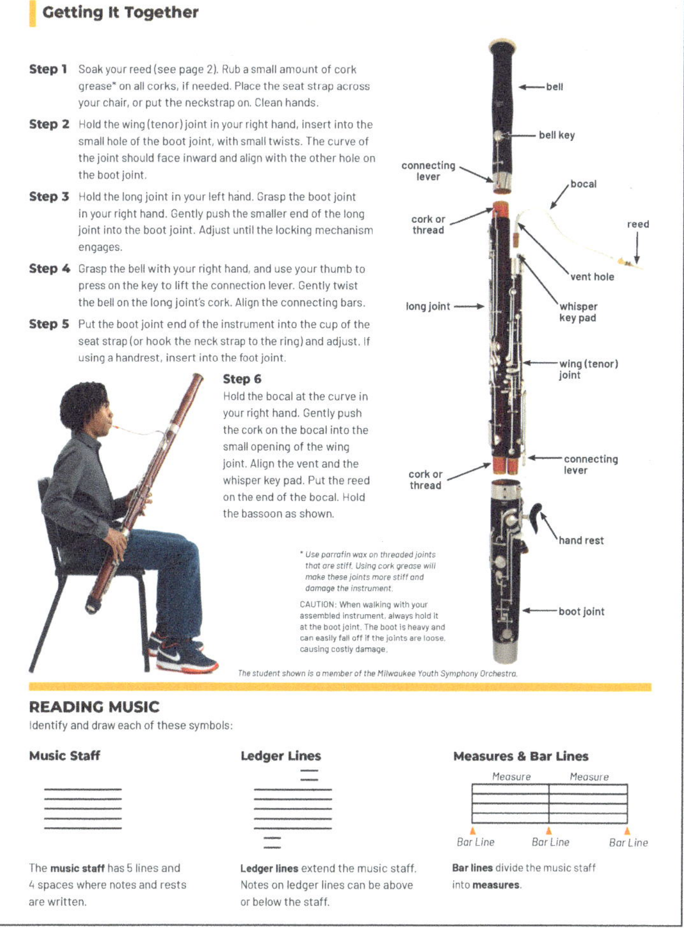

* Use parrafin wax on threaded joints that are stiff. Using cork grease will make these joints more stiff and damage the instrument.

CAUTION: When walking with your assembled instrument, always hold it at the boot joint. The boot is heavy and can easily fall off if the joints are loose, causing costly damage.

The student shown is a member of the Milwaukee Youth Symphony Orchestra.

READING MUSIC

Identify and draw each of these symbols:

Music Staff

The **music staff** has 5 lines and 4 spaces where notes and rests are written.

Ledger Lines

Ledger lines extend the music staff. Notes on ledger lines can be above or below the staff.

Measures & Bar Lines

Measure Measure

Bar Line Bar Line Bar Line

Bar lines divide the music staff into **measures**.

Clarinet

THE BASICS

Posture

Sit on the edge of your chair, and always keep your:

- Spine straight and tall
- Shoulders back and relaxed
- Feet flat on the floor

Breathing & Airstream

Breathing is a natural thing we all do constantly. To discover the correct airstream to play your instrument:

- Place the palm of your hand near your mouth.
- Inhale deeply through the corners of your mouth, keeping your shoulders steady. Your waist should expand like a balloon.
- Slowly whisper "too" as you gradually exhale air into your palm.

The air you feel is the airstream. It produces sound through the instrument. Your tongue is like a faucet or valve that releases the airstream.

Producing The Essential Tone

Your embouchure *(ohm'-bah-shure)* is your mouth's position on the mouthpiece of the instrument. A good embouchure takes time and effort, so carefully follow these steps for success:

REED PLACEMENT

- Put the thin end of the reed in your mouth to moisten it thoroughly.
- Looking at the flat side of the mouthpiece, the ligature screws extend to your right. Slide the ligature up with your thumb.
- Place the flat side of the reed against the mouthpiece under the ligature.
- Lower the ligature and position the reed so that only a hairline of the mouthpiece can be seen above the reed.
- Gently tighten the ligature screws.

EMBOUCHURE

- Moisten your lips and roll the lower lip over your bottom teeth.
- Firm the corners of your mouth like a slightly puckered smile.
- Stretch your chin downward.
- Place the mouthpiece on your lower lip so that the reed extends about 1/2 inch into your mouth. Place upper teeth on top of the mouthpiece.
- Close your mouth around the mouthpiece. Keep the corners of the mouth firm and the chin pointing downward.

Taking Care Of Your Instrument

Before putting your instrument back in its case after playing, do the following:

- Remove the reed, wipe off excess moisture and return it to the reed case.
- Remove the mouthpiece and wipe the inside with a clean cloth. Once a week, wash the mouthpiece with warm tap water. Dry thoroughly.
- Drop a weighted chamois or cotton swab into the bell and pull it out through the barrel.
- Carefully twist off the barrel and dry off any additional moisture. Place it in the case.
- Gently twist the upper and lower sections apart, with the bell still attached. Place the upper section in the case.
- Remove the bell and place the bell and lower section back into the case.
- As you put each piece back in the case, check to be sure they are dry.
- Your case is designed to hold only specific objects. If you try to force anything else into the case, it may damage your instrument.

MOUTHPIECE WORKOUT

Form your embouchure around the mouthpiece, and take a deep breath without raising your shoulders. Whisper "too" and gradually exhale your full airstream. Strive for an even tone.

REST

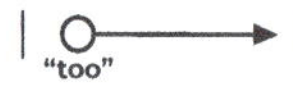

REST

Getting It Together

If you just played the MOUTHPIECE WORKOUT, begin by carefully removing the reed. Otherwise, take the reed from its case.

Step 1 Put the thin end of the reed into your mouth to moisten it thoroughly while assembling your instrument. If needed, rub a small amount of cork grease on all corks. Clean hands.

Step 2 Hold the lower section in the palm of your left hand, with the key work facing up. Do not put any pressure on the long rod. Pick up the bell with your right hand and gently twist it onto the cork of the lower section.

Step 3 Hold the upper section in your right hand so you can depress the lower of the two open rings with your second finger. Gently twist the upper section into the lower section. Check that the bridge key on the upper section crosses directly over its connector on the lower section. The tone holes of the two sections should be aligned.

Step 4 Hold your instrument in your left hand, near the top of the upper section. Pick up the barrel in your right hand and gently twist its larger end onto the top of the upper section.

Step 5 Twist the mouthpiece into the barrel. The flat side of the mouthpiece should form a straight line with the register key and thumb rest. Place the reed on the mouthpiece (see page 2).

Step 6 With your right thumb under the thumb rest and left thumb on the thumb key, use the pads of your fingers to cover the tone holes. Your fingers should curve naturally. Bring the clarinet up as shown on the left:

mouthpiece, ligature, cork, barrel, upper section, register key, thumb key, tone holes, cork, bridge keys, tone holes, lower section, cork, bell

The student shown is a member of the Milwaukee Youth Symphony Orchestra.

READING MUSIC

Identify and draw each of these symbols:

Music Staff

The **music staff** has 5 lines and 4 spaces where notes and rests are written.

Ledger Lines

Ledger lines extend the music staff. Notes on ledger lines can be above or below the staff.

Measures & Bar Lines

Measure Measure

Bar Line Bar Line Bar Line

Bar lines divide the music staff into **measures**.

Alto Clarinet

THE BASICS

Posture

Sit on the edge of your chair, and always keep your:

- Spine straight and tall
- Shoulders back and relaxed
- Feet flat on the floor

Breathing & Airstream

Breathing is a natural thing we all do constantly. To discover the correct airstream to play your instrument:

- Place the palm of your hand near your mouth.
- Inhale deeply through the corners of your mouth, keeping your shoulders steady. Your waist should expand like a balloon.
- Slowly whisper "too" as you gradually exhale air into your palm.

The air you feel is the airstream. It produces sound through the instrument. Your tongue is like a faucet or valve that releases the airstream.

Producing The Essential Tone

Your embouchure *(ohm'-bah-shure)* is your mouth's position on the mouthpiece of the instrument. A good embouchure takes time and effort, so carefully follow these steps for success:

REED PLACEMENT

- Put the thin end of the reed in your mouth to moisten it thoroughly.
- Looking at the flat side of the mouthpiece, the ligature screws extend to your right. Slide the ligature up with your thumb.
- Place the flat side of the reed against the mouthpiece under the ligature.
- Lower the ligature and position the reed so that only a hairline of the mouthpiece can be seen above the reed.
- Gently tighten the ligature screws.

EMBOUCHURE

- Moisten your lips and roll the lower lip over your bottom teeth.
- Firm the corners of your mouth like a slightly puckered smile.
- Stretch your chin downward.
- Place the mouthpiece on your lower lip so that the reed extends about 2/3 inch into your mouth. Place upper teeth on top of the mouthpiece.
- Close your mouth around the mouthpiece. Keep the corners of the mouth firm and the chin pointing downward.

Taking Care Of Your Instrument

Before putting your instrument back in its case after playing, do the following:

- Remove the reed, wipe off excess moisture and return it to the reed case.
- Remove the mouthpiece and wipe the inside with a clean cloth. Once a week, wash the mouthpiece with warm tap water. Dry thoroughly.
- Remove the neck and bell, and shake out excess moisture. Hold the upper section with your left hand and the lower section with your right hand. Gently twist the sections apart. Shake out the excess moisture.
- Drop a weighted chamois or cotton swab into the body of the instrument and pull it out the bottom.
- If the body of your alto clarinet has two sections, gently twist them apart. Return the body section(s) to the case.
- As you put each piece back in the case, check to be sure they are dry.
- Your case is designed to hold only specific objects. If you try to force anything else into the case, it may damage your instrument.

MOUTHPIECE WORKOUT

Form your embouchure around the mouthpiece, and take a deep breath without raising your shoulders. Whisper "too" and gradually exhale your full airstream. Strive for an even tone.

REST

REST

Getting It Together

If you just played the MOUTHPIECE WORKOUT, begin by carefully removing the reed. Otherwise, take the reed from its case.

Step 1 Put the thin end of the reed into your mouth to moisten it thoroughly while assembling your instrument. If needed, rub a small amount of cork grease on all corks. Clean hands.

Step 2 (If your instrument has one long body section, skip to Step 3.) Hold the upper section in your left hand and press your fingers on the round keys. The bridge keys **must** be raised. Grasp the lower section with your right hand, and press your fingers on the round keys. Gently twist upper and lower sections together. The upper section's bridge key must be directly over the lower section's bridge key. Be careful not to bend any keys or rods.

Step 3 Press the key on the bell to lift the lever, and twist the bell onto the cork of the lower section. Point the bell forward in line with the round keys.

Step 4 Put the neck into the upper section, and align with the register key. Twist the mouthpiece into the neck. Place the reed on the mouthpiece (see page 2).

Step 5 Put your neck strap on and place its hook through the ring on the back of the instrument. Put your left thumb across the thumb key. Place your right thumb under the thumb rest. Your fingers should curve naturally. Hold the instrument as shown:

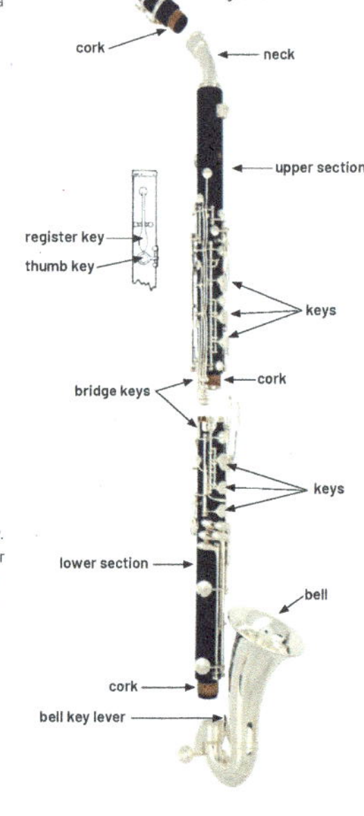

READING MUSIC

Identify and draw each of these symbols:

Music Staff

The **music staff** has 5 lines and 4 spaces where notes and rests are written.

Ledger Lines

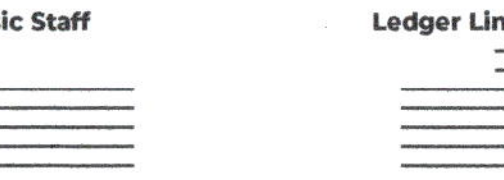

Ledger lines extend the music staff. Notes on ledger lines can be above or below the staff.

Measures & Bar Lines

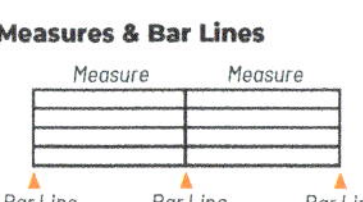

Bar lines divide the music staff into **measures**.

Bass Clarinet

2

THE BASICS

Posture

Sit on the edge of your chair, and always keep your:

- Spine straight and tall
- Shoulders back and relaxed
- Feet flat on the floor

Breathing & Airstream

Breathing is a natural thing we all do constantly. To discover the correct airstream to play your instrument:

- Place the palm of your hand near your mouth.
- Inhale deeply through the corners of your mouth, keeping your shoulders steady. Your waist should expand like a balloon.
- Slowly whisper "too" as you gradually exhale air into your palm.

The air you feel is the airstream. It produces sound through the instrument. Your tongue is like a faucet or valve that releases the airstream.

Producing The Essential Tone

Your embouchure *(ahm'-bah-shure)* is your mouth's position on the mouthpiece of the instrument. A good embouchure takes time and effort, so carefully follow these steps for success:

REED PLACEMENT

- Put the thin end of the reed in your mouth to moisten it thoroughly.
- Looking at the flat side of the mouthpiece, the ligature screws extend to your right. Slide the ligature up with your thumb.
- Place the flat side of the reed against the mouthpiece under the ligature.
- Lower the ligature and position the reed so that only a hairline of the mouthpiece can be seen above the reed.
- Gently tighten the ligature screws.

EMBOUCHURE

- Moisten your lips and roll the lower lip over your bottom teeth.
- Firm the corners of your mouth like a slightly puckered smile.
- Stretch your chin downward.
- Place the mouthpiece on your lower lip so that the reed extends about 3/4 inch into your mouth. Place upper teeth on top of the mouthpiece.
- Close your mouth around the mouthpiece. Keep the corners of the mouth firm and the chin pointing downward.

Taking Care Of Your Instrument

Before putting your instrument back in its case after playing, do the following:

- Remove the reed, wipe off excess moisture and return it to the reed case.
- Remove the mouthpiece and wipe the inside with a clean cloth. Once a week, wash the mouthpiece with warm tap water. Dry thoroughly.
- Remove the neck and bell, and shake out excess moisture. Return them to the case.
- Drop a weighted chamois or cotton swab into the body of the instrument and pull it out the top end.
- If the body of your bass clarinet has two sections, gently twist them apart. Return the body section(s) to the case.
- As you put each piece back in the case, check to be sure they are dry.
- Your case is designed to hold only specific objects. If you try to force anything else into the case, it may damage your instrument.

MOUTHPIECE WORKOUT

Form your embouchure around the mouthpiece, and take a deep breath without raising your shoulders. Whisper "too" and gradually exhale your full airstream. Strive for an even tone.

REST

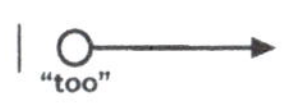

REST

3

Getting It Together

If you just played the MOUTHPIECE WORKOUT, begin by carefully removing the reed. Otherwise, take the reed from its case.

Step 1 Put the thin end of the reed into your mouth to moisten it thoroughly while assembling your instrument. If needed, rub a small amount of cork grease on all corks. Clean hands.

Step 2 (If your instrument has one body section, skip to Step 3.) Hold the upper section in your left hand. Press your fingers on the round keys. The bridge keys **must** be raised. Grasp the lower section with your right hand, and press your fingers on the round keys. Gently twist upper and lower sections together. The upper section's bridge key must be directly over the lower section's bridge key. Be careful not to bend any keys or rods.

Step 3 Press the key on the bell to lift the lever, and twist the bell onto the cork of the lower section. Point the bell forward in line with the round keys.

Step 4 Insert the end pin on the back of the bell. Tighten the screw and lower the instrument to the ground. If you use a neck strap, put it on.

Step 5 Twist the mouthpiece into the neck. Place the reed on the mouthpiece (see page 2).

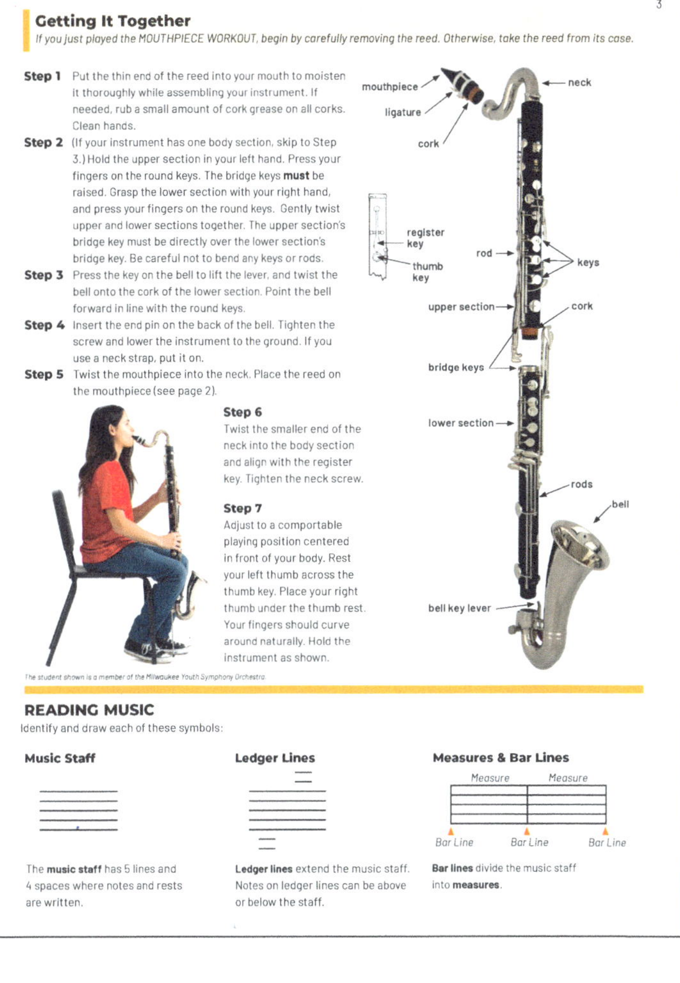

Step 6 Twist the smaller end of the neck into the body section and align with the register key. Tighten the neck screw.

Step 7 Adjust to a comportable playing position centered in front of your body. Rest your left thumb across the thumb key. Place your right thumb under the thumb rest. Your fingers should curve around naturally. Hold the instrument as shown.

The student shown is a member of the Milwaukee Youth Symphony Orchestra.

READING MUSIC

Identify and draw each of these symbols:

Music Staff

The **music staff** has 5 lines and 4 spaces where notes and rests are written.

Ledger Lines

Ledger lines extend the music staff. Notes on ledger lines can be above or below the staff.

Measures & Bar Lines

Measure Measure

Bar Line Bar Line Bar Line

Bar lines divide the music staff into **measures**.

Alto Saxophone

2

THE BASICS

Posture

Sit on the edge of your chair, and always keep your:

- Spine straight and tall
- Shoulders back and relaxed
- Feet flat on the floor

Breathing & Airstream

Breathing is a natural thing we all do constantly. To discover the correct airstream to play your instrument:

- Place the palm of your hand near your mouth.
- Inhale deeply through the corners of your mouth, keeping your shoulders steady. Your waist should expand like a balloon.
- Slowly whisper "too" as you gradually exhale air into your palm.

The air you feel is the airstream. It produces sound through the instrument. Your tongue is like a faucet or valve that releases the airstream.

Producing The Essential Tone

Your embouchure *(ahm'-bah-shure)* is your mouth's position on the mouthpiece of the instrument. A good embouchure takes time and effort, so carefully follow these steps for success:

REED PLACEMENT

- Put the thin end of the reed in your mouth to moisten it thoroughly.
- Looking at the flat side of the mouthpiece, the ligature screws extend to your right. Slide the ligature up with your thumb.
- Place the flat side of the reed against the mouthpiece under the ligature.
- Lower the ligature and position the reed so that only a hairline of the mouthpiece can be seen above the reed.
- Gently tighten the ligature screws.

EMBOUCHURE

- Moisten your lips and roll the lower lip over your bottom teeth.
- Center the mouthpiece on your lips and place it in your mouth about 1/2 inch.
- Place your upper teeth directly on the mouthpiece. The reed rests on the lower lip over the teeth.
- Close your mouth around the mouthpiece, like a rubber band. Your facial muscles all support and cushion your lips on the mouthpiece.
- Keep your chin down and slightly relaxed.

Taking Care Of Your Instrument

Before putting your instrument back in its case after playing, do the following:

- Remove the reed, wipe off excess moisture and return it to the reed case.
- Remove the mouthpiece and wipe the inside with a clean cloth. Once a week, wash the mouthpiece with warm tap water. Dry thoroughly.
- Loosen the neck screw and remove the neck. Shake out excess moisture and dry the neck with a neck cleaner.
- Drop the weight of a chamois or cotton swab into the bell. Pull the swab through the body several times. Return the instrument to its case.
- Your case is designed to hold only specific objects. If you try to force anything else into the case, it may damage your instrument.

MOUTHPIECE WORKOUT

Form your embouchure around the mouthpiece, and take a deep breath without raising your shoulders. Whisper "too" and gradually exhale your full airstream. Strive for an even tone.

REST

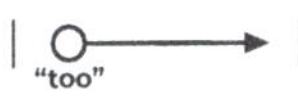

REST

See inside front cover for information on accessing instructional videos.

3

Getting It Together

If you just played the MOUTHPIECE WORKOUT, begin by carefully removing the reed. Otherwise, take the reed from its case.

Step 1 Carefully put the thin end of the reed in your mouth to moisten thoroughly. Rub a small amount of cork grease on the neck cork, if needed. Clean hands.

Step 2 Hold the body of the saxophone near its upper end and remove the end plug. Loosen the neck screw and gently twist the neck into the body. Be careful not to bend any keys. Tighten the neck screw.

Step 3 Carefully twist the mouthpiece on the neck so that approximately 1/2 of the cork remains uncovered. Place the reed on the mouthpiece (see page 2).

Step 4 Place the neck strap around your neck and attach the hook to the ring on the back of the saxophone. Adjust the length of the strap so you can comfortably put the mouthpiece in your mouth.

Step 5 Place your right thumb under the thumb rest. Put your left thumb diagonally across the left thumb rest. Your fingers should curve naturally. Hold the instrument as shown here:

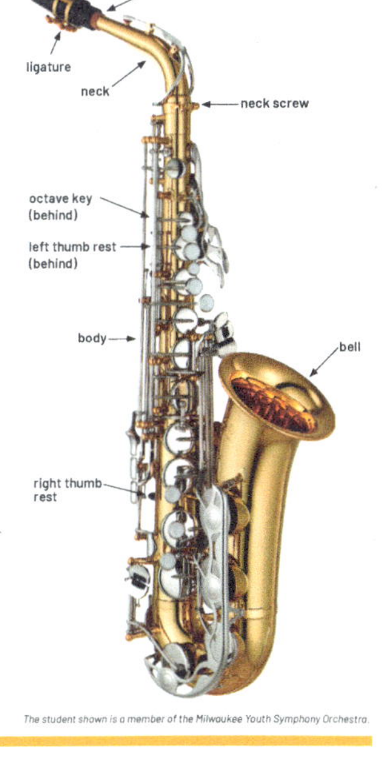

The student shown is a member of the Milwaukee Youth Symphony Orchestra.

READING MUSIC

Identify and draw each of these symbols:

Music Staff

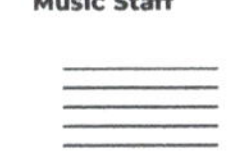

The **music staff** has 5 lines and 4 spaces where notes and rests are written.

Ledger Lines

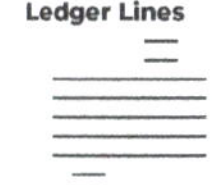

Ledger lines extend the music staff. Notes on ledger lines can be above or below the staff.

Measures & Bar Lines

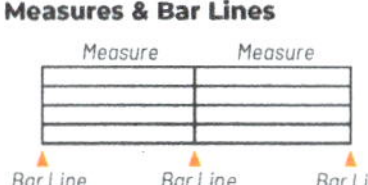

Bar lines divide the music staff into **measures**.

Tenor Saxophone

2

THE BASICS

Posture

Sit on the edge of your chair, and always keep your:

- Spine straight and tall
- Shoulders back and relaxed
- Feet flat on the floor

Breathing & Airstream

Breathing is a natural thing we all do constantly. To discover the correct airstream to play your instrument:

- Place the palm of your hand near your mouth.
- Inhale deeply through the corners of your mouth, keeping your shoulders steady. Your waist should expand like a balloon.
- Slowly whisper "too" as you gradually exhale air into your palm.

The air you feel is the airstream. It produces sound through the instrument. Your tongue is like a faucet or valve that releases the airstream.

Producing The Essential Tone

Your embouchure *(ohm'-bah-shure)* is your mouth's position on the mouthpiece of the instrument. A good embouchure takes time and effort, so carefully follow these steps for success:

REED PLACEMENT

- Put the thin end of the reed in your mouth to moisten it thoroughly.
- Looking at the flat side of the mouthpiece, the ligature screws extend to your right. Slide the ligature up with your thumb.
- Place the flat side of the reed against the mouthpiece under the ligature.
- Lower the ligature and position the reed so that only a hairline of the mouthpiece can be seen above the reed.
- Gently tighten the ligature screws.

EMBOUCHURE

- Moisten your lips and roll the lower lip over your bottom teeth.
- Center the mouthpiece on your lips and place it in your mouth about 2/3 inch.
- Place your upper teeth directly on the mouthpiece. The reed rests on the lower lip over the teeth.
- Close your mouth around the mouthpiece, like a rubber band. Your facial muscles all support and cushion your lips on the mouthpiece.
- Keep your chin down and slightly relaxed.

Taking Care Of Your Instrument

Before putting your instrument back in its case after playing, do the following:

- Remove the reed, wipe off excess moisture and return it to the reed case.
- Remove the mouthpiece and wipe the inside with a clean cloth. Once a week, wash the mouthpiece with warm tap water. Dry thoroughly.
- Loosen the neck screw and remove the neck. Shake out excess moisture and dry the neck with a neck cleaner.
- Drop the weight of a chamois or cotton swab into the bell. Pull the swab through the body several times. Return the instrument to its case.
- Your case is designed to hold only specific objects. If you try to force anything else into the case, it may damage your instrument.

MOUTHPIECE WORKOUT

Form your embouchure around the mouthpiece, and take a deep breath without raising your shoulders. Whisper "too" and gradually exhale your full airstream. Strive for an even tone.

See inside front cover for information on accessing instructional videos.

3

Getting It Together

If you just played the MOUTHPIECE WORKOUT, begin by carefully removing the reed. Otherwise, take the reed from its case.

Step 1 Carefully put the thin end of the reed in your mouth to moisten thoroughly. Rub a small amount of cork grease on the neck cork, if needed. Clean hands.

Step 2 Hold the body of the saxophone near its upper end and remove the end plug. Loosen the neck screw and gently twist the neck into the body. Be careful not to bend any keys. Tighten the neck screw.

Step 3 Carefully twist the mouthpiece on the neck so that approximately 1/2 of the cork remains uncovered. Place the reed on the mouthpiece (see page 2).

Step 4 Place the neck strap around your neck and attach the hook to the ring on the back of the saxophone. Adjust the length of the strap so you can comfortably put the mouthpiece in your mouth.

Step 5 Place your right thumb under the thumb rest. Put your left thumb diagonally across the left thumb rest. Your fingers should curve naturally. Hold the instrument as shown.

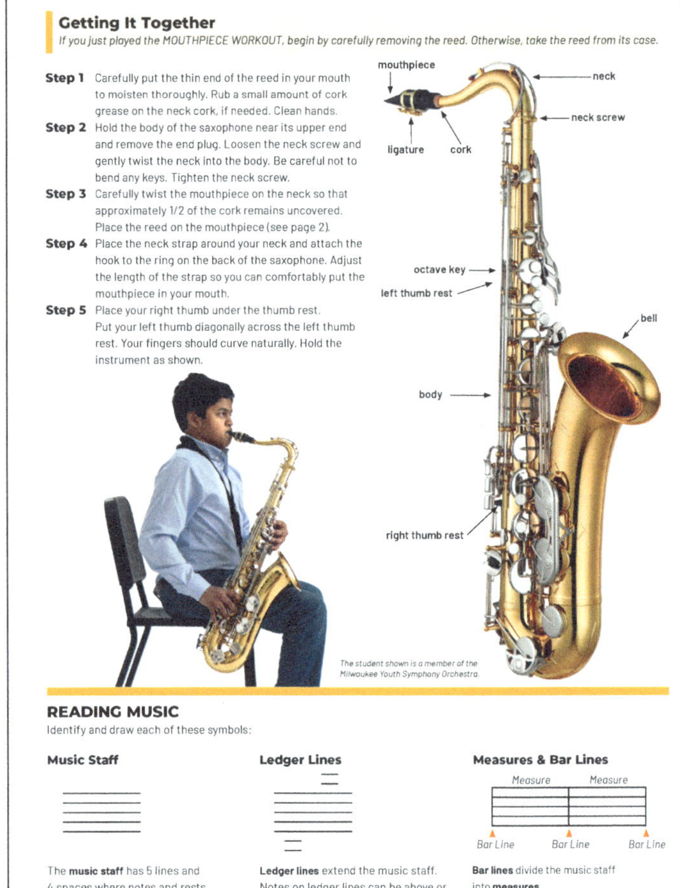

The student shown is a member of the Milwaukee Youth Symphony Orchestra.

READING MUSIC

Identify and draw each of these symbols:

Music Staff

The **music staff** has 5 lines and 4 spaces where notes and rests are written.

Ledger Lines

Ledger lines extend the music staff. Notes on ledger lines can be above or below the staff.

Measures & Bar Lines

Measure Measure

Bar Line Bar Line Bar Line

Bar lines divide the music staff into **measures**.

Baritone Saxophone

2

THE BASICS

Posture

Sit on the edge of your chair, and always keep your:

- Spine straight and tall
- Shoulders back and relaxed
- Feet flat on the floor

Breathing & Airstream

Breathing is a natural thing we all do constantly. To discover the correct airstream to play your instrument:

- Place the palm of your hand near your mouth.
- Inhale deeply through the corners of your mouth, keeping your shoulders steady. Your waist should expand like a balloon.
- Slowly whisper "too" as you gradually exhale air into your palm.

The air you feel is the airstream. It produces sound through the instrument. Your tongue is like a faucet or valve that releases the airstream.

Producing The Essential Tone

Your embouchure *(ohm'-bah-shure)* is your mouth's position on the mouthpiece of the instrument. A good embouchure takes time and effort, so carefully follow these steps for success:

REED PLACEMENT

- Put the thin end of the reed in your mouth to moisten it thoroughly.
- Looking at the flat side of the mouthpiece, the ligature screws extend to your right. Slide the ligature up with your thumb.
- Place the flat side of the reed against the mouthpiece under the ligature.
- Lower the ligature and position the reed so that only a hairline of the mouthpiece can be seen above the reed.
- Gently tighten the ligature screws.

EMBOUCHURE

- Moisten your lips and roll the lower lip over your bottom teeth.
- Center the mouthpiece on your lips and place it in your mouth about 3/4 inch.
- Place your upper teeth directly on the mouthpiece. The reed rests on the lower lip over the teeth.
- Close your mouth around the mouthpiece, like a rubber band. Your facial muscles all support and cushion your lips on the mouthpiece.
- Keep your chin down and slightly relaxed.

Taking Care Of Your Instrument

Before putting your instrument back in its case after playing, do the following:

- Remove the reed, wipe off excess moisture and return it to the reed case.
- Remove the mouthpiece and wipe the inside with a clean cloth. Once a week, wash the mouthpiece with warm tap water. Dry thoroughly.
- Loosen the neck screw and remove the neck. Shake out excess moisture and dry the neck with a neck cleaner.
- Use a body swab to dry the inside of your instrument. Or, drop the weight of a chamois or cotton swab into the bell. Pull the swab through the body several times. Return the instrument to its case.
- Your case is designed to hold only specific objects. If you try to force anything else into the case, it may damage your instrument.

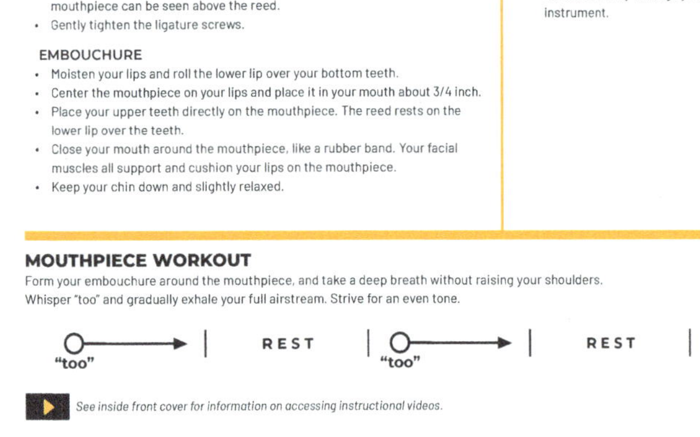

MOUTHPIECE WORKOUT

Form your embouchure around the mouthpiece, and take a deep breath without raising your shoulders. Whisper "too" and gradually exhale your full airstream. Strive for an even tone.

"too" REST "too" REST

See inside front cover for information on accessing instructional videos.

3

Getting It Together

If you just played the MOUTHPIECE WORKOUT, begin by carefully removing the reed. Otherwise, take the reed from its case.

Step 1 Carefully put the thin end of the reed in your mouth to moisten thoroughly. Rub a small amount of cork grease on the neck cork, if needed. Clean hands.

Step 2 Hold the body of the saxophone near its upper end and remove the end plug. Loosen the neck screw and gently twist the neck into the body. Be careful not to bend any keys.

Step 3 Carefully twist the mouthpiece on the neck so that approximately 1/2 of the cork remains uncovered. Place the reed on the mouthpiece (see page 2).

Step 4 Place the neck strap around your neck and attach the hook to the ring on the back of the saxophone. Adjust the length of the strap so you can comfortably put the mouthpiece in your mouth.

Step 5 Place your right thumb under the thumb rest. Put your left thumb diagonally across the left thumb rest. Your fingers should curve naturally. Hold the instrument as shown here:

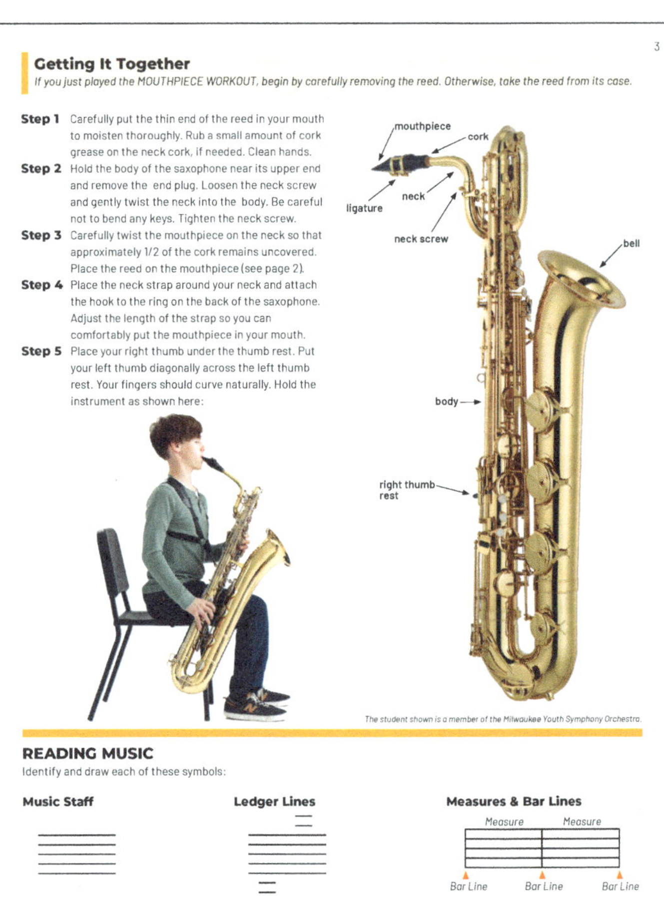

The student shown is a member of the Milwaukee Youth Symphony Orchestra.

READING MUSIC

Identify and draw each of these symbols:

Music Staff

The **music staff** has 5 lines and 4 spaces where notes and rests are written.

Ledger Lines

Ledger lines extend the music staff. Notes on ledger lines can be above or below the staff.

Measures & Bar Lines

Measure Measure

Bar Line Bar Line Bar Line

Bar lines divide the music staff into **measures**.

Trumpet

THE BASICS

Posture

Sit on the edge of your chair, and always keep your:
- Spine straight and tall
- Shoulders back and relaxed
- Feet flat on the floor

Breathing & Airstream

Breathing is a natural thing we all do constantly. To discover the correct airstream to play your instrument:
- Place the palm of your hand near your mouth.
- Inhale deeply through the corners of your mouth, keeping your shoulders steady. Your waist should expand like a balloon.
- Slowly whisper "tah" as you gradually exhale air into your palm.

The air you feel is the airstream. It produces sound through the instrument. Your tongue is like a faucet or valve that releases the airstream.

Producing The Essential Tone

"Buzzing" through the mouthpiece produces your tone. The buzz is a fast vibration in the center of your lips. Your embouchure *(ahm'-bah-shure)* is your mouth's position on the mouthpiece of the instrument. A good embouchure takes time and effort, so carefully follow these steps for success:

BUZZING
- Moisten your lips.
- Bring your lips together as if saying the letter "m."
- Relax your jaw to separate your upper and lower teeth.
- Form a slightly puckered smile to firm the corners of your mouth.
- Direct a full airstream through the center of your lips, creating a buzz.
- Buzz frequently without your mouthpiece.

MOUTHPIECE PLACEMENT
- Form your "buzzing" embouchure.
- Center the mouthpiece on your lips. Your teacher may suggest a slightly different mouthpiece placement.
- Take a full breath through the corners of your mouth.
- Start your buzz with the syllable "tah." Buzz through the center of your lips keeping a steady, even buzz. Your lips provide a cushion for the mouthpiece.

Taking Care Of Your Instrument

Before putting your instrument back in its case after playing, do the following:
- Use the water key to empty water from the instrument. Blow air through it.
- Remove the mouthpiece. Once a week, wash the mouthpiece with warm tap water. Dry thoroughly.
- Wipe off the instrument with a clean soft cloth. Return the instrument to its case.

Trumpet valves occasionally need oiling. To oil your trumpet valves:
- Unscrew the valve at the top of the casing.
- Lift the valve half-way out of the casing.
- Apply a few drops of special brass valve oil to the exposed valve.
- Carefully return the valve to its casing. When properly inserted, the top of the valve should easily screw back into place.

Be sure to grease the slides regularly. Your director will recommend special slide grease and valve oil, and will help you apply them when necessary.

MOUTHPIECE WORKOUT

Using only the mouthpiece, form your embouchure carefully. Take a deep breath without raising your shoulders. Begin buzzing your lips by whispering "tah" and gradually exhale your full airstream. Strive for an even tone.

REST

REST

See inside front cover for information on accessing instructional videos.

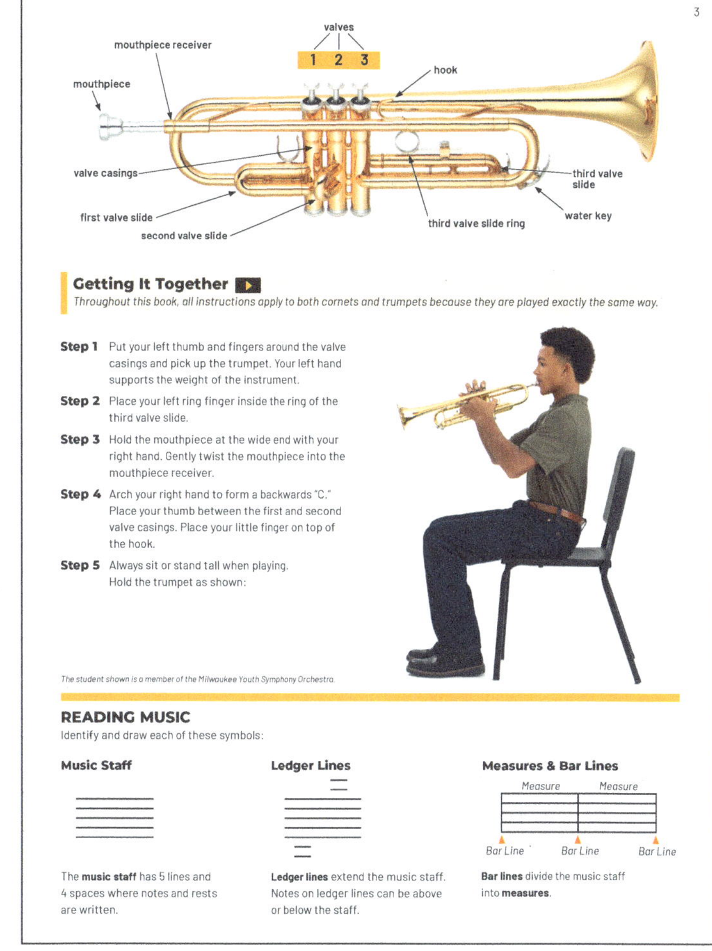

Getting It Together

Throughout this book, all instructions apply to both cornets and trumpets because they are played exactly the same way.

Step 1 Put your left thumb and fingers around the valve casings and pick up the trumpet. Your left hand supports the weight of the instrument.

Step 2 Place your left ring finger inside the ring of the third valve slide.

Step 3 Hold the mouthpiece at the wide end with your right hand. Gently twist the mouthpiece into the mouthpiece receiver.

Step 4 Arch your right hand to form a backwards "C." Place your thumb between the first and second valve casings. Place your little finger on top of the hook.

Step 5 Always sit or stand tall when playing. Hold the trumpet as shown:

The student shown is a member of the Milwaukee Youth Symphony Orchestra.

READING MUSIC

Identify and draw each of these symbols:

Music Staff

The **music staff** has 5 lines and 4 spaces where notes and rests are written.

Ledger Lines

Ledger lines extend the music staff. Notes on ledger lines can be above or below the staff.

Measures & Bar Lines

Measure Measure

Bar Line Bar Line Bar Line

Bar lines divide the music staff into **measures**.

F Horn

THE BASICS

Posture

Sit on the edge of your chair, and always keep your:
- Spine straight and tall
- Shoulders back and relaxed
- Feet flat on the floor

Breathing & Airstream

Breathing is a natural thing we all do constantly. To discover the correct airstream to play your instrument:
- Place the palm of your hand near your mouth.
- Inhale deeply through the corners of your mouth, keeping your shoulders steady. Your waist should expand like a balloon.
- Slowly whisper "tah" as you gradually exhale air into your palm.

The air you feel is the airstream. It produces sound through the instrument. Your tongue is like a faucet or valve that releases the airstream.

Producing The Essential Tone

"Buzzing" through the mouthpiece produces your tone. The buzz is a fast vibration in the center of your lips. Your embouchure *(ahm'-bah-shure)* is your mouth's position on the mouthpiece of the instrument. A good embouchure takes time and effort, so carefully follow these steps for success:

BUZZING
- Moisten your lips.
- Bring your lips together as if saying the letter "m."
- Relax your jaw to separate your upper and lower teeth.
- Form a slightly puckered smile to firm the corners of your mouth.
- Direct a full airstream through the center of your lips, creating a buzz.
- Buzz frequently without your mouthpiece.

MOUTHPIECE PLACEMENT

If you are switching from trumpet to horn, note that the horn mouthpiece placement is nearly the opposite as the trumpet mouthpiece placement.
- Form your "buzzing" embouchure.
- Place the mouthpiece approximately 2/3 on the upper lip and 1/3 on the lower lip. Your teacher may suggest a slightly different mouthpiece placement.
- Take a full breath through the corners of your mouth.
- Start your buzz with the syllable "tah." Buzz through the center of your lips keeping a steady, even buzz. Your lips provide a cushion for the mouthpiece.

Taking Care Of Your Instrument

Before putting your instrument back in its case after playing, do the following:
- Use the water key to empty water from the instrument. Blow air through it. If your horn does not have a water key, invert the instrument. You may also remove the main tuning slide, invert the instrument and remove excess water.
- Wipe the instrument off with a clean soft cloth. Return the instrument to its case.
- Remove the mouthpiece. Once a week, wash the mouthpiece with warm tap water. Dry thoroughly.

Horn valves and slides occasionally need lubricating. Your director will recommend valve oil and slide grease, and will help you apply them when necessary.

MOUTHPIECE WORKOUT

Using only the mouthpiece, form your embouchure carefully. Take a deep breath without raising your shoulders. Begin buzzing your lips by whispering "tah" and gradually exhale your full airstream. Strive for an even tone.

REST

REST

See inside front cover for information on accessing instructional videos.

Getting It Together

Step 1 Hold the horn in your left hand, and place the bell of the instrument on your right thigh. The bell should point backwards, slightly angled to the right.

Step 2 Use your right hand to gently twist the mouthpiece into the mouthpiece receiver.

Step 3 Place your left thumb inside the thumb ring. Your fingertips should rest on the valves. Place your little finger in the hook.

Step 4 Cup your right hand slightly. Keep your fingers together and put your thumb against your index finger as shown below. Place your hand inside the bell. The back of your fingers should touch the far side of the bell.

Step 5 Always sit up straight when playing. Hold the horn as shown.

Single Horn/Double Horn Fingerings

The fingerings used throughout the exercises in this book are intended for students who are playing a Single F Horn or a Double F/B♭ Horn. **Single F Horn** players should always use the fingerings that are indicated for F Horn.

For **Double Horn** players, notes commonly played on the "F side" of the horn are shown only with F Horn fingerings. For notes that are preferably played on the "B♭ side" of the horn, the B♭ Horn fingering is shown in addition to the F Horn fingering. Students with Double Horns should add the thumb key and use the B♭ fingering where indicated.

Students who may be playing a **Single B♭ Horn** will need to refer to the fingering chart in the back of this book for the proper fingerings for Single B♭ Horn.

The student shown is a member of the Milwaukee Youth Symphony Orchestra.

READING MUSIC

Identify and draw each of these symbols:

Music Staff

The **music staff** has 5 lines and 4 spaces where notes and rests are written.

Ledger Lines

Ledger lines extend the music staff. Notes on ledger lines can be above or below the staff.

Measures & Bar Lines

Measure Measure

Bar Line Bar Line Bar Line

Bar lines divide the music staff into **measures**.

Trombone

2

THE BASICS

Posture

Sit on the edge of your chair, and always keep your:

- Spine straight and tall
- Shoulders back and relaxed
- Feet flat on the floor

Breathing & Airstream

Breathing is a natural thing we all do constantly. To discover the correct airstream to play your instrument:

- Place the palm of your hand near your mouth.
- Inhale deeply through the corners of your mouth, keeping your shoulders steady. Your waist should expand like a balloon.
- Slowly whisper "tah" as you gradually exhale air into your palm.

The air you feel is the airstream. It produces sound through the instrument. Your tongue is like a faucet or valve that releases the airstream.

Producing The Essential Tone

"Buzzing" through the mouthpiece produces your tone. The buzz is a fast vibration in the center of your lips. Your embouchure *(ahm'-bah-shure)* is your mouth's position on the mouthpiece of the instrument. A good embouchure takes time and effort, so carefully follow these steps for success:

BUZZING

- Moisten your lips.
- Bring your lips together as if saying the letter "m."
- Relax your jaw to separate your upper and lower teeth.
- Form a slightly puckered smile to firm the corners of your mouth.
- Direct a full airstream through the center of your lips, creating a buzz.
- Buzz frequently without your mouthpiece.

MOUTHPIECE PLACEMENT

- Form your "buzzing" embouchure.
- Place the mouthpiece approximately 2/3 on the upper lip and 1/3 on the lower lip. Your teacher may suggest a slightly different mouthpiece placement.
- Take a full breath through the corners of your mouth.
- Start your buzz with the syllable "tah." Buzz through the center of your lips keeping a steady, even buzz. Your lips provide a cushion for the mouthpiece.

Taking Care Of Your Instrument

Before putting your instrument back in its case after playing, do the following:

- Use the water key to empty water from the instrument. Blow air through it.
- Remove the mouthpiece and slide assembly. Do not take the outer slide off the inner slide piece. Return the instrument to its case.
- Once a week, wash the mouthpiece with warm tap water. Dry thoroughly.

Trombone slides occasionally need oiling. To oil your slide, simply:

- Rest the tip of the slide on the floor and unlock the slide.
- Exposing the inner slide, put a few drops of oil on the inner slide.
- Rapidly move the slide back and forth. The oil will then lubricate the slide.
- Be sure to grease the tuning slide regularly. Your director will recommend special slide oil and grease, and will help you apply them when necessary.

MOUTHPIECE WORKOUT

Using only the mouthpiece, form your embouchure carefully. Take a deep breath without raising your shoulders. Begin buzzing your lips by whispering "tah" and gradually exhale your full air stream. Strive for an even tone.

REST

REST

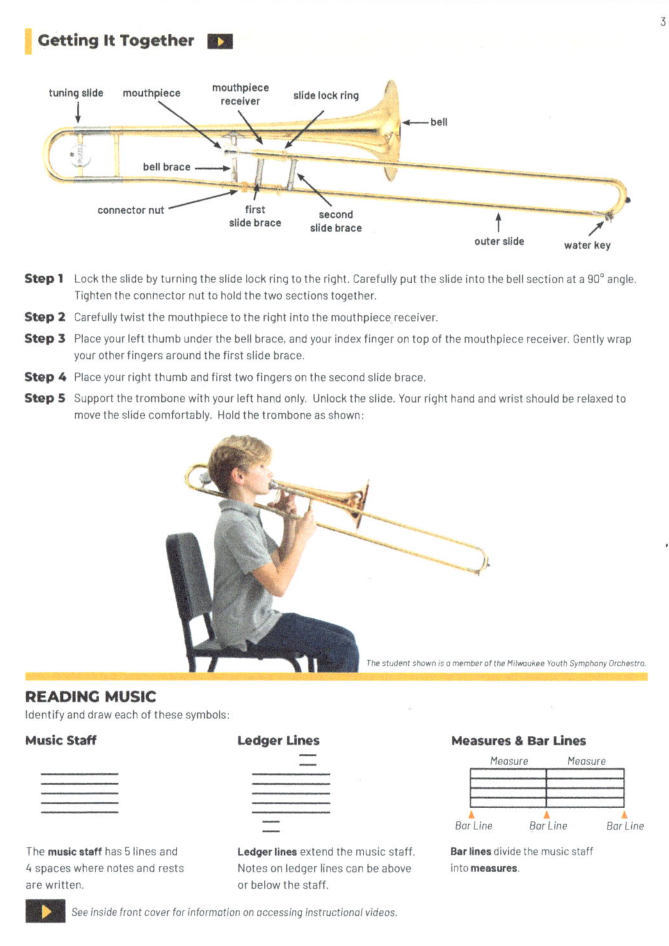

3

Getting It Together

Step 1 Lock the slide by turning the slide lock ring to the right. Carefully put the slide into the bell section at a 90° angle. Tighten the connector nut to hold the two sections together.

Step 2 Carefully twist the mouthpiece to the right into the mouthpiece receiver.

Step 3 Place your left thumb under the bell brace, and your index finger on top of the mouthpiece receiver. Gently wrap your other fingers around the first slide brace.

Step 4 Place your right thumb and first two fingers on the second slide brace.

Step 5 Support the trombone with your left hand only. Unlock the slide. Your right hand and wrist should be relaxed to move the slide comfortably. Hold the trombone as shown:

The student shown is a member of the Milwaukee Youth Symphony Orchestra.

READING MUSIC

Identify and draw each of these symbols:

Music Staff

The **music staff** has 5 lines and 4 spaces where notes and rests are written.

Ledger Lines

Ledger lines extend the music staff. Notes on ledger lines can be above or below the staff.

Measures & Bar Lines

Measure Measure

Bar Line Bar Line Bar Line

Bar lines divide the music staff into **measures**.

See inside front cover for information on accessing instructional videos.

Baritone

2

THE BASICS

Posture

Sit on the edge of your chair, and always keep your:

- Spine straight and tall
- Shoulders back and relaxed
- Feet flat on the floor

Breathing & Airstream

Breathing is a natural thing we all do constantly. To discover the correct airstream to play your instrument:

- Place the palm of your hand near your mouth.
- Inhale deeply through the corners of your mouth, keeping your shoulders steady. Your waist should expand like a balloon.
- Slowly whisper "tah" as you gradually exhale air into your palm.

The air you feel is the airstream. It produces sound through the instrument. Your tongue is like a faucet or valve that releases the airstream.

Producing The Essential Tone

"Buzzing" through the mouthpiece produces your tone. The buzz is a fast vibration in the center of your lips. Your embouchure *(ahm'-bah-shure)* is your mouth's position on the mouthpiece of the instrument. A good embouchure takes time and effort, so carefully follow these steps for success:

BUZZING

- Moisten your lips.
- Bring your lips together as if saying the letter "m."
- Relax your jaw to separate your upper and lower teeth.
- Form a slightly puckered smile to firm the corners of your mouth.
- Direct a full airstream through the center of your lips, creating a buzz.
- Buzz frequently without your mouthpiece.

MOUTHPIECE PLACEMENT

- Form your "buzzing" embouchure.
- Place the mouthpiece approximately 2/3 on the upper lip and 1/3 on the lower lip. Your teacher may suggest a slightly different mouthpiece placement.
- Take a full breath through the corners of your mouth.
- Start your buzz with the syllable "tah." Buzz through the center of your lips keeping a steady, even buzz. Your lips provide a cushion for the mouthpiece.

Taking Care Of Your Instrument

Before putting your instrument back in its case after playing, do the following:

- Use the water key to empty water from the instrument. Blow air through it.
- Remove the mouthpiece. Once a week, wash the mouthpiece with warm tap water. Dry thoroughly.
- Wipe off the instrument with a clean soft cloth. Return the instrument to its case.

Baritone valves occasionally need oiling. To oil your baritone valves:

- Unscrew the valve at the top of the casing.
- Lift the valve half-way out of the casing.
- Apply a few drops of special brass valve oil to the exposed valve.
- Carefully return the valve to its casing. When properly inserted, the top of the valve should easily screw back into place.

Be sure to grease the slides regularly. Your director will recommend special slide grease and valve oil, and will help you apply them when necessary.

MOUTHPIECE WORKOUT

Using only the mouthpiece, form your embouchure carefully. Take a deep breath without raising your shoulders. Begin buzzing your lips by whispering "tah" and gradually exhale your full airstream. Strive for an even tone.

REST

REST

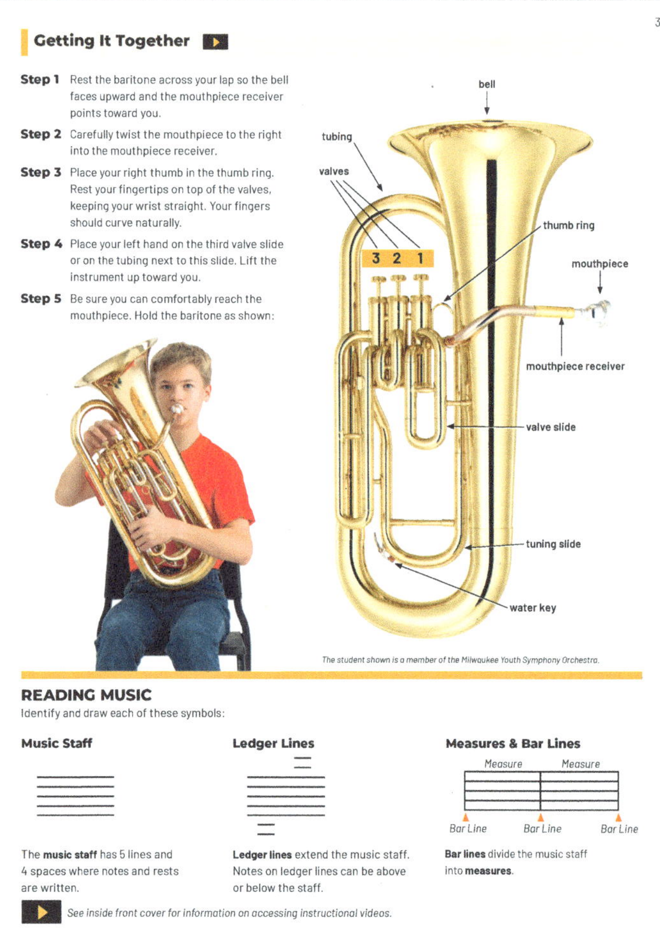

3

Getting It Together

Step 1 Rest the baritone across your lap so the bell faces upward and the mouthpiece receiver points toward you.

Step 2 Carefully twist the mouthpiece to the right into the mouthpiece receiver.

Step 3 Place your right thumb in the thumb ring. Rest your fingertips on top of the valves, keeping your wrist straight. Your fingers should curve naturally.

Step 4 Place your left hand on the third valve slide or on the tubing next to this slide. Lift the instrument up toward you.

Step 5 Be sure you can comfortably reach the mouthpiece. Hold the baritone as shown:

The student shown is a member of the Milwaukee Youth Symphony Orchestra.

READING MUSIC

Identify and draw each of these symbols:

Music Staff

The **music staff** has 5 lines and 4 spaces where notes and rests are written.

Ledger Lines

Ledger lines extend the music staff. Notes on ledger lines can be above or below the staff.

Measures & Bar Lines

Measure Measure

Bar Line Bar Line Bar Line

Bar lines divide the music staff into **measures**.

See inside front cover for information on accessing instructional videos.

Tuba

THE BASICS

Posture

Sit on the edge of your chair, and always keep your:

- Spine straight and tall
- Shoulders back and relaxed
- Feet flat on the floor

Breathing & Airstream

Breathing is a natural thing we all do constantly. To discover the correct airstream to play your instrument:

- Place the palm of your hand near your mouth.
- Inhale deeply through the corners of your mouth, keeping your shoulders steady. Your waist should expand like a balloon.
- Slowly whisper "tah" as you gradually exhale air into your palm.

The air you feel is the airstream. It produces sound through the instrument. Your tongue is like a faucet or valve that releases the airstream.

Producing The Essential Tone

"Buzzing" through the mouthpiece produces your tone. The buzz is a fast vibration in the center of your lips. Your embouchure (*ahm'-bah-shure*) is your mouth's position on the mouthpiece of the instrument. A good embouchure takes time and effort, so carefully follow these steps for success:

BUZZING

- Moisten your lips.
- Bring your lips together as if saying the letter "m."
- Relax your jaw to separate your upper and lower teeth.
- Form a slightly puckered smile to firm the corners of your mouth.
- Direct a full airstream through the center of your lips, creating a buzz.
- Buzz frequently without your mouthpiece.

MOUTHPIECE PLACEMENT

- Form your "buzzing" embouchure.
- Center the mouthpiece on your lips. Your teacher may suggest a slightly different mouthpiece placement.
- Take a full breath through the corners of your mouth.
- Start your buzz with the syllable "tah." Buzz through the center of your lips keeping a steady, even buzz. Your lips provide a cushion for the mouthpiece.

Taking Care Of Your Instrument

Before putting your instrument back in its case after playing, do the following:

- Use the water key to empty water from the instrument. Blow air through it.
- Remove the mouthpiece. Once a week, wash the mouthpiece with warm tap water. Dry thoroughly.
- Wipe off the instrument with a clean soft cloth. Return the instrument to its case.

Tuba valves occasionally need oiling. To oil your tuba valves:

- Unscrew the valve at the top of the casing.
- Lift the valve half-way out of the casing.
- Apply a few drops of special brass valve oil to the exposed valve.
- Carefully return the valve to its casing. When properly inserted, the top of the valve should easily screw back into place.

Be sure to grease the slides regularly. Your director will recommend special slide grease and valve oil, and will help you apply them when necessary.

MOUTHPIECE WORKOUT

Using only the mouthpiece, form your embouchure carefully. Take a deep breath without raising your shoulders. Begin buzzing your lips by whispering "tah" and gradually exhale your full airstream. Strive for an even tone.

Getting It Together

Step 1 If you are playing a TUBA, rest it across your lap with the mouthpiece receiver toward you. If you are playing a SOUSAPHONE, place the open circular section over your left shoulder. Rest your right arm comfortably on the tubing.

Step 2 Carefully twist the mouthpiece to the right into the mouthpiece receiver.

Step 3 Place your right thumb in the thumb ring. Rest your fingertips on top of the valves, keeping your wrist straight. Your fingers should curve naturally.

Step 4 For TUBAS, place your left hand on the first valve slide or on the tubing next to this slide. Lift the instrument up toward you and rest it in your lap.

Step 5 Be sure you can comfortably reach the mouthpiece. Hold the tuba as shown:

bell
tubing
valves
3 2 1
mouthpiece
mouthpiece receiver
water key
valve slide

The student shown is a member of the Milwaukee Youth Symphony Orchestra.

READING MUSIC

Identify and draw each of these symbols:

Music Staff

The **music staff** has 5 lines and 4 spaces where notes and rests are written.

Ledger Lines

Ledger lines extend the music staff. Notes on ledger lines can be above or below the staff.

Measures & Bar Lines

Measure Measure
Bar Line Bar Line Bar Line

Bar lines divide the music staff into **measures**.

Electric Bass

THE BASICS

Posture

Sit on the edge of your chair, and always keep your:

- Spine straight and tall
- Shoulders back and relaxed
- Feet flat on the floor

Instrument & Left Hand Position

Your instrument should be fully supported by the strap when standing, and rests on top of your right leg when seated. Point the instrument neck slightly upwards. Your left hand helps balance the instrument—place the pad of your left thumb on the back side of the neck and curve the fingers just above the strings.

Producing The Essential Tone

Good bass players learn to produce a clean sound with a clear start to each tone and an even volume between tones. Except for the 4 open strings, your left hand "selects" a note by pressing down a string just behind a fret, and holding it for the entire length of the note. Your right hand "plays" the note by pulling across the string to start it vibrating.

STARTING THE TONE

- Rest your thumb on the E (largest) string or on the top edge of the pickup.
- Pull across the G (smallest) string with your index finger so that the finger comes to rest on the next string (D).
- Make the same tone by playing the G string with your middle finger.
- Play 2 tones on each string, with alternating index finger/middle finger.
- Strive for an even volume and clear start to each tone.

STOPPING THE TONE (DAMPENING)

- Stop a tone by gently touching the string with either hand.
- Fretted tones can also be stopped by lifting the left hand finger which was pressing down the string, but keeping the finger on the string.

Taking Care Of Your Instrument

- Be sure your amplifier is turned off before plugging in or unplugging the audio cable connecting it to your instrument.
- When unplugging a cable, hold it by the plug (not by the wire).
- After playing, wipe off the instrument and strings with a clean soft cloth. Return the instrument to its case.
- Close all the latches on your case when the instrument is inside.
- Keep all 4 strings in tune (at normal tension) to prevent warping of the neck.
- Your case is designed to hold only specific objects. If you force anything else into the case, it may damage your instrument.

TUNING THE ELECTRIC BASS

Tuning means setting the correct pitch (higher or lower tone) of each string. This is adjusted by tightening or loosening the tuning keys on the head of the bass. Your teacher can help you tune to the 4 notes on the online audio, or to the notes on a piano:

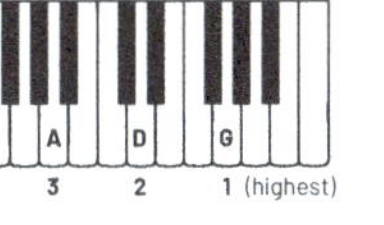

Many bass players use an **Electronic Tuner** which "listens" to each string and indicates whether it is too high or low. You can learn to use **Relative Tuning** by comparing one string with another. After one string is tuned, it is compared with the pitch of the next lower string played with the 5th fret. The two pitches should match exactly.

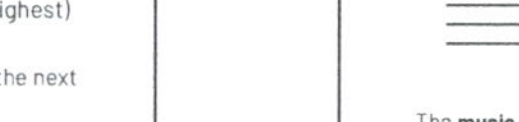

See inside front cover for information on accessing Instructional videos.

Getting It Together

Step 1 Securely attach the strap to the strap buttons, adjusting it so that the bass is at the correct height (approximately waist-high) and playing angle.

Step 2 With the amplifier off, plug the audio cable into the bass and the amplifier. Turn on the amplifier and set the volume.

Step 3 LEFT HAND: Place the pad of your left thumb on the back side of the neck. Your fingers should be relaxed and curved, just above the strings.

Step 4 RIGHT HAND: Rest your right thumb on the E (largest) string or on the top edge of the pickup. Rest the pad of your index finger on the G (smallest) string.

Step 5 Always sit or stand tall when playing, with feet flat on the floor and with arms and shoulders relaxed. Check your playing position with the illustrations:

Think of your fingers as being numbered 1 through 4.
1st 2nd 3rd 4th

head
tuning keys
strings
nut
frets
neck/ fingerboard
frets
position markers
strap button
body
pickups
tone/ volume controls
bridge
strap button
output jack

Fingerboard diagrams show where to play the notes. Circles are drawn on the diagram to indicate the fingers to be used to play the notes.

The student shown is a member of the Milwaukee Youth Symphony Orchestra.

READING MUSIC

Identify and draw each of these symbols:

Music Staff

The **music staff** has 5 lines and 4 spaces where notes and rests are written.

Ledger Lines

Ledger lines extend the music staff. Notes on ledger lines can be above or below the staff.

Measures & Bar Lines

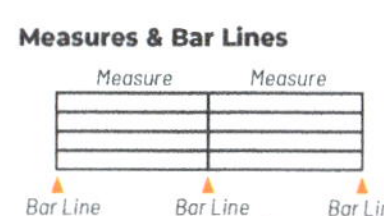

Bar lines divide the music staff into **measures**.

Percussion – Matched Grip

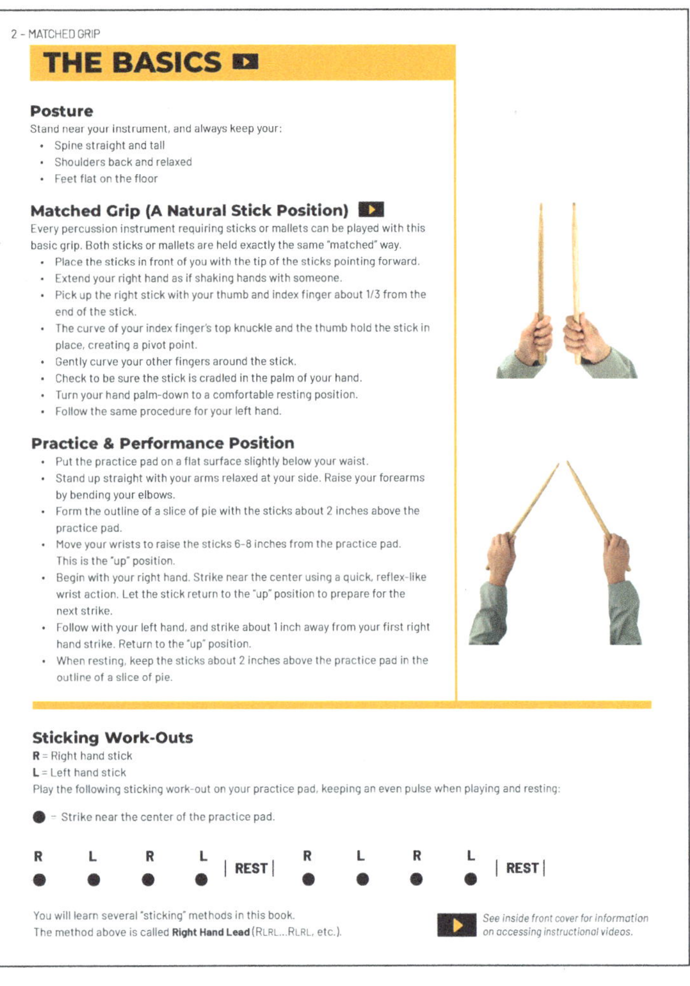

2 - MATCHED GRIP

THE BASICS

Posture
Stand near your instrument, and always keep your:
- Spine straight and tall
- Shoulders back and relaxed
- Feet flat on the floor

Matched Grip (A Natural Stick Position)
Every percussion instrument requiring sticks or mallets can be played with this basic grip. Both sticks or mallets are held exactly the same "matched" way.
- Place the sticks in front of you with the tip of the sticks pointing forward.
- Extend your right hand as if shaking hands with someone.
- Pick up the right stick with your thumb and index finger about 1/3 from the end of the stick.
- The curve of your index finger's top knuckle and the thumb hold the stick in place, creating a pivot point.
- Gently curve your other fingers around the stick.
- Check to be sure the stick is cradled in the palm of your hand.
- Turn your hand palm-down to a comfortable resting position.
- Follow the same procedure for your left hand.

Practice & Performance Position
- Put the practice pad on a flat surface slightly below your waist.
- Stand up straight with your arms relaxed at your side. Raise your forearms by bending your elbows.
- Form the outline of a slice of pie with the sticks about 2 inches above the practice pad.
- Move your wrists to raise the sticks 6-8 inches from the practice pad. This is the "up" position.
- Begin with your right hand. Strike near the center using a quick, reflex-like wrist action. Let the stick return to the "up" position to prepare for the next strike.
- Follow with your left hand, and strike about 1 inch away from your first right hand strike. Return to the "up" position.
- When resting, keep the sticks about 2 inches above the practice pad in the outline of a slice of pie.

Sticking Work-Outs
R = Right hand stick
L = Left hand stick
Play the following sticking work-out on your practice pad, keeping an even pulse when playing and resting:

● = Strike near the center of the practice pad.

R L R L | REST | R L R L | REST |

You will learn several "sticking" methods in this book.
The method above is called **Right Hand Lead** (RLRL...RLRL, etc.).

See inside front cover for information on accessing instructional videos.

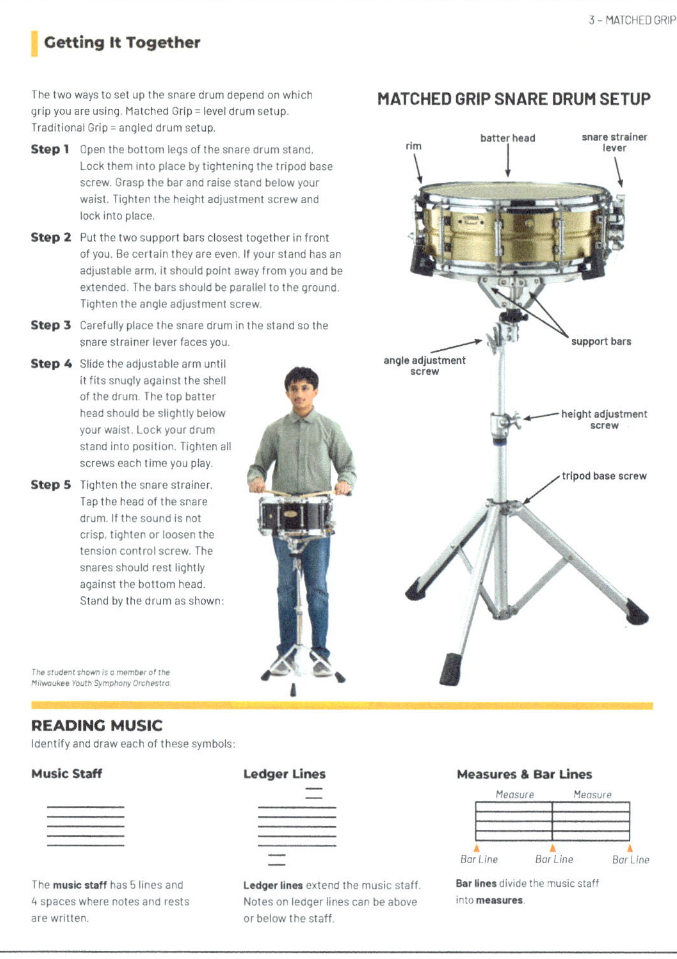

3 - MATCHED GRIP

Getting It Together
The two ways to set up the snare drum depend on which grip you are using. Matched Grip = level drum setup. Traditional Grip = angled drum setup.

Step 1 Open the bottom legs of the snare drum stand. Lock them into place by tightening the tripod base screw. Grasp the bar and raise stand below your waist. Tighten the height adjustment screw and lock into place.

Step 2 Put the two support bars closest together in front of you. Be certain they are even. If your stand has an adjustable arm, it should point away from you and be extended. The bars should be parallel to the ground. Tighten the angle adjustment screw.

Step 3 Carefully place the snare drum in the stand so the snare strainer lever faces you.

Step 4 Slide the adjustable arm until it fits snugly against the shell of the drum. The top batter head should be slightly below your waist. Lock your drum stand into position. Tighten all screws each time you play.

Step 5 Tighten the snare strainer. Tap the head of the snare drum. If the sound is not crisp, tighten or loosen the tension control screw. The snares should rest lightly against the bottom head. Stand by the drum as shown:

The student shown is a member of the Milwaukee Youth Symphony Orchestra.

MATCHED GRIP SNARE DRUM SETUP

READING MUSIC
Identify and draw each of these symbols:

Music Staff
The **music staff** has 5 lines and 4 spaces where notes and rests are written.

Ledger Lines
Ledger lines extend the music staff. Notes on ledger lines can be above or below the staff.

Measures & Bar Lines

Bar lines divide the music staff into **measures**.

Percussion – Traditional Grip

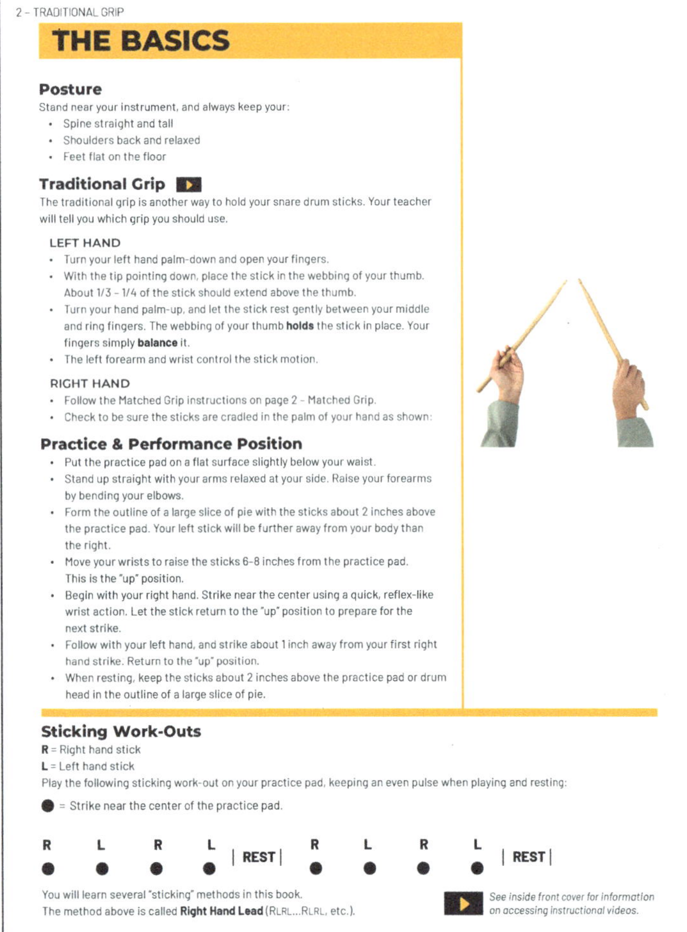

2 - TRADITIONAL GRIP

THE BASICS

Posture
Stand near your instrument, and always keep your:
- Spine straight and tall
- Shoulders back and relaxed
- Feet flat on the floor

Traditional Grip
The traditional grip is another way to hold your snare drum sticks. Your teacher will tell you which grip you should use.

LEFT HAND
- Turn your left hand palm-down and open your fingers.
- With the tip pointing down, place the stick in the webbing of your thumb. About 1/3 - 1/4 of the stick should extend above the thumb.
- Turn your hand palm-up, and let the stick rest gently between your middle and ring fingers. The webbing of your thumb **holds** the stick in place. Your fingers simply **balance** it.
- The left forearm and wrist control the stick motion.

RIGHT HAND
- Follow the Matched Grip instructions on page 2 - Matched Grip.
- Check to be sure the sticks are cradled in the palm of your hand as shown:

Practice & Performance Position
- Put the practice pad on a flat surface slightly below your waist.
- Stand up straight with your arms relaxed at your side. Raise your forearms by bending your elbows.
- Form the outline of a large slice of pie with the sticks about 2 inches above the practice pad. Your left stick will be further away from your body than the right.
- Move your wrists to raise the sticks 6-8 inches from the practice pad. This is the "up" position.
- Begin with your right hand. Strike near the center using a quick, reflex-like wrist action. Let the stick return to the "up" position to prepare for the next strike.
- Follow with your left hand, and strike about 1 inch away from your first right hand strike. Return to the "up" position.
- When resting, keep the sticks about 2 inches above the practice pad or drum head in the outline of a large slice of pie.

Sticking Work-Outs
R = Right hand stick
L = Left hand stick
Play the following sticking work-out on your practice pad, keeping an even pulse when playing and resting:

● = Strike near the center of the practice pad.

R L R L | REST | R L R L | REST |

You will learn several "sticking" methods in this book.
The method above is called **Right Hand Lead** (RLRL...RLRL, etc.).

See inside front cover for information on accessing instructional videos.

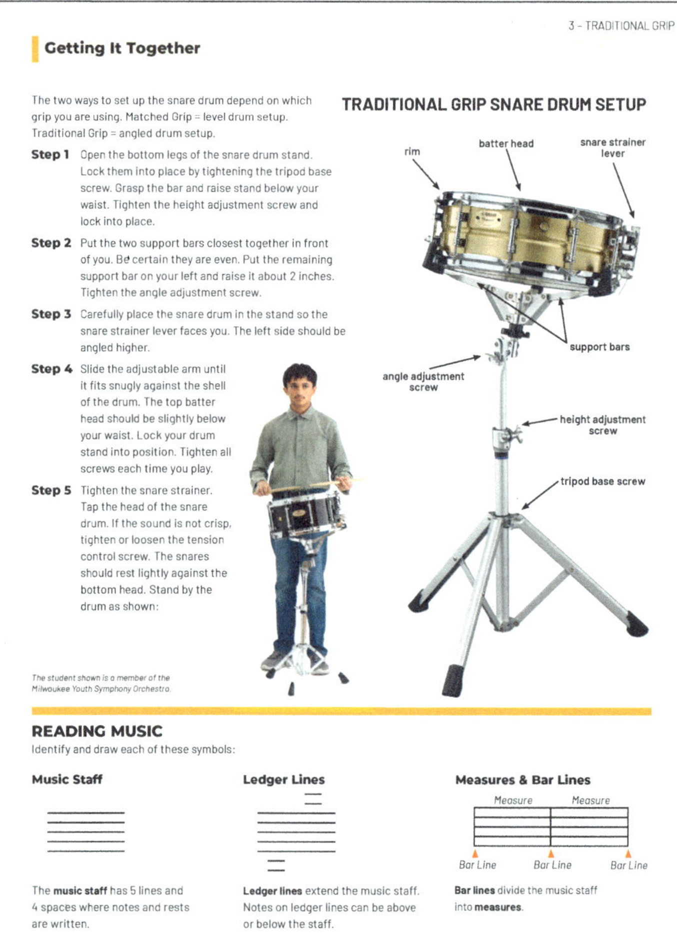

3 - TRADITIONAL GRIP

Getting It Together
The two ways to set up the snare drum depend on which grip you are using. Matched Grip = level drum setup. Traditional Grip = angled drum setup.

Step 1 Open the bottom legs of the snare drum stand. Lock them into place by tightening the tripod base screw. Grasp the bar and raise stand below your waist. Tighten the height adjustment screw and lock into place.

Step 2 Put the two support bars closest together in front of you. Be certain they are even. Put the remaining support bar on your left and raise it about 2 inches. Tighten the angle adjustment screw.

Step 3 Carefully place the snare drum in the stand so the snare strainer lever faces you. The left side should be angled higher.

Step 4 Slide the adjustable arm until it fits snugly against the shell of the drum. The top batter head should be slightly below your waist. Lock your drum stand into position. Tighten all screws each time you play.

Step 5 Tighten the snare strainer. Tap the head of the snare drum. If the sound is not crisp, tighten or loosen the tension control screw. The snares should rest lightly against the bottom head. Stand by the drum as shown:

The student shown is a member of the Milwaukee Youth Symphony Orchestra.

TRADITIONAL GRIP SNARE DRUM SETUP

READING MUSIC
Identify and draw each of these symbols:

Music Staff
The **music staff** has 5 lines and 4 spaces where notes and rests are written.

Ledger Lines
Ledger lines extend the music staff. Notes on ledger lines can be above or below the staff.

Measures & Bar Lines

Bar lines divide the music staff into **measures**.

Keyboard Percussion

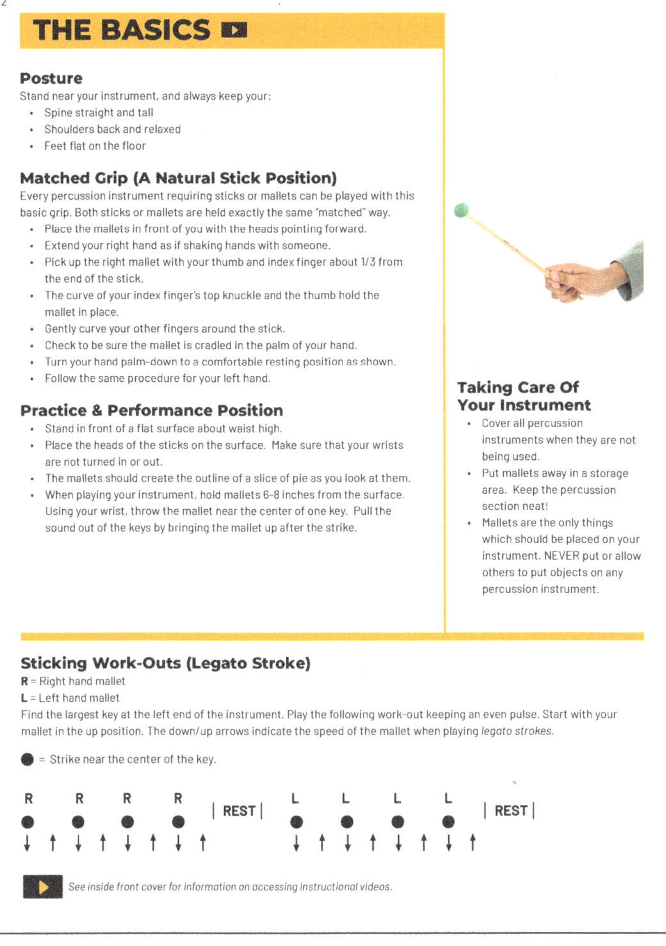

2

THE BASICS

Posture

Stand near your instrument, and always keep your:

- Spine straight and tall
- Shoulders back and relaxed
- Feet flat on the floor

Matched Grip (A Natural Stick Position)

Every percussion instrument requiring sticks or mallets can be played with this basic grip. Both sticks or mallets are held exactly the same "matched" way.

- Place the mallets in front of you with the heads pointing forward.
- Extend your right hand as if shaking hands with someone.
- Pick up the right mallet with your thumb and index finger about 1/3 from the end of the stick.
- The curve of your index finger's top knuckle and the thumb hold the mallet in place.
- Gently curve your other fingers around the stick.
- Check to be sure the mallet is cradled in the palm of your hand.
- Turn your hand palm-down to a comfortable resting position as shown.
- Follow the same procedure for your left hand.

Practice & Performance Position

- Stand in front of a flat surface about waist high.
- Place the heads of the sticks on the surface. Make sure that your wrists are not turned in or out.
- The mallets should create the outline of a slice of pie as you look at them.
- When playing your instrument, hold mallets 6-8 inches from the surface. Using your wrist, throw the mallet near the center of one key. Pull the sound out of the keys by bringing the mallet up after the strike.

Taking Care Of Your Instrument

- Cover all percussion instruments when they are not being used.
- Put mallets away in a storage area. Keep the percussion section neat!
- Mallets are the only things which should be placed on your instrument. NEVER put or allow others to put objects on any percussion instrument.

Sticking Work-Outs (Legato Stroke)

R = Right hand mallet
L = Left hand mallet

Find the largest key at the left end of the instrument. Play the following work-out keeping an even pulse. Start with your mallet in the up position. The down/up arrows indicate the speed of the mallet when playing *legato strokes*.

● = Strike near the center of the key.

R R R R | REST | L L L L | REST |

See inside front cover for information on accessing instructional videos.

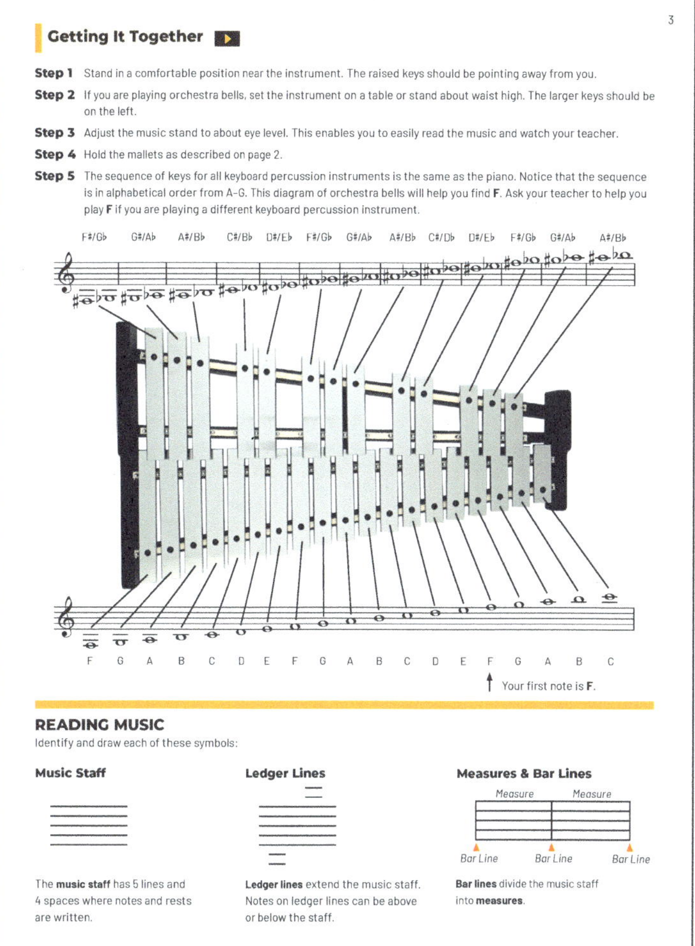

3

Getting It Together

Step 1 Stand in a comfortable position near the instrument. The raised keys should be pointing away from you.

Step 2 If you are playing orchestra bells, set the instrument on a table or stand about waist high. The larger keys should be on the left.

Step 3 Adjust the music stand to about eye level. This enables you to easily read the music and watch your teacher.

Step 4 Hold the mallets as described on page 2.

Step 5 The sequence of keys for all keyboard percussion instruments is the same as the piano. Notice that the sequence is in alphabetical order from A-G. This diagram of orchestra bells will help you find **F**. Ask your teacher to help you play **F** if you are playing a different keyboard percussion instrument.

READING MUSIC

Identify and draw each of these symbols:

Music Staff

The **music staff** has 5 lines and 4 spaces where notes and rests are written.

Ledger Lines

Ledger lines extend the music staff. Notes on ledger lines can be above or below the staff.

Measures & Bar Lines

Bar lines divide the music staff into **measures**.

Basic Percussion Instruments

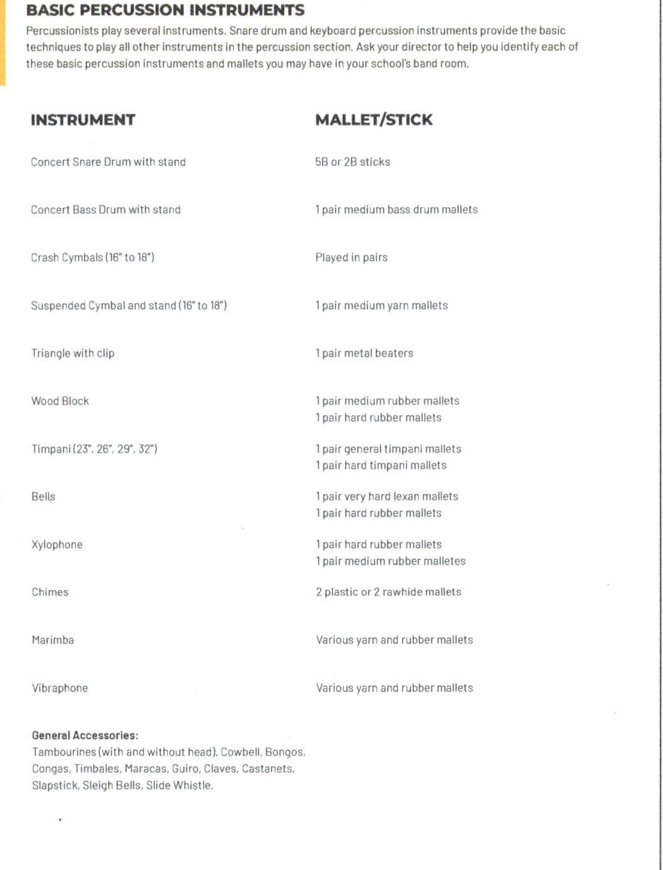

4-A

BASIC PERCUSSION INSTRUMENTS

Percussionists play several instruments. Snare drum and keyboard percussion instruments provide the basic techniques to play all other instruments in the percussion section. Ask your director to help you identify each of these basic percussion instruments and mallets you may have in your school's band room.

INSTRUMENT	MALLET/STICK
Concert Snare Drum with stand	5B or 2B sticks
Concert Bass Drum with stand	1 pair medium bass drum mallets
Crash Cymbals (16" to 18")	Played in pairs
Suspended Cymbal and stand (16" to 18")	1 pair medium yarn mallets
Triangle with clip	1 pair metal beaters
Wood Block	1 pair medium rubber mallets 1 pair hard rubber mallets
Timpani (23", 26", 29", 32")	1 pair general timpani mallets 1 pair hard timpani mallets
Bells	1 pair very hard lexan mallets 1 pair hard rubber mallets
Xylophone	1 pair hard rubber mallets 1 pair medium rubber malletes
Chimes	2 plastic or 2 rawhide mallets
Marimba	Various yarn and rubber mallets
Vibraphone	Various yarn and rubber mallets

General Accessories:
Tambourines (with and without head), Cowbell, Bongos, Congas, Timbales, Maracas, Guiro, Claves, Castanets, Slapstick, Sleigh Bells, Slide Whistle.

Long Tone

To begin, we'll use a special "Long Tone" note. Hold the tone until your teacher tells you to rest. Practice long tones each day to develop your sound.

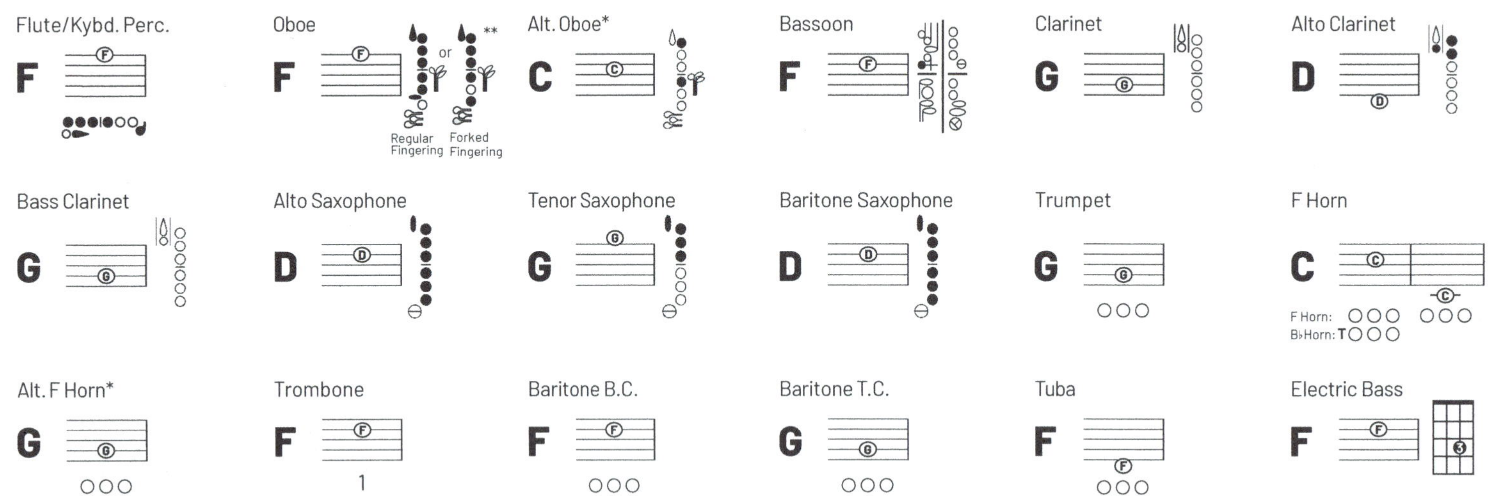

TEACHING TIP If your brass players are having difficulty in playing the Concert F, encourage them to use a faster airstream, or to place a bit more upper lip in the mouthpiece.

Oboe Practice this exercise using both the "regular" and the "forked" fingering for "F." **

F Horn Your teacher will tell you which line to play first, and how long to hold each note. Double Horn Players: add the thumb key and use the B♭ Horn fingering to play "C."

Percussion Play your quarter note as the band plays their long tone. Start with right-hand stick.

Kybd. Perc. Play a legato stroke for each new note.

***Alt. Oboe/Alt. F Horn** from Left-side (Oboes only/ Horns only) student pages 4A–11A. Notes sound a 4th lower than right side (Full Band) unison pages.

1. THE FIRST NOTE

Hold each long tone until your teacher tells you to rest.

Flute, Oboe: F — REST — F — REST

B♭ Clarinet, B♭ Bass Cl., B♭ Tenor Sax., B♭ Trumpet, Alt. F Horn*, Baritone T.C.: G — REST — G — REST (Tenor Sax. 8va)

E♭ Alto Sax., E♭ Bari. Sax.: D — REST — D — REST

E♭ Alto Cl.: D — D

Alt. Oboe*: C — REST — C — REST

F Horn: C — C

Trombone, Baritone B.C., Bassoon, Electric Bass: F — REST — F — REST

Tuba: F — F

Percussion (Snare Drum): R — REST — L — REST

Kybd. Perc.: F — REST — F — REST

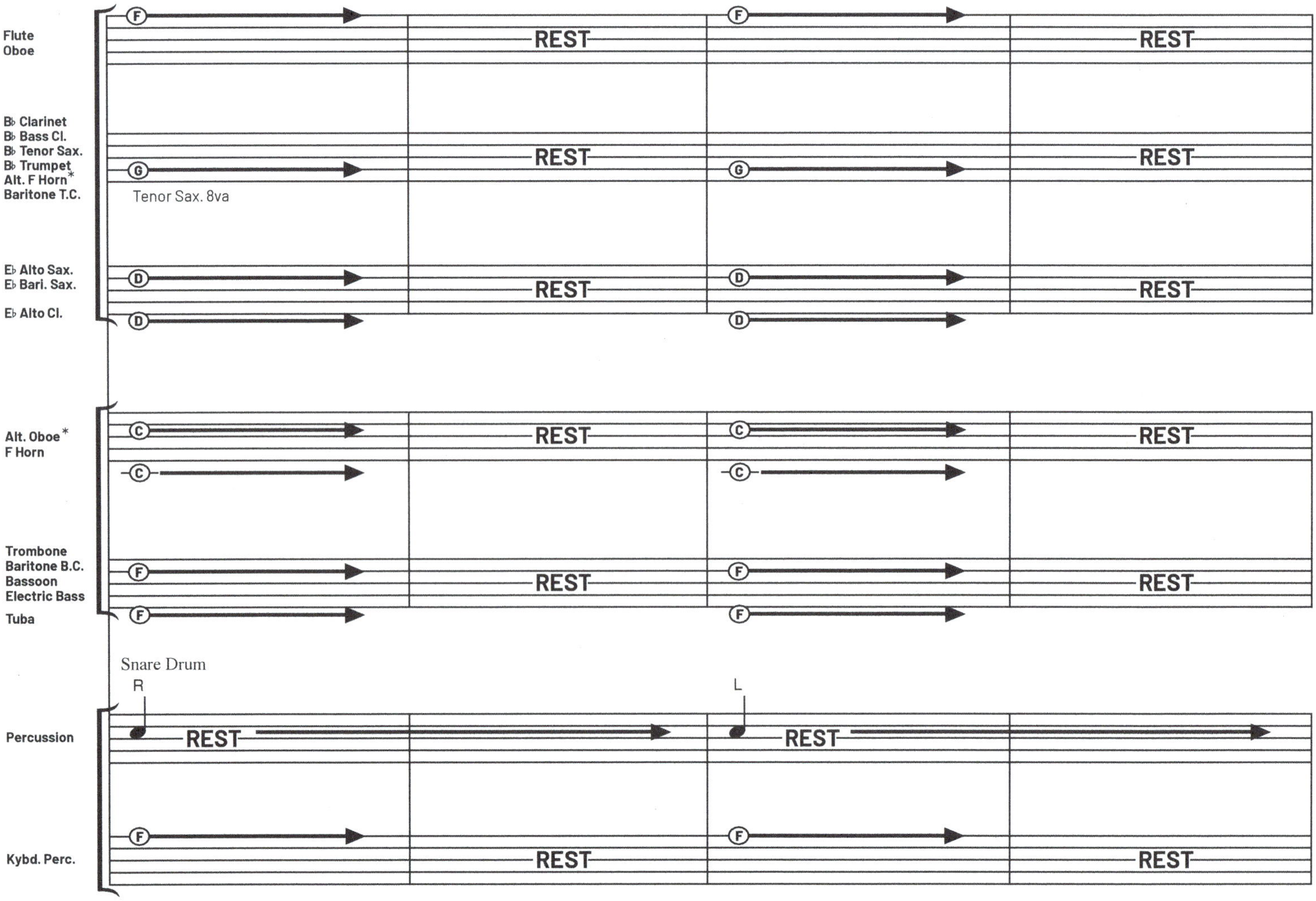

*** For more information about these fingerings, see the oboe fingering chart.*

The Beat

The **beat** is the pulse of music, and like your heartbeat it should remain very steady. Counting aloud and foot-tapping help us maintain a steady beat. Tap your foot **down** on each number and **up** on each "&."

One beat = 1 &

↓ ↑

Notes & Rests

Notes tell us how high or low to play by their placement on a line or space of the music staff, and how long to play by their shape. **Rests** tell us to count silent beats.

Quarter Note = 1 beat

Quarter Rest = 1 silent beat

TEACHING TIP Essential Elements uses a traditional counting system and teaches the subdivided beat from the beginning. It is helpful to count and clap exercises with your students before playing them.

Oboe Practice this exercise using both the "regular" and the "forked" fingering for "F." *

2. COUNT AND PLAY

Flute
Oboe

Count: 1 & 2 & 3 & 4 & | 1 & 2 & 3 & 4 & | 1 & 2 & 3 & 4 & | 1 & 2 & 3 & 4 &
Tap: ↓ ↑ ↓ ↑ ↓ ↑ ↓ ↑ | ↓ ↑ ↓ ↑ ↓ ↑ ↓ ↑ | ↓ ↑ ↓ ↑ ↓ ↑ ↓ ↑ | ↓ ↑ ↓ ↑ ↓ ↑ ↓ ↑

B♭ Clarinet
B♭ Bass Cl.
B♭ Tenor Sax.
B♭ Trumpet
Alt. F Horn
Baritone T.C.

Tenor Sax. 8va

E♭ Alto Sax.
E♭ Bari. Sax.
E♭ Alto Cl.

Alt. Oboe
F Horn

Trombone
Baritone B.C.
Bassoon
Electric Bass
Tuba

Percussion

R R R R | | R R R R |

Kybd. Perc.

R L R L | | R L R L |

Alt. Oboe/Alt. F Horn parts are from Left-side (Oboes only/Horns only) pages.

Kybd. Perc. Alternate Sticking A hand to hand sticking pattern usually beginning with the right hand.

** For more information about this fingering, see the oboe fingering chart.*

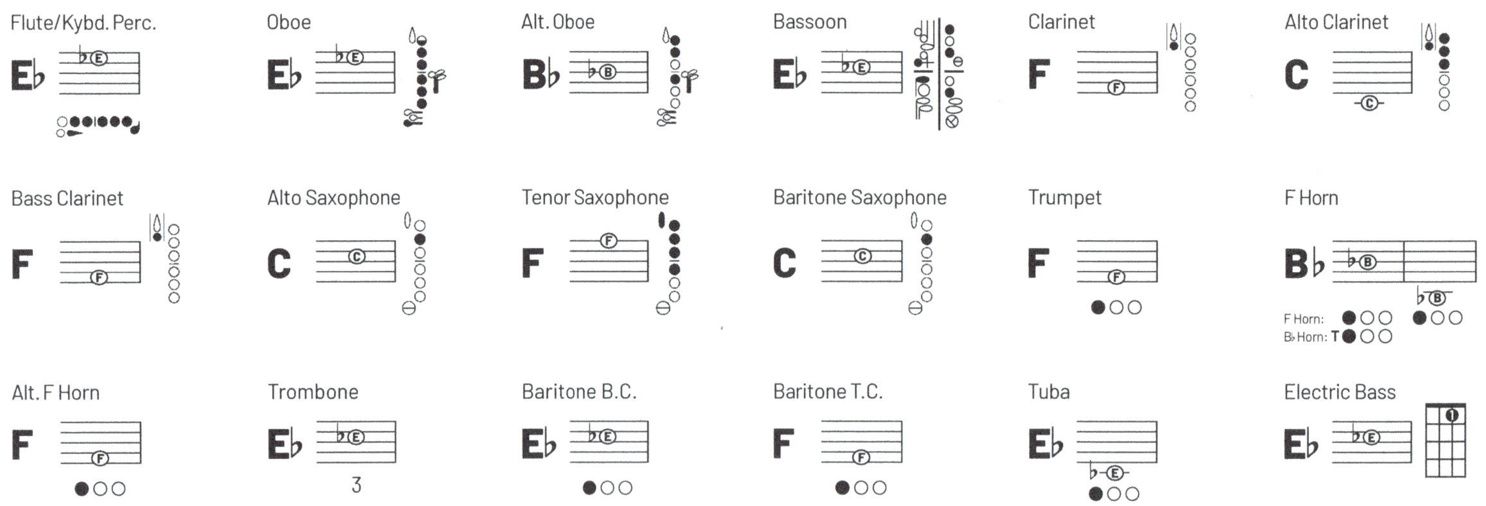

Make sure keys and valves are fully depressed. Clarinet – thumb must completely cover the hole.

Oboe Use the half-hole key on "E-flat."

F Horn Double Horn Players: add the thumb key and use the B♭ Horn fingering to play "B♭."

Percussion Play sticking as marked.

3. A NEW NOTE

Look for the fingering/slide position diagram with each new note.

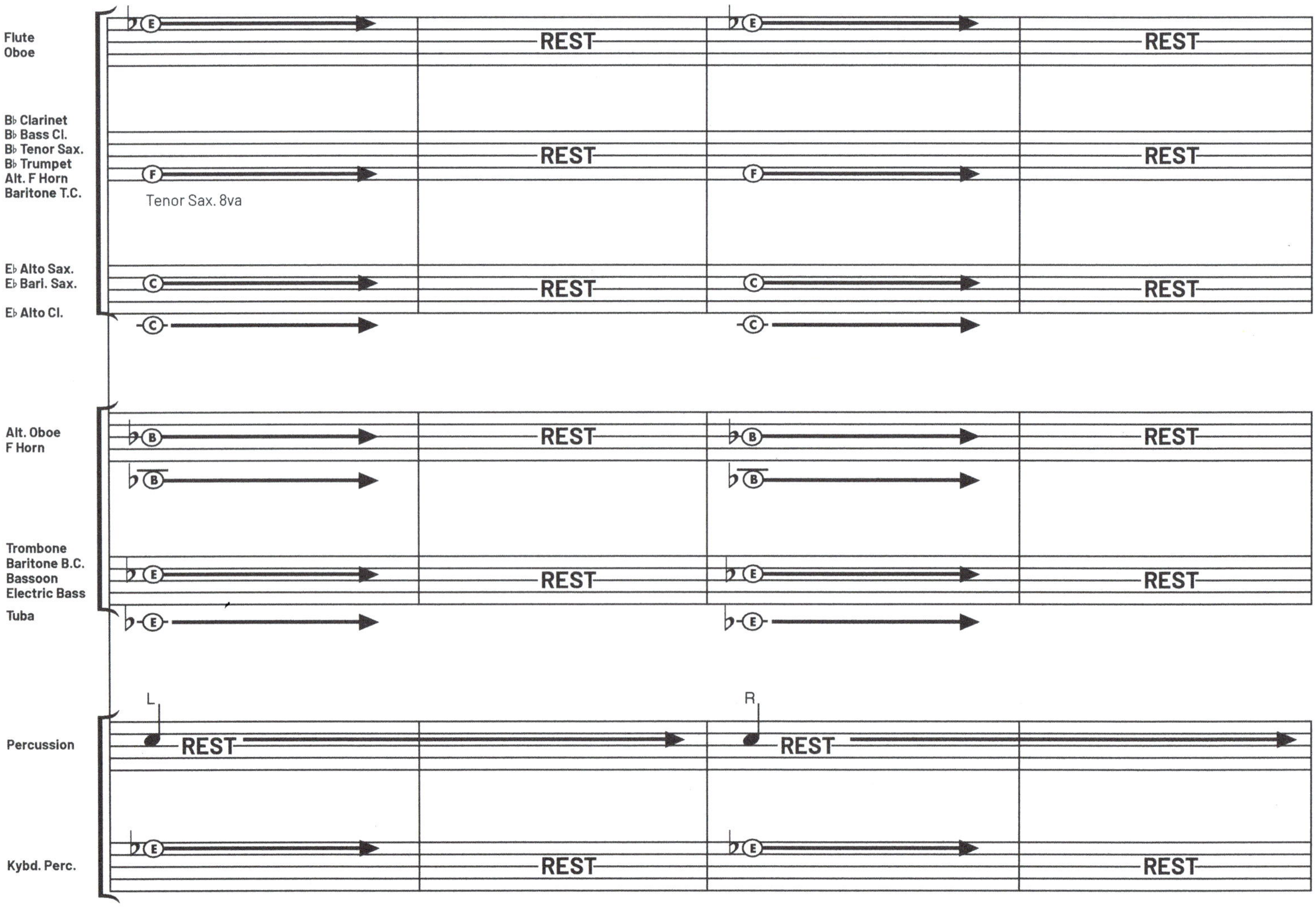

Flute
Oboe

REST REST

B♭ Clarinet
B♭ Bass Cl.
B♭ Tenor Sax.
B♭ Trumpet
Alt. F Horn
Baritone T.C.

Tenor Sax. 8va

REST REST

E♭ Alto Sax.
E♭ Bari. Sax.
E♭ Alto Cl.

REST REST

Alt. Oboe
F Horn

REST REST

Trombone
Baritone B.C.
Bassoon
Electric Bass
Tuba

REST REST

Percussion

L REST R REST

Kybd. Perc.

REST REST

Alt. Oboe/Alt. F Horn parts are from Left-side (Oboes only/Horns only) pages.

Encourage students to use a steady airstream while tonguing instead of using "puffs" of air.

Oboe Use the "forked" fingering to play "F." *

4. TWO'S A TEAM

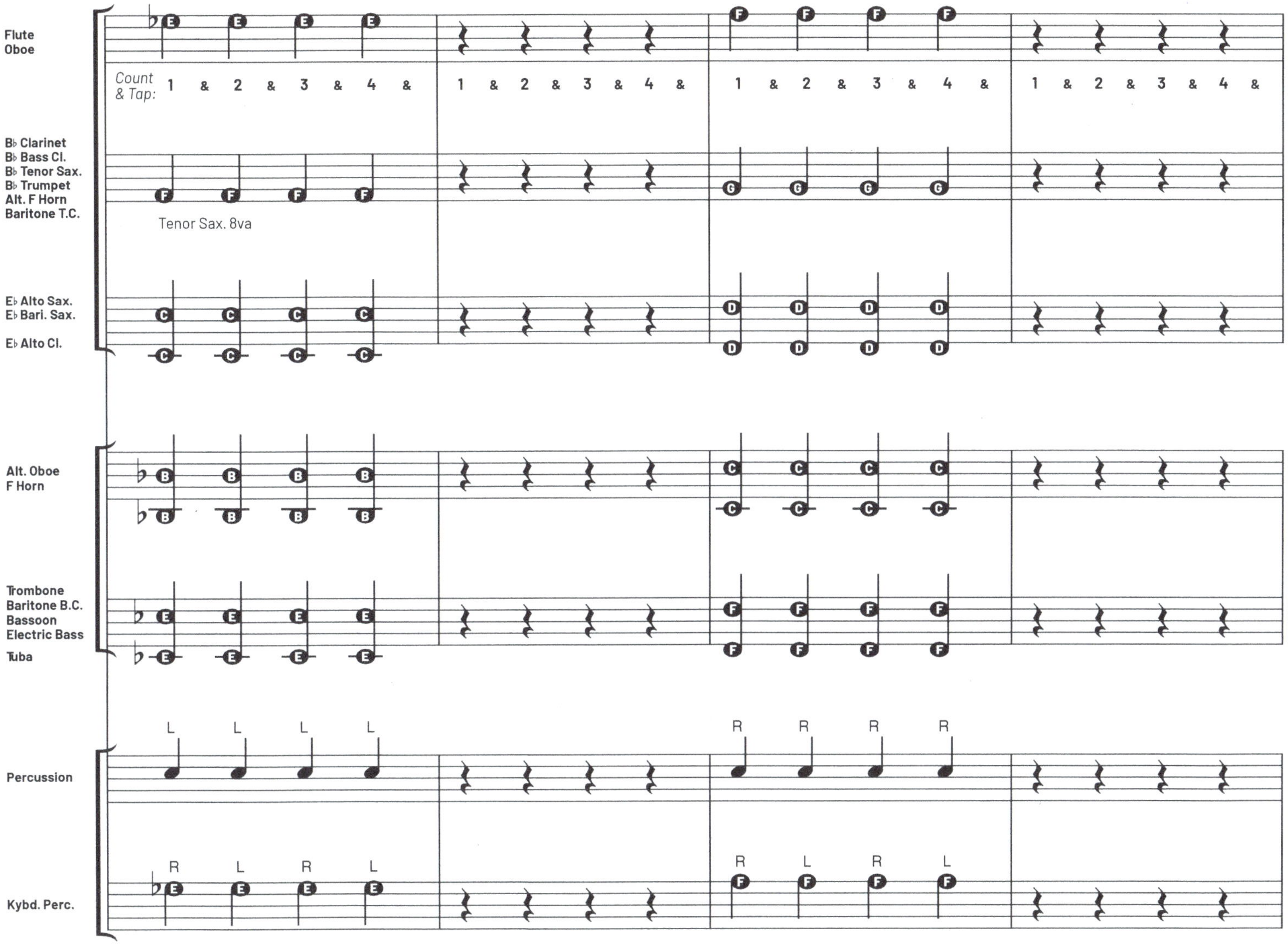

Alt. Oboe/Alt. F Horn parts are from Left-side (Oboes only/Horns only) pages.

** For more information about this fingering, see the oboe fingering chart.*

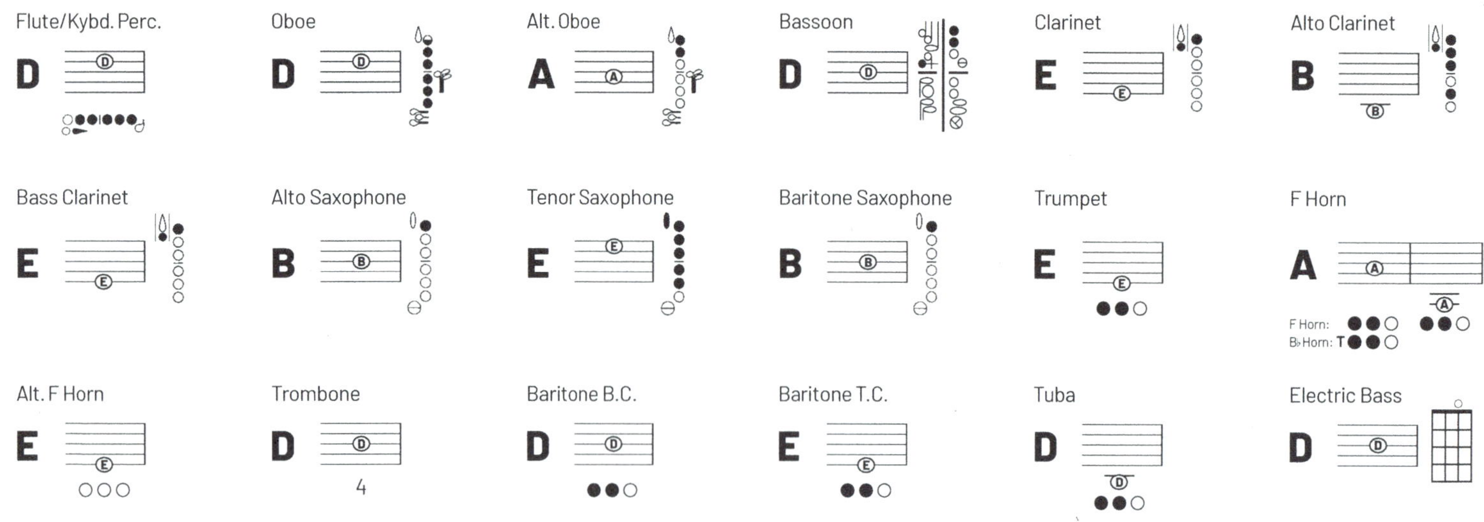

When giving a preparatory beat, it is important for the teacher to model correct breathing habits. As students inhale to play the note, breathe with them.

Oboe Use the half-hole key on "D."

F Horn Double Horn Players: add the thumb key and use the B♭ Horn fingering to play "A."

Percussion Always stand straight and tall with your shoulders relaxed.

5. HEADING DOWN

Practice long tones on each new note.

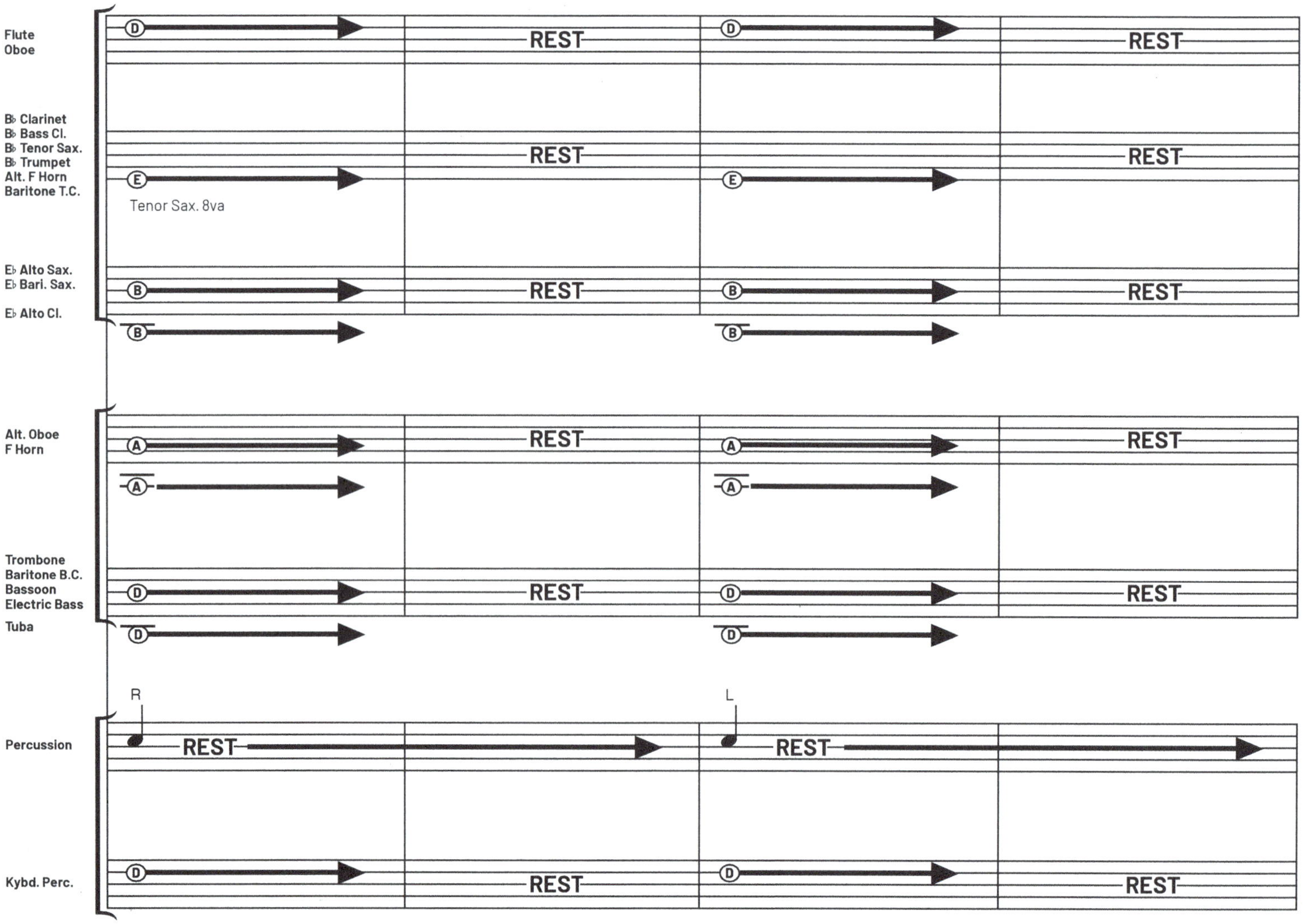

Flute
Oboe
D — REST — D — REST

B♭ Clarinet
B♭ Bass Cl.
B♭ Tenor Sax.
B♭ Trumpet
Alt. F Horn
Baritone T.C.
E — REST — E — REST

Tenor Sax. 8va

E♭ Alto Sax.
E♭ Bari. Sax.
B — REST — B — REST

E♭ Alto Cl.
B — B

Alt. Oboe
F Horn
A — REST — A — REST
A — A

Trombone
Baritone B.C.
Bassoon
Electric Bass
D — REST — D — REST

Tuba
D — D

Percussion
R — REST — L — REST

Kybd. Perc.
D — REST — D — REST

Alt. Oboe/Alt. F Horn parts are from Left-side (Oboes only/Horns only) pages.

Teach students to observe all rests. Say "rest" on each of the quarter rests found in measures 2 and 4.

Oboe The "forked" fingering makes it easier to play "F" when moving to or from "E♭" or "D." *

Kybd. Perc. **Double Sticking**

A pattern in which two consecutive notes are played with the same hand (RRLL, RRLL). This pattern may begin with either a double right or a double left sticking.

6. MOVING ON UP

Flute
Oboe

Count & Tap: 1 & 2 & 3 & 4 & | 1 & 2 & 3 & 4 & | 1 & 2 & 3 & 4 & | 1 & 2 & 3 & 4 &

B♭ Clarinet
B♭ Bass Cl.
B♭ Tenor Sax.
B♭ Trumpet
Alt. F Horn
Baritone T.C.

Tenor Sax. 8va

E♭ Alto Sax.
E♭ Bari. Sax.
E♭ Alto Cl.

Alt. Oboe
F Horn

Trombone
Baritone B.C.
Bassoon
Electric Bass
Tuba

Percussion: R R R R | R | R R L L | R

Kybd. Perc.: R R L L | R | R R L L | R

Alt. Oboe/Alt. F Horn parts are from Left-side (Oboes only/Horns only) pages.

** For more information about this fingering, see the oboe fingering chart.*

Double Bar indicates the end of a piece of music.

Repeat Sign Without stopping, play once again from the beginning.

Flute/Kybd. Perc.
C
Oboe
C
Alt. Oboe
G
Bassoon
C
Clarinet
D
Alto Clarinet
A
Bass Clarinet
D
Alto Saxophone
A
Tenor Saxophone
D
Baritone Saxophone
A
Trumpet
D
F Horn
G
F Horn:
Alt. F Horn
D
Trombone
C
6
Baritone B.C.
C
Baritone T.C.
D
Tuba
C
Electric Bass
C
3

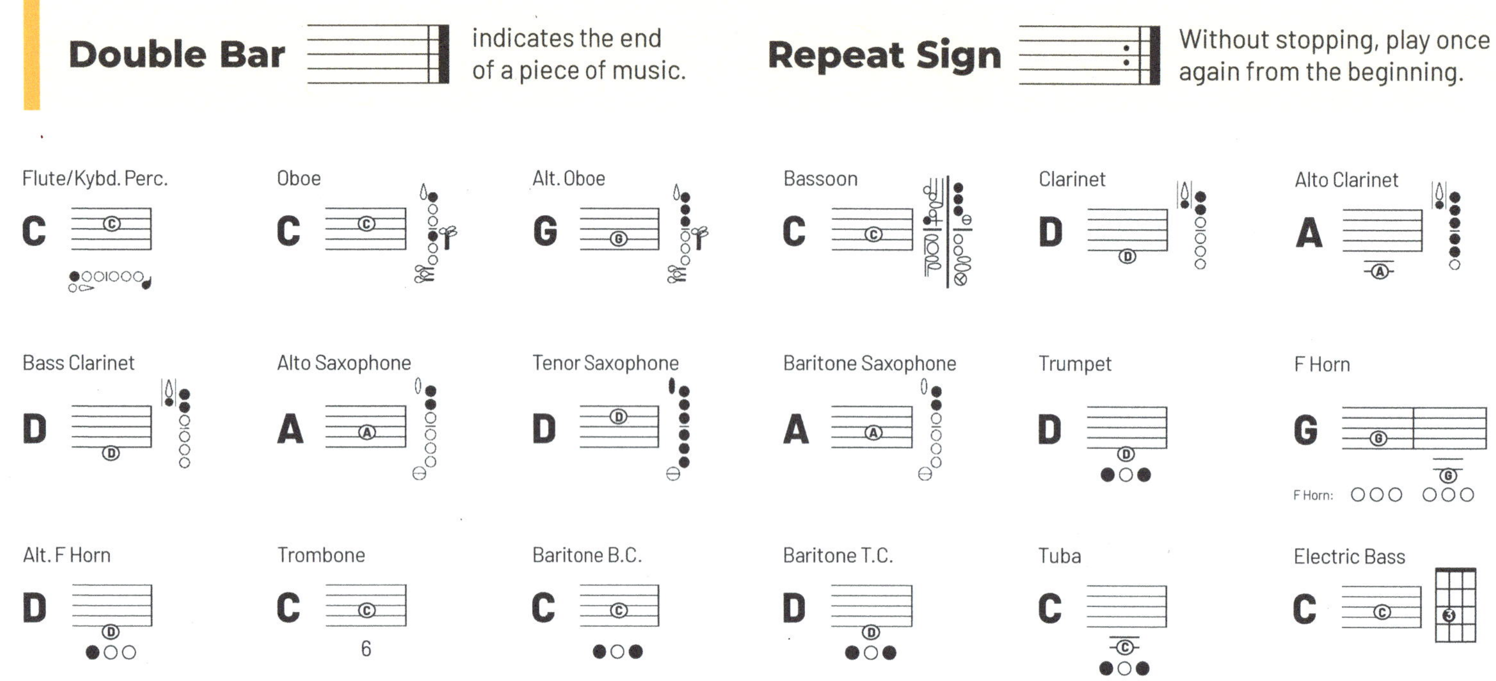

TEACHING TIP Be sure students take a full breath to play their new note with good tone.

7. THE LONG HAUL

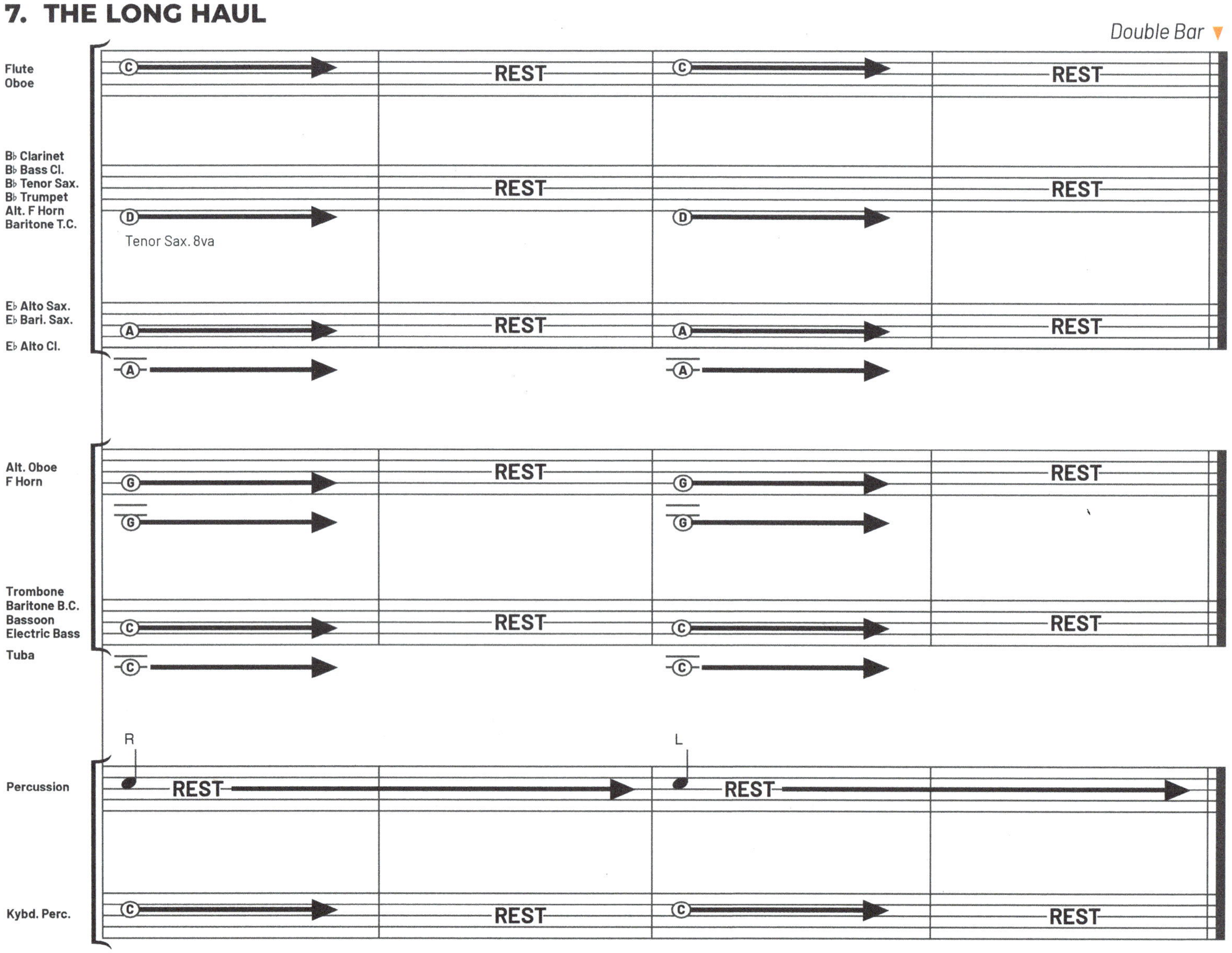
Double Bar
Flute
Oboe
REST
REST
B♭ Clarinet
B♭ Bass Cl.
B♭ Tenor Sax.
B♭ Trumpet
Alt. F Horn
Baritone T.C.
REST
REST
Tenor Sax. 8va
E♭ Alto Sax.
E♭ Bari. Sax.
E♭ Alto Cl.
REST
REST
Alt. Oboe
F Horn
REST
REST
Trombone
Baritone B.C.
Bassoon
Electric Bass
Tuba
REST
REST
R
L
Percussion
REST
REST
Kybd. Perc.
REST
REST

Alt. Oboe/Alt. F Horn parts are from Left-side (Oboes only/Horns only) pages.

Encourage students to play full value quarter notes.

Oboe Use "forked" fingering on "F." Roll your first finger to the half-hole key to play "E♭." *

Percussion Practice Right Hand Lead as marked.

Kybd. Perc. Use Alternate Sticking.

8. FOUR BY FOUR

Repeat Sign

Flute
Oboe

Count & Tap: 1 & 2 & 3 & 4 & 1 & 2 & 3 & 4 & 1 & 2 & 3 & 4 & 1 & 2 & 3 & 4 &

B♭ Clarinet
B♭ Bass Cl.
B♭ Tenor Sax.
B♭ Trumpet
Alt. F Horn
Baritone T.C.

Tenor Sax. 8va

E♭ Alto Sax.
E♭ Bari. Sax.
E♭ Alto Cl.

Alt. Oboe
F Horn

Trombone
Baritone B.C.
Bassoon
Electric Bass
Tuba

Percussion

R L R L R R L R L R

Kybd. Perc.

R L R L R R L R L R

Alt. Oboe/Alt. F Horn parts are from Left-side (Oboes only/Horns only) pages.

** For more information about this fingering, see the oboe fingering chart.*

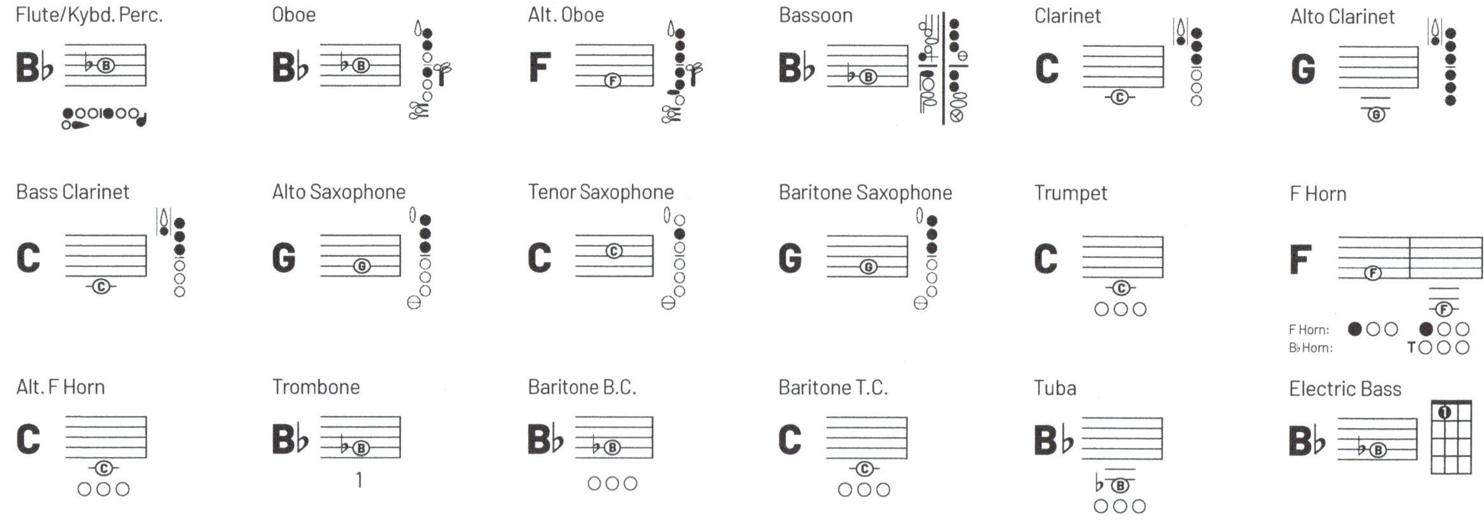

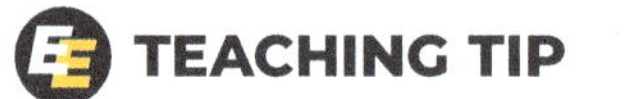

Flute/Kybd. Perc.
B♭
Oboe
B♭
Alt. Oboe
F
Bassoon
B♭
Clarinet
C
Alto Clarinet
G
Bass Clarinet
C
Alto Saxophone
G
Tenor Saxophone
C
Baritone Saxophone
G
Trumpet
C
F Horn
F
F Horn:
B♭ Horn:
T
Alt. F Horn
C
Trombone
B♭
1
Baritone B.C.
B♭
Baritone T.C.
C
Tuba
B♭
Electric Bass
B♭
0

TEACHING TIP When playing long notes, students should relax the tongue.

F Horn Double Horn Players: add the thumb key and use the B♭ Horn fingering to play "F."

9. TOUCHDOWN

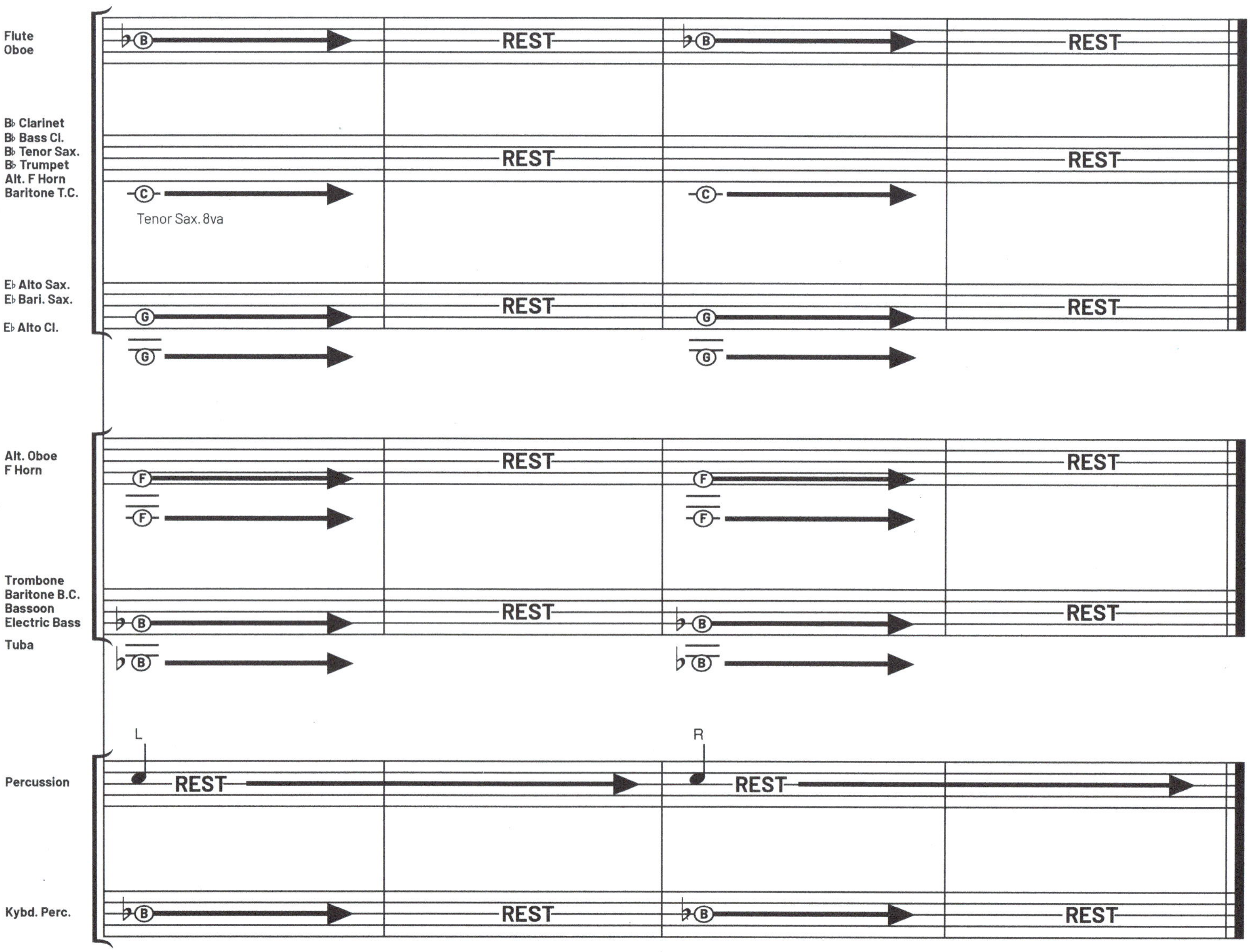

Flute
Oboe
REST
REST
B♭ Clarinet
B♭ Bass Cl.
B♭ Tenor Sax.
B♭ Trumpet
Alt. F Horn
Baritone T.C.
Tenor Sax. 8va
E♭ Alto Sax.
E♭ Bari. Sax.
E♭ Alto Cl.
Alt. Oboe
F Horn
Trombone
Baritone B.C.
Bassoon
Electric Bass
Tuba
L
R
Percussion
Kybd. Perc.

Alt. Oboe/Alt. F Horn parts are from Left-side (Oboes only/Horns only) pages.

Keep the embouchure steady while tonguing the notes.

Oboe Use "forked" fingering on "F." *

Percussion Right Hand Lead.

Kybd. Perc. Use Double Sticking.

10. THE FAB FIVE

Flute
Oboe

1 & 2 & 3 & 4 & | 1 & 2 & 3 & 4 & | 1 & 2 & 3 & 4 & | 1 & 2 & 3 & 4 &

B♭ Clarinet
B♭ Bass Cl.
B♭ Tenor Sax.
B♭ Trumpet
Alt. F Horn
Baritone T.C.

Tenor Sax. 8va

E♭ Alto Sax.
E♭ Bari. Sax.
E♭ Alto Cl.

Alt. Oboe
F Horn

Trombone
Baritone B.C.
Bassoon
Electric Bass
Tuba

Percussion

R R | R L R L | R R | R L R L

Kybd. Perc.

R R L L | R | R R L L | R

Alt. Oboe/Alt. F Horn parts are from Left-side (Oboes only/Horns only) pages.

** For more information about this fingering, see the oboe fingering chart.*

THEORY

Treble Clef

(G Clef) indicates the position of note names on a music staff: Second line is G.

Bass Clef

(F Clef) indicates the position of note names on a music staff: Fourth line is F.

Time Signature

indicates how many beats per measure and what kind of note gets one beat.

4/4 = **4 beats** per measure
= **Quarter** note gets one beat

Note Names

Each note is on a line or a space of the staff. These note names are indicated by the Clef.

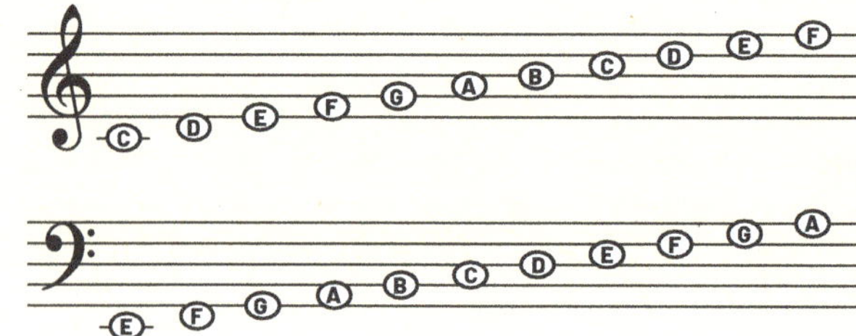

Sharp ♯ raises the note and remains in effect for the entire measure.

Flat ♭ lowers the note and remains in effect for the entire measure.

Natural ♮ cancels a flat (♭) or sharp (♯) and remains in effect for the entire measure.

Percussion Clefs indicate a new line of music and a set of note names. Percussion instruments use three common clefs:

Percussion Clef

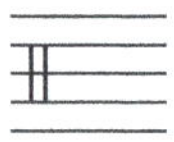

Snare Drum
Bass Drum
Cymbals
Drum Set
Accessory Instruments

Treble Clef

Bells
Xylophone
Marimba
Vibraphone
Chimes

Bass Clef

Timpani
Marimba
Older snare drum and bass drum publications often use the bass clef.

Kybd. Perc. This chart will help you play notes on orchestra bells. Practice all exercises with other percussionists using the keyboard percussion section at the end of this book. Switch parts often!

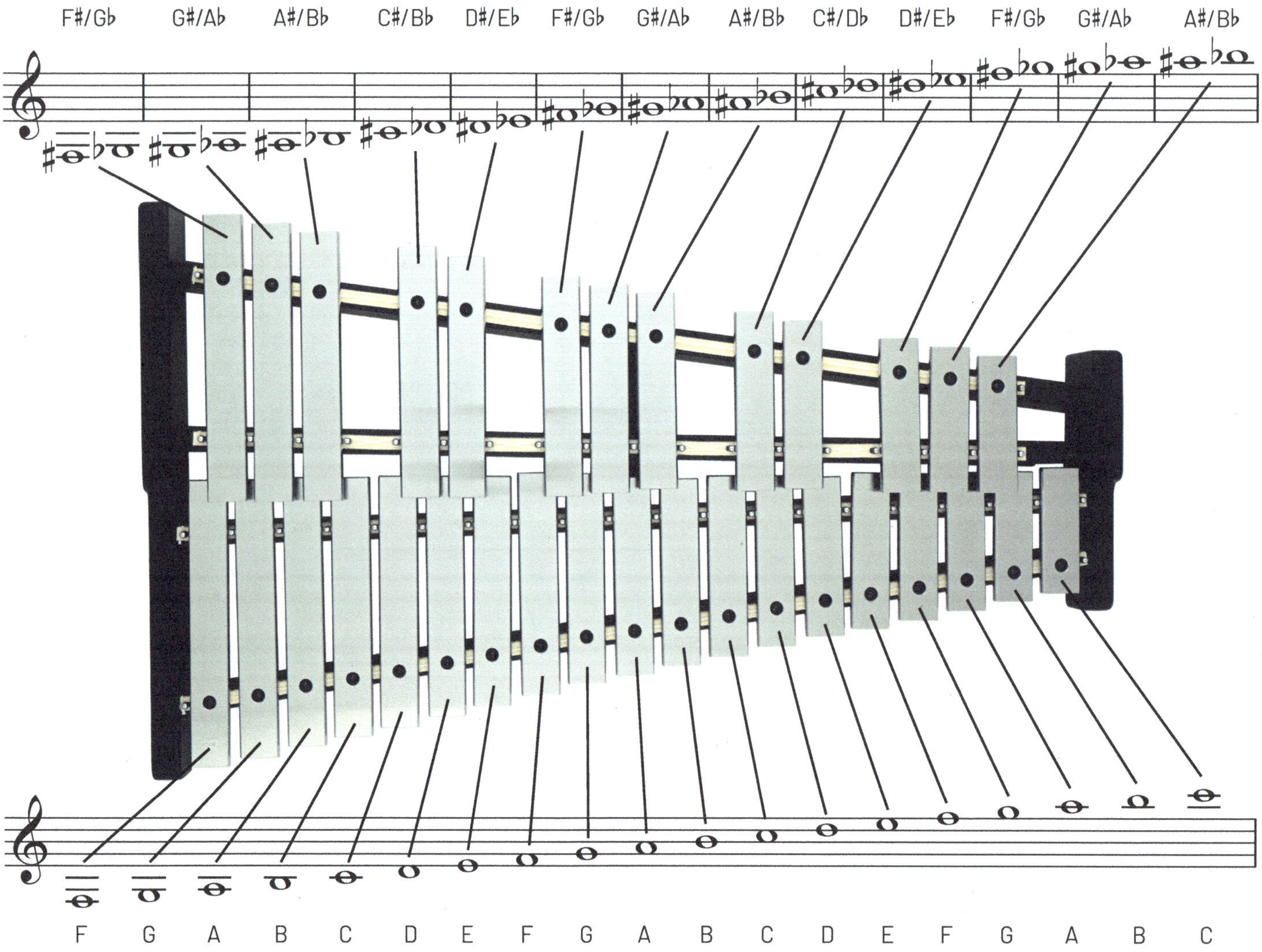

F♯/G♭ G♯/A♭ A♯/B♭ C♯/B♭ D♯/E♭ F♯/G♭ G♯/A♭ A♯/B♭ C♯/D♭ D♯/E♭ F♯/G♭ G♯/A♭ A♯/B♭

F G A B C D E F G A B C D E F G A B C

TEACHING TIP Have students say note names before playing this exercise.

Oboe Use "forked" fingering on "F." *

11. READING THE NOTES *Compare this to exercise 10, THE FAB FIVE.*

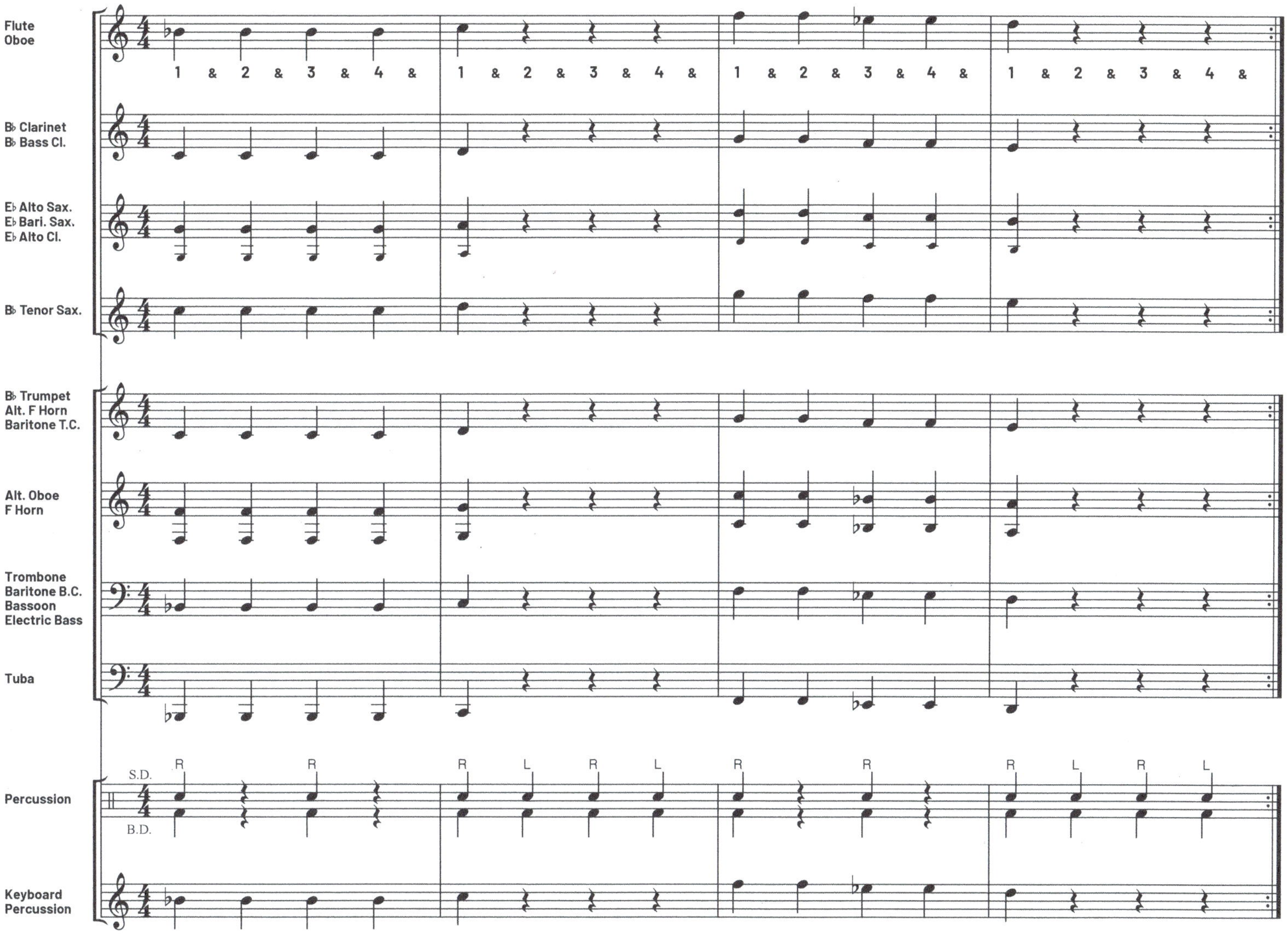

Alt. Oboe/Alt. F Horn parts are from Left-side (Oboes only/Horns only) pages.

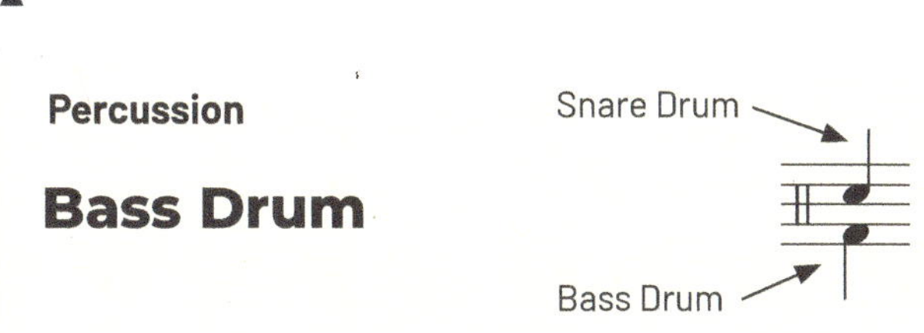

Percussion

Bass Drum

The bass drum is one of the most important instruments in band. Hold the bass drum mallet with your right hand (matched grip). Place your left hand on the head opposite the striking surface. Strike the bass drum half-way between the center and the top rim, pulling the sound out of the bass drum. **B.D.** is the abbreviation for bass drum.

** For more information about this fingering, see the oboe fingering chart.*

Oboe Ⓕ = Use "forked" fingering. For students whose oboe has a "left F" key, they can use "left F" for these notes as well.

12. FIRST FLIGHT

Flute / Oboe
B♭ Clarinet / B♭ Bass Cl.
E♭ Alto Sax. / E♭ Bari. Sax. / E♭ Alto Cl.
B♭ Tenor Sax.
B♭ Trumpet / Alt. F Horn / Baritone T.C.
Alt. Oboe / F Horn
Trombone / Baritone B.C. / Bassoon / Electric Bass
Tuba
Percussion (S.D. / B.D.)
Keyboard Percussion

*No sticking is printed, allowing students to mark their own appropriate sticking before playing.

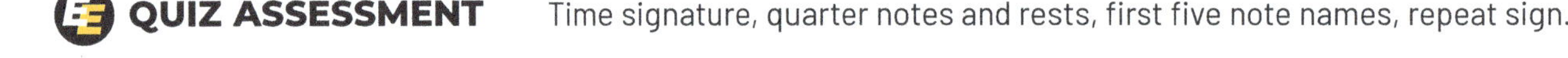

QUIZ ASSESSMENT Time signature, quarter notes and rests, first five note names, repeat sign.

13. ESSENTIAL ELEMENTS QUIZ *Fill in the remaining note names before playing.**

Flute / Oboe (B♭ C D ___ | ___ ___ ___ | ___ ___ ___ ___ | ___ ___ ___)
B♭ Clarinet / B♭ Bass Cl.
E♭ Alto Sax. / E♭ Bari. Sax. / E♭ Alto Cl.
B♭ Tenor Sax.
B♭ Trumpet / Alt. F Horn / Baritone T.C.
Alt. Oboe / F Horn
Trombone / Baritone B.C. / Bassoon / Electric Bass
Tuba
Percussion (S.D. / B.D.)
Keyboard Percussion

*Percussion can also do the written quiz.
Alt. Oboe/Alt. F Horn parts are from Left-side (Oboes only/Horns only) pages.

A **Notes In Review** fingering chart appears above exercise 14 in the student books. The first five notes learned: Concert F, E♭, D, C, and B♭ are shown on a staff along with their note names and fingerings/slide positions. Students are asked to memorize the fingerings for the notes they've learned.

TEACHING TIP Move fingers/slides with steady rhythm to help with accuracy.

Kybd. Perc. Use Alternate Sticking.

14. ROLLING ALONG

Alt. Oboe/Alt. F Horn parts are from Left-side (Oboes only/Horns only) pages.

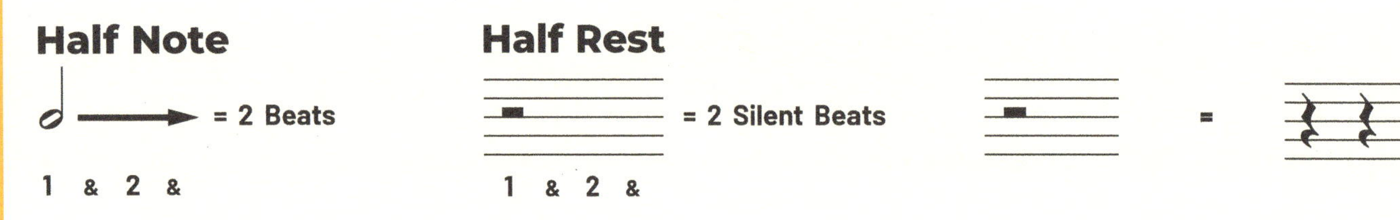

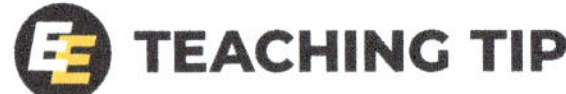

Half Note

= 2 Beats

1 & 2 &

Half Rest

= 2 Silent Beats

1 & 2 &

=

TEACHING TIP Encourage students to practice this exercise with the play-along track to internalize steady rhythm.

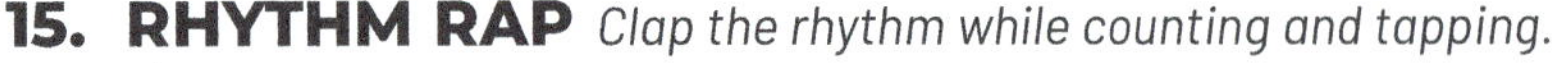

15. RHYTHM RAP *Clap the rhythm while counting and tapping.*

Clap
Repeat Sign

1 & 2 & 3 & 4 & 1 & 2 & 3 & 4 & 1 & 2 & 3 & 4 & 1 & 2 & 3 & 4 & 1 & 2 & 3 & 4 & 1 & 2 & 3 & 4 &

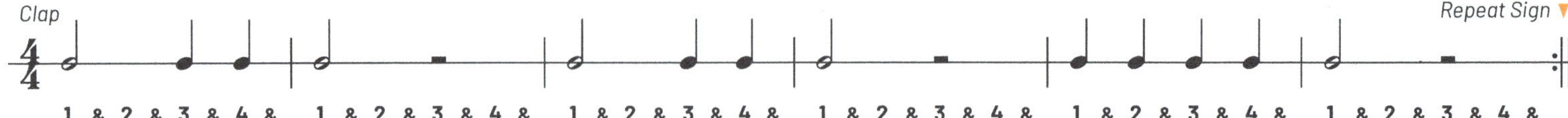

TEACHING TIP Ask students if they've seen this rhythm before. (Same as #15 Rhythm Rap.)

16. THE HALF COUNTS

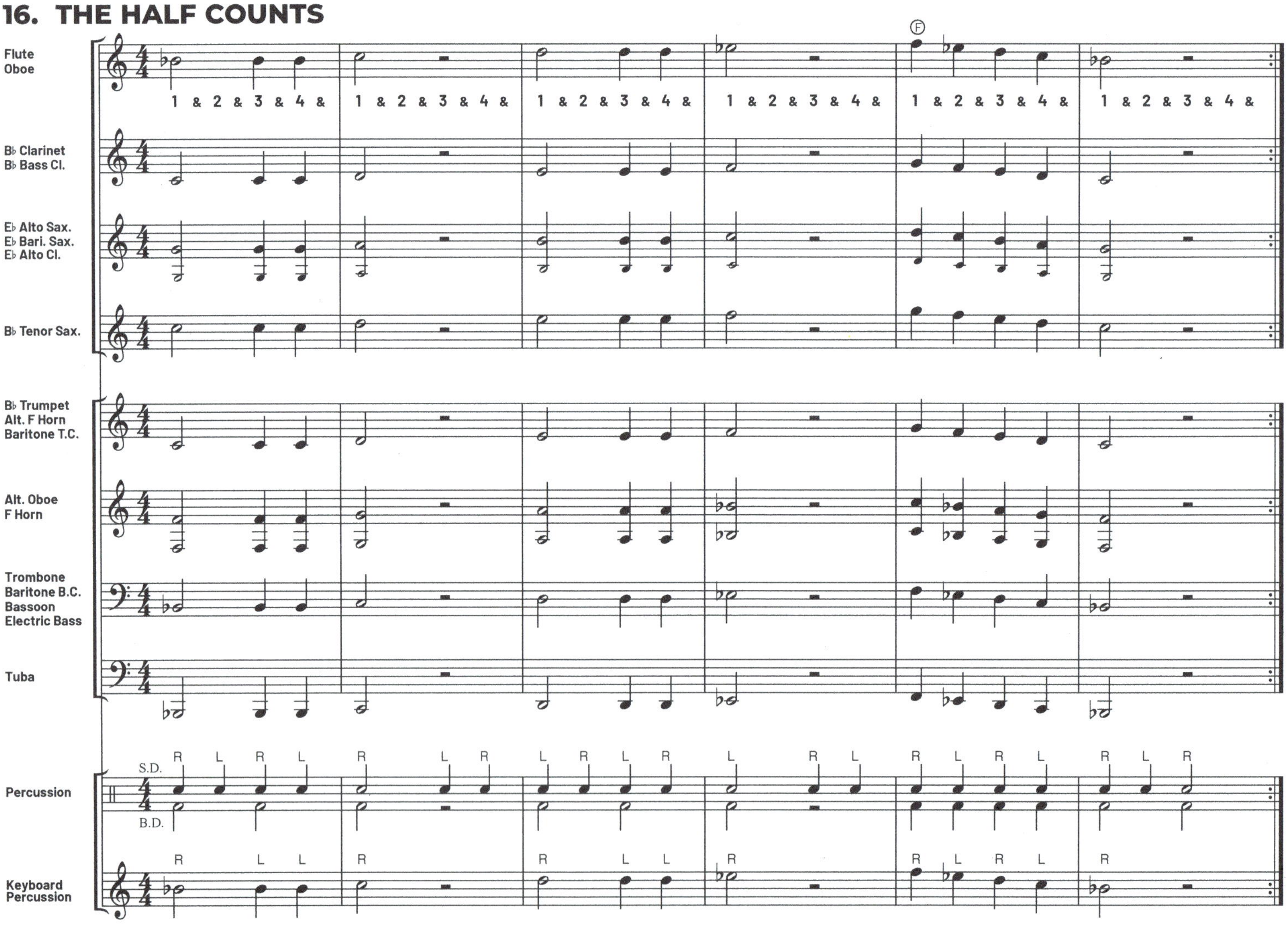
Flute
Oboe
B♭ Clarinet
B♭ Bass Cl.
E♭ Alto Sax.
E♭ Bari. Sax.
E♭ Alto Cl.
B♭ Tenor Sax.
B♭ Trumpet
Alt. F Horn
Baritone T.C.
Alt. Oboe
F Horn
Trombone
Baritone B.C.
Bassoon
Electric Bass
Tuba
Percussion
S.D.
B.D.
Keyboard Percussion
1 & 2 & 3 & 4 &
R L R L R L R L R L R L R L R L R L R L R L R
R L L R R L L R R L R L R

Alt. Oboe/Alt. F Horn parts are from Left-side (Oboes only/Horns only) pages.

Percussion **Alternate Sticking** A hand to hand sticking pattern usually beginning with the right hand.

Bass Drum When playing half notes, use a slower stroke to *pull* the sound out of the bass drum.

Kybd. Perc. **Combination Sticking** A sticking pattern that combines both alternate and double sticking.

 **TEACHING TIP** Remind students not to breathe after each half note.

17. HOT CROSS BUNS

WWs.: Check your embouchure and hand position.
Brass: Try this song on your mouthpiece only. Then play it on your instrument.

Breath Mark

, Take a deep breath through your mouth after you play a full-length note.

 **TEACHING TIP** Encourage students to take a quick breath at each breath mark.

18. GO TELL AUNT RHODIE

American Folk Song

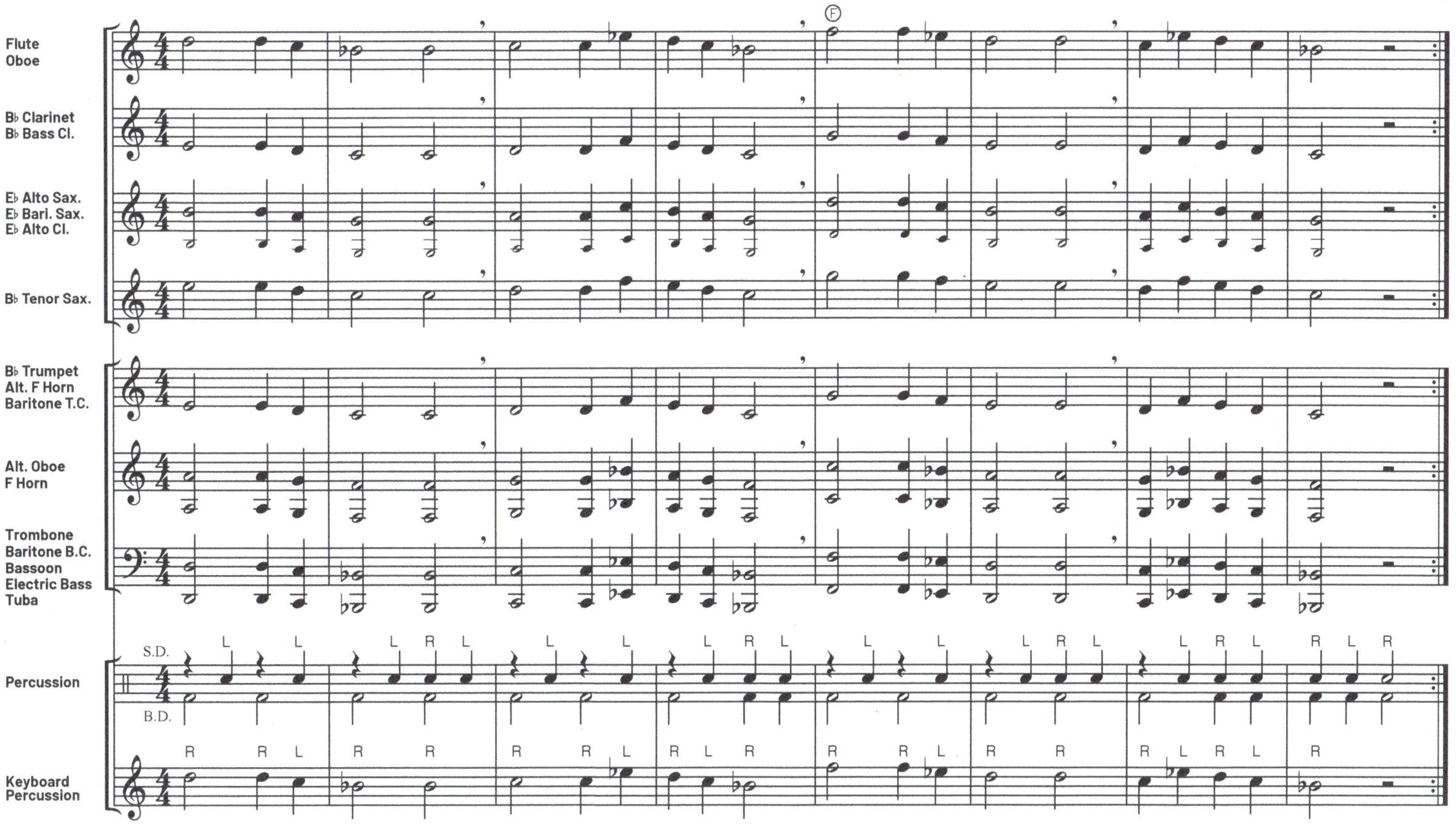

Flute
Oboe
B♭ Clarinet
B♭ Bass Cl.
E♭ Alto Sax.
E♭ Bari. Sax.
E♭ Alto Cl.
B♭ Tenor Sax.
B♭ Trumpet
Alt. F Horn
Baritone T.C.
Alt. Oboe
F Horn
Trombone
Baritone B.C.
Bassoon
Electric Bass
Tuba
Percussion
S.D.
B.D.
Keyboard
Percussion

Alt. Oboe/Alt. F Horn parts are from Left-side (Oboes only/Horns only) pages.

Drawing notes on staff, half notes, and quarter notes.

19. ESSENTIAL ELEMENTS QUIZ

*Using the note names and rhythms below, draw your notes on the staff before playing.**

Instrument	Measure 1	Measure 2	Measure 3	Measure 4
Flute, Oboe	E♭ F E♭ D	E♭ D C B♭	C D	E♭ D E♭
B♭ Clarinet, B♭ Bass Cl.	F G F E	F E D C	D E	F E F
E♭ Alto Sax., E♭ Bari. Sax., E♭ Alto Cl.	C D C B	C B A G	A B	C B C
B♭ Tenor Sax.	F G F E	F E D C	D E	F E F
B♭ Trumpet, Alt. F Horn, Baritone T.C.	F G F E	F E D C	D E	F E F
Alt. Oboe, F Horn	B♭ C B♭ A	B♭ A G F	G A	B♭ A B♭
Trombone, Baritone B.C., Bassoon, Electric Bass	E♭ F E♭ D	E♭ D C B♭	C D	E♭ D E♭
Tuba	E♭ F E♭ D	E♭ D C B♭	C D	E♭ D E♭
Percussion (S.D./B.D.)	R L L	L L	R L R L	L R
Keyboard Percussion	E♭ F E♭ D	E♭ D C B♭	C D	E♭ D E♭

**Percussion can also do the written quiz.*

Alt. Oboe/Alt. F Horn parts are from Left-side (Oboes only/Horns only) pages.

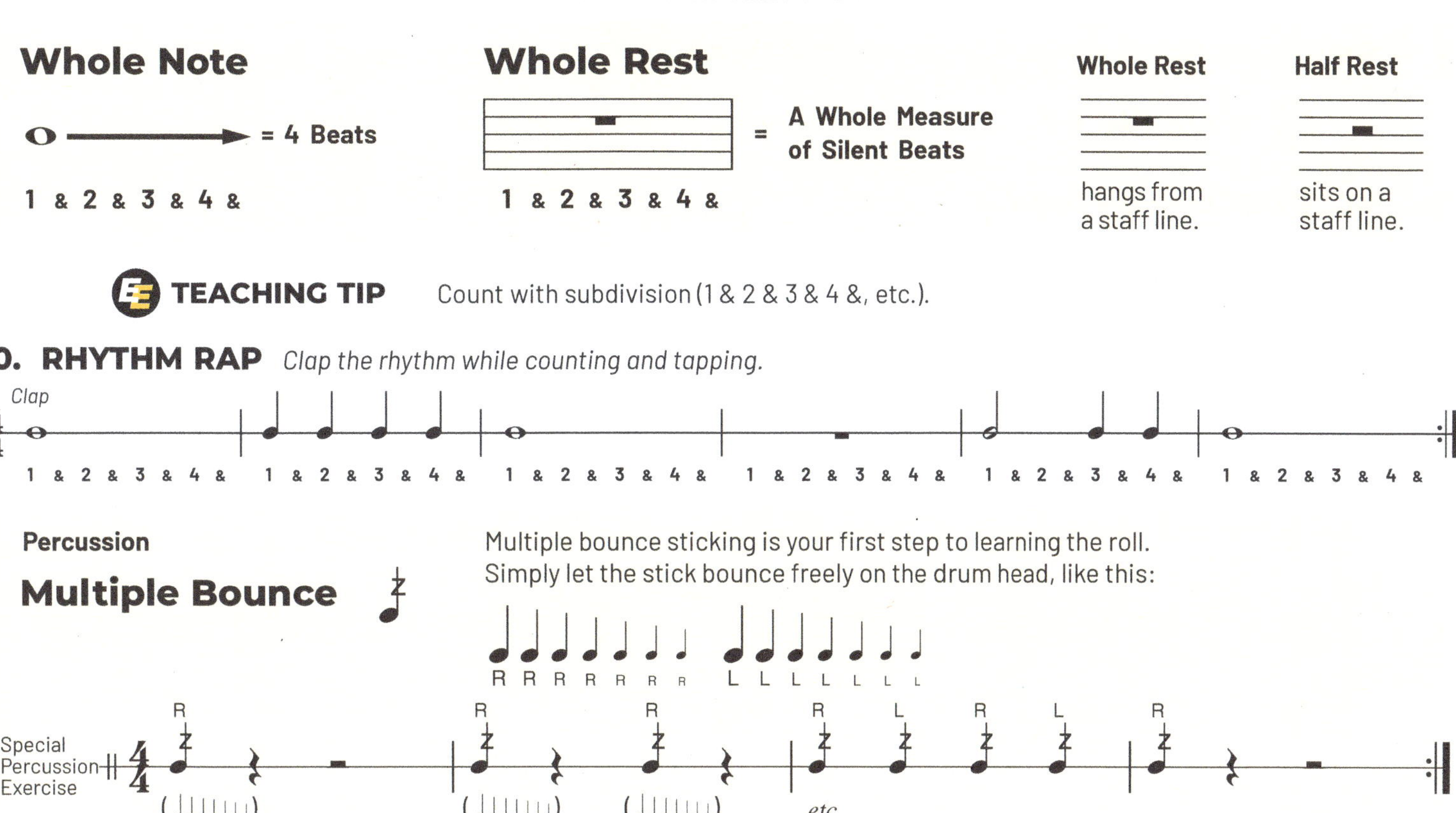

Whole Note

= 4 Beats

1 & 2 & 3 & 4 &

Whole Rest

= A Whole Measure of Silent Beats

1 & 2 & 3 & 4 &

Whole Rest hangs from a staff line.

Half Rest sits on a staff line.

TEACHING TIP Count with subdivision (1 & 2 & 3 & 4 &, etc.).

20. RHYTHM RAP *Clap the rhythm while counting and tapping.*

Percussion

Multiple Bounce

Multiple bounce sticking is your first step to learning the roll. Simply let the stick bounce freely on the drum head, like this:

Keep counting and maintain a steady tempo.

TEACHING TIP Have half of the class count and clap the Rhythm Rap (#20) while the other half plays this line. Then switch.

Percussion Practice this exercise with Alternate Sticking.

21. THE WHOLE THING

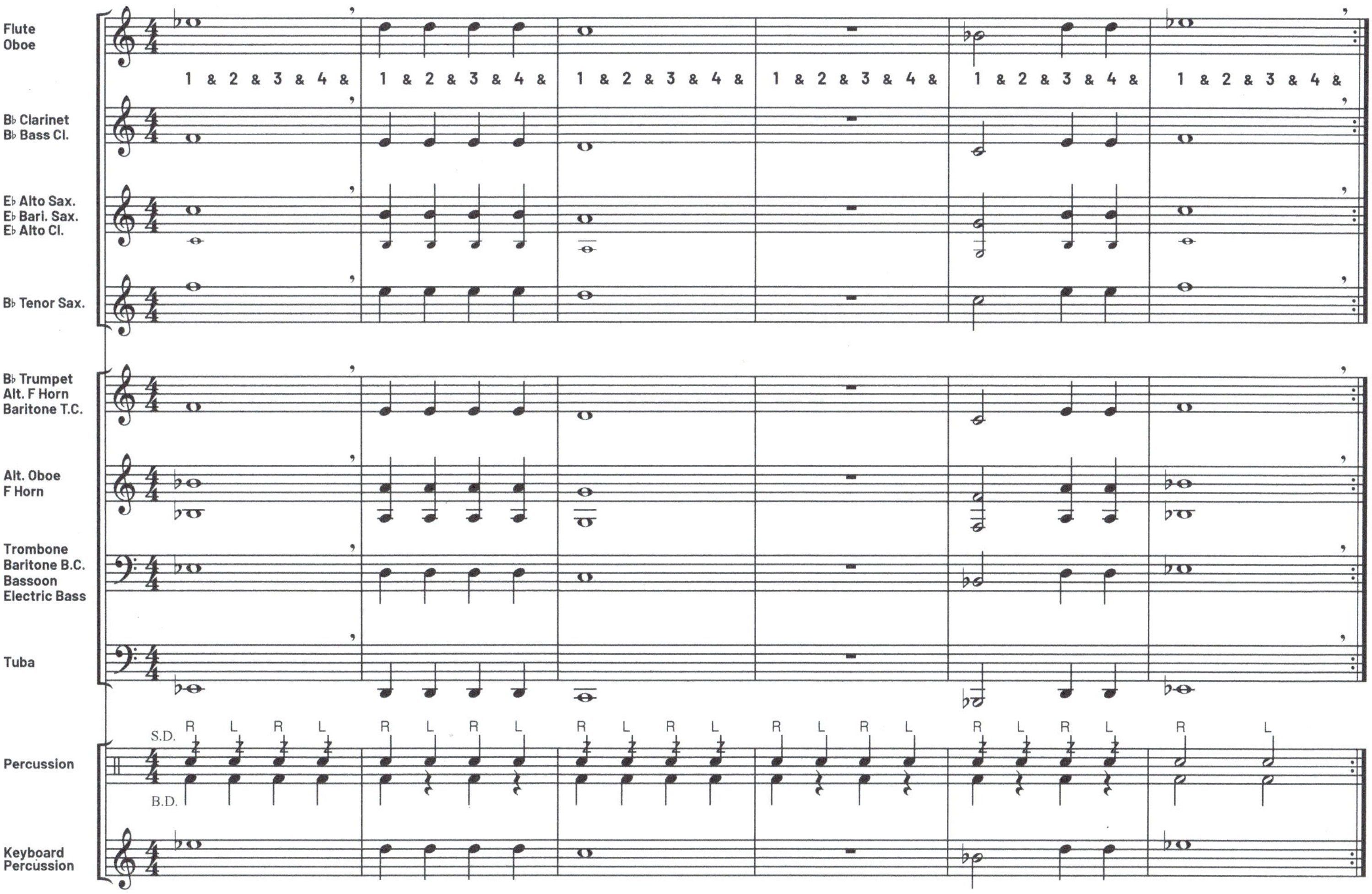

Flute
Oboe

1 & 2 & 3 & 4 &

B♭ Clarinet
B♭ Bass Cl.

E♭ Alto Sax.
E♭ Bari. Sax.
E♭ Alto Cl.

B♭ Tenor Sax.

B♭ Trumpet
Alt. F Horn
Baritone T.C.

Alt. Oboe
F Horn

Trombone
Baritone B.C.
Bassoon
Electric Bass

Tuba

Percussion

S.D. B.D.

R L R L

Keyboard Percussion

Alt. Oboe/Alt. F Horn parts are from Left-side (Oboes only/Horns only) pages.

Duet A composition with two different parts, played together.

This duet emphasizes the similarity of airstreams needed to play a whole note and 4 quarter notes. Practice lines A & B separately. Then divide the class and play as a duet.

22. SPLIT DECISION – Duet

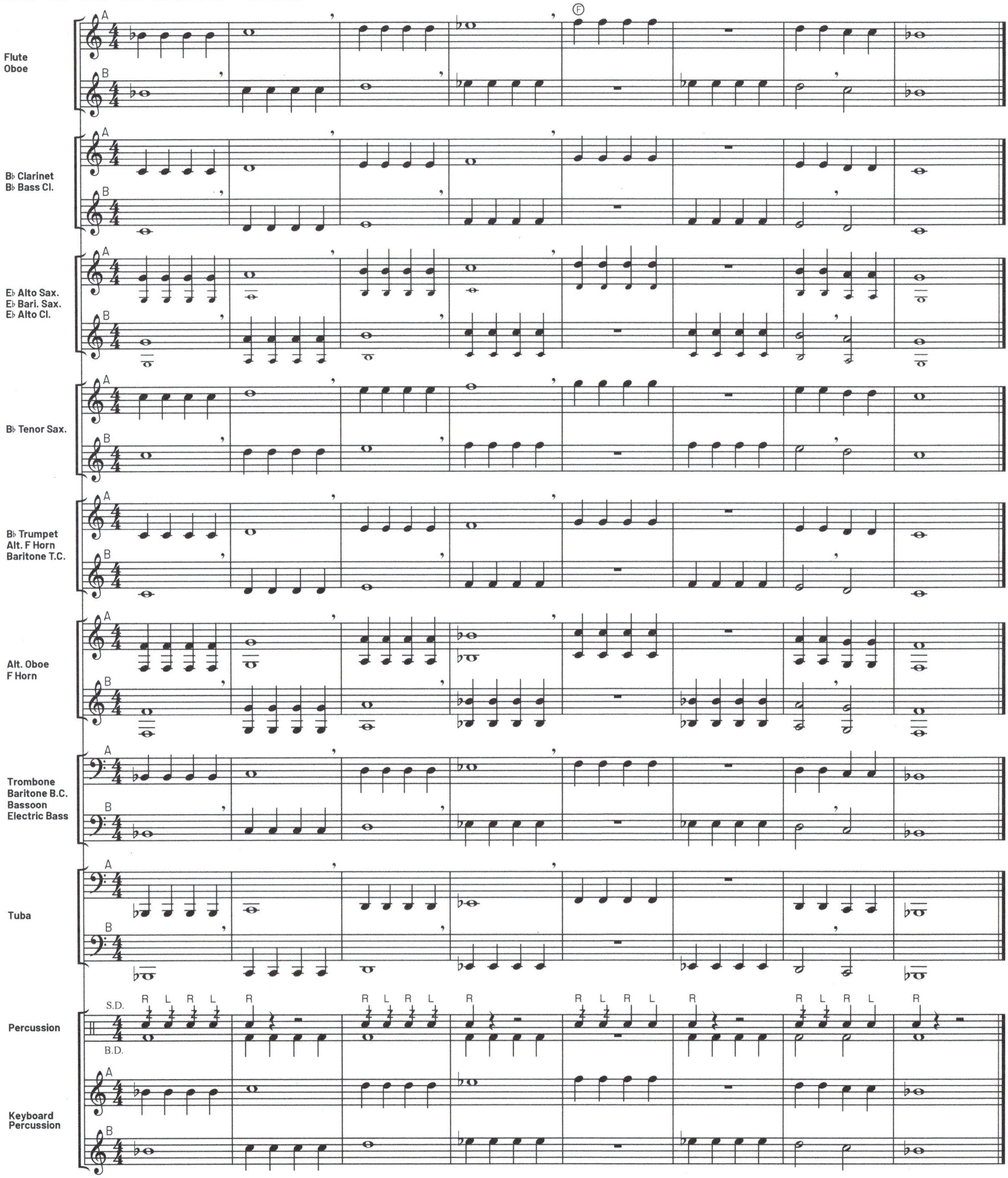

Flute
Oboe

B♭ Clarinet
B♭ Bass Cl.

E♭ Alto Sax.
E♭ Bari. Sax.
E♭ Alto Cl.

B♭ Tenor Sax.

B♭ Trumpet
Alt. F Horn
Baritone T.C.

Alt. Oboe
F Horn

Trombone
Baritone B.C.
Bassoon
Electric Bass

Tuba

Percussion

Keyboard Percussion

Alt. Oboe/Alt. F Horn parts are from Left-side (Oboes only/Horns only) pages.

Percussion Bass Drum When playing half notes, use a slower stroke to *pull* the sound out. Play your percussion part as the brass and woodwinds play their "duet" parts.

Keyboard Percussion Practice this duet with a friend or play both parts yourself.

Key Signature

The **Key Signature** tells us which notes to play with sharps (♯) or flats (♭) throughout the music.

C Instruments  or  Your Key Signature indicates the *Key of B♭* – play all B's as B-flats and all E's as E-flats.

B♭ Instruments  Your Key Signature indicates the *Key of C* (no sharps or flats).

E♭ Instruments  Your Key Signature indicates the *Key of G* – play all F's as F-sharps.

F Horn, Alt. Oboe  Your Key Signature indicates the *Key of F* – play all B's as B-flats.

TEACHING TIP Have students say the note names while performing the fingerings in rhythm before playing.

23. MARCH STEPS

Flute
Oboe

B♭ Clarinet
B♭ Bass Cl.

E♭ Alto Sax.
E♭ Bari. Sax.
E♭ Alto Cl.

B♭ Tenor Sax.

B♭ Trumpet
Alt. F Horn
Baritone T.C.

Alt. Oboe
F Horn

Trombone
Baritone B.C.
Bassoon
Electric Bass

Tuba

Percussion (S.D., B.D.)

Keyboard Percussion

Alt. Oboe/Alt. F Horn parts are from Left-side (Oboes only/Horns only) pages.

Kybd. Perc. **Left Hand Lead** A sticking pattern that begins with the left hand and keeps the left hand on strong beats.

Students must count carefully during rests. Cueing entrances will help students to start together.

24. LISTEN TO OUR SECTIONS

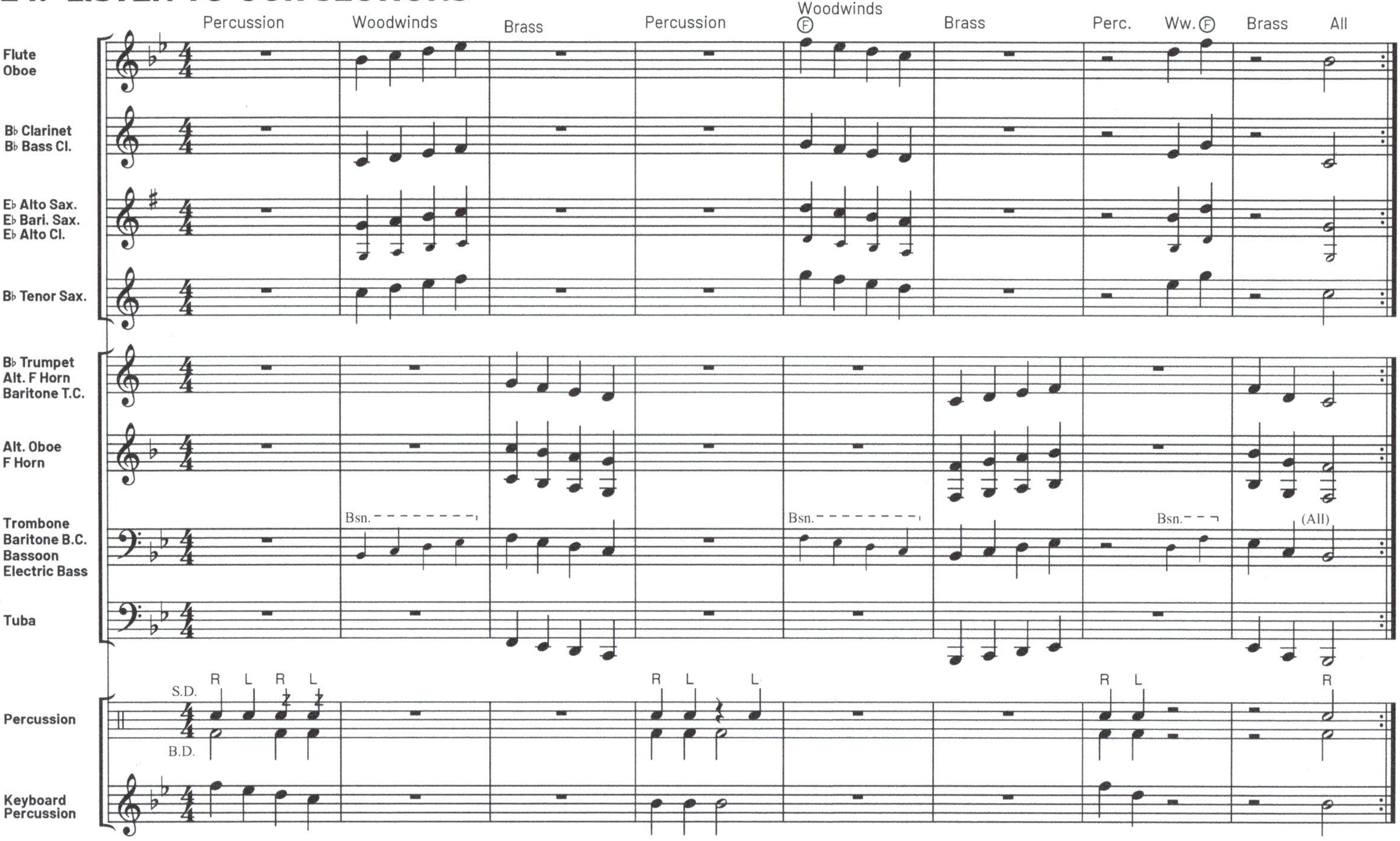

Percussion | Woodwinds | Brass | Percussion | Woodwinds (F) | Brass | Perc. | Ww. (F) | Brass | All

Flute / Oboe
B♭ Clarinet / B♭ Bass Cl.
E♭ Alto Sax. / E♭ Bari. Sax. / E♭ Alto Cl.
B♭ Tenor Sax.
B♭ Trumpet / Alt. F Horn / Baritone T.C.
Alt. Oboe / F Horn
Trombone / Baritone B.C. / Bassoon / Electric Bass (Bsn. … (All))
Tuba
Percussion (S.D., B.D.; R L R L … R L L … R L … R)
Keyboard Percussion

Alt. Oboe/Alt. F Horn parts are from Left-side (Oboes only/Horns only) pages.

Teach this exercise in segments to build endurance.

25. LIGHTLY ROW

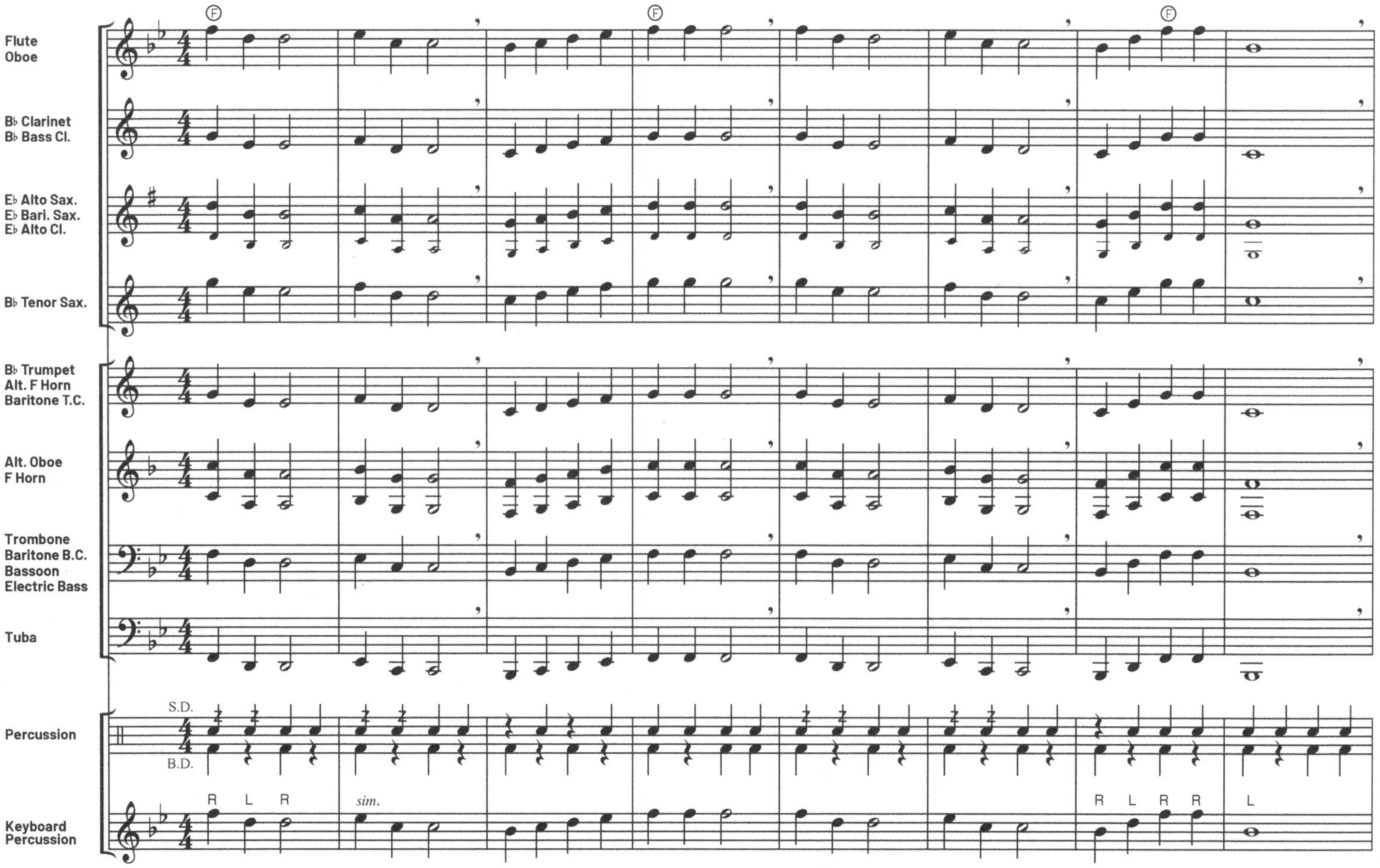

Flute / Oboe
B♭ Clarinet / B♭ Bass Cl.
E♭ Alto Sax. / E♭ Bari. Sax. / E♭ Alto Cl.
B♭ Tenor Sax.
B♭ Trumpet / Alt. F Horn / Baritone T.C.
Alt. Oboe / F Horn
Trombone / Baritone B.C. / Bassoon / Electric Bass
Tuba
Percussion (S.D., B.D.)
Keyboard Percussion (R L R *sim.* … R L R R L)

Percussion Mark your own sticking before you play.

Kybd. Perc. Right Hand Lead.

Flute Oboe
B♭ Clarinet B♭ Bass Cl.
E♭ Alto Sax. E♭ Bari. Sax. E♭ Alto Cl.
B♭ Tenor Sax.
B♭ Trumpet Alt. F Horn Baritone T.C.
Alt. Oboe F Horn
Trombone Baritone B.C. Bassoon Electric Bass
Tuba
Percussion
Keyboard Percussion

R L R R L

Kybd. Perc. **Simile** *(sim.)* Continue playing in the same style. Use right Hand Lead.

QUIZ ASSESSMENT Counting (drawing bar lines), whole note, half rest, key signature (Concert B♭).

26. ESSENTIAL ELEMENTS QUIZ *Draw in the bar lines before you play.*

Flute Oboe
B♭ Clarinet B♭ Bass Cl.
E♭ Alto Sax. E♭ Bari. Sax. E♭ Alto Cl.
B♭ Tenor Sax.
B♭ Trumpet Alt. F Horn Baritone T.C.
Alt. Oboe F Horn
Trombone Baritone B.C. Bassoon Electric Bass
Tuba
Percussion S.D. B.D.
Keyboard Percussion

Alt. Oboe/Alt. F Horn parts are from Left-side (Oboes only/Horns only) pages.

Fermata

Hold the note (or rest) longer than normal.

Percussion

Rudiments

Rudiments are the basic techniques of playing snare drum. You should practice and memorize rudiments to improve your skill. The flam is your first rudiment.

Flam

The small note is a grace note. It has no rhythmic value and sounds just ahead of the regular sized, or primary note. The primary note sounds on the beat.

Right Hand Flam

Hold the left stick about 2 inches above the drum head. Hold the right stick in the "up" position. Move both sticks at the same speed. The left stick will hit the drum just before the right stick. Let the left stick rebound to the "up" position and the right stick rebound to the 2 inch position.

Left Hand Flam

Hold the right stick about 2 inches above the drum head. Hold the left stick in the "up" position. Move both sticks at the same speed. The right stick will hit the drum just before the left stick. Let the right stick rebound to the "up" position and the left stick rebound to the 2 inch position.

A flam produces a sound that is slightly longer than a regular note (a tap). Listen to the difference between flams and taps.

Flute/Kybd. Perc.

Oboe

Alt. Oboe

Bassoon

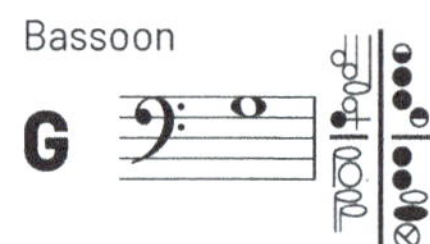

Clarinet

Alto Clarinet

Bass Clarinet

Alto Saxophone

Tenor Saxophone

Baritone Saxophone

Trumpet

F Horn

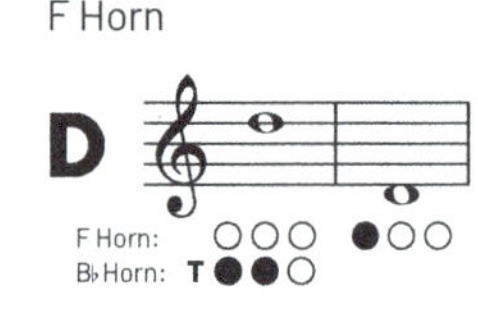

Alt. F Horn

A

F Horn:
B♭ Horn: T

Trombone

Baritone B.C.

Baritone T.C.

Tuba

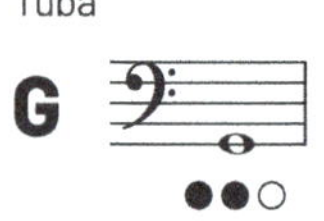

Electric Bass

G

Having brass players buzz "sirens" on their mouthpiece will help build range.

Alt. Oboe Use the half-hole key on "D."

Oboe Ⓡ = "regular" fingering. Use the "regular" fingering for "F." See student page 4B to review this fingering.

Bassoon Use the half-hole key on "G."

Alt. F Horn Double Horn Players: add the thumb key and use the B♭ Horn fingering to play "A."

F Horn Double Horn Players: add the thumb key and use the B♭ Horn fingering for the upper "D."

27. REACHING HIGHER – New Note *Practice long tones on each new note.*

Fermata

Flute
Oboe

B♭ Clarinet
B♭ Bass Cl.

E♭ Alto Sax.
E♭ Bari. Sax.
E♭ Alto Cl.

B♭ Tenor Sax.

B♭ Trumpet
Alt. F Horn
Baritone T.C.

Alt. Oboe
F Horn

Trombone
Baritone B.C.
Bassoon
Electric Bass

Tuba

Percussion

Keyboard
Percussion

Alt. Oboe/Alt. F Horn parts are from Left-side (Oboes only/Horns only) pages.

Student Book Page 8

TEACHING TIP Encourage brass players to increase airspeed as they approach the higher notes.

Oboe Use the "forked" fingering for all "F's" in this exercise. The "forked" fingering makes it easier to play "F" when moving to or from "E♭" or "D." *

Kybd. Perc. Use Left Hand Lead.

28. AU CLAIRE DE LA LUNE

French Folk Song

Flute
Oboe

B♭ Clarinet
B♭ Bass Cl.

E♭ Alto Sax.
E♭ Bari. Sax.
E♭ Alto Cl.

B♭ Tenor Sax.

B♭ Trumpet
Alt. F Horn
Baritone T.C.

Alt. Oboe
F Horn

Trombone
Baritone B.C.
Bassoon
Electric Bass

Tuba

Percussion

Keyboard
Percussion

L R R L L R R L L R L R L L R L L R R L L R R L L R L R L L R L R

L R L R L R *sim.*

TEACHING TIP Breathe only at the breath marks.

29. REMIX

Alt. Oboe/Alt. F Horn parts are from Left-side (Oboes only/Horns only) pages.

** For more information about this fingering, see the oboe fingering chart.*

Harmony Two or more notes played together. Each combination forms a *chord*.

TEACHING TIP Practice lines A & B separately. Then divide the class and play as a duet.

Percussion Mark your own sticking before you play.

30. LONDON BRIDGE – Duet

English Folk Song

Alt. Oboe/Alt. F Horn parts are from Left-side (Oboes only/Horns only) pages.

HISTORY

Austrian composer **Wolfgang Amadeus Mozart** (1756-1791) was a child prodigy who started playing professionally at age six, and lived during the time of the American Revolution. Mozart's music is melodic and imaginative. He wrote more than 600 compositions during his short life, including a piano piece based on the famous song, "Twinkle, Twinkle, Little Star."

TEACHING TIP Say note names while practicing fingerings in rhythm before playing.

Kybd. Perc. Use Double Sticking.

31. A MOZART MELODY

Adaptation

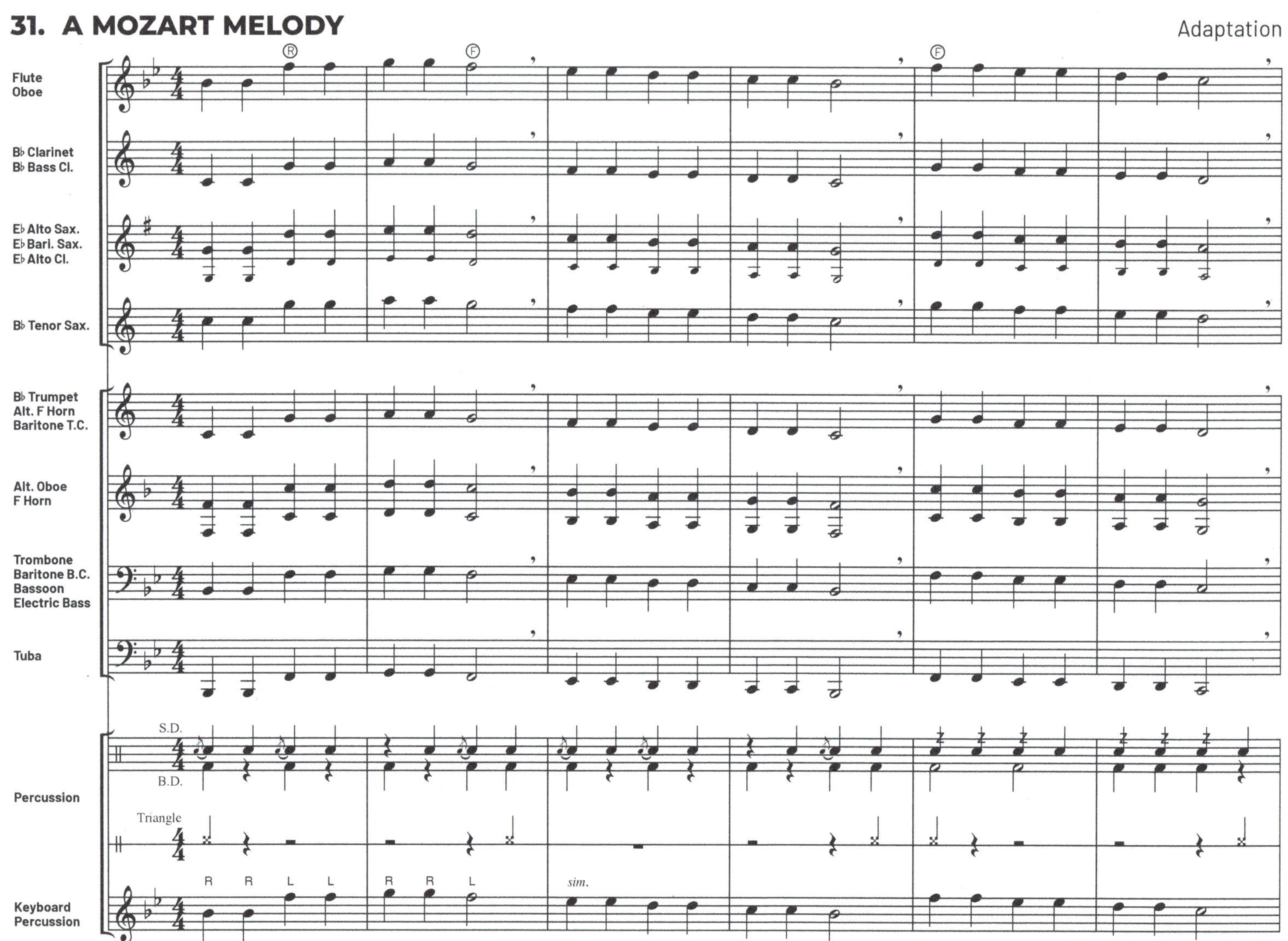

Alt. Oboe/Alt. F Horn parts are from Left-side (Oboes only/Horns only) pages.

Percussion
Triangle

The triangle should be suspended on a clip and held at eye level. Use a metal triangle beater and hit the triangle opposite the open end. To stop the sound, touch the instrument with your fingers. **Tri.** is the abbreviation for triangle.

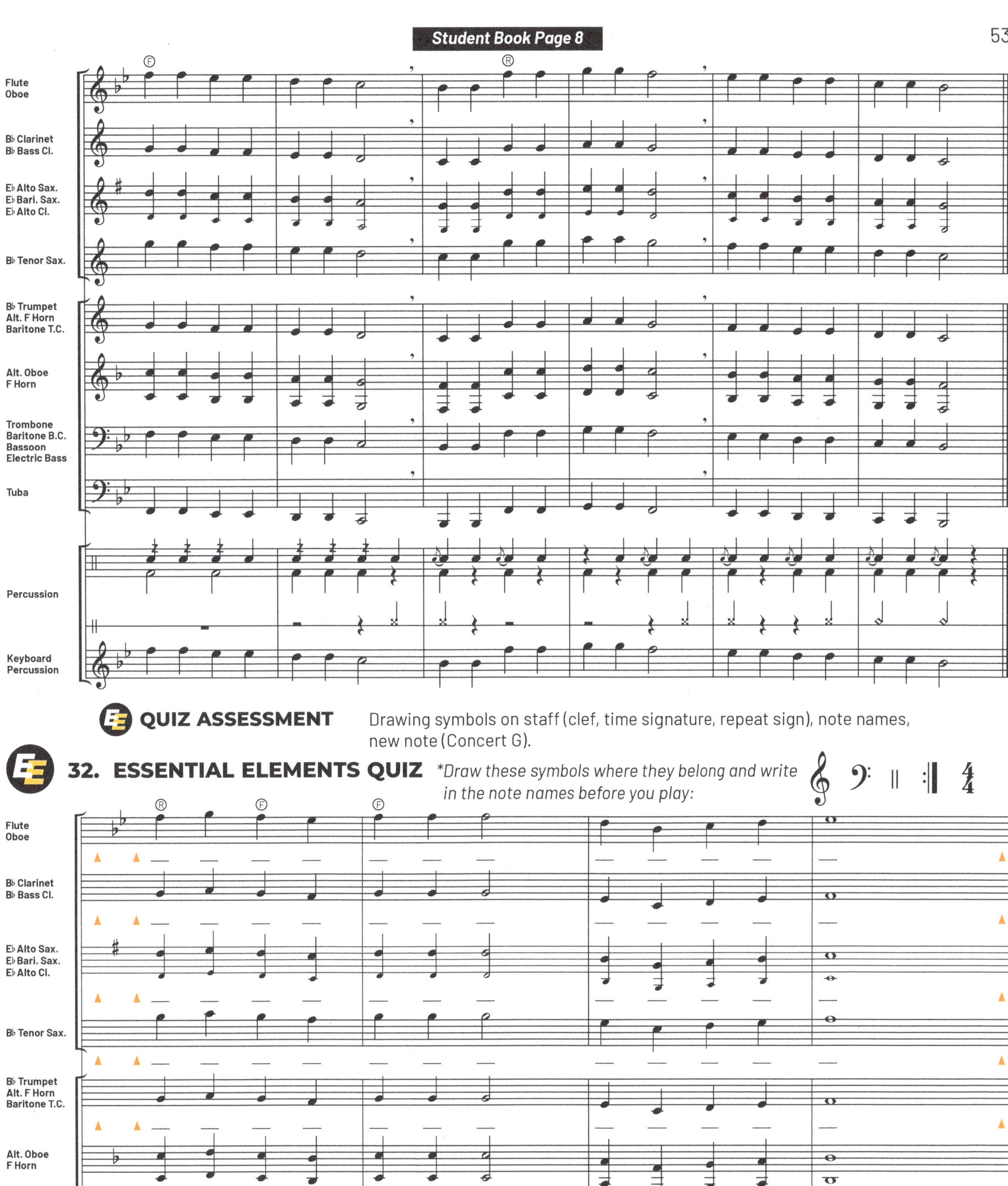

QUIZ ASSESSMENT Drawing symbols on staff (clef, time signature, repeat sign), note names, new note (Concert G).

32. ESSENTIAL ELEMENTS QUIZ

**Draw these symbols where they belong and write in the note names before you play:*

**Percussion can also do the written quiz.*
Alt. Oboe/Alt. F Horn parts are from Left-side (Oboes only/Horns only) pages.

Percussion

Eighth Note & Eighth Rest

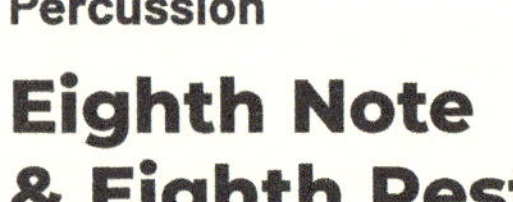

Each Eighth Note or Rest = ½ Beat
2 Eighth Notes or Rests = 1 Beat

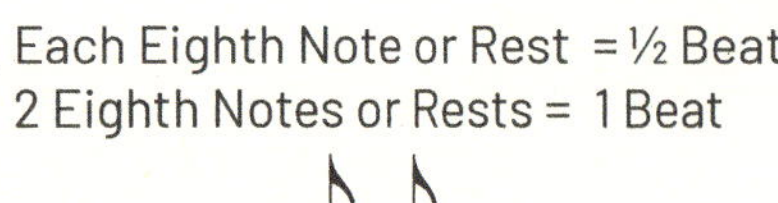

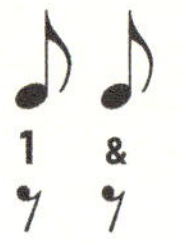

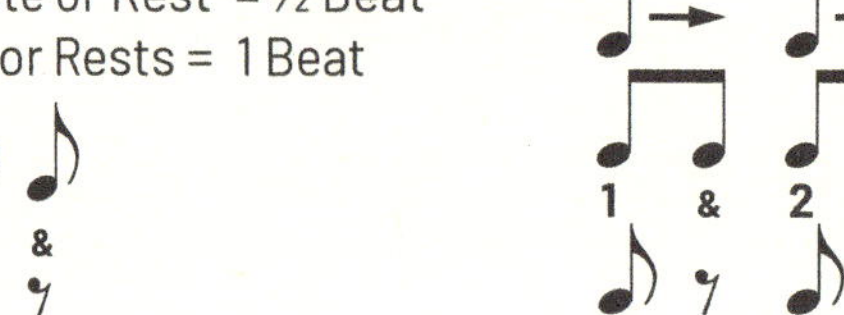

Eighth Note groups have a beam.

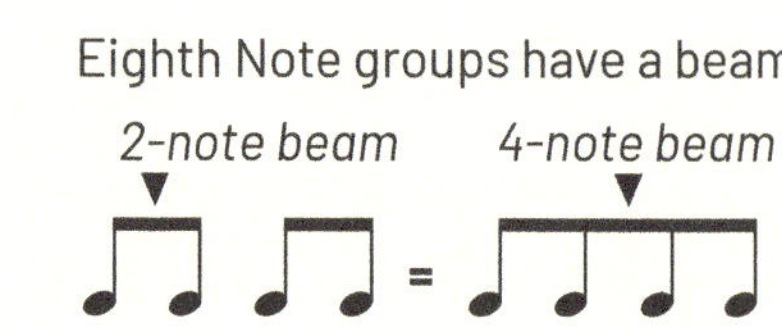

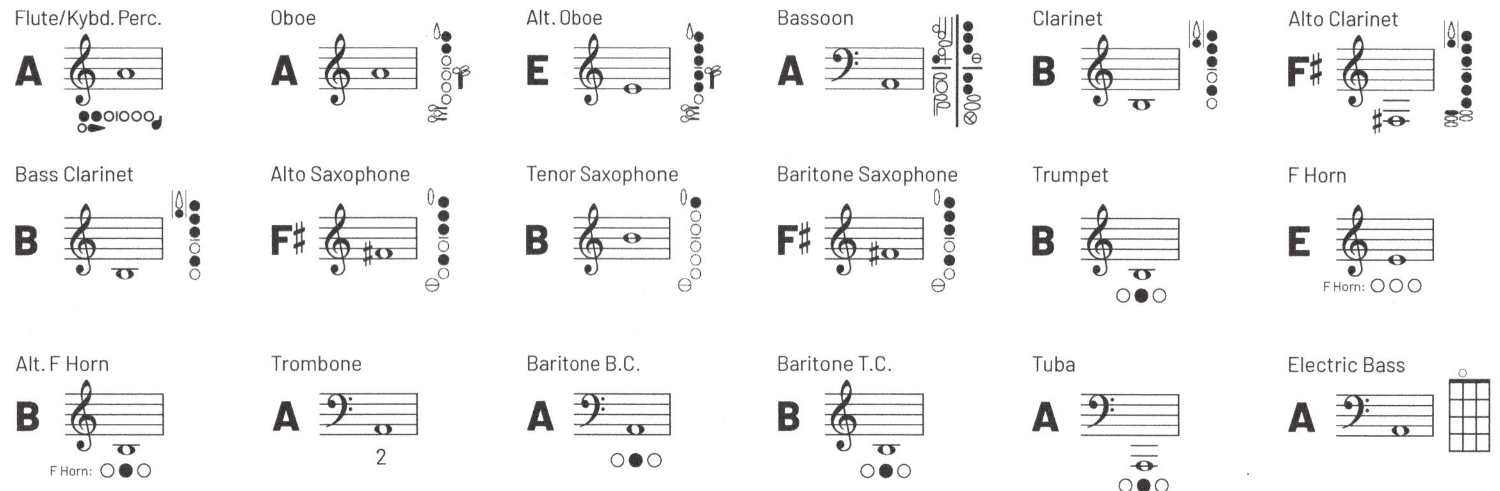

Play the new note before playing this exercise.

33. DEEP POCKETS – New Note

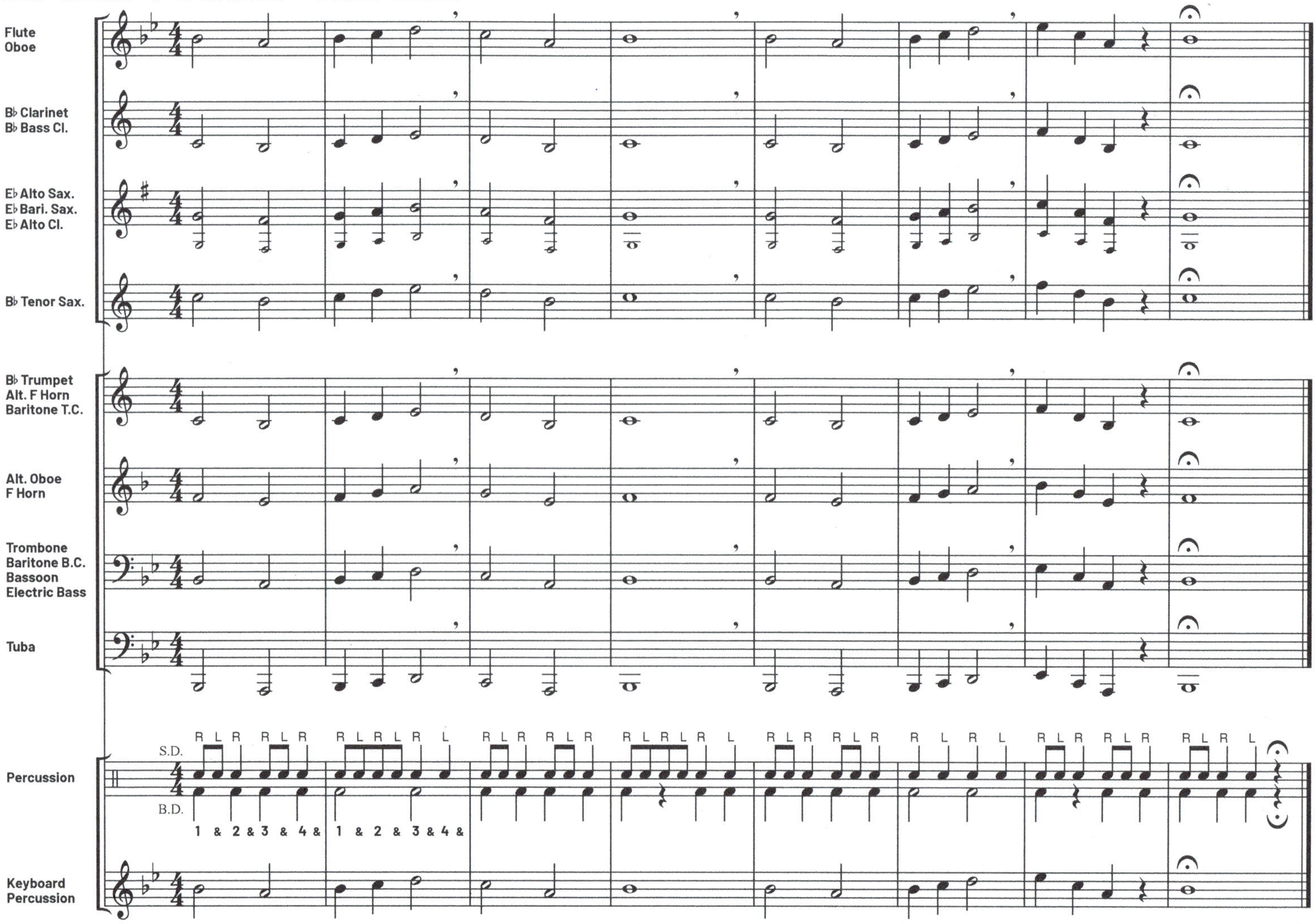

Flute
Oboe

B♭ Clarinet
B♭ Bass Cl.

E♭ Alto Sax.
E♭ Bari. Sax.
E♭ Alto Cl.

B♭ Tenor Sax.

B♭ Trumpet
Alt. F Horn
Baritone T.C.

Alt. Oboe
F Horn

Trombone
Baritone B.C.
Bassoon
Electric Bass

Tuba

Percussion

S.D.
B.D.

R L R R L R | R L R L R L | R L R R L R | R L R L R L | R L R R L R | R L R L | R L R R L R | R L R L

1 & 2 & 3 & 4 & | 1 & 2 & 3 & 4 &

Keyboard
Percussion

Alt. Oboe/Alt. F Horn parts are from Left-side (Oboes only/Horns only) pages.

TEACHING TIP Practice measures 5 and 6 slowly to improve note accuracy.

Percussion Mark the sticking before you play.

Kybd. Perc. Combination Sticking.

34. DOODLE ALL DAY

Flute
Oboe

B♭ Clarinet
B♭ Bass Cl.

E♭ Alto Sax.
E♭ Bari. Sax.
E♭ Alto Cl.

B♭ Tenor Sax.

B♭ Trumpet
Alt. F Horn
Baritone T.C.

Alt. Oboe
F Horn

Trombone
Baritone B.C.
Bassoon
Electric Bass

Tuba

Percussion (S.D., B.D.)

Keyboard Percussion

R R L L | R R L | R R L R | L | R R L L | R R L | R R L R | L

Alt. Oboe/Alt. F Horn parts are from Left-side (Oboes only/Horns only) pages.

Students need to take a very quick breath at the breath mark in measure 6.

Percussion Follow the Double Sticking carefully and strive for a consistent sound.

35. JUMP ROPE

Flute / Oboe; B♭ Clarinet / B♭ Bass Cl.; E♭ Alto Sax. / E♭ Bari. Sax. / E♭ Alto Cl.; B♭ Tenor Sax.; B♭ Trumpet / Alt. F Horn / Baritone T.C.; Alt. Oboe / F Horn; Trombone / Baritone B.C. / Bassoon / Electric Bass / Tuba; Percussion (S.D., B.D.); Keyboard Percussion

R L L R L L R L L R L L R R L R R L R L L R L

R L L R L L R L L R L L R R L R R L R L L R

Alt. Oboe/Alt. F Horn parts are from Left-side (Oboes only/Horns only) pages.

Percussion

Doubling or Double Sticking

A pattern in which two consecutive notes are played with the same hand (R R L L, R R L L). Double Sticking, or Doubling, is an important skill for snare drum.

Pick-Up Notes

One or more notes that come before the first *full* measure.
The beats of Pick-Up Notes are subtracted from the last measure.

TEACHING TIP Conduct 3 preparatory beats and have students count and clap 4 & 1.

Oboe Use the "forked" fingering for all "F's" in this exercise. *

36. A-TISKET, A-TASKET

Pick-up note

Flute Oboe

4 & 1 & 2 & 3 & 4 &

B♭ Clarinet B♭ Bass Cl.

E♭ Alto Sax. E♭ Bari. Sax. E♭ Alto Cl.

B♭ Tenor Sax.

B♭ Trumpet Alt. F Horn Baritone T.C.

Alt. Oboe F Horn

Trombone Baritone B.C. Bassoon Electric Bass Tuba

Percussion S.D. B.D. R R L R L R R *continue*

Keyboard Percussion

Flute Oboe

1 & 2 & 3 &

B♭ Clarinet B♭ Bass Cl.

E♭ Alto Sax. E♭ Bari. Sax. E♭ Alto Cl.

B♭ Tenor Sax.

B♭ Trumpet Alt. F Horn Baritone T.C.

Alt. Oboe F Horn

Trombone Baritone B.C. Bassoon Electric Bass Tuba

Paradiddles R L R R L R L L

Percussion

Keyboard Percussion

Alt. Oboe/Alt. F Horn parts are from Left-side (Oboes only/Horns only) pages.

Percussion Rudiments

Paradiddle

A snare drum rudiment (see measure 7).

** For more information about this fingering, see the oboe fingering chart.*

Dynamics

f - *forte* (play loudly) ***mf*** - *mezzo forte* (play moderately loud) ***p*** - *piano* (play softly)

Remember to use full breath support to control your tone at all dynamic levels.

TEACHING TIP Encourage students to keep a steady beat as they clap and count at various dynamic levels.

37. LOUD AND SOFT

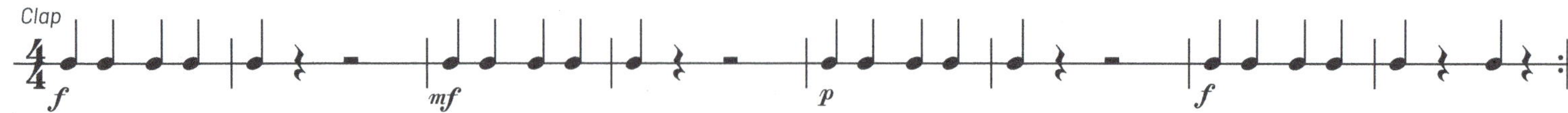

TEACHING TIP Be sure students play familiar melodies "as written" – not as they remember hearing them.

38. JINGLE BELLS

WWs.: Keep your fingers close to the keys, curved naturally.
Brass: Also practice new music on your mouthpiece only.

J. S. Pierpont

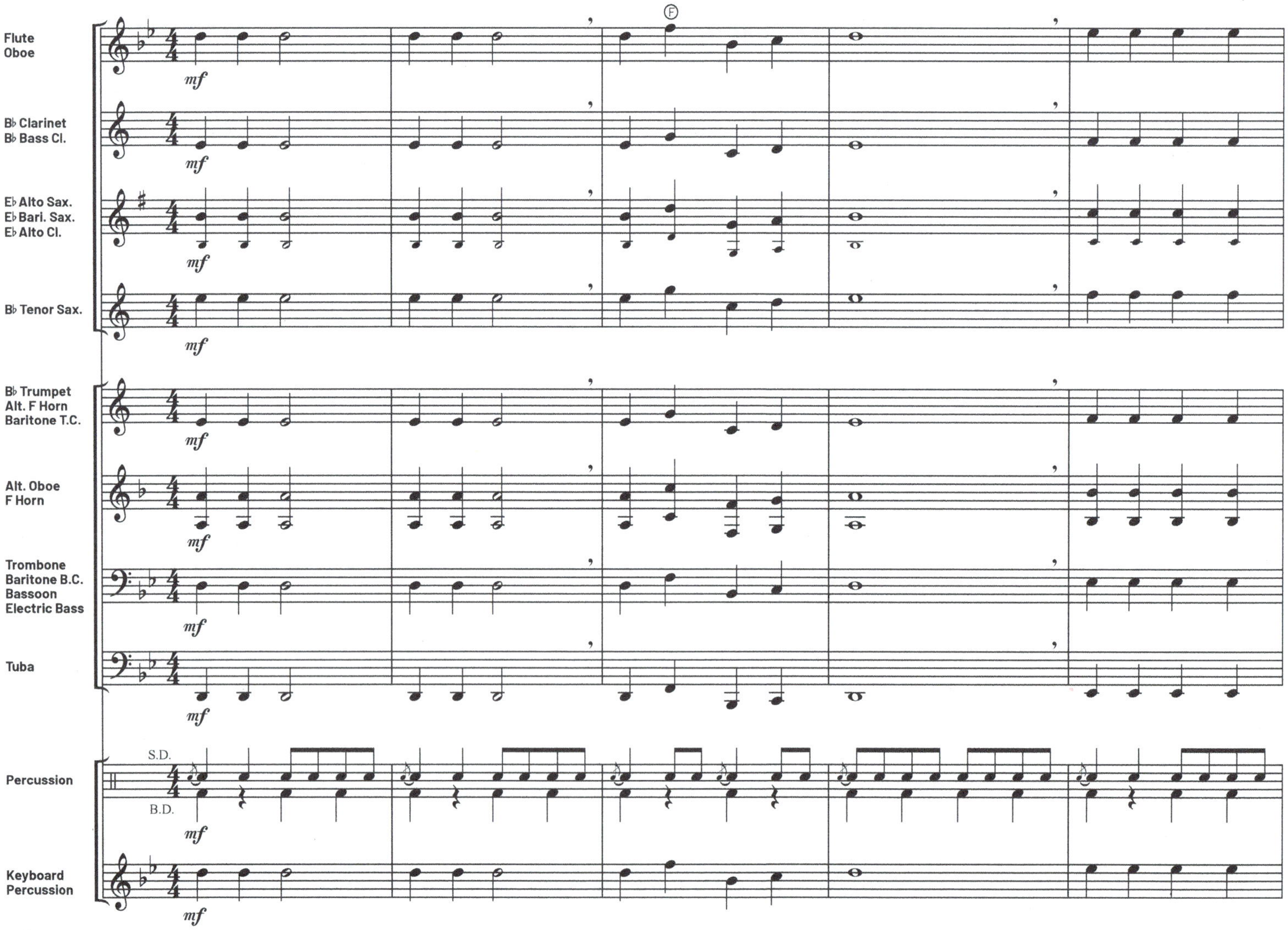

Flute
Oboe

B♭ Clarinet
B♭ Bass Cl.

E♭ Alto Sax.
E♭ Bari. Sax.
E♭ Alto Cl.

B♭ Tenor Sax.

B♭ Trumpet
Alt. F Horn
Baritone T.C.

Alt. Oboe
F Horn

Trombone
Baritone B.C.
Bassoon
Electric Bass

Tuba

Percussion

S.D.
B.D.

Keyboard
Percussion

mf

F

Alt. Oboe/Alt. F Horn parts are from Left-side (Oboes only/Horns only) pages.

Flute
Oboe

B♭ Clarinet
B♭ Bass Cl.

E♭ Alto Sax.
E♭ Bari. Sax.
E♭ Alto Cl.

B♭ Tenor Sax.

B♭ Trumpet
Alt. F Horn
Baritone T.C.

Alt. Oboe
F Horn

Trombone
Baritone B.C.
Bassoon
Electric Bass

Tuba

Percussion

Keyboard
Percussion

Flute
Oboe

B♭ Clarinet
B♭ Bass Cl.

E♭ Alto Sax.
E♭ Bari. Sax.
E♭ Alto Cl.

B♭ Tenor Sax.

B♭ Trumpet
Alt. F Horn
Baritone T.C.

Alt. Oboe
F Horn

Trombone
Baritone B.C.
Bassoon
Electric Bass

Tuba

Percussion

Keyboard
Percussion

Student Book Page 9

Percussion Practice "Doubling" in this exercise.

39. MY DREYDL *Use full breath support at all dynamic levels.*

Traditional Hanukkah Song

Alt. Oboe/Alt. F Horn parts are from Left-side (Oboes only/Horns only) pages.

Flute
Oboe
B♭ Clarinet
B♭ Bass Cl.
E♭ Alto Sax.
E♭ Bari. Sax.
E♭ Alto Cl.
B♭ Tenor Sax.
B♭ Trumpet
Alt. F Horn
Baritone T.C.
Alt. Oboe
F Horn
Trombone
Baritone B.C.
Bassoon
Electric Bass
Tuba
Percussion
Keyboard
Percussion
F
L R L R L R L R L R R L L R

Eighth Notes

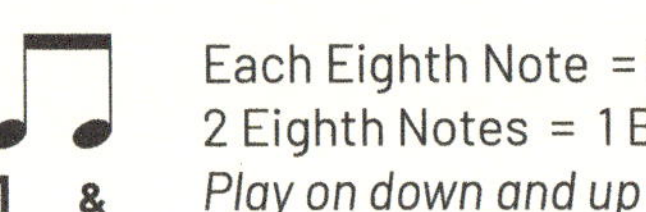

Each Eighth Note = ½ Beat
2 Eighth Notes = 1 Beat
Play on down and up taps.

Two or more Eighth Notes have a *beam* across the stems.

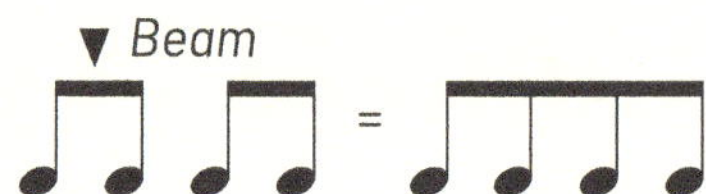

TEACHING TIP Teach this clapping exercise one measure at a time, counting and tapping the beats.

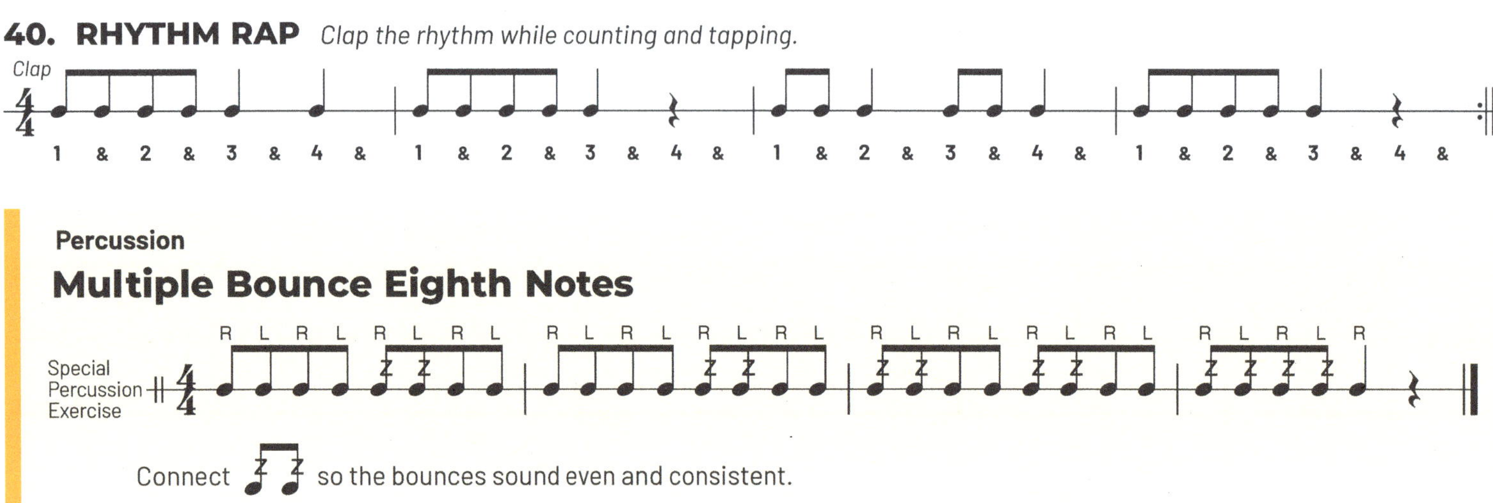

TEACHING TIP Have half the class count and tap while the other half plays – then switch.

41. EIGHTH NOTE JAM

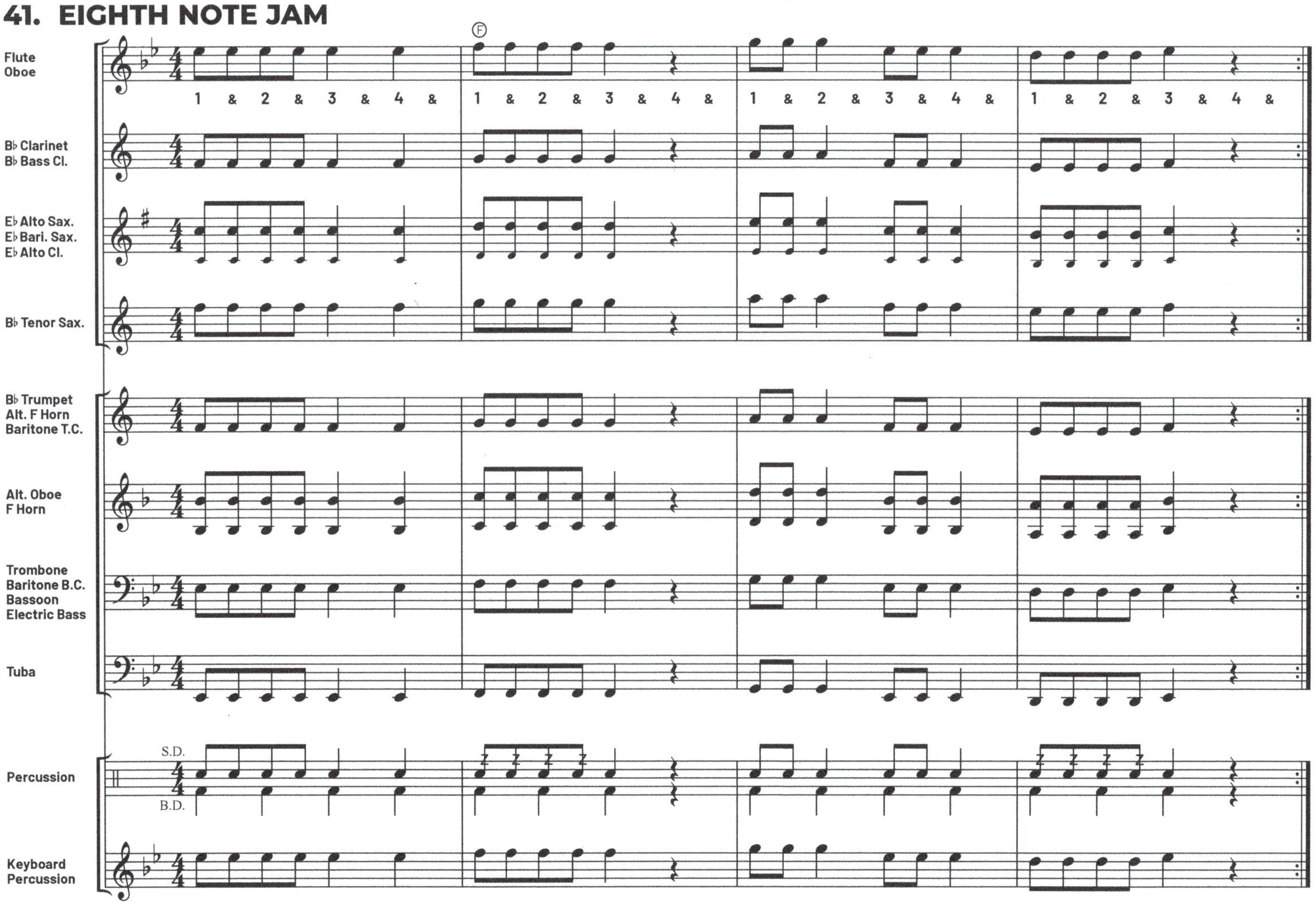

F

Flute
Oboe

1 & 2 & 3 & 4 & 1 & 2 & 3 & 4 & 1 & 2 & 3 & 4 & 1 & 2 & 3 & 4 &

B♭ Clarinet
B♭ Bass Cl.

E♭ Alto Sax.
E♭ Bari. Sax.
E♭ Alto Cl.

B♭ Tenor Sax.

B♭ Trumpet
Alt. F Horn
Baritone T.C.

Alt. Oboe
F Horn

Trombone
Baritone B.C.
Bassoon
Electric Bass

Tuba

Percussion
S.D.
B.D.

Keyboard
Percussion

Alt. Oboe/Alt. F Horn parts are from Left-side (Oboes only/Horns only) pages.

TEACHING TIP Have students write in the counting for this exercise.

Kybd. Perc. Use Alternate Sticking.

42. SKIP TO MY LOU

American Folk Song

Alt. Oboe/Alt. F Horn parts are from Left-side (Oboes only/Horns only) pages.

Percussion **Suspended Cymbal** One single cymbal suspended on a stand. Always use yarn mallets, not timpani mallets. **Sus. Cym.** is the abbreviation for suspended cymbal.

TEACHING TIP When students play soft dynamics, encourage them to use a steady airstream and good tone.

43. LONG, LONG AGO

Good posture improves your sound. Always sit straight and tall.

Flute
Oboe

B♭ Clarinet
B♭ Bass Cl.

E♭ Alto Sax.
E♭ Bari. Sax.
E♭ Alto Cl.

B♭ Tenor Sax.

B♭ Trumpet
Alt. F Horn
Baritone T.C.

Alt. Oboe
F Horn

Trombone
Baritone B.C.
Bassoon
Electric Bass

Tuba

Percussion (S.D., B.D.)

Keyboard
Percussion

Alt. Oboe/Alt. F Horn parts are from Left-side (Oboes only/Horns only) pages.

Percussion

Wood Block
(Ex.44)

Cup your palm to form a resonating chamber under the wood block.

Curved wood block—strike on top near the center using a hard rubber mallet or snare drum stick if necessary.

Flat wood block—the best sound is toward the edge of the top surface near the side with the open slit. You should use a hard rubber mallet or a wooden xylophone mallet. A drumstick does not produce a good sound on a flat wood block.

Wd. Blk. is the abbreviation for wood block.

TEACHING TIP Review pick-up notes before playing this exercise.

44. CANDY MOUNTAIN ROCK

Flute
Oboe

B♭ Clarinet
B♭ Bass Cl.

E♭ Alto Sax.
E♭ Bari. Sax.
E♭ Alto Cl.

B♭ Tenor Sax.

B♭ Trumpet
Alt. F Horn
Baritone T.C.

Alt. Oboe
F Horn

Trombone
Baritone B.C.
Bassoon
Electric Bass

Tuba

Percussion
S.D.
B.D.
Wood Block

Keyboard
Percussion

f

Flute
Oboe

B♭ Clarinet
B♭ Bass Cl.

E♭ Alto Sax.
E♭ Bari. Sax.
E♭ Alto Cl.

B♭ Tenor Sax.

B♭ Trumpet
Alt. F Horn
Baritone T.C.

Alt. Oboe
F Horn

Trombone
Baritone B.C.
Bassoon
Electric Bass

Tuba

Percussion

Keyboard
Percussion

Alt. Oboe/Alt. F Horn parts are from Left-side (Oboes only/Horns only) pages.

HISTORY

Italian composer **Gioachino Rossini** (1792–1868) began composing as a teenager and was very proficient on the piano, viola and horn. He wrote "William Tell" at age 37 as the last of his forty operas, and its familiar theme is still heard today on radio and television.

QUIZ ASSESSMENT

Eighth notes, pick-up notes, dynamic (*mf*, *f*), breath mark, reading two lines of music.

45. ESSENTIAL ELEMENTS QUIZ — WILLIAM TELL

Gioachino Rossini

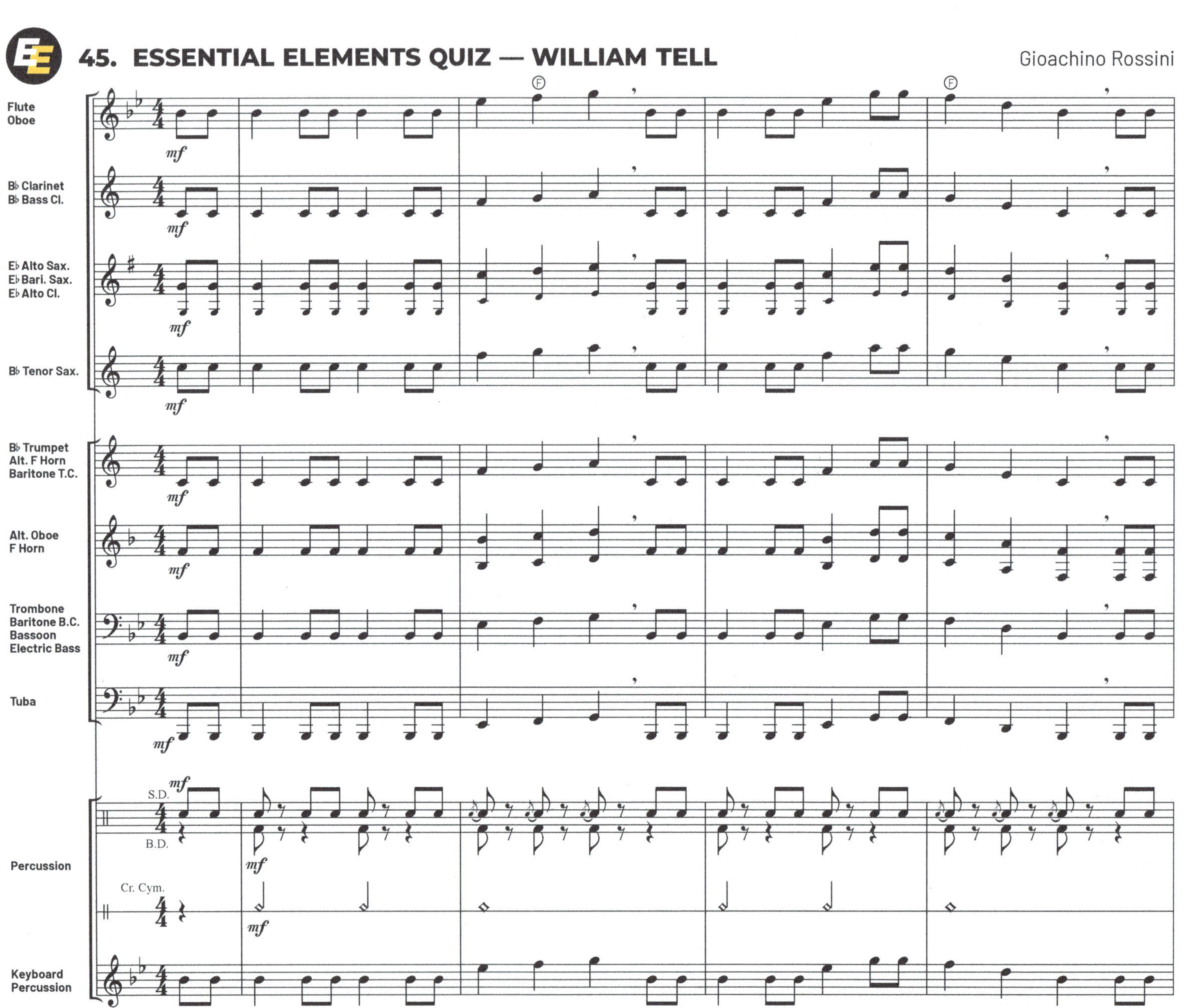

Alt. Oboe/Alt. F Horn parts are from Left-side (Oboes only/Horns only) pages.

Percussion
Crash Cymbals

Hold the left cymbal in front of you at a slight angle. Allow the right cymbal to be positioned slightly above and slightly in front of the left cymbal.

Learn the basic stroke for a quarter note. Using a glancing stroke (and gravity), allow the right cymbal to drop into the left cymbal and follow through. This same motion is used for half notes, but slower in speed. For whole notes, the same motion is slower than for half notes.

To stop the sound of the cymbals, bring both edges of the plates against your body.

Choke = muffle (or stop) the sound immediately.

Cr. Cym. is the abbreviation for crash cymbals.

THEORY

$\frac{2}{4}$ Time Signature

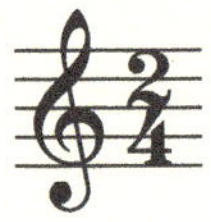

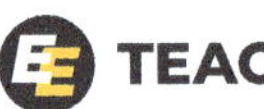

= **2 beats** per measure
= **Quarter** note gets one beat

Conducting

Practice conducting this two-beat pattern.

1
2

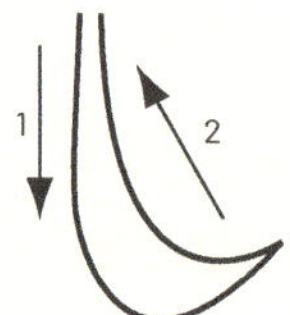

TEACHING TIP Have students say "rest and" during the quarter rests in measures 5 and 6.

46. RHYTHM RAP

Clap
1 & 2 & 1 & 2 & 1 & 2 & 1 & 2 & 1 & 2 & 1 & 2 & 1 & 2 & 1 & 2 &

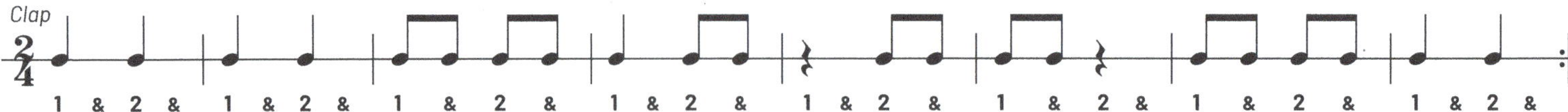

Percussion

Rudiment

Flam Tap

R R L L

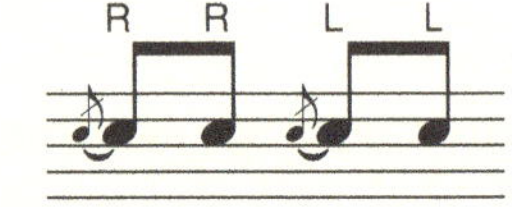

After you play a flam, play a tap, always with the low hand. This will keep your hands correctly positioned for the rest of the exercise. Remember, a tap is played with the stick closest to the drum head.

Be careful to maintain the same tempo when going from flam taps (measures 1 and 2) to the regular flams in measure 3.

Solo In ensemble music, *Solo* marks a passage where one instrument takes a leading part. In the next exercise, the Bass Drum is featured in the places marked *Solo*.

TEACHING TIP Remind students to play the same rhythm they clapped in exercise 46.

47. TWO BY TWO

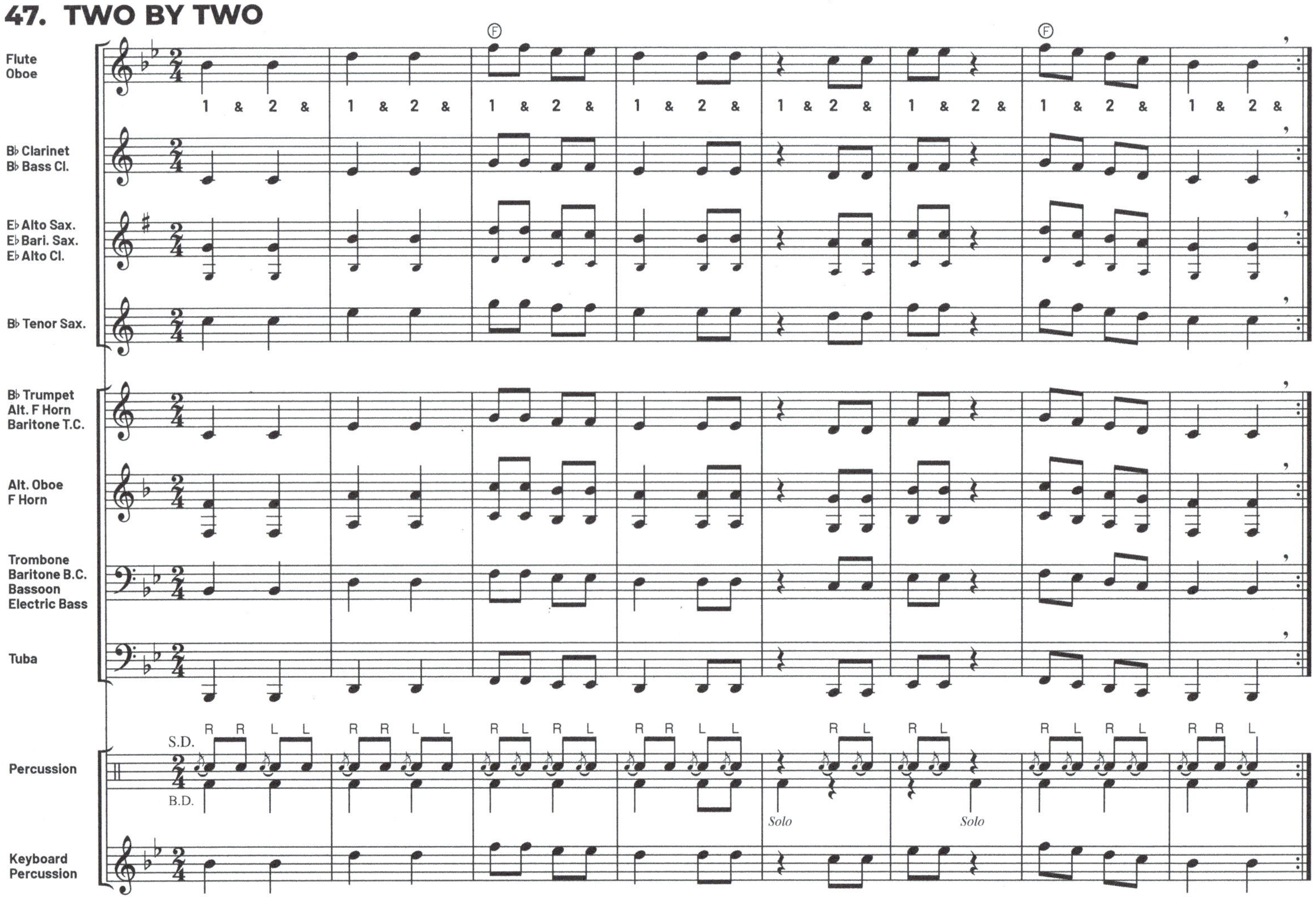
Flute
Oboe
B♭ Clarinet
B♭ Bass Cl.
E♭ Alto Sax.
E♭ Bari. Sax.
E♭ Alto Cl.
B♭ Tenor Sax.
B♭ Trumpet
Alt. F Horn
Baritone T.C.
Alt. Oboe
F Horn
Trombone
Baritone B.C.
Bassoon
Electric Bass
Tuba
Percussion
S.D.
B.D.
Solo
Solo
Keyboard Percussion

Alt. Oboe/Alt. F Horn parts are from Left-side (Oboes only/Horns only) pages.

Tempo Markings

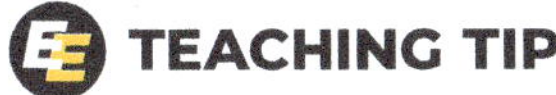

Tempo is the speed of music. Tempo markings are usually written above the staff, in Italian.
Allegro – Fast tempo **Moderato** – Medium tempo **Andante** – Slower walking tempo

TEACHING TIP

Play this exercise at a slower tempo, gradually increasing to allegro.

Percussion Use a slower motion on half note crashes.

48. HIGH SCHOOL CADETS – March

John Philip Sousa

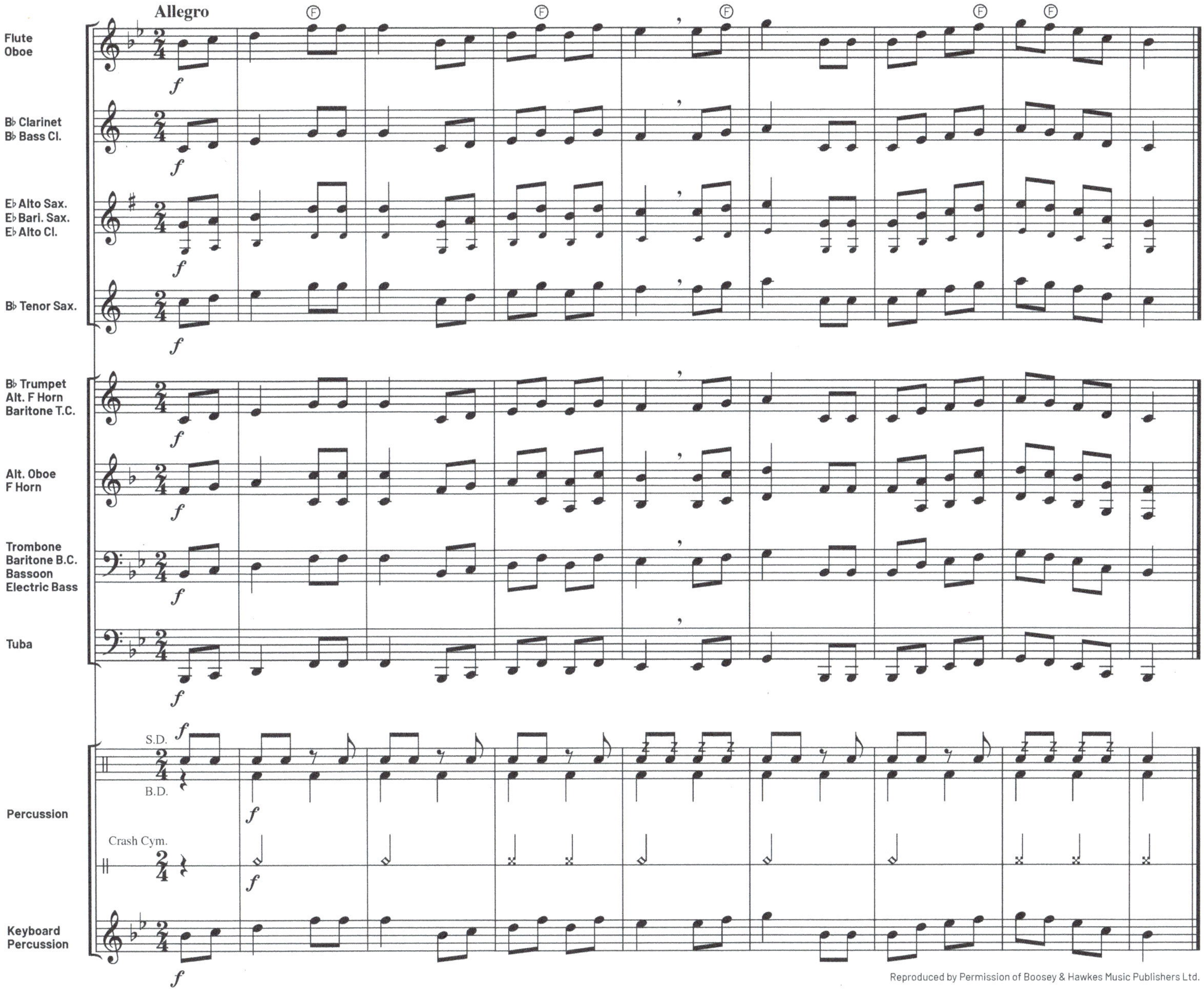
Allegro
Flute
Oboe
B♭ Clarinet
B♭ Bass Cl.
E♭ Alto Sax.
E♭ Bari. Sax.
E♭ Alto Cl.
B♭ Tenor Sax.
B♭ Trumpet
Alt. F Horn
Baritone T.C.
Alt. Oboe
F Horn
Trombone
Baritone B.C.
Bassoon
Electric Bass
Tuba
S.D.
B.D.
Percussion
Crash Cym.
Keyboard
Percussion

Alt. Oboe/Alt. F Horn parts are from Left-side (Oboes only/Horns only) pages.

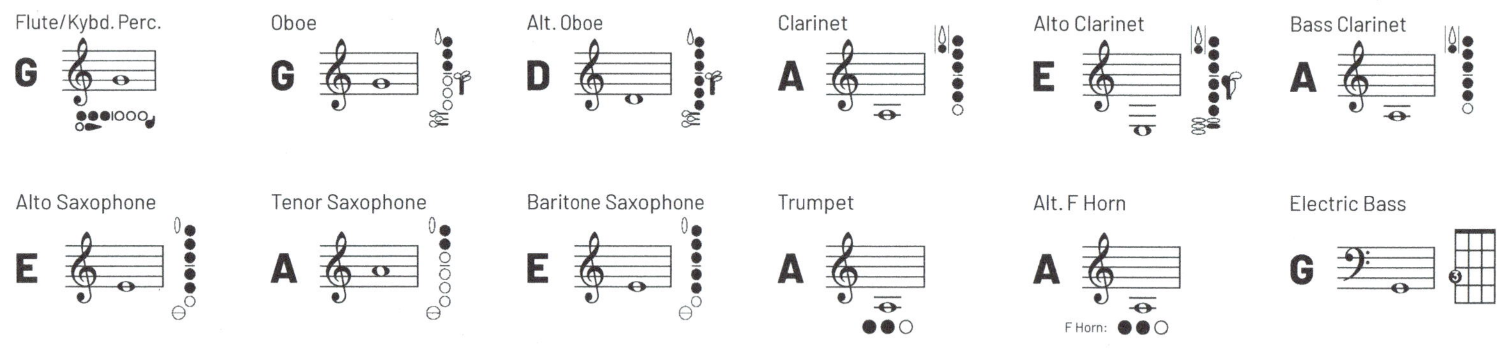

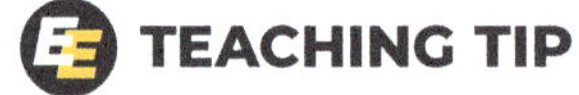

Flute/Kybd. Perc.
G
Oboe
G
Alt. Oboe
D
Clarinet
A
Alto Clarinet
E
Bass Clarinet
A
Alto Saxophone
E
Tenor Saxophone
A
Baritone Saxophone
E
Trumpet
A
Alt. F Horn
A
F Horn:
Electric Bass
G

TEACHING TIP Play the new note before playing this exercise.

49. HEY, HO! NOBODY'S HOME – New Note

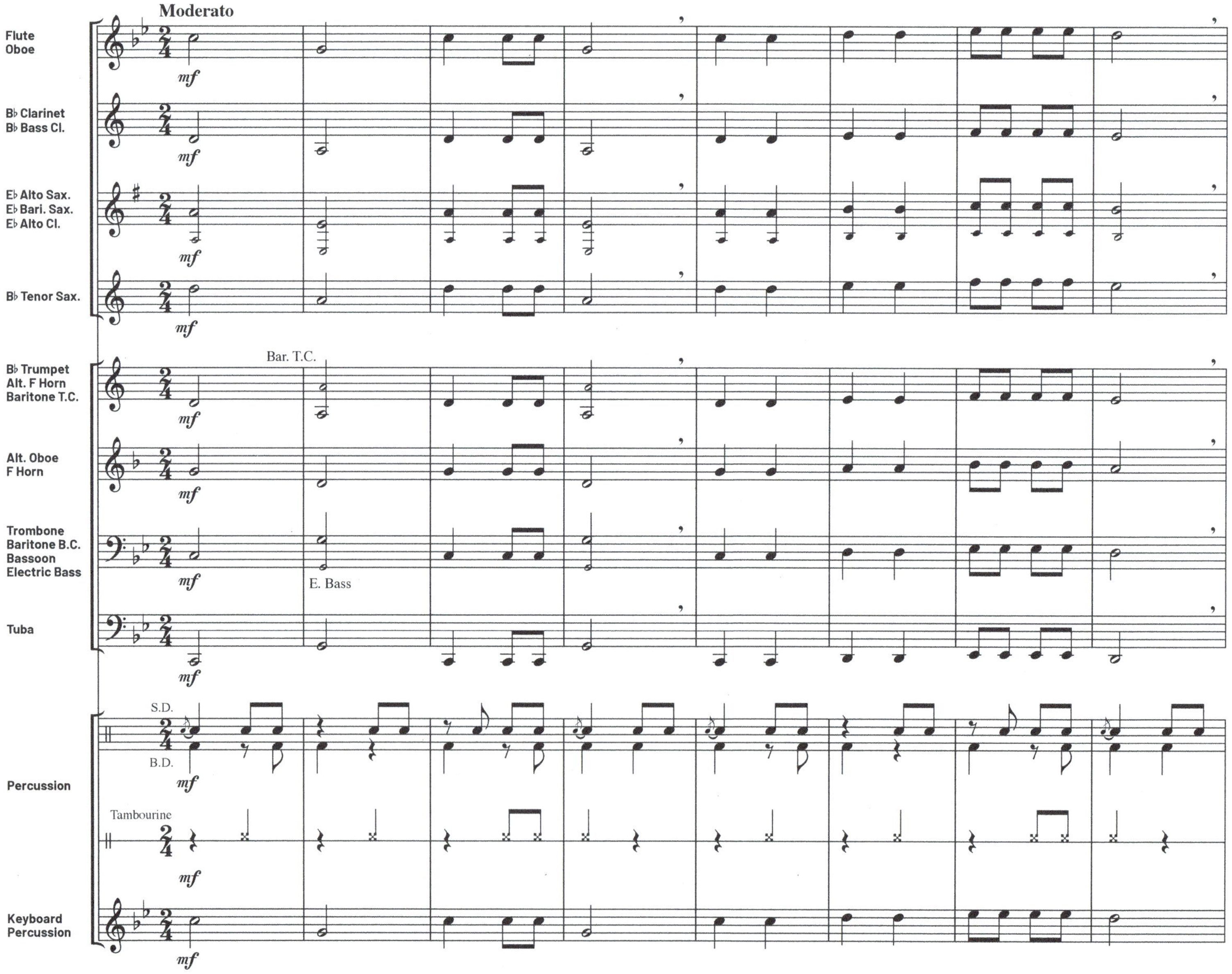
Moderato
Flute
Oboe
B♭ Clarinet
B♭ Bass Cl.
E♭ Alto Sax.
E♭ Bari. Sax.
E♭ Alto Cl.
B♭ Tenor Sax.
B♭ Trumpet
Alt. F Horn
Baritone T.C.
Bar. T.C.
Alt. Oboe
F Horn
Trombone
Baritone B.C.
Bassoon
Electric Bass
E. Bass
Tuba
S.D.
B.D.
Percussion
Tambourine
Keyboard
Percussion
mf

Alt. Oboe/Alt. F Horn parts are from Left-side (Oboes only/Horns only) pages.

Percussion
Tambourine

Hold the tambourine steady in your left hand at a slight upward angle.
Your right hand strikes the head of the instrument according to the written dynamics:

Soft light sounds use one or two fingertips near the edge of the head.

Medium loud sounds use tips of all fingers one-third of the way from the edge to the center.

Loud sounds knuckles on head, half-way between edge and the center.
Use a motion similar to knocking on a door.

Dynamics

Crescendo (gradually louder) **_Decrescendo_** or **_Diminuendo_** (gradually softer)

Remind students to keep a steady tempo as they gradually change the volume.

50. CLAP THE DYNAMICS

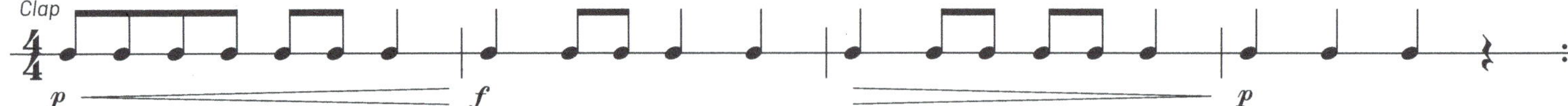

Percussion
Suspended Cymbal Roll

With yarn mallets on a suspended cymbal, use a rapid series of alternate strokes on the opposite edges of the cymbal (3 o'clock and 9 o'clock). Increase the speed of the roll to build an effective crescendo.

TEACHING TIP Encourage students to play with a good tone at all dynamic levels.

51. PLAY THE DYNAMICS

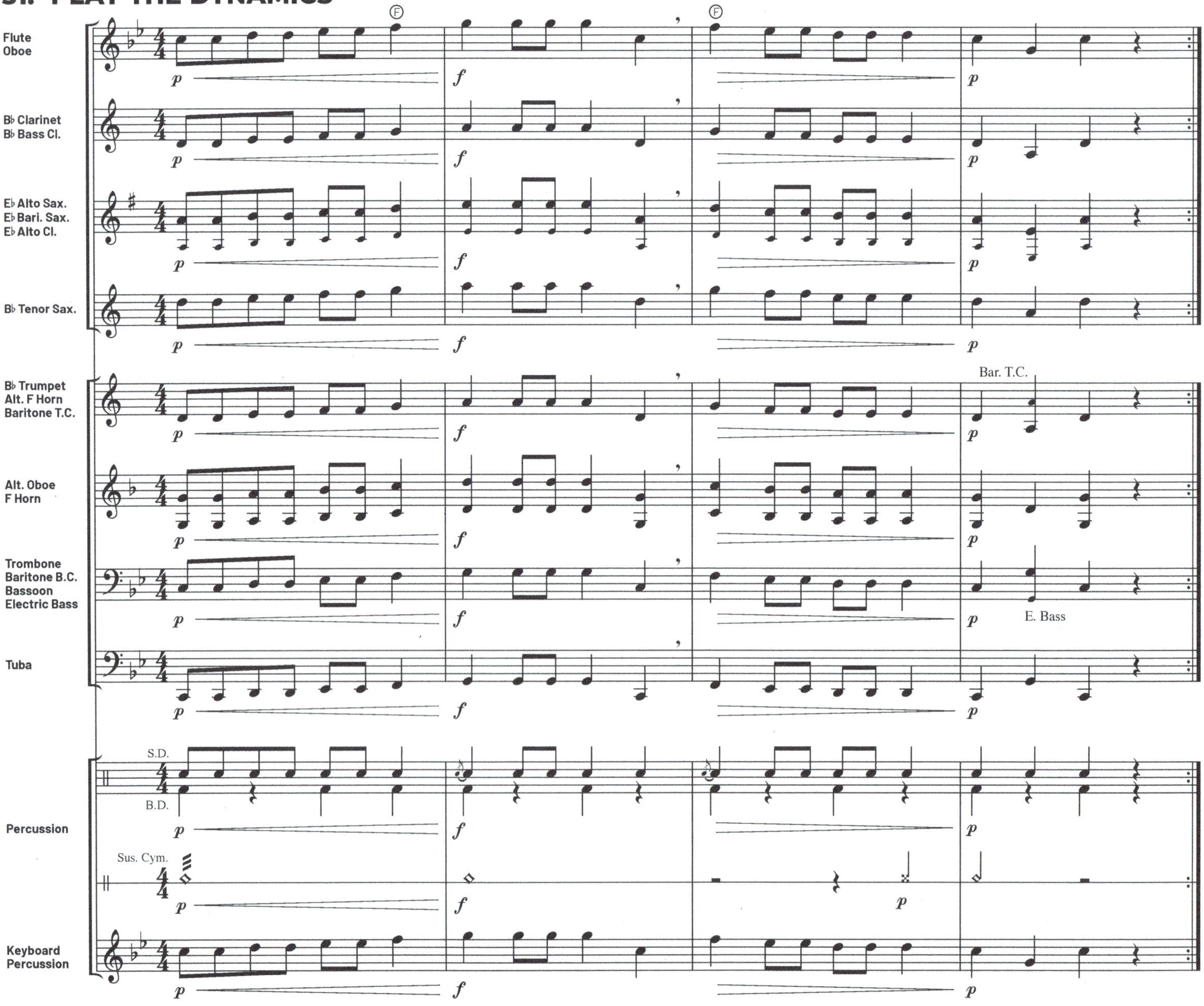

Flute
Oboe

B♭ Clarinet
B♭ Bass Cl.

E♭ Alto Sax.
E♭ Bari. Sax.
E♭ Alto Cl.

B♭ Tenor Sax.

B♭ Trumpet
Alt. F Horn
Baritone T.C.

Alt. Oboe
F Horn

Trombone
Baritone B.C.
Bassoon
Electric Bass

Tuba

Percussion

Keyboard
Percussion

S.D.
B.D.
Sus. Cym.
Bar. T.C.
E. Bass

Alt. Oboe/Alt. F Horn parts are from Left-side (Oboes only/Horns only) pages.

Looking for some more fun music to play?
See the inside front cover for instructions on accessing recent popular Bonus Songs.

The following special pages appear just before
page 12 in the Oboe and F Horn books:
11C, 11D - Oboes only
11C, 11D - Horns only
For students who have followed the Left-side
(Oboes only/Horns only) pages 4A through 11A,
these "Range Builder" pages introduce the new notes
and key signature needed to play with the full band
from page 12 to the end.

Director For those oboe students who have followed the "Left-side" pages (4A–11A), exercises 52C–61D teach the four remaining notes necessary to play with the full band from student book page 12 to the end. Accompaniments for exercises 52C–61D appear in the "Left-side" (Oboes only) play-along tracks.

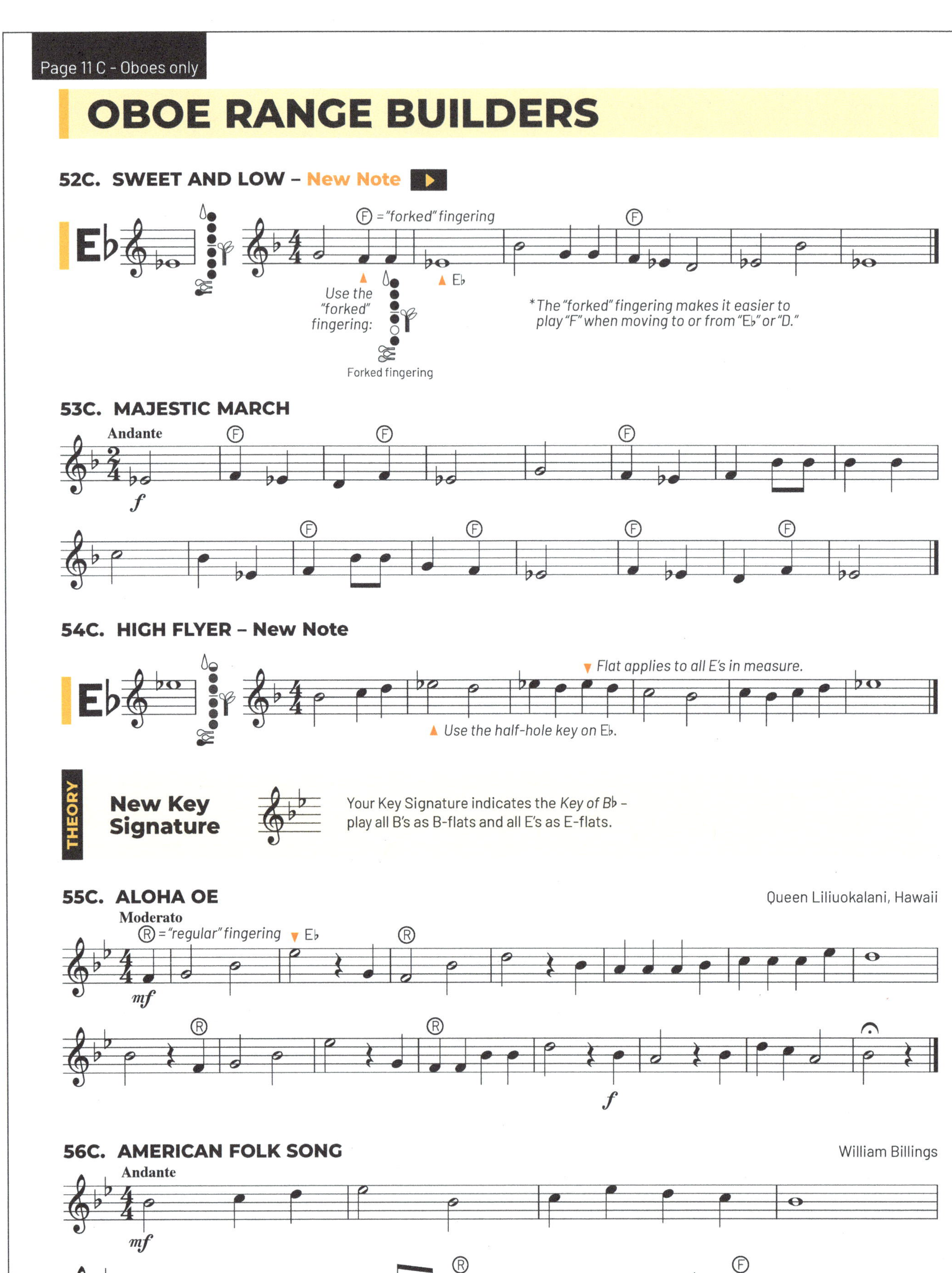

Page 11 D - Oboes only

OBOE RANGE BUILDERS

57D. HIGH SEAS – New Note

Ⓕ = "forked" fingering.
Ⓡ = "regular" fingering.

*The "forked" fingering makes it easier to play "F" when moving to or from "E♭" or "D."

58D. MARIANNE

Jamaican Folk Song

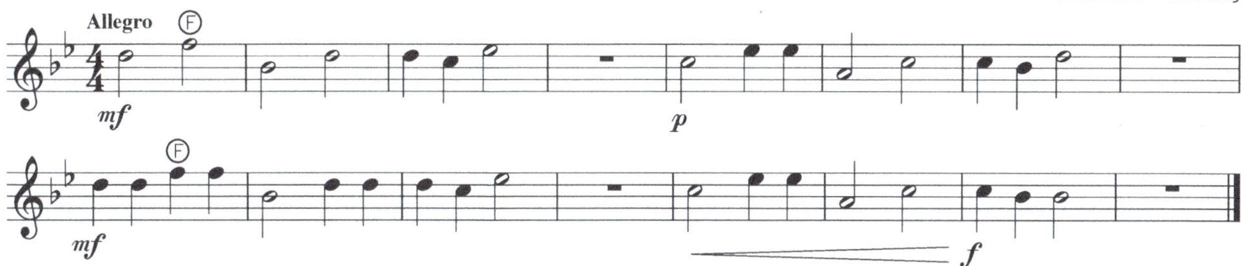

59D. BILL GROGAN'S GOAT

American Folk Song

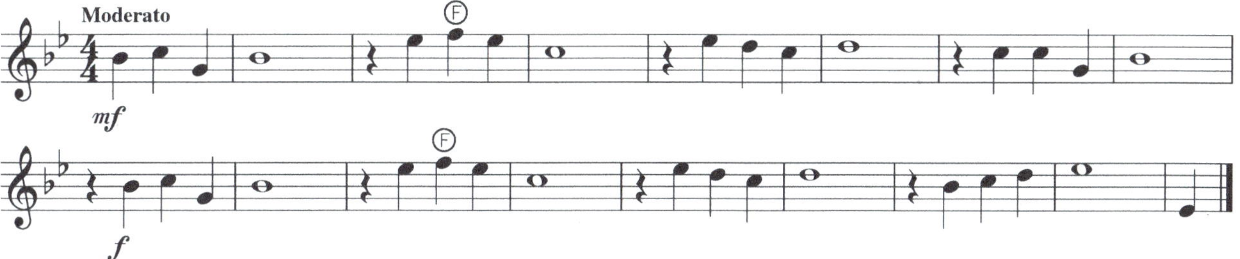

60D. HI-DEE-HO – New Note

61D. THE GREAT GATE OF KIEV – Duet

Modeste Moussorgsky

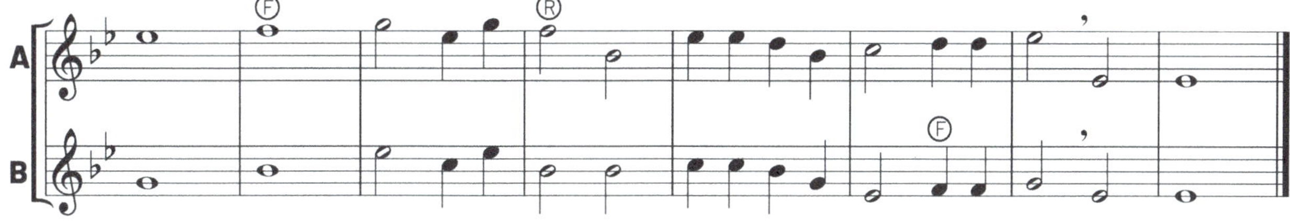

* For more information about this fingering, see the fingering chart on page 47.

Director For those horn students who have followed the "Left-side" pages (4A–11A), exercises 52C–61D teach the four remaining notes necessary to play with the full band from student book page 12 to the end. Accompaniments for exercises 52C–61D appear in the "Left-side" (Horns only) play-along tracks.

HORN RANGE BUILDERS

Flat ♭

A **flat** sign lowers the pitch of a note by a half-step. The note B-flat sounds a half-step below B, and all B's become B-flats for the rest of the measure where they occur.

52C. SWEET AND LOW – New Note

53C. MAJESTIC MARCH

54C. HIGH FLYER – New Note

Double Horn Players: add the thumb key and use the B♭ Horn fingering.

New Key Signature

Your Key Signature indicates the *Key of F* – play all B's as B-flats.

55C. ALOHA OE

Queen Liliuokalani, Hawaii

56C. AMERICAN FOLK SONG

William Billings

Page 11 D - Horns only

HORN RANGE BUILDERS

57D. HIGH SEAS – New Note

58D. MARIANNE

Jamaican Folk Song

59D. BILL GROGAN'S GOAT

American Folk Song

60D. HI-DEE-HO – New Note

61D. THE GREAT GATE OF KIEV – Duet

Modeste Moussorgsky

Student Book Page 12

PERFORMANCE SPOTLIGHT

Exercises 52 – 58 can be used as a cumulative review of all previous material and/or as a pre-planned first band concert. Other items which could be added to the concert include demonstrations of the various instrument families and highlights from the earlier material in the book.

52. PERFORMANCE WARM-UPS

TONE BUILDER

Flute Oboe

B♭ Clarinet

E♭ Alto Sax.

B♭ Tenor Sax.

B♭ Trumpet

F Horn

Low Brass & Woodwinds

Percussion

S.D.

B.D.

Keyboard Percussion

Flute Oboe

B♭ Clarinet

E♭ Alto Sax.

B♭ Tenor Sax.

B♭ Trumpet

F Horn

Low Brass & Woodwinds

Percussion

Keyboard Percussion

RHYTHM ETUDE

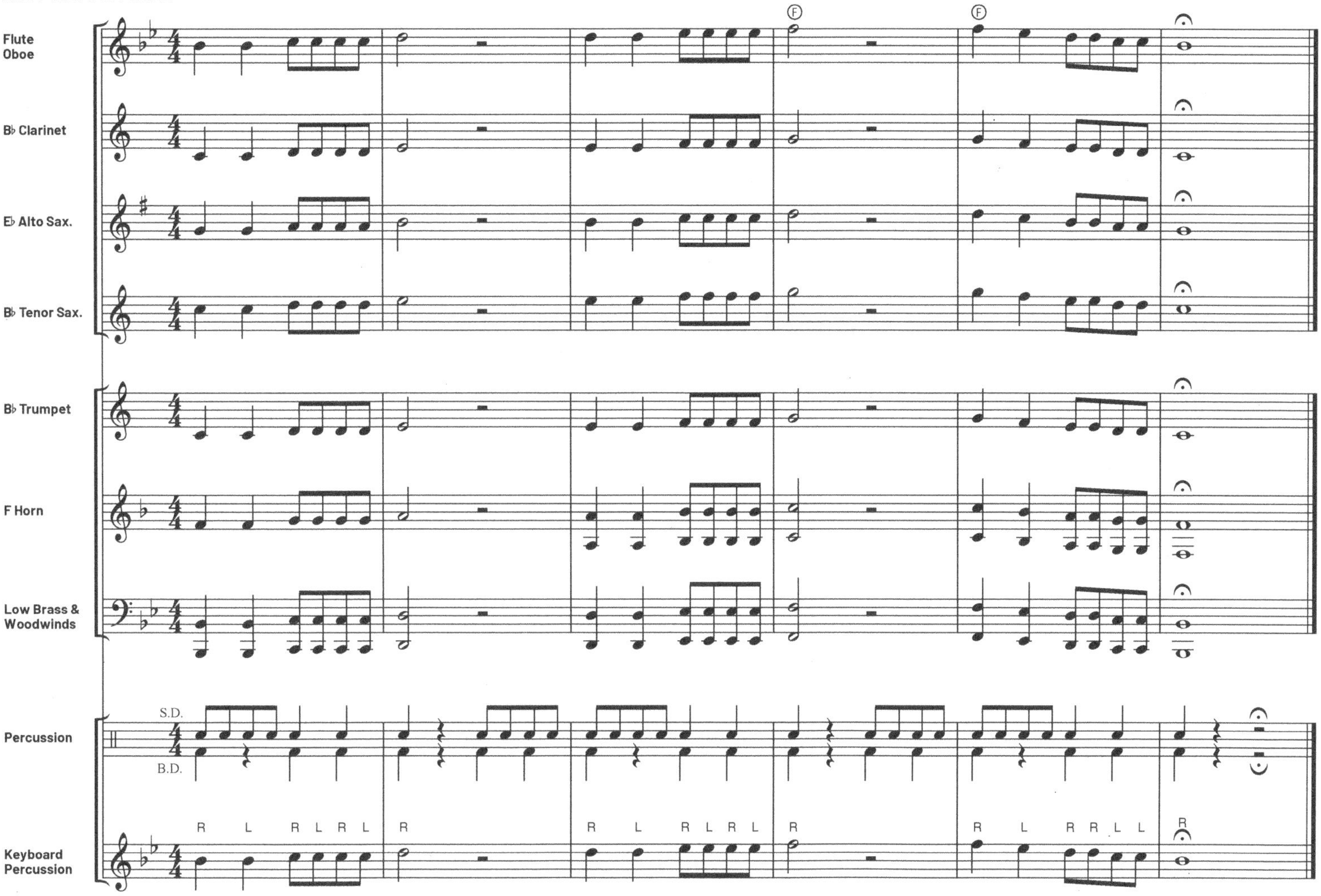

Flute Oboe
B♭ Clarinet
E♭ Alto Sax.
B♭ Tenor Sax.
B♭ Trumpet
F Horn
Low Brass & Woodwinds
Percussion
S.D.
B.D.
Keyboard Percussion
R L R L R L
R
R L R L R L
R
R L R R L L
R
F
F

Kybd. Perc. Use Combination Sticking.

RHYTHM RAP

Clap
Stomp!
S.D.
B.D.
Percussion
Tambourine

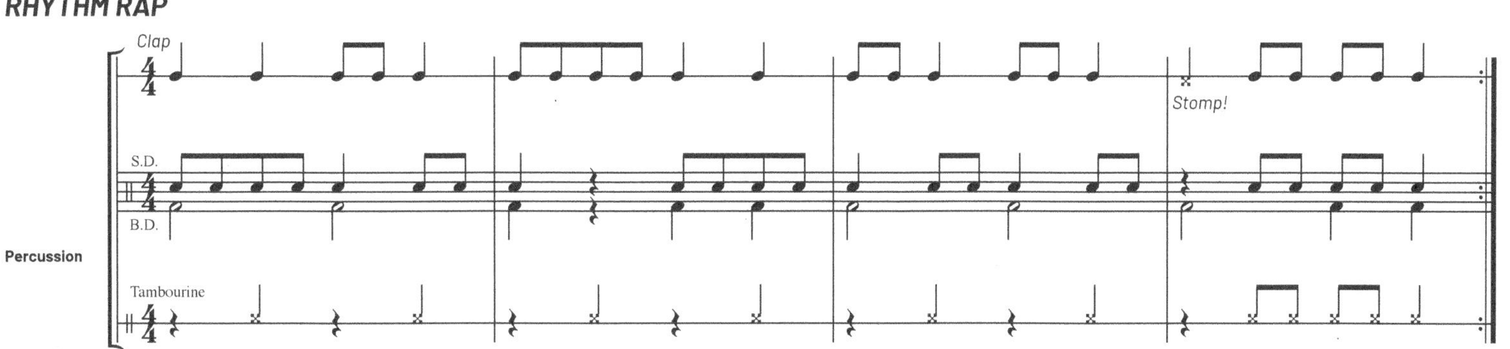

Percussion Remember: how your hand strikes the tambourine is determined by the dynamics.

Student Book Page 12

CHORALE

Andante

Flute Oboe

B♭ Clarinet

E♭ Alto Sax.

B♭ Tenor Sax.

B♭ Trumpet

F Horn

Low Brass & Woodwinds

Percussion (Sus. Cym.)

Keyboard Percussion

p — *mf* — *p*

Percussion Remember: start softly to make an effective crescendo.

Percussion

Let Ring

(Chorale)

Let the sound continue to "ring" without stopping. It is a common indication for triangle or cymbals. The same effect is sometimes marked *l.v.* (let vibrate) or *l.r.* (let ring).

Percussion

Triangle

(Ex. 53)

Striking the side opposite the open end will produce a "fundamental" sound.
Striking the bottom leg will produce a sound with more overtones (ringing).
Listen to the band and decide which sound works best with the music. It's your choice!

Kybd. Perc.

Melodic Sticking

(Ex. 53)

An approach that combines all the various stickings to create the best performance of the melodic line.

53. AURA LEE – Duet or Band Arrangement

George R. Poulton

(Part A = Melody, Part B = Harmony)

Student Book Page 12

54. FRÈRE JACQUES – Round *(When group A reaches ②, group B begins at ①)*

French Folk Song

Kybd. Perc. Use Melodic Sticking

Student Book Page 13

PERFORMANCE SPOTLIGHT

55. WHEN THE SAINTS GO MARCHING IN – Band Arrangement

Arr. by John Higgins

11
Flute
Oboe
B♭ Clarinet
E♭ Alto Sax.
B♭ Tenor Sax.
B♭ Trumpet
F Horn
Low Brass &
Woodwinds
Percussion
p
Keyboard
Percussion
19
mf
f
mf
f
Choke
f

56. OLD MACDONALD HAD A BAND – Section Feature

Percussion **Sus. Cym. with Sticks**

When playing sus. cym. with sticks, the best sound is usually one third or one half the distance from the edge to the dome.

57. ODE TO JOY (from Symphony No. 9)

Ludwig van Beethoven
Arr. by John Higgins

Percussion Triangle (Remember: Fundamental or overtones – your choice.)

Student Book Page 13

58. HARD ROCK BLUES – Encore

John Higgins

Tie A curved line connecting notes of the same pitch. Play one note for the combined counts of the tied notes.

TEACHING TIP Count and clap this exercise before playing.

59. FIT TO BE TIED

2 beats

Flute Oboe

B♭ Clarinet B♭ Bass Cl.

E♭ Alto Sax. E♭ Bari. Sax. E♭ Alto Cl.

B♭ Tenor Sax.

B♭ Trumpet Baritone T.C.

F Horn

Trombone Baritone B.C. Bassoon Electric Bass

Tuba

Percussion S.D. B.D.

Keyboard Percussion

Flute Oboe

B♭ Clarinet B♭ Bass Cl.

E♭ Alto Sax. E♭ Bari. Sax. E♭ Alto Cl.

B♭ Tenor Sax.

B♭ Trumpet

F Horn

Trombone Baritone B.C. Bassoon Electric Bass

Tuba

Percussion

Keyboard Percussion

Student Book Page 14

60. ALOUETTE

French-Canadian Folk Song

A dot adds half the value of the note.

TEACHING TIP The sounding rhythms of *Alouette* and *Alouette – The Sequel* are identical. Ask the students to identify the tied notes and the corresponding single notes of equal rhythmic value.

61. ALOUETTE – THE SEQUEL

French-Canadian Folk Song

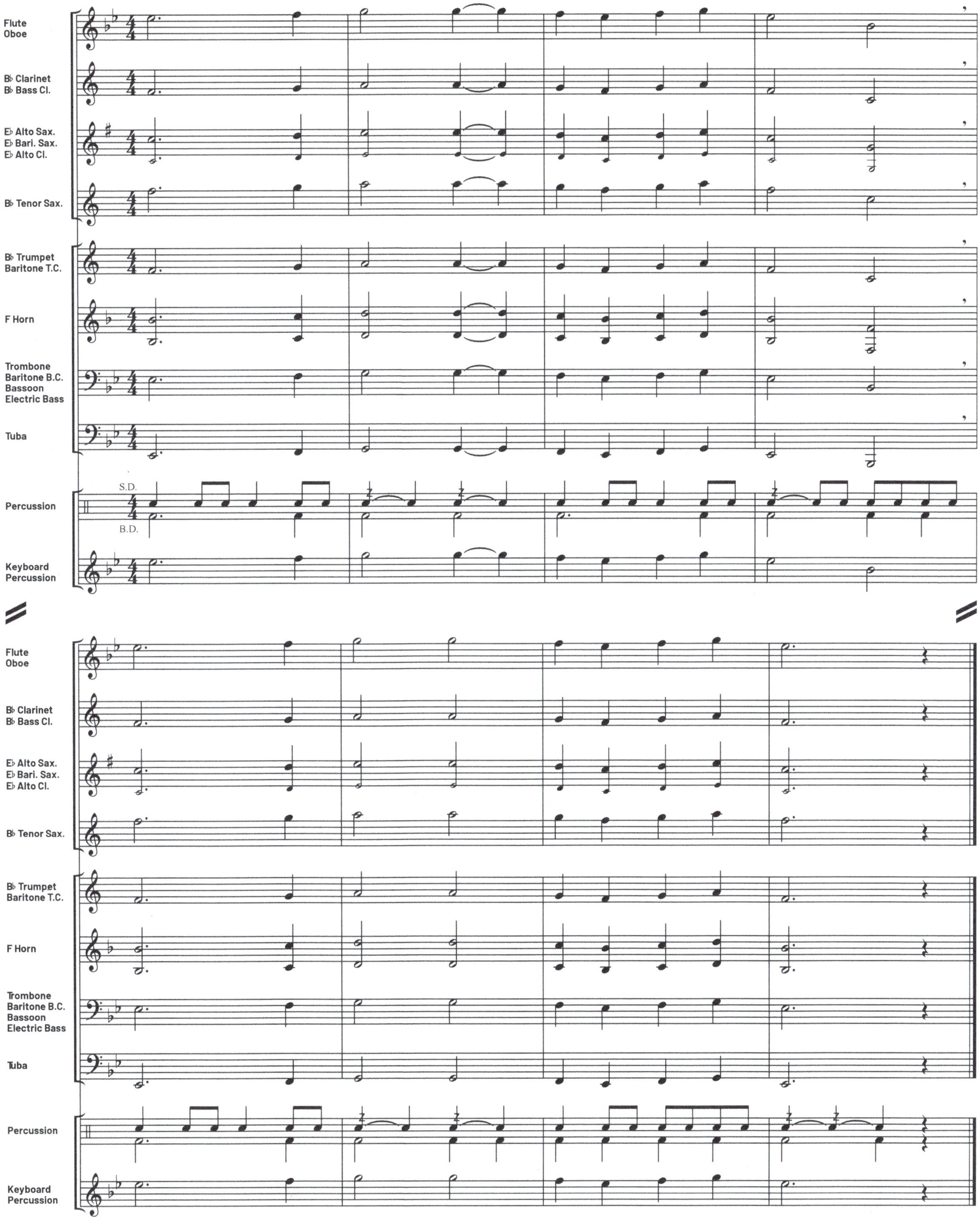

Flute
Oboe

B♭ Clarinet
B♭ Bass Cl.

E♭ Alto Sax.
E♭ Bari. Sax.
E♭ Alto Cl.

B♭ Tenor Sax.

B♭ Trumpet
Baritone T.C.

F Horn

Trombone
Baritone B.C.
Bassoon
Electric Bass

Tuba

Percussion

S.D.

B.D.

Keyboard
Percussion

Flute
Oboe

B♭ Clarinet
B♭ Bass Cl.

E♭ Alto Sax.
E♭ Bari. Sax.
E♭ Alto Cl.

B♭ Tenor Sax.

B♭ Trumpet
Baritone T.C.

F Horn

Trombone
Baritone B.C.
Bassoon
Electric Bass

Tuba

Percussion

Keyboard
Percussion

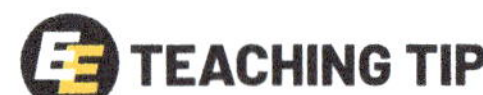

TEACHING TIP Observing the written breath marks is preferred, but some students may need to take additional breaths to maintain good tone quality.

Percussion Practice Flam Taps in this exercise.

62. IT'S RAINING

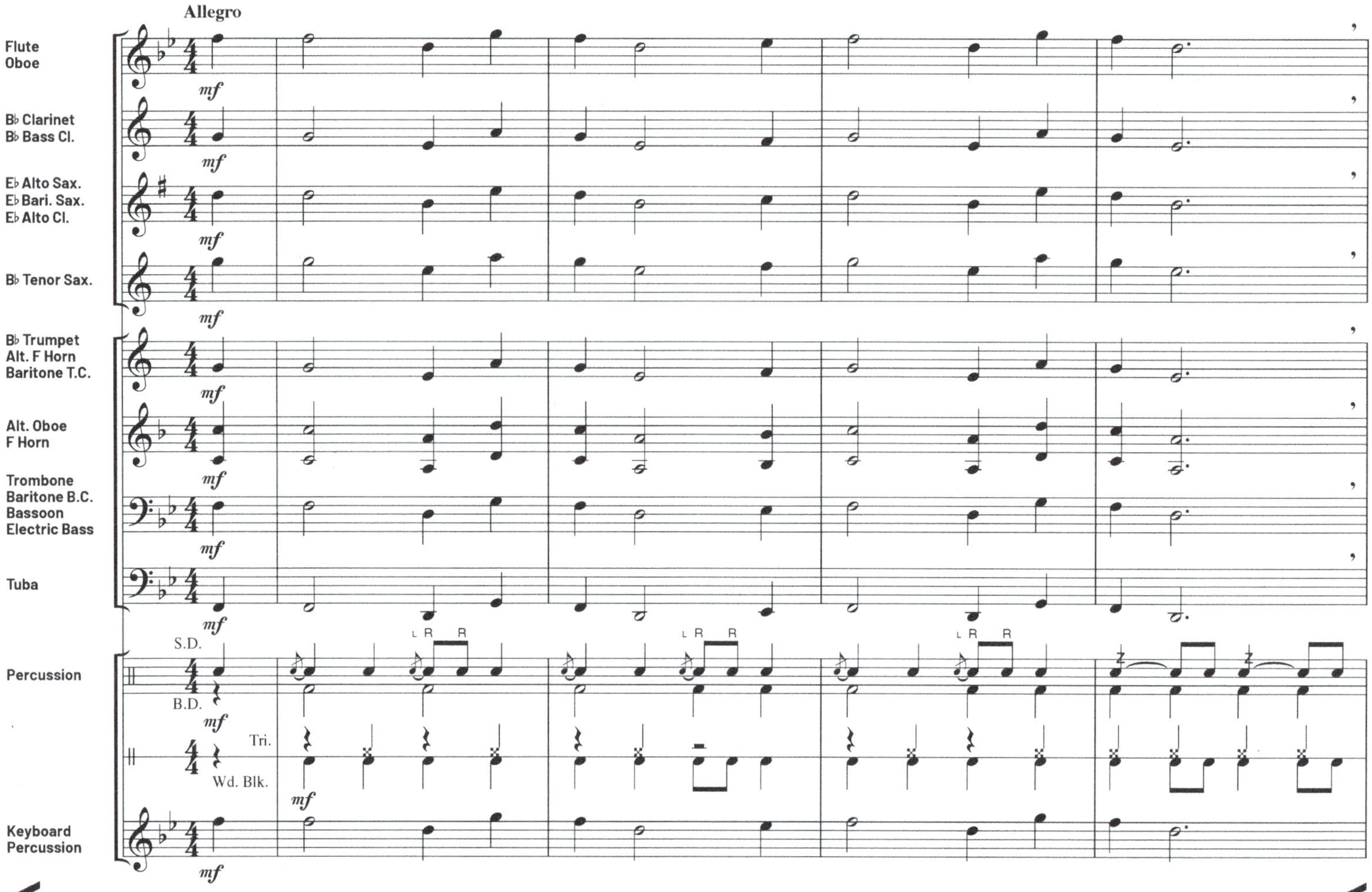
Allegro
Flute
Oboe
B♭ Clarinet
B♭ Bass Cl.
E♭ Alto Sax.
E♭ Bari. Sax.
E♭ Alto Cl.
B♭ Tenor Sax.
B♭ Trumpet
Alt. F Horn
Baritone T.C.
Alt. Oboe
F Horn
Trombone
Baritone B.C.
Bassoon
Electric Bass
Tuba
Percussion
S.D.
B.D.
Tri.
Wd. Blk.
Keyboard
Percussion
mf
L R R

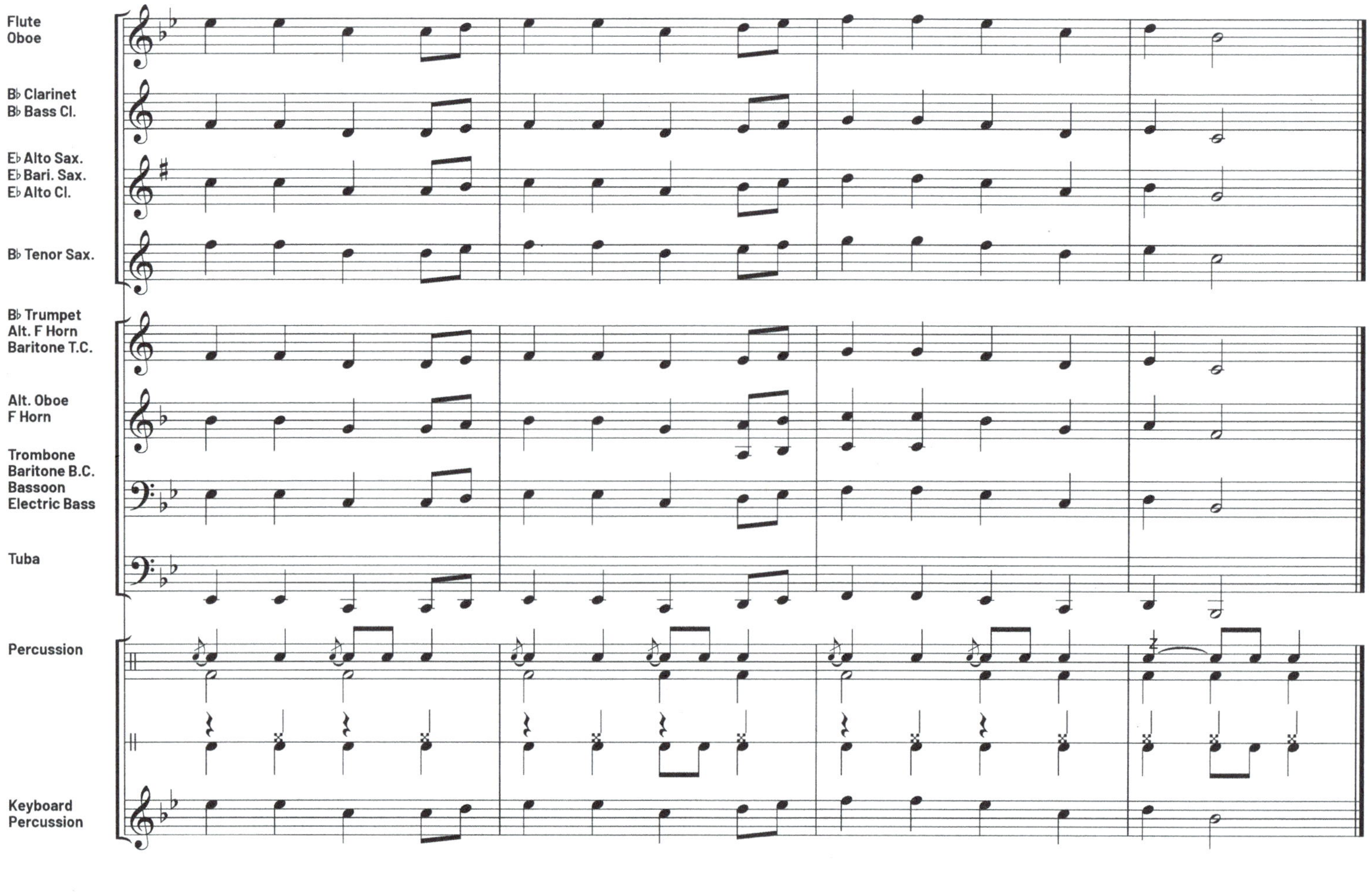
Flute
Oboe
B♭ Clarinet
B♭ Bass Cl.
E♭ Alto Sax.
E♭ Bari. Sax.
E♭ Alto Cl.
B♭ Tenor Sax.
B♭ Trumpet
Alt. F Horn
Baritone T.C.
Alt. Oboe
F Horn
Trombone
Baritone B.C.
Bassoon
Electric Bass
Tuba
Percussion
Keyboard
Percussion

Flute/Kybd. Perc. Oboe Clarinet/Bass Clarinet Alto Saxophone Tenor Saxophone Baritone Saxophone

F
F
or
Regular fingering
Forked fingering
G
D
G
D

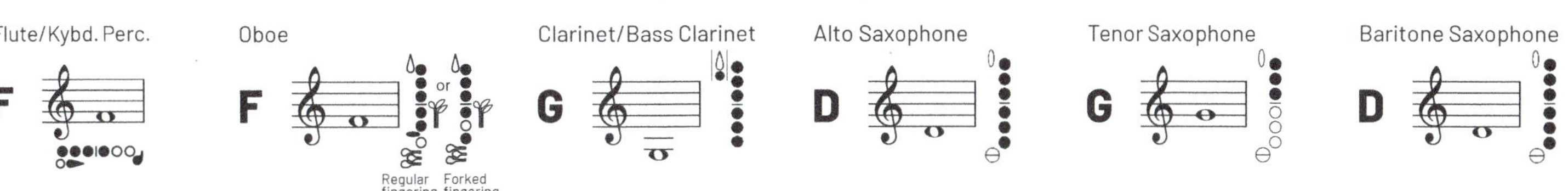

TEACHING TIP Be prepared to spend extra time with the woodwinds as they learn new notes.

Flute To play lower notes, blow softly and direct the airstream lower into the embouchure hole.

Oboe The "forked" fingering makes it easier to play "F" when moving to or from "E♭" or "D." *

Tenor Sax. For the best possible tone, keep your chin flat, cheeks in and the corners of your mouth firm.

63. NEW DIRECTIONS – New Note

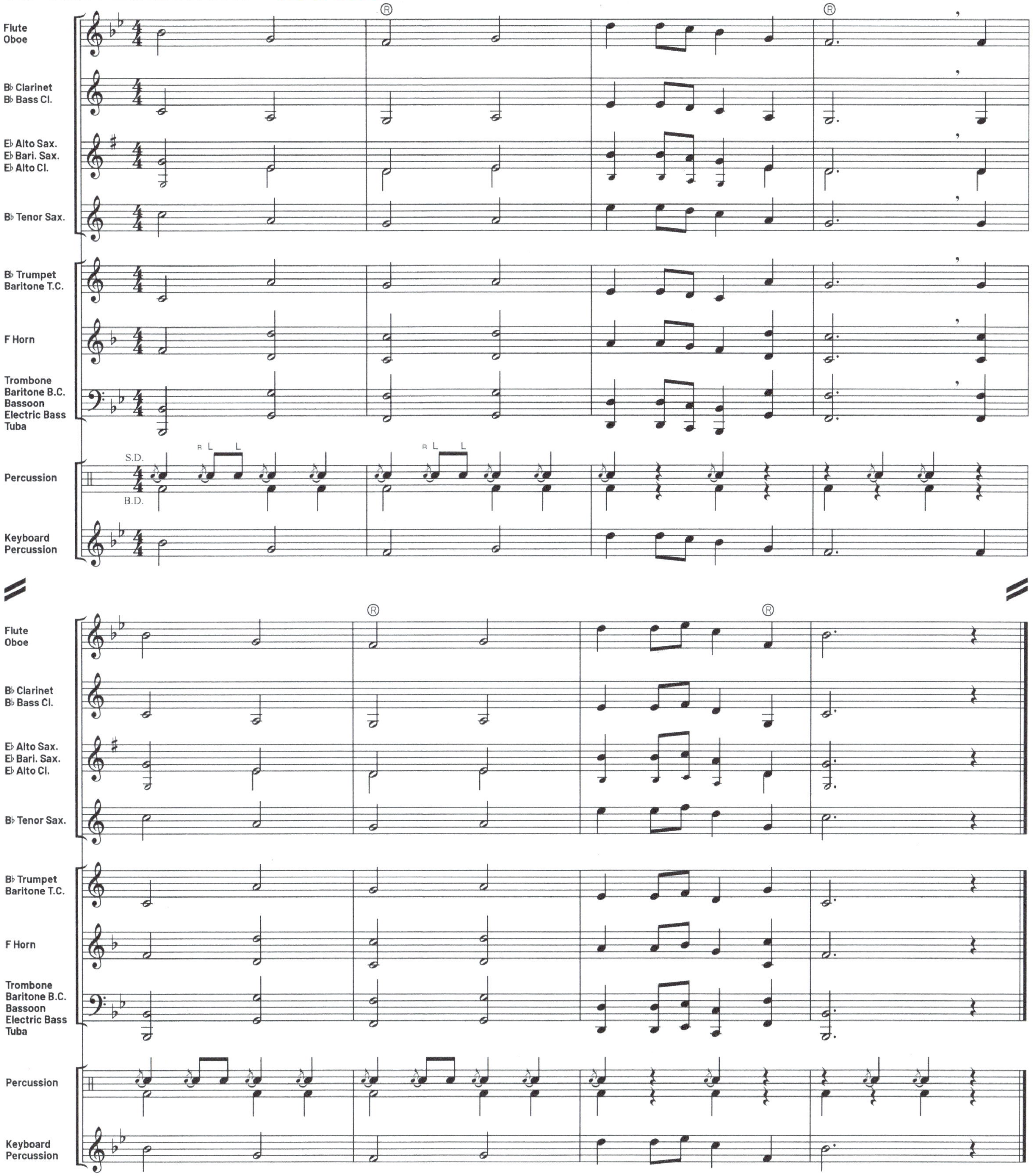
Flute
Oboe
B♭ Clarinet
B♭ Bass Cl.
E♭ Alto Sax.
E♭ Bari. Sax.
E♭ Alto Cl.
B♭ Tenor Sax.
B♭ Trumpet
Baritone T.C.
F Horn
Trombone
Baritone B.C.
Bassoon
Electric Bass
Tuba
Percussion
S.D.
B.D.
R L L
Keyboard
Percussion

For more information about this fingering, see the oboe fingering chart.

Student Book Page 14

Review the first note with the woodwinds before playing this exercise.

Clarinets Always use a full airstream. Keep fingers above the tone holes, curved naturally.
Trombone Always use a full airstream and maintain good posture.

64. THE NOBLES

Always use a full airstream. Keep fingers close to the keys/on top of the valves, curved/arched naturally.

Ⓡ 3 beats

Flute Oboe
B♭ Clarinet B♭ Bass Cl.
E♭ Alto Sax. E♭ Bari. Sax. E♭ Alto Cl.
B♭ Tenor Sax.
B♭ Trumpet Baritone T.C.
F Horn
Trombone Baritone B.C. Bassoon Electric Bass
Tuba
Percussion S.D. B.D.
Keyboard Percussion

Ⓕ Ⓡ

Flute Oboe
B♭ Clarinet B♭ Bass Cl.
E♭ Alto Sax. E♭ Bari. Sax. E♭ Alto Cl.
B♭ Tenor Sax.
B♭ Trumpet Baritone T.C.
F Horn
Trombone Baritone B.C. Bassoon Electric Bass
Tuba
Percussion
Keyboard Percussion

QUIZ ASSESSMENT Tie, dotted half note.

65. ESSENTIAL ELEMENTS QUIZ

THEORY

3/4 Time Signature

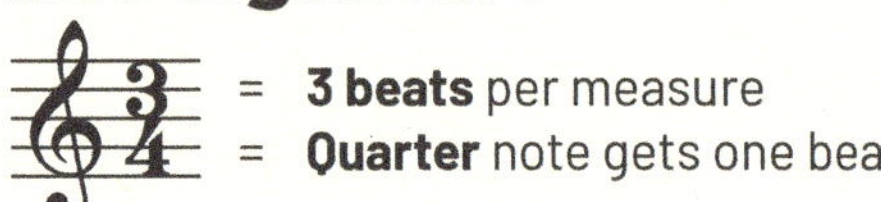

= **3 beats** per measure
= **Quarter** note gets one beat

Conducting

Practice conducting this three-beat pattern.

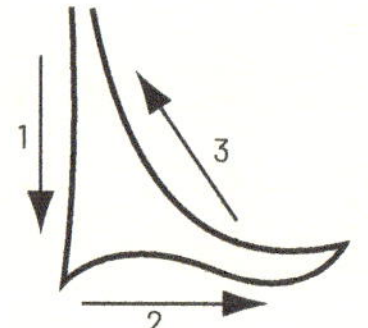

Students should count aloud while conducting in 3/4 time.

66. RHYTHM RAP

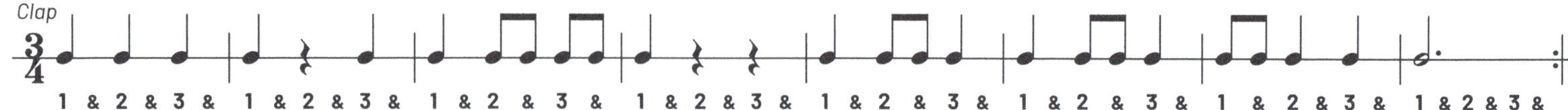

TEACHING TIP Have half of the band conduct while the other half plays the exercise. Switch.

67. THREE BEAT JAM

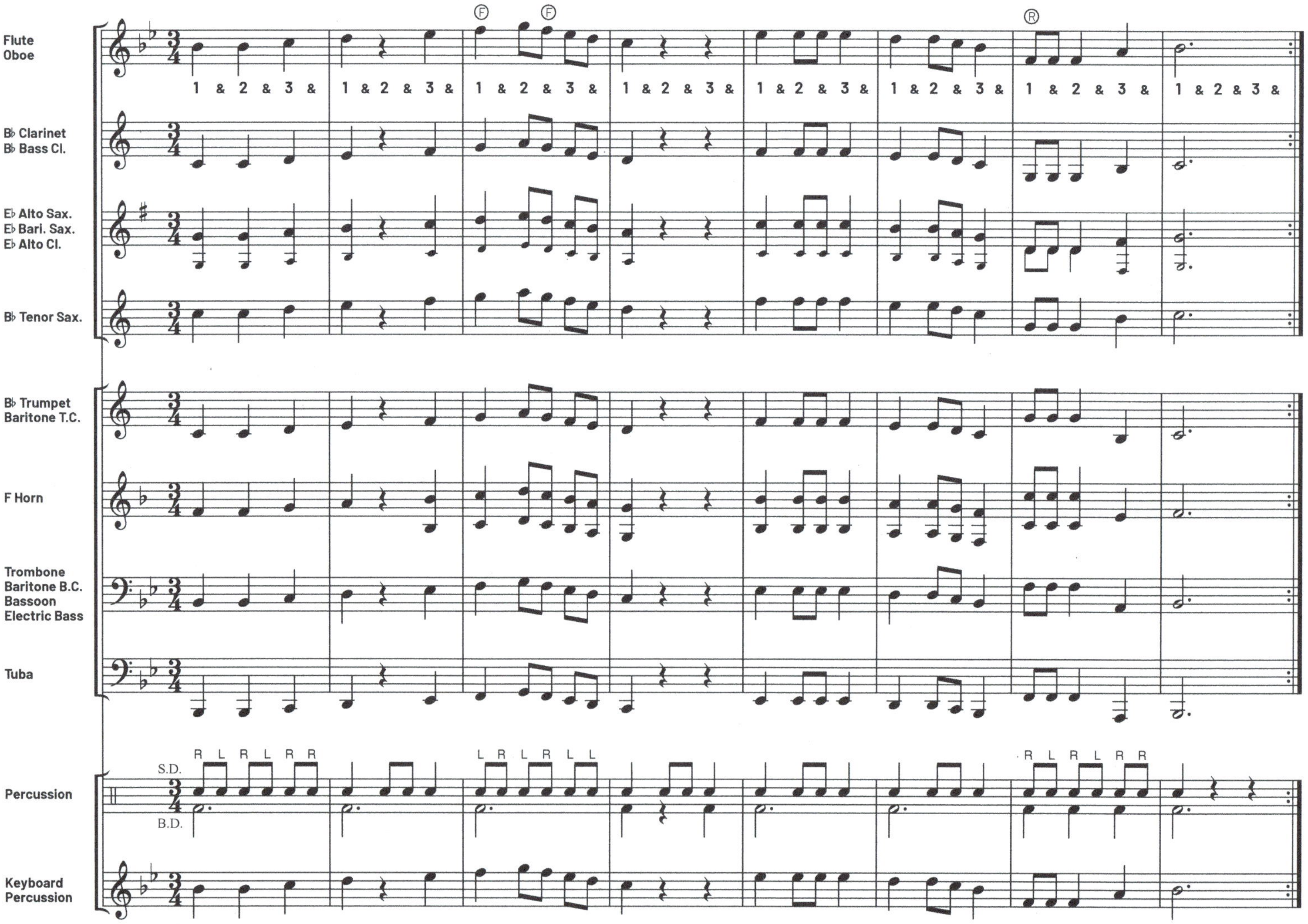

Flute
Oboe

1 & 2 & 3 & 1 & 2 & 3 & 1 & 2 & 3 & 1 & 2 & 3 & 1 & 2 & 3 & 1 & 2 & 3 & 1 & 2 & 3 & 1 & 2 & 3 &

B♭ Clarinet
B♭ Bass Cl.

E♭ Alto Sax.
E♭ Bari. Sax.
E♭ Alto Cl.

B♭ Tenor Sax.

B♭ Trumpet
Baritone T.C.

F Horn

Trombone
Baritone B.C.
Bassoon
Electric Bass

Tuba

Percussion

S.D.
B.D.

R L R L R R L R L R L L R L R L R R

Keyboard
Percussion

Percussion **Rudiment**

Double Paradiddle

Encourage students to use a steady stream of air.

68. BARCAROLLE

Jacques Offenbach

Moderato

Flute
Oboe

B♭ Clarinet
B♭ Bass Cl.

E♭ Alto Sax.
E♭ Bari. Sax.
E♭ Alto Cl.

B♭ Tenor Sax.

B♭ Trumpet
Baritone T.C.

F Horn

Trombone
Baritone B.C.
Bassoon
Electric Bass

Tuba

Percussion (S.D., B.D.)

Keyboard Percussion

mf

Percussion

Rudiment

Flam Accent

After you play a flam, play two strokes, always with the high hand. This will keep your hands properly positioned.

Student Book Page 15

HISTORY

Norwegian composer **Edvard Grieg** (1843–1907) wrote *Peer Gynt Suite* for a play by Henrik Ibsen in 1875, the year before the telephone was invented by Alexander Graham Bell. "Morning" is a melody from *Peer Gynt Suite*. Music used in plays, or in films and television, is called **incidental music**.

TEACHING TIP Make sure keys and valves are depressed completely when playing soft, slow music.

Oboe Use the "forked" fingering for all "F's" in this exercise. *

69. MORNING (from Peer Gynt)

Edvard Grieg

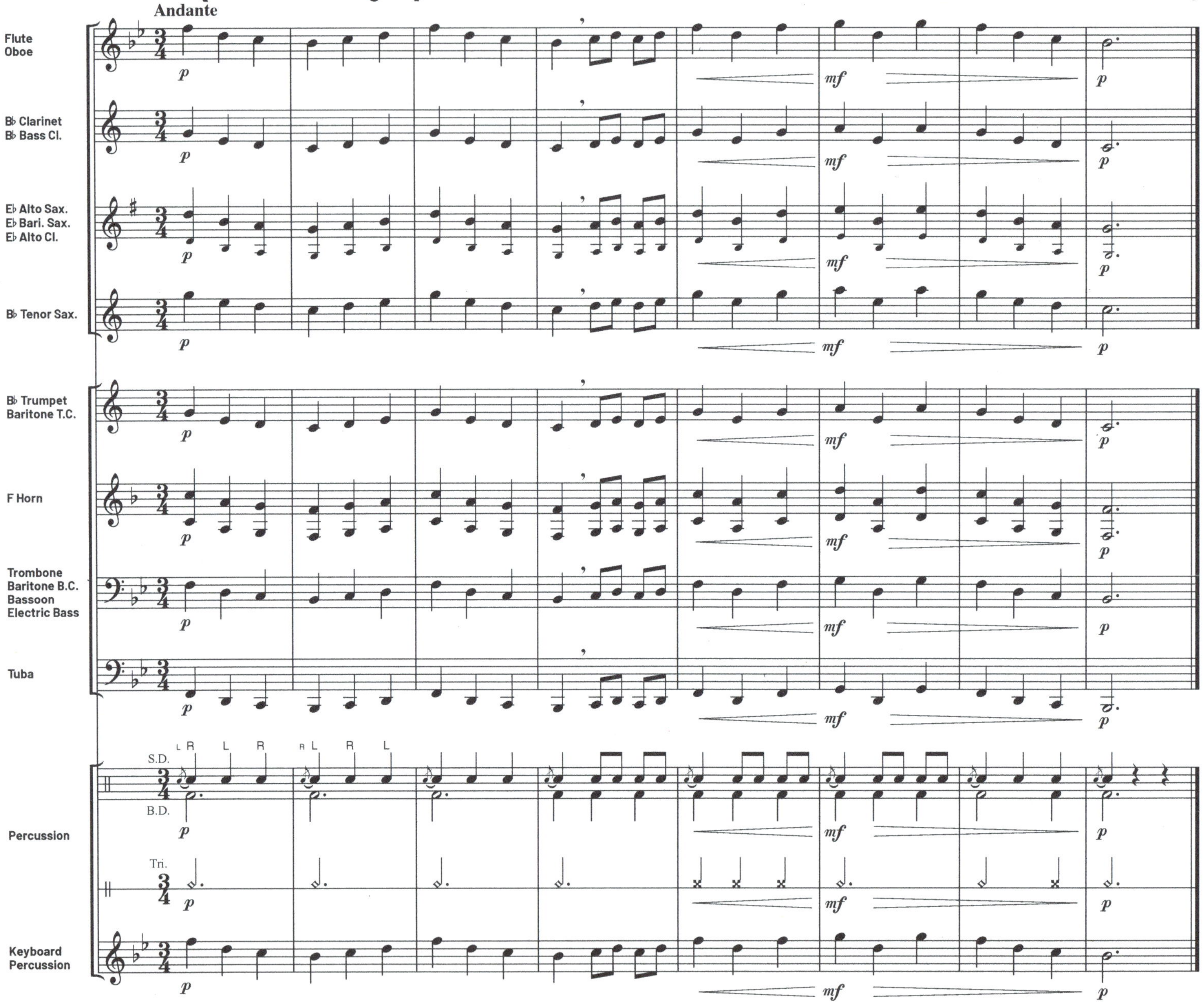

Andante
Flute
Oboe
B♭ Clarinet
B♭ Bass Cl.
E♭ Alto Sax.
E♭ Bari. Sax.
E♭ Alto Cl.
B♭ Tenor Sax.
B♭ Trumpet
Baritone T.C.
F Horn
Trombone
Baritone B.C.
Bassoon
Electric Bass
Tuba
Percussion
S.D.
B.D.
Tri.
L R L R R L R L
Keyboard Percussion
p
mf
p

Accent

Emphasize the note.

TEACHING TIP Be certain students do not rush the accented notes.

70. ACCENT YOUR TALENT

Clap

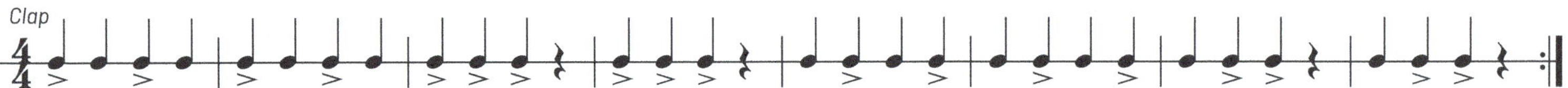

* *For more information about this fingering, see the oboe fingering chart.*

Latin American music has its roots in the African, Native American, Spanish and Portuguese cultures. This diverse music features lively accompaniments by drums and other percussion instruments such as maracas and claves. Music from Latin America continues to influence jazz, classical and popular styles of music. "Chiapanecas" is a popular children's dance and game song.

Play exercise 71 with steady rhythm, making sure that students do not rush the accented notes.

Oboe Choose the best fingering whenever you play "F."

71. MEXICAN CLAPPING SONG ("Chiapanecas")

Latin American Folk Song

Flute / Oboe

B♭ Clarinet / B♭ Bass Cl.

E♭ Alto Sax. / E♭ Bari. Sax. / E♭ Alto Cl.

B♭ Tenor Sax.

B♭ Trumpet / Baritone T.C.

F Horn

Trombone / Baritone B.C. / Bassoon / Electric Bass

Tuba

Percussion (S.D., B.D., R.S., Solo; Maracas, Claves)

Keyboard Percussion

Percussion

Maracas Hold maracas by the handles. Use a short, precise wrist motion to shake maracas. Maintain a steady tempo.

Claves Cup your left hand to form a resonating chamber. Hold the lower pitched clave in your left hand. Use the clave in your right hand to strike the center of the left clave.

Rim Shot

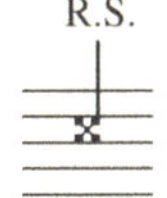

Place tip of left stick on center of drum. Rest stick on rim and hold fimly. Strike with right stick about 1/3 away from tip of left stick. **R.S.** is the abbreviation for rim shot.

CREATIVITY TIP This exercise introduces music composition. Check for accurate rhythms in measures 3 and 4, and be sure the notes are ones they have already learned. How many students ended this exercise on the tonic (Concert B♭)? As each student plays their exercise, ask the class if they feel this composition's last note is one that gives the music a feeling of finality, or is one that makes the listener want to hear more.

72. ESSENTIAL CREATIVITY

**Compose your own music for measures 3 and 4 using this rhythm:*

Flute
Oboe

B♭ Clarinet
B♭ Bass Cl.

E♭ Alto Sax.
E♭ Bari. Sax.
E♭ Alto Cl.

B♭ Tenor Sax.

B♭ Trumpet
Baritone T.C.

F Horn

Trombone
Baritone B.C.
Bassoon
Electric Bass

Tuba

Percussion
S.D.
B.D.

Keyboard
Percussion

Percussion This percussion part can be played to accompany a band member's melody.
*Percussion can also do the written quiz.

Accidental

Any sharp, flat or natural sign which appears in the music without being in the key signature is called an **accidental**.

Flat ♭ A **flat** sign lowers the pitch of a note by a half-step. The note A-flat (C inst.) sounds a half-step below A, and all A's become A-flats for the rest of the measure where they occur.

Natural ♮ A **natural** sign cancels a flat (♭) or sharp (♯) and remains in effect for the entire measure.

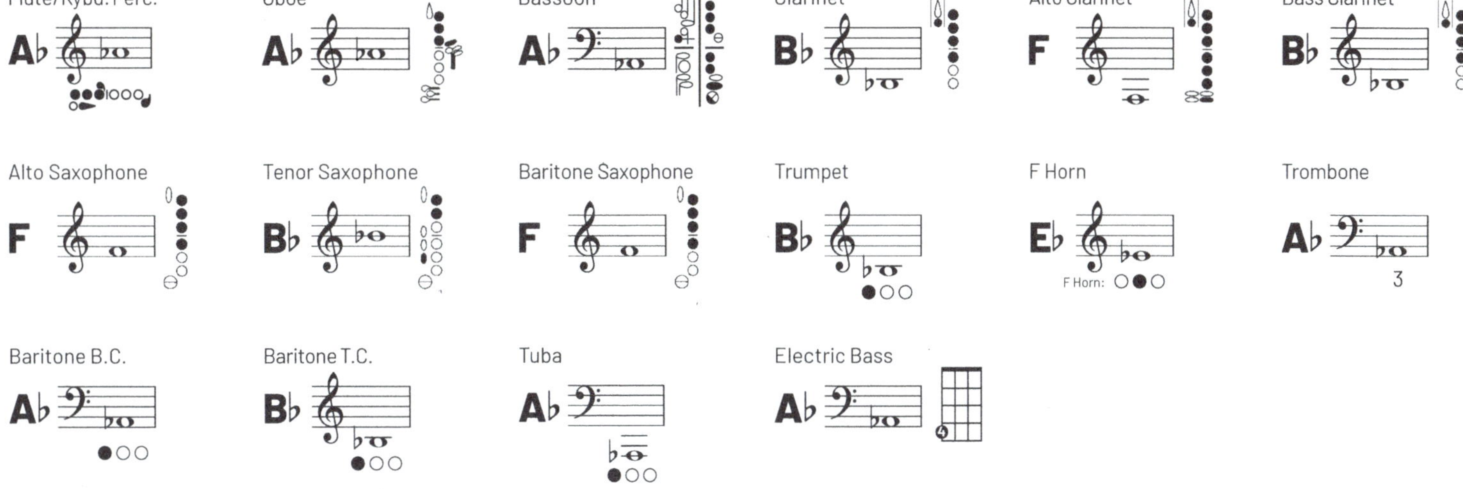

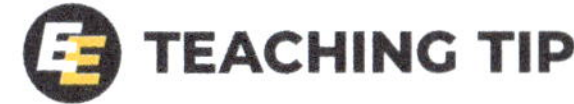

Flute/Kybd. Perc.
A♭
Oboe
A♭
Bassoon
A♭
Clarinet
B♭
Alto Clarinet
F
Bass Clarinet
B♭
Alto Saxophone
F
Tenor Saxophone
B♭
Baritone Saxophone
F
Trumpet
B♭
F Horn
E♭
F Horn:
Trombone
A♭
3
Baritone B.C.
A♭
Baritone T.C.
B♭
Tuba
A♭
Electric Bass
A♭

TEACHING TIP Play their new note before playing this exercise.

73. HOT MUFFINS – New Note

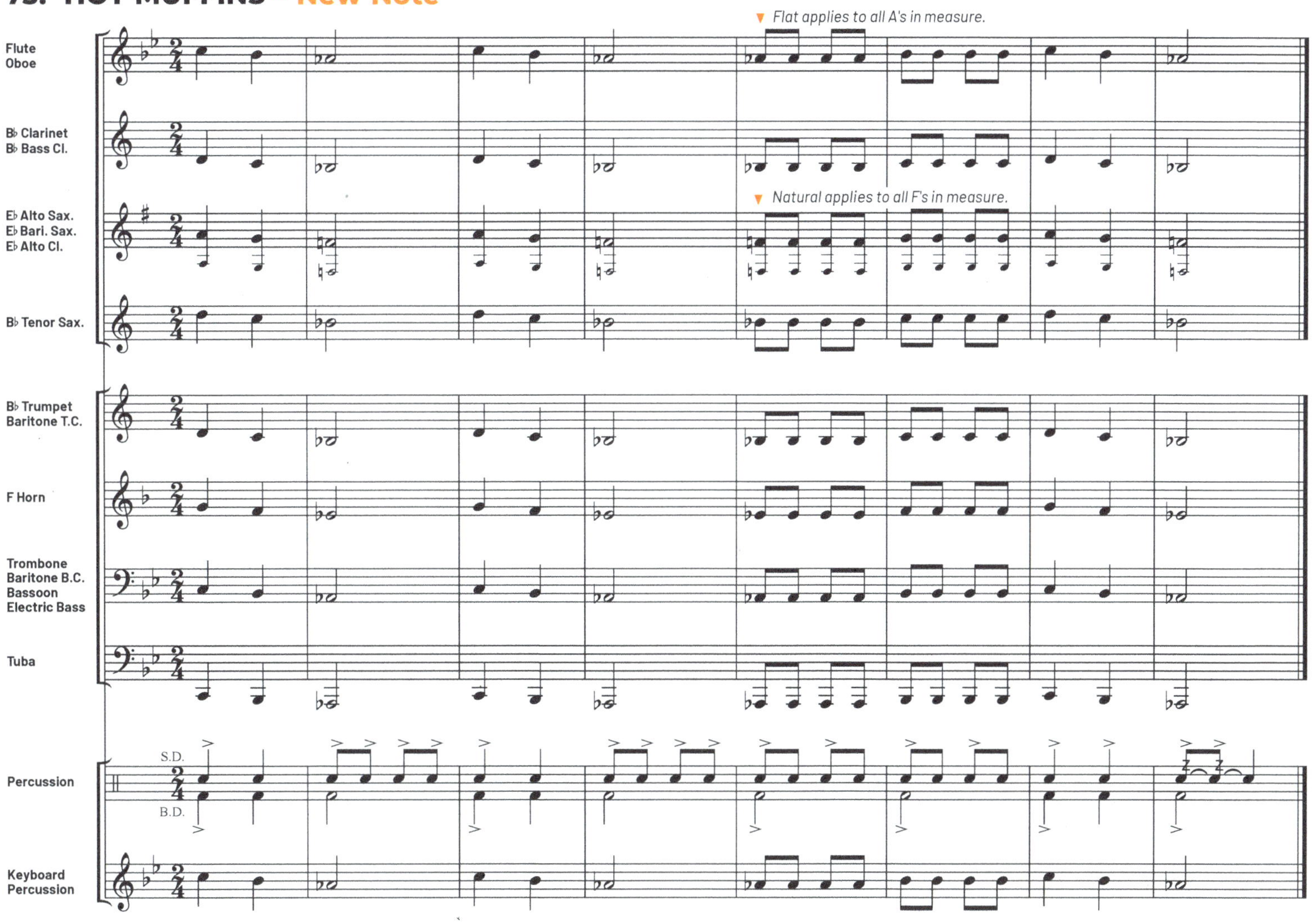
Flat applies to all A's in measure.
Flute
Oboe
B♭ Clarinet
B♭ Bass Cl.
Natural applies to all F's in measure.
E♭ Alto Sax.
E♭ Bari. Sax.
E♭ Alto Cl.
B♭ Tenor Sax.
B♭ Trumpet
Baritone T.C.
F Horn
Trombone
Baritone B.C.
Bassoon
Electric Bass
Tuba
Percussion
S.D.
B.D.
Keyboard
Percussion

Review the repeat sign.

74. COSSACK DANCE

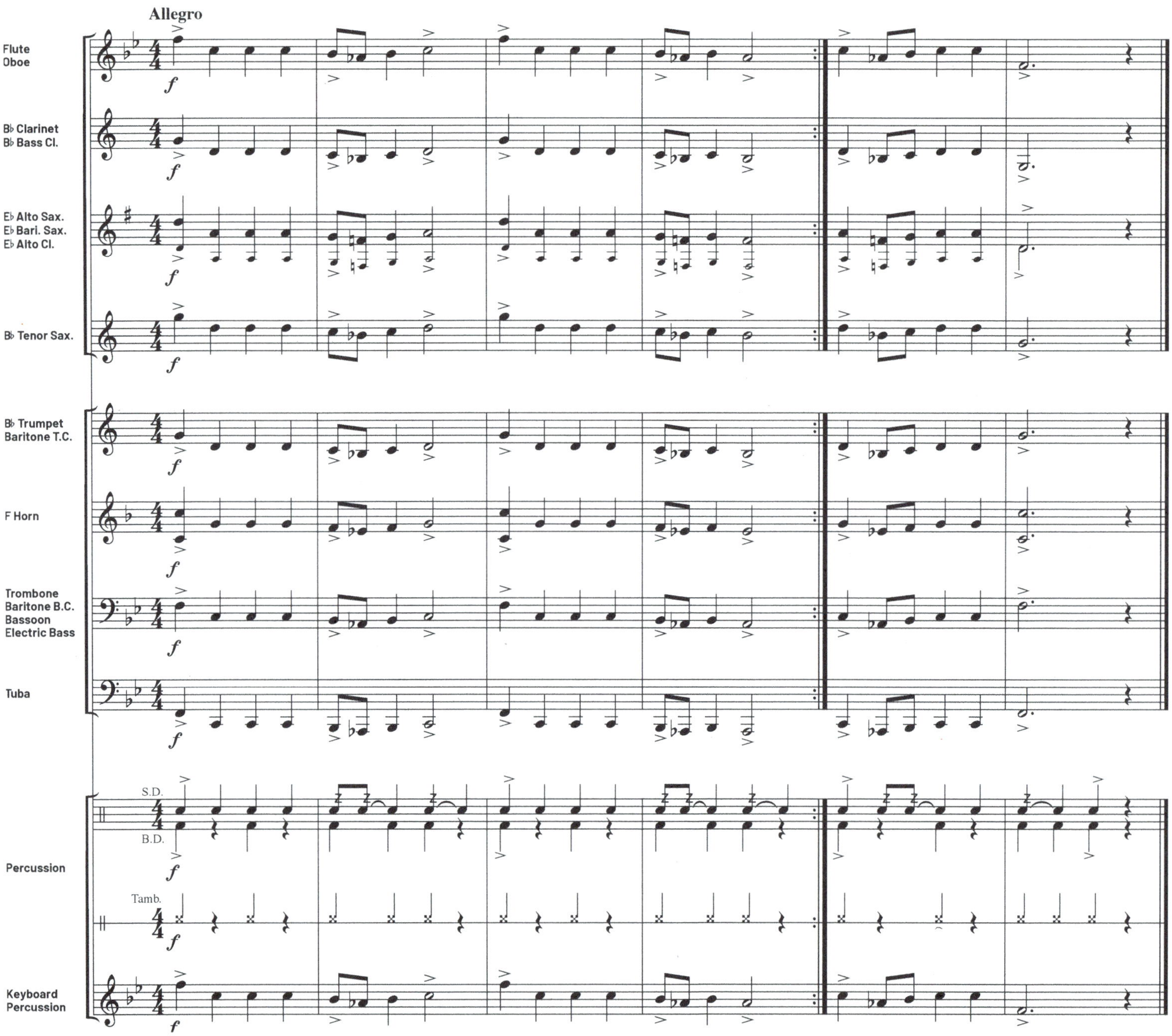

Allegro

Flute
Oboe

B♭ Clarinet
B♭ Bass Cl.

E♭ Alto Sax.
E♭ Bari. Sax.
E♭ Alto Cl.

B♭ Tenor Sax.

B♭ Trumpet
Baritone T.C.

F Horn

Trombone
Baritone B.C.
Bassoon
Electric Bass

Tuba

Percussion

S.D.
B.D.
Tamb.

Keyboard
Percussion

Flute/Kybd. Perc.
A♭
Oboe
A♭
Bassoon
A♭
Clarinet
B♭
Alto Clarinet
F
Bass Clarinet
B♭
Alto Saxophone
F
Tenor Saxophone
B♭
Baritone Saxophone
F
Trumpet
B♭
F Horn
E♭
F Horn:
B♭ Horn: T
Trombone
A♭
3
Baritone B.C.
A♭
Baritone T.C.
B♭
Tuba
A♭
Electric Bass
A♭

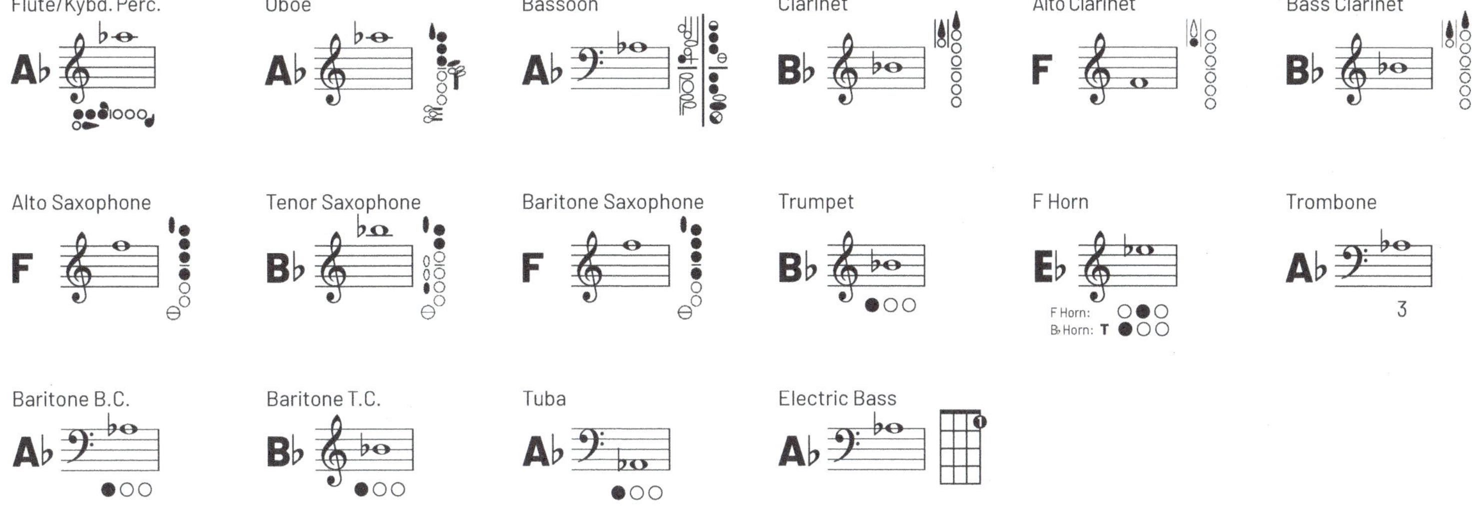

TEACHING TIP Play the new note before playing this exercise.

F Horn Double Horn Players: add the thumb key and use the B♭ Horn fingering to play "E♭."

75. BASIC BLUES – New Note

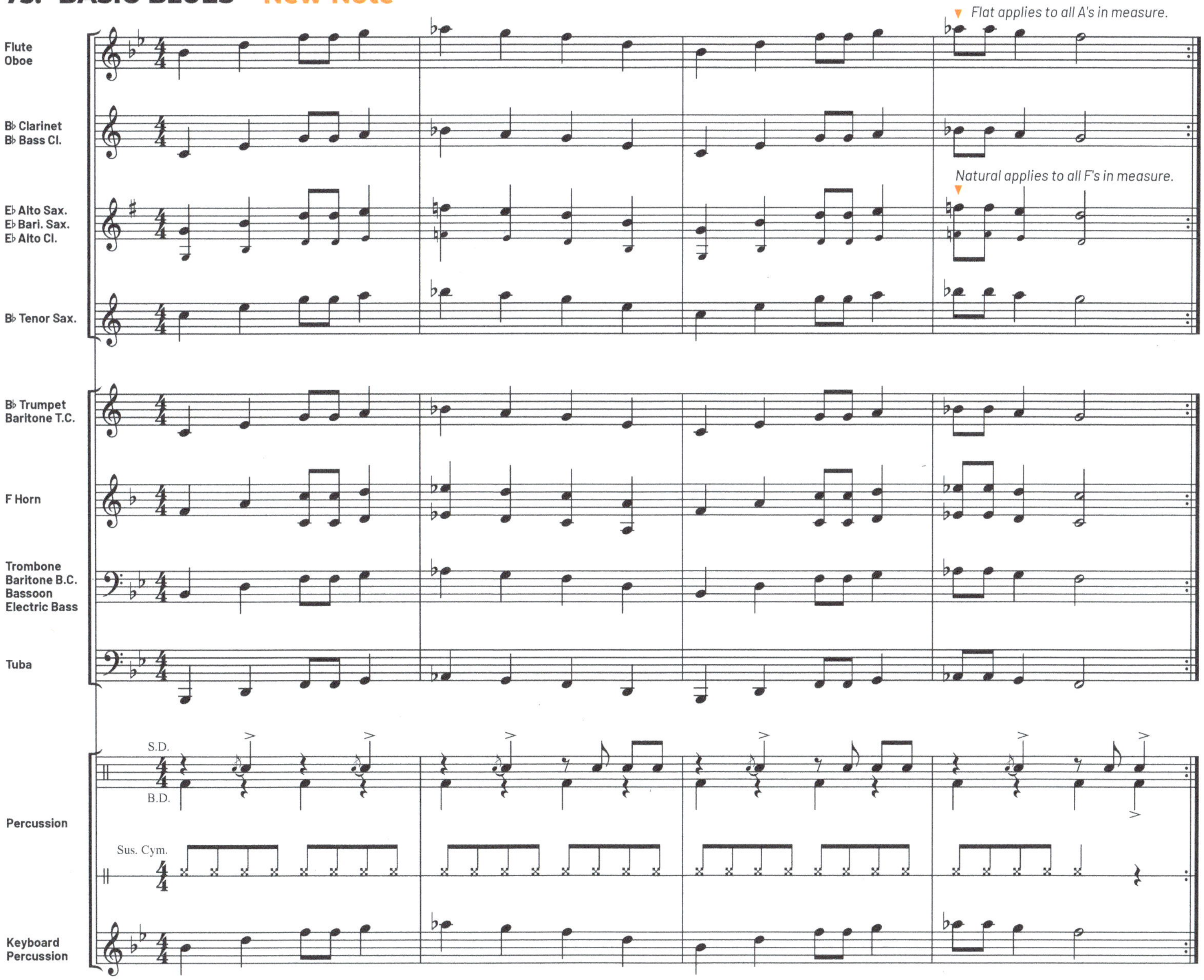
Flat applies to all A's in measure.
Flute
Oboe
B♭ Clarinet
B♭ Bass Cl.
Natural applies to all F's in measure.
E♭ Alto Sax.
E♭ Bari. Sax.
E♭ Alto Cl.
B♭ Tenor Sax.
B♭ Trumpet
Baritone T.C.
F Horn
Trombone
Baritone B.C.
Bassoon
Electric Bass
Tuba
S.D.
B.D.
Percussion
Sus. Cym.
Keyboard
Percussion

THEORY

New Key Signature

C Instruments  or — This Key Signature indicates the *Key of E♭* - play all B's as B-flats, all E's as E-flats, and all A's as A-flats.

B♭ Instruments  This Key Signature indicates the *Key of F* - play all B's as B-flats.

E♭ Instruments  This Key Signature indicates the *Key of C* (no sharps or flats).

F Horn  This Key Signature indicates the *Key of B♭* - play all B's as B-flats and all E's as E-flats.

1st & 2nd Endings

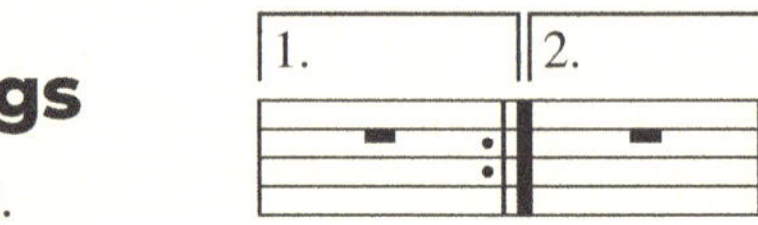

Play through the 1st Ending.
Then play the repeated section of music, **skipping** the 1st Ending and playing the 2nd Ending.

TEACHING TIP Give students a visual example to make sure they understand 1st and 2nd endings.

76. HIGH FLYING

Moderato

Flute
Oboe

B♭ Clarinet
B♭ Bass Cl.

E♭ Alto Sax.
E♭ Bari. Sax.
E♭ Alto Cl.

B♭ Tenor Sax.

B♭ Trumpet
Baritone T.C.

F Horn

Trombone
Baritone B.C.
Bassoon
Electric Bass

Tuba

Percussion (S.D., B.D., Triangle)

Keyboard
Percussion

mf

2nd time
1.
2.
Flute
Oboe
B♭ Clarinet
B♭ Bass Cl.
E♭ Alto Sax.
E♭ Bari. Sax.
E♭ Alto Cl.
B♭ Tenor Sax.
B♭ Trumpet
Baritone T.C.
F Horn
Trombone
Baritone B.C.
Bassoon
Electric Bass
Tuba
Percussion
Keyboard
Percussion

HISTORY

Japanese folk music actually has its origins in ancient China. "Sakura, Sakura" was performed on instruments such as the **koto**, a 13-string instrument that is more than 4000 years old, and the **shakuhachi** or bamboo flute. The unique sound of this ancient Japanese melody results from the pentatonic (or five-note) sequence used in this tonal system.

Before playing the entire arrangement, play the first three notes slowly, listening for balance.

77. SAKURA, SAKURA – Band Arrangement

Japanese Folk Song
Arr. by John Higgins

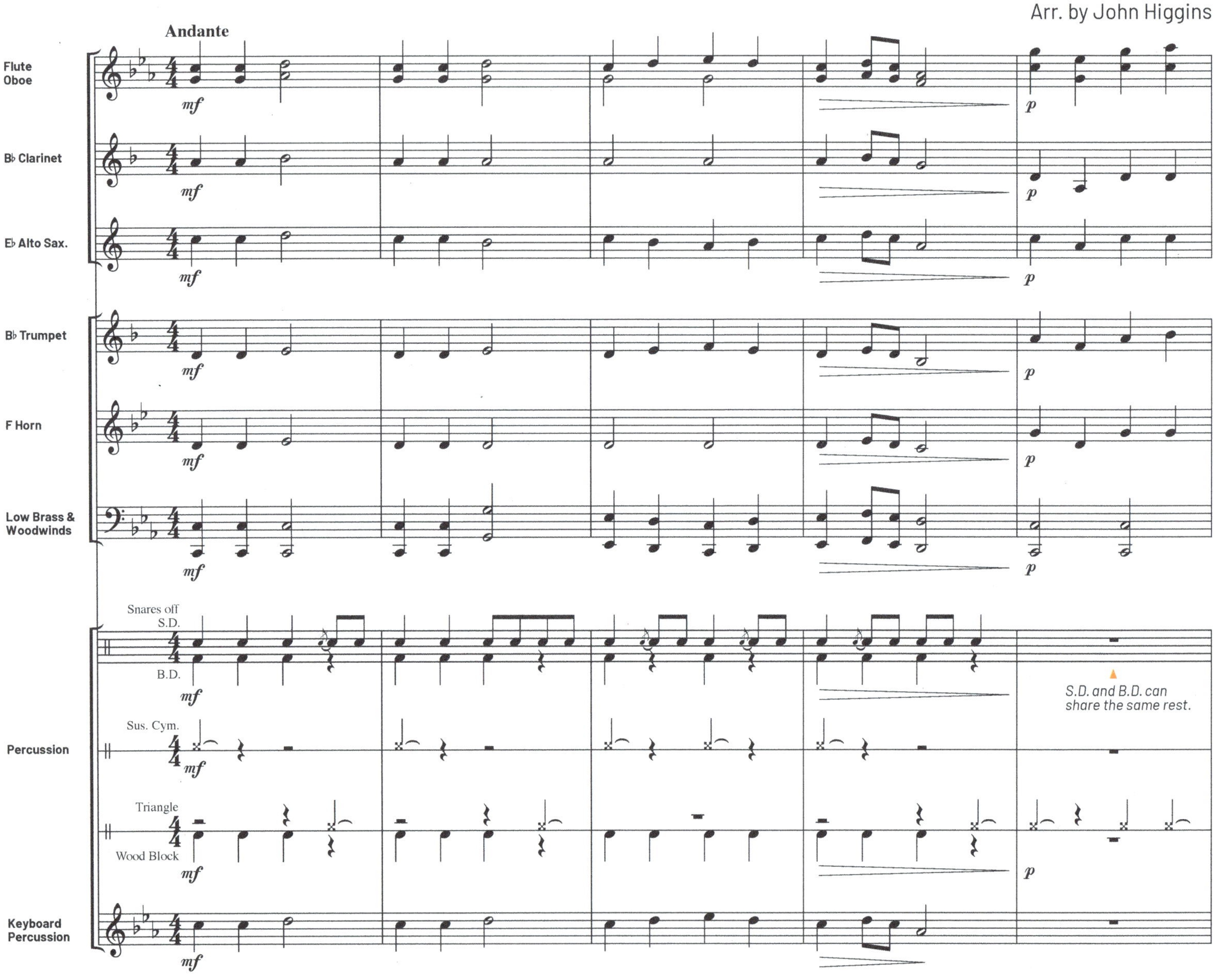

Andante

Flute Oboe

B♭ Clarinet

E♭ Alto Sax.

B♭ Trumpet

F Horn

Low Brass & Woodwinds

Percussion: Snares off S.D., B.D., Sus. Cym., Triangle, Wood Block

S.D. and B.D. can share the same rest.

Keyboard Percussion

Flute
Oboe
B♭ Clarinet
E♭ Alto Sax.
B♭ Trumpet
F Horn
Low Brass &
Woodwinds
Percussion
Keyboard
Percussion
mf
p
f
Shared rest
Choke

Percussion

Sleigh Bells

Sleigh bells are usually shaken on the rhythm indicated. However, handle-mounted sleigh bells can be tapped gently in time with the fist by holding the instrument perpendicular to the floor.

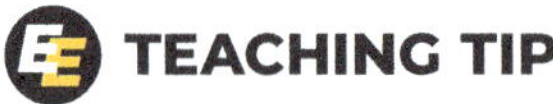

TEACHING TIP Review the 1st and 2nd ending concept.

78. UP ON A HOUSETOP

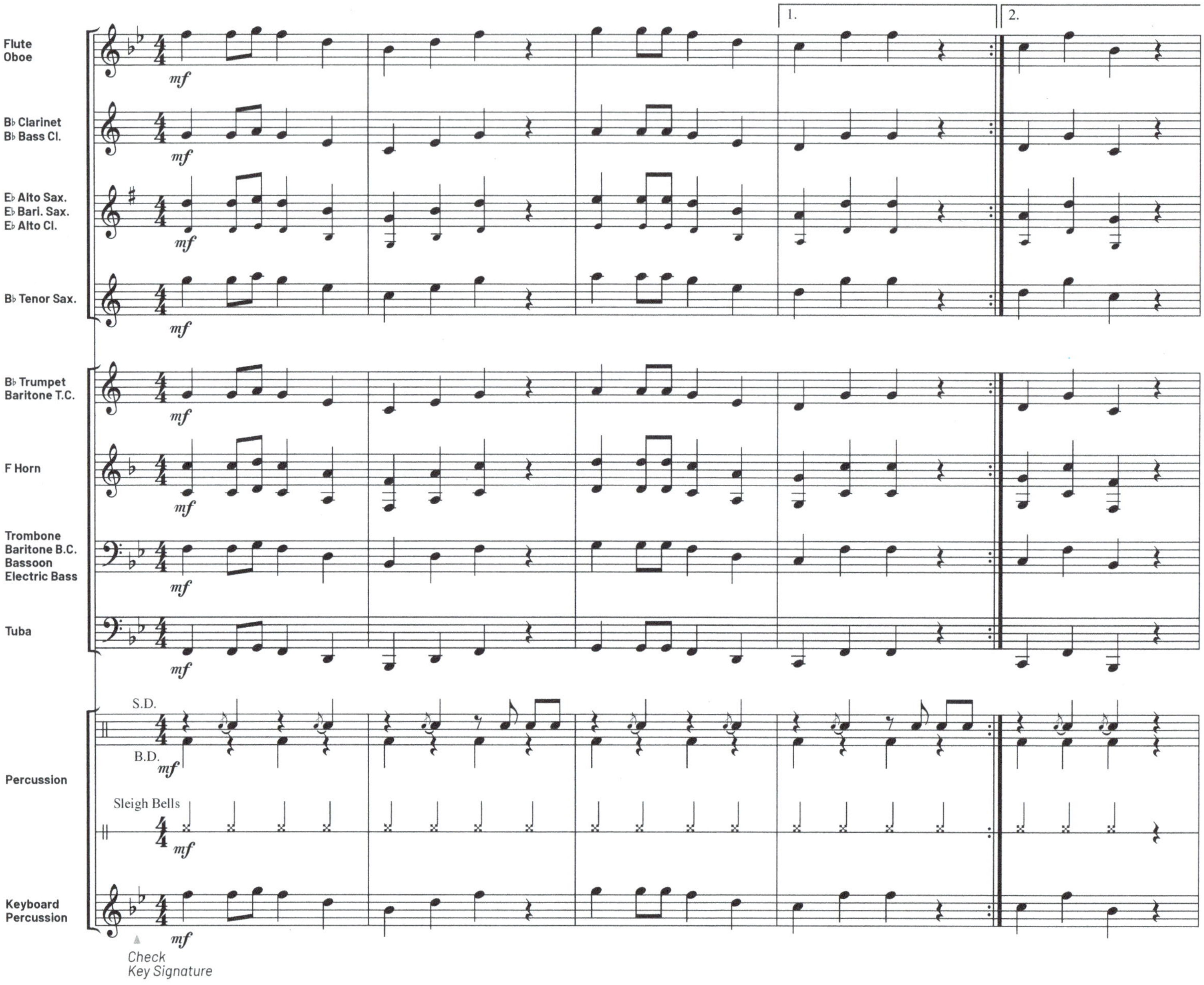
1.
2.
Flute
Oboe
B♭ Clarinet
B♭ Bass Cl.
E♭ Alto Sax.
E♭ Bari. Sax.
E♭ Alto Cl.
B♭ Tenor Sax.
B♭ Trumpet
Baritone T.C.
F Horn
Trombone
Baritone B.C.
Bassoon
Electric Bass
Tuba
Percussion
S.D.
B.D.
Sleigh Bells
Keyboard
Percussion
mf
Check
Key Signature

Flute
Oboe
B♭ Clarinet
B♭ Bass Cl.
E♭ Alto Sax.
E♭ Bari. Sax.
E♭ Alto Cl.
B♭ Tenor Sax.
B♭ Trumpet
Baritone T.C.
F Horn
Trombone
Baritone B.C.
Bassoon
Electric Bass
Tuba
Percussion
Keyboard
Percussion
f

Practice lines A and B separately. The 1st and 2nd ending markings above line A apply to both duet parts.

79. JOLLY OLD ST. NICK – Duet

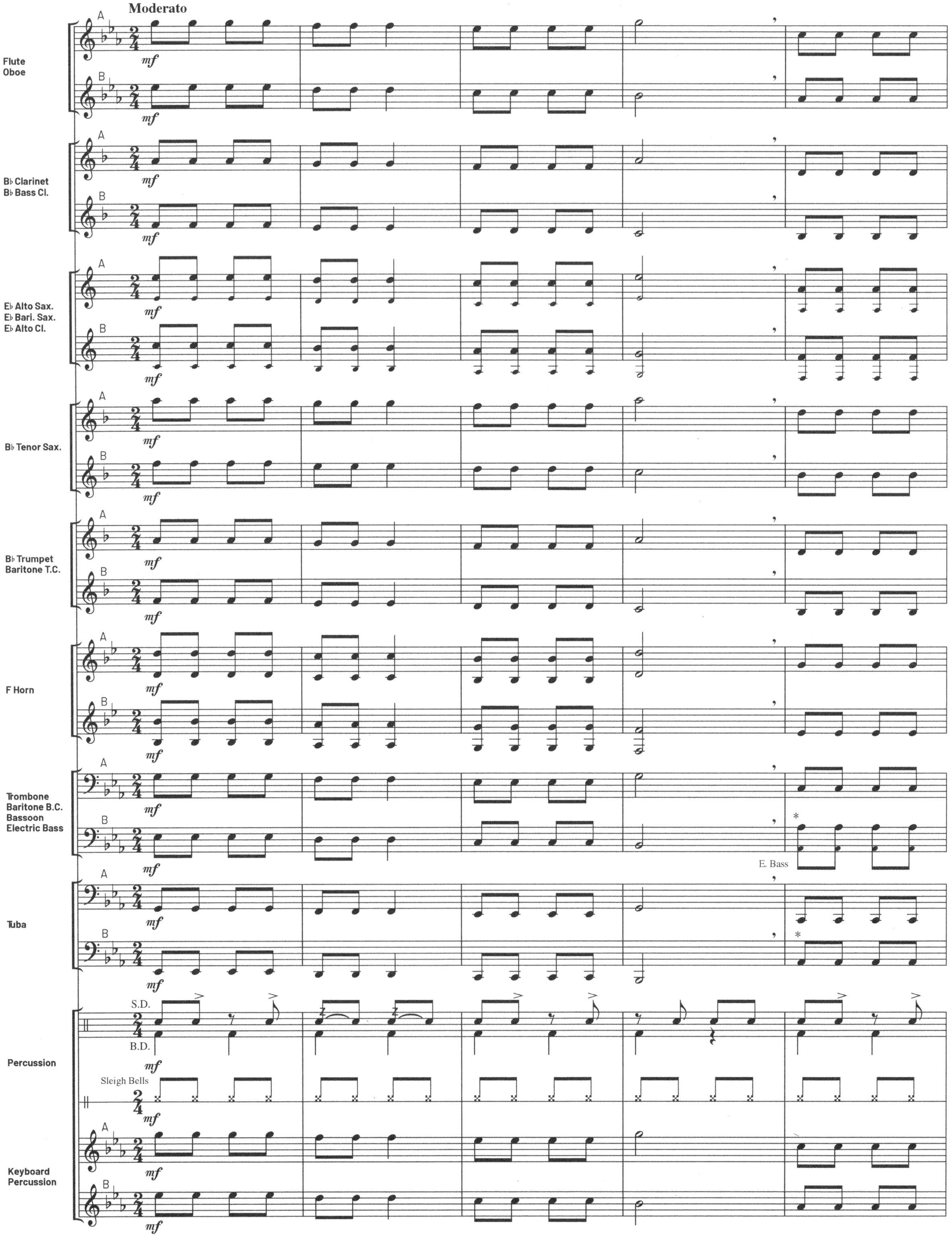

Moderato

Flute
Oboe

B♭ Clarinet
B♭ Bass Cl.

E♭ Alto Sax.
E♭ Bari. Sax.
E♭ Alto Cl.

B♭ Tenor Sax.

B♭ Trumpet
Baritone T.C.

F Horn

Trombone
Baritone B.C.
Bassoon
Electric Bass

E. Bass

Tuba

Percussion

S.D.

B.D.

Sleigh Bells

Keyboard
Percussion

* Conductor note: At times the B part may be higher than the A part.

Percussion Remember to emphasize the accented notes.

See page 9 for additional holiday music, MY DREYDL and JINGLE BELLS.

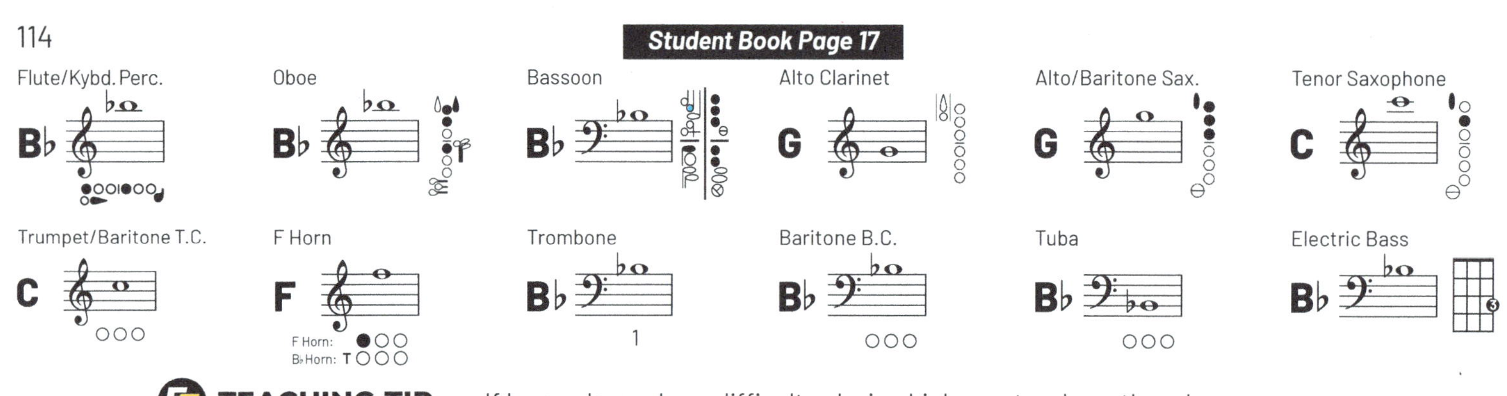

TEACHING TIP If brass players have difficulty playing higher notes, have them buzz a "siren" pattern on their mouthpiece. Stress breath support.

F Horn Double Horn Players: add the thumb key and use the B♭ Horn fingering to play "F." (High "F" is optional.)

80. THE BIG AIRSTREAM – New Note

Flute
Oboe

B♭ Clarinet
B♭ Bass Cl.

E♭ Alto Sax.
E♭ Bari. Sax.
E♭ Alto Cl.

B♭ Tenor Sax.

B♭ Trumpet
Baritone T.C.

F Horn

Trombone
Baritone B.C.
Bassoon
Electric Bass
Tuba

Percussion
S.D.
B.D.

Keyboard
Percussion

Flute
Oboe

B♭ Clarinet
B♭ Bass Cl.

E♭ Alto Sax.
E♭ Bari. Sax.
E♭ Alto Cl.

B♭ Tenor Sax.

B♭ Trumpet
Baritone T.C.

F Horn

Trombone
Baritone B.C.
Bassoon
Electric Bass
Tuba

Percussion

Keyboard
Percussion

81. WALTZ THEME (THE MERRY WIDOW WALTZ)

Franz Lehar

Oboe

E♭

Clarinet

F

Bass Clarinet

F

Tenor Saxophone

F

Percussion

Sixteenth Notes

1 e & a

Each Sixteenth Note = 1/4 Beat
4 Sixteenth Notes = 1 Beat

1 e & a 2 e & a

Special Percussion Exercise

R L R L R L R L R L R L R L R L R L R L R L R L R L R L R L R L R L R L R L R
1 & 2 & 3 & 4 & 1 & 2 & 3 & 4 & 1 e & a 2 & 3 e & a 4 & 1 & 2 e & a 3 & 4 &

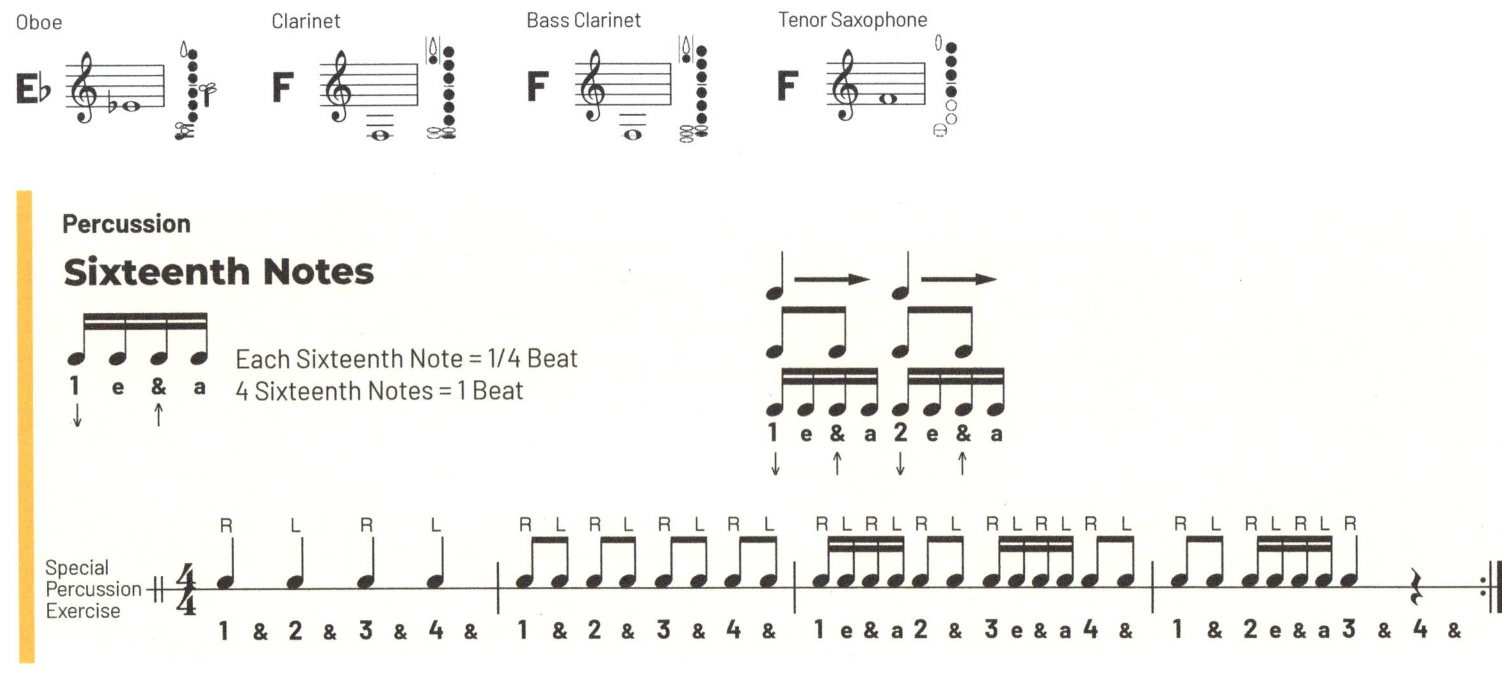

TEACHING TIP Be prepared to spend extra time with the woodwinds on their new note.

Percussion Count carefully and maintain a steady tempo.

82. AIR TIME – New Note

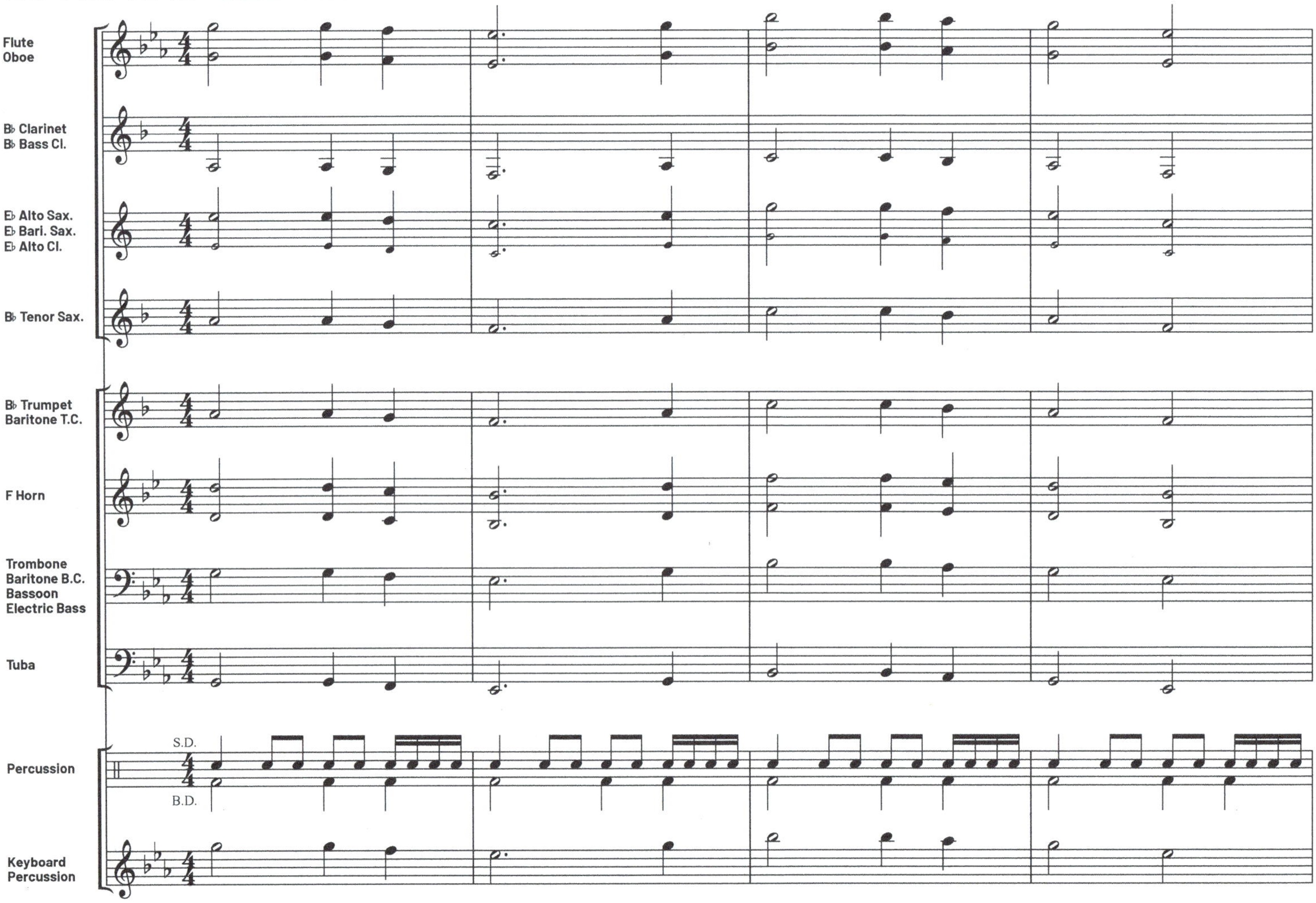
Flute
Oboe
B♭ Clarinet
B♭ Bass Cl.
E♭ Alto Sax.
E♭ Bari. Sax.
E♭ Alto Cl.
B♭ Tenor Sax.
B♭ Trumpet
Baritone T.C.
F Horn
Trombone
Baritone B.C.
Bassoon
Electric Bass
Tuba
Percussion
S.D.
B.D.
Keyboard
Percussion

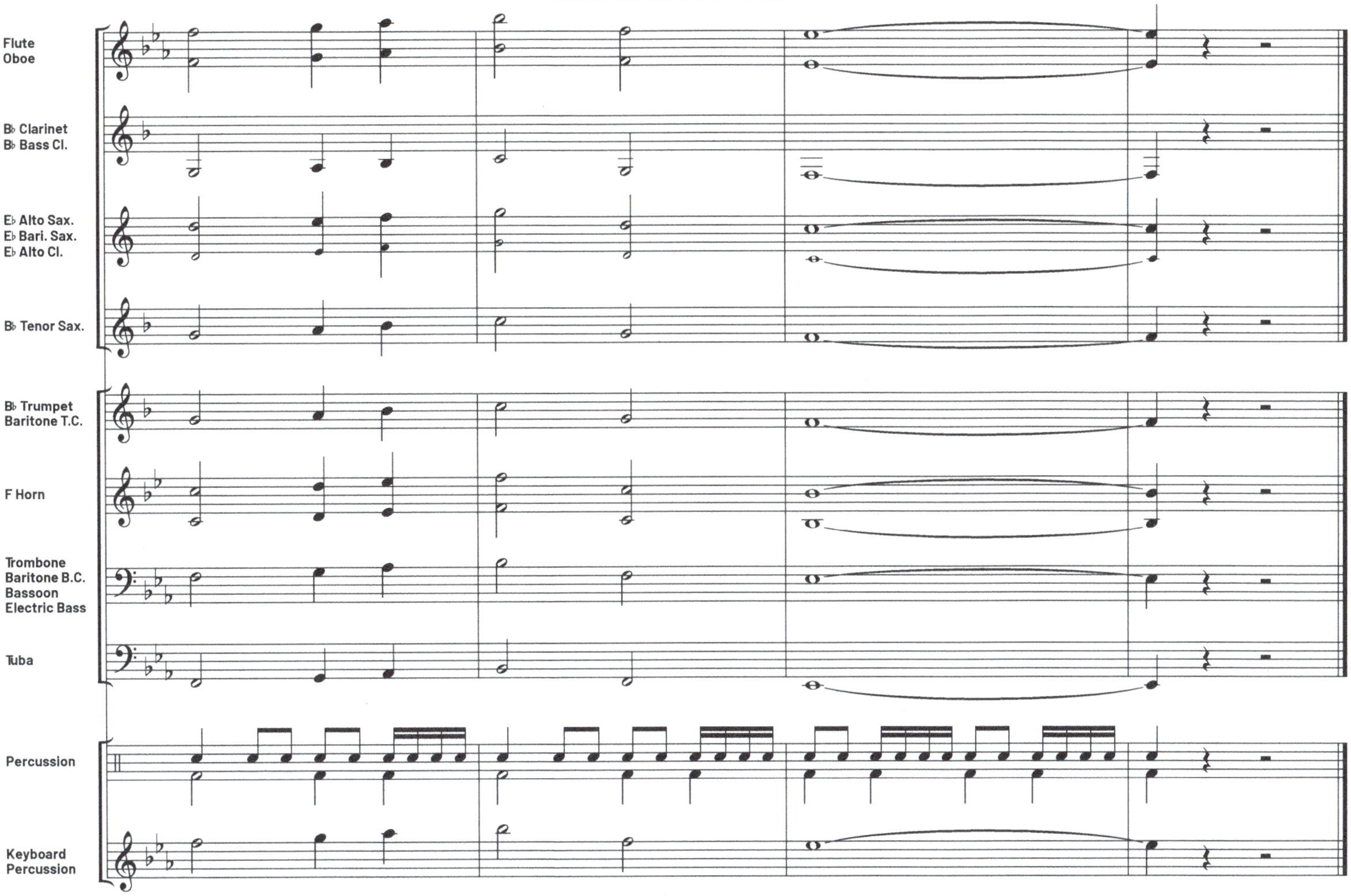

Flute
Oboe

B♭ Clarinet
B♭ Bass Cl.

E♭ Alto Sax.
E♭ Bari. Sax.
E♭ Alto Cl.

B♭ Tenor Sax.

B♭ Trumpet
Baritone T.C.

F Horn

Trombone
Baritone B.C.
Bassoon
Electric Bass

Tuba

Percussion

Keyboard
Percussion

Review the first note with the woodwinds before playing this exercise.

83. DOWN BY THE STATION

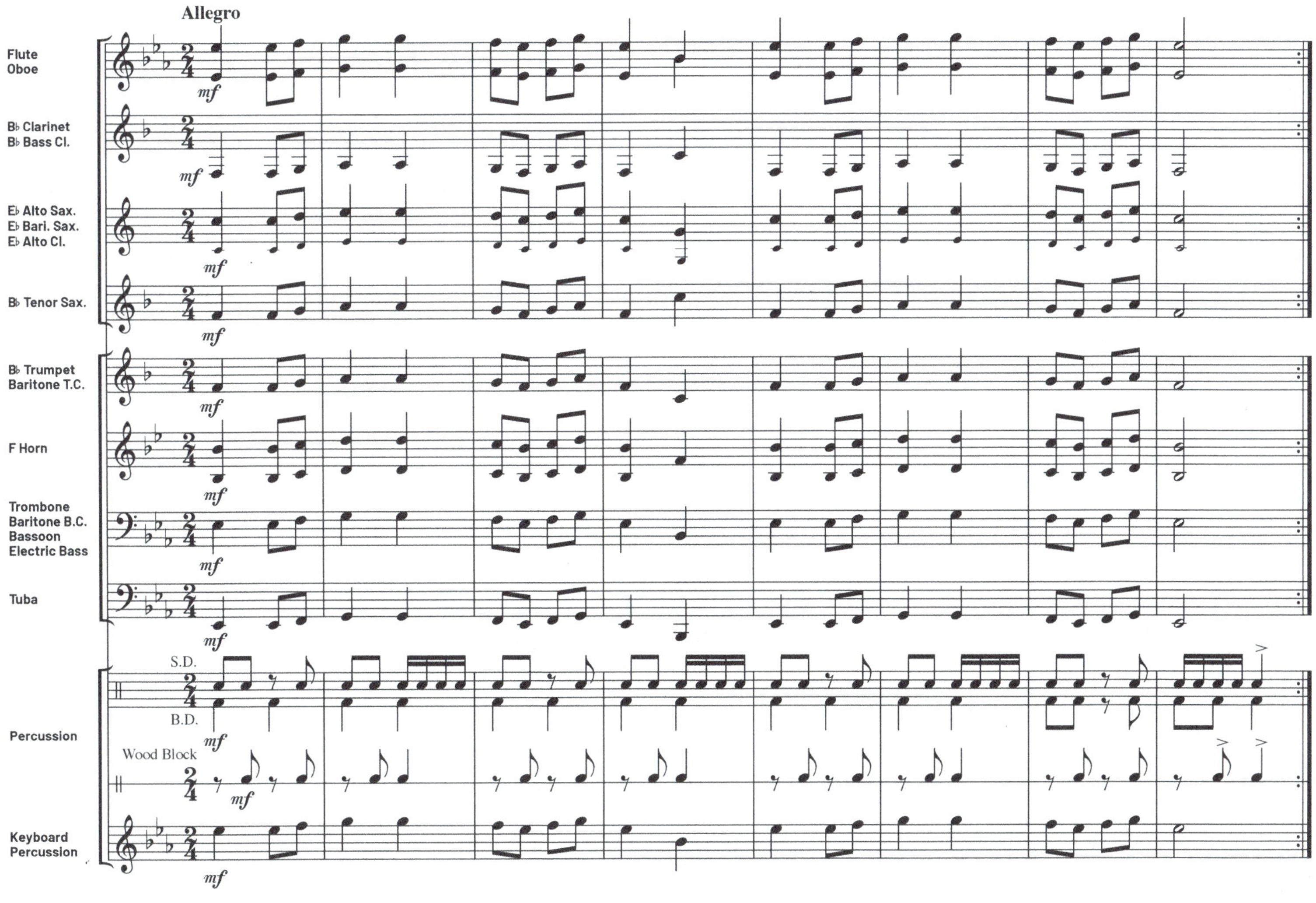

Allegro

Flute
Oboe

B♭ Clarinet
B♭ Bass Cl.

E♭ Alto Sax.
E♭ Bari. Sax.
E♭ Alto Cl.

B♭ Tenor Sax.

B♭ Trumpet
Baritone T.C.

F Horn

Trombone
Baritone B.C.
Bassoon
Electric Bass

Tuba

Percussion

S.D.

B.D.

Wood Block

Keyboard
Percussion

mf

Key signature (Concert E♭), 3/4 Time signature, Moderato, new notes (Concert A♭, B♭), crescendo, accent, decrescendo, dynamic (*p*).

84. ESSENTIAL ELEMENTS QUIZ

Moderato

Flute
Oboe

B♭ Clarinet
B♭ Bass Cl.

E♭ Alto Sax.
E♭ Bari. Sax.
E♭ Alto Cl.

B♭ Tenor Sax.

B♭ Trumpet
Baritone T.C.

F Horn

Trombone
Baritone B.C.
Bassoon
Electric Bass
Tuba

Percussion

S.D.

B.D.

Keyboard
Percussion

a2 *mf* *f*

Flute
Oboe

B♭ Clarinet
B♭ Bass Cl.

E♭ Alto Sax.
E♭ Bari. Sax.
E♭ Alto Cl.

B♭ Tenor Sax.

B♭ Trumpet

F Horn

Trombone
Baritone B.C.
Bassoon
Electric Bass
Tuba

Percussion

Cr. Cym. *Solo* *f*

Solo

Keyboard
Percussion

a2 *p*

CREATIVITY TIP Before beginning this exercise, review the rhythms the students have learned. If your students are having difficulty with this exercise, encourage them to write out a rhythm (which totals 4 beats) for each measure before playing. Then try to vary the rhythms.

Percussion Improvise your own part for measures 3–8 using these rhythms: ♩, ♫, ♬♬

85. ESSENTIAL CREATIVITY *Using these notes, improvise your own rhythms:*

Flute
Oboe

B♭ Clarinet
B♭ Bass Cl.

E♭ Alto Sax.
E♭ Bari. Sax.
E♭ Alto Cl.

B♭ Tenor Sax.

B♭ Trumpet
Baritone T.C.

F Horn

Trombone
Baritone B.C.
Bassoon
Electric Bass

Tuba

Percussion
S.D.
B.D.

Keyboard
Percussion

Flute
Oboe

B♭ Clarinet
B♭ Bass Cl.

E♭ Alto Sax.
E♭ Bari. Sax.
E♭ Alto Cl.

B♭ Tenor Sax.

B♭ Trumpet
Baritone T.C.

F Horn

Trombone
Baritone B.C.
Bassoon
Electric Bass

Tuba

Percussion

Keyboard
Percussion

Student Book Page 18

DAILY WARM-UPS

WORK-OUTS FOR TONE & TECHNIQUE

TEACHING TIP These Warm-Ups will help develop the student's tone, technique, rhythm, and ensemble listening skills. They should be used daily until student book page 30.

86. TONE BUILDER *Use a steady stream of air.*

Flute
Oboe

B♭ Clarinet
B♭ Bass Cl.

E♭ Alto Sax.
E♭ Bari. Sax.
E♭ Alto Cl.

B♭ Tenor Sax.

B♭ Trumpet
Baritone T.C.

F Horn

Trombone
Baritone B.C.
Bassoon
Electric Bass

Tuba

Percussion

S.D.
B.D.

Keyboard
Percussion

Flute
Oboe

B♭ Clarinet
B♭ Bass Cl.

E♭ Alto Sax.
E♭ Bari. Sax.
E♭ Alto Cl.

B♭ Tenor Sax.

B♭ Trumpet
Baritone T.C.

F Horn

Trombone
Baritone B.C.
Bassoon
Electric Bass

Tuba

Percussion

Keyboard
Percussion

87. RHYTHM BUILDER

Alto Sax., Bari. Sax. Roll your thumb up to the octave key. Always keep your thumb on the left thumb rest.

88. TECHNIQUE TRAX

89. CHORALE *(Adapted from Cantata 147)*

Johann Sebastian Bach

THEORY

Theme and Variations

A musical form featuring a **theme**, or primary melody, followed by **variations**, or altered versions of the theme.

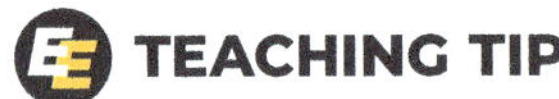

TEACHING TIP Once learned, divide the group and have one section play the theme while another plays Variation 1. Do the same with Variation 2.

90. VARIATIONS ON A FAMILIAR THEME

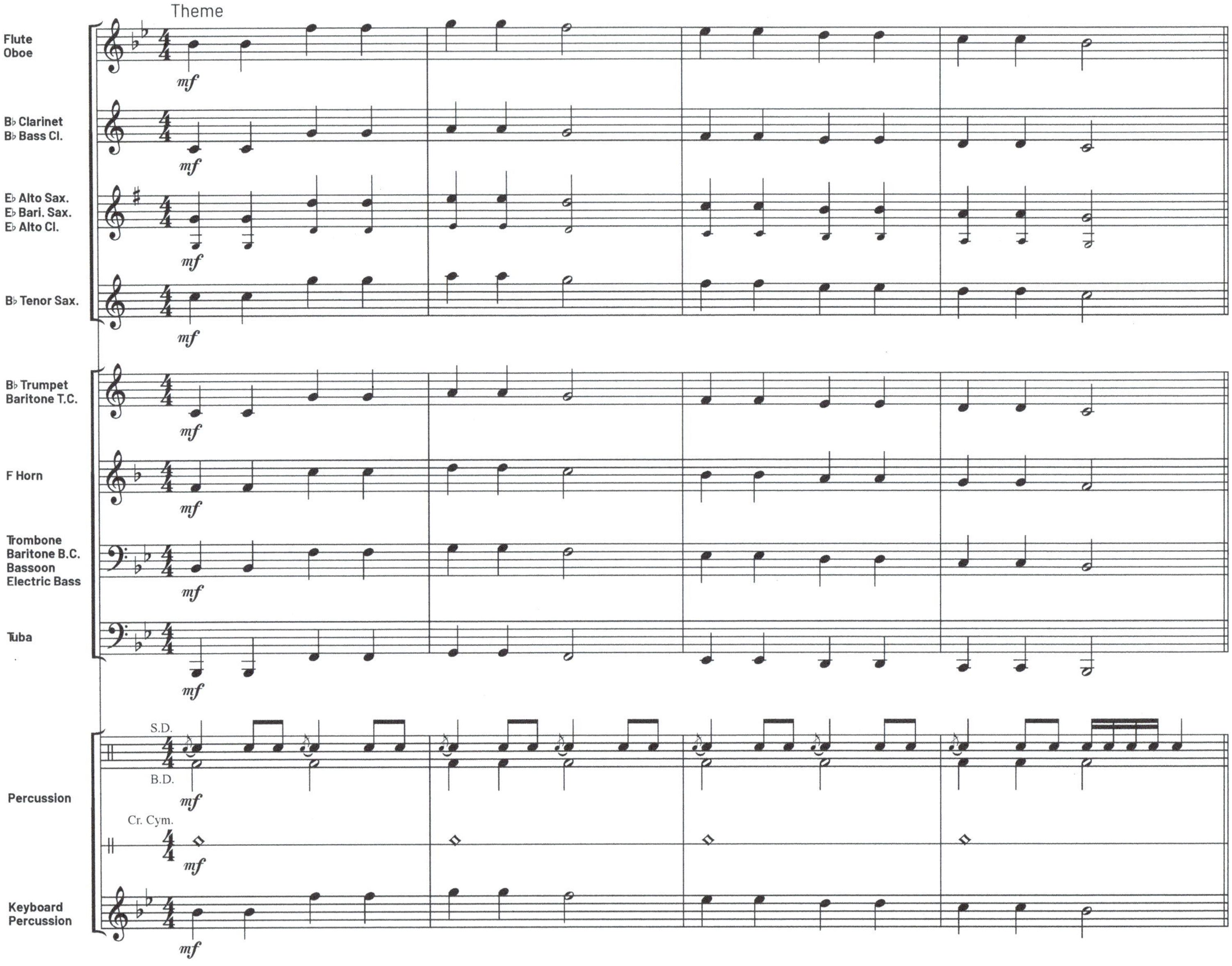
Theme
Flute
Oboe
B♭ Clarinet
B♭ Bass Cl.
E♭ Alto Sax.
E♭ Bari. Sax.
E♭ Alto Cl.
B♭ Tenor Sax.
B♭ Trumpet
Baritone T.C.
F Horn
Trombone
Baritone B.C.
Bassoon
Electric Bass
Tuba
Percussion
S.D.
B.D.
Cr. Cym.
Keyboard
Percussion
mf

Variation 1
Flute
Oboe
B♭ Clarinet
B♭ Bass Cl.
E♭ Alto Sax.
E♭ Bari. Sax.
E♭ Alto Cl.
B♭ Tenor Sax.
B♭ Trumpet
Baritone T.C.
F Horn
Trombone
Baritone B.C.
Bassoon
Electric Bass
Tuba
Percussion
Change to Triangle
Tri.
mf
Keyboard
Percussion
Variation 2
Change to Cr. Cym.
Cr. Cym.
mf

D.C. al Fine

At the **D.C. al Fine** play again from the beginning, stopping at **Fine** *(fee'- nay)*.
D.C. is the abbreviation for **Da Capo**, or "to the beginning," and **Fine** means "the end."

Percussion

Eighth Note Two Sixteenths

1 e & a

= 1 Beat
Subdivide each beat into 4 equal parts.

=
1 e & a

1 e & a 2 e & a

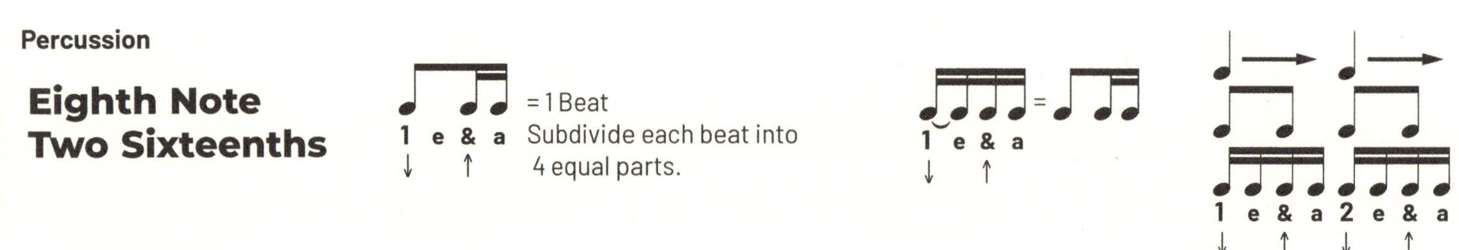

TEACHING TIP Say note names while practicing fingerings in rhythm.

91. BANANA BOAT SONG

Caribbean Folk Song

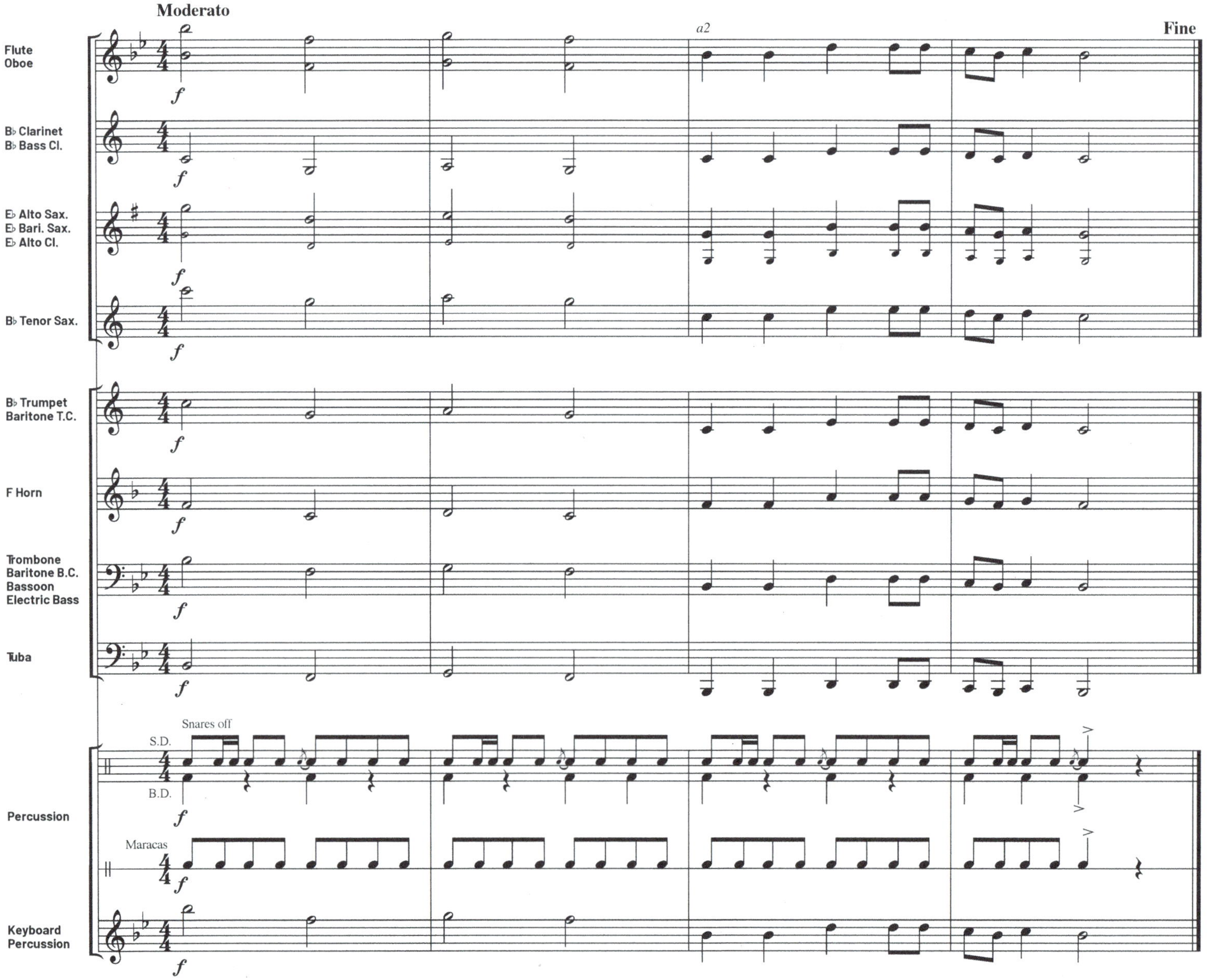

Moderato
a2
Fine
Flute
Oboe
B♭ Clarinet
B♭ Bass Cl.
E♭ Alto Sax.
E♭ Bari. Sax.
E♭ Alto Cl.
B♭ Tenor Sax.
B♭ Trumpet
Baritone T.C.
F Horn
Trombone
Baritone B.C.
Bassoon
Electric Bass
Tuba
Snares off
S.D.
B.D.
Percussion
Maracas
Keyboard
Percussion

Flute
Oboe
mf

B♭ Clarinet
B♭ Bass Cl.
mf

E♭ Alto Sax.
E♭ Bari. Sax.
E♭ Alto Cl.
mf

B♭ Tenor Sax.
mf

B♭ Trumpet
Baritone T.C.
mf

F Horn
mf

Trombone
Baritone B.C.
Bassoon
Electric Bass
mf

Tuba
mf

Percussion
mf
mf
mf

Keyboard
Percussion
mf

D.C. al Fine

Flute
Oboe

B♭ Clarinet
B♭ Bass Cl.

E♭ Alto Sax.
E♭ Bari. Sax.
E♭ Alto Cl.

B♭ Tenor Sax.

B♭ Trumpet
Baritone T.C.

F Horn

Trombone
Baritone B.C.
Bassoon
Electric Bass

Tuba

Percussion

Keyboard
Percussion

THEORY

Natural ♮
A **natural** sign cancels a flat (♭) or sharp (♯) and remains in effect for the entire measure.

Sharp ♯
A sharp sign raises the pitch of a note by a half-step. The note F-sharp (C-sharp) sounds a half-step above F (C), and all F's (C's) become F-sharps (C-sharps) for the rest of the measure where they occur.

Flute/Kybd. Perc. E
Oboe E
Bassoon E
Clarinet F♯
Alto Clarinet C♯
Bass Clarinet F♯
Alto Saxophone C♯
Tenor Saxophone F♯
Baritone Saxophone C♯
Trumpet F♯
F Horn B
F Horn:
B♭ Horn: T
Trombone E
2
Baritone B.C. E
Baritone T.C. F♯
Tuba E
Electric Bass E

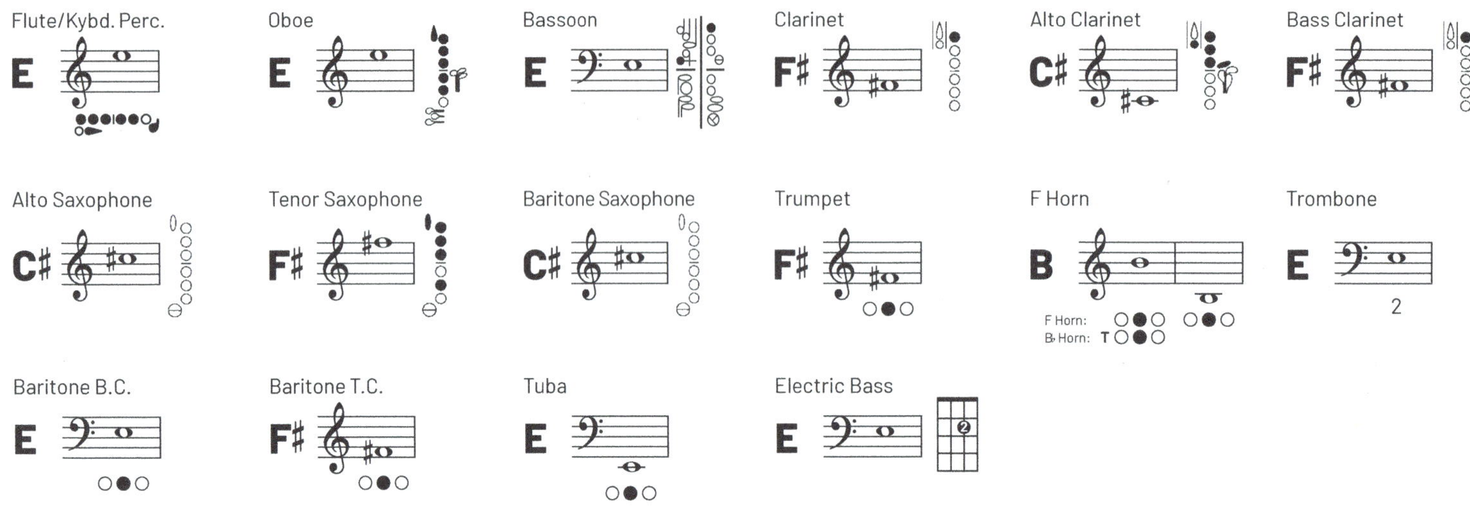

TEACHING TIP Play the new note before playing this exercise.

F Horn Double Horn Players: add the thumb key and use the B♭ Horn fingering for the upper "B-natural."

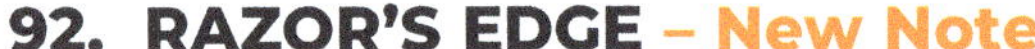

92. RAZOR'S EDGE – New Note

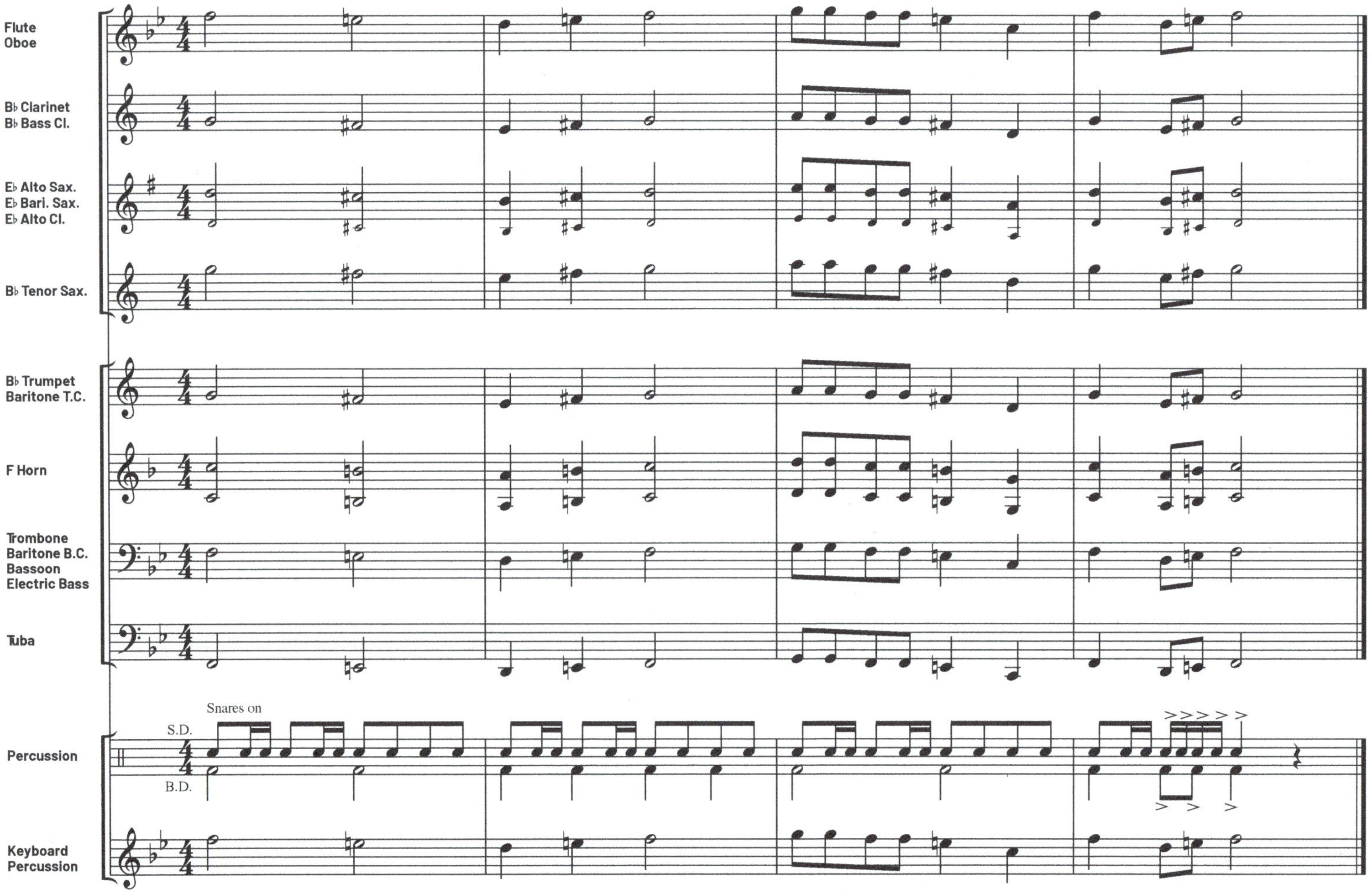
Flute
Oboe
B♭ Clarinet
B♭ Bass Cl.
E♭ Alto Sax.
E♭ Bari. Sax.
E♭ Alto Cl.
B♭ Tenor Sax.
B♭ Trumpet
Baritone T.C.
F Horn
Trombone
Baritone B.C.
Bassoon
Electric Bass
Tuba
Snares on
S.D.
B.D.
Percussion
Keyboard
Percussion

Remind students that an accidental applies to the entire measure.

93. THE MUSIC BOX

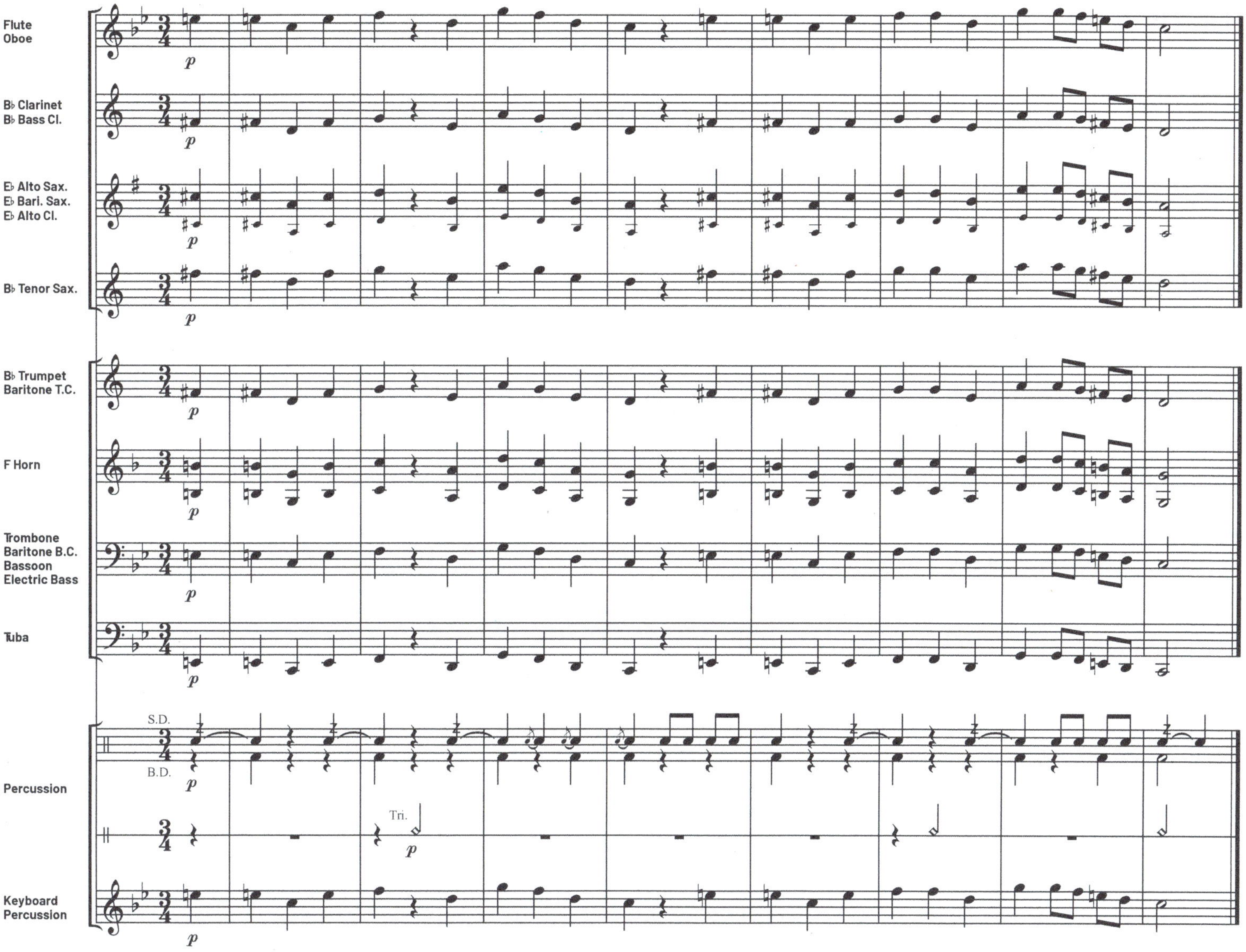

Flute
Oboe

B♭ Clarinet
B♭ Bass Cl.

E♭ Alto Sax.
E♭ Bari. Sax.
E♭ Alto Cl.

B♭ Tenor Sax.

B♭ Trumpet
Baritone T.C.

F Horn

Trombone
Baritone B.C.
Bassoon
Electric Bass

Tuba

Percussion

S.D.
B.D.
Tri.

Keyboard
Percussion

p

HISTORY

African-American spirituals originated in the 1700's, midway through the period of slavery in the United States. One of the largest categories of true American folk music, these primarily religious songs were sung and passed on for generations without being written down. The first collection of spirituals was published in 1867, four years after The Emancipation Proclamation was signed into law.

94. EZEKIEL SAW THE WHEEL

African-American Spiritual

Slur

A curved line which connects notes of different pitch. Tongue only the first note in a **slur**.

Trombone Tongue the first note normally. Then, play the slurred note(s) using "dah", a legato toguing syllalble. *Legato* – An Italian word for smooth and connected.

TEACHING TIP Move their fingers or slides quickly from one note to the next. Play the first two measures and measure 5 several times before playing this exercise.

Trombone Slur 2 notes. Tongue the first note. Use "dah" on the second note.

95. SMOOTH OPERATOR

Slur 2 notes – tongue only the first.

Flute
Oboe

B♭ Clarinet
B♭ Bass Cl.

E♭ Alto Sax.
E♭ Bari. Sax.
E♭ Alto Cl.

B♭ Tenor Sax.

B♭ Trumpet
Baritone T.C.

F Horn

Trombone
Baritone B.C.
Bassoon
Electric Bass

Tuba

Percussion (S.D., B.D., Rim Shot)

Keyboard Percussion

Note how the pattern changed.

Remind students to use adequate breath support during the 4-note slurs.

Trombone Slur 4 notes. Tongue the first note. Use "dah" on all notes connected by a slur.

Percussion Practice "Doubling" in this exercise.

96. GLIDING ALONG

Slur 4 notes – tongue only the first.

Flute / Oboe

B♭ Clarinet / B♭ Bass Cl.

E♭ Alto Sax. / E♭ Bari. Sax. / E♭ Alto Cl.

B♭ Tenor Sax.

B♭ Trumpet / Baritone T.C.

F Horn

Trombone / Baritone B.C. / Bassoon / Electric Bass

Tuba

Percussion (S.D., B.D.) — R L L R L R L R L L R L R L; Rim Shot R

Keyboard Percussion

Ragtime is an American music style that was popular from the 1890's until the time of World War I. This early form of jazz brought fame to pianists like "Jelly Roll" Morton and Scott Joplin, who wrote "The Entertainer" and "Maple Leaf Rag." Surprisingly, the style was incorporated into some orchestral music by Igor Stravinsky and Claude Debussy. The trombones now learn to play a *glissando*, a technique used in ragtime and other styles of music.

This exercise features the trombone "glissando." Trombones – use a steady stream of air to get the maximum effect.

97. TROMBONE RAG

Allegro

Flute / Oboe / Kybd. Perc.

B♭ Clarinet / B♭ Bass Cl.

E♭ Alto Sax. / E♭ Bari. Sax. / E♭ Alto Cl.

B♭ Tenor Sax.

B♭ Trumpet

F Horn

Trombone / Baritone B.C. / Bassoon / Electric Bass / Tuba

Percussion — S.D. (On Rim), B.D., Wood Block

f

1. 2.

Tbn. gliss.

Solo

Trombone A special trombone technique used in ragtime and other styles of music is called a *glissando*, which looks like this: To play a *glissando*, move your slide without tonguing and use a full airstream. Remember that *glissandos* are different from *legato* tonguing (slurs).

Student Book Page 19

QUIZ ASSESSMENT Andante, slur, sharp, new note (Concert E), D.C. al fine.

98. ESSENTIAL ELEMENTS QUIZ

Andante

Fine

Flute
Oboe

B♭ Clarinet
B♭ Bass Cl.

E♭ Alto Sax.
E♭ Bari. Sax.
E♭ Alto Cl.

B♭ Tenor Sax.

B♭ Trumpet
Baritone T.C.

F Horn

Trombone
Baritone B.C.
Bassoon
Electric Bass

Tuba

Percussion

S.D.

B.D.

Keyboard Percussion

p

D.C. al Fine

Flute
Oboe

B♭ Clarinet
B♭ Bass Cl.

E♭ Alto Sax.
E♭ Bari. Sax.
E♭ Alto Cl.

B♭ Tenor Sax.

B♭ Trumpet
Baritone T.C.

F Horn

Trombone
Baritone B.C.
Bassoon
Electric Bass

Tuba

Percussion

Keyboard Percussion

Flute/Kybd. Perc.
A
Oboe
A
Bassoon
A
Alto Clarinet
F♯
Alto Saxophone
F♯
Tenor Saxophone
B
Baritone Saxophone
F♯
Trumpet
B
F Horn
E
F Horn:
B♭ Horn: T
Trombone
A
2
Baritone B.C.
A
Baritone T.C.
B
Tuba
A
Electric Bass
A

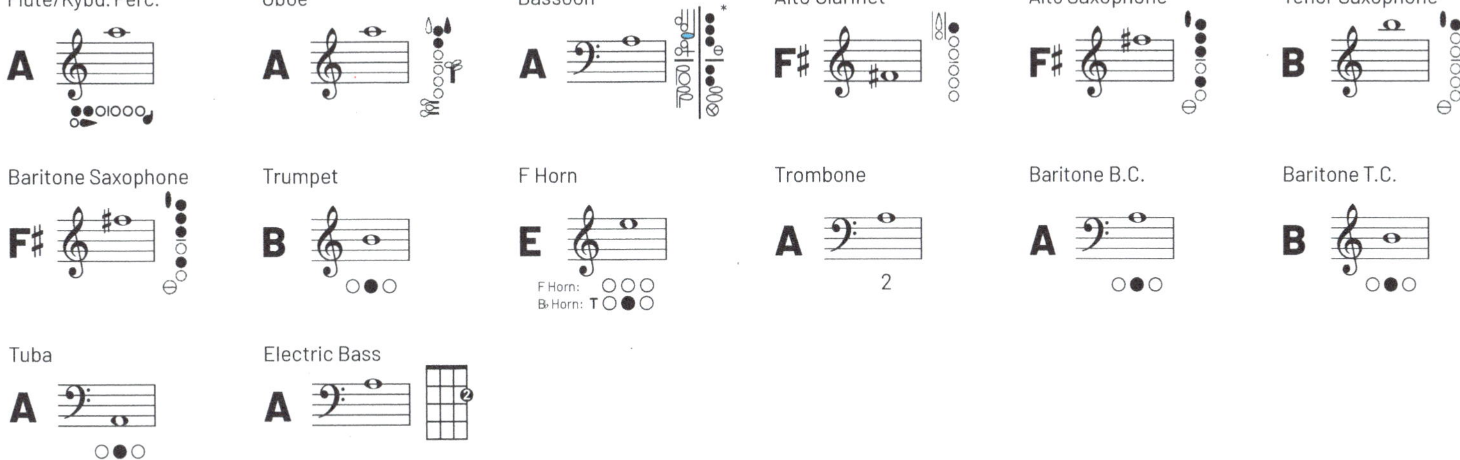

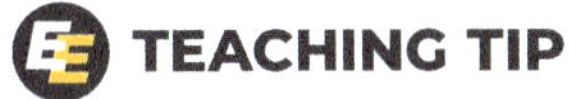

TEACHING TIP While introducing Concert A to other instruments, this is an excellent exercise to develop the chalameau register of the clarinet. Encourage everyone to play with good breath support and a full tone.

Cl., A. Cl., Bs. Cl. Always cover the tone holes completely.

F Horn Double Horn Players: add the thumb key and use the B♭ Horn fingering.
See student book page 9B if you wish to review the fingering for low "E-natural." High "E" is optional.

Percussion Practice Right Hand Lead in this exercise.

99. TAKE THE LEAD – New Note

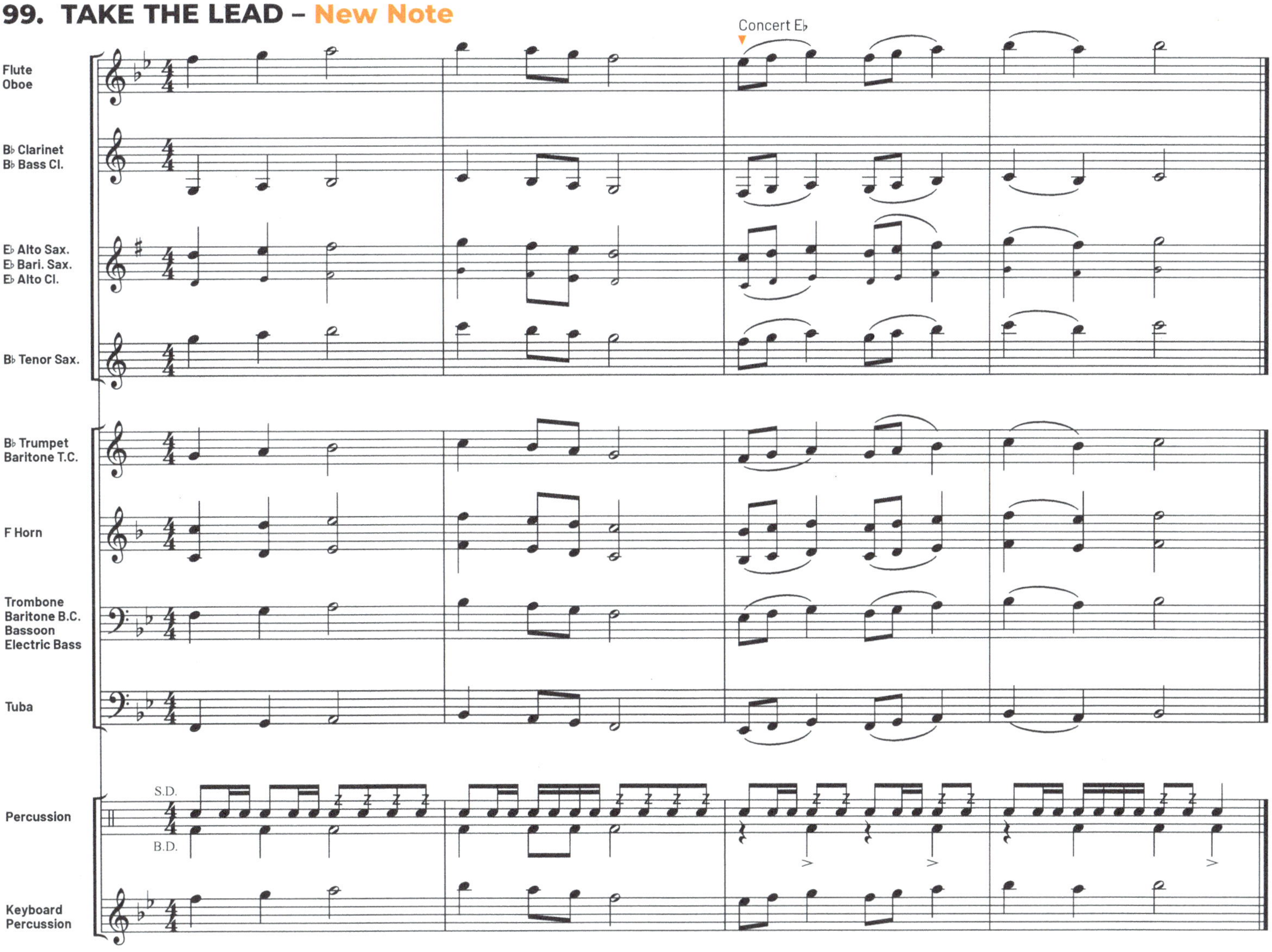
Concert E♭
Flute
Oboe
B♭ Clarinet
B♭ Bass Cl.
E♭ Alto Sax.
E♭ Bari. Sax.
E♭ Alto Cl.
B♭ Tenor Sax.
B♭ Trumpet
Baritone T.C.
F Horn
Trombone
Baritone B.C.
Bassoon
Electric Bass
Tuba
S.D.
Percussion
B.D.
Keyboard
Percussion

** For more information about this fingering, see the bassoon fingering chart.*

Phrase

A musical "sentence" which is often 2 or 4 measures long. Try to play a **phrase** in one breath.

Point out that a phrase is more than just "breathing at the right time." Also note dynamic markings.

Percussion Percussionists should match the dynamics of the band.

100. THE COLD WIND

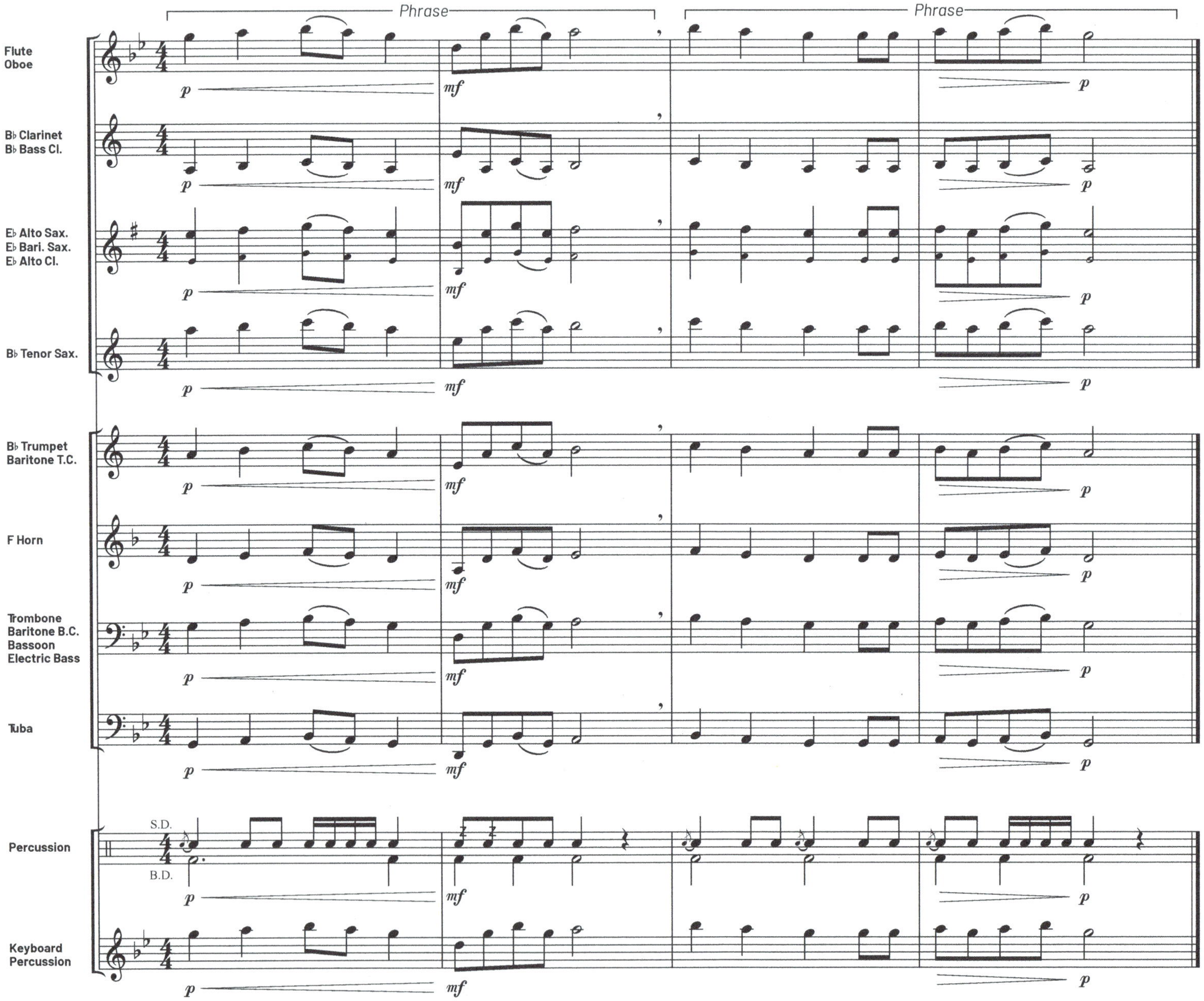

Phrase Phrase

Flute
Oboe

B♭ Clarinet
B♭ Bass Cl.

E♭ Alto Sax.
E♭ Bari. Sax.
E♭ Alto Cl.

B♭ Tenor Sax.

B♭ Trumpet
Baritone T.C.

F Horn

Trombone
Baritone B.C.
Bassoon
Electric Bass

Tuba

Percussion
S.D.
B.D.

Keyboard
Percussion

p mf p

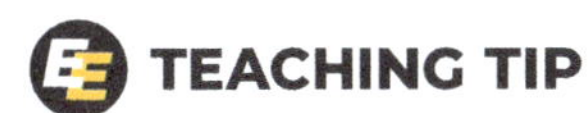

TEACHING TIP Ask for volunteers to perform this exercise alone. Have the rest of the class identify the performer's phrases.

101. PHRASEOLOGY *Write in the breath mark(s) between the phrases.*

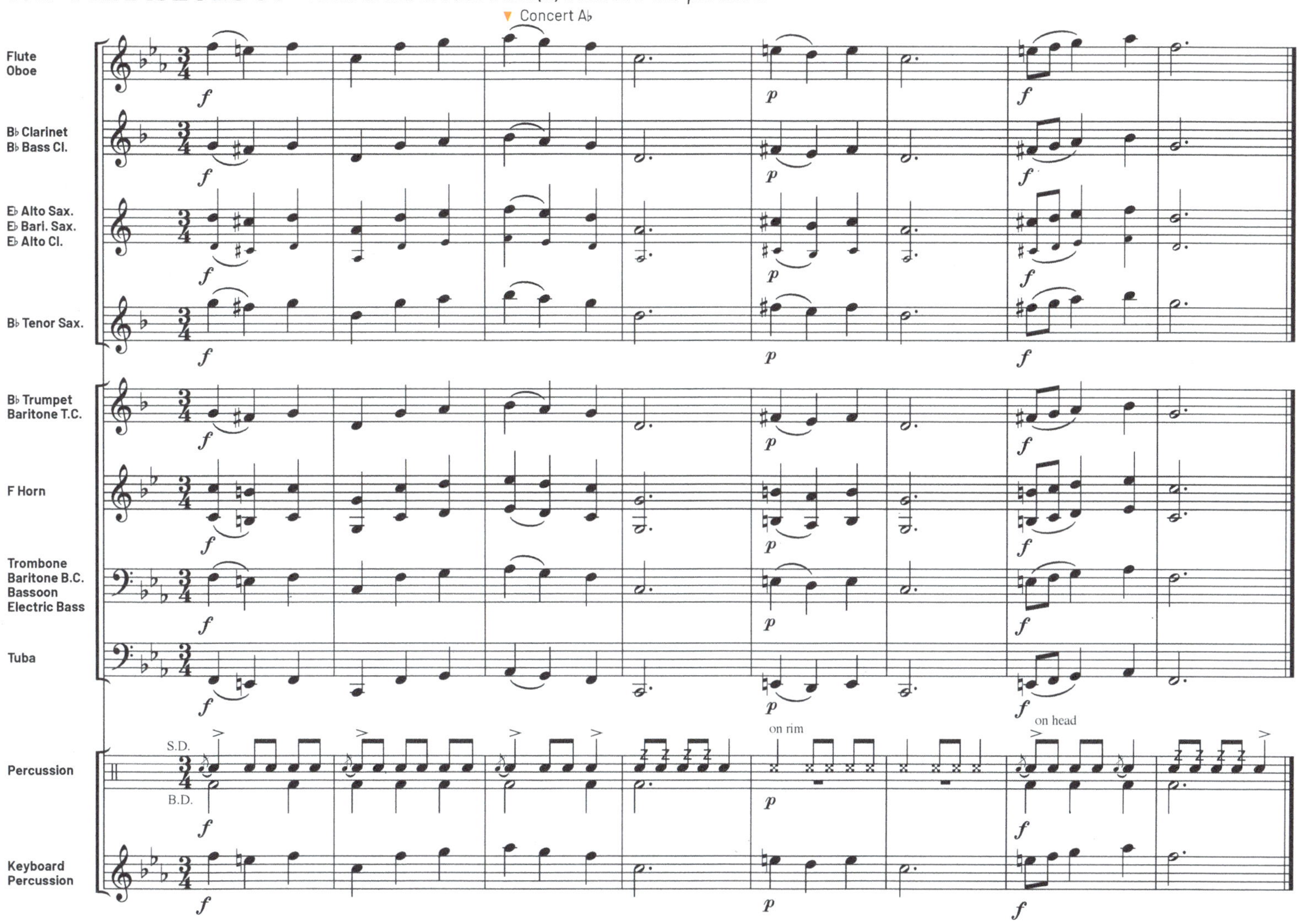

Concert A♭
Flute
Oboe
B♭ Clarinet
B♭ Bass Cl.
E♭ Alto Sax.
E♭ Bari. Sax.
E♭ Alto Cl.
B♭ Tenor Sax.
B♭ Trumpet
Baritone T.C.
F Horn
Trombone
Baritone B.C.
Bassoon
Electric Bass
Tuba
Percussion
S.D.
B.D.
on rim
on head
Keyboard
Percussion
f
p
f

New Key Signature (Ex. 102)

C Instruments or This **Key Signature** indicates the *Key of F* – play all B's as B-flats.

B♭ Instruments This **Key Signature** indicates the *Key of G* – play all F's as F-sharps.

E♭ Instruments This **Key Signature** indicates the *Key of D* – play all F's as F-sharps, and all C's as C-sharps.

F Horn This **Key Signature** indicates the *Key of C* (no sharps or flats).

Multiple Measure Rest
(Ex. 102)

The number above the staff tells you how many full measures to rest. Count each measure of rest in sequence.

2

1-2-3-4 **2**-2-3-4

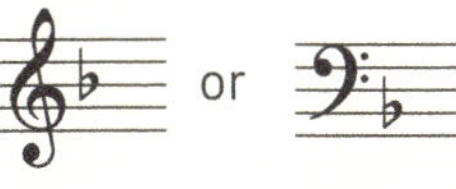

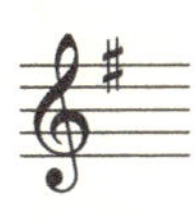

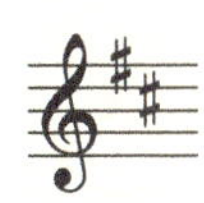

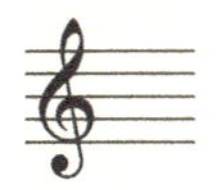

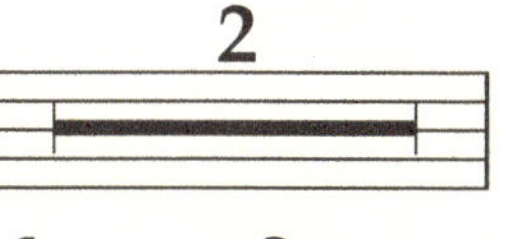

THEORY

Percussion (Ex. 102)

Simile *(sim.)*

Continue playing in the same style.

Kybd. Perc. (Ex. 102)

Roll

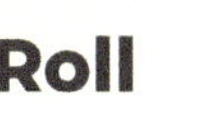

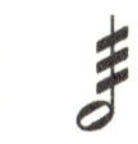

Rapidly alternate single strokes as smoothly as possible. Release the roll on the tied note or final beat with the same hand that started the roll. Rolls are usually found in xylophone and marimba music.

Have all students count their two measure rest in unison before playing this exercise.

Percussion Practice Double Sticking in this exercise.

102. SATIN LATIN

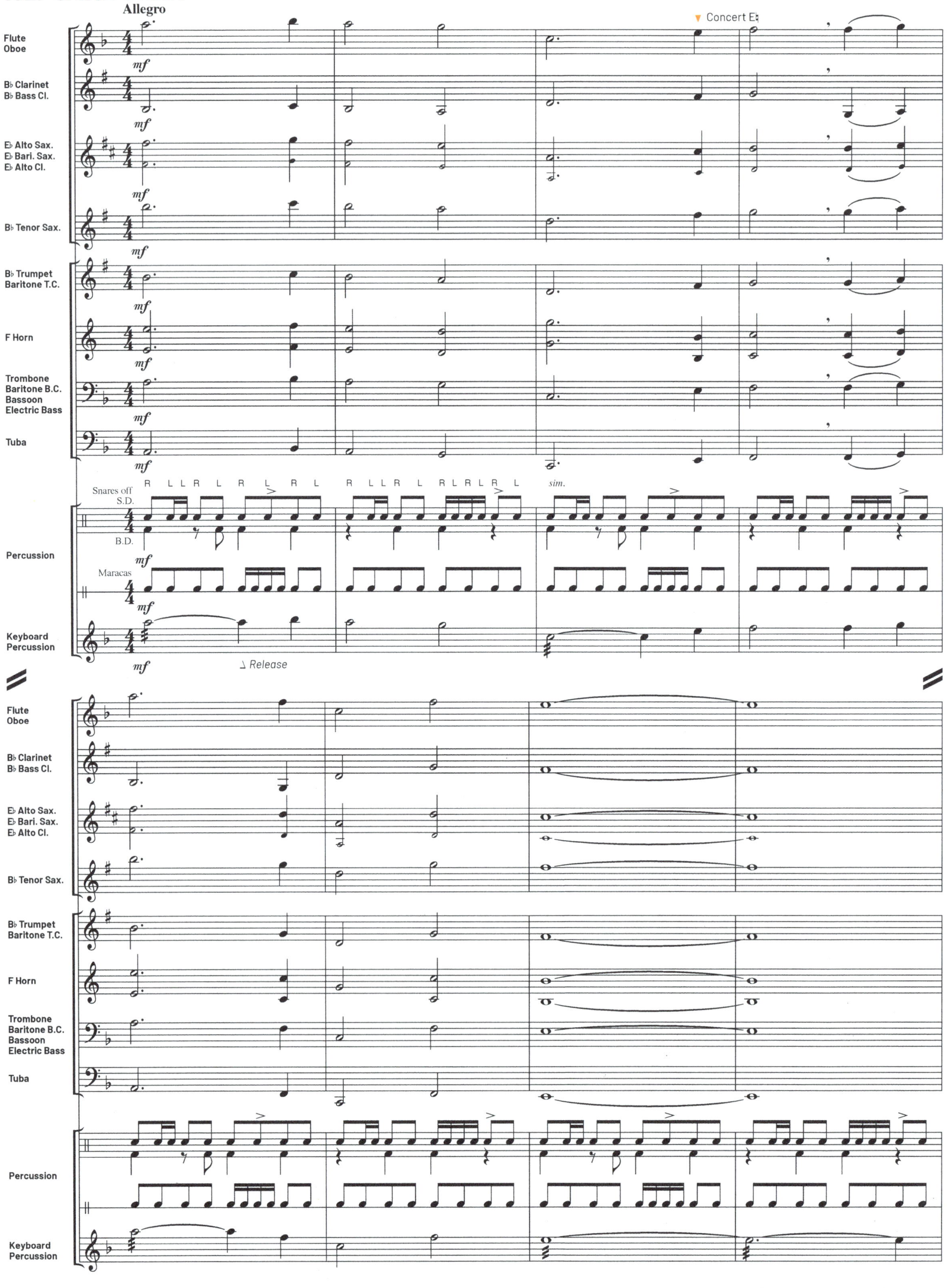

Allegro

Flute Oboe

B♭ Clarinet B♭ Bass Cl.

E♭ Alto Sax. E♭ Bari. Sax. E♭ Alto Cl.

B♭ Tenor Sax.

B♭ Trumpet Baritone T.C.

F Horn

Trombone Baritone B.C. Bassoon Electric Bass

Tuba

Percussion

Snares off S.D.

B.D.

Maracas

R L L R L R L R L R L L R L R L R L R L sim.

Keyboard Percussion

mf

Concert E♮

Release

Flute
Oboe
B♭ Clarinet
B♭ Bass Cl.
E♭ Alto Sax.
E♭ Bari. Sax.
E♭ Alto Cl.
B♭ Tenor Sax.
B♭ Trumpet
Baritone T.C.
F Horn
Trombone
Baritone B.C.
Bassoon
Electric Bass
Tuba
Percussion
Keyboard
Percussion
1 - 2 - 3 - 4 2 - 2 - 3 - 4
mf
Soli
Fl.
Ob.
a2
R L L R L R L R L R L L R L R L R L R

HISTORY

German composer **Johann Sebastian Bach** (1685–1750) was part of a large family of famous musicians and became the most recognized composer of the Baroque era. Beginning as a choir member, Bach soon became an organist, a teacher, and a prolific composer, writing more than 600 masterworks. This *Minuet*, or dance in 3/4 time, was written as a teaching piece for use with an early form of the piano.

TEACHING TIP Practice lines A and B separately. Then, divide the class and play.

103. MINUET – Duet

Johann Sebastian Bach

Flute
Oboe
B♭ Clarinet
B♭ Bass Cl.
E♭ Alto Sax.
E♭ Bari. Sax.
E♭ Alto Cl.
B♭ Tenor Sax.
B♭ Trumpet
Baritone T.C.
F Horn
Trombone
Baritone B.C.
Bassoon
Electric Bass
Tuba
Percussion
Keyboard
Percussion

This exercise should be played in both 3/4 and 4/4 time signatures. It demonstrates the effect that meter has on the feeling of the music.

104. ESSENTIAL CREATIVITY

This melody can be played in 3/4 or 4/4. Pencil in either time signature, draw the bar lines and play. Now erase the bar lines and try the other time signature. Do the phrases sound different?

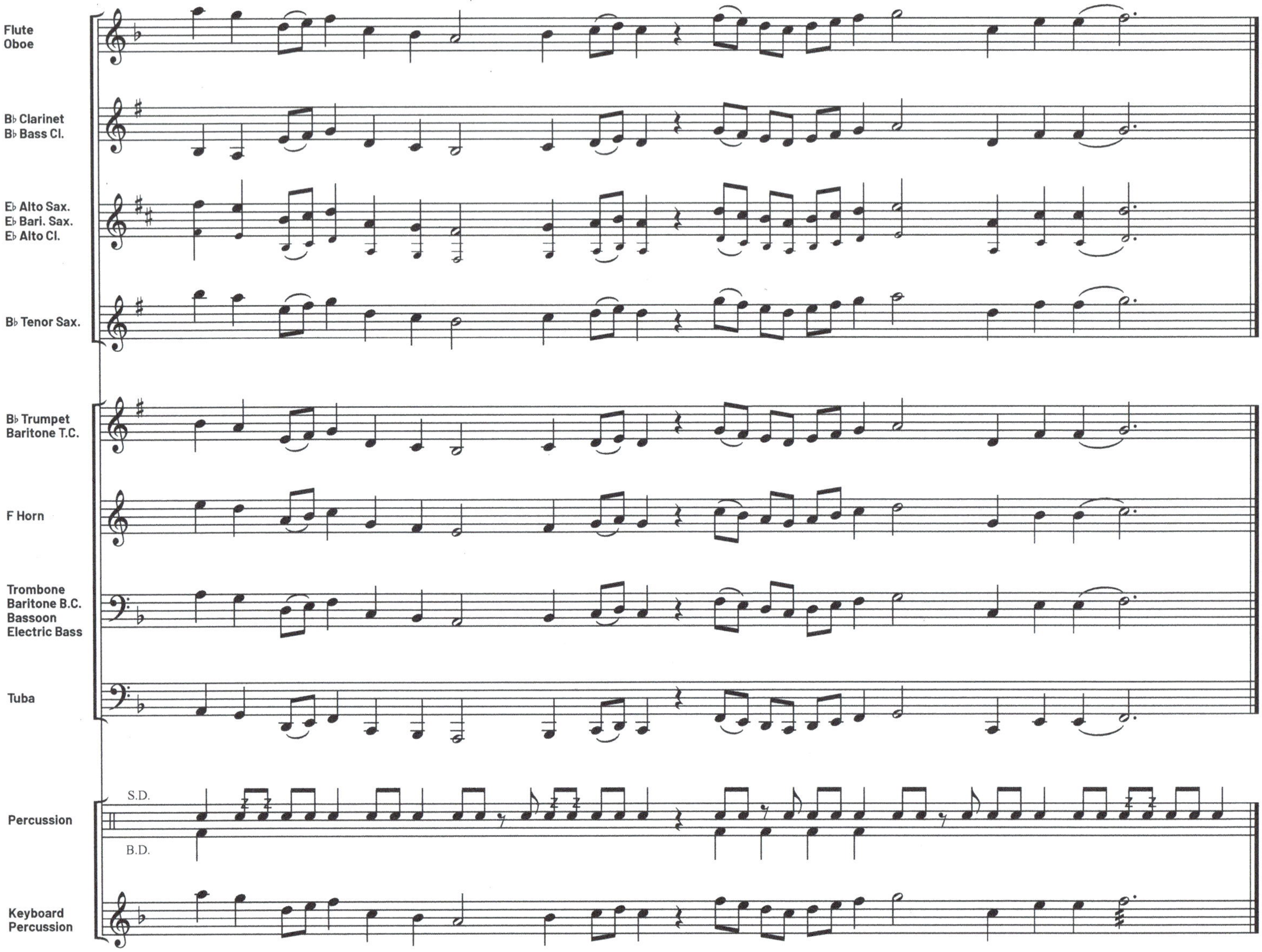

Flute
Oboe

B♭ Clarinet
B♭ Bass Cl.

E♭ Alto Sax.
E♭ Bari. Sax.
E♭ Alto Cl.

B♭ Tenor Sax.

B♭ Trumpet
Baritone T.C.

F Horn

Trombone
Baritone B.C.
Bassoon
Electric Bass

Tuba

Percussion
S.D.
B.D.

Keyboard
Percussion

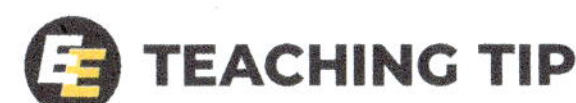

TEACHING TIP Point out the Concert E in measure 1 and the accidental in measure 3 before playing this exercise.

Percussion Right Hand Lead.

105. NATURALLY

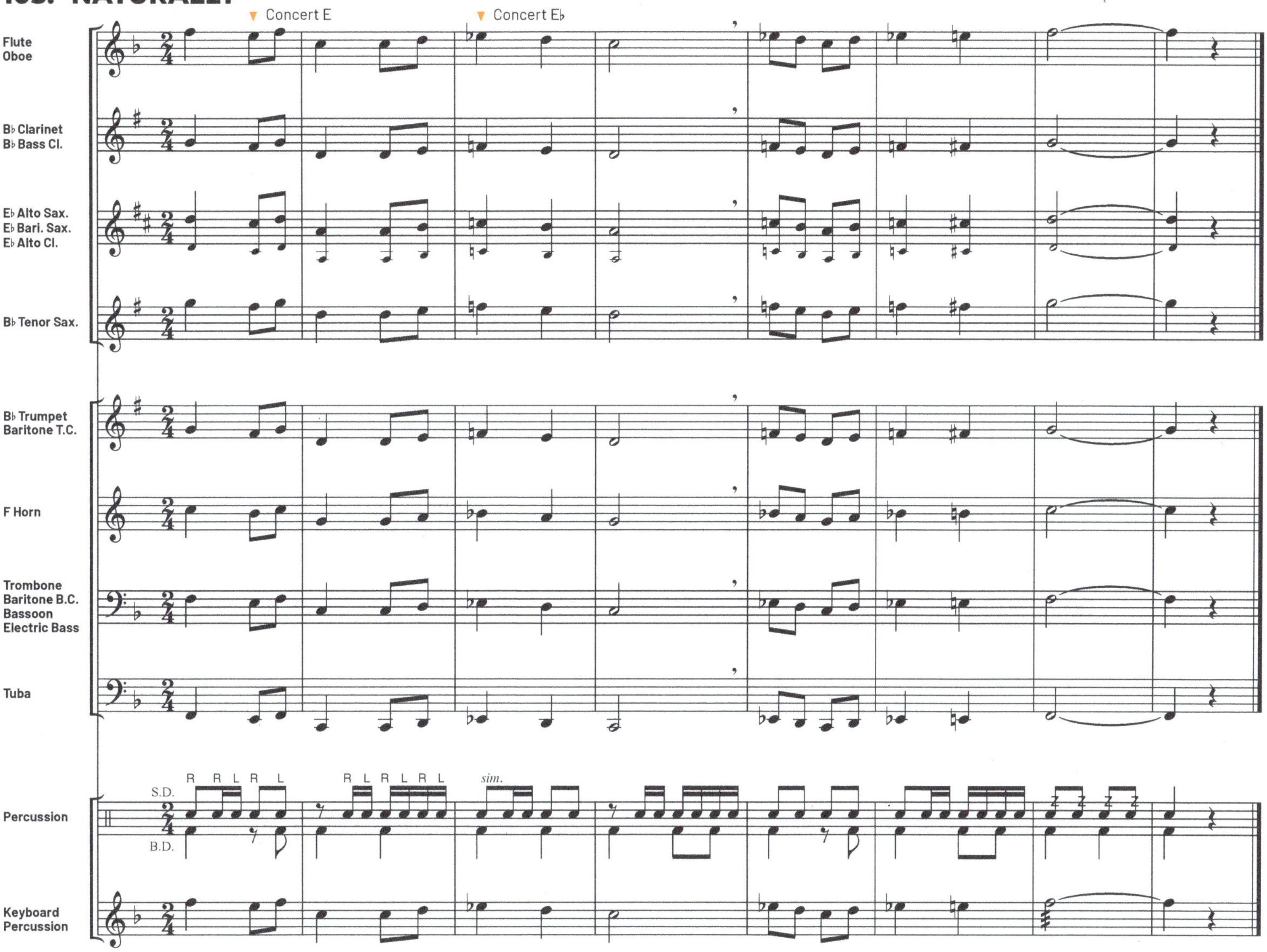
Concert E
Concert E♭
Flute
Oboe
B♭ Clarinet
B♭ Bass Cl.
E♭ Alto Sax.
E♭ Bari. Sax.
E♭ Alto Cl.
B♭ Tenor Sax.
B♭ Trumpet
Baritone T.C.
F Horn
Trombone
Baritone B.C.
Bassoon
Electric Bass
Tuba
R R L R L
R L R L R L
sim.
S.D.
B.D.
Percussion
Keyboard
Percussion

HISTORY

Austrian composer **Franz Peter Schubert** (1797–1828) lived a shorter life than any other great composer, but he created an incredible amount of music: more than 600 art-songs (concert music for voice and accompaniment), ten symphonies, chamber music, operas, choral works and piano pieces. His "March Militaire" was originally a piano duet.

THEORY

Percussion

One Measure Repeat

Repeat the previous measure.

TEACHING TIP Practice this exercise slowly and accurately before gradually increasing to an "allegro" tempo.

Percussion Practice "Doubling" in this exercise.

106. MARCH MILITAIRE – New Note

Franz Schubert

Allegro

Flute
Oboe

B♭ Clarinet
B♭ Bass Cl.

E♭ Alto Sax.
E♭ Bari. Sax.
E♭ Alto Cl.

B♭ Tenor Sax.

B♭ Trumpet
Baritone T.C.

F Horn

Trombone
Baritone B.C.
Bassoon
Electric Bass

Tuba

Percussion

S.D.
B.D.
Cr. Cym.

R L L R L R L L R L L R R R L L R L L R L

Keyboard
Percussion

f *mf*

Flute
Oboe
B♭ Clarinet
B♭ Bass Cl.
E♭ Alto Sax.
E♭ Bari. Sax.
E♭ Alto Cl.
B♭ Tenor Sax.
B♭ Trumpet
Baritone T.C.
F Horn
Trombone
Baritone B.C.
Bassoon
Electric Bass
Tuba
Percussion
Keyboard
Percussion
R L L R L

Flute/Kybd. Perc.
D♭
Oboe
D♭
Oboe
E♭
Alternate fingering
Bassoon
D♭
Clarinet
E♭
Alto Clarinet
B♭
Bass Clarinet
E♭
Alto Saxophone
B♭
Tenor Saxophone
E♭
Baritone Saxophone
B♭
Trumpet
E♭
F Horn
A♭
F Horn:
B♭ Horn: T
Trombone
D♭
5
Baritone B.C.
D♭
Baritone T.C.
E♭
Tuba
D♭
Electric Bass
D♭

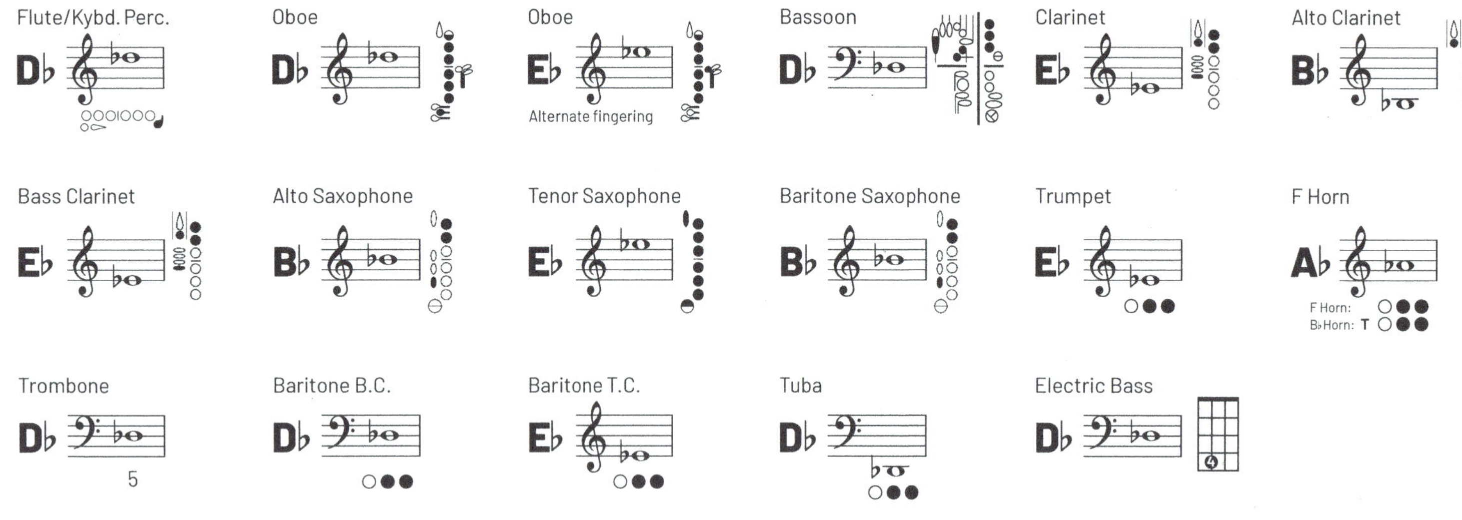

TEACHING TIP Play the new note before playing this exercise.

Oboe Use alternate E♭ when moving to or from D♭. Use the half-hole key on D♭.

Alto Cl., Alto Sax., Bari. Sax. These instruments learn flat for the first time for their new note "B♭."

F Horn **Double Horn Players:** add the thumb key and use the B♭ Horn fingering to play "A♭."

107. THE FLAT ZONE – New Note

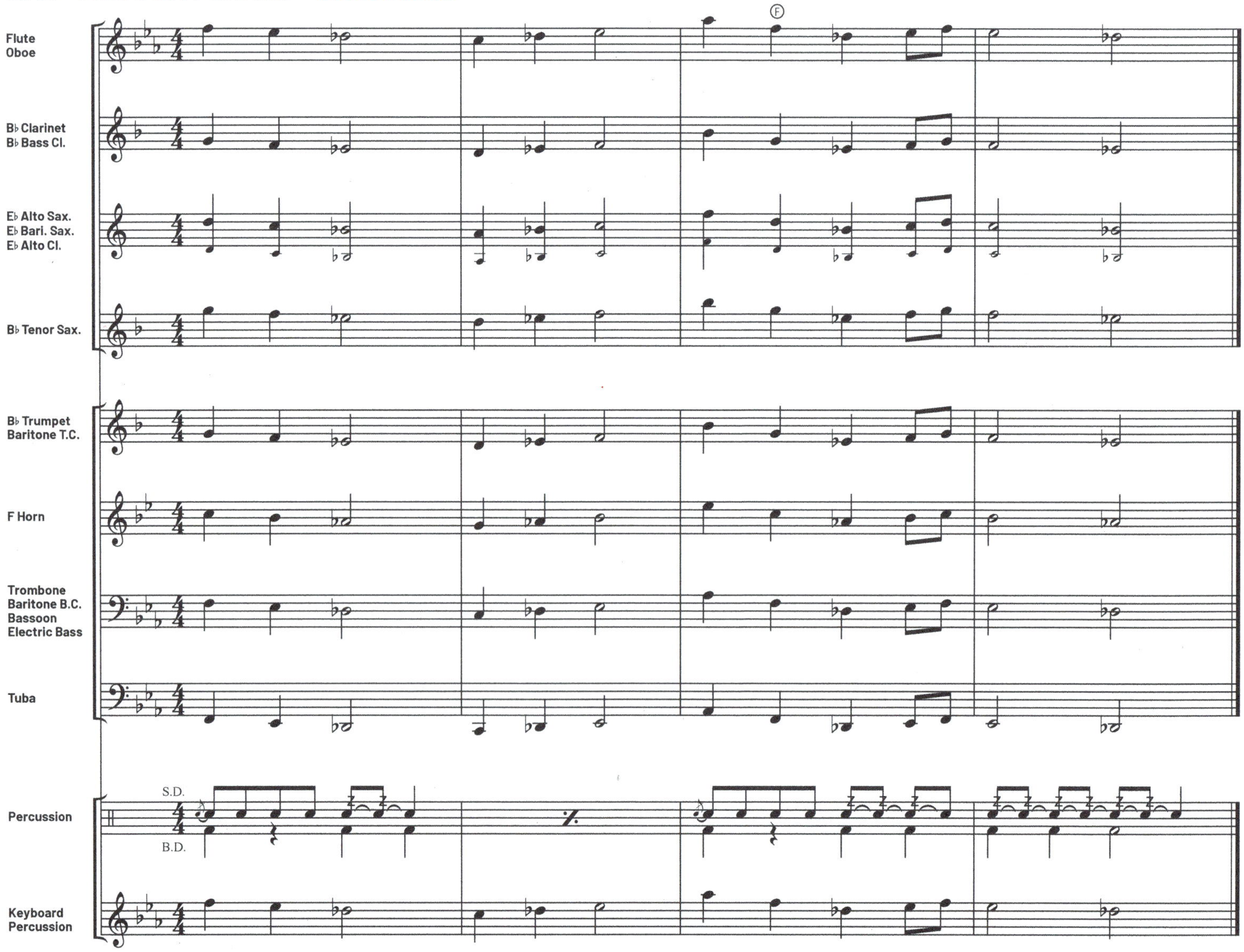
Flute
Oboe
B♭ Clarinet
B♭ Bass Cl.
E♭ Alto Sax.
E♭ Bari. Sax.
E♭ Alto Cl.
B♭ Tenor Sax.
B♭ Trumpet
Baritone T.C.
F Horn
Trombone
Baritone B.C.
Bassoon
Electric Bass
Tuba
Percussion
S.D.
B.D.
Keyboard
Percussion
F

Have students count and clap this exercise before playing. Keep hands together for the duration of the ties.

108. ON TOP OF OLD SMOKEY

American Folk Song

Allegro

Flute
Oboe

B♭ Clarinet
B♭ Bass Cl.

E♭ Alto Sax.
E♭ Bari. Sax.
E♭ Alto Cl.

B♭ Tenor Sax.

B♭ Trumpet
Baritone T.C.

F Horn

Trombone
Baritone B.C.
Bassoon
Electric Bass

Tuba

S.D.

B.D.

Percussion

Tri.

Keyboard
Percussion

Flute
Oboe

B♭ Clarinet
B♭ Bass Cl.

E♭ Alto Sax.
E♭ Bari. Sax.
E♭ Alto Cl.

B♭ Tenor Sax.

B♭ Trumpet
Baritone T.C.

F Horn

Trombone
Baritone B.C.
Bassoon
Electric Bass

Tuba

Percussion

Keyboard
Percussion

HISTORY

Boogie-woogie is a style of the **blues**, and it was first recorded by pianist Clarence "Pine Top" Smith in 1928, one year after Charles Lindbergh's solo flight across the Atlantic. A form of jazz, blues music features altered notes and is usually written in 12-measure verses, like "Bottom Bass Boogie."

Make sure everyone gets a chance to play both lines.

109. BOTTOM BASS BOOGIE – Duet

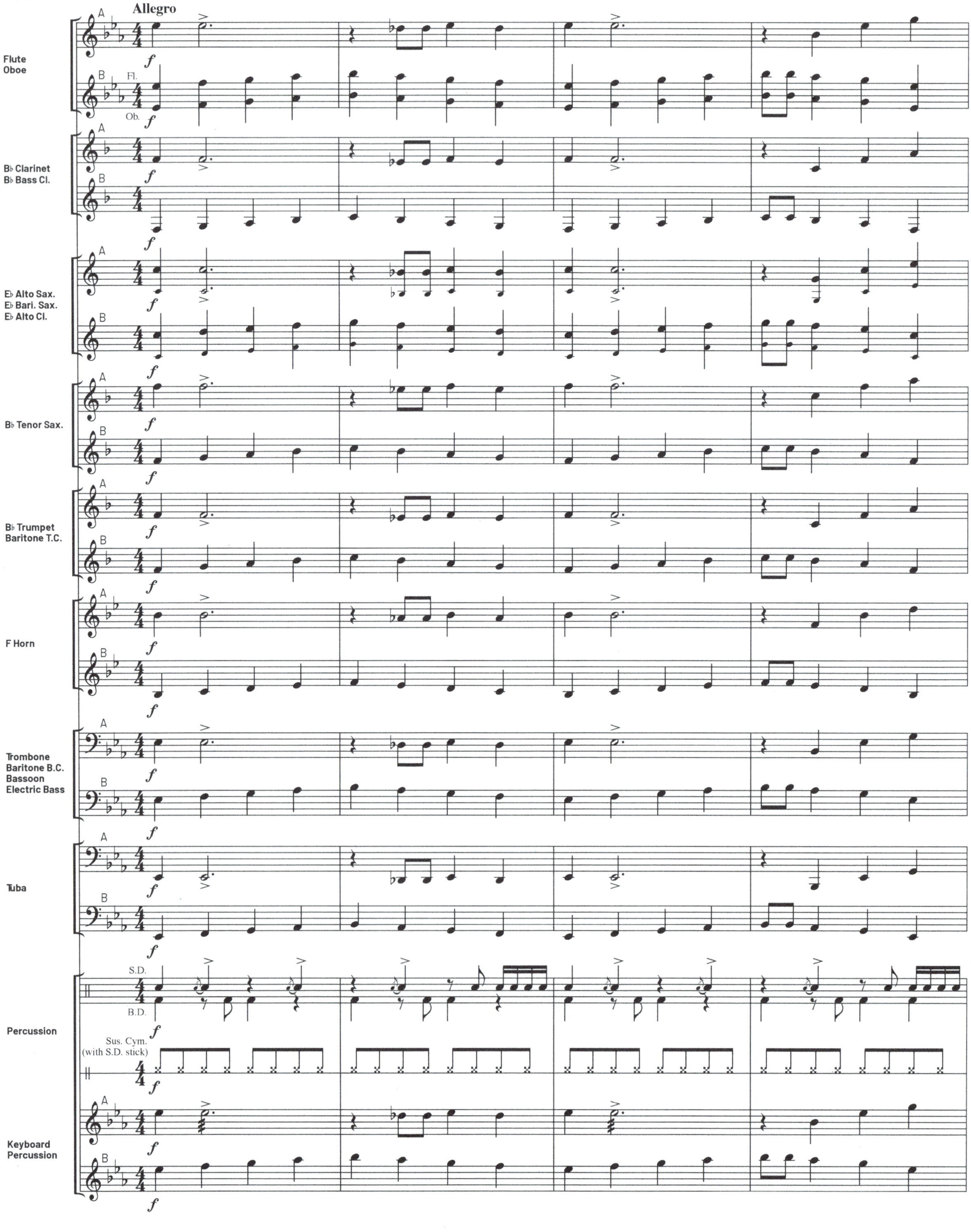

Allegro

Flute
Oboe

Fl.
Ob.

B♭ Clarinet
B♭ Bass Cl.

E♭ Alto Sax.
E♭ Bari. Sax.
E♭ Alto Cl.

B♭ Tenor Sax.

B♭ Trumpet
Baritone T.C.

F Horn

Trombone
Baritone B.C.
Bassoon
Electric Bass

Tuba

Percussion

S.D.
B.D.
Sus. Cym.
(with S.D. stick)

Keyboard
Percussion

Flute
Oboe
a2
B♭ Clarinet
B♭ Bass Cl.
E♭ Alto Sax.
E♭ Bari. Sax.
E♭ Alto Cl.
B♭ Tenor Sax.
B♭ Trumpet
Baritone T.C.
F Horn
Trombone
Baritone B.C.
Bassoon
Electric Bass
Tuba
Percussion
Keyboard
Percussion

Student Book Page 21

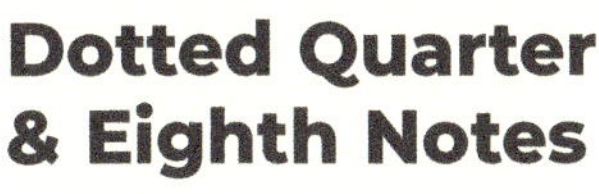

Dotted Quarter & Eighth Notes

= 2 Beats
1 & 2 &

A **dot** adds half the value of the quarter note.

1 & 2 &

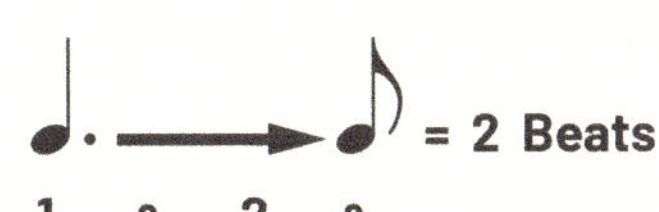

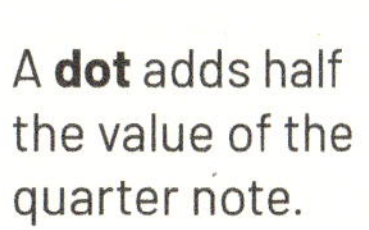

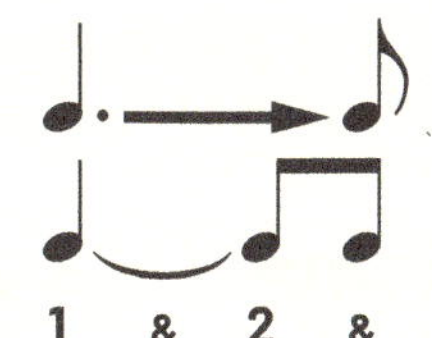

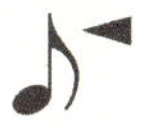

A single **eighth note** has a **flag** on the stem.

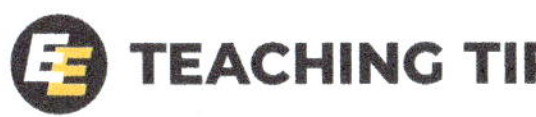

TEACHING TIP Make sure students hear that measures 2, 3, and 4 all sound the same.

110. RHYTHM RAP

Clap
1 & 2 & 3 & 4 &
1 & 2 & 3 & 4 &
1 & 2 & 3 & 4 &
1 & 2 & 3 & 4 &

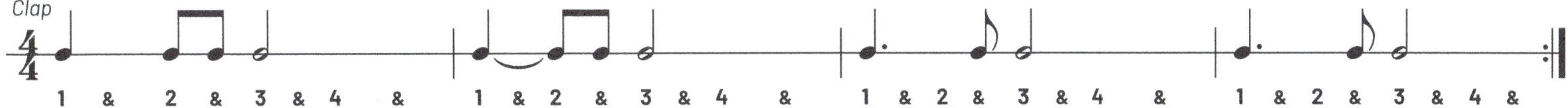

TEACHING TIP These rhythms are identical to #110 Rhythm Rap.

111. THE DOT ALWAYS COUNTS

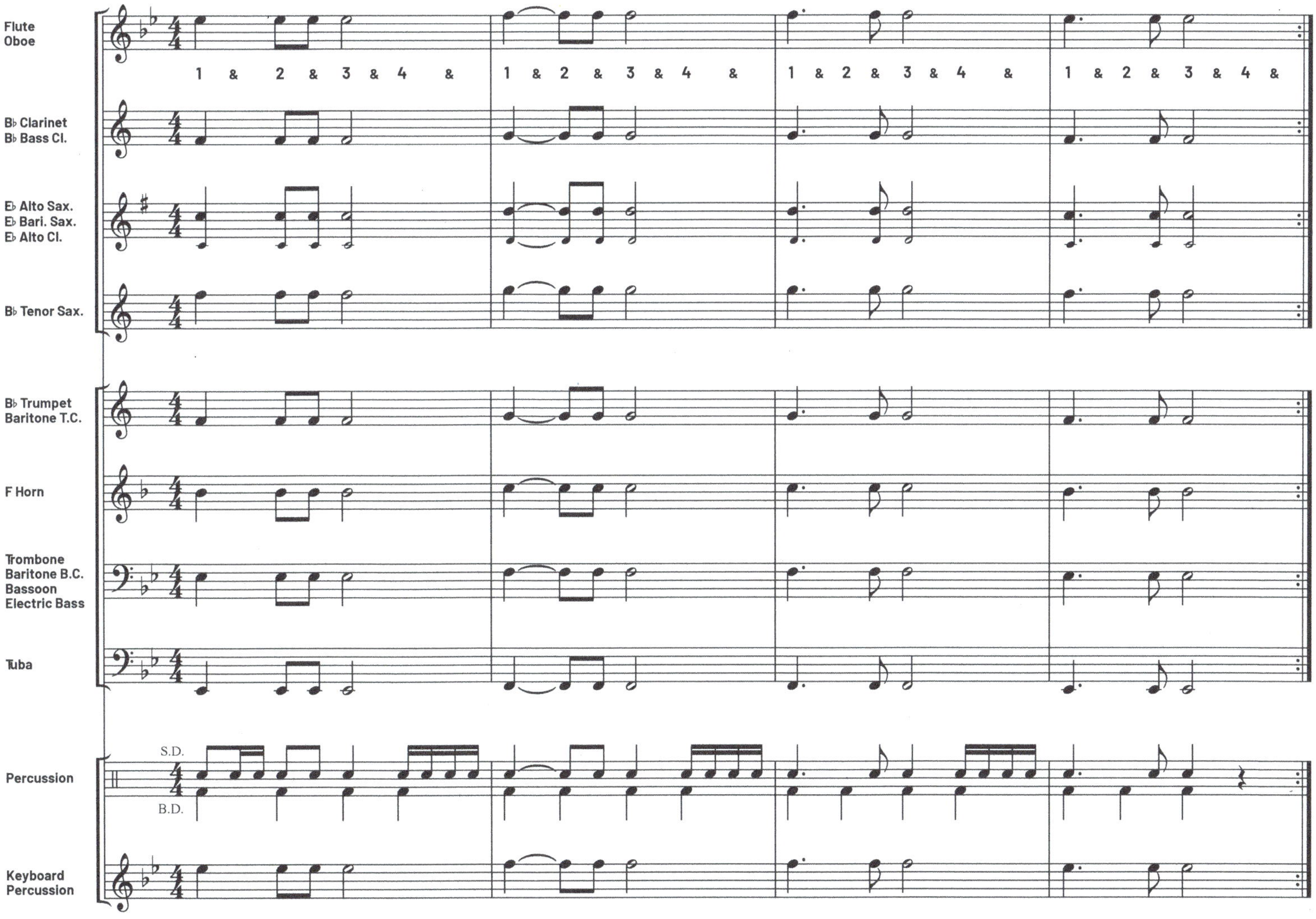
Flute
Oboe
1 & 2 & 3 & 4 &
1 & 2 & 3 & 4 &
1 & 2 & 3 & 4 &
1 & 2 & 3 & 4 &
B♭ Clarinet
B♭ Bass Cl.
E♭ Alto Sax.
E♭ Bari. Sax.
E♭ Alto Cl.
B♭ Tenor Sax.
B♭ Trumpet
Baritone T.C.
F Horn
Trombone
Baritone B.C.
Bassoon
Electric Bass
Tuba
Percussion
S.D.
B.D.
Keyboard
Percussion

Percussion
Closed Roll

Subdivide each [roll] into 4 equal strokes, and connect the multiple bounces as smoothly as possible. Closed rolls fill each beat with a buzzing sound.

TEACHING TIP Remind students of the D.C. al Fine. Review #91 Banana Boat Song if needed.

112. ALL THROUGH THE NIGHT

TEACHING TIP Have students count and clap the first phrase before playing.

113. SEA CHANTY *Always use a full airstream.*

English Folk Song

TEACHING TIP Students should continue the crescendo through the breath mark in measure 8.

114. SCARBOROUGH FAIR

English Folk Song

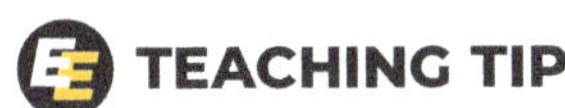

TEACHING TIP Compare measures 2 and 3.

115. RHYTHM RAP

Clap
1 & 2 & 3 & 4 &
1 & 2 & 3 & 4 &
1 & 2 & 3 & 4 &
1 & 2 & 3 & 4 &

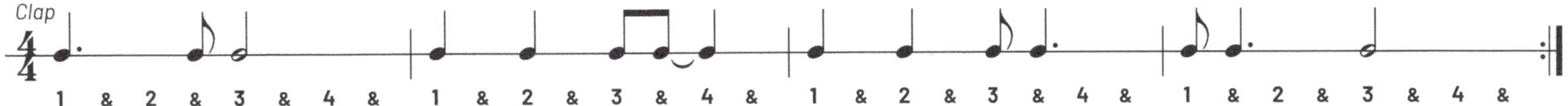

TEACHING TIP These rhythms are identical to #115 Rhythm Rap.

116. THE TURNAROUND

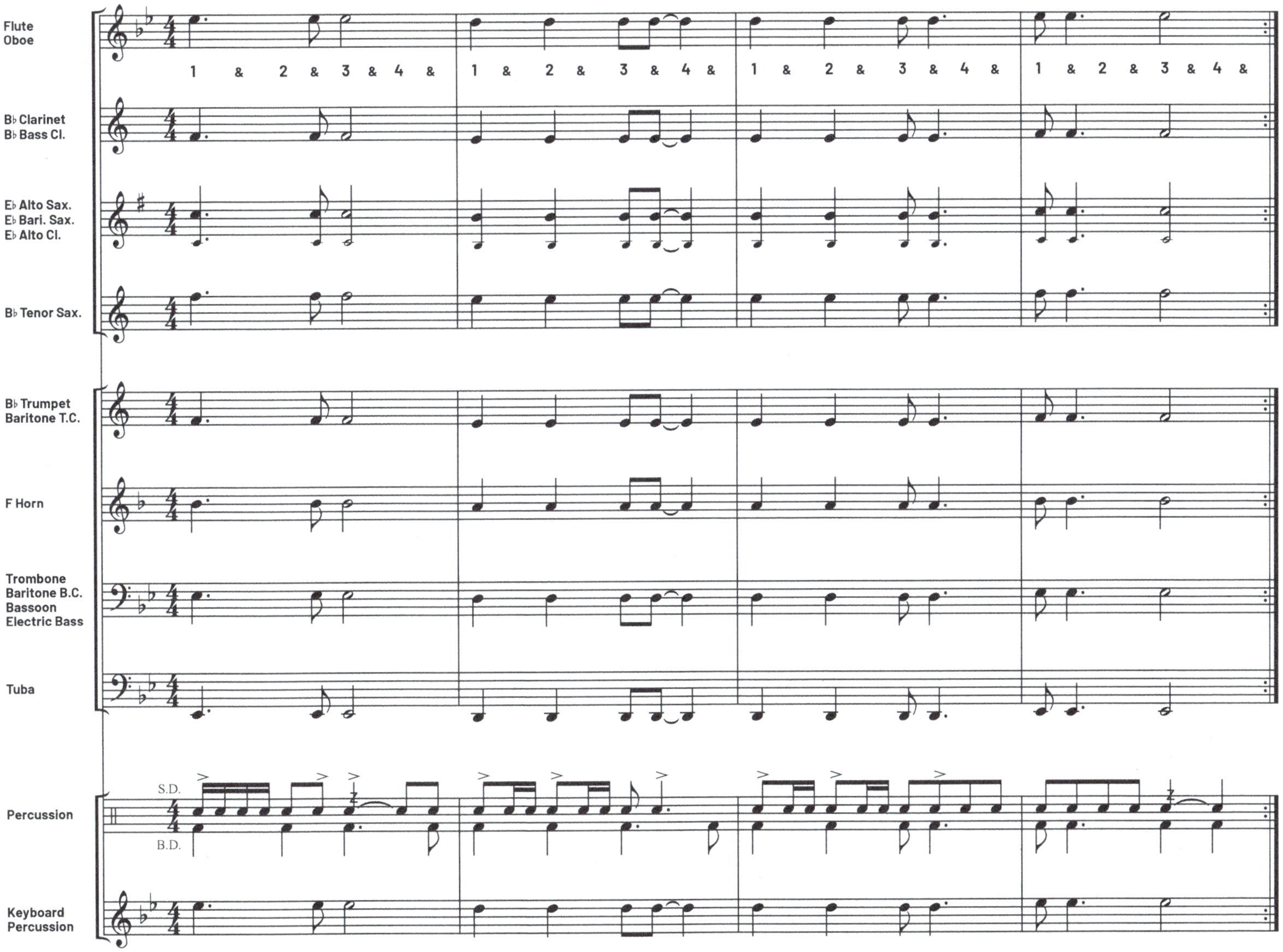
Flute
Oboe
1 & 2 & 3 & 4 &
1 & 2 & 3 & 4 &
1 & 2 & 3 & 4 &
1 & 2 & 3 & 4 &
B♭ Clarinet
B♭ Bass Cl.
E♭ Alto Sax.
E♭ Bari. Sax.
E♭ Alto Cl.
B♭ Tenor Sax.
B♭ Trumpet
Baritone T.C.
F Horn
Trombone
Baritone B.C.
Bassoon
Electric Bass
Tuba
Percussion
S.D.
B.D.
Keyboard
Percussion

Student Book Page 22

QUIZ ASSESSMENT Dotted quarter and eighth note rhythms.

117. ESSENTIAL ELEMENTS QUIZ – AULD LANG SYNE

Scottish Folk Song

TEACHING TIP This solo with piano accompaniment appears in each student book. A solo for snare drum is found on Conductor pages 158–159.

PERFORMANCE SPOTLIGHT

Solo with Piano Accompaniment

You can perform this solo with or without a piano accompanist. Play it for the band, the school or your family. It is part of **Symphony No. 9 ("From The New World")** by Czech composer **Antonin Dvorák** (1841–1904). He wrote it while visiting America in 1893, and was inspired to include melodies from American folksongs and spirituals. This is the **Largo** (or "very slow tempo") theme.

118. THEME FROM "NEW WORLD SYMPHONY"

Antonin Dvorák

Largo

5 Measure number

Flute*

Piano

13

21

29 Slower

*Transposed for all instruments in student books.

Student Book Page 23

PERFORMANCE SPOTLIGHT

Solo with Piano Accompaniment

You can perform this snare drum solo with a piano accompiment. Play it for the band, the school or your family. The theme in the piano part is a well-known melody from a set of orchestral works called **Hungarian Dances**, by the German composer **Johannes Brahms** (1833–1897). Many of Brahms' works include dance and folk styles he learned from touring Europe as a young man.

118. HUNGARIAN DANCE NO. 5 – Snare Drum Solo

Johannes Brahms
Arr. by Will Rapp

*Hit sticks together.

L R L R R L R L L R
33
R L R R L R L R R L
f
f
R L R L R R L R L R L L R

Great musicians give encouragement to fellow performers. On this page, clarinetists learn their instruments' upper register in the "Grenadilla Gorilla Jumps" (named after the grenadilla wood used to make clarinets). Brass players learn lip slurs, a new warm-up pattern, and percussionists combine new sticking patterns.. The success of your band depends on everyone's effort and encouragement.

SPECIAL CLARINET TECHNIQUE – Register Key

Notes above B♭ require the **Register Key** and are called "upper register" notes.

Remember the following:
1. Maintain a steady, fast stream of air.
2. Keep your embouchure firm and your chin flat.
3. Roll your thumb up slightly to open the register key.

Lip Slur

Lip Slurs are notes that are slurred without changing positions. Brass players practice these to develop a stronger airstream and embouchure, and to increase range. Add this pattern to your daily Warm-Ups:

SPECIAL TRUMPET/BARITONE T.C. EXERCISE – Lip Slurs

SPECIAL HORN EXERCISE – Lip Slurs

SPECIAL TROMBONE/BARITONE B.C. EXERCISE – Lip Slurs

SPECIAL TUBA EXERCISE – Lip Slurs

Percussion **Snare Drum**

The following exercises will help you develop important skills.
Follow the written sticking very carefully to help build your snare drum technique.

While a clarinet player holds a low "A," push the register key for him/her. Point out to clarinets that no embouchure movement is used when moving the upper register. Brass - don't allow airstream to "sag" when slurring to low note.

119. GRENADILLA GORILLA JUMP No. 1 – New Note

Flute
Oboe

Add register key

B♭ Clarinet
B♭ Bass Cl.

E♭ Alto Sax.
E♭ Bari. Sax.
E♭ Alto Cl.

B♭ Tenor Sax.

B♭ Trumpet
Baritone T.C.

F Horn

Trombone
Baritone B.C.
Bassoon
Electric Bass

Tuba

R L L R L L R L R R L L R L L R L L R L R L L R L L R L R R L L R L L R L L R L

S.D.
Percussion
B.D.

Keyboard
Percussion

a2 a2

Flute
Oboe

B♭ Clarinet
B♭ Bass Cl.

E♭ Alto Sax.
E♭ Bari. Sax.
E♭ Alto Cl.

B♭ Tenor Sax.

B♭ Trumpet
Baritone T.C.

F Horn

Trombone
Baritone B.C.
Bassoon
Electric Bass

Tuba

sim.

Percussion

Keyboard
Percussion

Student Book Page 24

EE TEACHING TIP Check clarinet finger and hand positions. Squeaks indicate tone holes not completely covered.

120. JUMPIN' UP AND DOWN

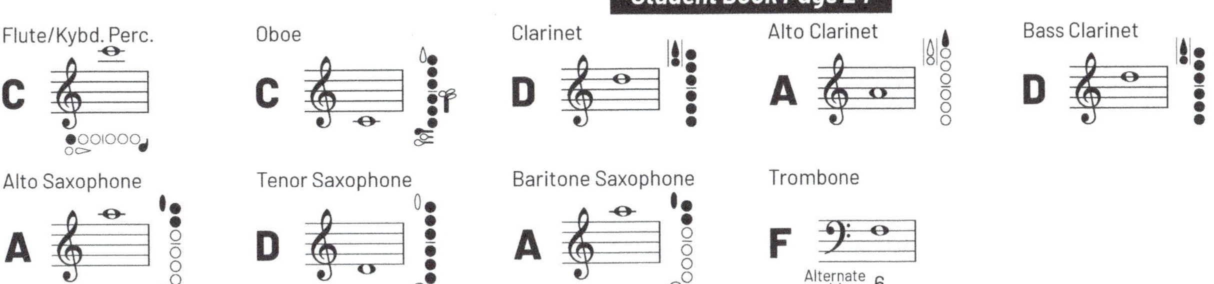

TEACHING TIP Make sure the clarinet low "G" is well established before making the skip to high "D."

Flute Higher notes are easier when you aim your airstream higher across the embouchure hole.

Trombone Play all "F's" in 6th position in this exercise.

121. GRENADILLA GORILLA JUMP No. 2 – New Note

Flute
Oboe

B♭ Clarinet
B♭ Bass Cl.

▲ *Add register key*

E♭ Alto Sax.
E♭ Bari. Sax.
E♭ Alto Cl.

B♭ Tenor Sax.

B♭ Trumpet
Baritone T.C.

F Horn

Trombone
Baritone B.C.
Bassoon
Electric Bass
Tuba

Percussion

S.D. R R L R R L R L R R L L *sim.*

B.D.

Keyboard
Percussion

Flute
Oboe

B♭ Clarinet
B♭ Bass Cl.

E♭ Alto Sax.
E♭ Bari. Sax.
E♭ Alto Cl.

B♭ Tenor Sax.

B♭ Trumpet
Baritone T.C.

F Horn

Trombone
Baritone B.C.
Bassoon
Electric Bass
Tuba

Percussion

R R L R R L L R L R L *sim.* L R R R L L R L R L

Keyboard
Percussion

Student Book Page 24

122. JUMPIN' FOR JOY

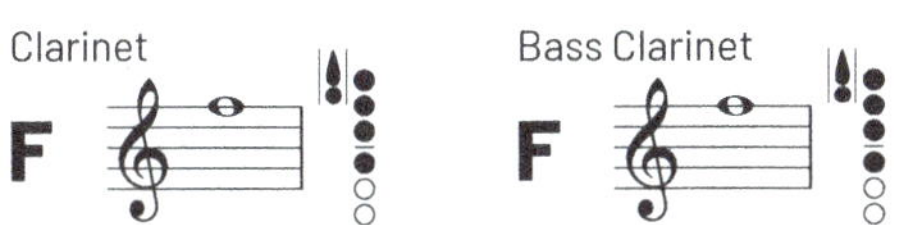

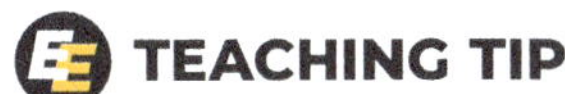

Clarinet

F

Bass Clarinet

F

TEACHING TIP Clarinets – maintain good breath support when adding register key. Don't pinch embouchure.

123. GRENADILLA GORILLA JUMP No. 3 – New Note

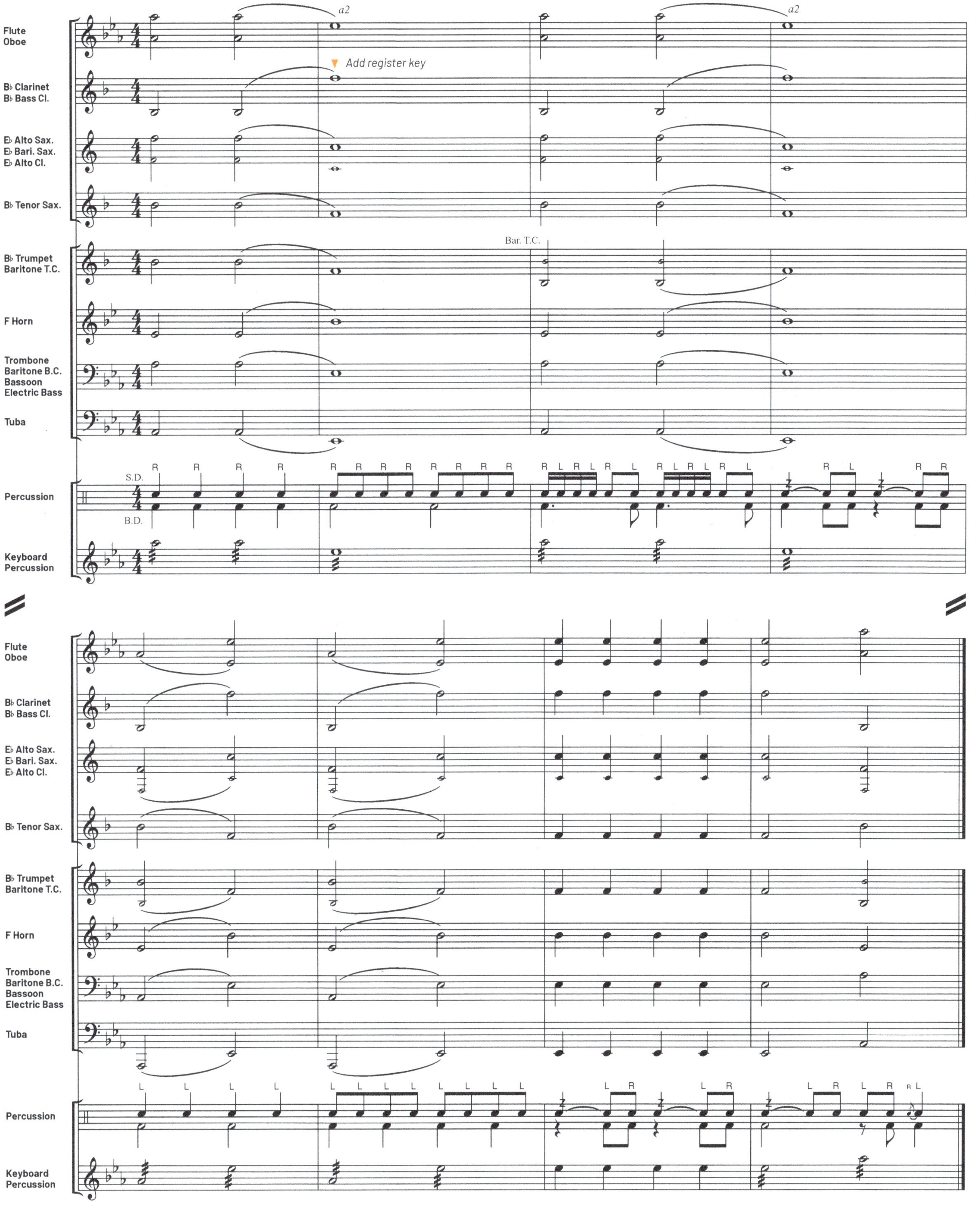
a2
Flute
Oboe
Add register key
B♭ Clarinet
B♭ Bass Cl.
E♭ Alto Sax.
E♭ Bari. Sax.
E♭ Alto Cl.
B♭ Tenor Sax.
Bar. T.C.
B♭ Trumpet
Baritone T.C.
F Horn
Trombone
Baritone B.C.
Bassoon
Electric Bass
Tuba
S.D.
B.D.
Percussion
Keyboard
Percussion

Student Book Page 24

124. JUMPIN' JACKS

Interval

The distance between two pitches is an **interval**. Starting with "1" on the lower note, count each line and space between the notes. The number of the higher note is the distance of the interval.

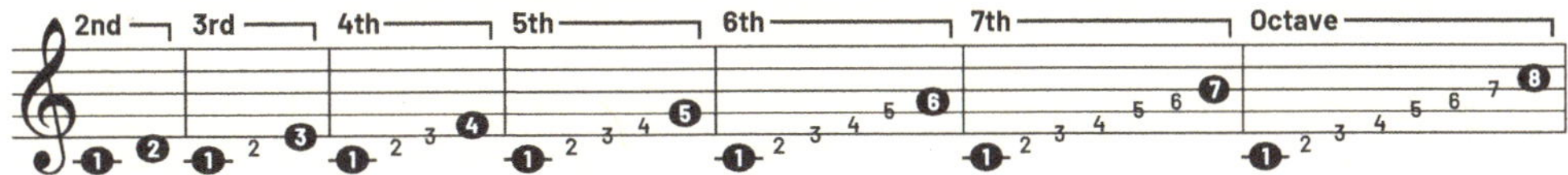

Percussion A quiz on intervals appears in the keyboard section (page 24)

QUIZ ASSESSMENT Interval numbers, new notes (clarinets).

125. ESSENTIAL ELEMENTS QUIZ

Write in the numbers of the intervals, counting up from the lower notes.

Flute Oboe
a2
B♭ Clarinet B♭ Bass Cl.
E♭ Alto Sax. E♭ Bari. Sax. E♭ Alto Cl.
B♭ Tenor Sax.
B♭ Trumpet Baritone T.C.
F Horn
Trombone Baritone B.C. Bassoon Electric Bass Tuba
Percussion
S.D.
B.D.
Keyboard Percussion

Flute Oboe
Intervals: 2nd
B♭ Clarinet B♭ Bass Cl.
E♭ Alto Sax. E♭ Bari. Sax. E♭ Alto Cl.
B♭ Tenor Sax.
B♭ Trumpet Baritone T.C.
F Horn
Trombone Baritone B.C. Bassoon Electric Bass Tuba
Percussion
Keyboard Percussion

Additional Bonus Songs are available online. See the inside front cover for details.

Clarinet

Bass Clarinet

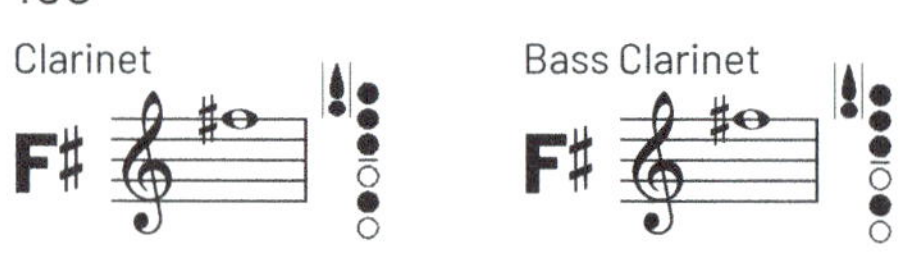

Percussion Practice Alternate Sticking as marked.

126. GRENADILLA GORILLA JUMP No. 4 – New Note

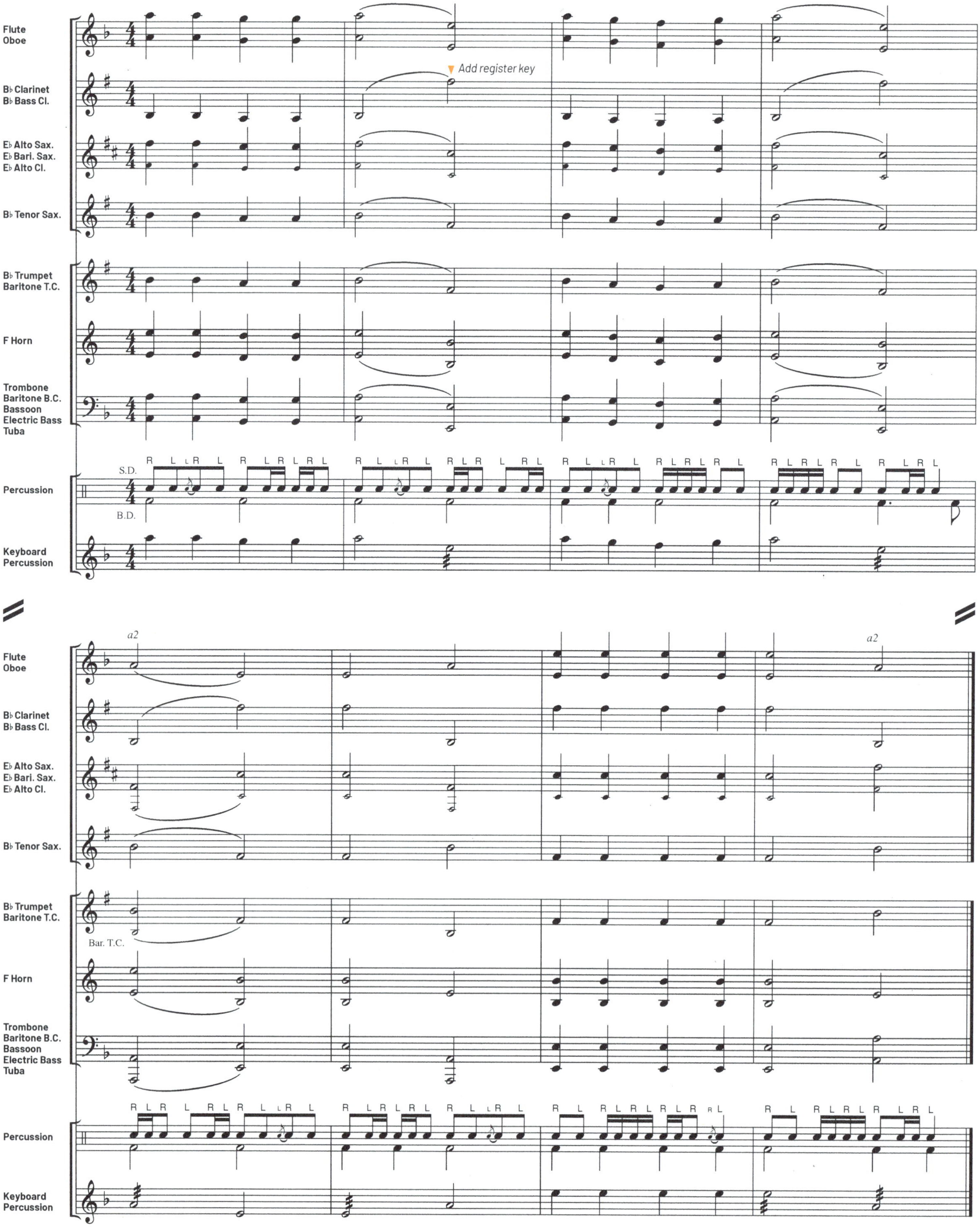

Review 3/4 time signature and accidentals.

127. THREE IS THE COUNT

Flute
Oboe

B♭ Clarinet
B♭ Bass Cl.

E♭ Alto Sax.
E♭ Bari. Sax.
E♭ Alto Cl.

B♭ Tenor Sax.

B♭ Trumpet
Baritone T.C.

F Horn

Trombone
Baritone B.C.
Bassoon
Electric Bass

Tuba

Percussion

Keyboard
Percussion

Flute
Oboe

B♭ Clarinet
B♭ Bass Cl.

E♭ Alto Sax.
E♭ Bari. Sax.
E♭ Alto Cl.

B♭ Tenor Sax.

B♭ Trumpet
Baritone T.C.

F Horn

Trombone
Baritone B.C.
Bassoon
Electric Bass

Tuba

R R L L L R R R L R

Percussion

Keyboard
Percussion

Student Book Page 25

Make sure the clarinet low "F" is well established before adding the register key.

128. GRENADILLA GORILLA JUMP No. 5 – New Note

Flute Oboe
B♭ Clarinet B♭ Bass Cl.
▼ Add register key
E♭ Alto Sax. E♭ Bari. Sax. E♭ Alto Cl.
B♭ Tenor Sax.
B♭ Trumpet Baritone T.C.
F Horn
Trombone Baritone B.C. Bassoon Electric Bass
Tuba
Percussion
S.D.
B.D.
Keyboard Percussion

Flute Oboe
Ob.
B♭ Clarinet B♭ Bass Cl.
E♭ Alto Sax. E♭ Bari. Sax. E♭ Alto Cl.
B♭ Tenor Sax.
B♭ Trumpet Baritone T.C.
F Horn
Trombone Baritone B.C. Bassoon Electric Bass
Tuba
Percussion
Keyboard Percussion

Percussion
Closed Roll

Subdivide each into 2 equal strokes, and connect the multiple bounces as smoothly as possible.

TEACHING TIP Note accidentals.

129. TECHNIQUE TRAX

Flute
Oboe

B♭ Clarinet
B♭ Bass Cl.

E♭ Alto Sax.
E♭ Bari. Sax.
E♭ Alto Cl.

B♭ Tenor Sax.

B♭ Trumpet
Baritone T.C.

F Horn

Trombone
Baritone B.C.
Bassoon
Electric Bass

Tuba

Percussion

S.D.
B.D.

Keyboard
Percussion

Flute
Oboe

B♭ Clarinet
B♭ Bass Cl.

E♭ Alto Sax.
E♭ Bari. Sax.
E♭ Alto Cl.

B♭ Tenor Sax.

B♭ Trumpet
Baritone T.C.

F Horn

Trombone
Baritone B.C.
Bassoon
Electric Bass

Tuba

Percussion

Keyboard
Percussion

Clarinet, Bass Clarinet

Crossing the Break

*When alternating between high and low registers, you can keep your **right hand fingers down** on G, A and Bb:*

Bassoon
C
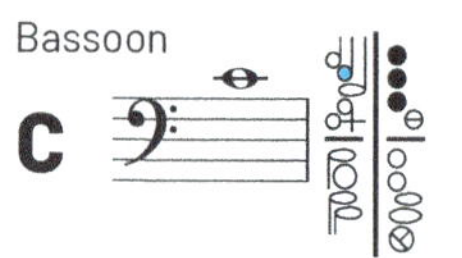

Trumpet
D

Trombone
C

Baritone B.C.
C

Baritone T.C.
D

Tuba
C
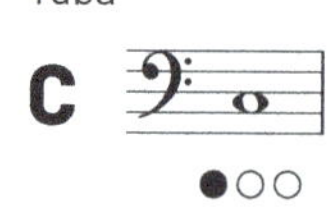

Electric Bass
C

Clarinets - play long tones on G, A, and Bb with right hand fingers down to prepare for this exercise. Explain why and when to use (for smoother technique when alternating between high and low registers). Brass - use plenty of air for new note.

130. CROSSING OVER – New Note

Flute Oboe
Bb Clarinet Bb Bass Cl.
Right hand down: (4 fingers down)
Eb Alto Sax. Eb Bari. Sax. Eb Alto Cl.
Bb Tenor Sax.
Bb Trumpet
F Horn
Trombone Baritone B.C. Bassoon Electric Bass
Tuba
Percussion
S.D.
B.D.
Keyboard Percussion

Flute Oboe
Bb Clarinet Bb Bass Cl.
(3 fingers down)
Eb Alto Sax. Eb Bari. Sax. Eb Alto Cl.
Bb Tenor Sax.
Bb Trumpet
F Horn
Trombone Baritone B.C. Bassoon Electric Bass
Tuba
Percussion
Keyboard Percussion

Trio A **trio** is a composition with three parts played together. Practice this trio with two other players and listen for 3-part harmony.

TEACHING TIP When playing this trio with full band, have low instruments all play their bottom (C) part.

Percussion This percussion part can accompany a trio of players or the full band.

131. KUM BAH YAH – Trio *Always check the key signature.*

African Folk Song

Flute
Oboe
B♭ Clarinet
E♭ Alto Sax.
B♭ Trumpet
F Horn
Low Brass &
Woodwinds
Tuba
Percussion
Keyboard
Percussion

Flute
Oboe
B♭ Clarinet
E♭ Alto Sax.
B♭ Trumpet
F Horn
Low Brass &
Woodwinds
T. Sax.
Tuba
Percussion
Keyboard
Percussion
p

Repeat Signs

Repeat the section of music enclosed by the **repeat signs**. *(If 1st and 2nd endings are used, they are played as usual – but go back only to the first repeat sign, not to the beginning.)*

Review 1st and 2nd endings before playing.

Percussion Flam accents can also apply to eighth notes.

132. MICHAEL ROW THE BOAT ASHORE

African-American Spiritual

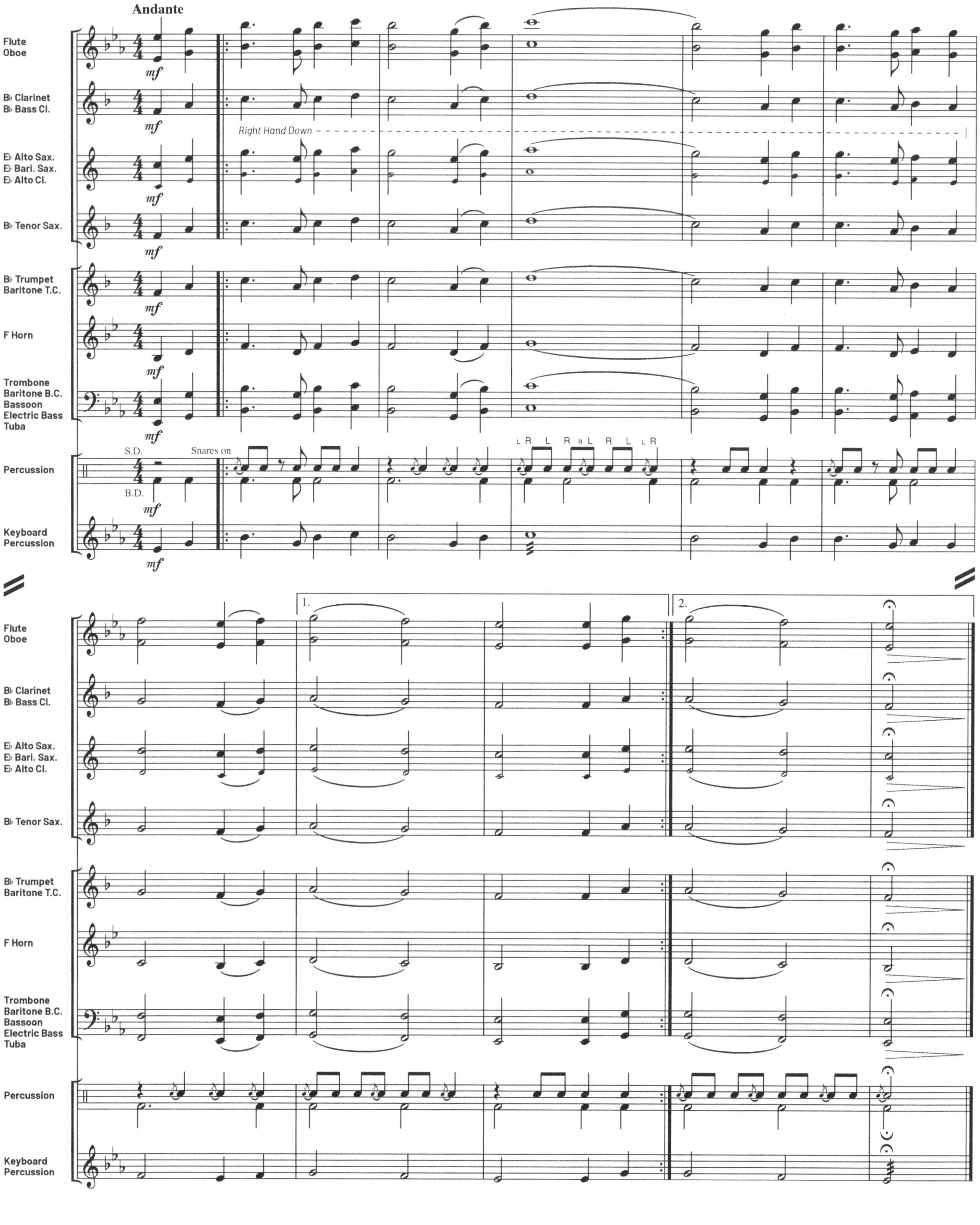

Andante

Flute / Oboe

B♭ Clarinet / B♭ Bass Cl.

Right Hand Down

E♭ Alto Sax. / E♭ Bari. Sax. / E♭ Alto Cl.

B♭ Tenor Sax.

B♭ Trumpet / Baritone T.C.

F Horn

Trombone / Baritone B.C. / Bassoon / Electric Bass / Tuba

Percussion

S.D. Snares on

B.D.

L R L R R L R L L R

Keyboard Percussion

mf

1. 2.

TEACHING TIP Have the students count and practice fingerings in rhythm before they play.

133. AUSTRIAN WALTZ

Austrian Folk Song

134. BOTANY BAY

Australian Folk Song

C Time Signature

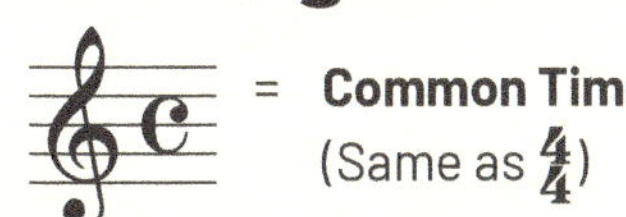

= Common Time (Same as 4/4)

Conducting

Practice conducting this four-beat pattern.

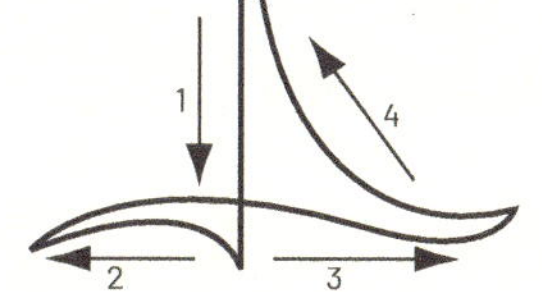

TEACHING TIP Introduction of common time notation is an excellent time to learn the 4/4 conducting pattern.

135. TECHNIQUE TRAX *Practice at all dynamic levels.*

Flute
Oboe

B♭ Clarinet
B♭ Bass Cl.

E♭ Alto Sax.
E♭ Bari. Sax.
E♭ Alto Cl.

B♭ Tenor Sax.

B♭ Trumpet
Baritone T.C.

F Horn

Trombone
Baritone B.C.
Bassoon
Electric Bass

Tuba

Percussion

S.D.
B.D.

Keyboard
Percussion

Review repeat signs and endings.

136. FINLANDIA

Jean Sibelius

Andante

Flute
Oboe

B♭ Clarinet
B♭ Bass Cl.

E♭ Alto Sax.
E♭ Bari. Sax.
E♭ Alto Cl.

B♭ Tenor Sax.

B♭ Trumpet
Baritone T.C.

F Horn

Trombone
Baritone B.C.
Bassoon
Electric Bass

Tuba

Percussion

S.D.

B.D.

Keyboard
Percussion

Flute
Oboe

B♭ Clarinet
B♭ Bass Cl.

E♭ Alto Sax.
E♭ Bari. Sax.
E♭ Alto Cl.

B♭ Tenor Sax.

B♭ Trumpet
Baritone T.C.

F Horn

Trombone
Baritone B.C.
Bassoon
Electric Bass

Tuba

Percussion

Keyboard
Percussion

Flute
Oboe

B♭ Clarinet
B♭ Bass Cl.

E♭ Alto Sax.
E♭ Bari. Sax.
E♭ Alto Cl.

B♭ Tenor Sax.

B♭ Trumpet
Baritone T.C.

F Horn

Trombone
Baritone B.C.
Bassoon
Electric Bass

Tuba

Percussion

Keyboard
Percussion

CREATIVITY TIP This exercise demonstrates how rhythm affects music. As students play their compositions, ask class members to identify which measures were changed.

137. ESSENTIAL CREATIVITY

Create your own variations by penciling in a dot and a flag to change the rhythm of any measure from ♩ ♩ | *to* | ♩. ♪

Flute
Oboe

B♭ Clarinet
B♭ Bass Cl.

E♭ Alto Sax.
E♭ Bari. Sax.
E♭ Alto Cl.

B♭ Tenor Sax.

B♭ Trumpet
Baritone T.C.

F Horn

Trombone
Baritone B.C.
Bassoon
Electric Bass

Tuba

Percussion

Keyboard
Percussion

TEACHING TIP Note special part for clarinets on this exercise.

138. EASY GORILLA JUMPS – New Note

Flute
Oboe

B♭ Clarinet
B♭ Bass Cl.

Add register key

E♭ Alto Sax.
E♭ Bari. Sax.
E♭ Alto Cl.

B♭ Tenor Sax.

B♭ Trumpet
Baritone T.C.

F Horn

Trombone
Baritone B.C.
Bassoon
Electric Bass

Tuba

Percussion
S.D.
B.D.

Keyboard
Percussion

Flute
Oboe

B♭ Clarinet
B♭ Bass Cl.

E♭ Alto Sax.
E♭ Bari. Sax.
E♭ Alto Cl.

B♭ Tenor Sax.

B♭ Trumpet
Baritone T.C.

F Horn

Trombone
Baritone B.C.
Bassoon
Electric Bass

Tuba

Percussion

Keyboard
Percussion

139. TECHNIQUE TRAX *Always check the key signature.*

140. MORE TECHNIQUE TRAX

Stress dynamics.

141. GERMAN FOLK SONG

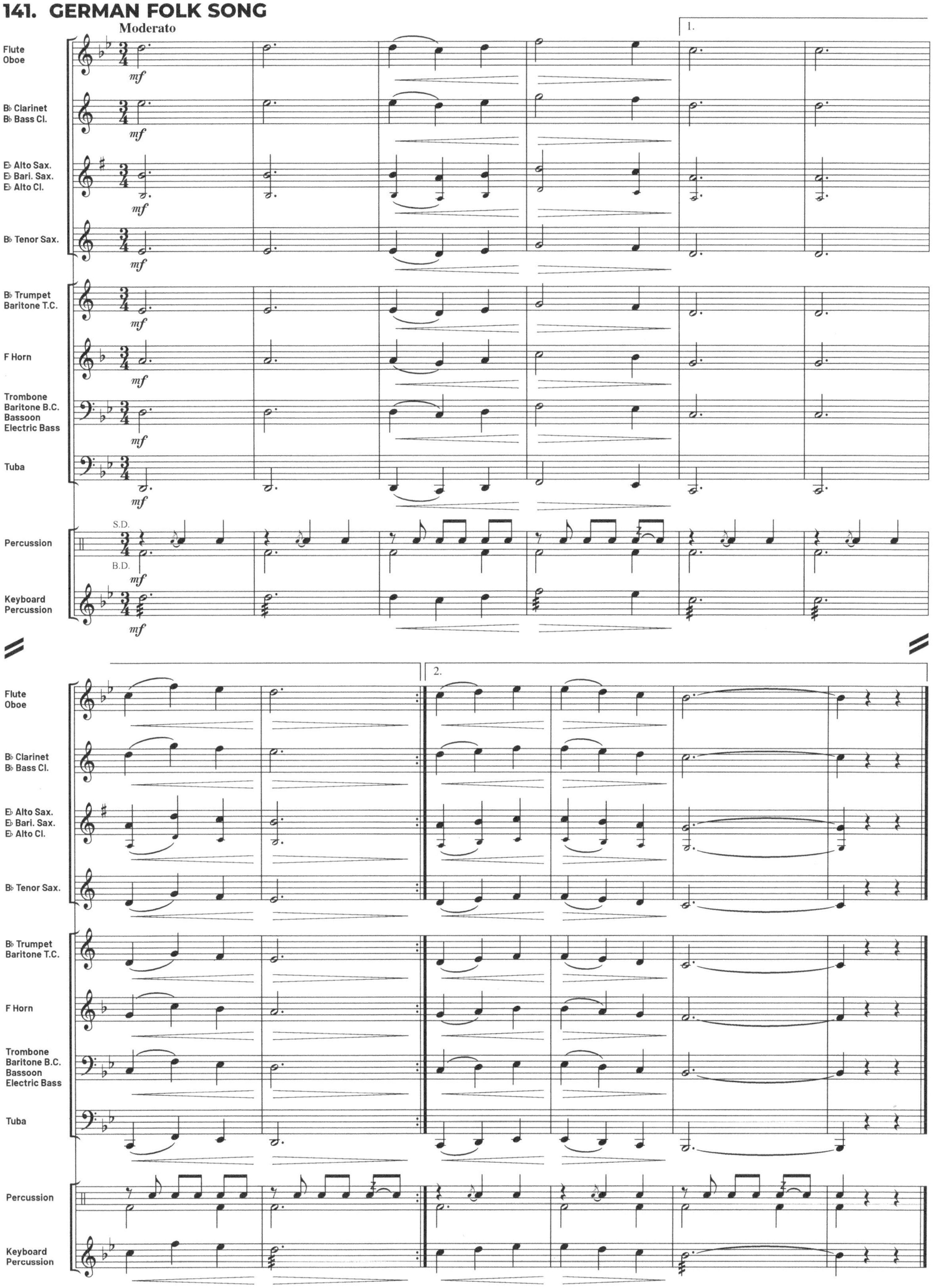

Moderato

Flute
Oboe

B♭ Clarinet
B♭ Bass Cl.

E♭ Alto Sax.
E♭ Bari. Sax.
E♭ Alto Cl.

B♭ Tenor Sax.

B♭ Trumpet
Baritone T.C.

F Horn

Trombone
Baritone B.C.
Bassoon
Electric Bass

Tuba

Percussion

S.D.

B.D.

Keyboard
Percussion

mf

1.

2.

Student Book Page 27

142. THE SAINTS GO MARCHIN' AGAIN

James Black and Katherine Purvis

Flute
Oboe
B♭ Clarinet
B♭ Bass Cl.
E♭ Alto Sax.
E♭ Bari. Sax.
E♭ Alto Cl.
B♭ Tenor Sax.
B♭ Trumpet
Baritone T.C.
F Horn
Trombone
Baritone B.C.
Bassoon
Electric Bass
Tuba
Percussion
Keyboard
Percussion
1.
2.
R.S.

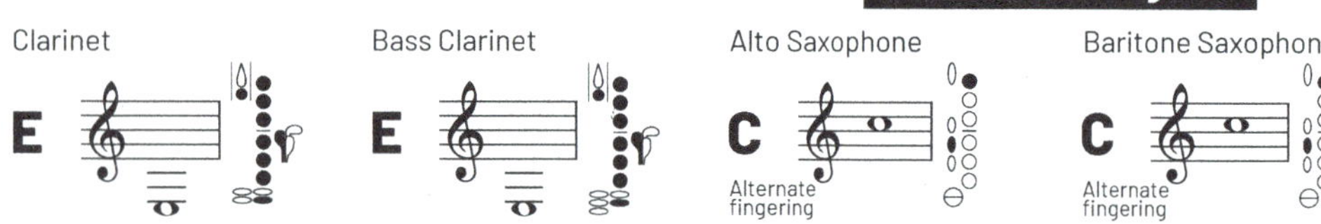

TEACHING TIP Check the clarinet low "E" to be sure the tone holes are completely covered.

Clarinet, Bs. Cl. Be sure the pads of your fingers cover the holes completely.

143. LOWLAND GORILLA WALK – New Note

Flute
Oboe

B♭ Clarinet
B♭ Bass Cl.

Use Alt. C fingering

Alt. C

E♭ Alto Sax.
E♭ Bari. Sax.
E♭ Alto Cl.

B♭ Tenor Sax.

B♭ Trumpet
Baritone T.C.

F Horn

Trombone
Baritone B.C.
Bassoon
Electric Bass
Tuba

On rim

S.D.

B.D.

Percussion

Keyboard Percussion

Low D

Flute
Oboe

B♭ Clarinet
B♭ Bass Cl.

Alt. C

Alt. C

E♭ Alto Sax.
E♭ Bari. Sax.
E♭ Alto Cl.

B♭ Tenor Sax.

B♭ Trumpet
Baritone T.C.

F Horn

Trombone
Baritone B.C.
Bassoon
Electric Bass
Tuba

Percussion

Keyboard Percussion

Percussion
Two Measure Repeat

Repeat the previous two measures.

144. SMOOTH SAILING

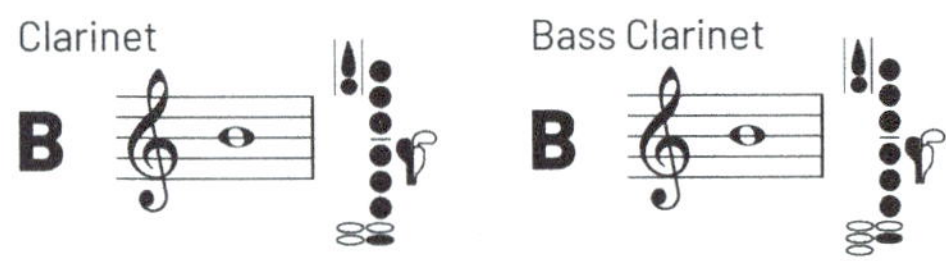

TEACHING TIP Note special part for clarinets.

145. MORE GORILLA JUMPS – New Note

Flute
Oboe

B♭ Clarinet
B♭ Bass Cl.

Add register key

E♭ Alto Sax.
E♭ Bari. Sax.
E♭ Alto Cl.

B♭ Tenor Sax.

B♭ Trumpet
Baritone T.C.

F Horn

Trombone
Baritone B.C.
Bassoon
Electric Bass

Tuba

S.D.
Percussion
B.D.

Keyboard
Percussion

Flute
Oboe

B♭ Clarinet
B♭ Bass Cl.

E♭ Alto Sax.
E♭ Bari. Sax.
E♭ Alto Cl.

B♭ Tenor Sax.

B♭ Trumpet
Baritone T.C.

F Horn

Trombone
Baritone B.C.
Bassoon
Electric Bass

Tuba

Percussion

Keyboard
Percussion

Tenor Saxophone

Clarinet Be sure to cover the holes completely.
Alto Sax. Use alternate C fingering.

146. FULL COVERAGE

Scale

A **scale** is a sequence of notes in ascending or descending order. Like a musical "ladder," each step is the next consecutive note in the key. (C inst.) This scale is in your Key of B♭ (two flats), so the top and bottom notes are both B♭'s. The interval between the B♭'s is an octave.

TEACHING TIP Teaching the scale steps by numbers will make chords and arpeggios easier to understand.

147. CONCERT B♭ SCALE

Chord & Arpeggio

When two or more notes are played together, they form a **chord** or **harmony**. (C inst.) This B♭ chord is built from the 1st, 3rd and 5th steps of the B♭ scale. The 8th step is the same as the 1st, but it is an octave higher. An **arpeggio** is a "broken" chord whose notes are played individually.

Quickly assign each student to play the top, middle, or bottom notes of the chords. Keep bass instruments in unison.

148. IN HARMONY

Divide the notes of the chords between band members and play together. Does the arpeggio sound like a chord?

Percussion

Extended Roll

Subdivide each beat into 4 equal strokes and connect the multiple bounces as smoothly as possible. Extended rolls are closed rolls which fill all beats with a buzzing sound.

TEACHING TIP Review the definitions of scales and arpeggios.

149. SCALE AND ARPEGGIO

HISTORY

Austrian composer **Franz Joseph Haydn** (1732–1809) wrote 104 symphonies. Many of these works had nicknames and included brilliant, unique effects for their time. His *Symphony No. 94* was named "The Surprise Symphony" because the soft second movement included a sudden loud dynamic, intended to wake up an often sleepy audience. Pay special attention to dynamics when you play this famous theme.

TEACHING TIP Stress the importance of dynamics.

150. THEME FROM "SURPRISE SYMPHONY"

Franz Josef Haydn

Andante

Flute
Oboe

B♭ Clarinet
B♭ Bass Cl.

E♭ Alto Sax.
E♭ Bari. Sax.
E♭ Alto Cl.

B♭ Tenor Sax.

B♭ Trumpet
Baritone T.C.

F Horn

Trombone
Baritone B.C.
Bassoon
Electric Bass

Tuba

Percussion

Keyboard
Percussion

a2 *p*

On rim S.D.

B.D.

f

Flute
Oboe
B♭ Clarinet
B♭ Bass Cl.
E♭ Alto Sax.
E♭ Bari. Sax.
E♭ Alto Cl.
B♭ Tenor Sax.
B♭ Trumpet
Baritone T.C.
F Horn
Trombone
Baritone B.C.
Bassoon
Electric Bass
Tuba
Percussion
Keyboard
Percussion
p
mf
a2

QUIZ ASSESSMENT Note names, 1st and 2nd endings, clarinet and bs. cl. - low E.

151. ESSENTIAL ELEMENTS QUIZ – THE STREETS OF LAREDO

American Folk Song

Write in the note names before you play.

PERFORMANCE SPOTLIGHT

Have students check the key signature, time signature, repeats, accidentals, and dynamics before they play the piece.

152. SCHOOL SPIRIT – Band Arrangement

W.T. Purdy
Arr. by John Higgins

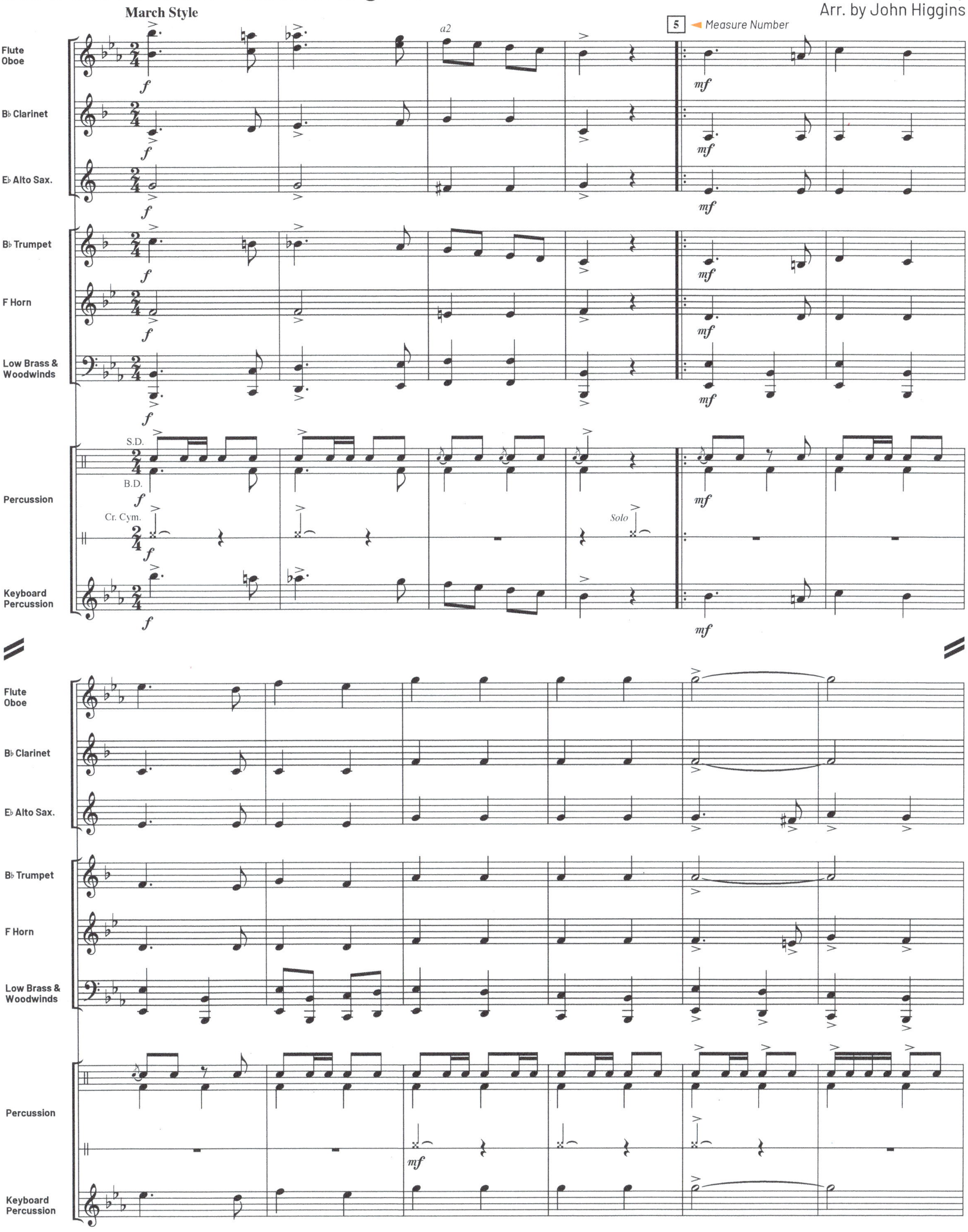

March Style

5 ◄ Measure Number

Flute Oboe

B♭ Clarinet

E♭ Alto Sax.

B♭ Trumpet

F Horn

Low Brass & Woodwinds

Percussion

S.D.

B.D.

Cr. Cym.

Solo

Keyboard Percussion

a2

f

mf

13
Flute
Oboe
B♭ Clarinet
E♭ Alto Sax.
B♭ Trumpet
F Horn
Low Brass &
Woodwinds
Percussion
Keyboard
Percussion
21
Flute
Oboe
B♭ Clarinet
E♭ Alto Sax.
B♭ Trumpet
F Horn
Low Brass &
Woodwinds
Percussion
mf
Keyboard
Percussion

29
Flute
Oboe
B♭ Clarinet
E♭ Alto Sax.
B♭ Trumpet
F Horn
Low Brass &
Woodwinds
Percussion
Keyboard
Percussion
a2
1.
2.

PERFORMANCE SPOTLIGHT

Soli

When playing music marked **Soli**, you are part of a group "solo" or group feature. Listen carefully in "Carnival of Venice," and name the instruments that play the Soli part at each indicated measure number.

TEACHING TIP Review multiple measure rests (Ex. 102) and practice counting them.

153. CARNIVAL OF VENICE – Band Arrangement

Julius Benedict
Arr. by John Higgins

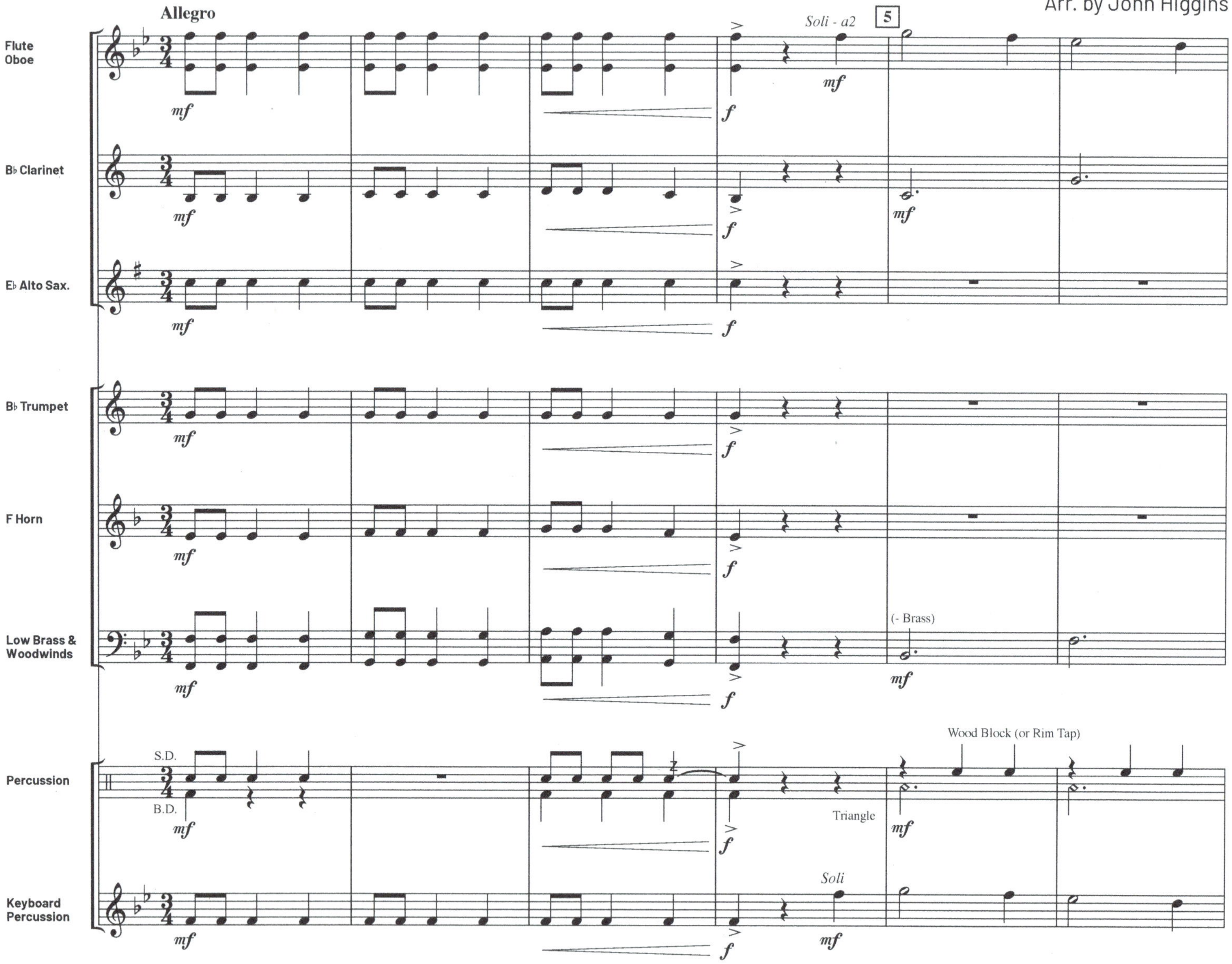

Allegro

Soli - a2

5

Flute
Oboe

B♭ Clarinet

E♭ Alto Sax.

B♭ Trumpet

F Horn

Low Brass & Woodwinds

(- Brass)

Percussion

S.D.

B.D.

Triangle

Wood Block (or Rim Tap)

Keyboard Percussion

Soli

mf *f*

end Soli
Flute
Oboe
B♭ Clarinet
E♭ Alto Sax.
Soli
mf
B♭ Trumpet
F Horn
Low Brass &
Woodwinds
Percussion
Keyboard
Percussion
end Soli
13
Flute
Oboe
B♭ Clarinet
E♭ Alto Sax.
B♭ Trumpet
F Horn
mf
All (- Ww.'s, Tuba)
Low Brass &
Woodwinds
Sus. Cym. (with S.D. stick)
Percussion
Tambourine
Keyboard
Percussion

*In some printed music, cymbals appear with the bass drum.

Flute Oboe
B♭ Clarinet
E♭ Alto Sax.
B♭ Trumpet
F Horn
end Soli
Low Brass & Woodwinds
end Soli
Percussion
Soli
mf
Keyboard Percussion
Soli
f
37
Flute Oboe
B♭ Clarinet
E♭ Alto Sax.
B♭ Trumpet
F Horn
Low Brass & Woodwinds
Percussion
Keyboard Percussion

45
a2
Flute Oboe
B♭ Clarinet
E♭ Alto Sax.
B♭ Trumpet
F Horn
Low Brass & Woodwinds
Percussion
Keyboard Percussion
p
mf
f

DAILY WARM-UPS

WORK-OUTS FOR TONE & TECHNIQUE

Use these daily warm-ups to help develop tone, range, technique, and flexibility.

154. RANGE AND FLEXIBILITY BUILDER

Flute
Oboe

B♭ Clarinet
B♭ Bass Cl.

E♭ Alto Sax.
E♭ Bari. Sax.
E♭ Alto Cl.

B♭ Tenor Sax.

B♭ Trumpet
Baritone T.C.

F Horn

Trombone
Baritone B.C.
Bassoon
Electric Bass

Tuba

Percussion

S.D.

B.D.

Keyboard
Percussion

Flute
Oboe

B♭ Clarinet
B♭ Bass Cl.

E♭ Alto Sax.
E♭ Bari. Sax.
E♭ Alto Cl.

B♭ Tenor Sax.

B♭ Trumpet
Baritone T.C.

F Horn

Trombone
Baritone B.C.
Bassoon
Electric Bass

Tuba

Percussion

Keyboard
Percussion

Percussion Emphasize the accents.
Rudiment
Triple Paradiddle
R L R L R L R R L R L R L R L L
155. TECHNIQUE TRAX
Flute
Oboe
B♭ Clarinet
B♭ Bass Cl.
E♭ Alto Sax.
E♭ Bari. Sax.
E♭ Alto Cl.
B♭ Tenor Sax.
B♭ Trumpet
Baritone T.C.
F Horn
Trombone
Baritone B.C.
Bassoon
Electric Bass
Tuba
S.D.
B.D.
Percussion
Keyboard
Percussion

Hold the first note of this chorale, listening for balance, blend, and good tone. Then play on, striving to maintain these qualities.

156. CHORALE

Johann Sebastian Bach

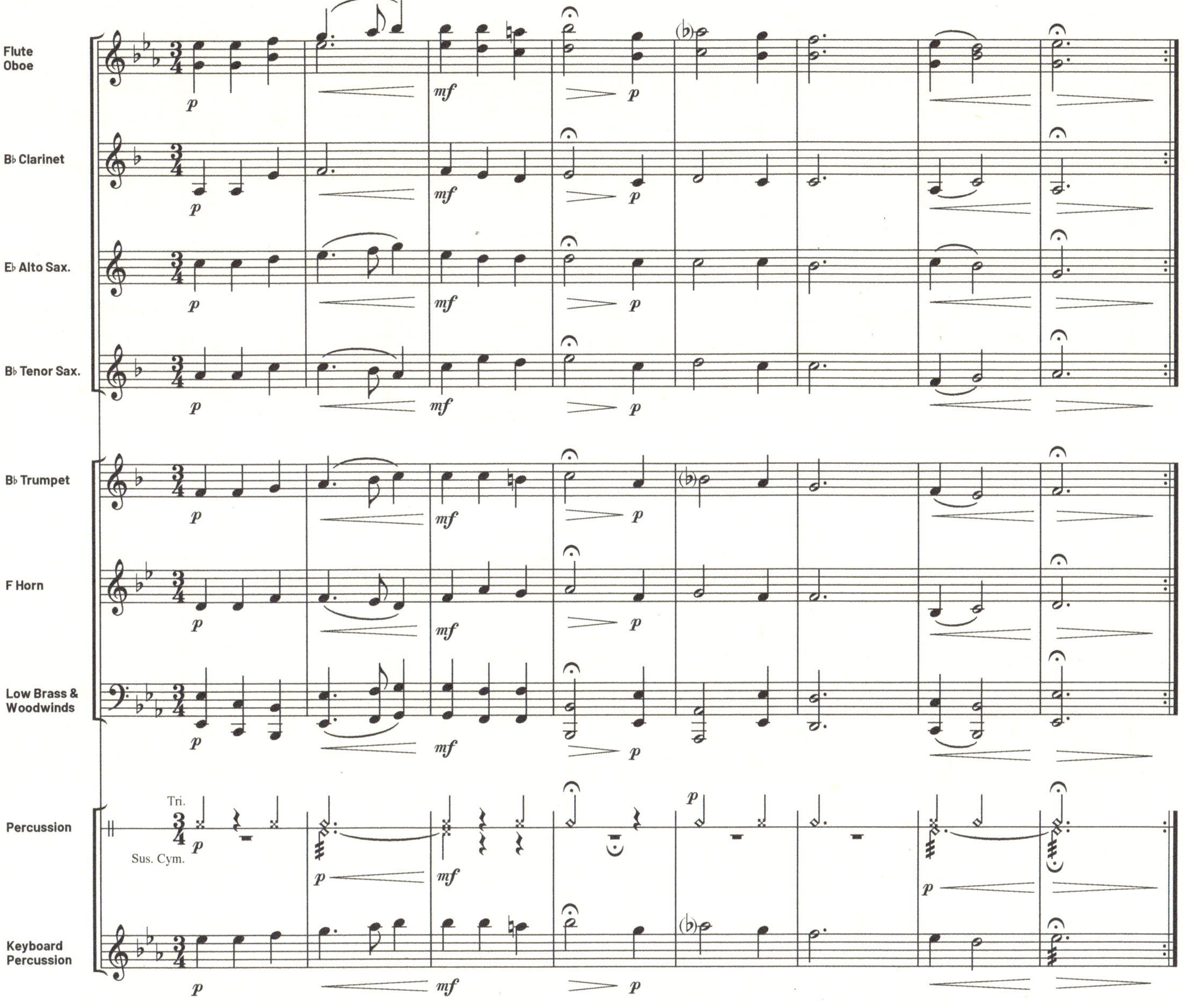

Flute
Oboe

B♭ Clarinet

E♭ Alto Sax.

B♭ Tenor Sax.

B♭ Trumpet

F Horn

Low Brass &
Woodwinds

Percussion

Tri.

Sus. Cym.

Keyboard
Percussion

HISTORY

The traditional Hebrew melody "Hatikvah" has been Israel's national anthem since the nation's inception. At the Declaration of State in 1948, it was sung by the gathered assembly during the opening ceremony and played by members of the Palestine Symphony Orchestra at its conclusion.

157. HATIKVAH

Israeli National Anthem

Flute
Oboe
B♭ Clarinet
B♭ Bass Cl.
E♭ Alto Sax.
E♭ Bari. Sax.
E♭ Alto Cl.
B♭ Tenor Sax.
B♭ Trumpet
Baritone T.C.
F Horn
Trombone
Baritone B.C.
Bassoon
Electric Bass
Tuba
Percussion
Keyboard
Percussion
a2
f
Sus. Cym.
Wd. Blk.
14
mf
Tri

Eighth Note & Eighth Rest

♪ = 1/2 beat of sound

𝄾 = 1/2 beat of silence

TEACHING TIP Be sure students are counting with subdivision.

158. RHYTHM RAP

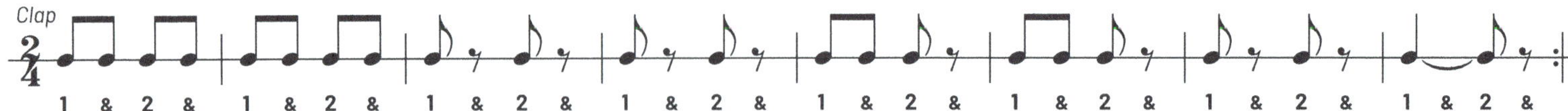

TEACHING TIP Note that rhythms are identical with #158 Rhythm Rap.

Percussion Practice "Doubling" and Paradiddles.

159. EIGHTH NOTE MARCH

Flute / Oboe — 1 & 2 & 1 & 2 & 1 & 2 & 1 & 2 & 1 & 2 & 1 & 2 & 1 & 2 & 1 & 2 &

B♭ Clarinet / B♭ Bass Cl.

E♭ Alto Sax. / E♭ Bar. Sax. / E♭ Alto Clar.

B♭ Tenor Sax.

B♭ Trumpet / Baritone T.C.

F Horn

Trombone / Baritone B.C. / Bassoon / Electric Bass

Tuba

Percussion — S.D. / B.D. — R R L R R L R R L R R L R L R R L R L L R R L L R R L L R R L R R L R L R R L; Cr. Cym.

Keyboard Percussion

TEACHING TIP Practice measure 2 slowly, comparing the full quarter note to the eighth notes and rests.

160. MINUET

Johann Sebastian Bach

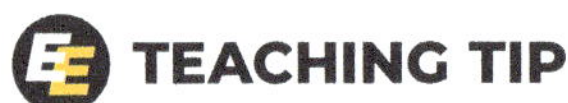

TEACHING TIP Stress subdivisions in counting.

161. RHYTHM RAP

Clap
1 & 2 & 3 & 4 & 1 & 2 & 3 & 4 & 1 & 2 & 3 & 4 & 1 & 2 & 3 & 4 &

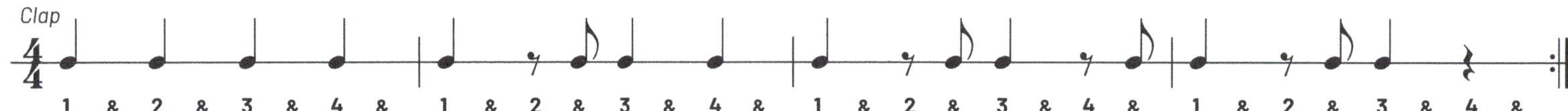

TEACHING TIP Note that rhythms are identical with #161 Rhythm Rap.

162. EIGHTH NOTES OFF THE BEAT

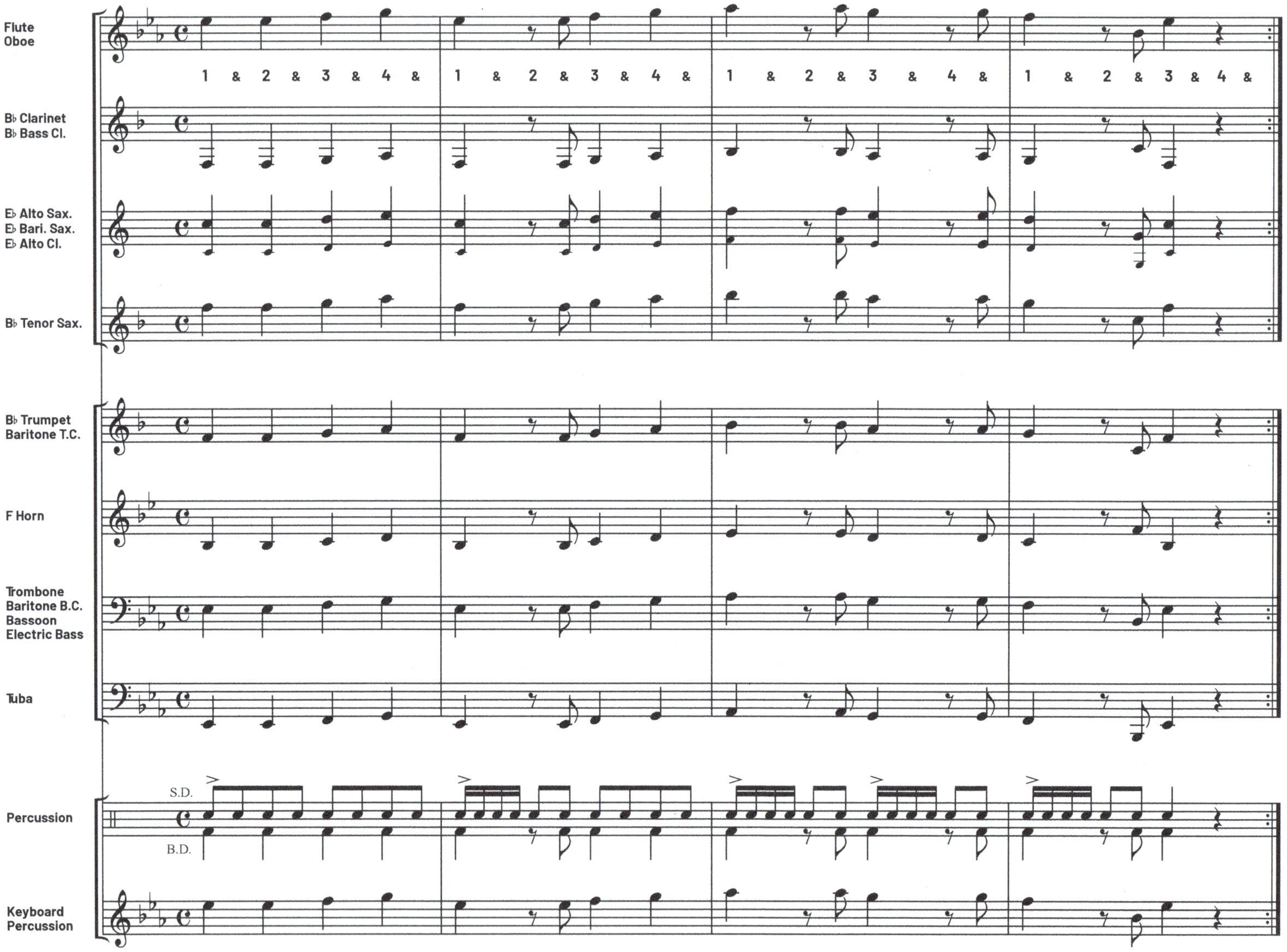
Flute
Oboe
1 & 2 & 3 & 4 & 1 & 2 & 3 & 4 & 1 & 2 & 3 & 4 & 1 & 2 & 3 & 4 &
B♭ Clarinet
B♭ Bass Cl.
E♭ Alto Sax.
E♭ Bari. Sax.
E♭ Alto Cl.
B♭ Tenor Sax.
B♭ Trumpet
Baritone T.C.
F Horn
Trombone
Baritone B.C.
Bassoon
Electric Bass
Tuba
Percussion
S.D.
B.D.
Keyboard
Percussion

Percussion
Cowbell

Hold the open end of the cowbell away from you, and play on the front edge of the open end with a stick.

TEACHING TIP Remind students to play full quarter notes before the eighth rests in measures 1–7.

163. EIGHTH NOTE SCRAMBLE

QUIZ ASSESSMENT 2/4 Time signature, Key signature (Concert F), eighth note, eighth rest.

164. ESSENTIAL ELEMENTS QUIZ

Flute/Kybd. Perc.
G♭
Oboe
G♭
Bassoon
G♭
Clarinet
A♭
Alto Clarinet
E♭
Bass Clarinet
A♭
Alto Saxophone
E♭
Tenor Saxophone
A♭
Baritone Saxophone
E♭
Trumpet
A♭
F Horn
D♭
F Horn:
B♭ Horn: T
Trombone
G♭
5
Baritone B.C.
G♭
Baritone T.C.
A♭
Tuba
G♭
Electric Bass
G♭

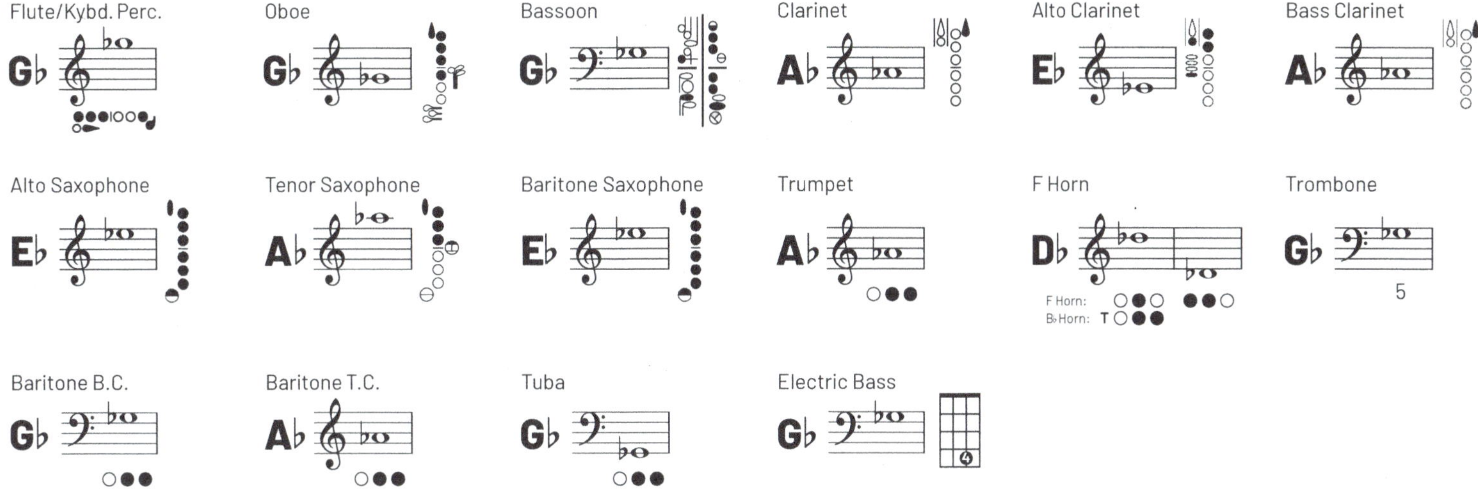

TEACHING TIP Play the new note before playing the exercise.

F Horn Double Horn Players: add the thumb key and use the B♭ Horn fingering for the upper "D♭."

165. DANCING MELODY – New Note

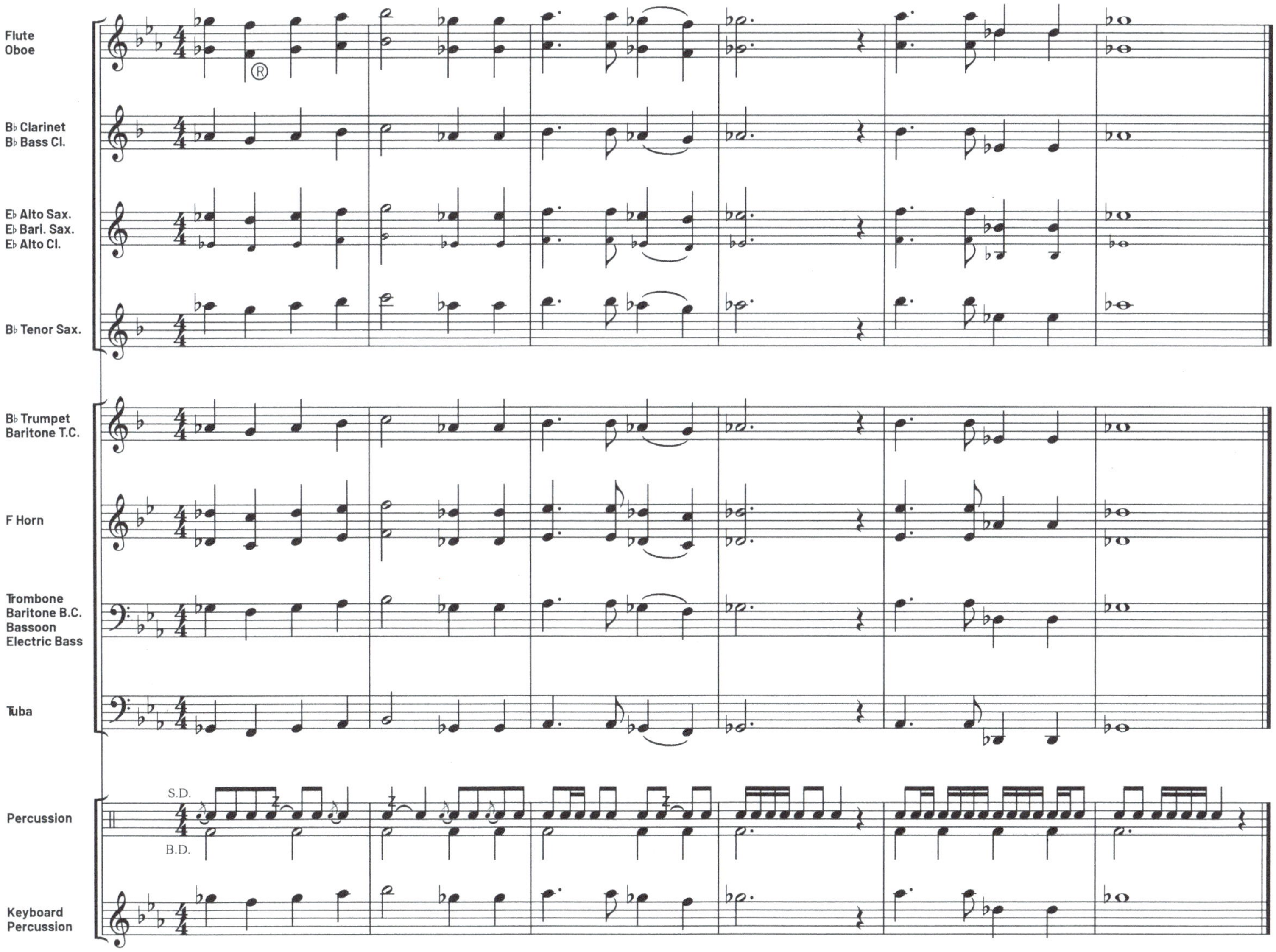
Flute
Oboe
B♭ Clarinet
B♭ Bass Cl.
E♭ Alto Sax.
E♭ Bari. Sax.
E♭ Alto Cl.
B♭ Tenor Sax.
B♭ Trumpet
Baritone T.C.
F Horn
Trombone
Baritone B.C.
Bassoon
Electric Bass
Tuba
Percussion
S.D.
B.D.
Keyboard
Percussion

HISTORY

American composer and conductor **John Philip Sousa** (1854–1932) wrote 136 marches. Known as "The March King," Sousa wrote *The Stars And Stripes Forever*, *Semper Fidelis*, *The Washington Post* and many other patriotic works. Sousa's band performed all over the country, and his fame helped boost the popularity of bands in America. Here is a melody from his famous *El Capitan* operetta and march.

Review 1st and 2nd endings. Students should identify the slur—how is it different from the ties?

166. EL CAPITAN

John Philip Sousa

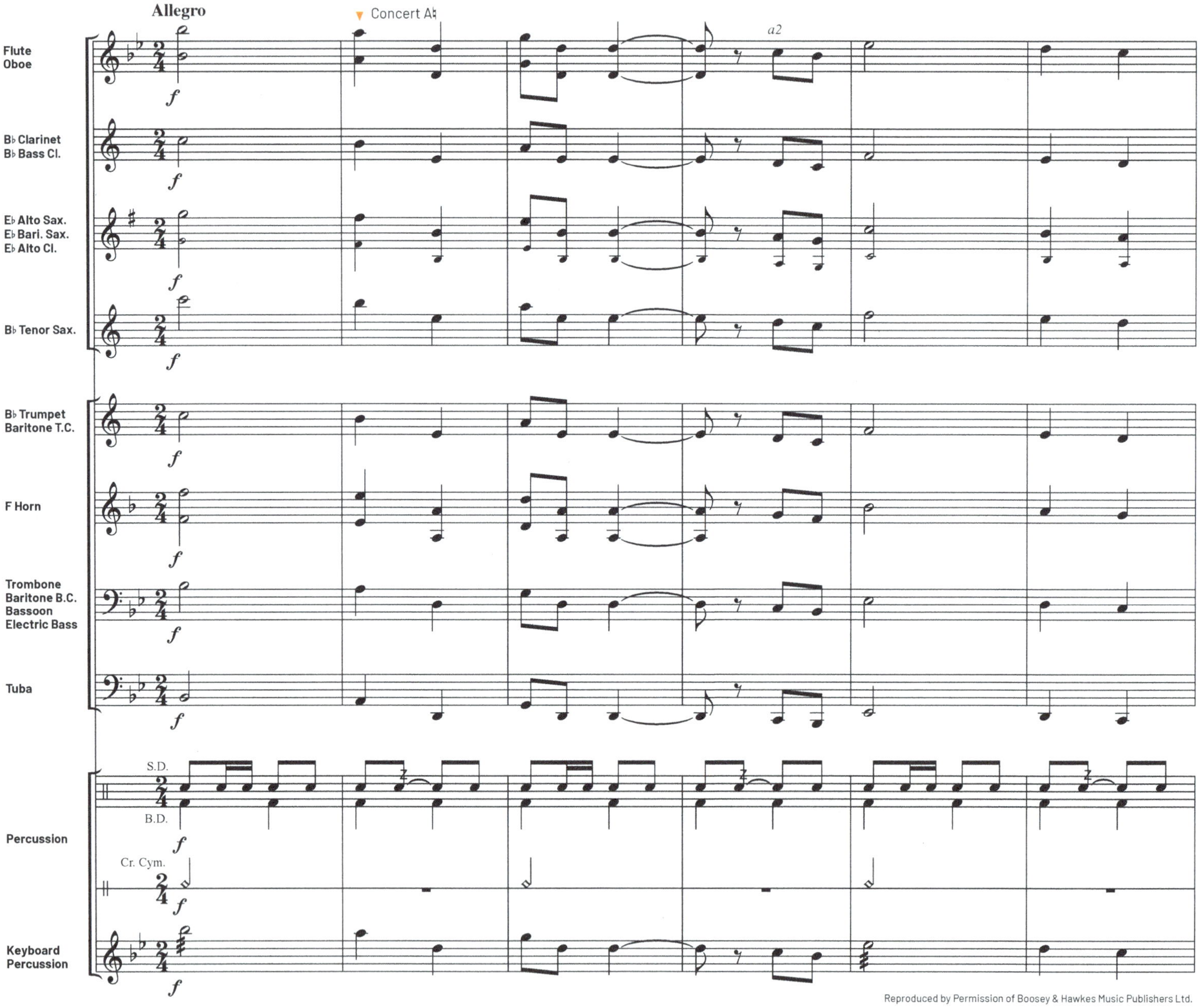

Allegro

▼ Concert A♮

a2

Flute
Oboe

B♭ Clarinet
B♭ Bass Cl.

E♭ Alto Sax.
E♭ Bari. Sax.
E♭ Alto Cl.

B♭ Tenor Sax.

B♭ Trumpet
Baritone T.C.

F Horn

Trombone
Baritone B.C.
Bassoon
Electric Bass

Tuba

Percussion

S.D.
B.D.
Cr. Cym.

Keyboard
Percussion

Flute
Oboe
a2
B♭ Clarinet
B♭ Bass Cl.
E♭ Alto Sax.
E♭ Bari. Sax.
E♭ Alto Cl.
B♭ Tenor Sax.
B♭ Trumpet
Baritone T.C.
F Horn
Trombone
Baritone B.C.
Bassoon
Electric Bass
Tuba
Percussion
Keyboard
Percussion

Flute
Oboe
a2
1.
2.
B♭ Clarinet
B♭ Bass Cl.
E♭ Alto Sax.
E♭ Bari. Sax.
E♭ Alto Cl.
B♭ Tenor Sax.
B♭ Trumpet
Baritone T.C.
F Horn
Trombone
Baritone B.C.
Bassoon
Electric Bass
Tuba
Percussion
Keyboard
Percussion

HISTORY

"O Canada," formerly known as the "National Song," was first performed during 1880 in French Canada. Robert Stanley Weir translated the English language version in 1908, but it was not adopted as the national anthem of Canada until 1980, one hundred years after its premiere.

167. O CANADA

Calixa Lavallee,
l'Hon. Judge Routhier and Justice R.S. Weir

9
Flute
Oboe
B♭ Clarinet
B♭ Bass Cl.
E♭ Alto Sax.
E♭ Bari. Sax.
E♭ Alto Cl.
B♭ Tenor Sax.
B♭ Trumpet
Baritone T.C.
F Horn
Trombone
Baritone B.C.
Bassoon
Electric Bass
Tuba
Percussion
Keyboard
Percussion
p
17
mf
f

Flute
Oboe
B♭ Clarinet
B♭ Bass Cl.
E♭ Alto Sax.
E♭ Bari. Sax.
E♭ Alto Cl.
B♭ Tenor Sax.
B♭ Trumpet
Baritone T.C.
F Horn
Trombone
Baritone B.C.
Bassoon
Electric Bass
Tuba
Percussion
Keyboard
Percussion
a2

QUIZ ASSESSMENT Playing mixed meters (4/4, 3/4).

168. ESSENTIAL ELEMENTS QUIZ – METER MANIA *Count and clap before playing. Can you conduct this?*

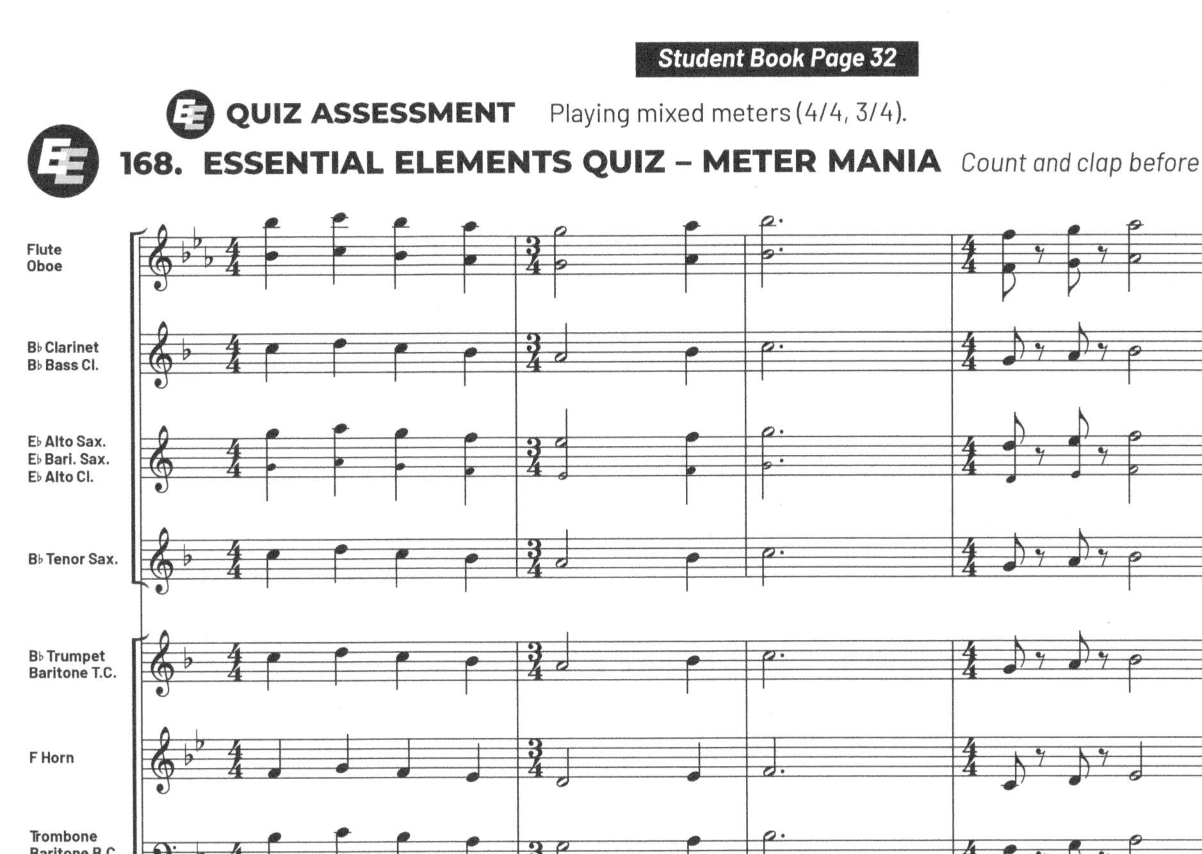

Flute
Oboe
B♭ Clarinet
B♭ Bass Cl.
E♭ Alto Sax.
E♭ Bari. Sax.
E♭ Alto Cl.
B♭ Tenor Sax.
B♭ Trumpet
Baritone T.C.
F Horn
Trombone
Baritone B.C.
Bassoon
Electric Bass
Tuba
Percussion
Keyboard
Percussion

THEORY

Enharmonics

Two notes that are written differently, but sound the same (and played with the same fingering) are called **enharmonics**. Your fingering chart on student book pages 46–47 shows the fingerings for the enharmonic notes on your instrument.

C instruments:
(Other student books are transposed.)

On a piano keyboard, each black key is both a flat and a sharp:

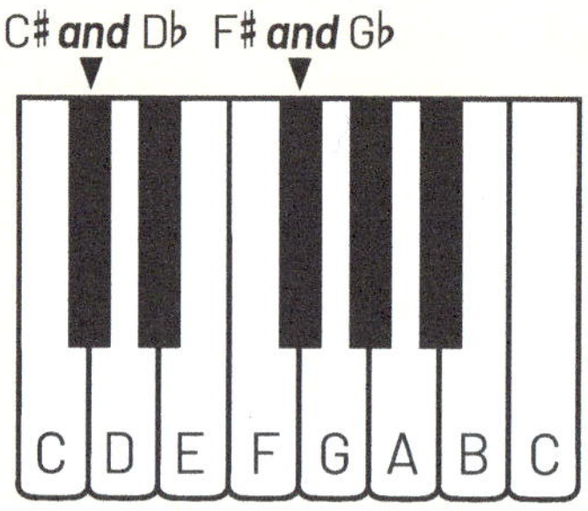
C♯ *and* D♭
F♯ *and* G♭
C D E F G A B C

Flute/Kybd. Perc.
G♭/F♯
Oboe
G♭/F♯
Bassoon
G♭/F♯
Clarinet
A♭/G♯
Alto Clarinet
E♭/D♯
Bass Clarinet
A♭/G♯
Alto Saxophone
E♭/D♯
Tenor Saxophone
A♭/G♯
Baritone Saxophone
E♭/D♯
Trumpet
A♭/G♯
F Horn
D♭/C♯
F Horn:
B♭ Horn:
T
Trombone
G♭/F♯
5
Baritone B.C.
G♭/F♯
Baritone T.C.
A♭/G♯
Tuba
G♭/F♯
Electric Bass
G♭/F♯
4

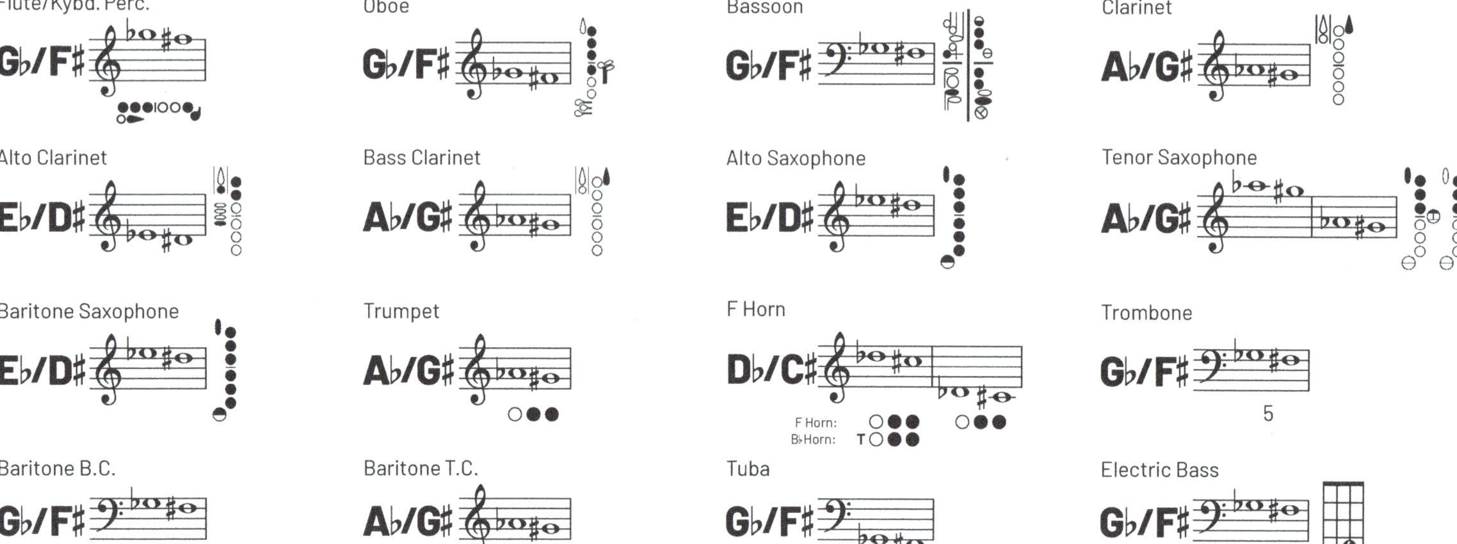

TEACHING TIP Play the enharmonic notes before playing the exercise.

F Horn Double Horn Players: add the thumb key and use the B♭ Horn fingering for the upper "D♭/C♯."

169. SNAKE CHARMER *Enharmonic notes use the same fingering/position.*

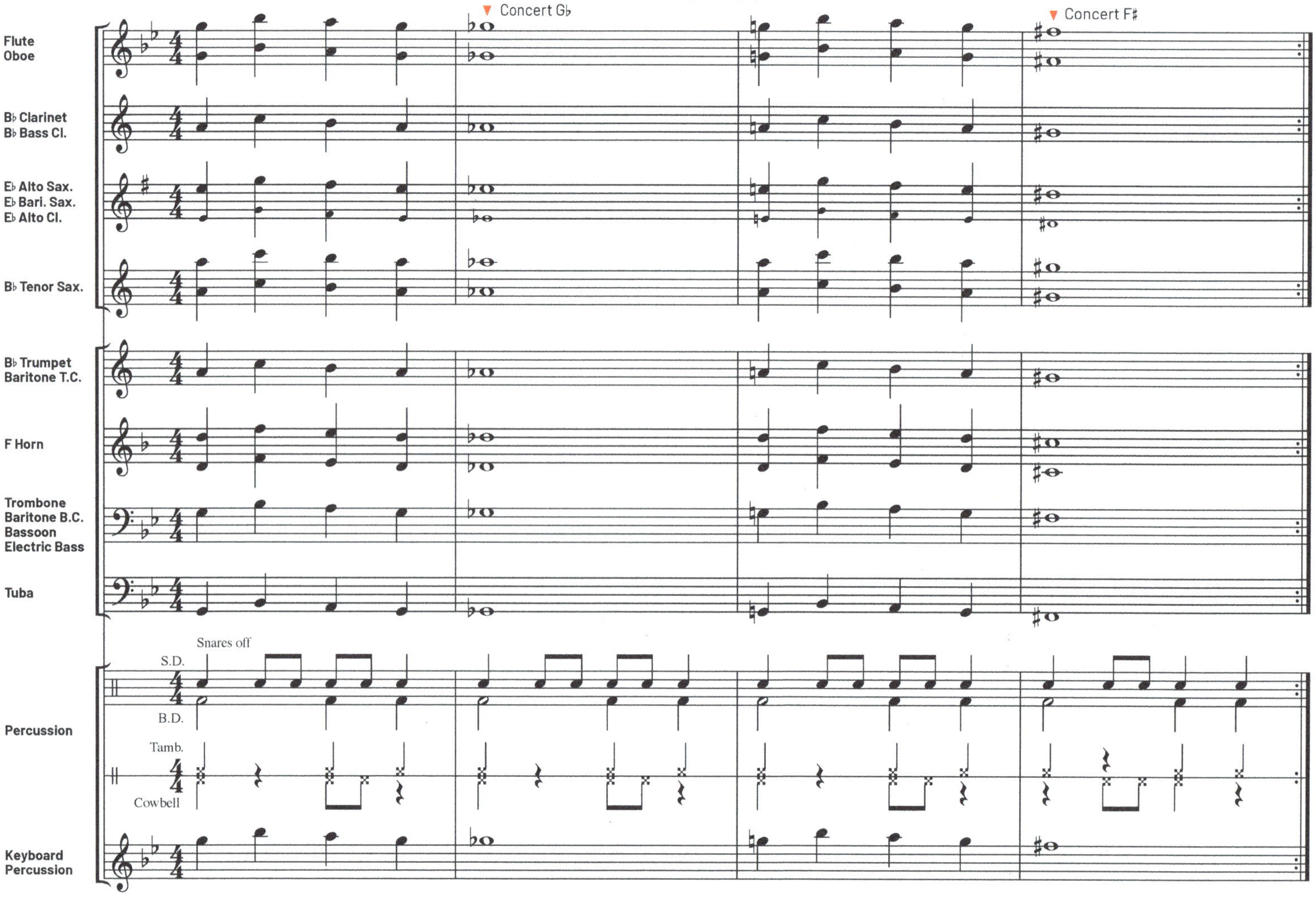
Concert G♭
Concert F♯
Flute
Oboe
B♭ Clarinet
B♭ Bass Cl.
E♭ Alto Sax.
E♭ Bari. Sax.
E♭ Alto Cl.
B♭ Tenor Sax.
B♭ Trumpet
Baritone T.C.
F Horn
Trombone
Baritone B.C.
Bassoon
Electric Bass
Tuba
Snares off
S.D.
B.D.
Percussion
Tamb.
Cowbell
Keyboard
Percussion

Review pick-up notes, and be sure students subdivide your preparatory beats. Ask students to identify the enharmonic notes.

170. DARK SHADOWS

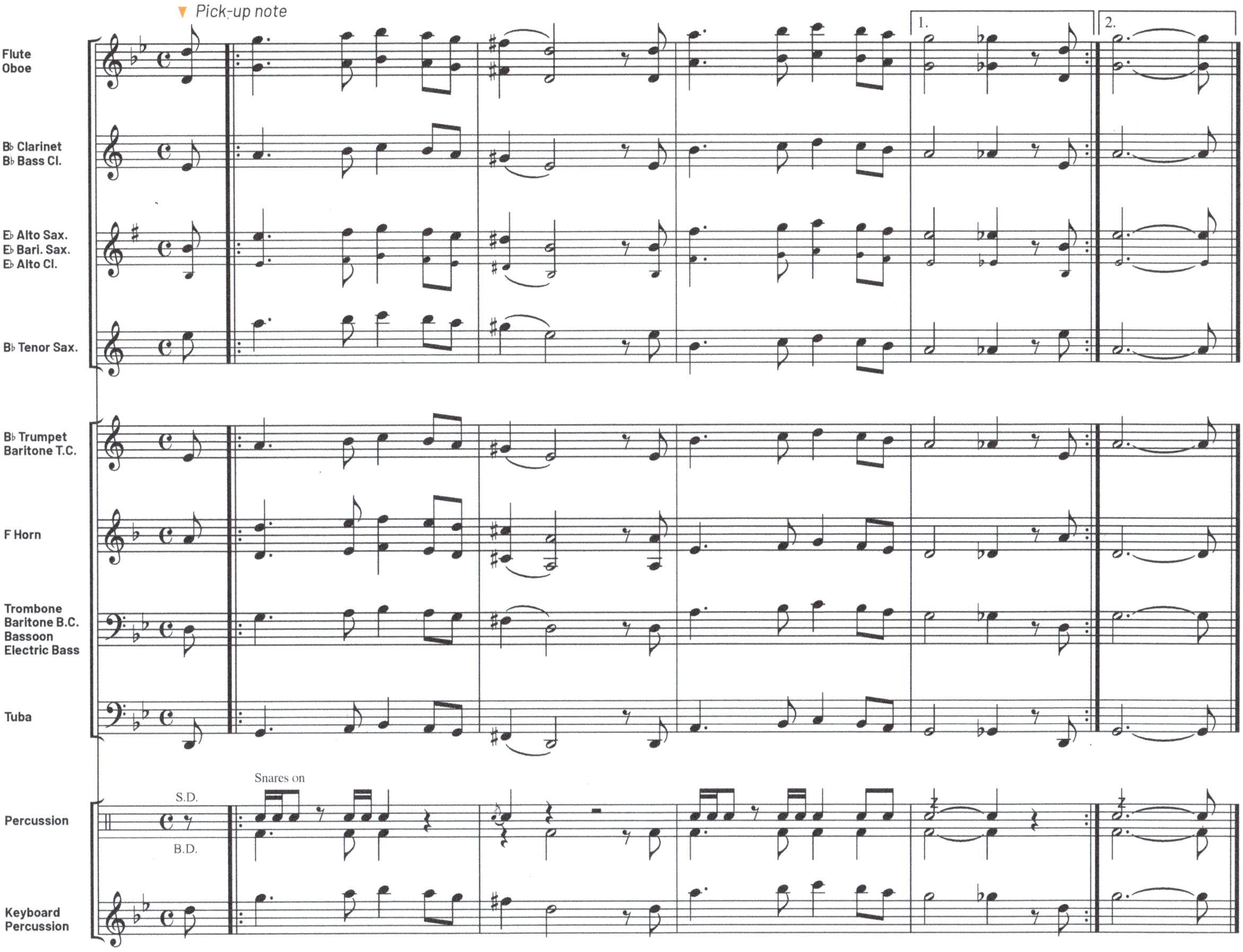

▼ *Pick-up note*

1. 2.

Flute
Oboe

B♭ Clarinet
B♭ Bass Cl.

E♭ Alto Sax.
E♭ Bari. Sax.
E♭ Alto Cl.

B♭ Tenor Sax.

B♭ Trumpet
Baritone T.C.

F Horn

Trombone
Baritone B.C.
Bassoon
Electric Bass

Tuba

Percussion

S.D.

B.D.

Snares on

Keyboard
Percussion

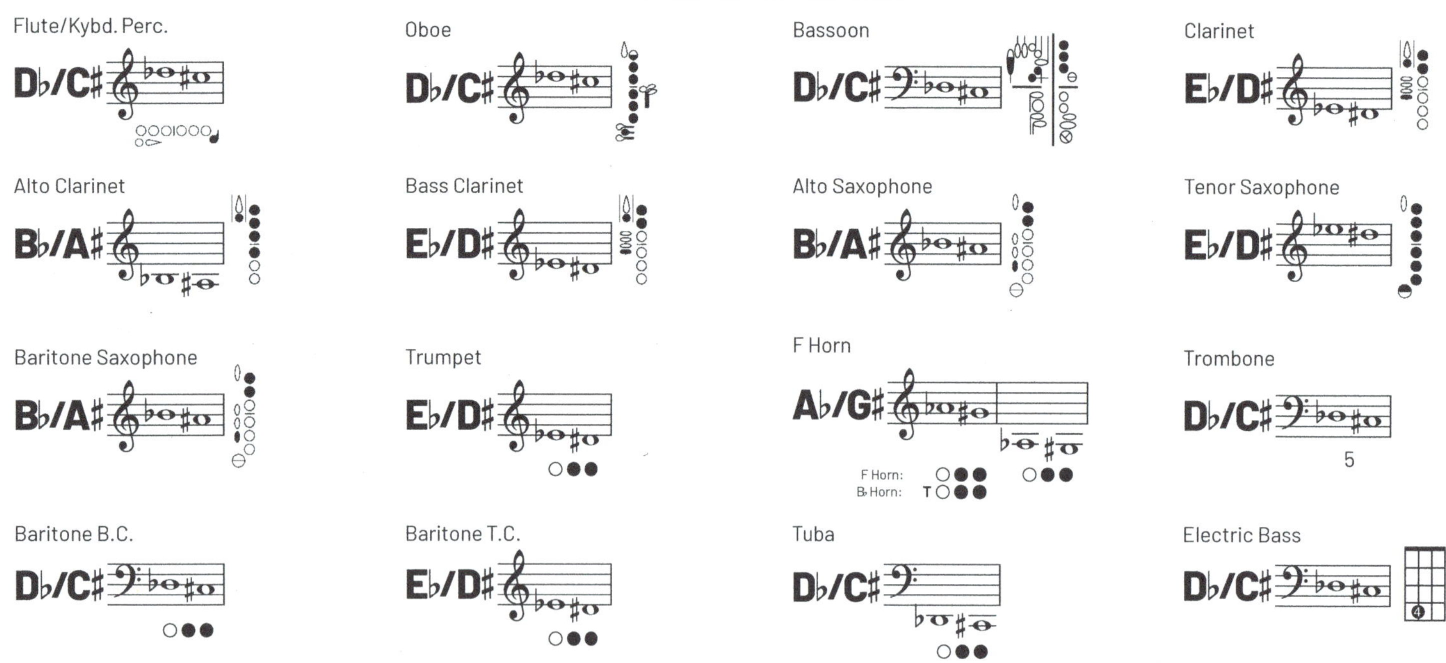

TEACHING TIP Play the enharmonic notes before playing the exercise.

F Horn Double Horn Players: add the thumb key and use the B♭ Horn fingering for the upper "A♭/G♯."

171. CLOSE ENCOUNTERS *Enharmonic notes use the same fingering/position.*

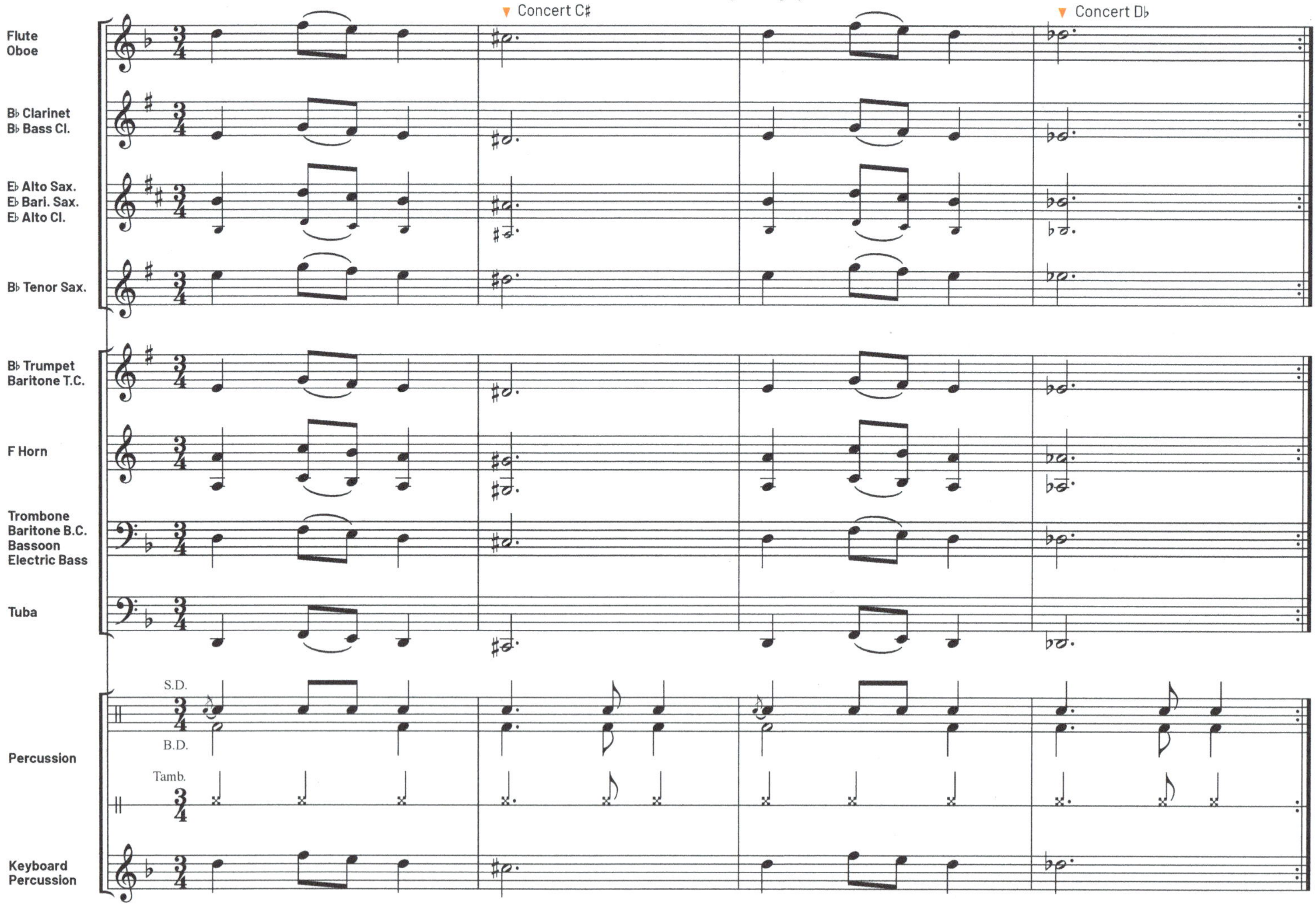

▼ Concert C♯ ▼ Concert D♭

Flute
Oboe

B♭ Clarinet
B♭ Bass Cl.

E♭ Alto Sax.
E♭ Bari. Sax.
E♭ Alto Cl.

B♭ Tenor Sax.

B♭ Trumpet
Baritone T.C.

F Horn

Trombone
Baritone B.C.
Bassoon
Electric Bass

Tuba

Percussion S.D. B.D. Tamb.

Keyboard Percussion

Timpani (Ex.172)

One of the most dramatic instruments in the percussion section, *Timpani* combines the rhythms of percussion with the pitch of other instruments. Use felt timpani mallets. For **March Slav** tune the larger drum to F and the smaller drum to B♭.

Percussion (Ex.172) Snare Drum is *tacet* (do not play). An optional timpani part appears on student book page 33-B.

Ask students—how long is an accidental in effect?

172. MARCH SLAV

Peter Ilyich Tchaikovsky

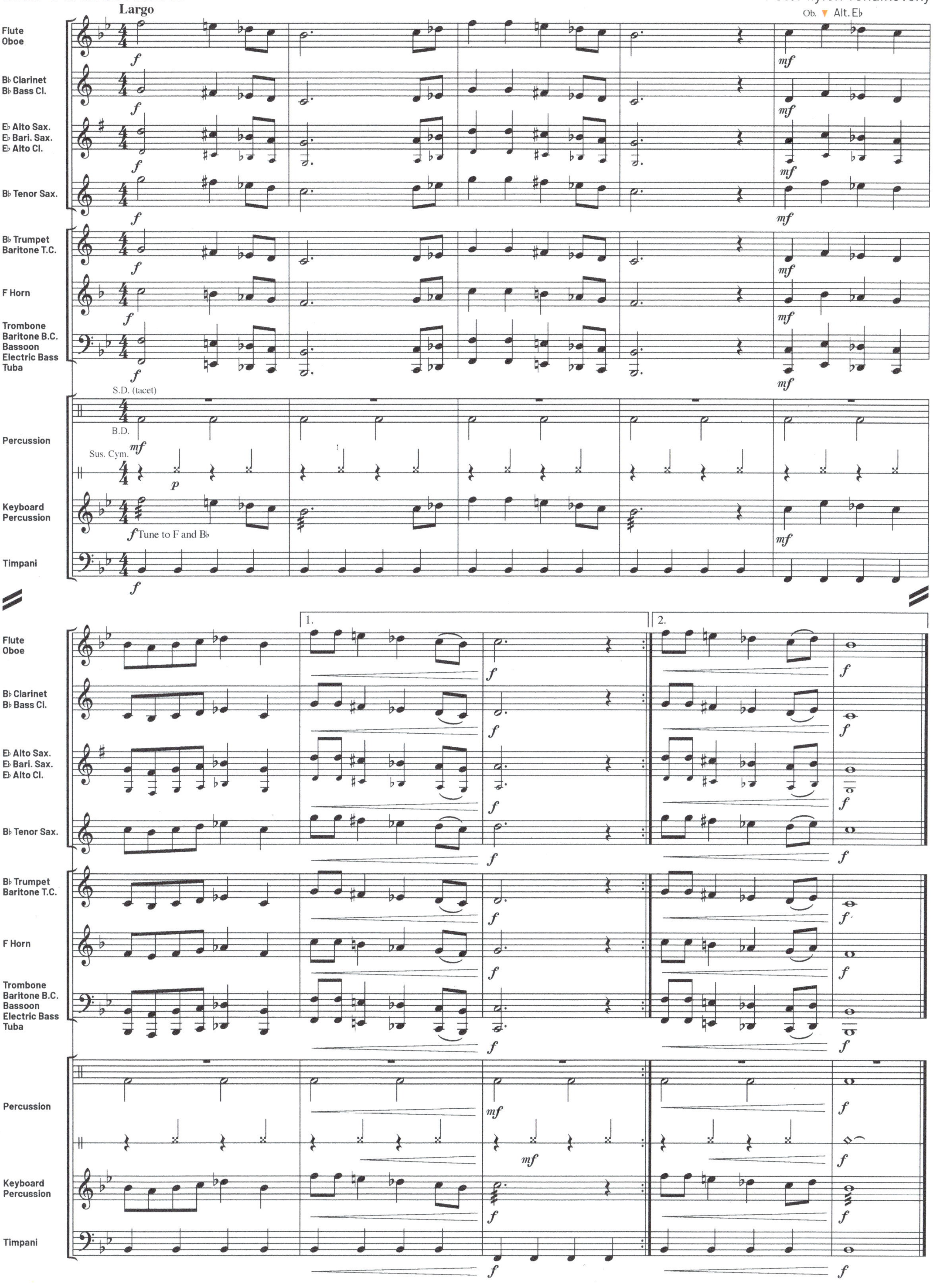

Largo

Flute
Oboe
B♭ Clarinet
B♭ Bass Cl.
E♭ Alto Sax.
E♭ Bari. Sax.
E♭ Alto Cl.
B♭ Tenor Sax.
B♭ Trumpet
Baritone T.C.
F Horn
Trombone
Baritone B.C.
Bassoon
Electric Bass
Tuba
Percussion
S.D. (tacet)
B.D.
Sus. Cym.
Keyboard Percussion
Tune to F and B♭
Timpani
Ob. ▼ Alt. E♭

1. 2.

TEACHING TIP This exercise features both pairs of enharmonics learned on student book page 33.

Oboe Enharmonic notes use the same fingering.

173. NOTES IN DISGUISE

Flute
Oboe

B♭ Clarinet
B♭ Bass Cl.

E♭ Alto Sax.
E♭ Bari. Sax.
E♭ Alto Cl.

Alt. B Alt. B Alt. B

B♭ Tenor Sax.

B♭ Trumpet
Baritone T.C.

F Horn

Trombone
Baritone B.C.
Bassoon
Electric Bass

Tuba

Percussion
S.D.
B.D.
Tri.
l.v.

Keyboard
Percussion

Chromatic Notes

Chromatic notes are altered with sharps, flats and natural signs which are not in the key signature. The smallest distance between two notes is a half-step, and a scale made up of consecutive half-steps is called a **chromatic scale**.

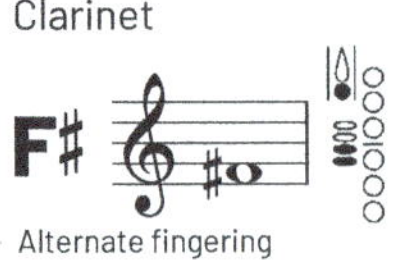

TEACHING TIP Play the alternate fingering before playing this chromatic scale.

174. HALF-STEPPIN'

HISTORY

French composer **Camille Saint-Saëns** (1835-1921) wrote music for virtually every medium: operas, suites, symphonies and chamber works. The "Egyptian Dance" is one of the main themes from his famous opera *Samson et Delilah*. The opera was written in the same year that Thomas Edison invented the phonograph—1877.

Percussion

Tambourine Shake

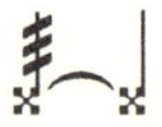

Shake the tambourine in your left hand. Stop the shake on the release (tied) note with the fist of your right hand.

Timpani Tune the larger drum to A and the smaller drum to E. Watch for accidentals. Use a light stroke to achieve a dance-like quality in your sound.

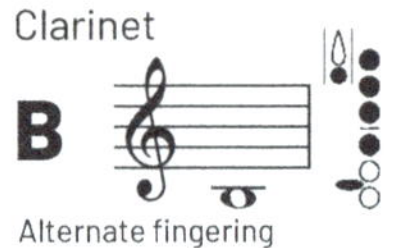

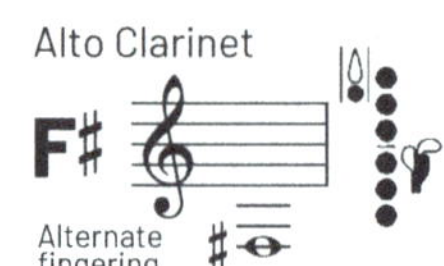

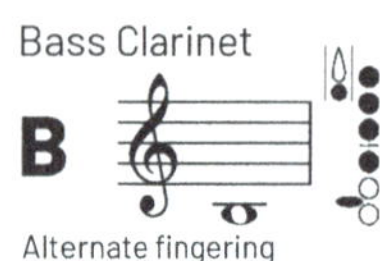

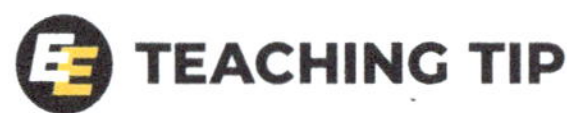

Clarinet

B

Alternate fingering

Alto Clarinet

F♯

Alternate fingering

Bass Clarinet

B

Alternate fingering

TEACHING TIP Ask students to identify the enharmonic notes and play the alternate fingering before playing this exercise.

175. EGYPTIAN DANCE *Watch for enharmonics.*

Camille Saint-Saëns

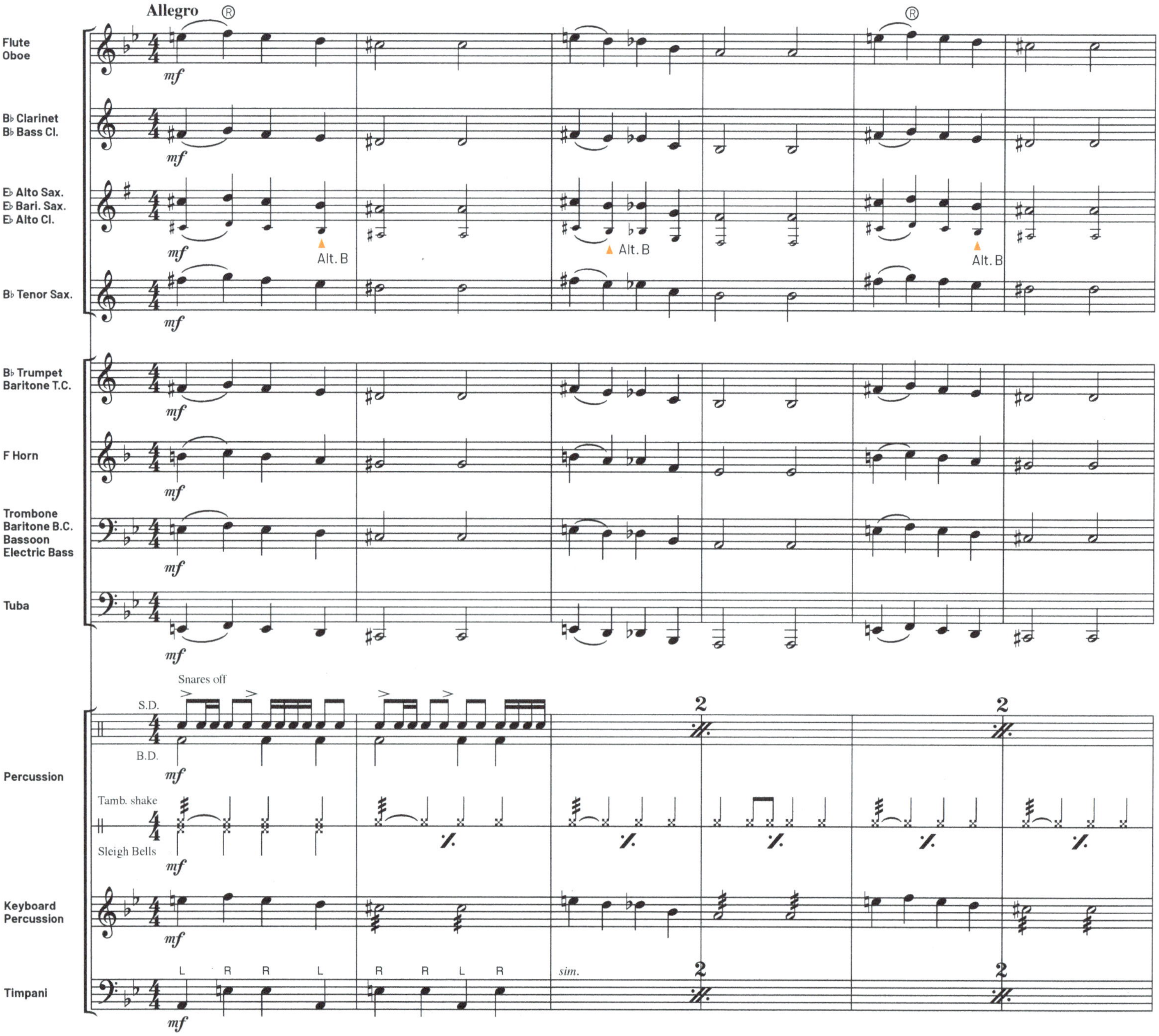
Allegro
Flute
Oboe
B♭ Clarinet
B♭ Bass Cl.
E♭ Alto Sax.
E♭ Bari. Sax.
E♭ Alto Cl.
Alt. B
Alt. B
Alt. B
B♭ Tenor Sax.
B♭ Trumpet
Baritone T.C.
F Horn
Trombone
Baritone B.C.
Bassoon
Electric Bass
Tuba
mf
Snares off
S.D.
B.D.
Percussion
Tamb. shake
Sleigh Bells
Keyboard
Percussion
Timpani
L R R L R R L R
sim.
2
2

Flute
Oboe
B♭ Clarinet
B♭ Bass Cl.
E♭ Alto Sax.
E♭ Bari. Sax.
E♭ Alto Cl.
B♭ Tenor Sax.
B♭ Trumpet
Baritone T.C.
F Horn
Trombone
Baritone B.C.
Bassoon
Electric Bass
Tuba
Percussion
Keyboard Percussion
Timpani
Alt. B
Alt. F♯
2

TEACHING TIP Review D.C. al Fine. Stress good tone and breath support. Don't allow rushing.

176. SILVER MOON BOAT

Chinese Folk Song

German composer **Ludwig van Beethoven** (1770–1827) is considered to be one of the world's greatest composers, despite becoming completely deaf in 1802. Although he could not hear his music the way we can, he could "hear" it in his mind. As a testament to his greatness, his *Symphony No. 9* (student book p. 13) was performed as the finale to the ceremony celebrating the reunification of Germany in 1990. This is the theme from his *Symphony No. 7*, second movement.

Assign parts to play this duet as a band arrangement. Bass instruments should play Part B. Review repeat signs and endings.

Percussion While this part looks easy, it is difficult because it is slow. Strive for an even consistent sound.

177. THEME FROM SYMPHONY NO. 7 – Duet

Ludwig van Beethoven

Allegro (moderately fast)

Flute / Oboe (A, B) — *p* — Ob. ▲ Alt. E♭ — ▲ Alt. E♭

B♭ Clarinet / B♭ Bass Cl. (A, B) — *p* — ▲ Alt. F♯

E♭ Alto Sax. / E♭ Bari. Sax. / E♭ Alto Cl. (A, B) — *p*

B♭ Tenor Sax. (A, B) — *p* — ▲ Alt. F♯

B♭ Trumpet / Baritone T.C. (A, B) — *p*

F Horn (A, B) — *p*

Trombone / Baritone B.C. / Bassoon / Electric Bass (A, B) — *p*

Tuba (A, B) — *p*

Percussion — S.D. / B.D. — *p* — Snares off

Keyboard Percussion (A, B) — *p*

Timpani — Tune to E♭ and A♭ — *p*

9
Flute
Oboe
Bb Clarinet
Bb Bass Cl.
Alt. F#
Eb Alto Sax.
Eb Bari. Sax.
Eb Alto Cl.
Alt. B
Bb Tenor Sax.
Alt. F#
Bb Trumpet
Baritone T.C.
F Horn
Trombone
Baritone B.C.
Bassoon
Electric Bass
Tuba
Percussion
Keyboard
Percussion
Timpani
mf

1.
2.
Flute
Oboe
Alt. E♭
Alt. E♭
Alt. E♭
B♭ Clarinet
B♭ Bass Cl.
E♭ Alto Sax.
E♭ Bari. Sax.
E♭ Alto Cl.
B♭ Tenor Sax.
B♭ Trumpet
Baritone T.C.
F Horn
Trombone
Baritone B.C.
Bassoon
Electric Bass
Tuba
Percussion
Keyboard
Percussion
Timpani

HISTORY

Russian composer **Peter Ilyich Tchaikovsky** (1840–1893) wrote six symphonies and hundreds of other works including *The Nutcracker* ballet. He was a master at writing brilliant settings of folk music, and his original melodies are among the most popular of all time. His *1812 Overture* and *Capriccio Italien* were both written in 1880, the year after Thomas Edison developed the practical electric light bulb.

This exercise features 2 repeated sections, each with a 1st and 2nd ending. Also review alternate fingering.

Percussion Timpani: Use a slow stroke to "pull" the sound out of the timpani. Tune F and B♭.

178. CAPRICCIO ITALIEN *Always check the key signature.*

Peter Ilyich Tchaikovsky

Allegro

1.

Flute
Oboe

B♭ Clarinet
B♭ Bass Cl.

Alt. F♯

E♭ Alto Sax.
E♭ Bari. Sax.
E♭ Alto Cl.

B♭ Tenor Sax.

Alt. F♯

B♭ Trumpet
Baritone T.C.

F Horn

Trombone
Baritone B.C.
Bassoon
Electric Bass
Tuba

Snares on
S.D.
B.D.

Percussion

Cr. Cym.

Keyboard
Percussion

Timpani

2.
Flute
Oboe
B♭ Clarinet
B♭ Bass Cl.
E♭ Alto Sax.
E♭ Bari. Sax.
E♭ Alto Cl.
B♭ Tenor Sax.
B♭ Trumpet
Baritone T.C.
F Horn
Trombone
Baritone B.C.
Bassoon
Electric Bass
Tuba
Percussion
Keyboard
Percussion
Timpani
1.
2.

Student Book Page 35

Practice at slower tempos and progress to an allegro.

A snare drum rudiment. Emphasize the

179. AMERICAN PATROL

F.W. Meacham

Allegro

Flute
Oboe

B♭ Clarinet
B♭ Bass Cl.

E♭ Alto Sax.
E♭ Bari. Sax.
E♭ Alto Cl.

B♭ Tenor Sax.

B♭ Trumpet
Baritone T.C.

F Horn

Trombone
Baritone B.C.
Bassoon
Electric Bass

Tuba

Percussion

S.D.
B.D.
L R L R L L R
sim.

Keyboard
Percussion

mf

Flute
Oboe

B♭ Clarinet
B♭ Bass Cl.

E♭ Alto Sax.
E♭ Bari. Sax.
E♭ Alto Cl.

B♭ Tenor Sax.

B♭ Trumpet
Baritone T.C.

F Horn

Trombone
Baritone B.C.
Bassoon
Electric Bass

Tuba

Percussion

L R L R L L R L R L
sim.

Keyboard
Percussion

Flute
Oboe
B♭ Clarinet
B♭ Bass Cl.
E♭ Alto Sax.
E♭ Bari. Sax.
E♭ Alto Cl.
B♭ Tenor Sax.
B♭ Trumpet
Baritone T.C.
F Horn
Trombone
Baritone B.C.
Bassoon
Electric Bass
Tuba
Percussion
Keyboard
Percussion
Alt. C

Student Book Page 35

TEACHING TIP Stress breath support at the soft dynamic level.

180. WAYFARING STRANGER

African-American Spiritual

Flute
Oboe
B♭ Clarinet
B♭ Bass Cl.
E♭ Alto Sax.
E♭ Bari. Sax.
E♭ Alto Cl.
B♭ Tenor Sax.
B♭ Trumpet
Baritone T.C.
F Horn
Trombone
Baritone B.C.
Bassoon
Electric Bass
Tuba
Percussion
Keyboard
Percussion
Low B♭

Student Book Page 35

QUIZ ASSESSMENT Counting, B♭ Concert Scale.

181. ESSENTIAL ELEMENTS QUIZ – SCALE* COUNTING CONQUEST

*Percussion **RUDIMENT COUNTING CONQUEST**

Additional Bonus Songs are available online. See the inside front cover for details.

Student Book Page 36

PERFORMANCE SPOTLIGHT

182. AMERICA THE BEAUTIFUL – Band Arrangement

Samuel A. Ward
Arr. by John Higgins

*T. Sax. use F♯ alternate fingering.

Flute
Oboe
B♭ Clarinet
E♭ Alto Sax.
B♭ Trumpet
F Horn
Low Brass &
Woodwinds
Percussion
Keyboard
Percussion
Timpani
15
Alt. F♯
Alt. F♯
Tri.
Sus. Cym.
Sus. Cym.
Tri.
a2

Percussion

Timpani Roll

Rapidly alternate single strokes as smoothly as possible. For the best sound, play about one third of the way from the edge to the center of the head.

PERFORMANCE SPOTLIGHT

183. LA CUCARACHA – Band Arrangement

Latin American Folk Song
Arr. by John Higgins

Flute Oboe
B♭ Clarinet
E♭ Alto Sax.
B♭ Trumpet
F Horn
Low Brass & Woodwinds
Percussion
Keyboard Percussion
a2
a2
13
mf

Flute
Oboe
B♭ Clarinet
E♭ Alto Sax.
B♭ Trumpet
F Horn
Low Brass &
Woodwinds
Percussion
Keyboard
Percussion
Flute
Oboe
a2
p
B♭ Clarinet
p
E♭ Alto Sax.
p
B♭ Trumpet
p
F Horn
p
Low Brass &
Woodwinds
p
Percussion
p
p
(To Tri.)
Tri.
(To Claves)
Keyboard
Percussion
p

25
Flute
Oboe
B♭ Clarinet
E♭ Alto Sax.
B♭ Trumpet
F Horn
Low Brass &
Woodwinds
Percussion
Claves
Keyboard
Percussion
f
a2
1.

2.
a2
Flute
Oboe
B♭ Clarinet
E♭ Alto Sax.
B♭ Trumpet
F Horn
Low Brass &
Woodwinds
Percussion
Keyboard
Percussion

PERFORMANCE SPOTLIGHT

184. THEME FROM 1812 OVERTURE – Band Arrangement

Peter Ilyich Tchaikovsky
Arr. by John Higgins

10
a2
p
detached
Flute
Oboe
B♭ Clarinet
E♭ Alto Sax.
B♭ Trumpet
F Horn
Low Brass & Woodwinds
Percussion
Keyboard Percussion
Timpani

*Stop sound with fingertips.

26

Flute
Oboe

B♭ Clarinet

E♭ Alto Sax.

B♭ Trumpet

F Horn

Low Brass &
Woodwinds

Percussion

Keyboard
Percussion

Timpani

f

Flute
Oboe

a2

B♭ Clarinet

E♭ Alto Sax.

B♭ Trumpet

F Horn

Low Brass &
Woodwinds

Percussion

Keyboard
Percussion

Timpani

34
Flute
Oboe
B♭ Clarinet
E♭ Alto Sax.
B♭ Trumpet
F Horn
Low Brass &
Woodwinds
Percussion
Keyboard
Percussion
Timpani
dampen
sim.
a2

42
Flute
Oboe
B♭ Clarinet
E♭ Alto Sax.
B♭ Trumpet
F Horn
Low Brass &
Woodwinds
Percussion
Keyboard
Percussion
Low D♭
Timpani
Flute
Oboe
B♭ Clarinet
E♭ Alto Sax.
B♭ Trumpet
F Horn
Low Brass &
Woodwinds
Percussion
Keyboard
Percussion
Timpani
a2

Student Book Page 37

Flute Oboe
a2
Bb Clarinet
Eb Alto Sax.
Bb Trumpet
F Horn
Low Brass & Woodwinds
Percussion
Keyboard Percussion
Timpani

The following solos with piano accompaniment appear in the student books on page 38:
EINE KLEINE NACHTMUSIK *(Concert E♭ version)* - Flute, Alto Sax.
EINE KLEINE NACHTMUSIK *(Concert B♭ version)* - Oboe, Clarinet
THEME FROM SYMPHONY NO. 1 *(Concert E♭ version)* - Trumpet, Trombone, Baritone, Tuba, Bassoon, Alto Cl., Bari. Sax.
THEME FROM SYMPHONY NO. 1 *(Concert B♭ version)* - F Horn, Bass Cl., T. Sax.
CAN - CAN *(Percussion Ensemble)* - Percussion

PERFORMANCE SPOTLIGHT

Solo with Piano Accompaniment

Performing for an audience is an exciting part of being involved in music. This solo is based on *Serenade in G Major*, K. 525, also known as "Eine Kleine Nachtmusik" ("A Little Night Music"). **Wolfgang Amadeus Mozart** wrote this piece in 1787, the same year the American Constitution was signed into law. You and a piano accompanist can perform this for the band or at other school and community events.

185. EINE KLEINE NACHTMUSIK – Solo *(Concert E♭ version: Flute, Alto Sax.)*

Wolfgang Amadeus Mozart
Arr. by John Higgins

PERFORMANCE SPOTLIGHT

Solo with Piano Accompaniment

Performing for an audience is an exciting part of being involved in music. This solo is based on *Serenade in G Major*, K. 525, also known as "Eine Kleine Nachtmusik" ("A Little Night Music"). **Wolfgang Amadeus Mozart** wrote this piece in 1787, the same year the American Constitution was signed into law. You and a piano accompanist can perform this for the band or at other school and community events.

185. EINE KLEINE NACHTMUSIK – Solo *(Concert B♭ version: Oboe, Clarinet)*

Wolfgang Amadeus Mozart
Arr. by John Higgins

PERFORMANCE SPOTLIGHT

Solo with Piano Accompaniment

Performing for an audience is an exciting part of being involved in music. This solo is based on *Symphony No. 1* by German composer **Johannes Brahms** (1833-1897). He completed his first symphony in 1876, the same year that the telephone was invented by Alexander Graham Bell. You and a piano accompanist can perform this for the band or at other school and community events.

185. THEME FROM SYMPHONY NO. 1 – Solo

(Concert E♭ version, Bsn., Alto Cl., Bar. Sax., Tpt.) Tbn., Bar. B.C., Bar. T.C., Tuba)

Johannes Brahms
Arr. by John Higgins

PERFORMANCE SPOTLIGHT

Solo with Piano Accompaniment

Performing for an audience is an exciting part of being involved in music. This solo is based on *Symphony No. 1* by German composer **Johannes Brahms** (1833–1897). He completed his first symphony in 1876, the same year that the telephone was invented by Alexander Graham Bell. You and a piano accompanist can perform this for the band or at other school and community events.

185. THEME FROM SYMPHONY NO. 1 – Solo *(Concert B♭ version, Bs. Cl., Ten. Sax., F Horn.)*

Johannes Brahms
Arr. by John Higgins

PERFORMANCE SPOTLIGHT

Solo for Percussion Ensemble

Performing for an audience is an exciting part of being involved in music. Percussion ensembles provide a unique solo performing opportunity for all members of the percussion section. This percussion ensemble is written for 5 or more players. It is based on the famous "Can-Can" dance from Jacques Offenbach's operetta *Orpheus in the Underworld*, completed in 1858. Your percussion ensemble can perform for the band or at other school and community events.

185. CAN-CAN

Jacques Offenbach
Arr. by Kevin Lepper

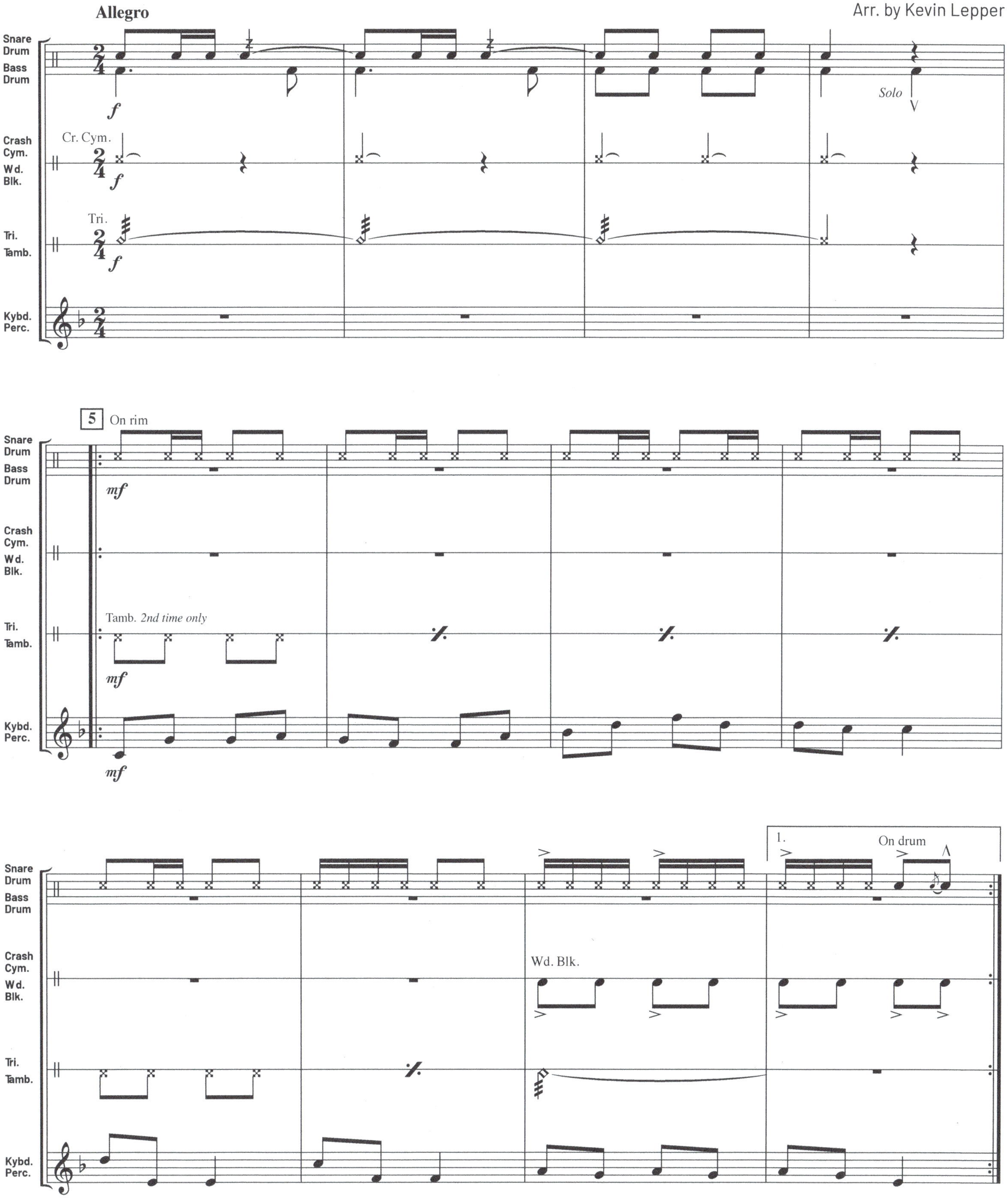

Allegro
Snare Drum
Bass Drum
Crash Cym.
Wd. Blk.
Tri.
Tamb.
Kybd. Perc.
Cr. Cym.
Tri.
f
Solo
5
On rim
mf
Tamb. 2nd time only
Wd. Blk.
1.
On drum

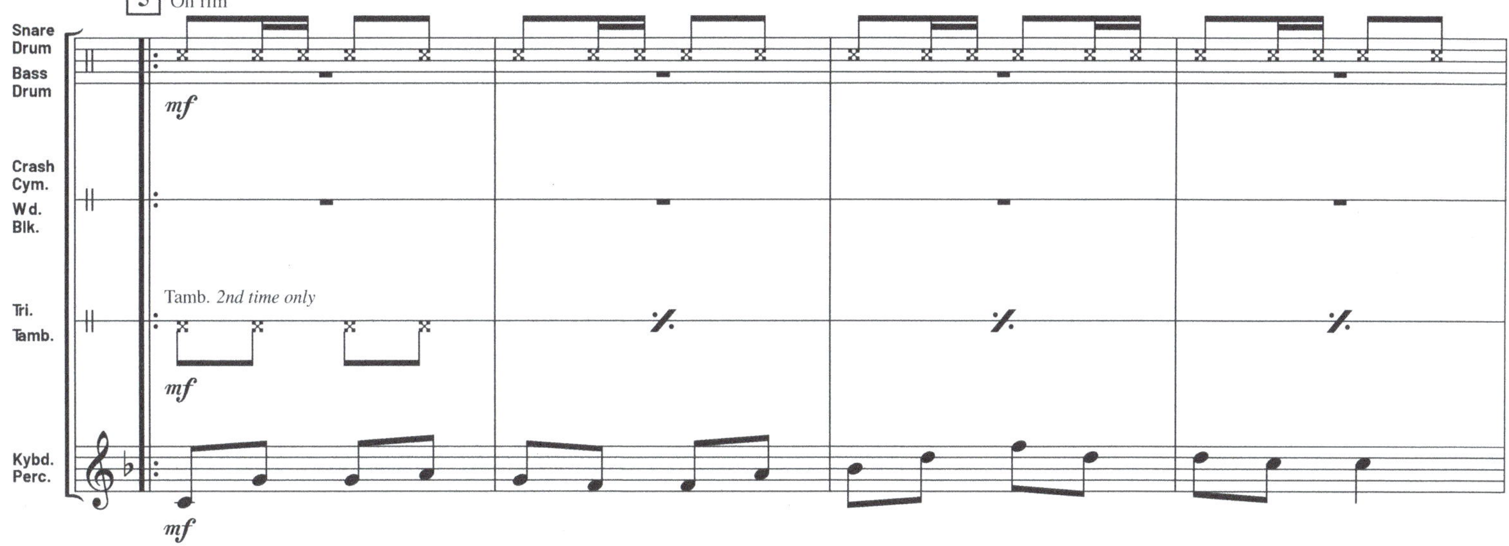

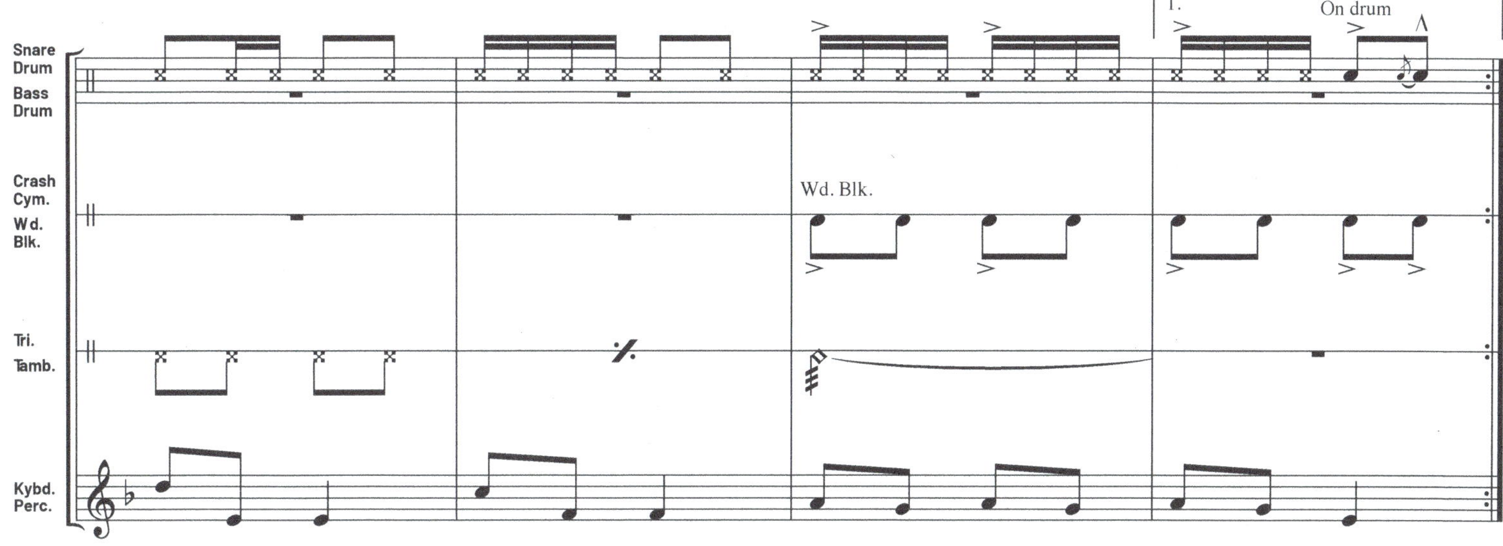

Snare Drum
Bass Drum
Crash Cym.
Wd. Blk.
Tri.
Tamb.
Kybd. Perc.
2.
14
Cr. Cym.
To Triangle
Solo
Choke
Tri.
Solo
To Tamb.
Choke
Solo
Choke
Wd. Blk.
Solo
Cr. Cym.
Soli - with Cym.
30
Tamb.

Snare Drum
Bass Drum
Crash Cym.
Wd. Blk.
Tri.
Tamb.
Kybd. Perc.
Choke

DUETS

Here is an opportunity to get together with a friend and enjoy playing music. The other player does not have to play the same instrument as you. Try to exactly match each other's rhythm, pitch and tone quality. Eventually, it may begin to sound like the two parts are being played by one person! Later, try switching parts.

186. SWING LOW, SWEET CHARIOT – Duet

African-American Spiritual

*These percussion parts can accompany two or more players playing the duet parts.

a2
Fine
Flute
Oboe
B♭ Clarinet
B♭ Bass Cl.
E♭ Alto Sax.
E♭ Bari. Sax.
E♭ Alto Cl.
B♭ Tenor Sax.
B♭ Trumpet
Baritone T.C.
F Horn
Trombone
Baritone B.C.
Bassoon
Electric Bass
Tuba
Percussion
Keyboard
Percussion

Flute
Oboe

a2

mf

Bb Clarinet
Bb Bass Cl.

Eb Alto Sax.
Eb Bari. Sax.
Eb Alto Cl.

Bb Tenor Sax.

Bb Trumpet
Baritone T.C.

F Horn

Trombone
Baritone B.C.
Bassoon
Electric Bass

Tuba

Solo

L R L R R L R L L R

Percussion

Keyboard
Percussion

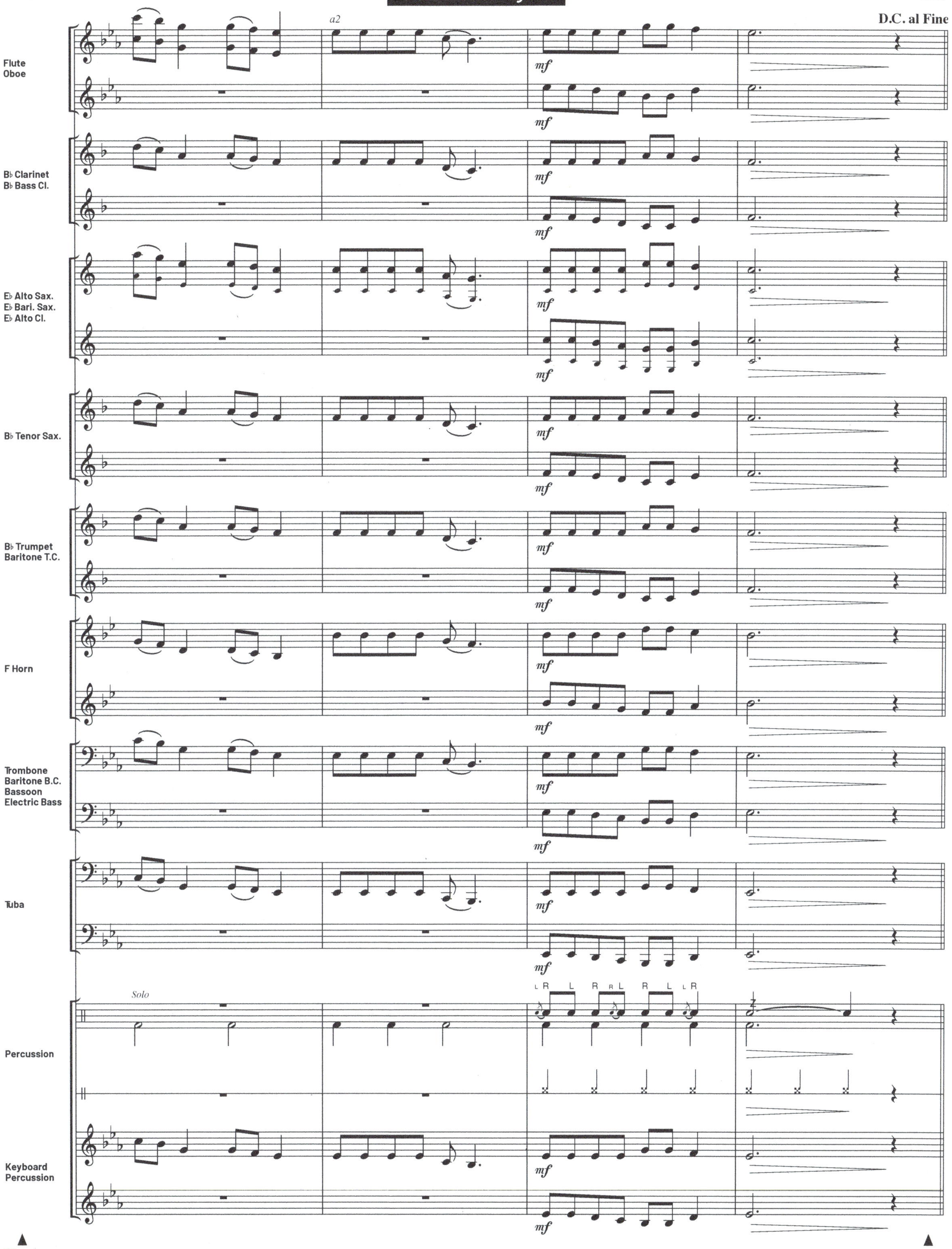
D.C. al Fine
a2
Flute
Oboe
mf
B♭ Clarinet
B♭ Bass Cl.
E♭ Alto Sax.
E♭ Bari. Sax.
E♭ Alto Cl.
B♭ Tenor Sax.
B♭ Trumpet
Baritone T.C.
F Horn
Trombone
Baritone B.C.
Bassoon
Electric Bass
Tuba
Solo
L R L R R L R L L R
Percussion
Keyboard
Percussion

Percussion

Rudiment Review

Flam Accent
(Eighth Notes)

L R L R
R L R L

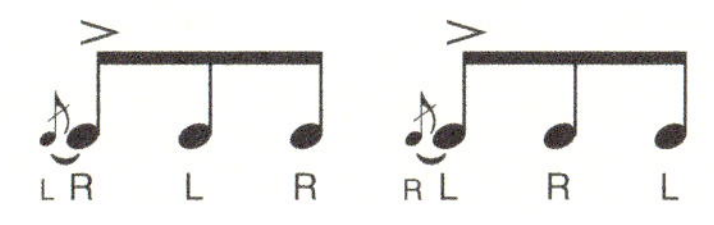

The snare drum rudiment used in measures 11 and 15. Follow the sticking carefully.

Percussion

Rim Knock

Hold left stick with butt end facing out. Place tip of stick about 1/3 away from the rim and *knock* the butt end of the stick on the rim. A rim knock is usually written with an on the snare drum space. The regular notes are played on the drum head with the right hand.

187. LA BAMBA – Duet

Mexican Folk Song

Allegro

Flute
Oboe

B♭ Clarinet
B♭ Bass Cl.

E♭ Alto Sax.
E♭ Bari. Sax.
E♭ Alto Cl.

B♭ Tenor Sax.

B♭ Trumpet
Baritone T.C.

F Horn

Trombone
Baritone B.C.
Bassoon
Electric Bass

Tuba

Percussion*

Rim Knock

S.D.

B.D.

Sus. Cym. dome with stick

Claves

Keyboard Percussion

*These percussion parts can accompany two or more players playing the duet parts.

Fine
Flute
Oboe
B♭ Clarinet
B♭ Bass Cl.
E♭ Alto Sax.
E♭ Bari. Sax.
E♭ Alto Cl.
B♭ Tenor Sax.
B♭ Trumpet
Baritone T.C.
F Horn
Trombone
Baritone B.C.
Bassoon
Electric Bass
Tuba
Percussion
Keyboard
Percussion

Student Book Page 39

D.C. al Fine
Flute
Oboe
B♭ Clarinet
B♭ Bass Cl.
E♭ Alto Sax.
E♭ Bari. Sax.
E♭ Alto Cl.
B♭ Tenor Sax.
B♭ Trumpet
Baritone T.C.
F Horn
Trombone
Baritone B.C.
Bassoon
Electric Bass
Tuba
Percussion
Keyboard
Percussion
p

Student Book Page 40

RUBANK® SCALE AND ARPEGGIO STUDIES
(With Rudimental Studies for Snare Drum)

These supplemental exercises can have multiple uses as needed. They are excellent for expanding individual technical skills, and may be introduced as extra challenges when appropriate for individual players. If the entire band has reached this page sequentially, they can also be used as full band warm-ups and technique builders. Additional performance skills can be reinforced by varying the tempo, dynamics, etc.

KEY OF CONCERT B♭ MAJOR

1.

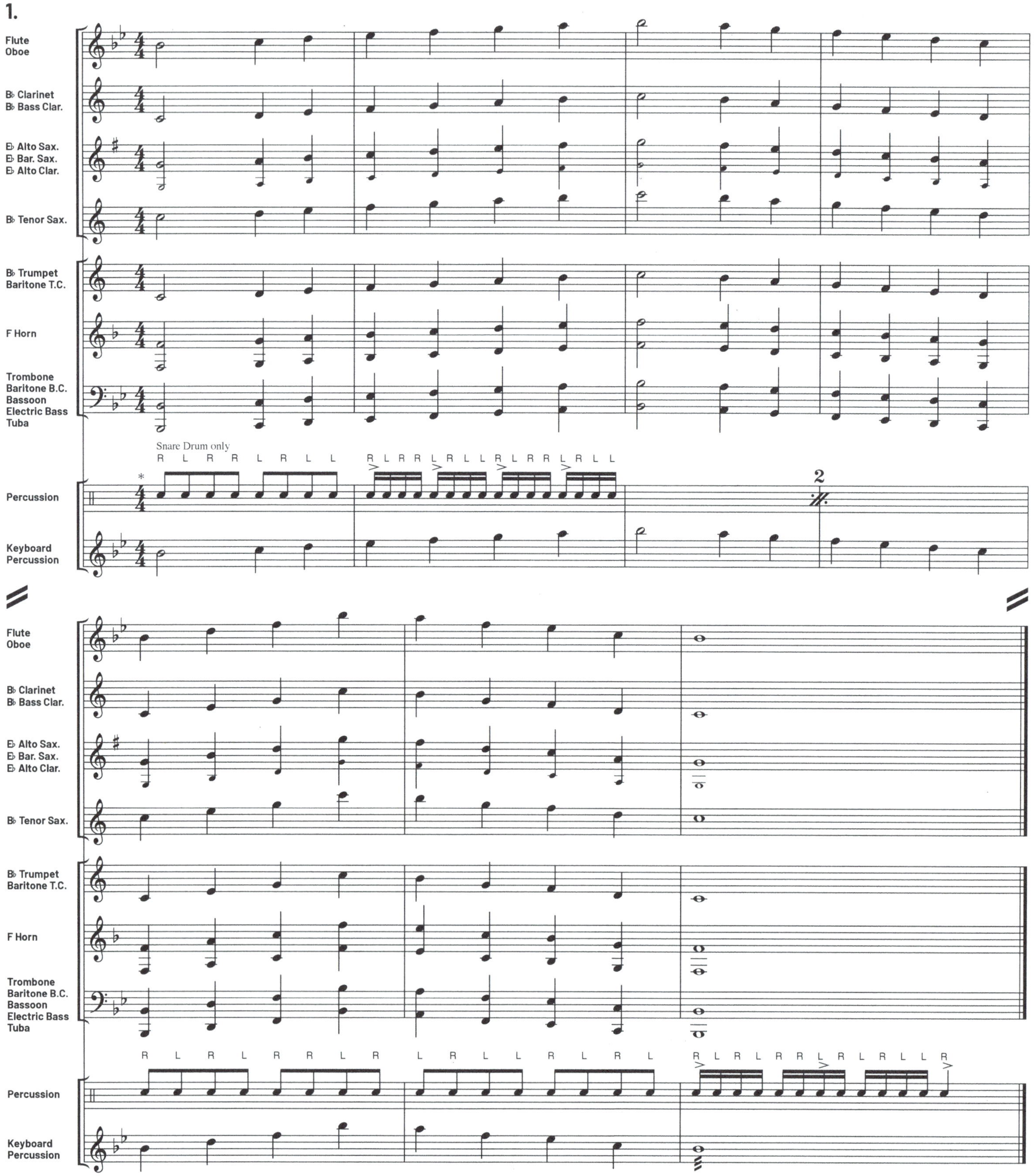

Flute
Oboe

B♭ Clarinet
B♭ Bass Clar.

E♭ Alto Sax.
E♭ Bar. Sax.
E♭ Alto Clar.

B♭ Tenor Sax.

B♭ Trumpet
Baritone T.C.

F Horn

Trombone
Baritone B.C.
Bassoon
Electric Bass
Tuba

Snare Drum only

Percussion*

Keyboard
Percussion

*These Snare Drum parts (1.–4.) are the same as E♭ major (indicated in student book).

RUBANK® SCALE AND ARPEGGIO STUDIES

(With Rudimental Studies for Snare Drum)

KEY OF B♭

2.

RUBANK® SCALE AND ARPEGGIO STUDIES

(With Rudimental Studies for Snare Drum)

KEY OF B♭

3.

RUBANK® SCALE AND ARPEGGIO STUDIES
(With Rudimental Studies for Snare Drum)

RUBANK® SCALE AND ARPEGGIO STUDIES
(With Rudimental Studies for Snare Drum)

KEY OF B♭

RUBANK® SCALE AND ARPEGGIO STUDIES
(With Rudimental Studies for Snare Drum)

RUBANK® SCALE AND ARPEGGIO STUDIES
(With Rudimental Studies for Snare Drum)

KEY OF CONCERT E♭ MAJOR

1.

*Cl., Bs. Cl. have both octaves.

**These Snare Drum parts (1.–4.) are the same as B♭ major (indicated in student book).

RUBANK® SCALE AND ARPEGGIO STUDIES
(With Rudimental Studies for Snare Drum)

KEY OF E♭

2.

Flute
Oboe

B♭ Clarinet
B♭ Bass Clar.

E♭ Alto Sax.
E♭ Bar. Sax.
E♭ Alto Clar.

B♭ Tenor Sax.

B♭ Trumpet
Baritone T.C.

F Horn

Trombone
Baritone B.C.
Bassoon
Electric Bass

Tuba

S.D.

Percussion

Keyboard
Percussion

RUBANK® SCALE AND ARPEGGIO STUDIES
(With Rudimental Studies for Snare Drum)

KEY OF E♭

3.

RUBANK® SCALE AND ARPEGGIO STUDIES
(With Rudimental Studies for Snare Drum)

RUBANK® SCALE AND ARPEGGIO STUDIES
(With Rudimental Studies for Snare Drum)

KEY OF E♭

4.

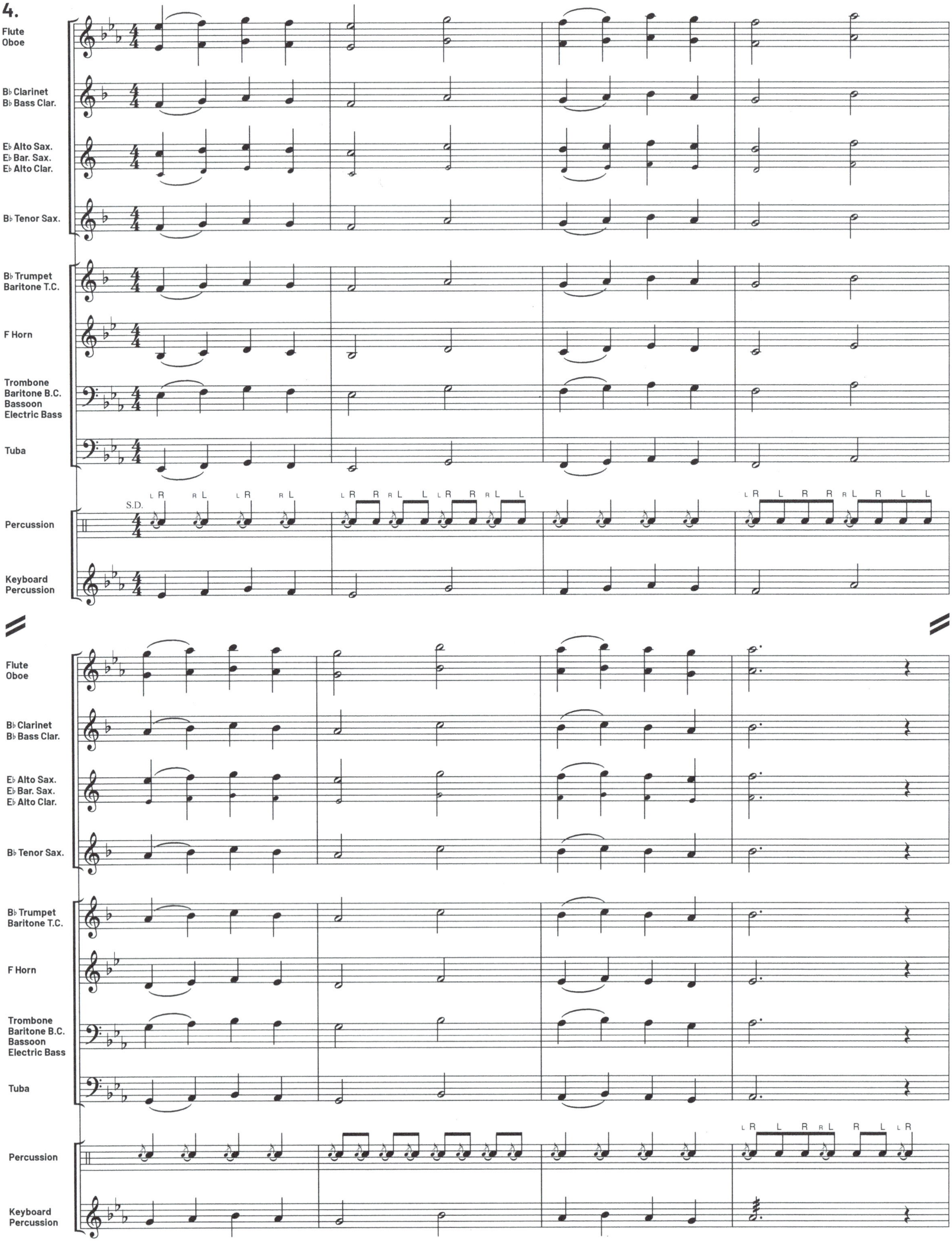
Flute
Oboe
B♭ Clarinet
B♭ Bass Clar.
E♭ Alto Sax.
E♭ Bar. Sax.
E♭ Alto Clar.
B♭ Tenor Sax.
B♭ Trumpet
Baritone T.C.
F Horn
Trombone
Baritone B.C.
Bassoon
Electric Bass
Tuba
S.D.
Percussion
Keyboard
Percussion
L R R L L R R L
L R R R L L L R R R L L
L R L R R L R L L
Flute
Oboe
B♭ Clarinet
B♭ Bass Clar.
E♭ Alto Sax.
E♭ Bar. Sax.
E♭ Alto Clar.
B♭ Tenor Sax.
B♭ Trumpet
Baritone T.C.
F Horn
Trombone
Baritone B.C.
Bassoon
Electric Bass
Tuba
Percussion
Keyboard
Percussion
L R L R L R L L R

RUBANK® SCALE AND ARPEGGIO STUDIES
(With Rudimental Studies for Snare Drum)

RUBANK® SCALE AND ARPEGGIO STUDIES
(With Rudimental Studies for Snare Drum)

KEY OF CONCERT F MAJOR

1.

*Cl., Bs. Cl. have both octaves.
**These Snare Drum parts (1.–4.) are the same as A♭ major (indicated in student book).

RUBANK® SCALE AND ARPEGGIO STUDIES
(With Rudimental Studies for Snare Drum)

KEY OF F

2.

RUBANK® SCALE AND ARPEGGIO STUDIES
(With Rudimental Studies for Snare Drum)

KEY OF F

3.

RUBANK® SCALE AND ARPEGGIO STUDIES
(With Rudimental Studies for Snare Drum)

RUBANK® SCALE AND ARPEGGIO STUDIES
(With Rudimental Studies for Snare Drum)

KEY OF F

4.

RUBANK® SCALE AND ARPEGGIO STUDIES
(With Rudimental Studies for Snare Drum)

RUBANK® SCALE AND ARPEGGIO STUDIES
(With Rudimental Studies for Snare Drum)

KEY OF CONCERT A♭ MAJOR

*These Snare Drum parts (1.–4.) are the same as F major (indicated in student book).

RUBANK® SCALE AND ARPEGGIO STUDIES
(With Rudimental Studies for Snare Drum)

KEY OF A♭

2.

RUBANK® SCALE AND ARPEGGIO STUDIES

(With Rudimental Studies for Snare Drum)

KEY OF A♭

3.

RUBANK® SCALE AND ARPEGGIO STUDIES
(With Rudimental Studies for Snare Drum)

RUBANK® SCALE AND ARPEGGIO STUDIES
(With Rudimental Studies for Snare Drum)

KEY OF A♭

RUBANK® SCALE AND ARPEGGIO STUDIES
(With Rudimental Studies for Snare Drum)

Student Book Page 42

RHYTHM STUDIES

The use of these supplementary rhythm exercises should be started in the early stages of a student's development. They advance sequentially, and can be used in any length of measure groupings. By specifying how often to change pitch, they can become very challenging.

1 2 3 4

5 6 7 8

9 10 11 12

13 14 15 16

17 18 19 20

21 22 23 24

25 26 27 28

29 30 31 32

33 34 35 36

RHYTHM STUDIES

CREATING MUSIC

TEACHING TIP This student page can be used as a culmination activity which follows the Essential Creativity exercises spread throughout the book.

THEORY

Composition

Composition is the art of writing original music. A composer often begins by creating a melody made up of individual **phrases**, like short musical "sentences." Some melodies have phrases that seem to answer or respond to "question" phrases, as in Beethoven's *Ode To Joy*. Play this melody and listen to how phrases 2 and 4 give slightly different answers to the same question (phrases 1 and 3).

1. ODE TO JOY

Ludwig van Beethoven

1. Question *2. Answer*

Flute
Oboe

B♭ Clarinet
B♭ Bass Clar.

E♭ Alto Sax.
E♭ Bar. Sax.
E♭ Alto Clar.

B♭ Tenor Sax.

B♭ Trumpet
Baritone T.C.

F Horn

Trombone
Baritone B.C.
Bassoon
Electric Bass
Tuba

Percussion

Keyboard
Percussion

3. Question *4. Answer*

Flute
Oboe

B♭ Clarinet
B♭ Bass Clar.

E♭ Alto Sax.
E♭ Bar. Sax.
E♭ Alto Clar.

B♭ Tenor Sax.

B♭ Trumpet
Baritone T.C.

F Horn

Trombone
Baritone B.C.
Bassoon
Electric Bass
Tuba

Percussion

Keyboard
Percussion

2. Q. AND A. *Write your own "answer" phrases in this melody.*

3. PHRASE BUILDERS *Write 4 different phrases using the rhythms below each staff.*

4. YOU NAME IT: ___________

Pick phrase A, B, C, or D from above, and write it as the "Question" for phrases 1 and 3 below. Then write 2 different "Answers" for phrases 2 and 4.

THEORY

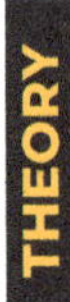

Improvisation

Improvisation is the art of freely creating your own melody *as you play*. Use these notes to play your own melody (Line A), to go with the accompaniment (Line B).

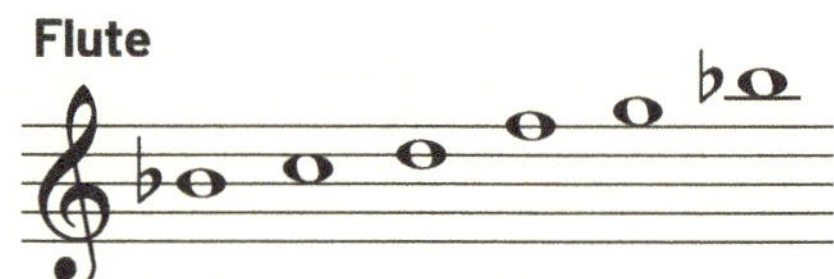

Flute

5. INSTANT MELODY

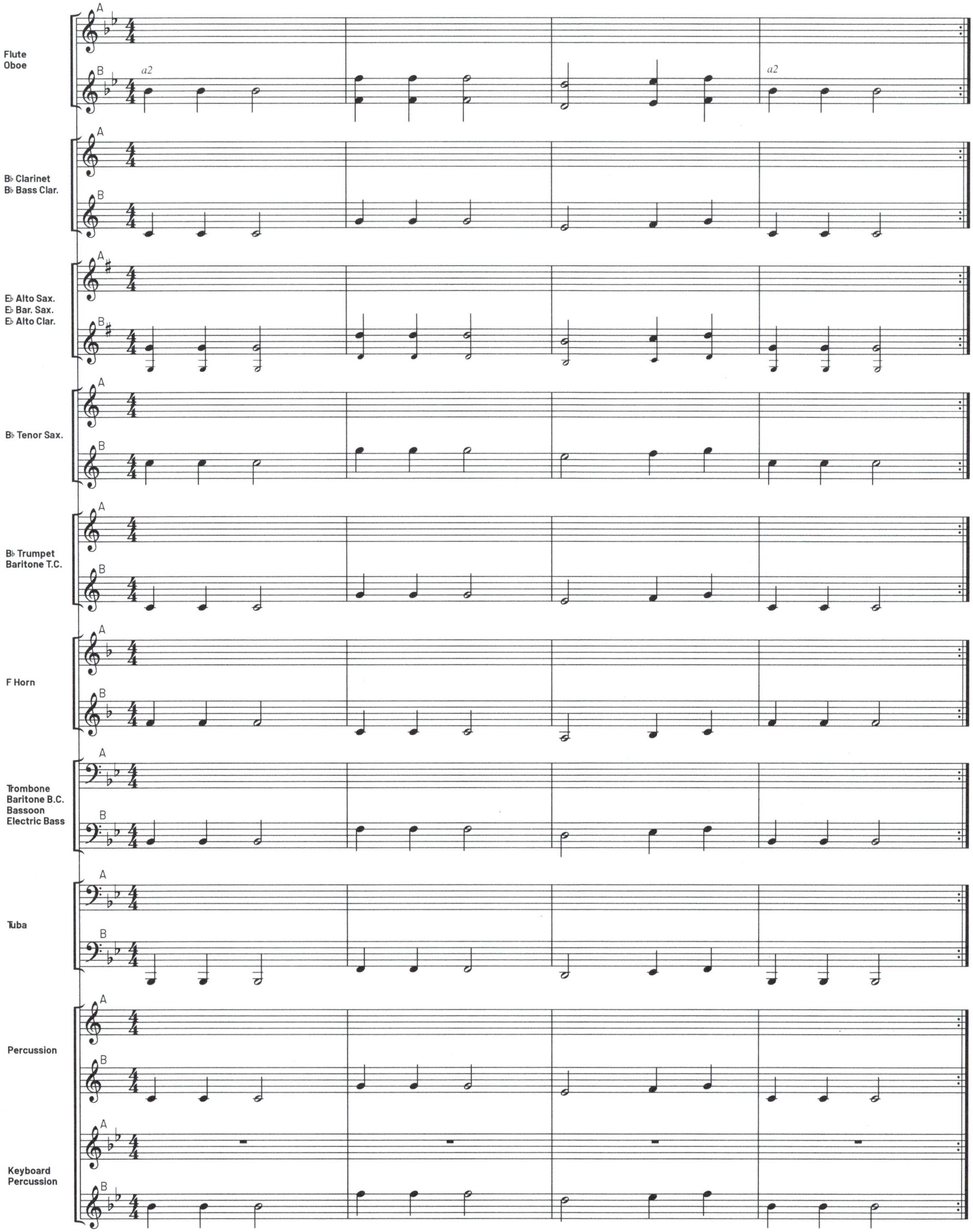
A
B
a2
Flute
Oboe
B♭ Clarinet
B♭ Bass Clar.
E♭ Alto Sax.
E♭ Bar. Sax.
E♭ Alto Clar.
B♭ Tenor Sax.
B♭ Trumpet
Baritone T.C.
F Horn
Trombone
Baritone B.C.
Bassoon
Electric Bass
Tuba
Percussion
Keyboard
Percussion

You can mark your progress through the book on this page.
Fill in the stars as instructed by your band director.

1. Page 2-3, The Basics
2. Page 5, EE Quiz, No. 13
3. Page 6, EE Quiz, No. 19
4. Page 7, EE Quiz, No. 26
5. Page 8, EE Quiz, No. 32
6. Page 10, EE Quiz, No. 45
7. Page 12-13, Performance Spotlight
8. Page 14, EE Quiz, No. 65
9. Page 15, Essential Creativity, No. 72
10. Page 17, EE Quiz, No. 84
11. Page 17, Essential Creativity, No. 85
12. Page 19, EE Quiz, No. 98
13. Page 20, Essential Creativity, No. 104
14. Page 21, No. 109
15. Page 22, EE Quiz, No. 117
16. Page 23, Performance Spotlight
17. Page 24, EE Quiz, No. 125
18. Page 26, Essential Creativity, No. 137
19. Page 28, No. 149
20. Page 28, EE Quiz, No. 151
21. Page 29, Performance Spotlight
22. Page 31, EE Quiz, No. 164
23. Page 32, EE Quiz, No. 168
24. Page 33, No. 174
25. Page 35, EE Quiz, No. 181
26. Page 36, Performance Spotlight
27. Page 37, Performance Spotlight
28. Page 38, Performance Spotlight

MUSIC — AN ESSENTIAL ELEMENT OF LIFE

FINGERING CHART

FLUTE

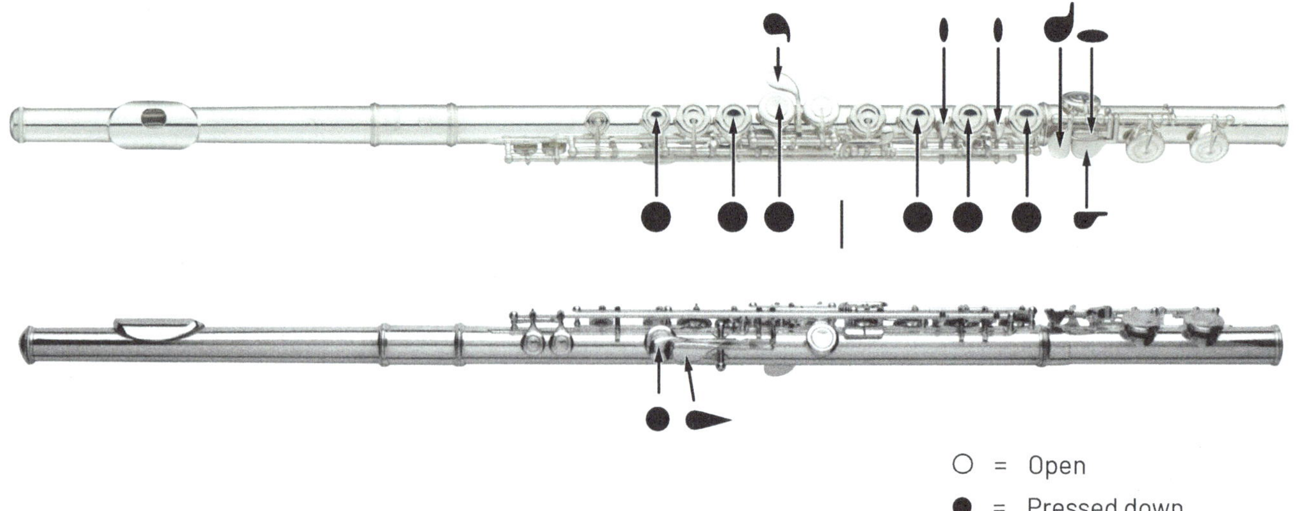

○ = Open

● = Pressed down

The most common fingering appears first when two fingerings are shown.

Instrument Care Reminders

Before putting your instrument back in its case after playing, do the following:

- Carefully remove the head joint.
- Put a clean soft cloth on the end of your cleaning rod and swab out the head joint.
- Twist the middle and foot joints apart and draw the cleaning rod through each joint.
- Carefully wipe the outside of each section to keep the finish clean.

Instruments and photos courtesy of Yamaha.

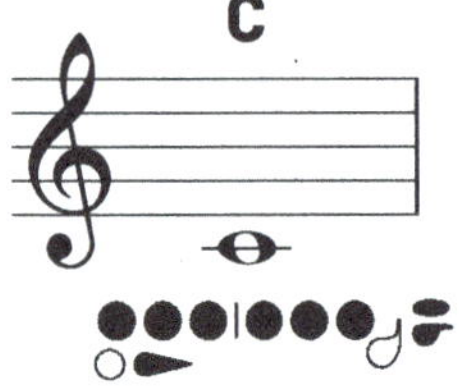

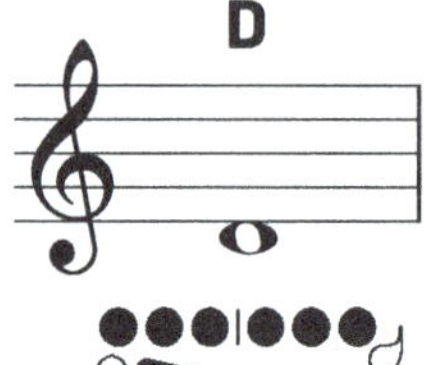

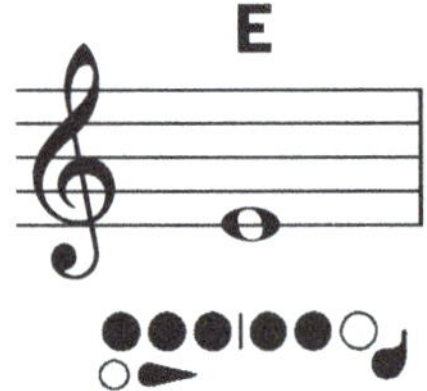

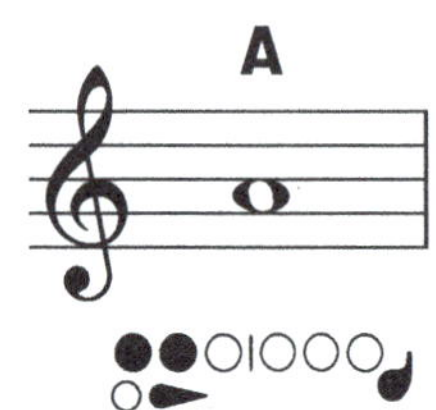

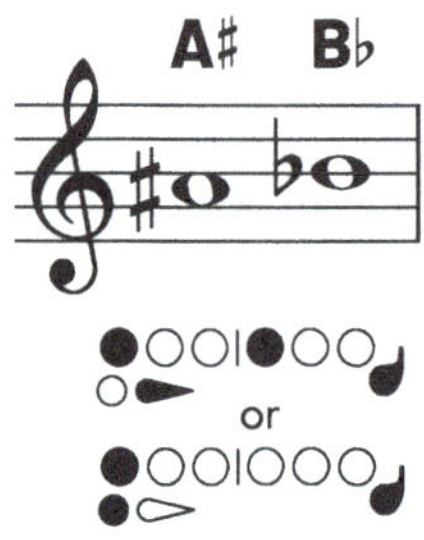

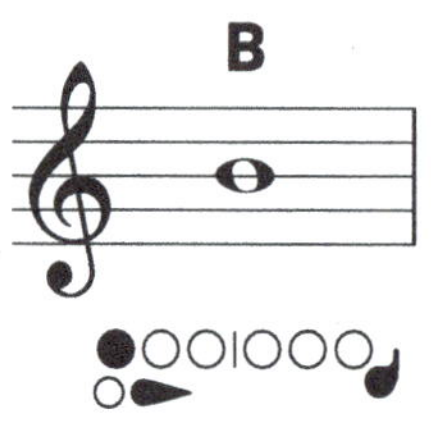

FINGERING CHART FLUTE

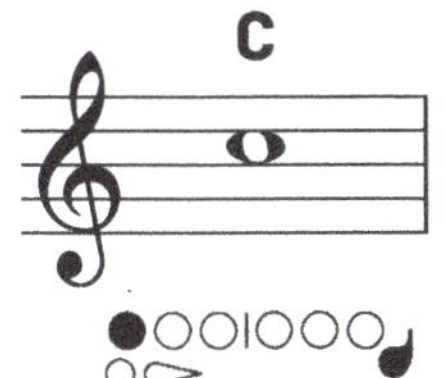

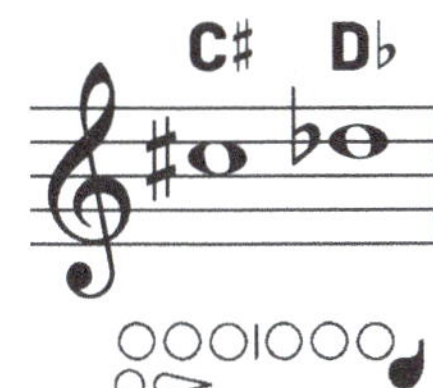

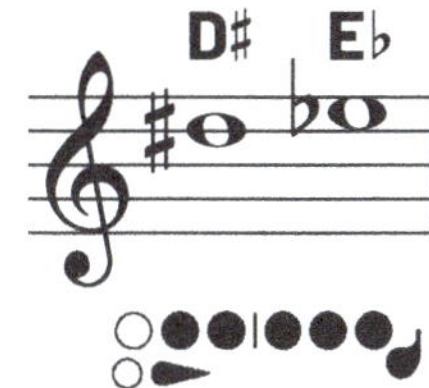

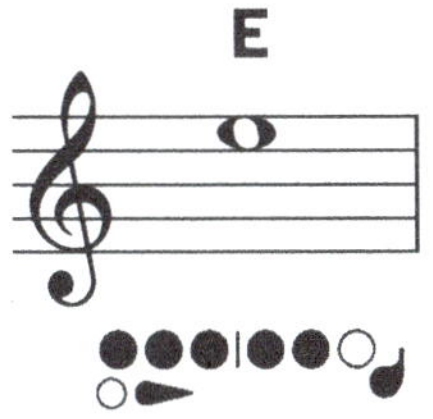

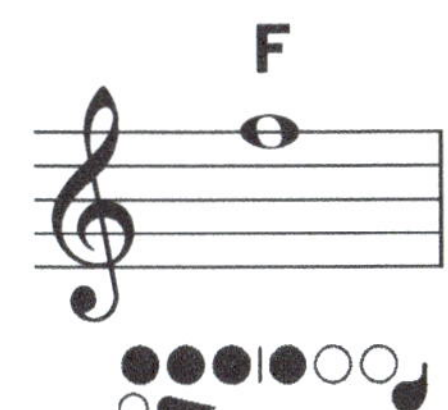

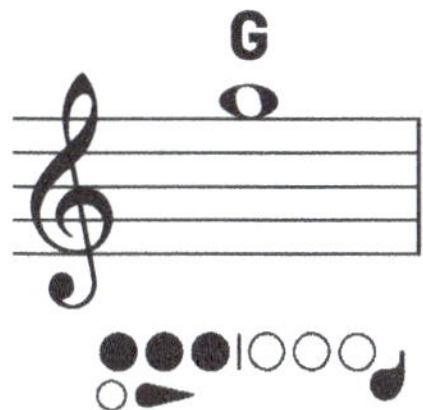

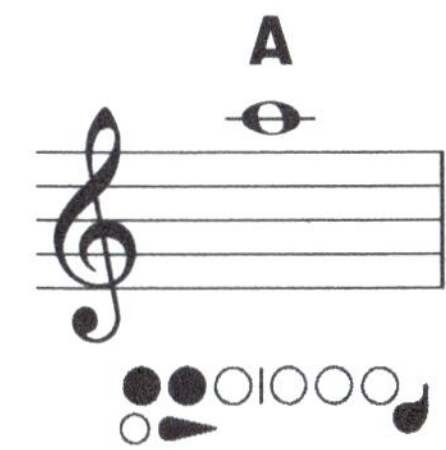

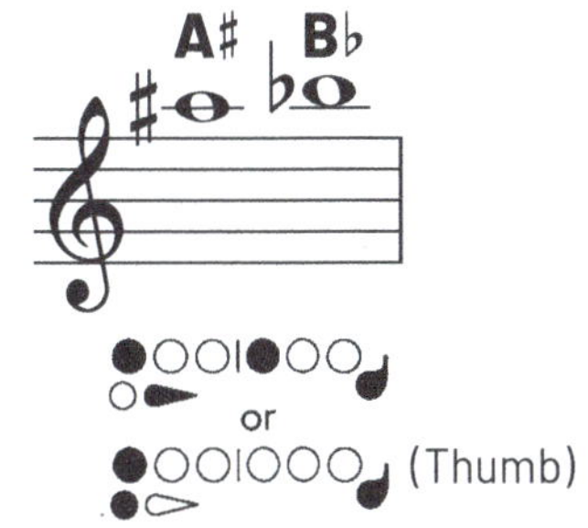

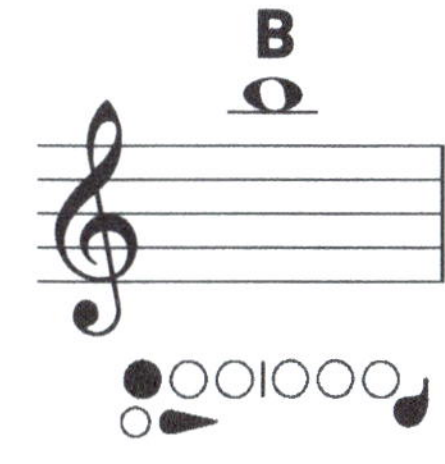

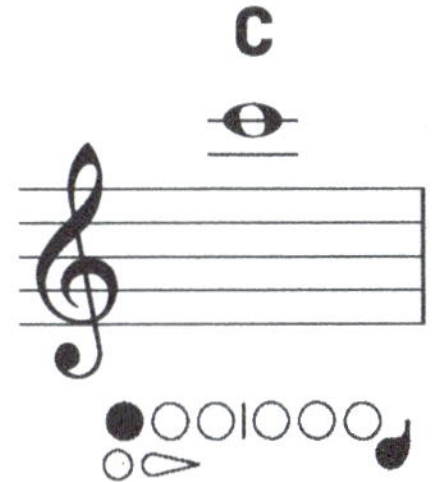

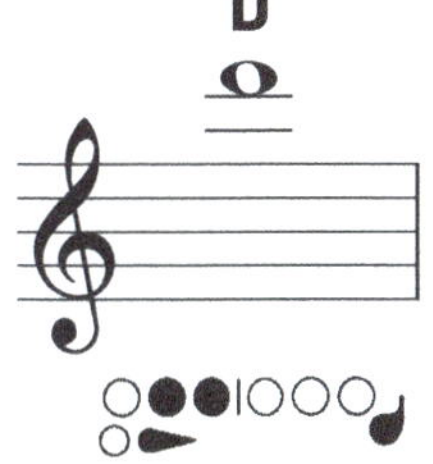

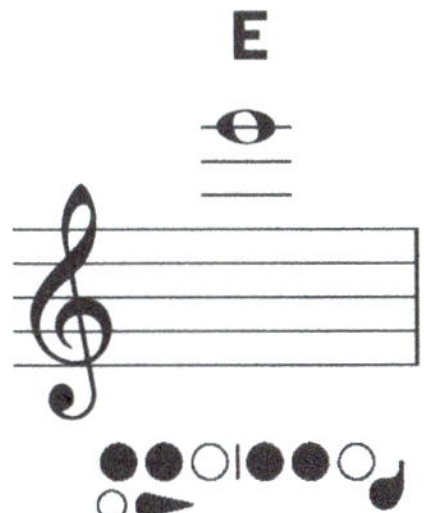

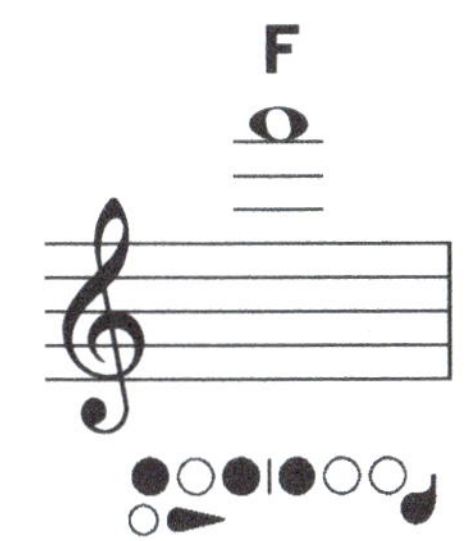

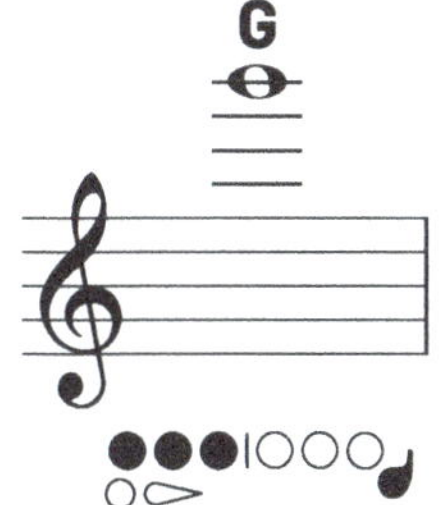

FINGERING CHART

OBOE

Instrument Care Reminders

Before putting your instrument back in its case after playing, do the following:

- Carefully remove the reed and blow air through it. Return to reed case.
- Gently twist apart the upper and lower sections. Drop a weighted swab through the lower section and pull it out the bell. Return the lower section and the bell to the case.
- Swab out the upper section or clean it with an oboe feather and return it to the case.

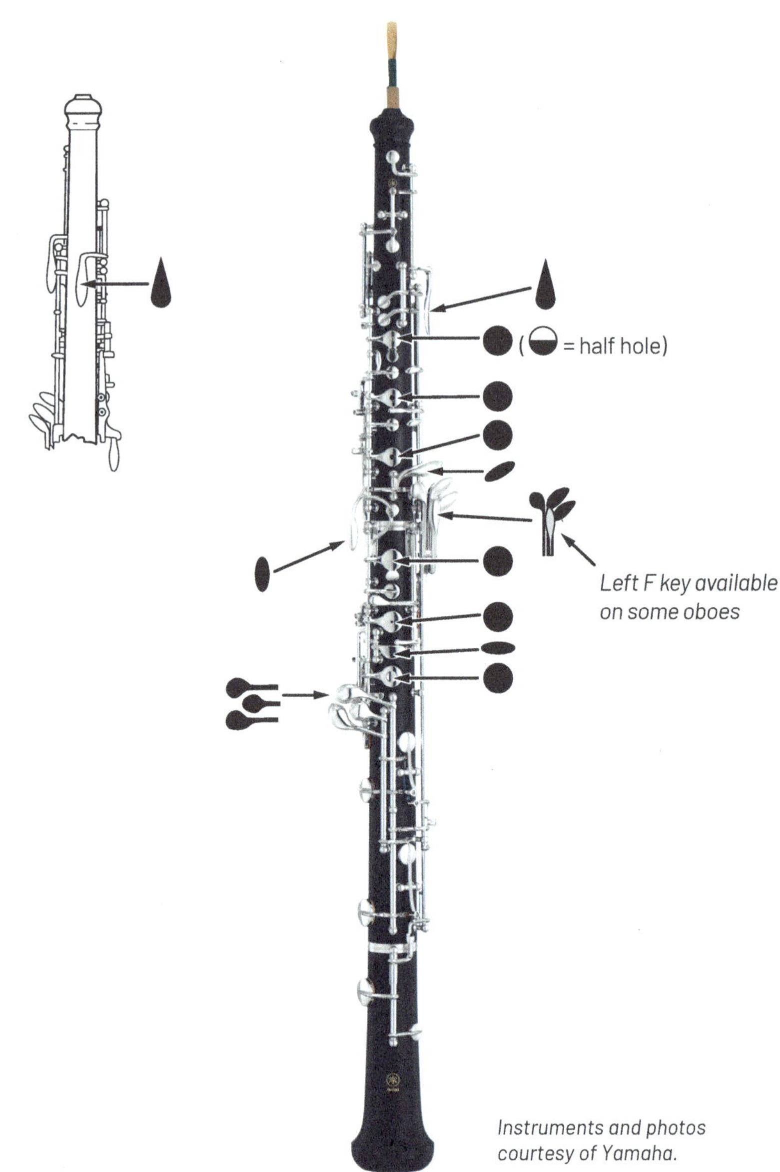

Instruments and photos courtesy of Yamaha.

○ = Open

● = Pressed down

◒ = Half hole covered

○ = Optional

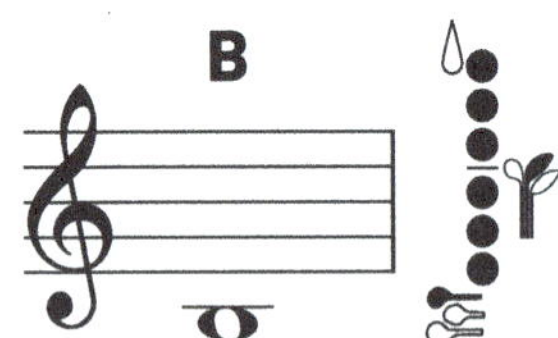

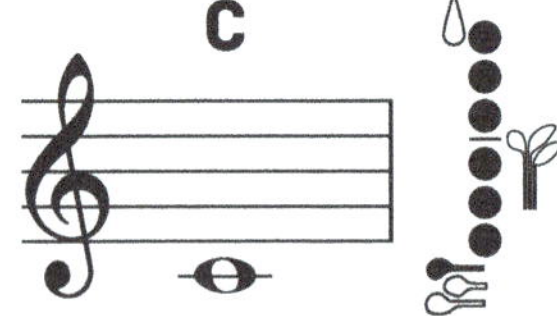

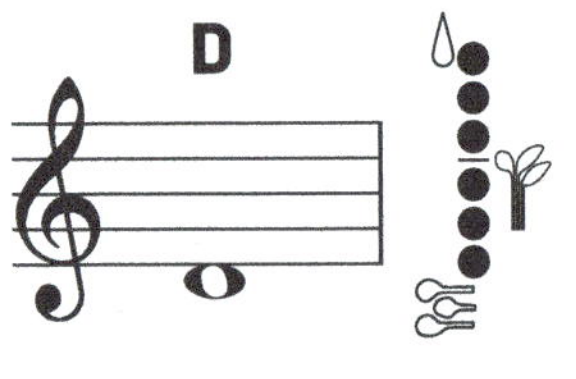

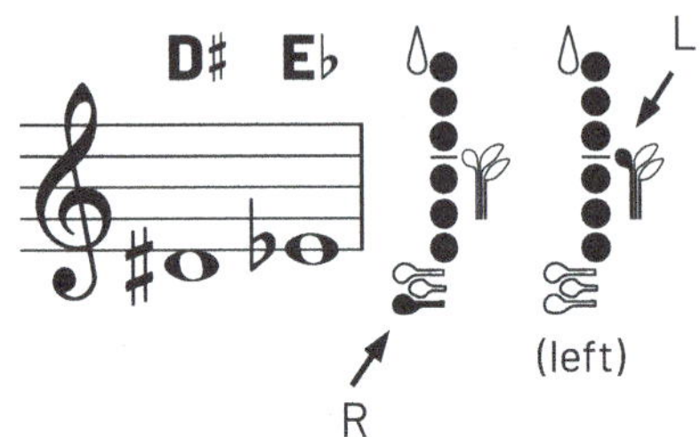

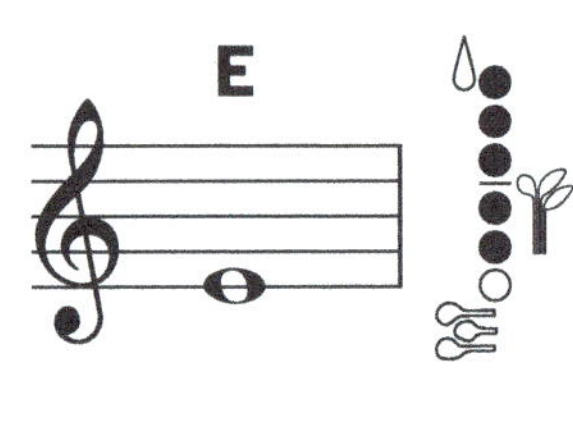

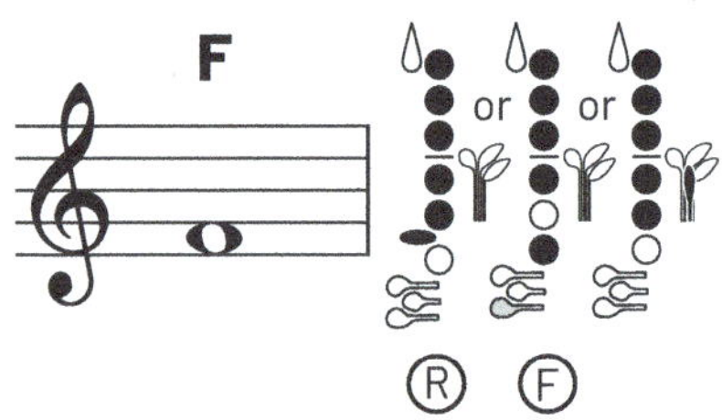

E♭ key raises pitch on Forked F. Only use if needed.

FINGERING CHART OBOE

* *If you play an oboe with a "Left F Key," you may prefer to use the left F in place of the forked fingering.*

FINGERING CHART

BASSOON

Taking Care Of Your Instrument

Before putting your instrument back in its case after playing, do the following:

- Carefully remove the reed and blow air through it. Return to reed case.
- Remove the bocal and blow air through the larger end to remove excess moisture.
- Take the instrument apart in the reverse order of assembly. Swab out each section with a cloth swab or cleaning rod. Drop the weight of the swab through each section and pull it through. Return each section to the correct spot in the case.

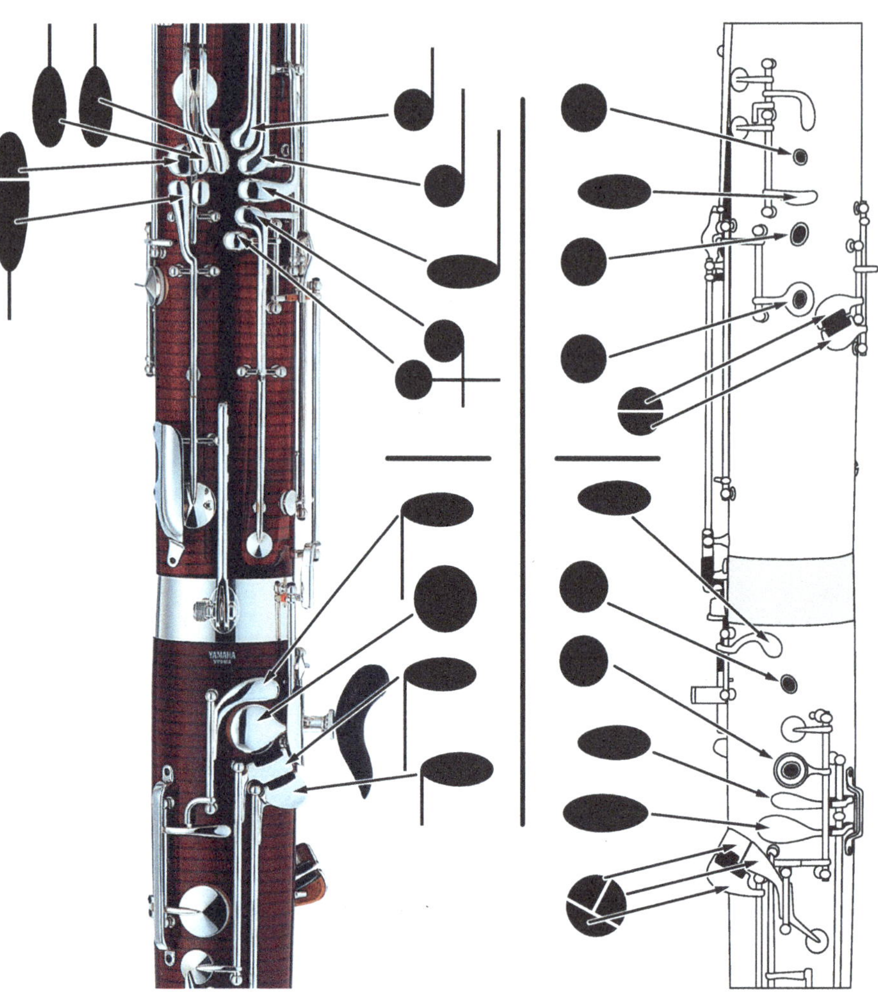

○ = Open
● = Pressed down
◒ = Half-hole covered
◕ = Quarter-hole open
○ = Flicked
○ = Optional

The most common fingering appears first when two fingerings are shown.

Instruments and photos courtesy of Yamaha.

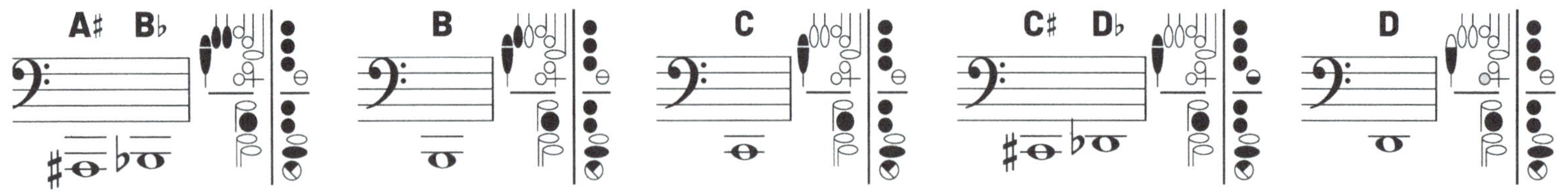

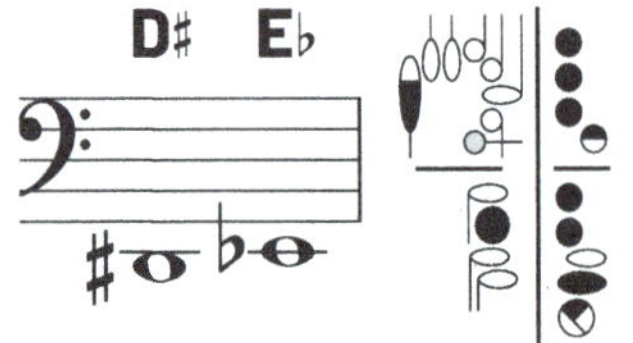

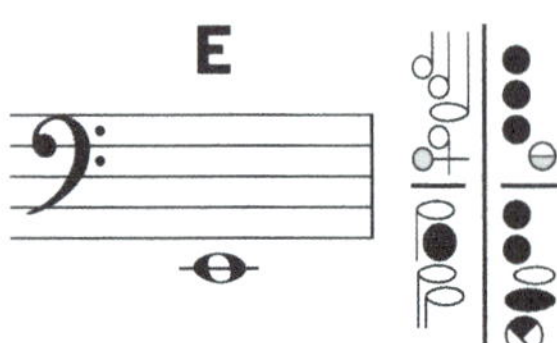

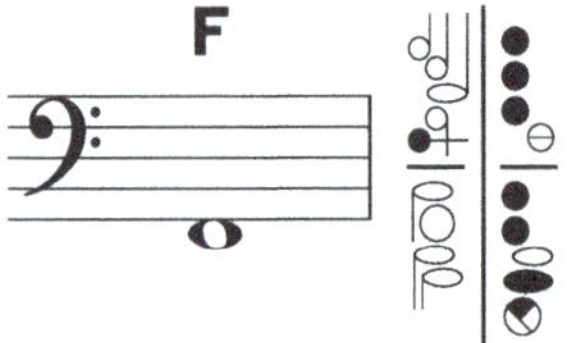

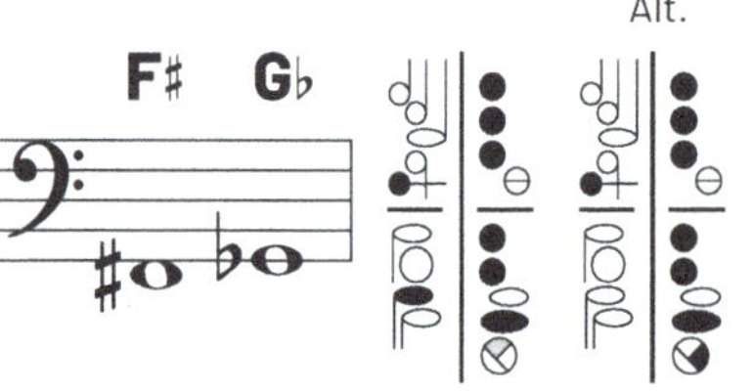

FINGERING CHART

BASSOON

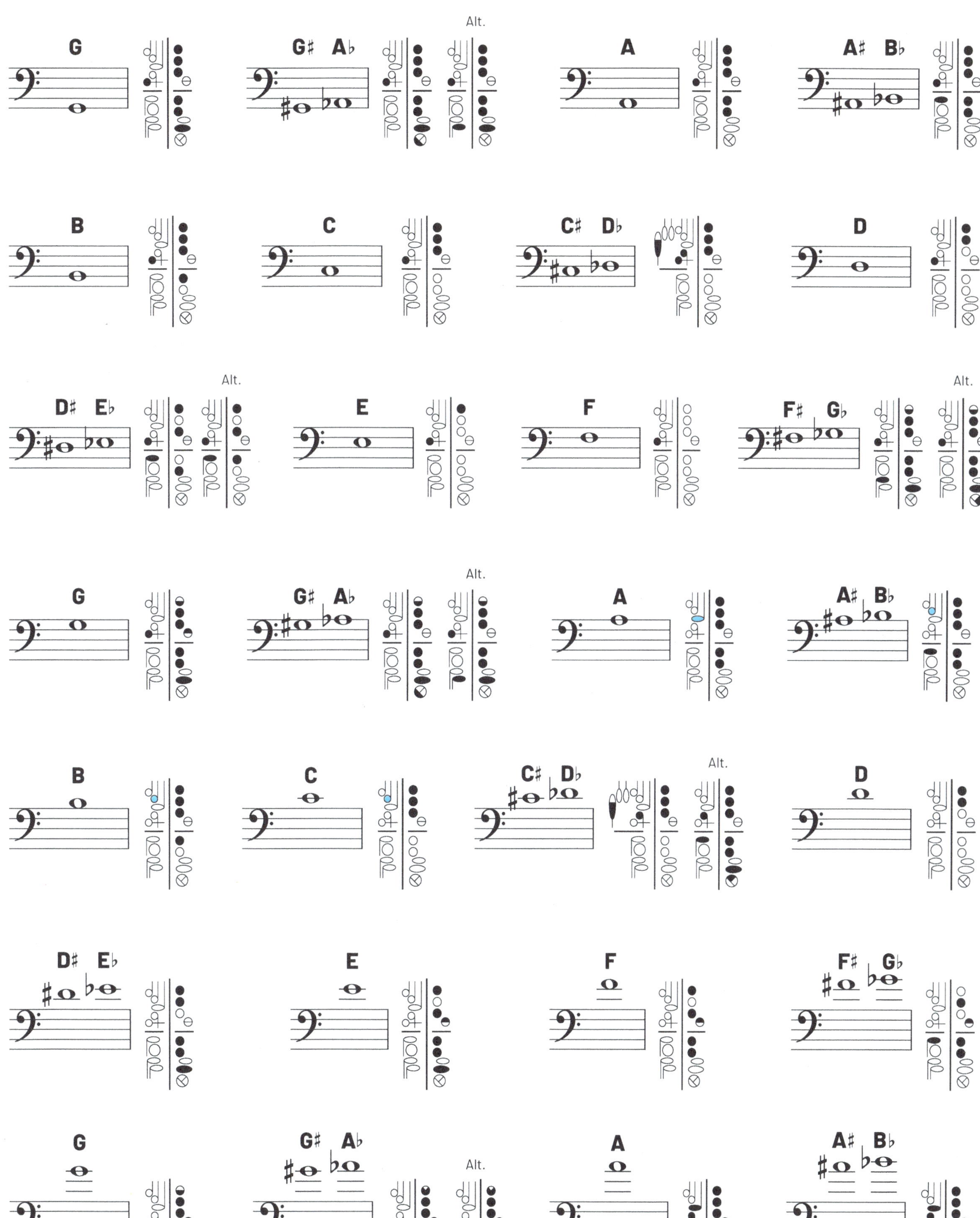

FINGERING CHART

B♭ CLARINET

Instrument Care Reminders

Before putting your instrument back in its case after playing, do the following:

- Remove the reed, wipe off excess moisture and return it to the reed case.
- Remove the mouthpiece and wipe the inside with a clean cloth. Once a week, wash the mouthpiece with warm tap water. Dry thoroughly.
- Drop a weighted chamois or cotton swab into the bell and pull it out through the barrel.
- Carefully twist off the barrel and dry off any additional moisture. Place it in the case.
- Gently twist the upper and lower sections apart, with the bell still attached. Place the upper section in the case.
- Remove the bell and place the bell and lower section back into the case.
- As you put each piece back in the case, check to be sure they are dry.
- Your case is designed to hold only specific objects. If you try to force anything else into the case, it may damage your instrument.

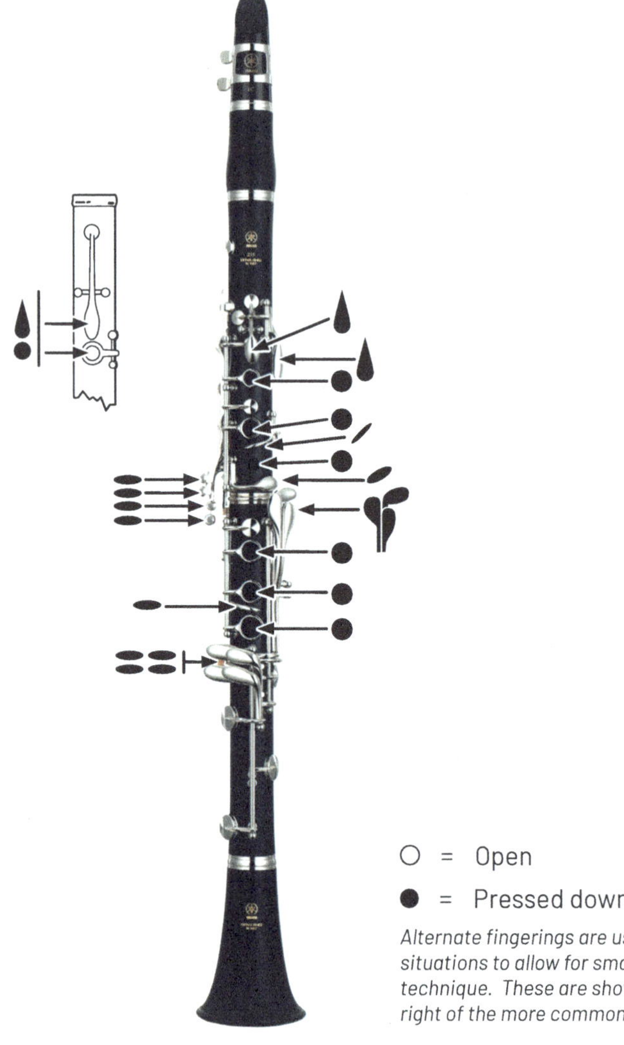

○ = Open

● = Pressed down

Alternate fingerings are used in certain situations to allow for smoother technique. These are shown to the right of the more common fingerings.

Instruments and photos courtesy of Yamaha.

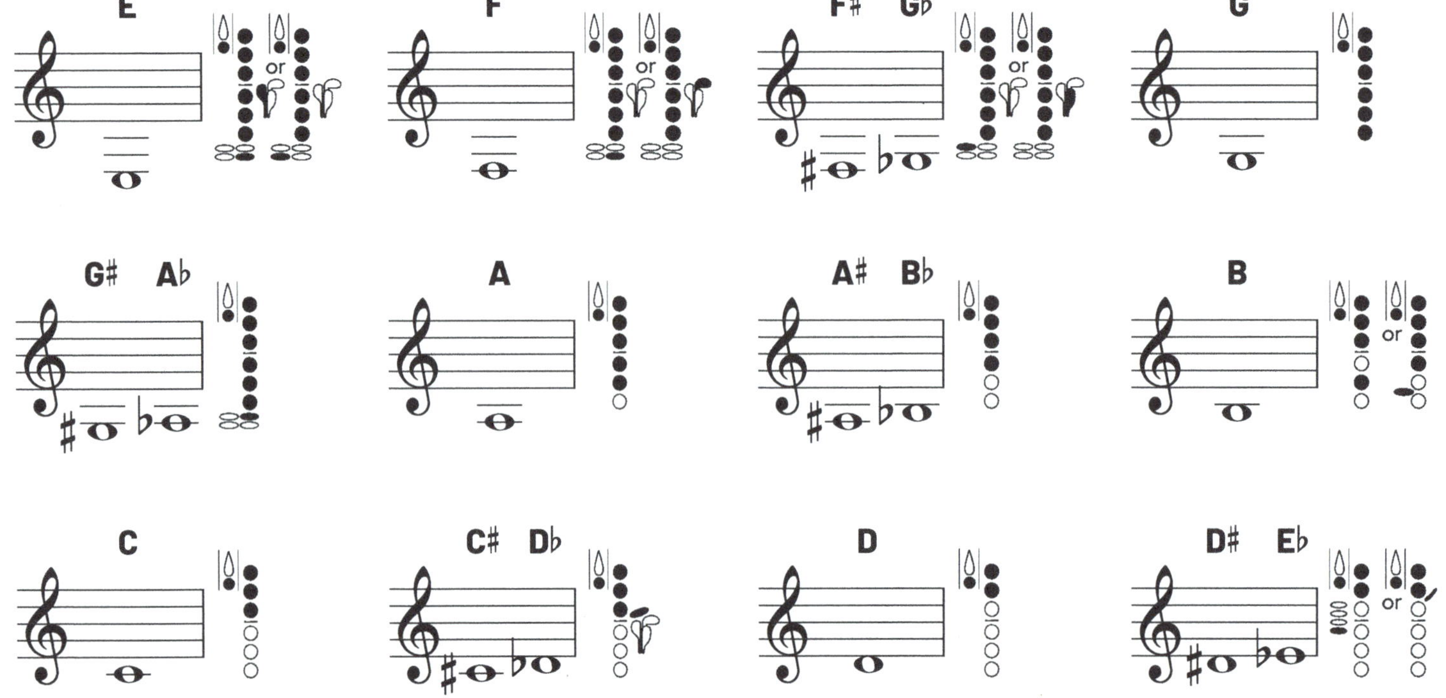

FINGERING CHART

B♭ CLARINET

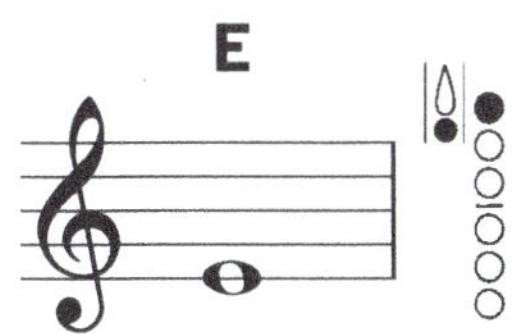

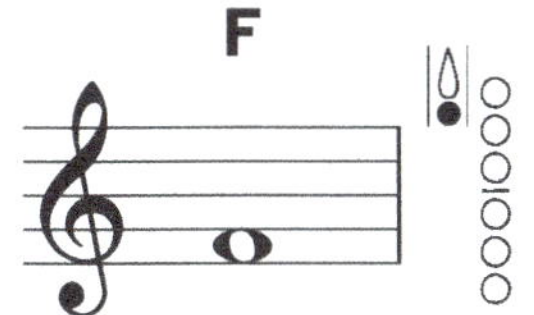

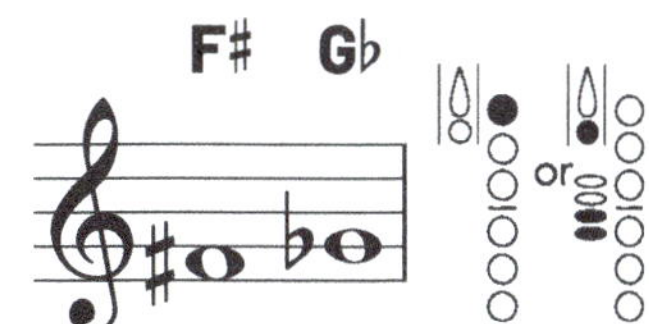

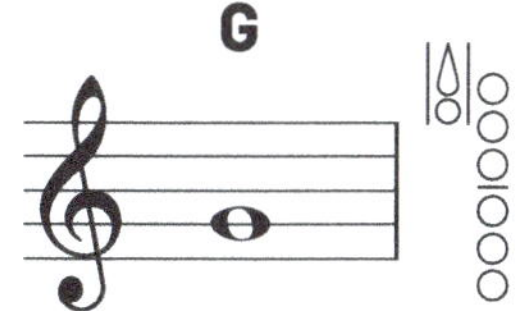

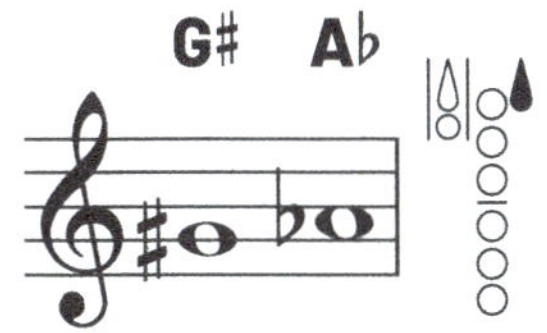

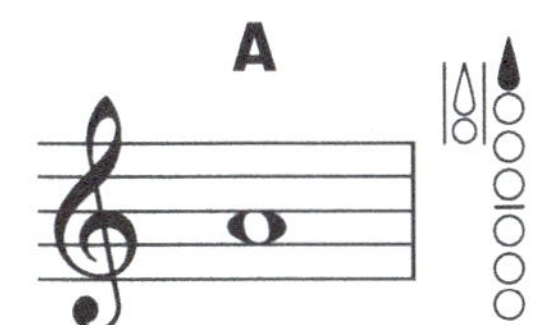

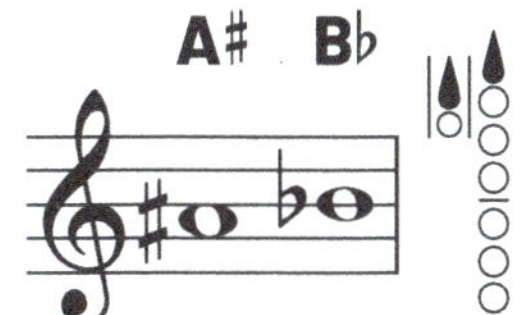

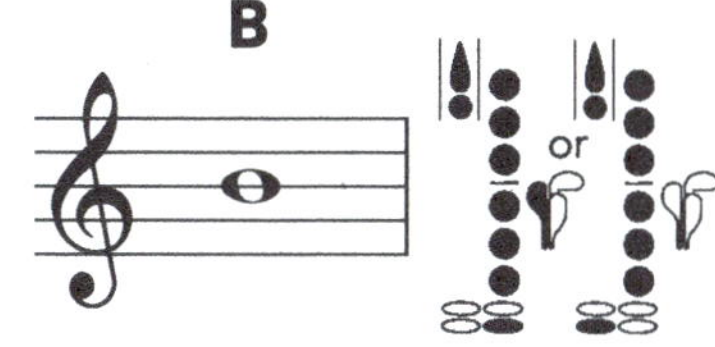

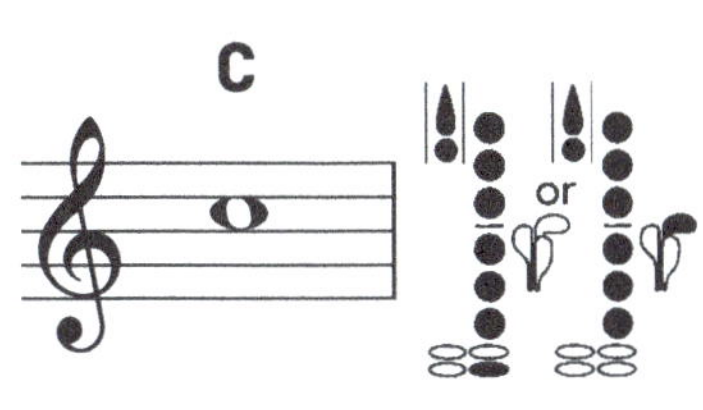

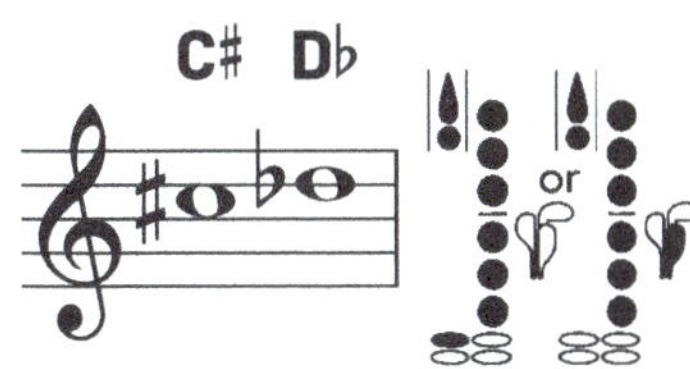

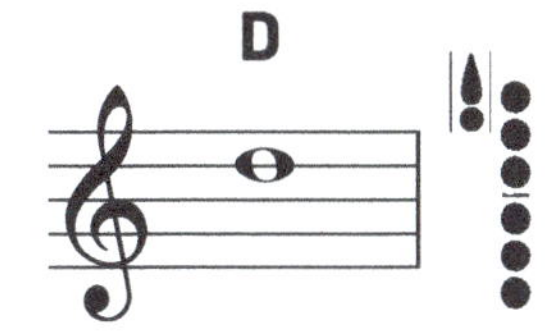

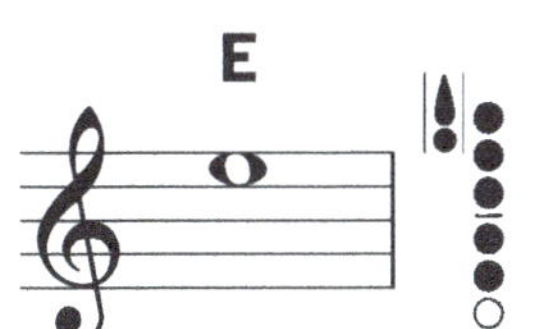

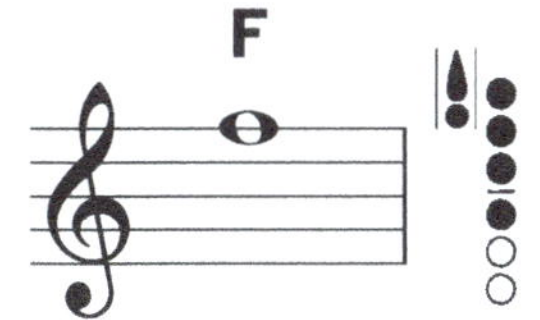

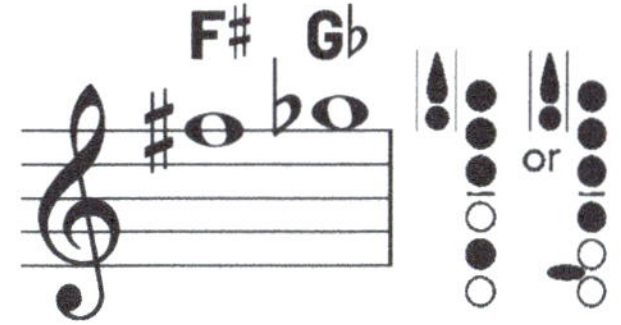

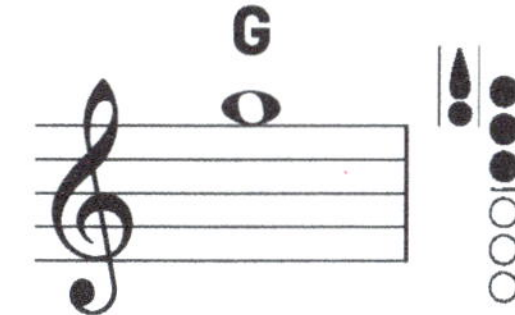

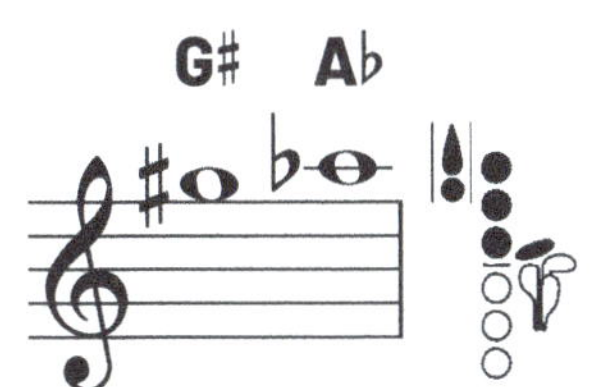

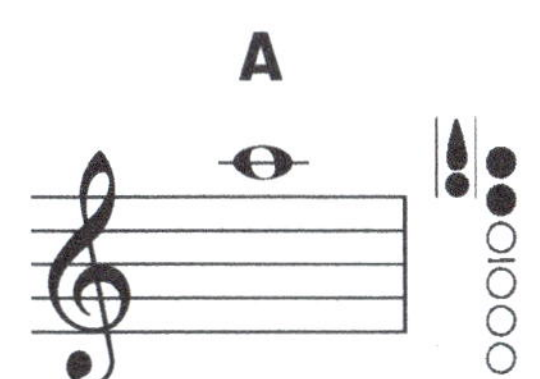

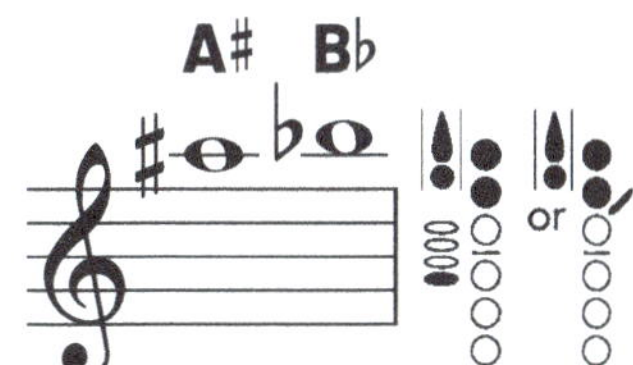

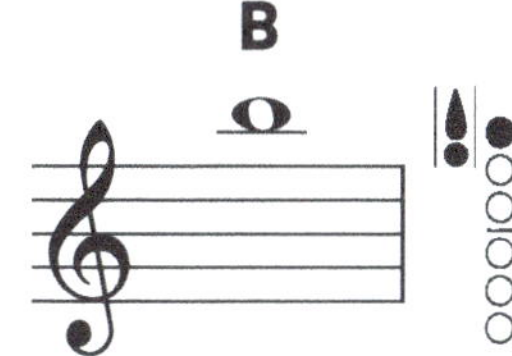

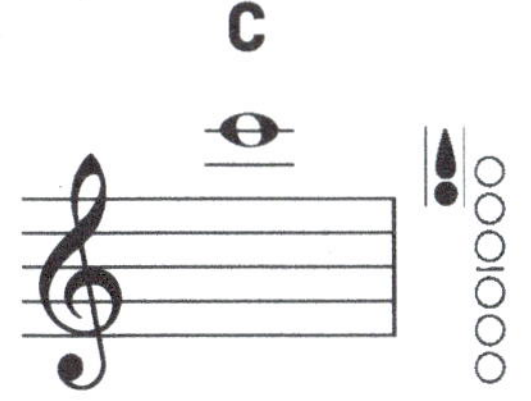

FINGERING CHART

E♭ ALTO CLARINET

Instrument Care Reminders

Before putting your instrument back in its case after playing, do the following:

- Remove the reed, wipe off excess moisture and return it to the reed case.
- Remove the mouthpiece and wipe the inside with a clean cloth. Once a week, wash the mouthpiece with warm tap water. Dry thoroughly.
- Remove the neck and bell, and shake out excess moisture. Hold the upper section with your left hand and the lower section with your right hand. Gently twist the sections apart. Shake out the excess moisture.
- Drop a weighted chamois or cotton swab into the body of the instrument and pull it out the bottom.
- If the body of your alto clarinet has two sections, gently twist them apart. Return the body section(s) to the case.
- As you put each piece back in the case, check to be sure they are dry.
- Your case is designed to hold only specific objects. If you try to force anything else into the case, it may damage your instrument.

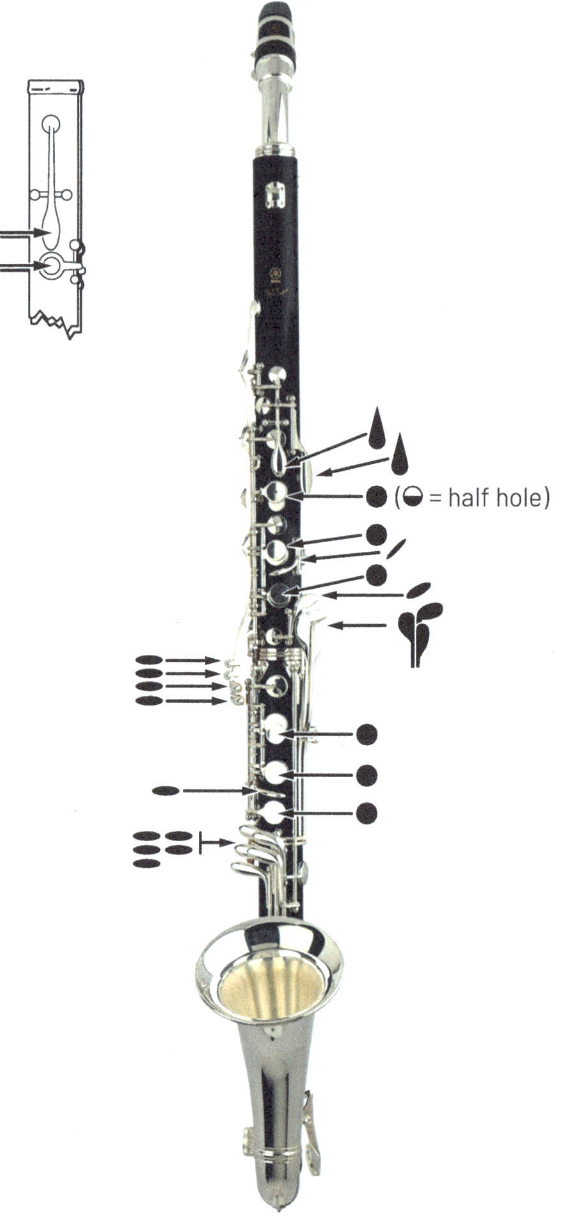

○ = Open

● = Pressed down

Alternate fingerings are used in certain situations to allow for smoother technique. These are shown to the right of the more common fingerings.

Instruments and photos courtesy of Yamaha.

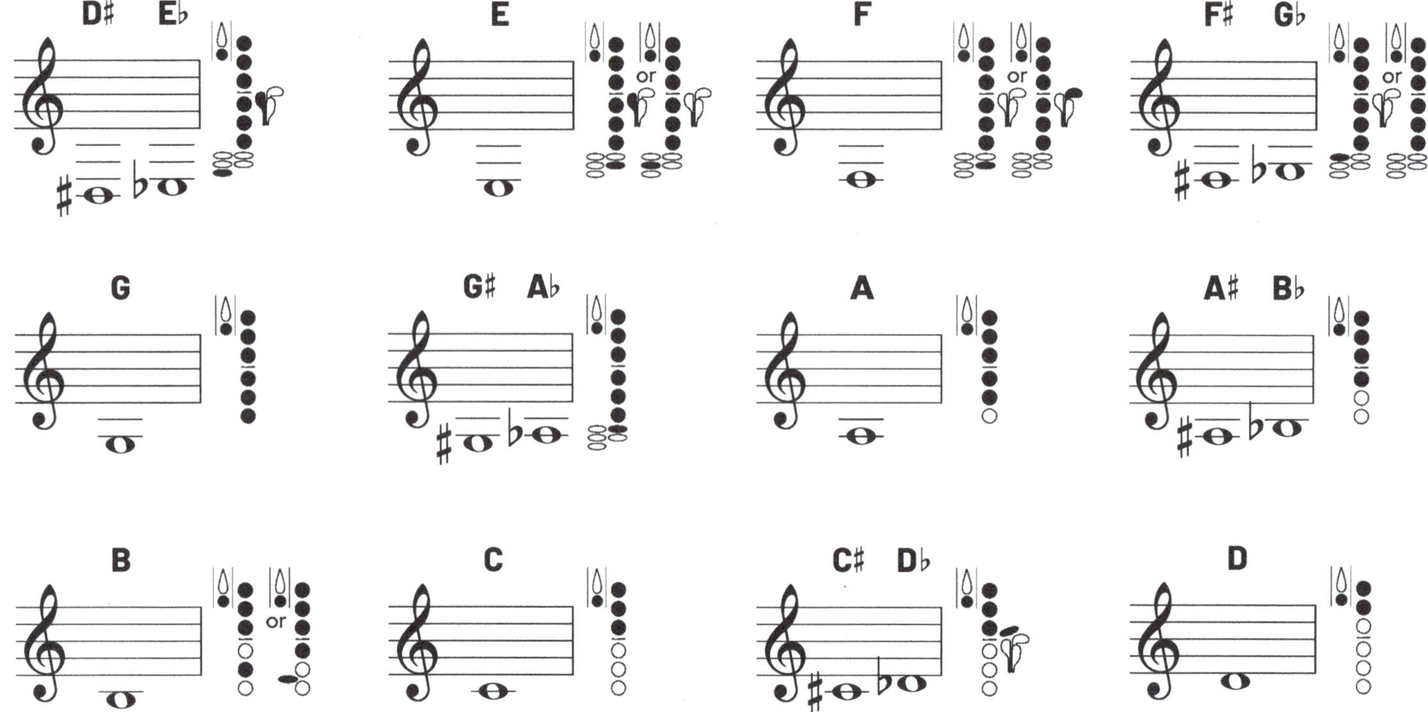

FINGERING CHART

E♭ ALTO CLARINET

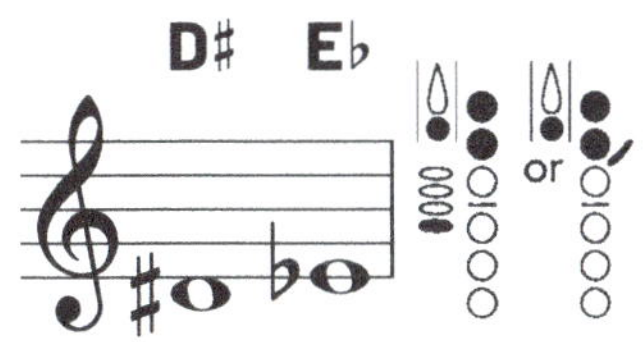

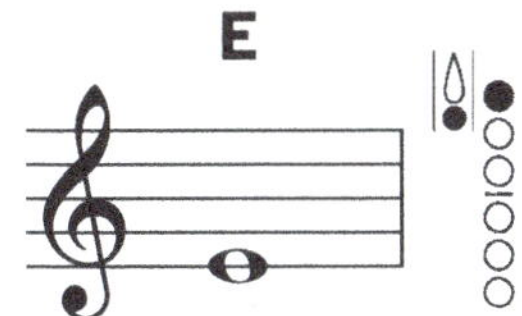

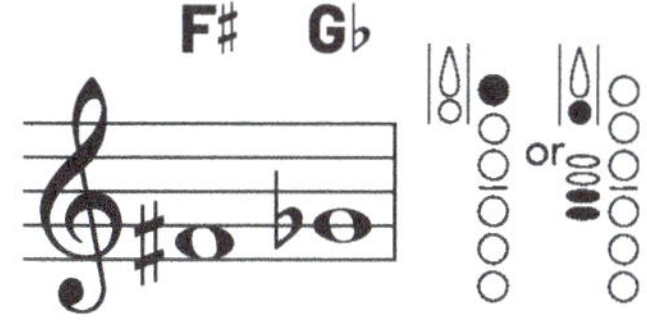

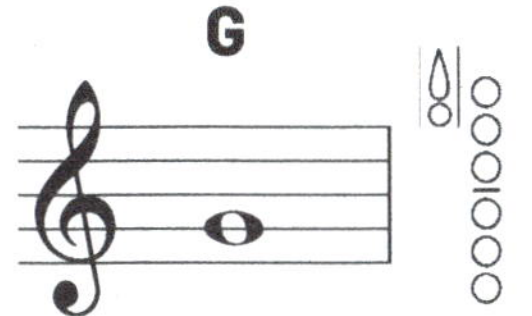

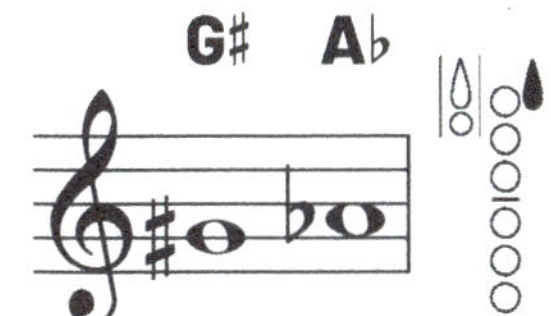

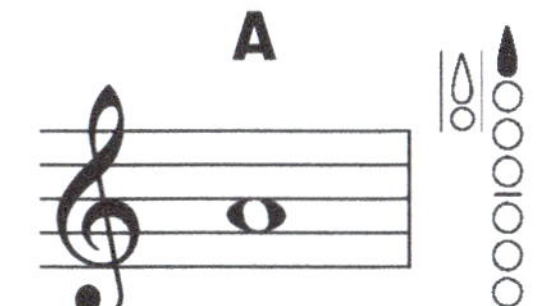

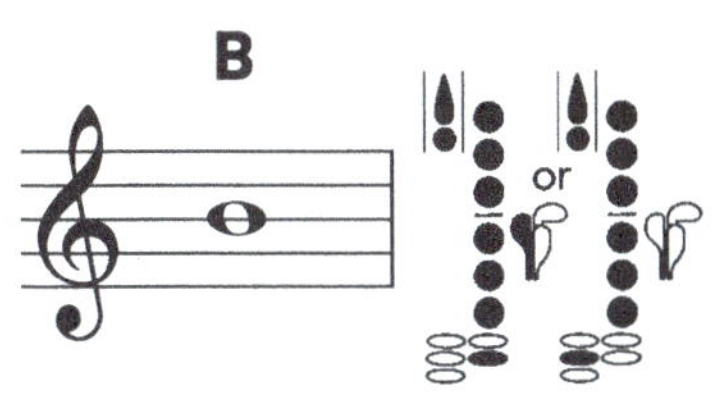

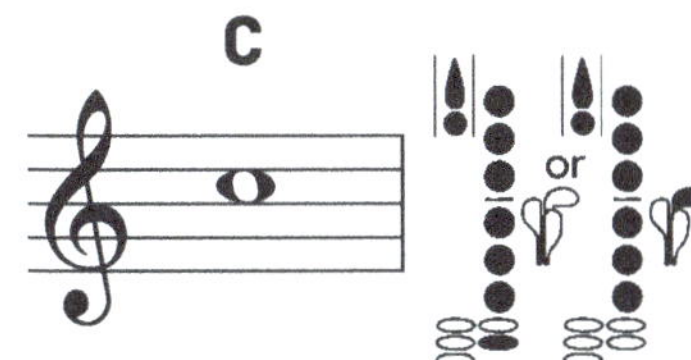

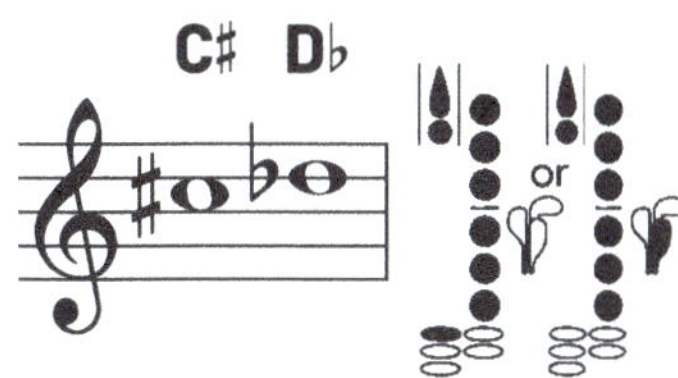

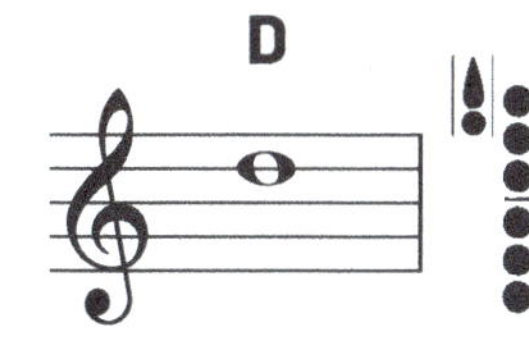

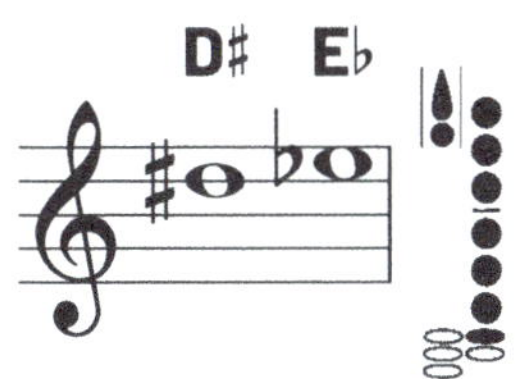

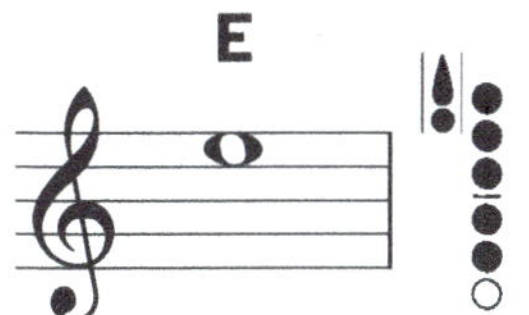

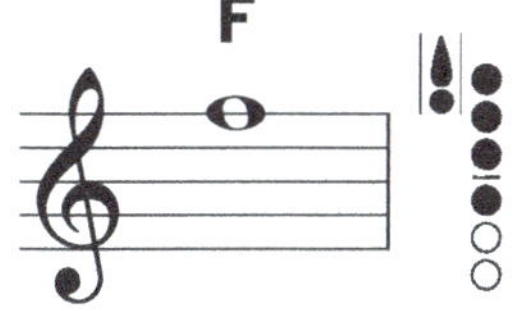

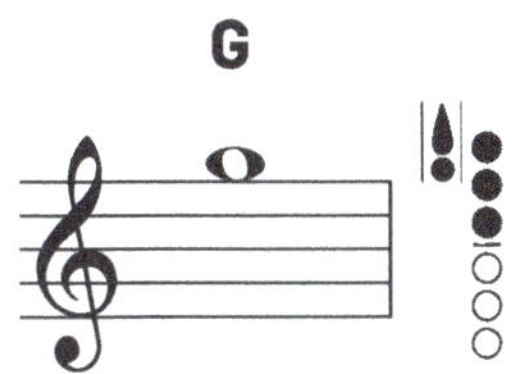

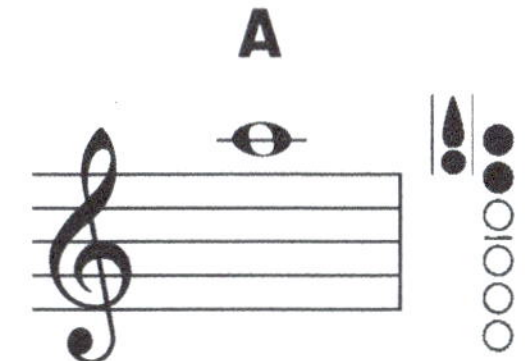

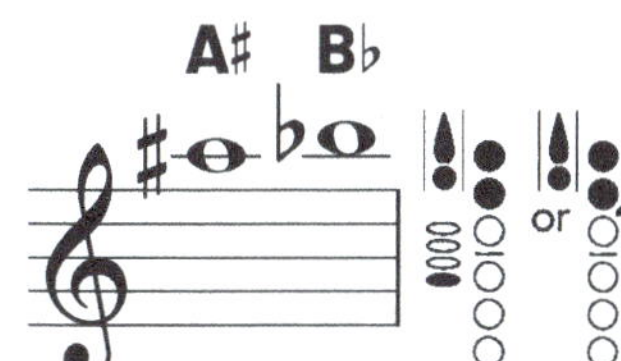

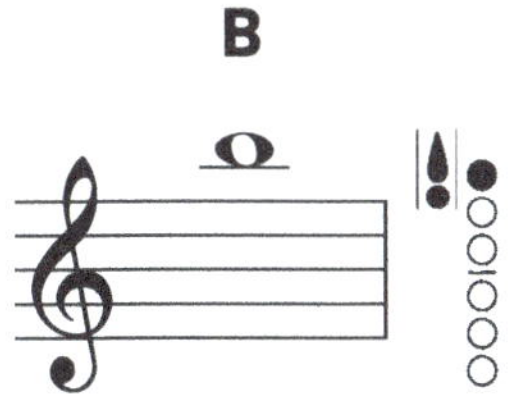

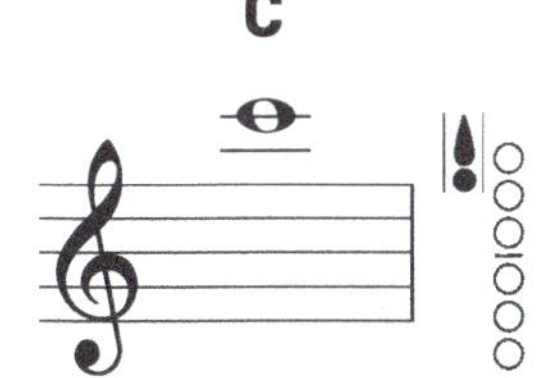

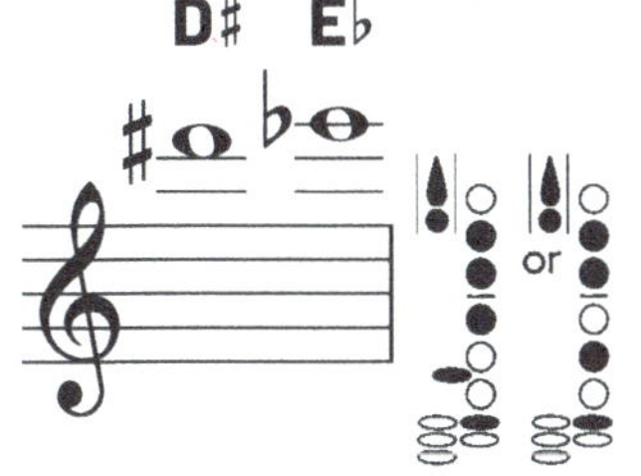

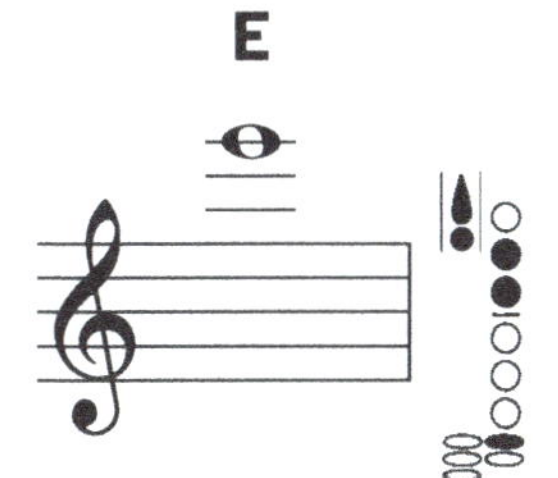

Student Book Page 46

FINGERING CHART

B♭ BASS CLARINET

Instrument Care Reminders

Before putting your instrument back in its case after playing, do the following:

- Remove the reed, wipe off excess moisture and return it to the reed case.
- Remove the mouthpiece and wipe the inside with a clean cloth. Once a week, wash the mouthpiece with warm tap water. Dry thoroughly.
- Remove the neck and bell, and shake out excess moisture. Hold the upper section with your left hand and the lower section with your right hand. Gently twist the sections apart. Shake out the excess moisture.
- Drop a weighted chamois or cotton swab into each section and pull it out the bottom.
- As you put each piece back in the case, check to be sure they are dry.
- Your case is designed to hold only specific objects. If you try to force anything else into the case, it may damage your instrument.

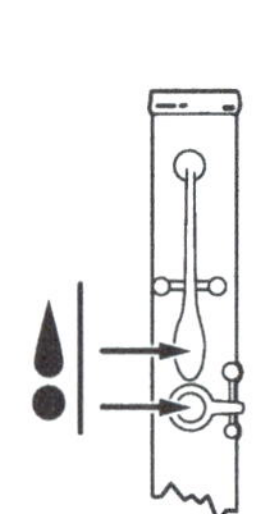

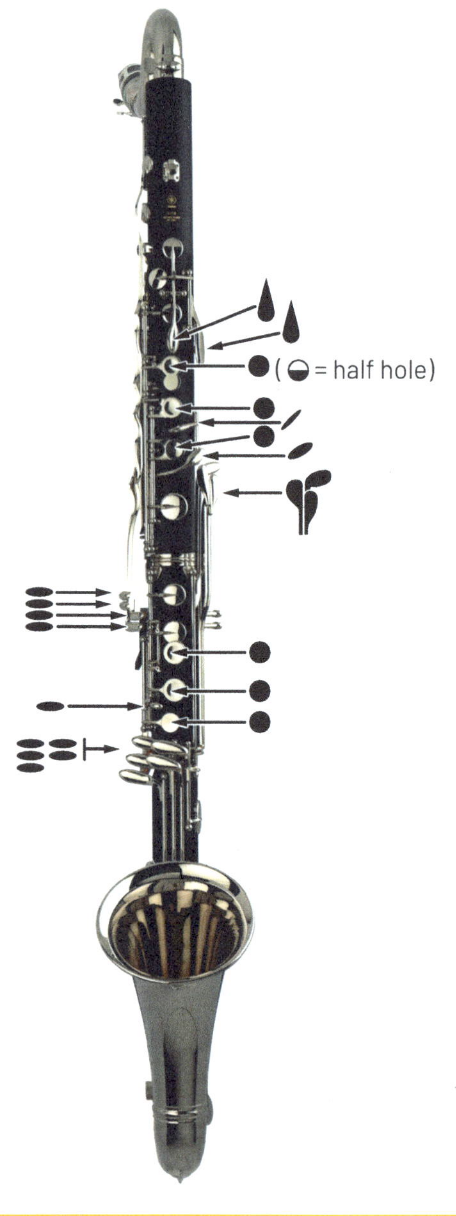

○ = Open

● = Pressed down

Alternate fingerings are used in certain situations to allow for smoother technique. These are shown to the right of the more common fingerings.

Instruments and photos courtesy of Yamaha.

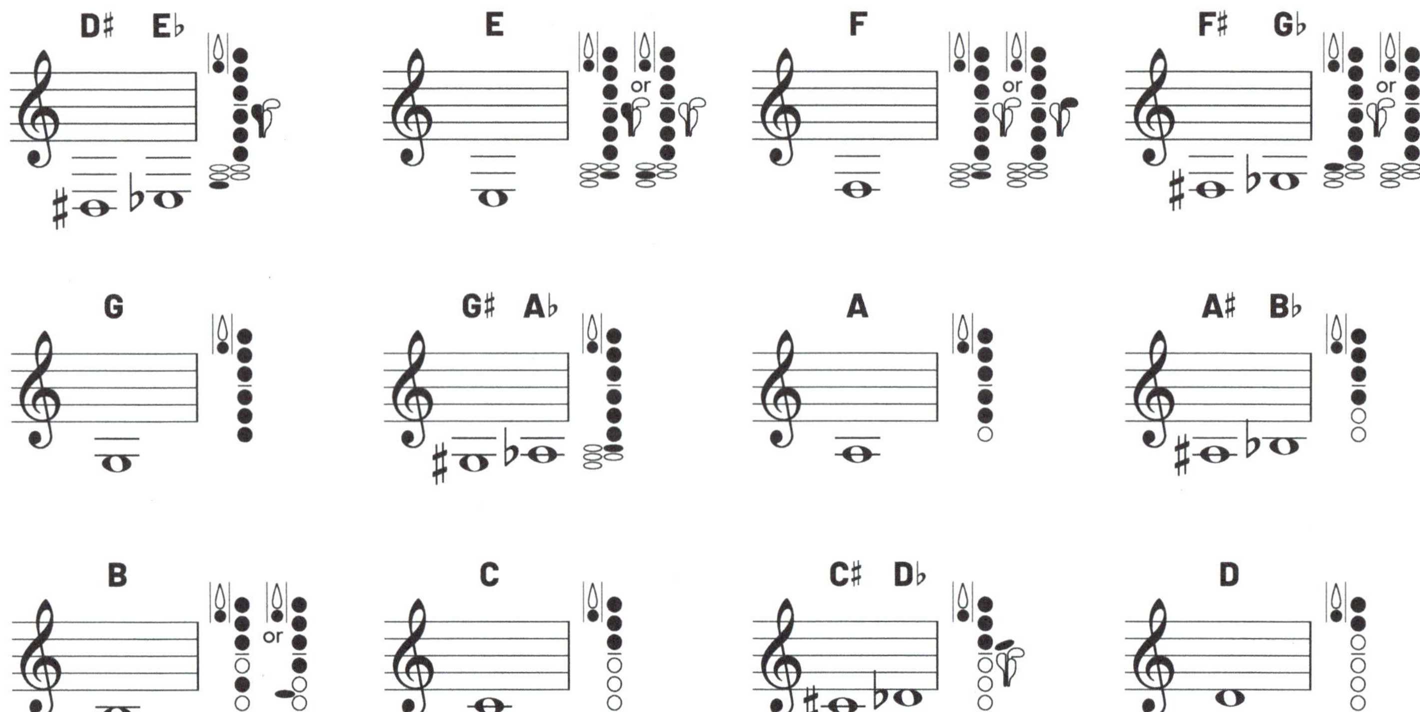

FINGERING CHART

B♭ BASS CLARINET

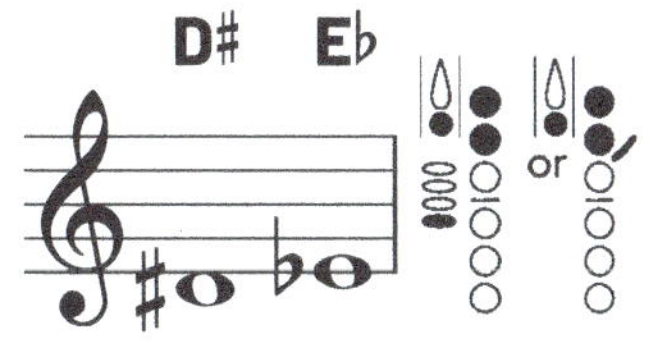

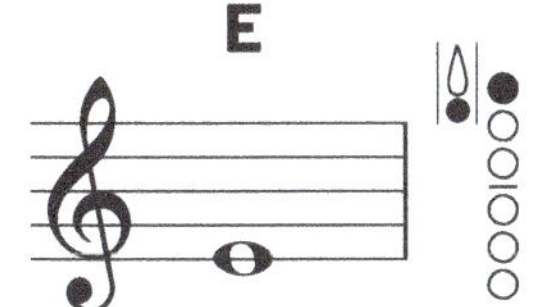

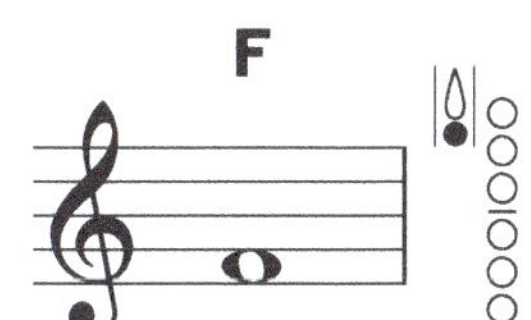

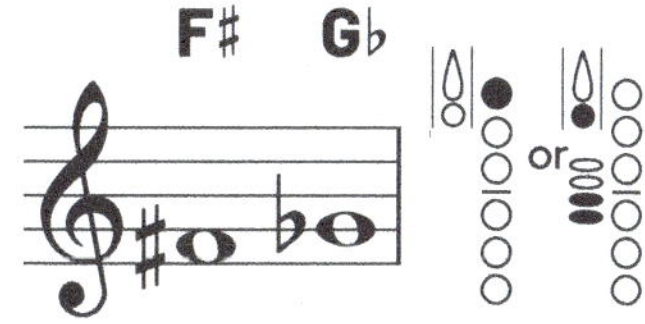

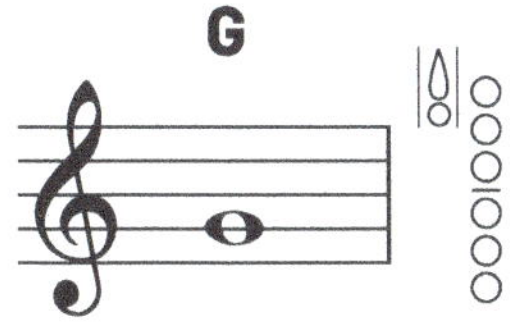

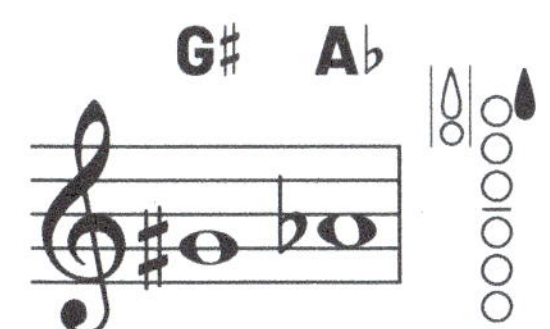

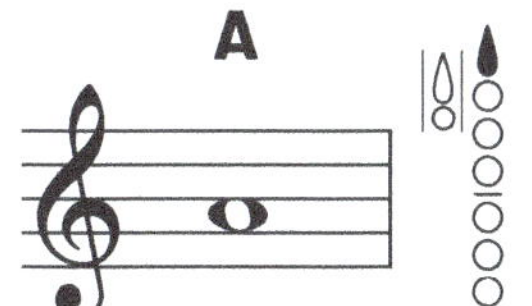

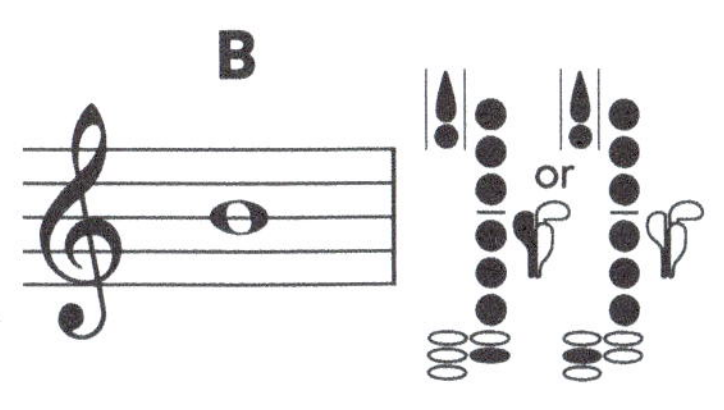

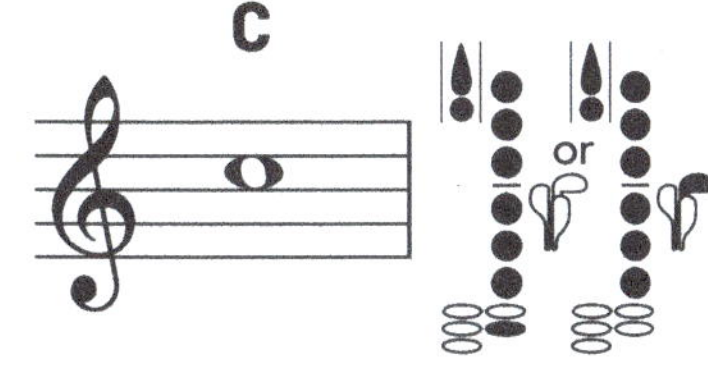

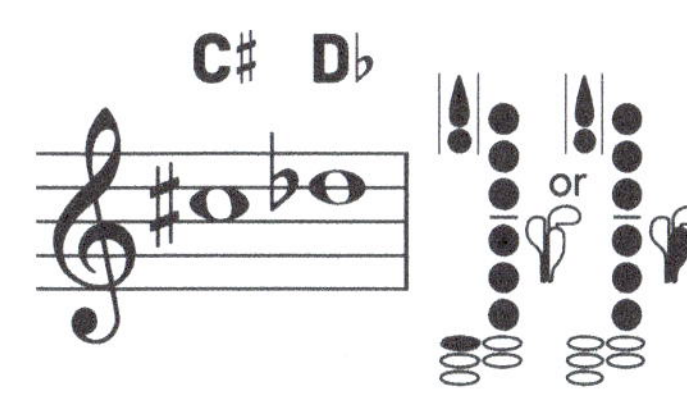

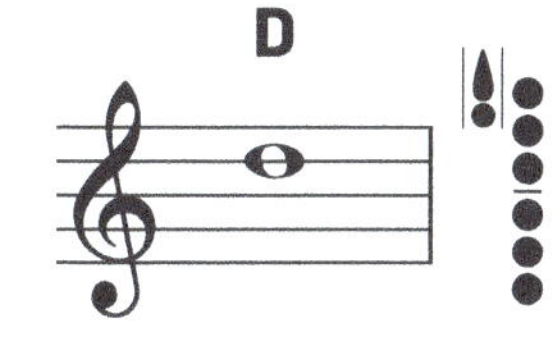

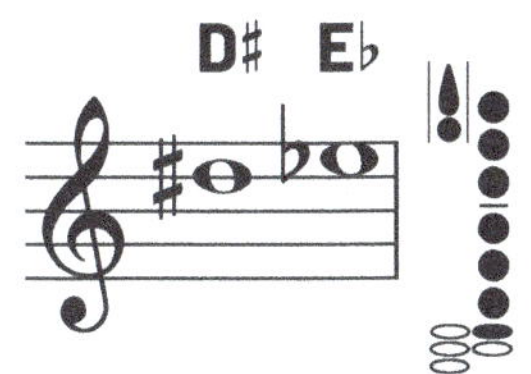

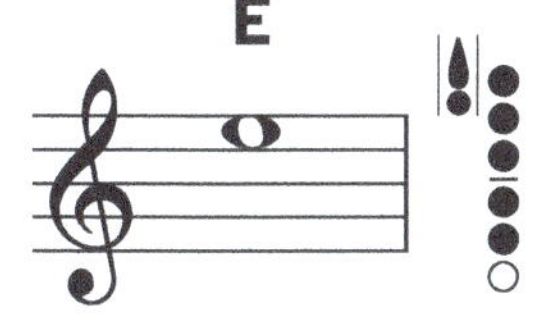

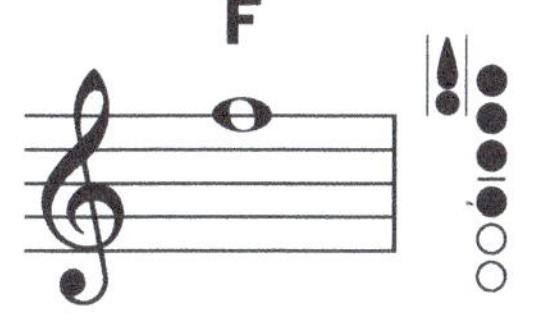

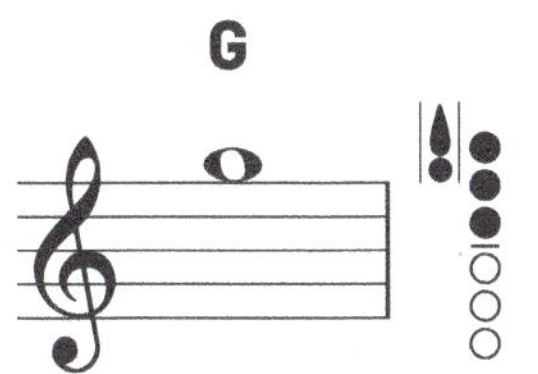

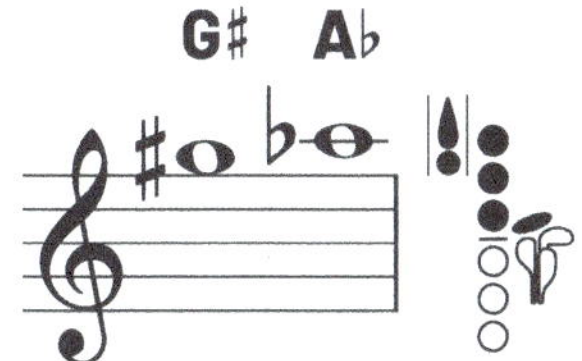

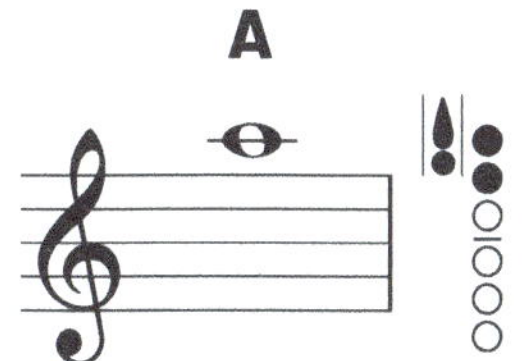

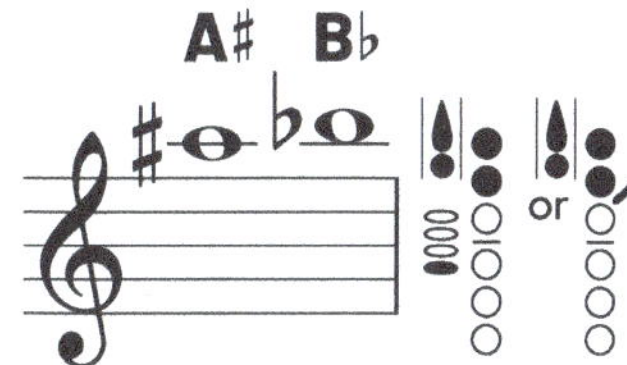

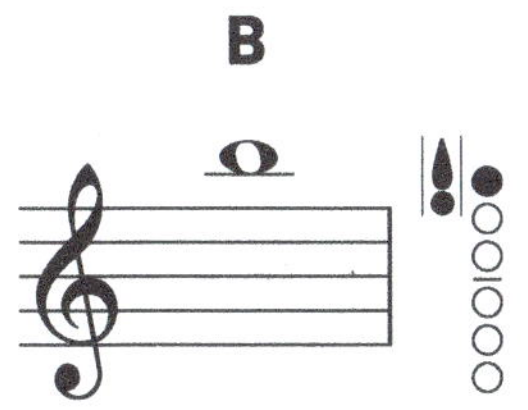

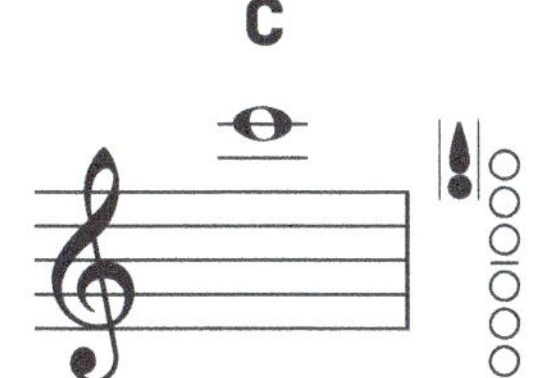

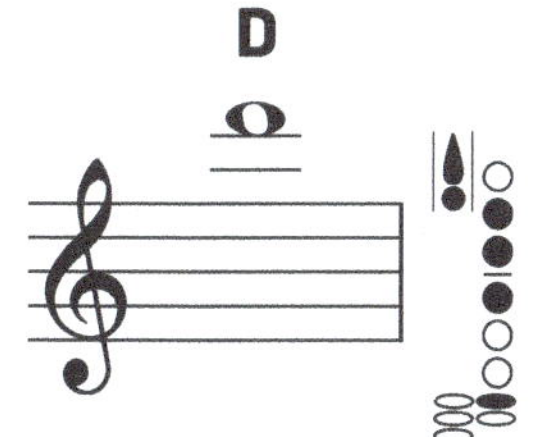

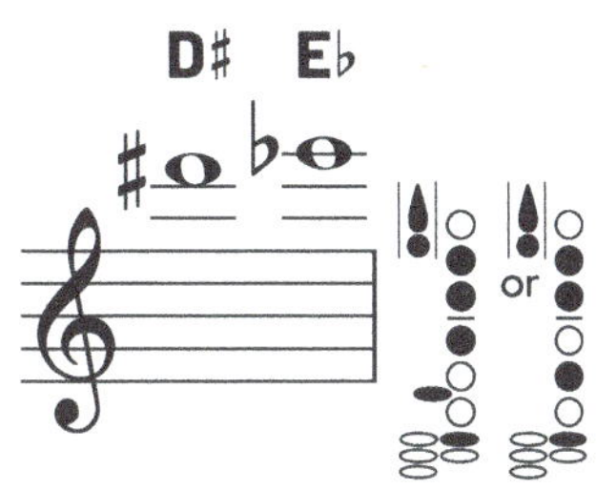

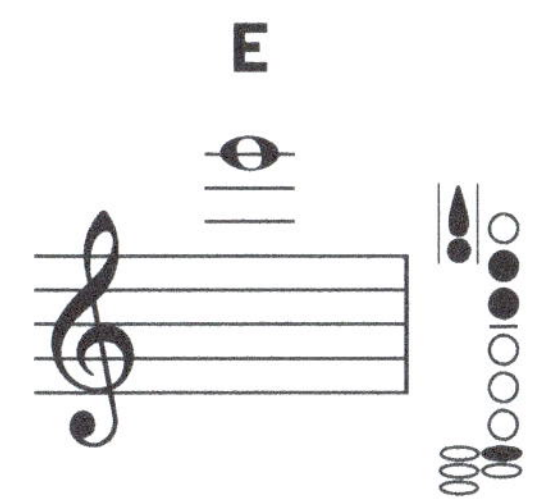

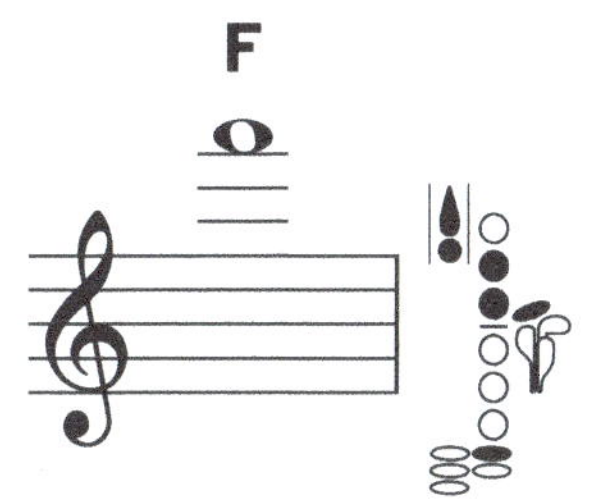

Student Book Page 46

FINGERING CHART

E♭ ALTO SAXOPHONE

Instrument Care Reminders

Before putting your instrument back in its case after playing, do the following:

- Remove the reed, wipe off excess moisture and return it to the reed case.
- Remove the mouthpiece and wipe the inside with a clean cloth. Once a week, wash the mouthpiece with warm tap water. Dry thoroughly.
- Loosen the neck screw and remove the neck. Shake out excess moisture and dry the neck with a neck cleaner.
- Drop the weight of a chamois or cotton swab into the bell. Pull the swab through the body several times. Return the instrument to its case.
- Your case is designed to hold only specific objects. If you try to force anything else into the case, it may damage your instrument.

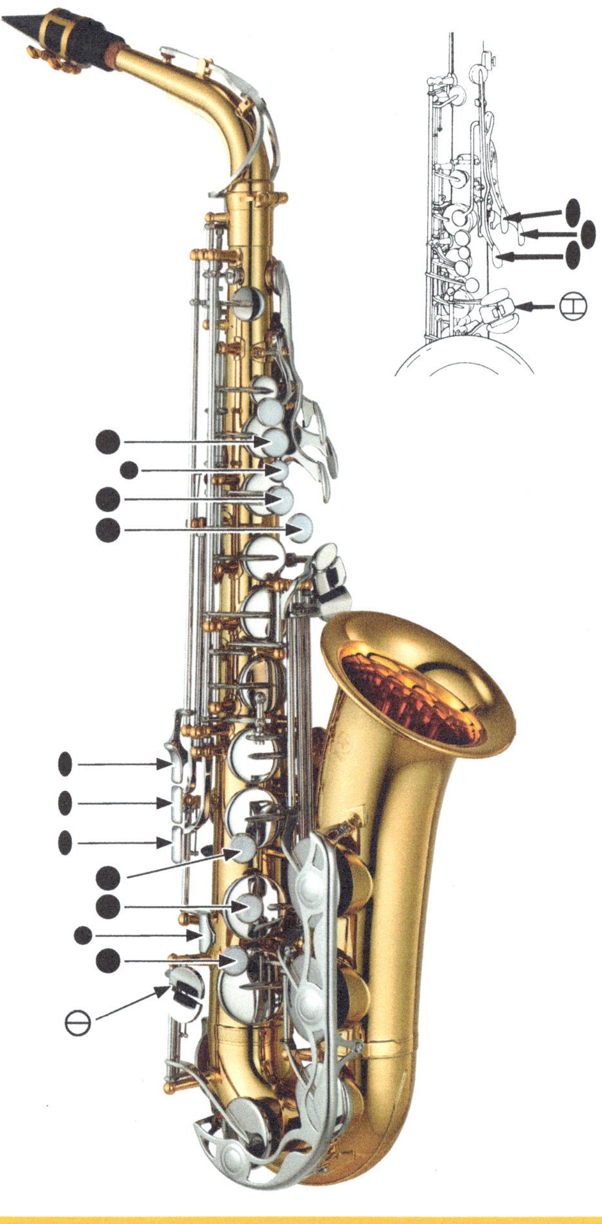

○ = Open

● = Pressed down

The most common fingering appears first when two fingerings are shown.

Instruments and photos courtesy of Yamaha.

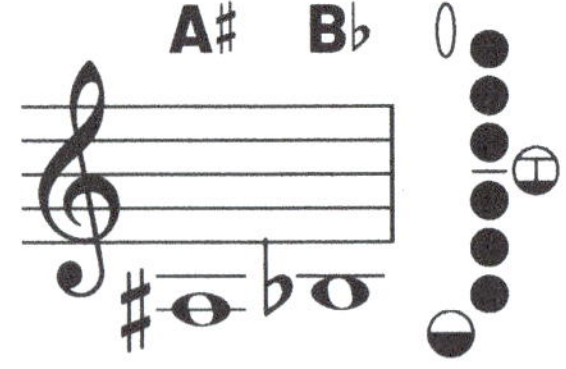

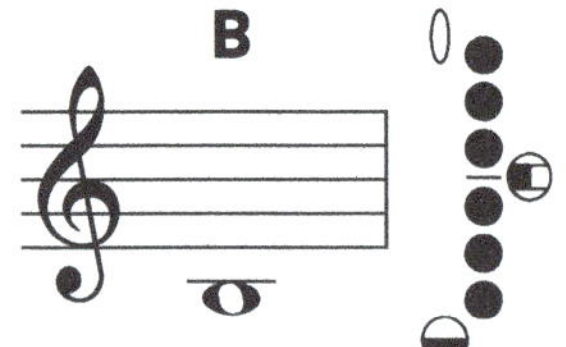

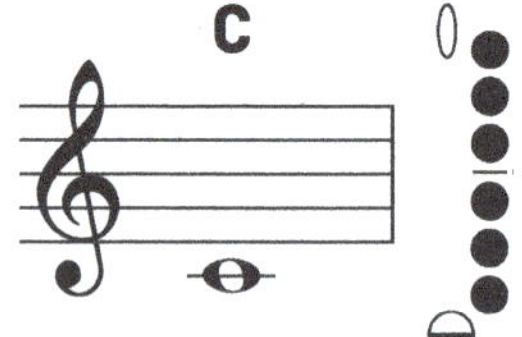

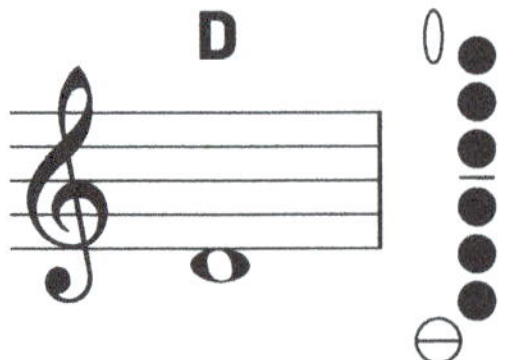

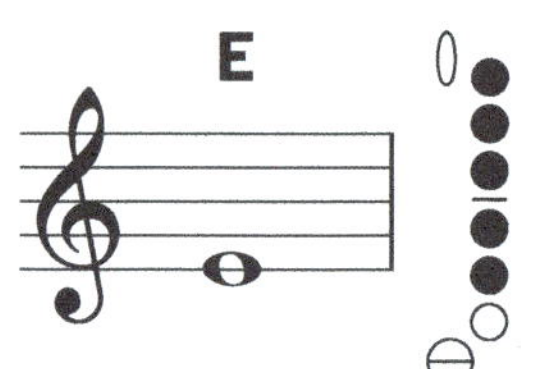

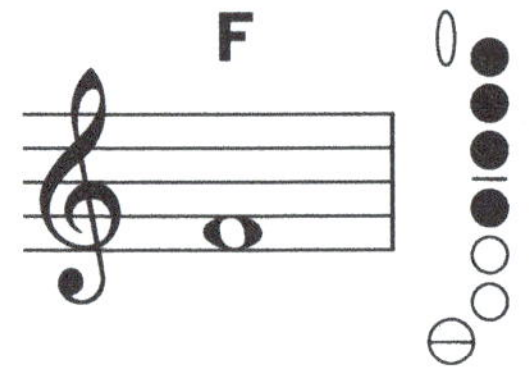

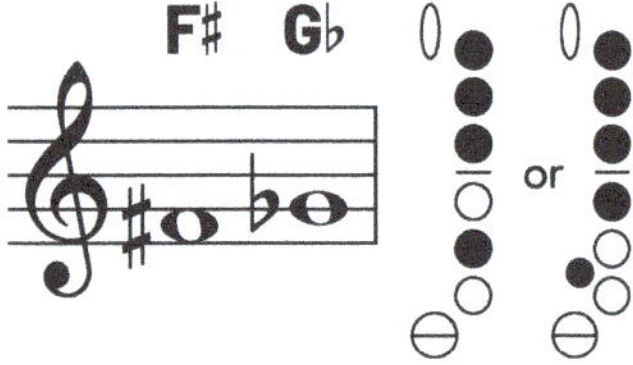

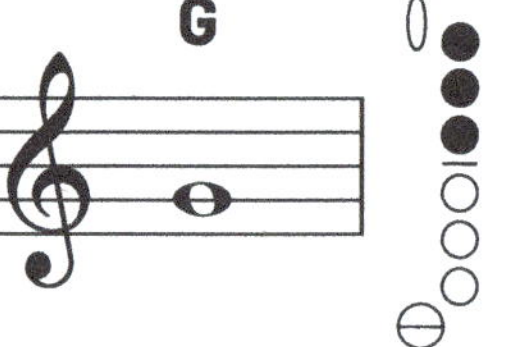

FINGERING CHART

E♭ ALTO SAXOPHONE

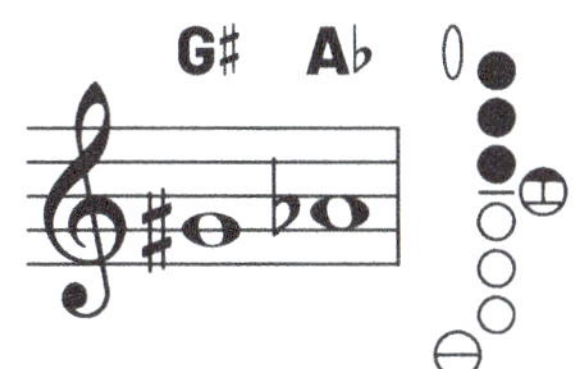

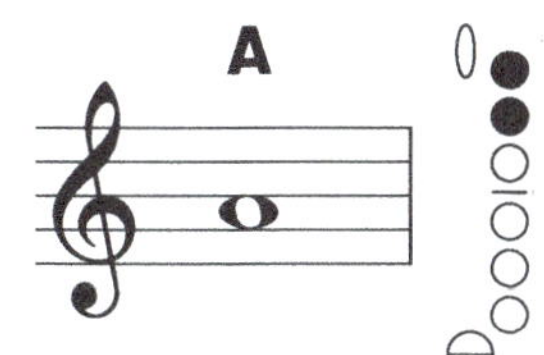

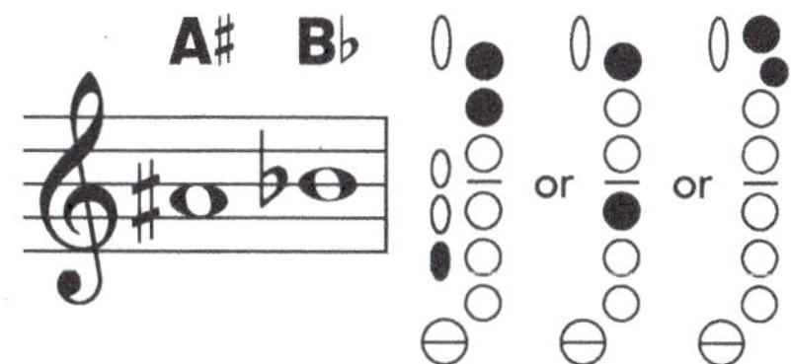

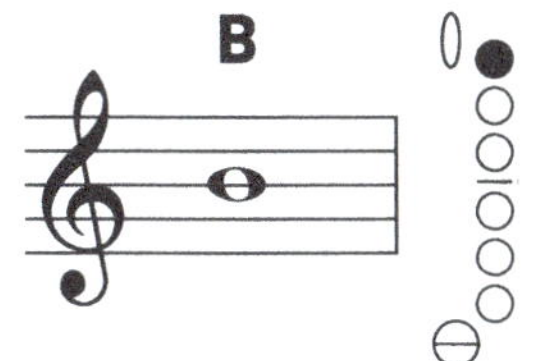

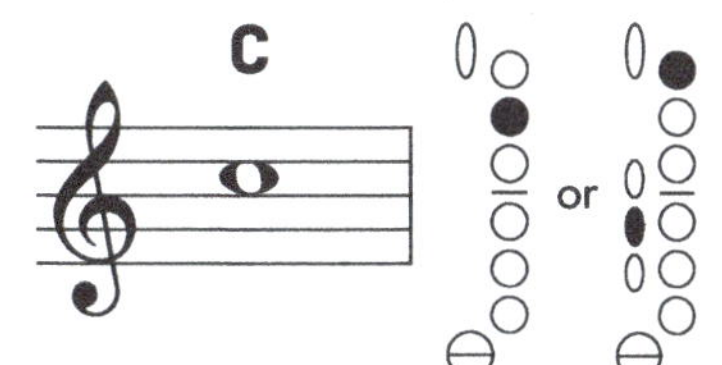

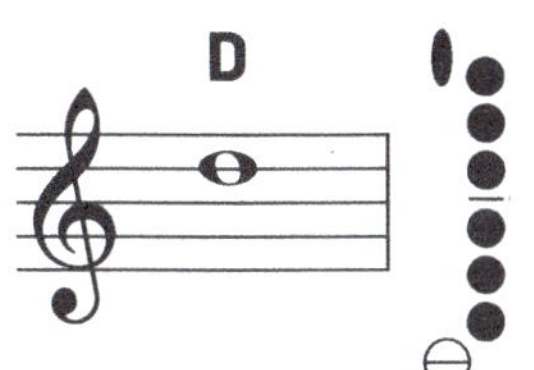

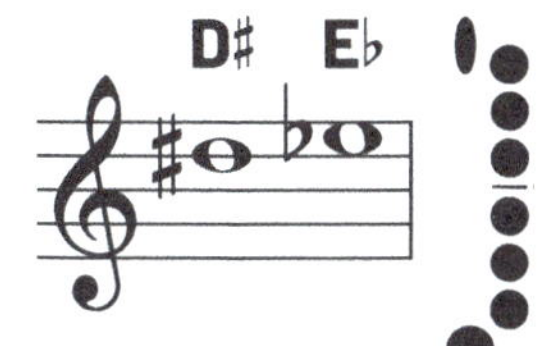

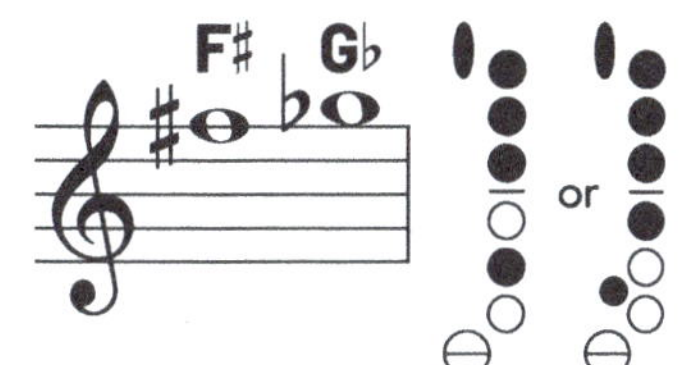

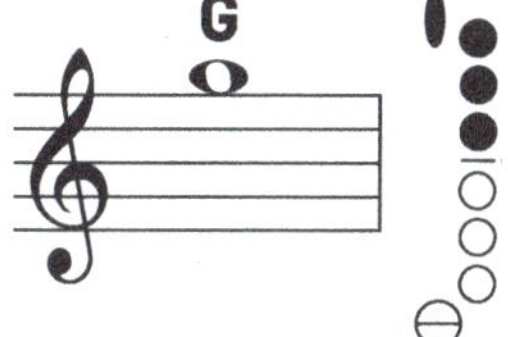

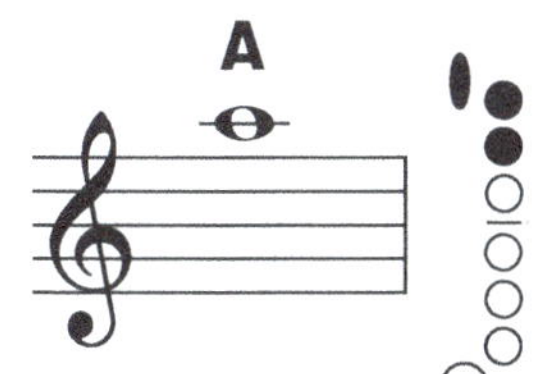

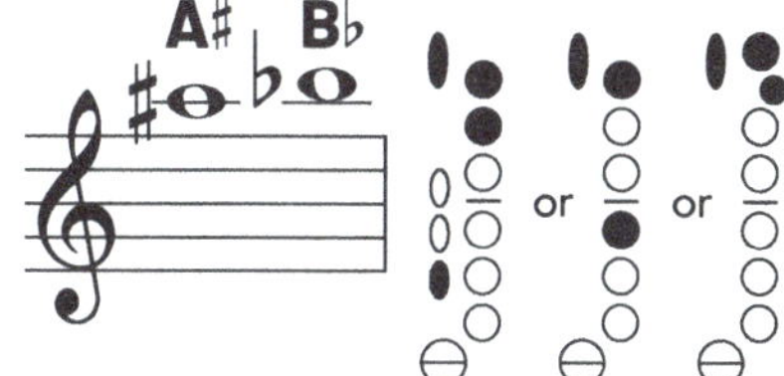

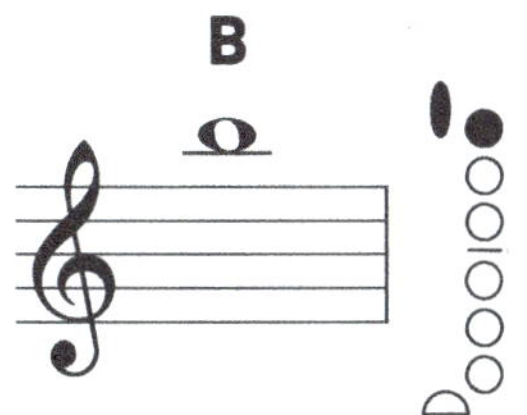

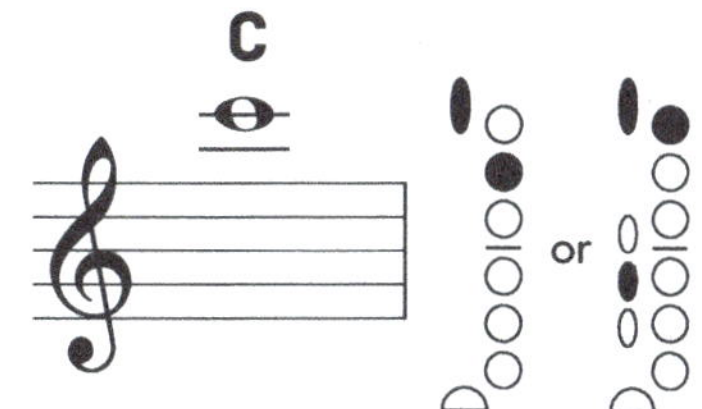

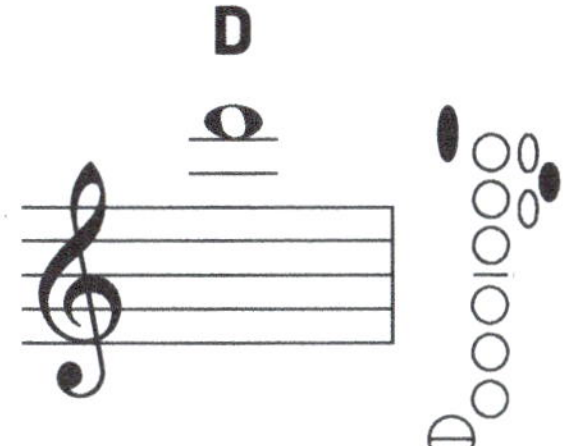

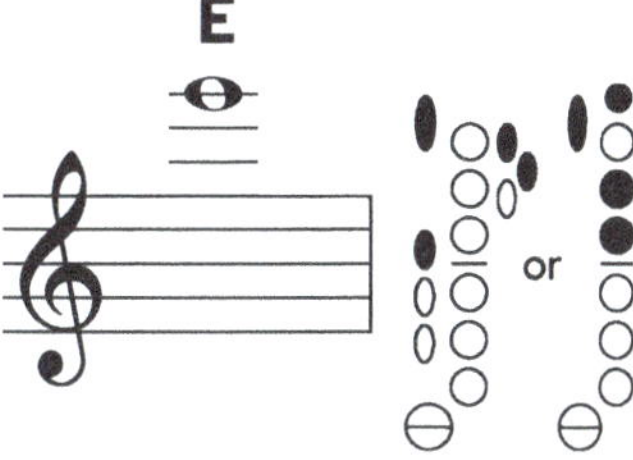

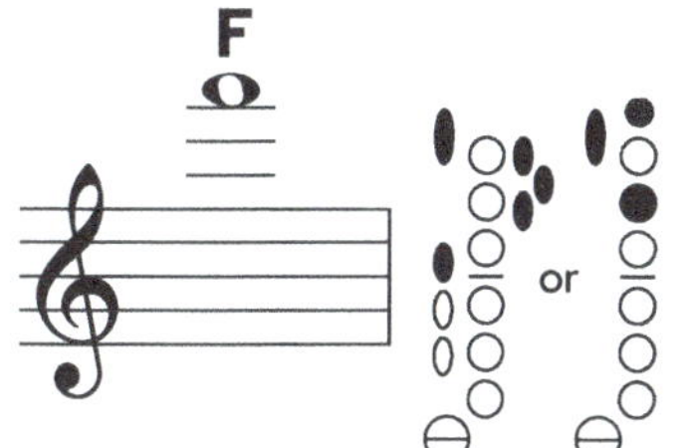

FINGERING CHART

B♭ TENOR SAXOPHONE

Instrument Care Reminders

Before putting your instrument back in its case after playing, do the following:

- Remove the reed, wipe off excess moisture and return it to the reed case.
- Remove the mouthpiece and wipe the inside with a clean cloth. Once a week, wash the mouthpiece with warm tap water. Dry thoroughly.
- Loosen the neck screw and remove the neck. Shake out excess moisture and dry the neck with a neck cleaner.
- Drop the weight of a chamois or cotton swab into the bell. Pull the swab through the body several times. Return the instrument to its case.
- Your case is designed to hold only specific objects. If you try to force anything else into the case, it may damage your instrument.

○ = Open

● = Pressed down

The most common fingering appears first when two fingerings are shown.

Instruments and photos courtesy of Yamaha.

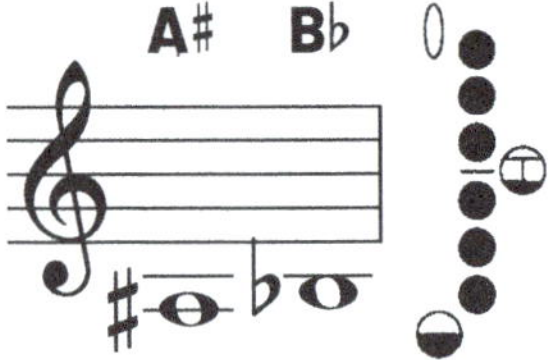

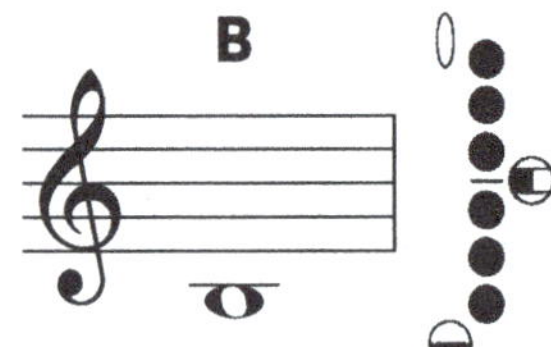

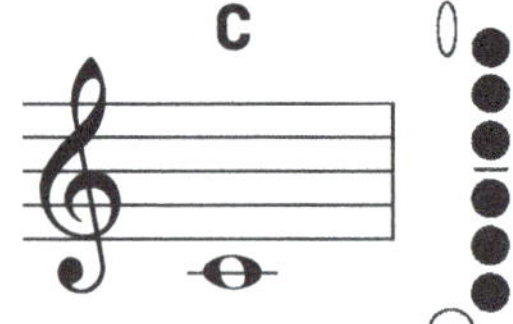

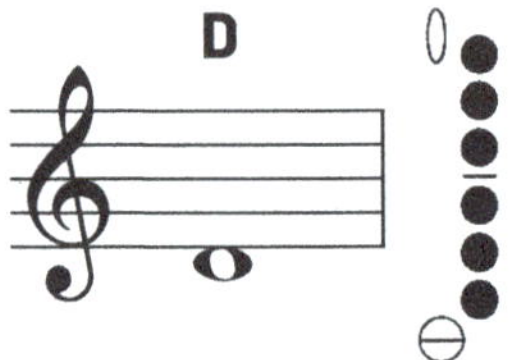

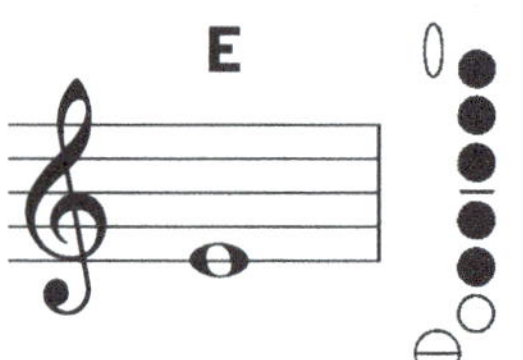

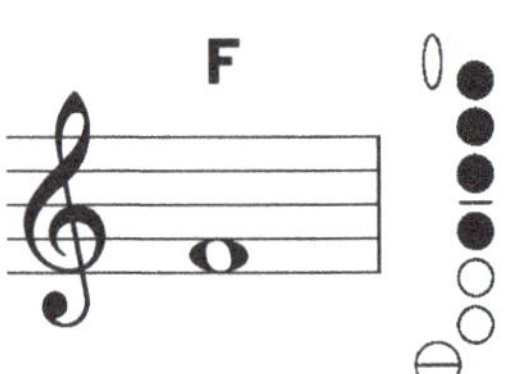

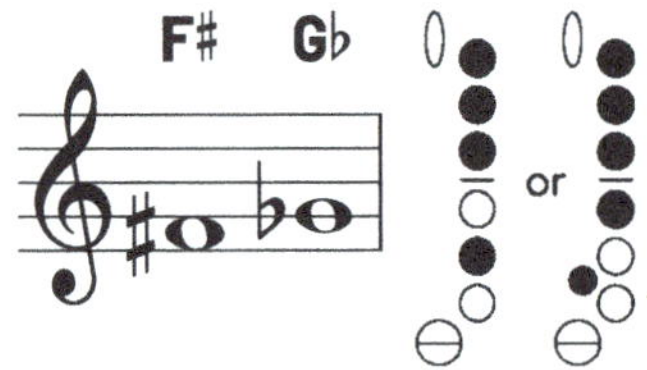

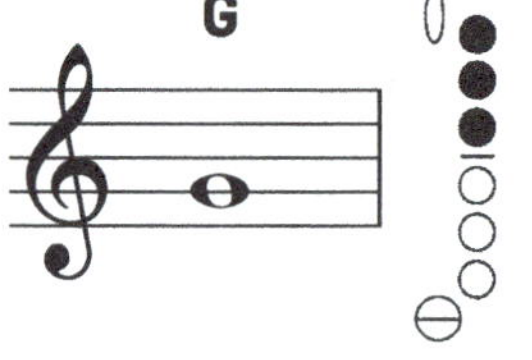

FINGERING CHART

B♭ TENOR SAXOPHONE

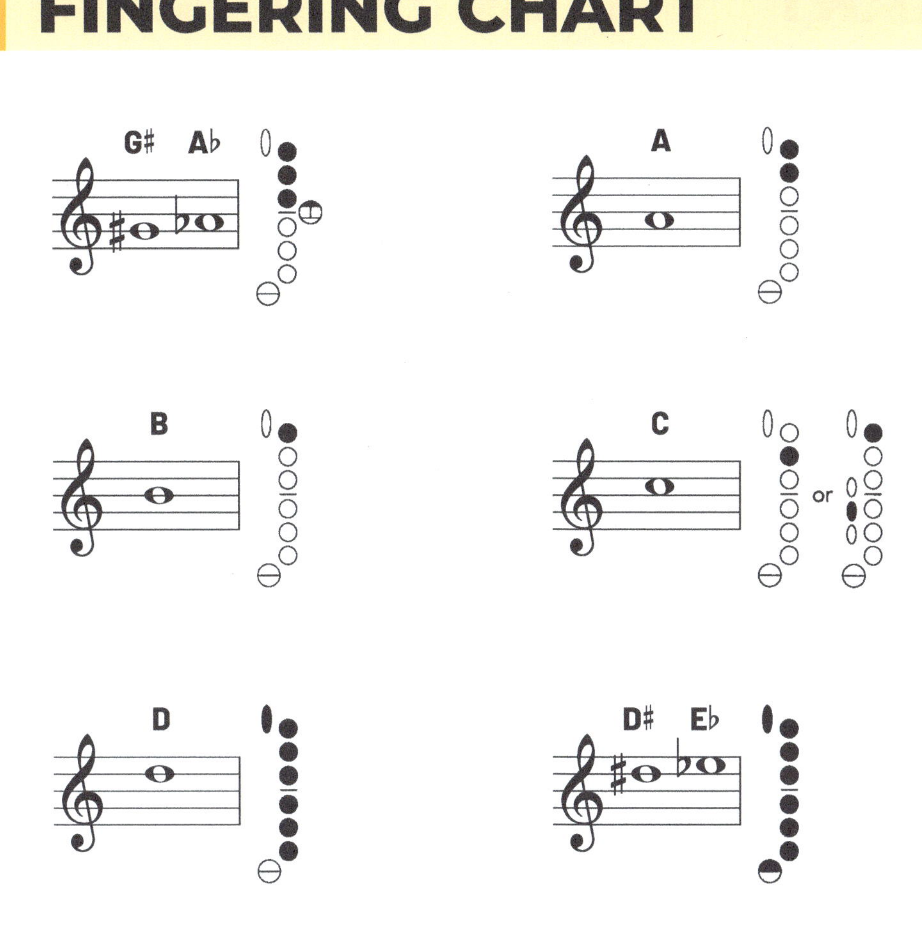

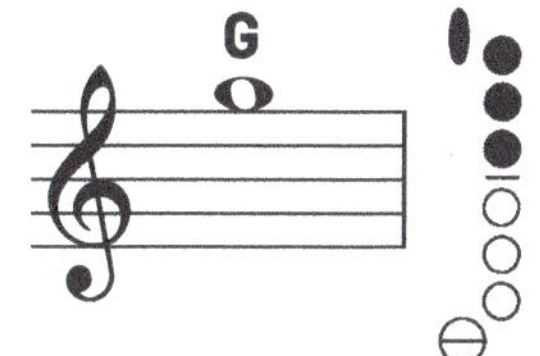

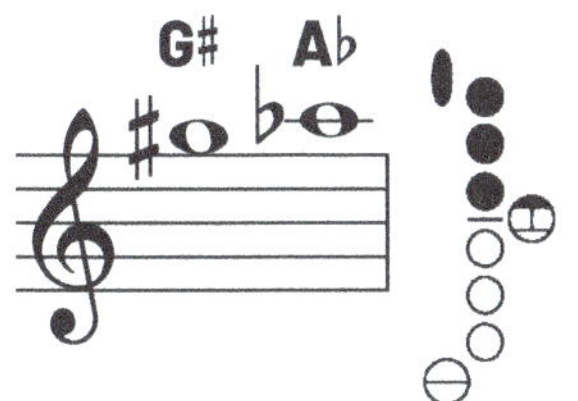

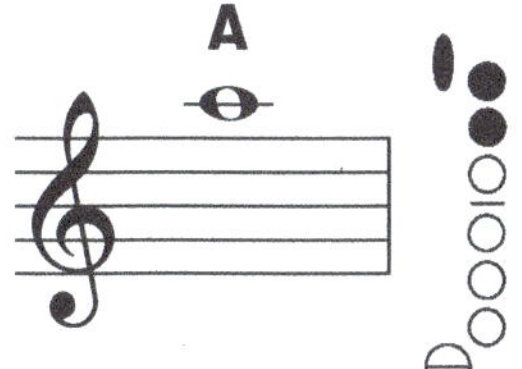

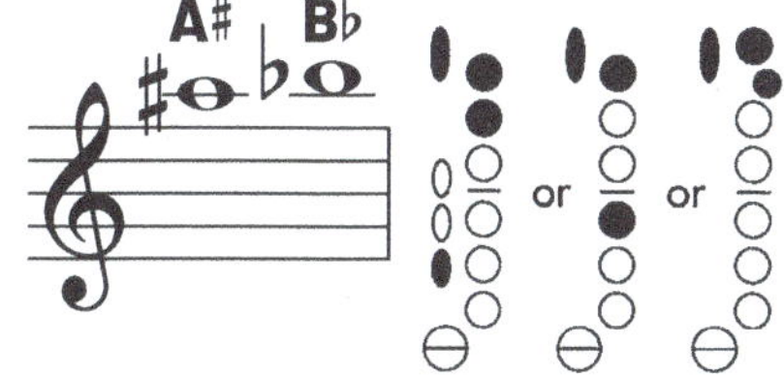

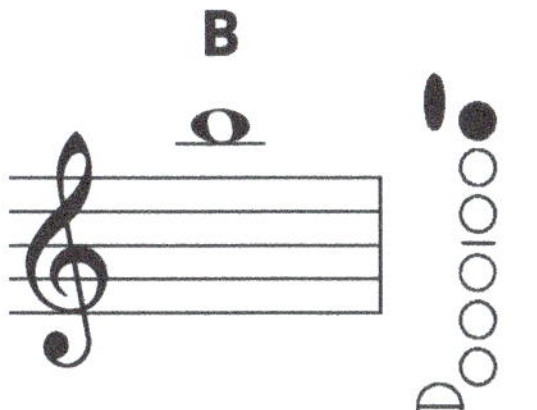

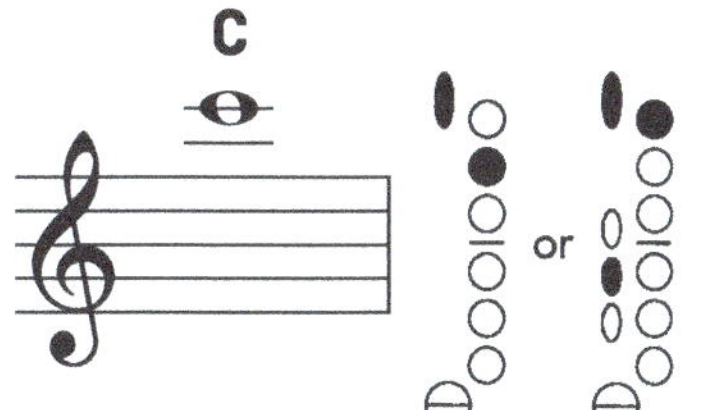

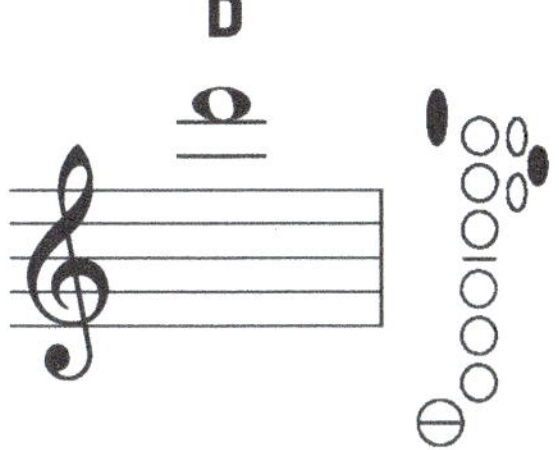

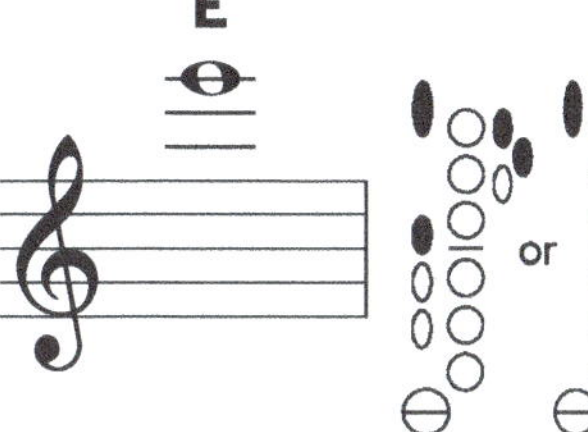

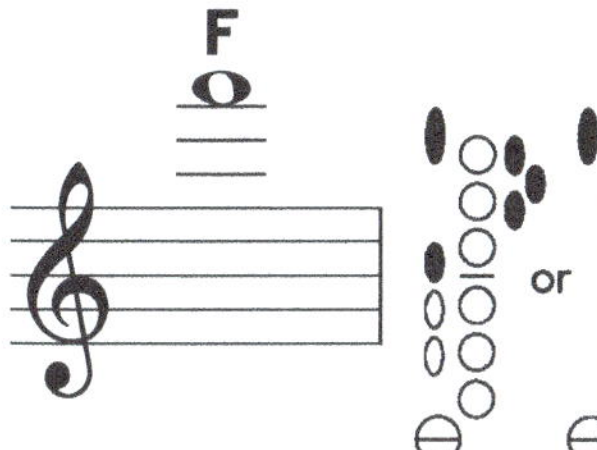

Student Book Page 46

FINGERING CHART

E♭ BARITONE SAXOPHONE

Instrument Care Reminders

Before putting your instrument back in its case after playing, do the following:

- Remove the reed, wipe off excess moisture and return it to the reed case.
- Remove the mouthpiece and wipe the inside with a clean cloth. Once a week, wash the mouthpiece with warm tap water. Dry thoroughly.
- Loosen the neck screw and remove the neck. Shake out excess moisture and dry the neck with a neck cleaner.
- Use a body swab to dry the inside of your instrument. Or, drop the weight of a chamois or cotton swab into the bell. Pull the swab through the body several times. Return the instrument to its case.
- Your case is designed to hold only specific objects. If you try to force anything else into the case, it may damage your instrument.

○ = Open

● = Pressed down

The most common fingering appears first when two fingerings are shown.

Instruments and photos courtesy of Yamaha.

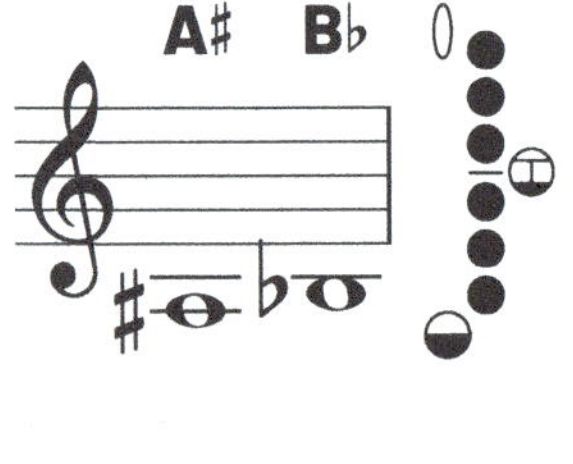

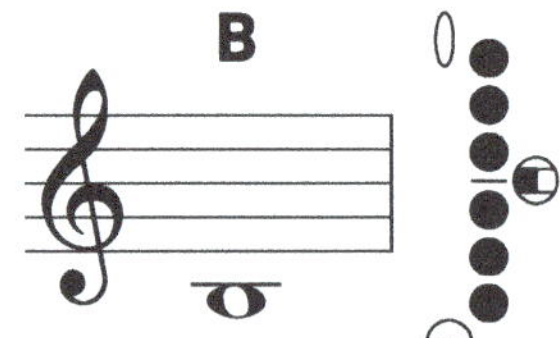

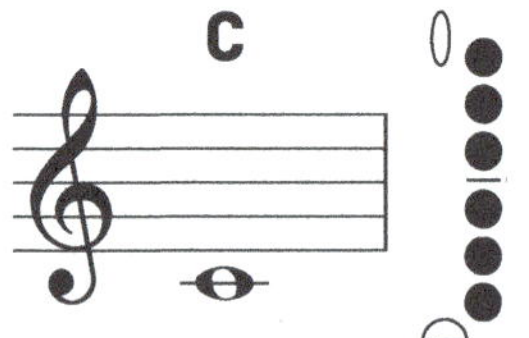

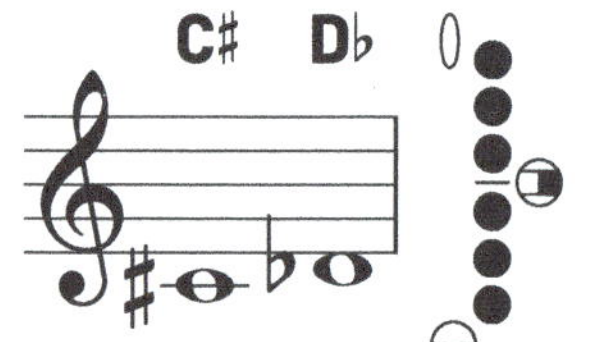

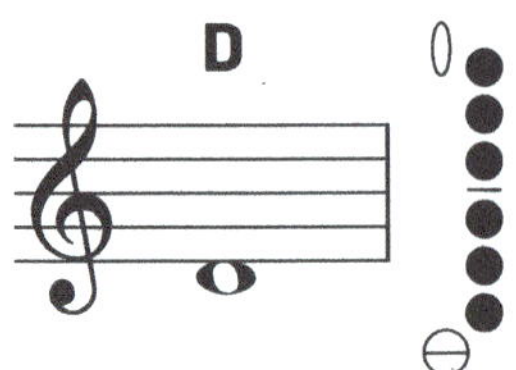

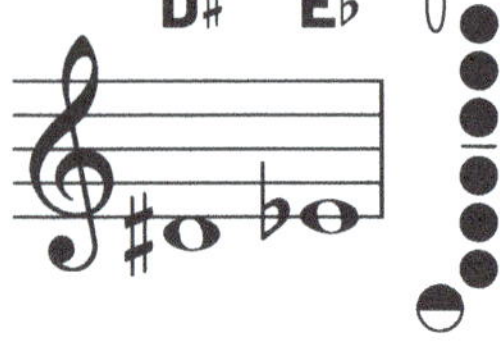

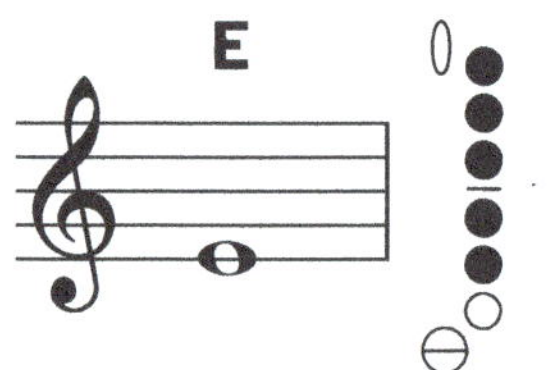

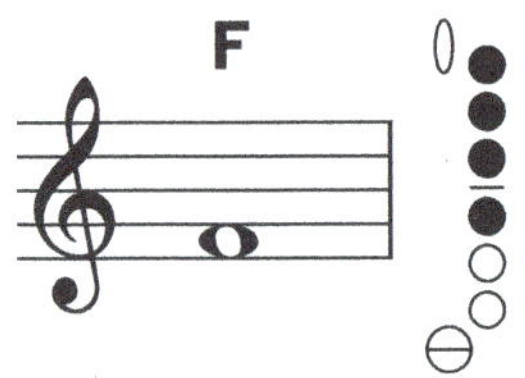

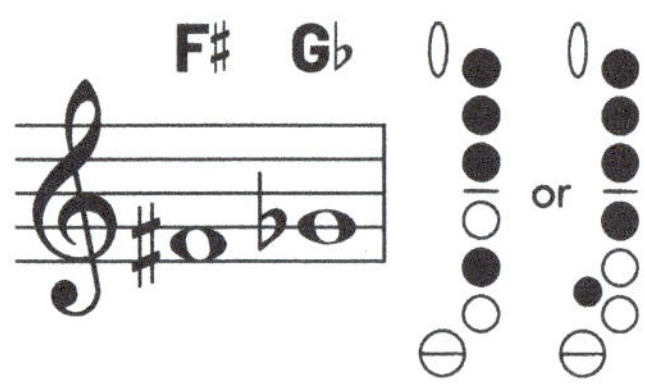

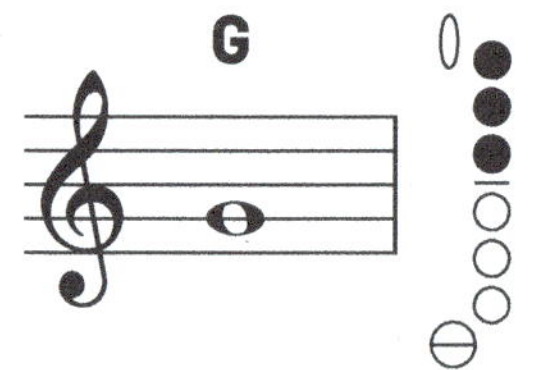

FINGERING CHART

E♭ BARITONE SAXOPHONE

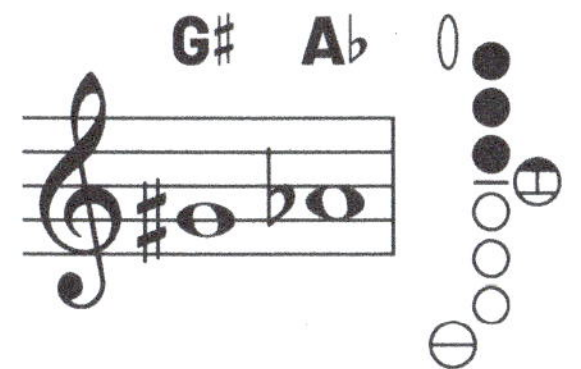

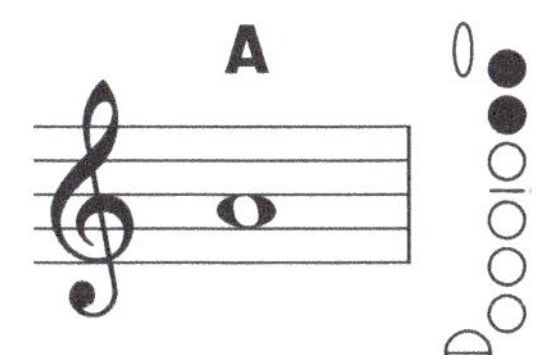

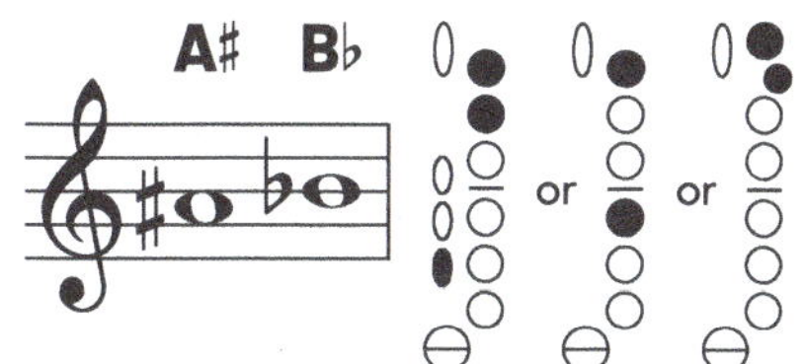

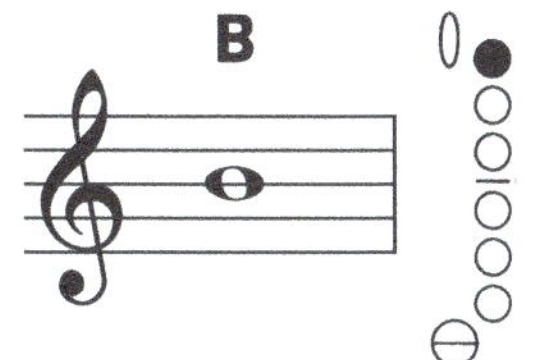

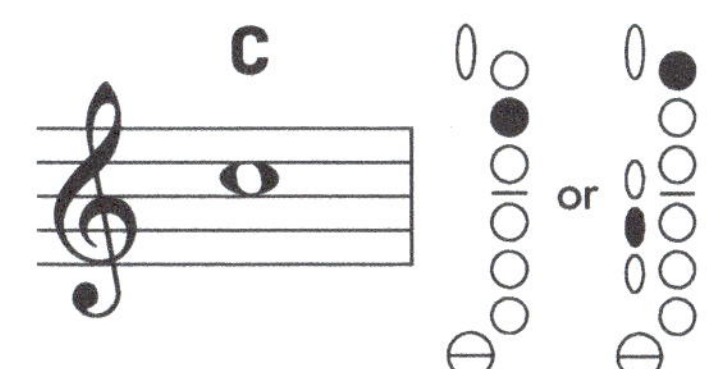

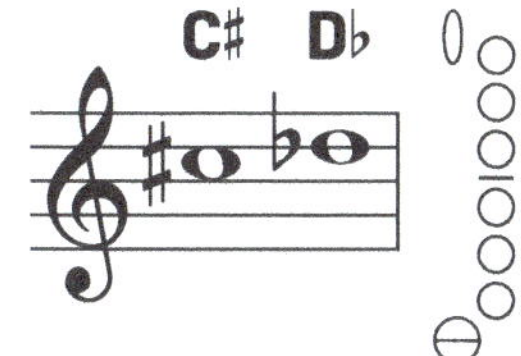

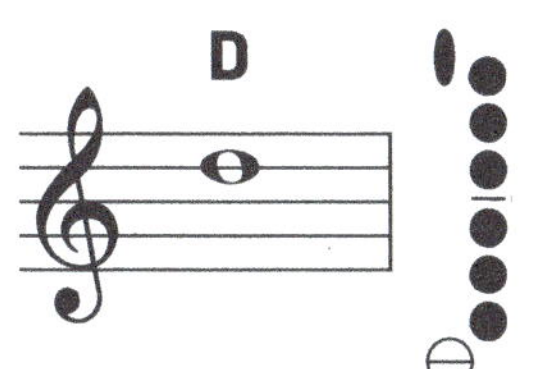

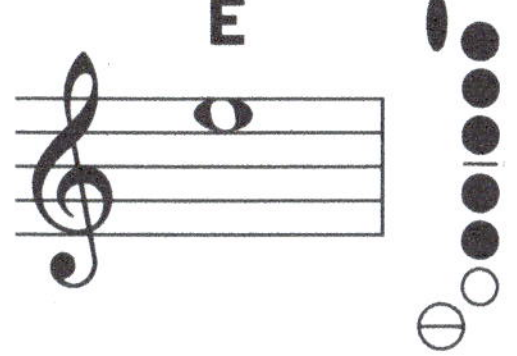

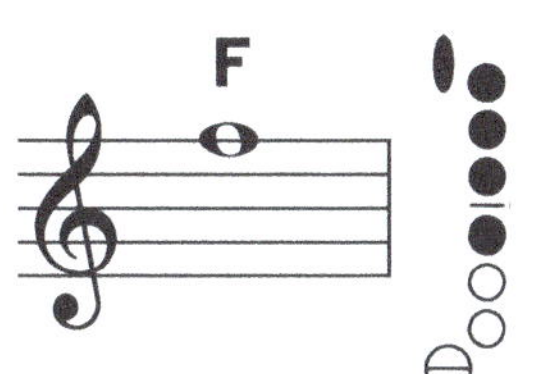

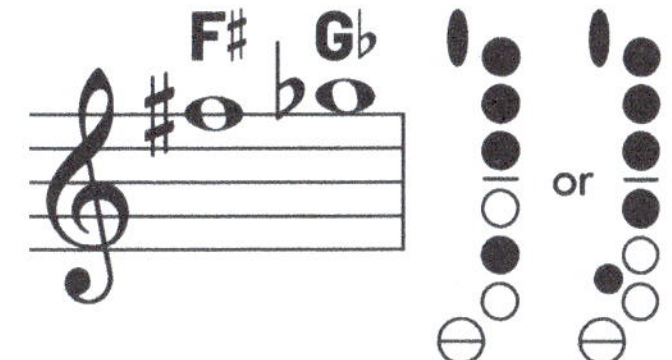

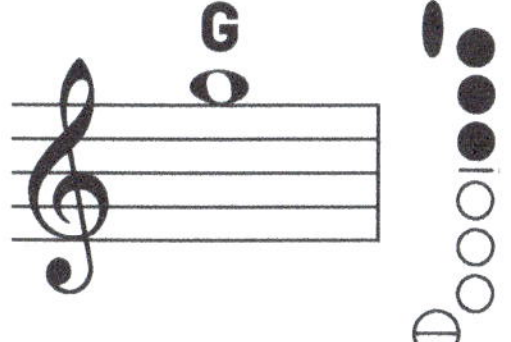

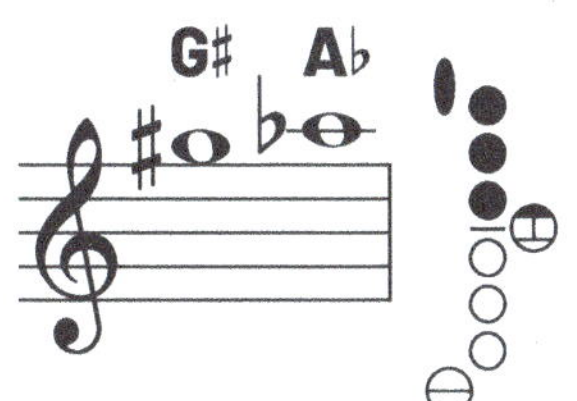

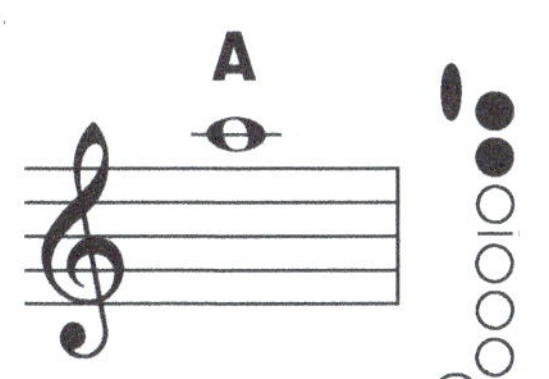

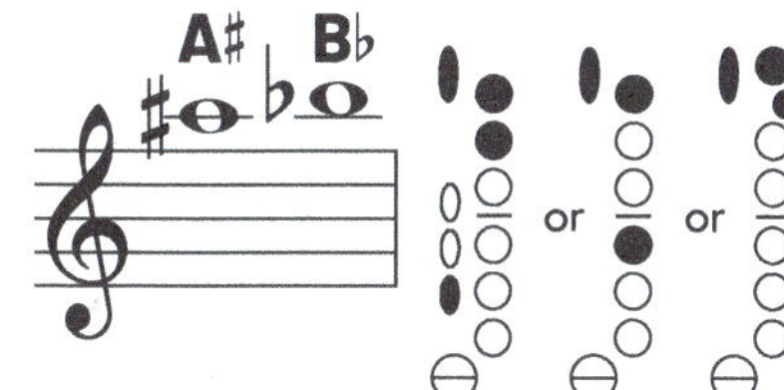

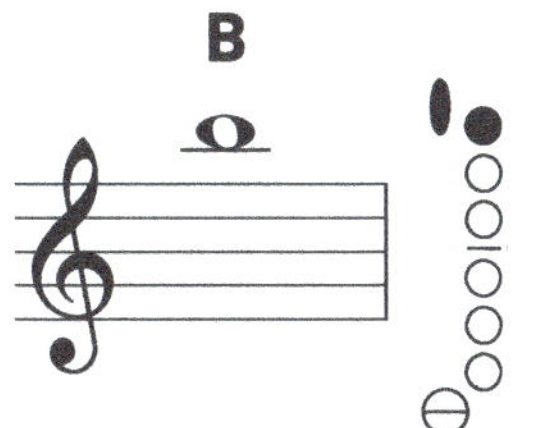

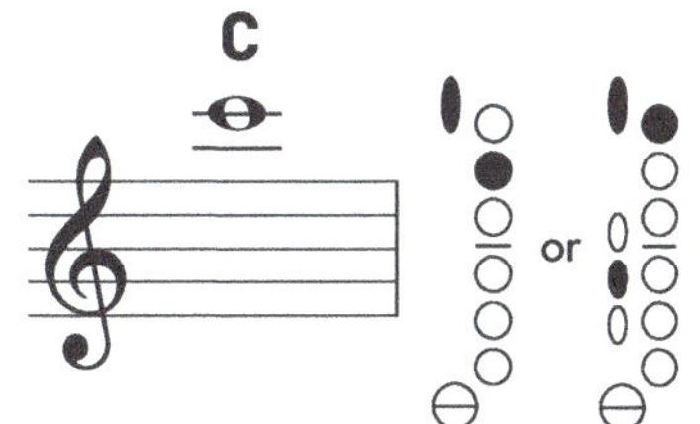

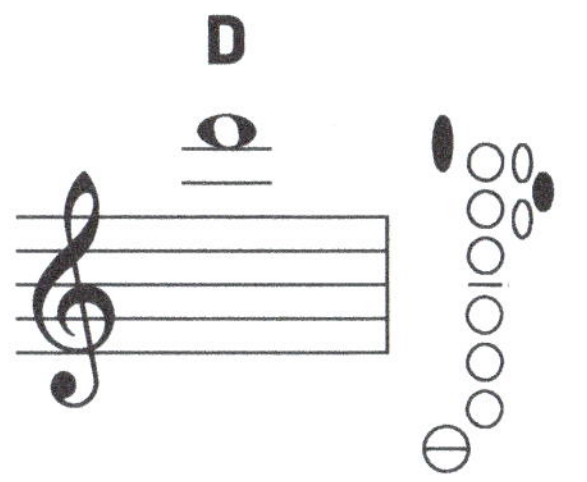

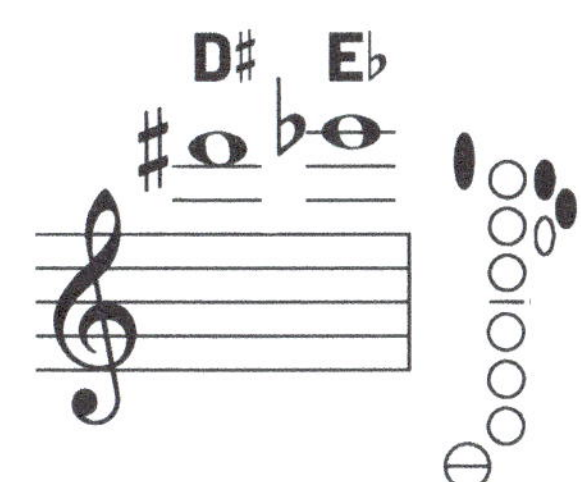

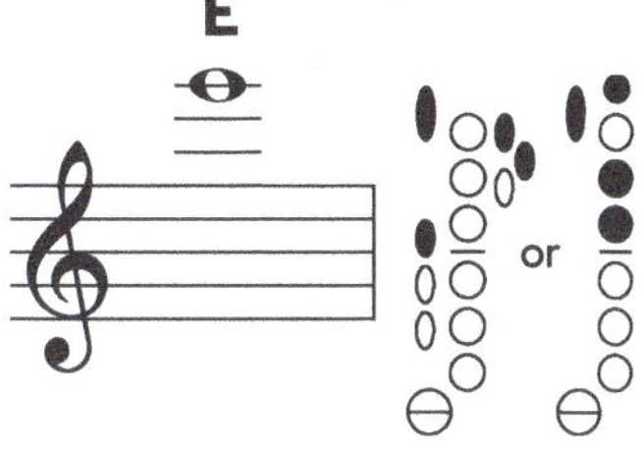

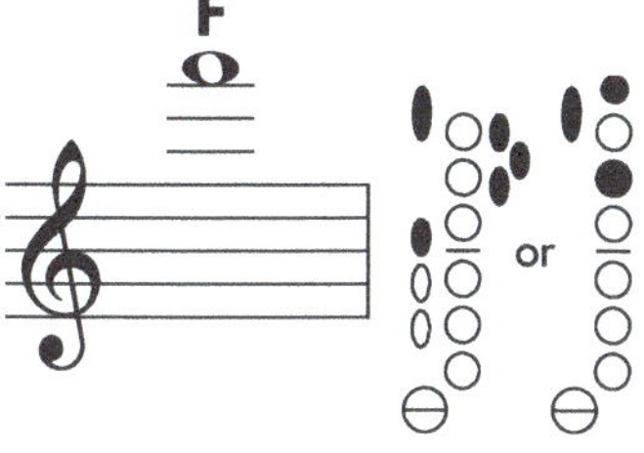

Student Book Page 46

FINGERING CHART

B♭ TRUMPET/ B♭ CORNET

Instrument Care Reminders

Before putting your instrument back in its case after playing, do the following:

- Use the water key to empty water from the instrument. Blow air through it.
- Remove the mouthpiece. Once a week, wash the mouthpiece with warm tap water. Dry thoroughly.
- Wipe off the instrument with a clean soft cloth. Return the instrument to its case.

Trumpet valves occasionally need oiling. To oil your trumpet valves:

- Unscrew the valve at the top of the casing.
- Lift the valve half-way out of the casing.
- Apply a few drops of special brass valve oil to the exposed valve.
- Carefully return the valve to its casing. When properly inserted, the top of the valve should easily screw back into place.

Be sure to grease the slides regularly. Your director will recommend special slide grease and valve oil, and will help you apply them when necessary.

CAUTION: If a slide, a valve or your mouthpiece becomes stuck, ask for help from your band director or music dealer. Special tools should be used to prevent damage to your instrument.

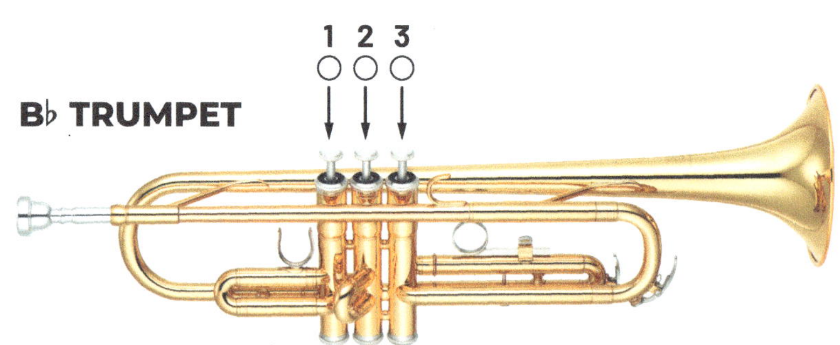

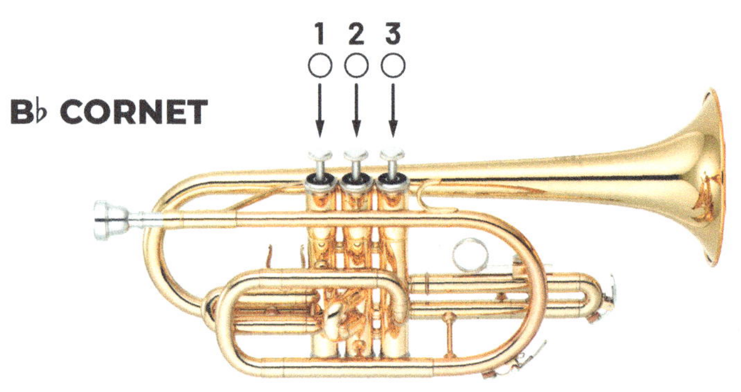

○ = Open

● = Pressed down

Instruments and photos courtesy of Yamaha.

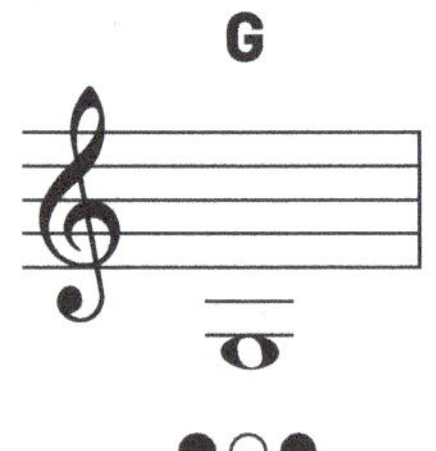

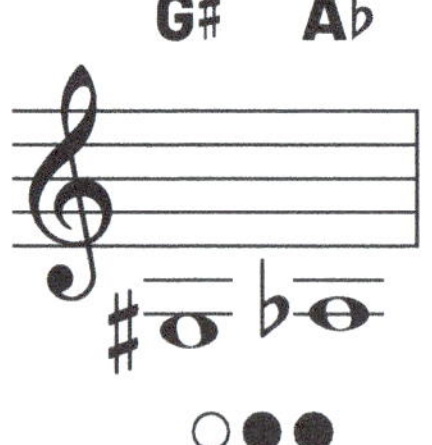

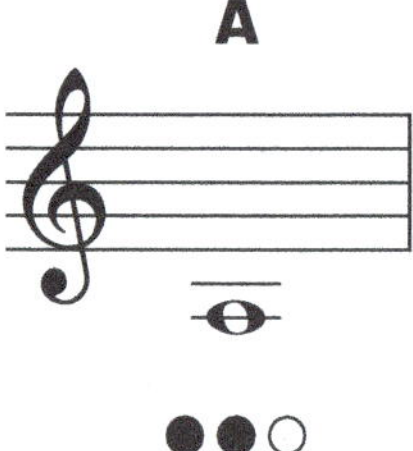

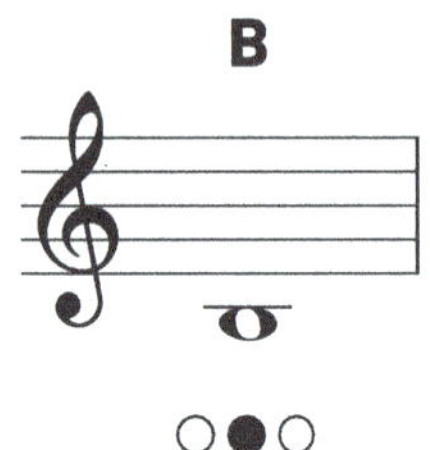

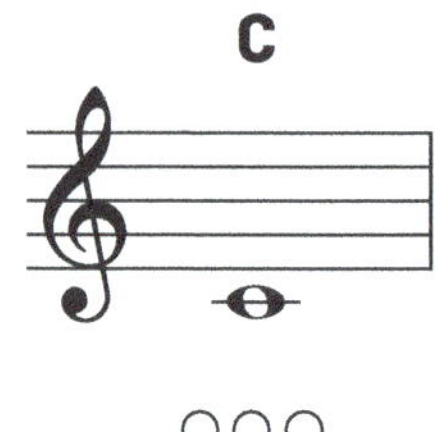

FINGERING CHART

B♭ TRUMPET/ B♭ CORNET

D

D♯ E♭

E

F

F♯ G♭

G

G♯ A♭

A

A♯ B♭

B

C

C♯ D♭

D

D♯ E♭

E

F

F♯ G♭

G

G♯ A♭

A

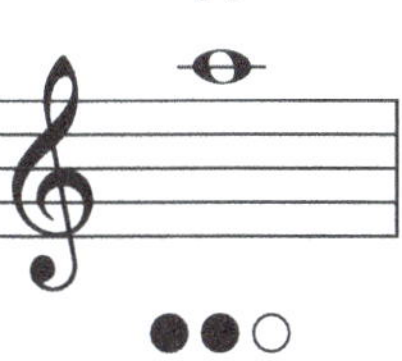

A♯ B♭

B

C

Student Book Page 46

FINGERING CHART

F HORN

Instrument Care Reminders

Before putting your instrument back in its case after playing, do the following:

- Use the water key to empty water from the instrument. Blow air through it. If your horn does not have a water key, invert the instrument. You may also remove the main tuning slide, invert the instrument and remove excess water.
- Wipe the instrument off with a clean soft cloth. Return the instrument to its case.
- Remove the mouthpiece. Once a week, wash the mouthpiece with warm tap water. Dry thoroughly.

Be sure to grease the slides regularly. Your director will recommend special slide grease and valve oil, and will help you apply them when necessary.

CAUTION: If a slide, a valve or your mouthpiece becomes stuck, ask for help from your band director or music dealer. Special tools should be used to prevent damage to your instrument.

Using the Correct Fingering

Single Horn Players

- F Horn players use the upper fingerings - marked "F Horn"
- B♭ Horn players use the lower fingerings - marked "B♭ Horn"
  *The trigger key (**T**) is only used on double horns.

Double Horn Players

- The trigger key (**T**) allows double horn players to switch between F and B♭ Horn
- Use the "F Horn" fingering when the trigger key is not pressed.
  *For notes without a "**T**" fingering, the F Horn fingering is the recommended double horn fingering for that note.
- Use the "B♭ Horn" fingering when the trigger key is pressed.
  *For notes with a "**T**" fingering, the B♭ Horn fingering is the recommended double horn fingering for that note.

○ = Open
● = Pressed down
T = Trigger (Double Horn Only)

Instruments and photos courtesy of Yamaha.

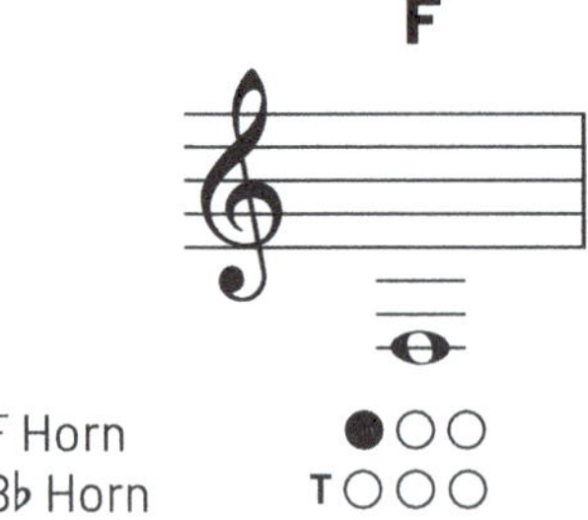

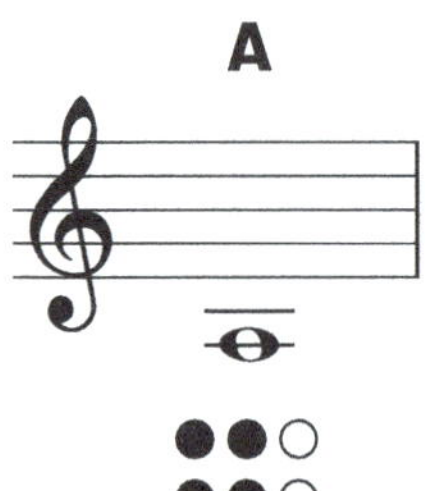

F Horn
B♭ Horn

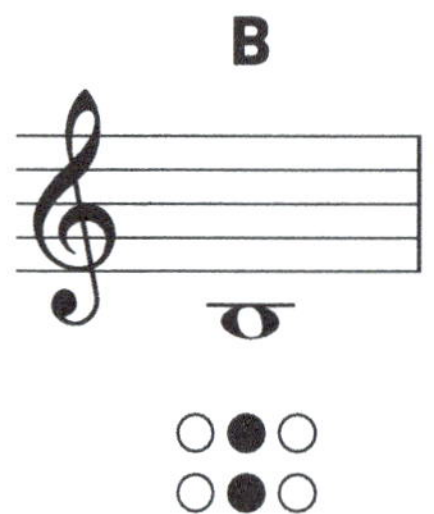

FINGERING CHART

F HORN

C♯ D♭

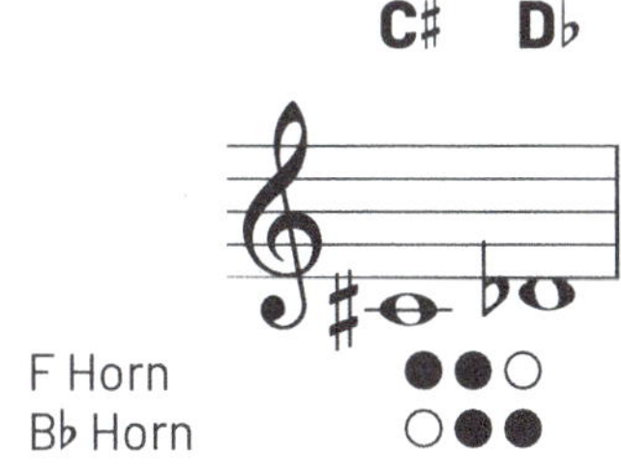

D

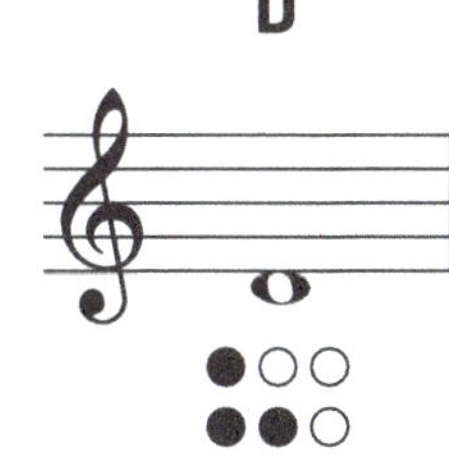

D♯ E♭

E

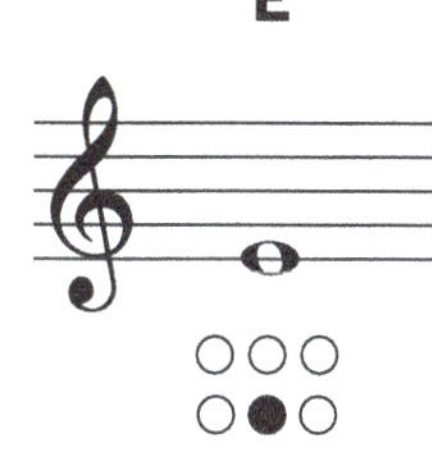

F

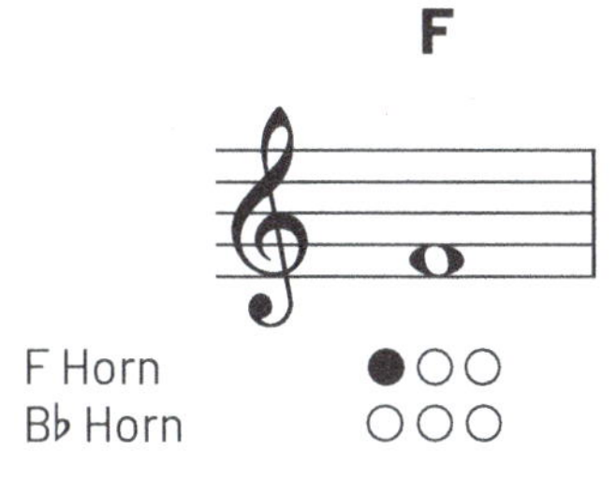

F♯ G♭

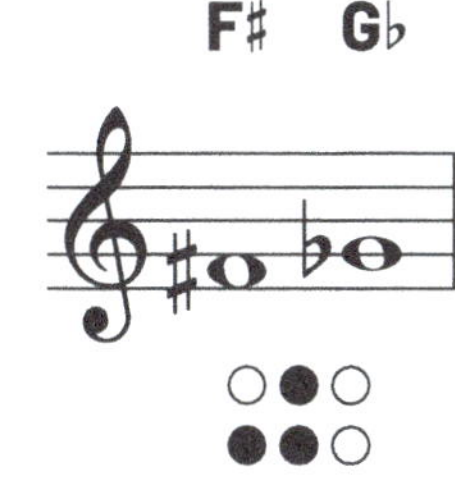

G

G♯ A♭

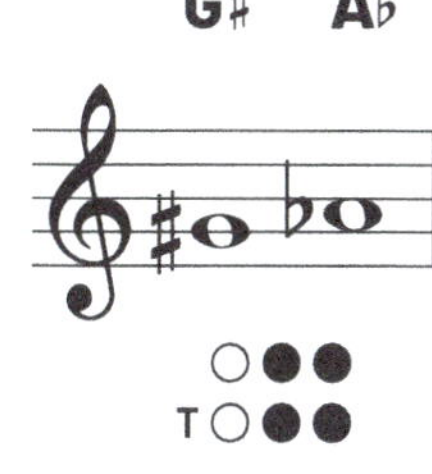

A

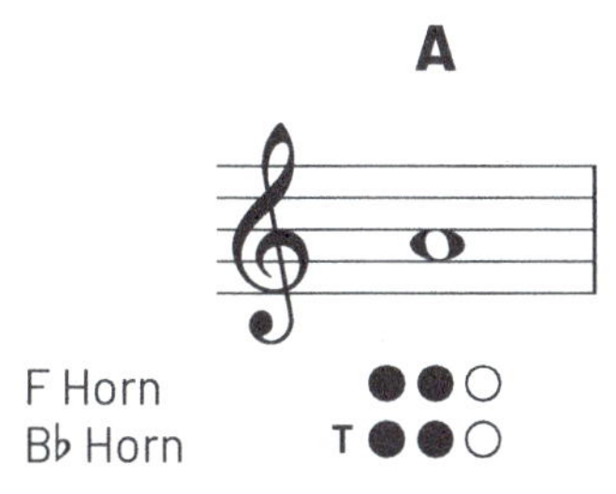

A♯ B♭

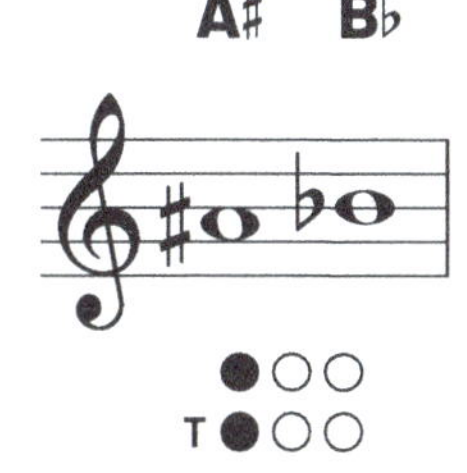

B

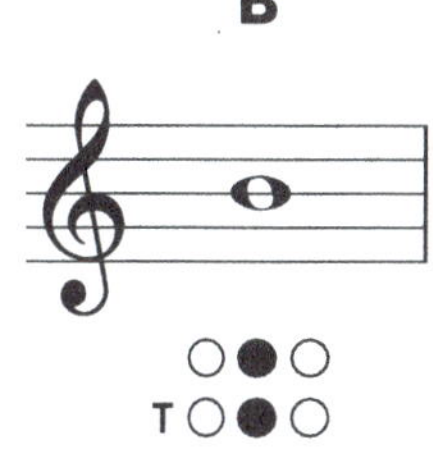

C

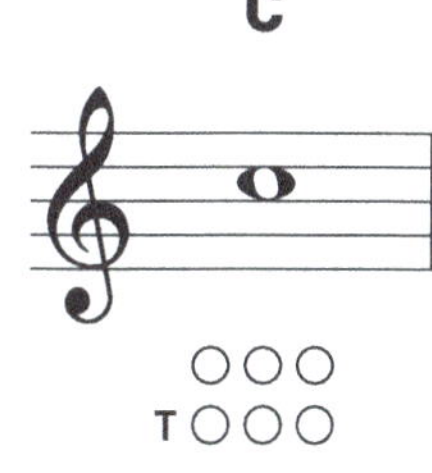

C♯ D♭

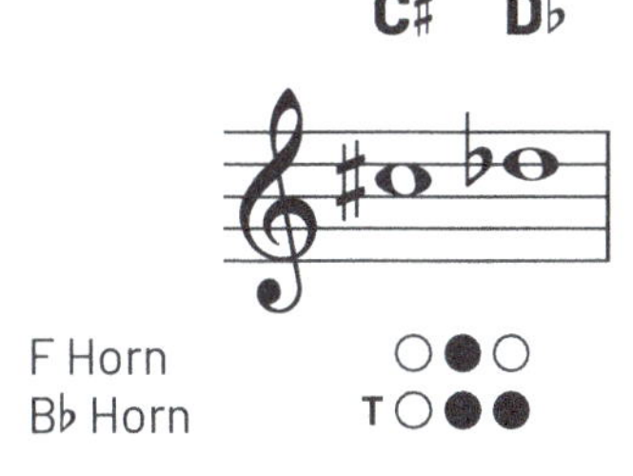

D

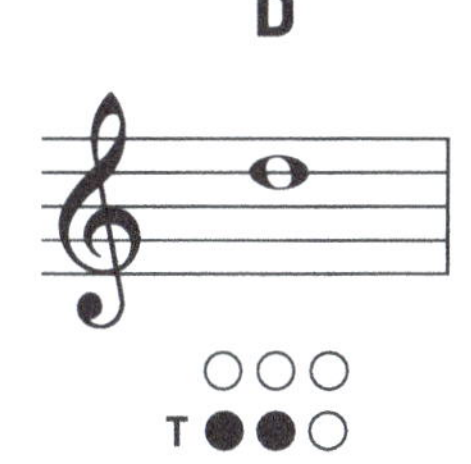

D♯ E♭

E

F

F♯ G♭

G

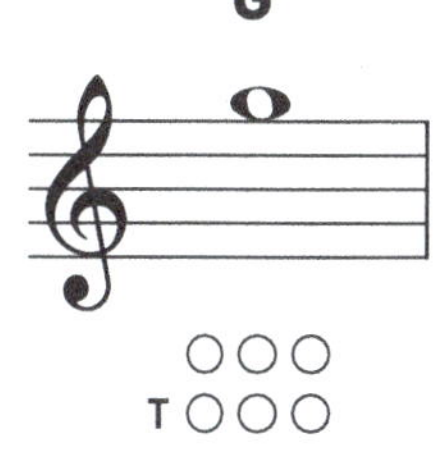

G♯ A♭

A

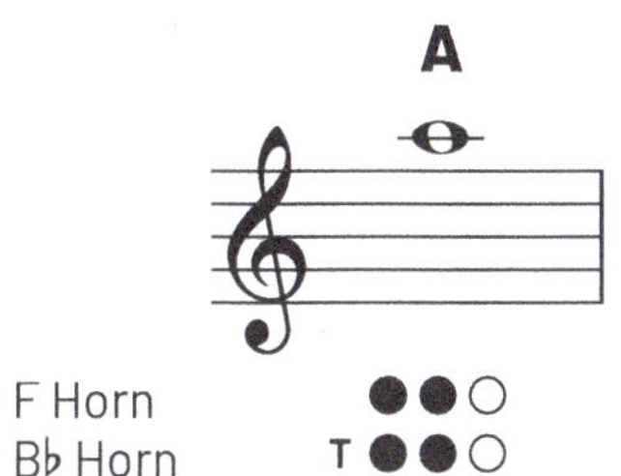

A♯ B♭

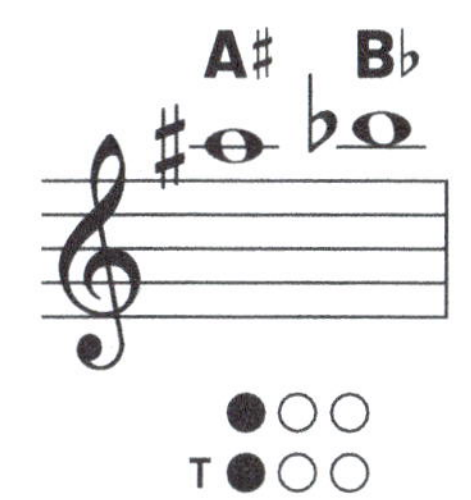

B

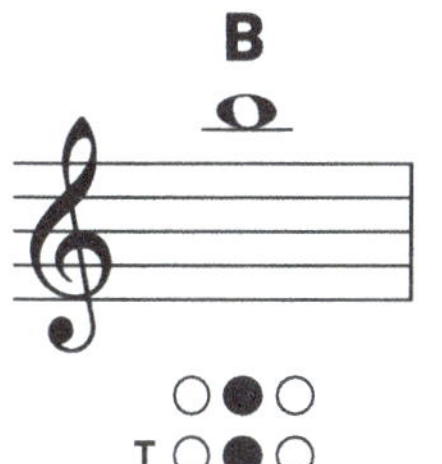

C

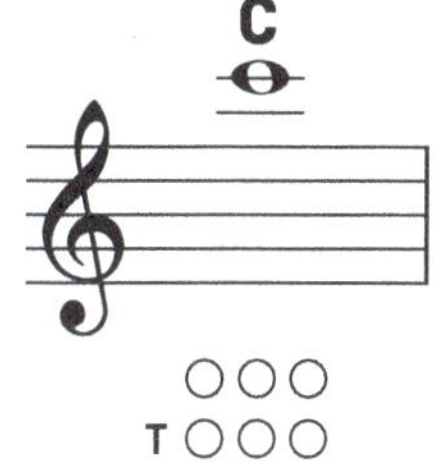

POSITION CHART

TROMBONE

Numbers below the notes = Slide positions

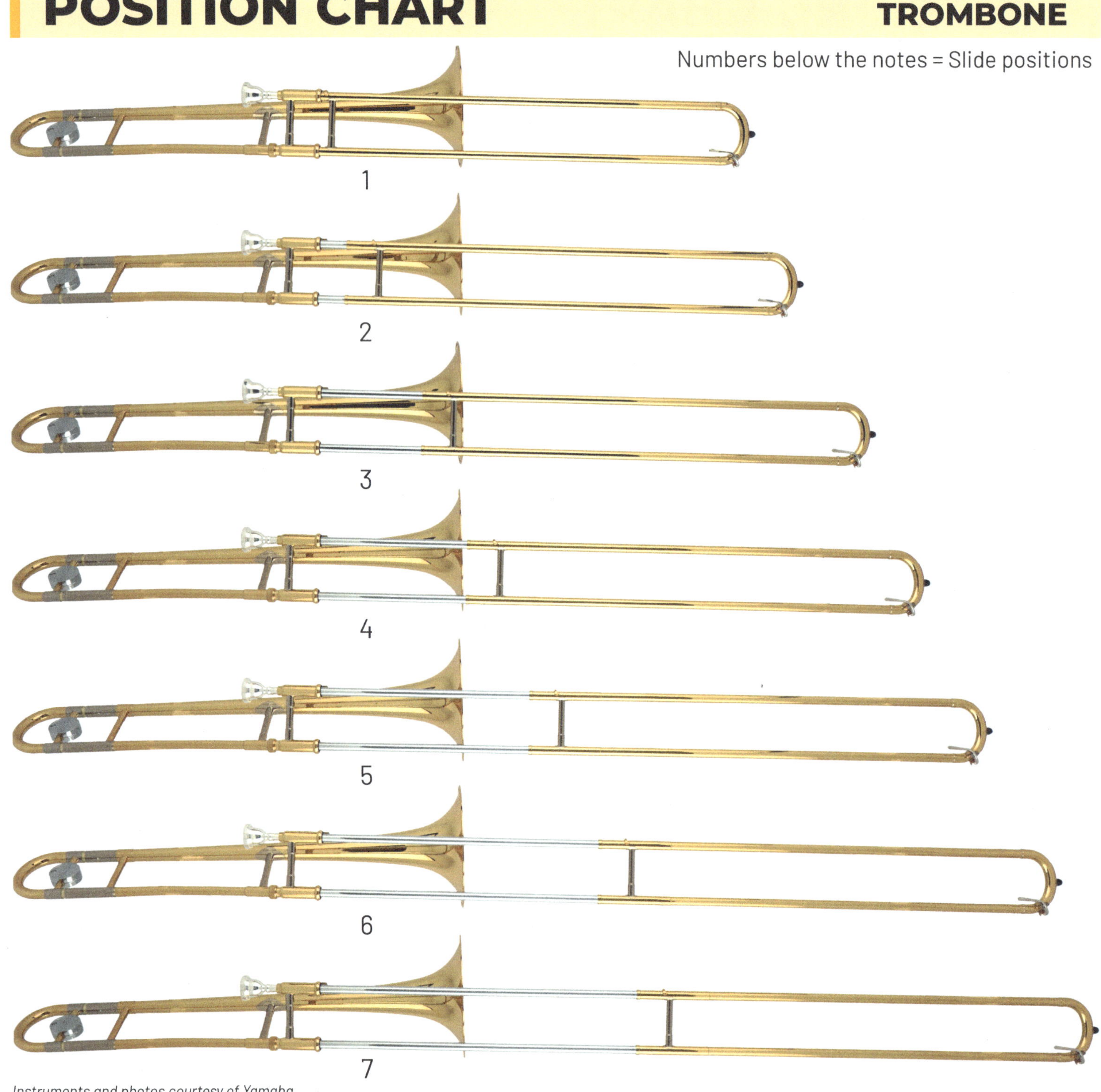

Instruments and photos courtesy of Yamaha.

Instrument Care Reminders

Before putting your instrument back in its case after playing, do the following:

- Use the water key to empty water from the instrument. Blow air through it.
- Remove the mouthpiece and slide assembly. Do not take the outer slide off the inner slide piece. Return the instrument to its case.
- Once a week, wash the mouthpiece with warm tap water. Dry thoroughly.

Trombone slides occasionally need oiling. To oil your slide, simply:

- Rest the tip of the slide on the floor and unlock the slide.
- Exposing the inner slide, put a few drops of oil on the inner slide.
- Rapidly move the slide back and forth. The oil will then lubricate the slide.
- Be sure to grease the tuning slide regularly. Your director will recommend special slide oil and grease, and will help you apply them when necessary.

CAUTION: If a slide or your mouthpiece becomes stuck, ask for help from your band director or music dealer. Special tools should be used to prevent damage to your instrument.

POSITION CHART

TROMBONE

E
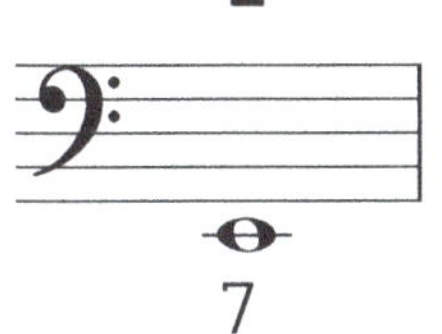
7

F

6

F♯ G♭

5

G

4

G♯ A♭
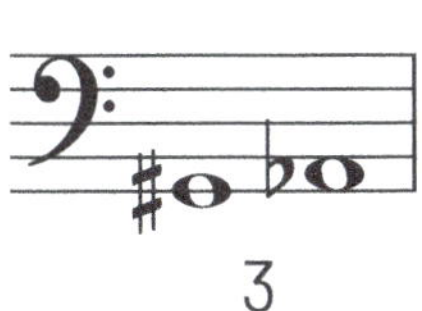
3

A

2

A♯ B♭
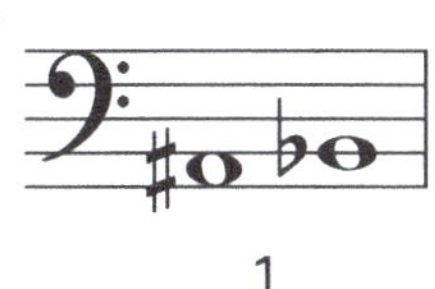
1

B

7

C
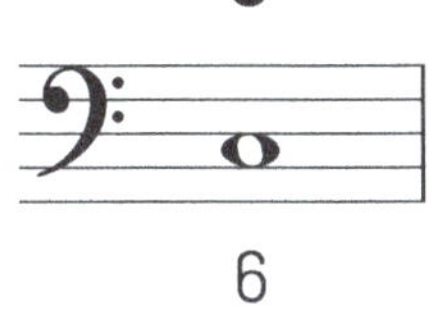
6

C♯ D♭
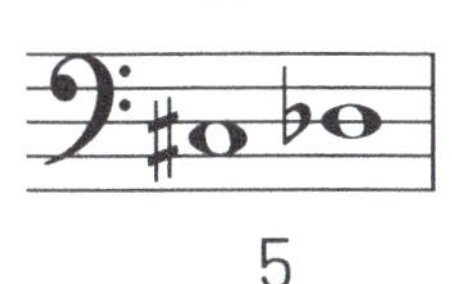
5

D
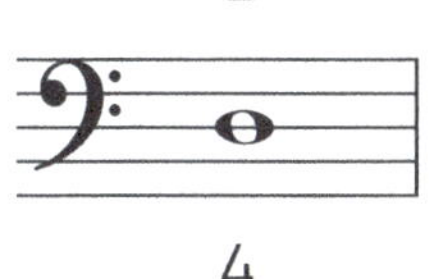
4

D♯ E♭
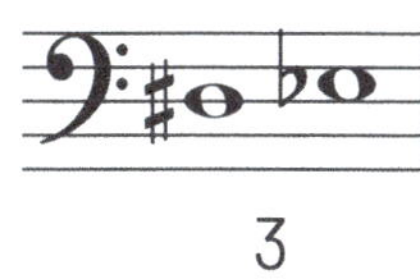
3

E
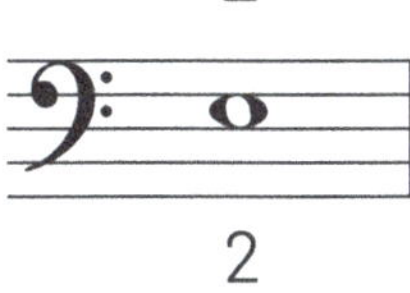
2

F
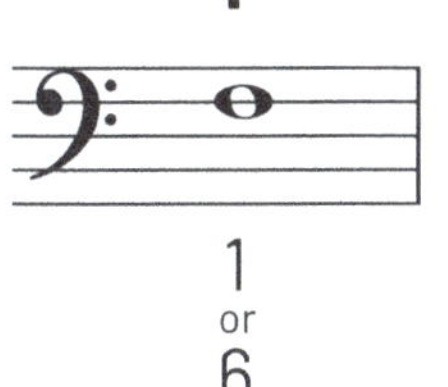
1 or 6

F♯ G♭
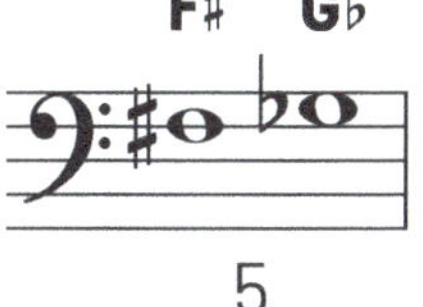
5

G
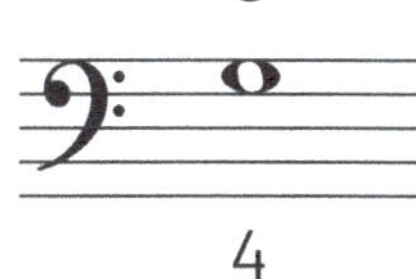
4

G♯ A♭
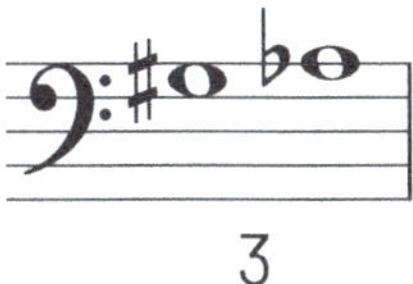
3

A
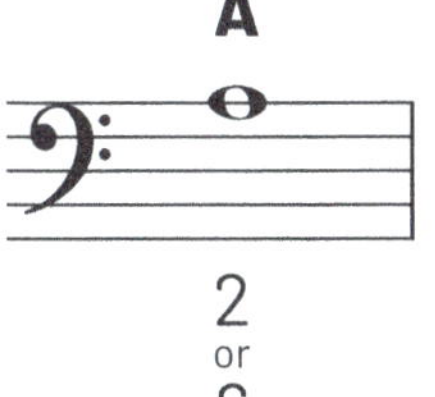
2 or 6

A♯ B♭
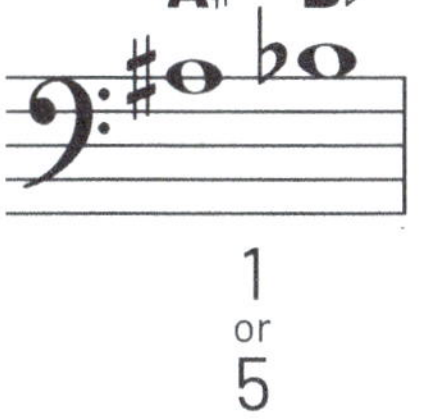
1 or 5

B
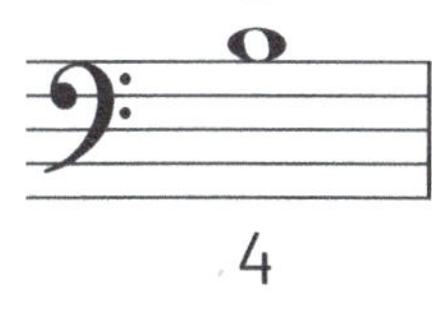
4

C

3

C♯ D♭

2

D
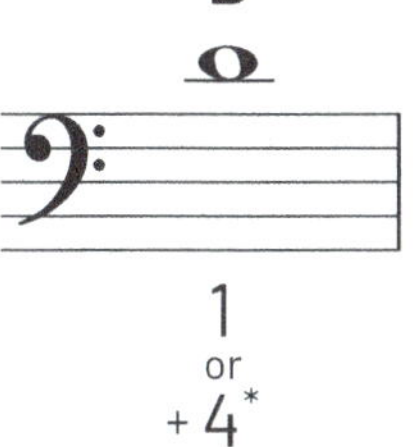
1 or +4*

D♯ E♭

3

E

2

F
1

F♯ G♭

-3**

G
-2

* + = Make the slide a little longer.
** - = Make the slide a little shorter.

FINGERING CHART

BARITONE B.C.

Instrument Care Reminders

Before putting your instrument back in its case after playing, do the following:

- Use the water key to empty water from the instrument. Blow air through it.
- Remove the mouthpiece. Once a week, wash the mouthpiece with warm tap water. Dry thoroughly.
- Wipe off the instrument with a clean soft cloth. Return the instrument to its case.

Baritone valves occasionally need oiling. To oil your baritone valves:

- Unscrew the valve at the top of the casing.
- Lift the valve half-way out of the casing.
- Apply a few drops of special brass valve oil to the exposed valve.
- Carefully return the valve to its casing. When properly inserted, the top of the valve should easily screw back into place.

Be sure to grease the slides regularly. Your director will recommend special slide grease and valve oil, and will help you apply them when necessary.

CAUTION: If a slide, a valve or your mouthpiece becomes stuck, ask for help from your band director or music dealer. Special tools should be used to prevent damage to your instrument.

Instruments and photos courtesy of Yamaha.

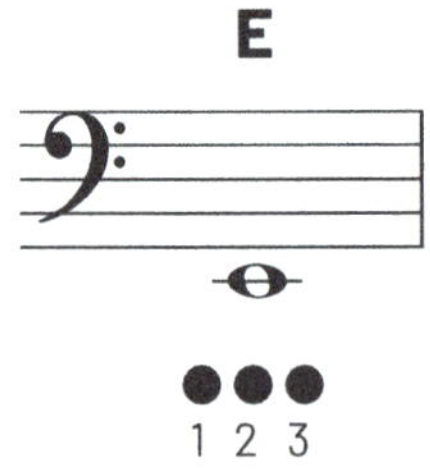

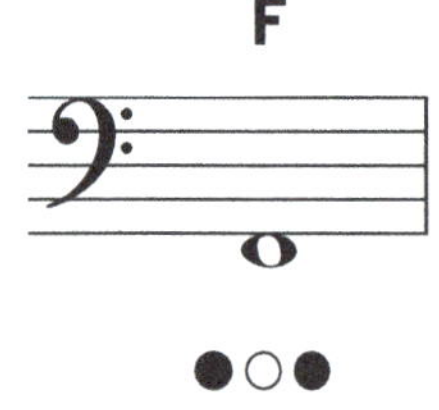

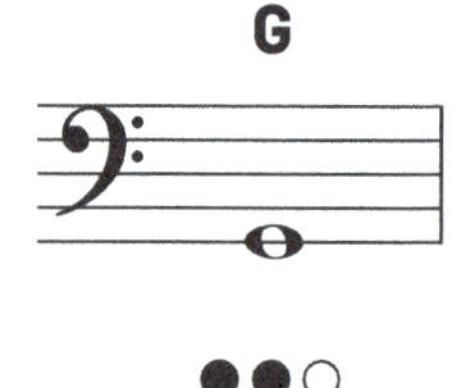

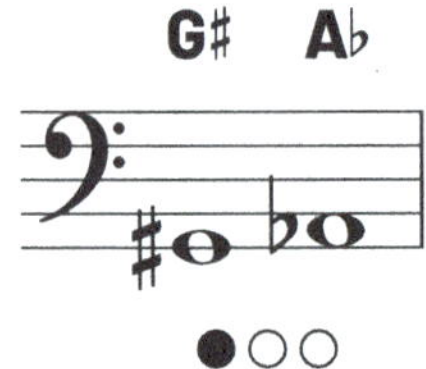

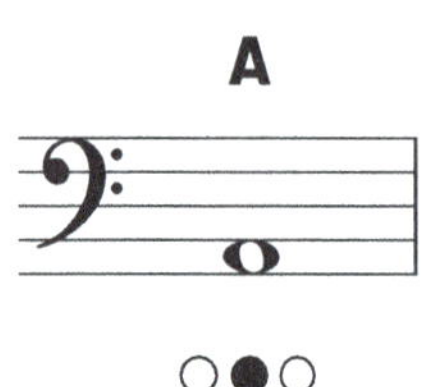

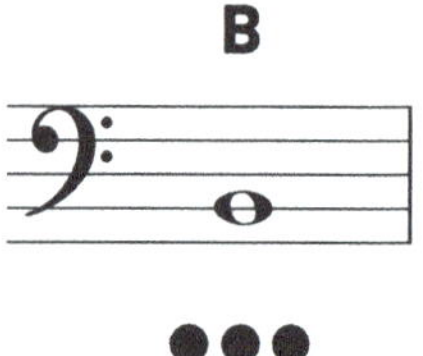

FINGERING CHART

BARITONE B.C.

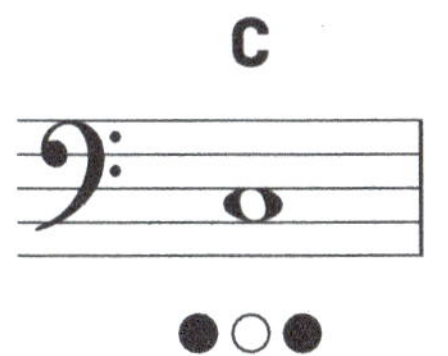

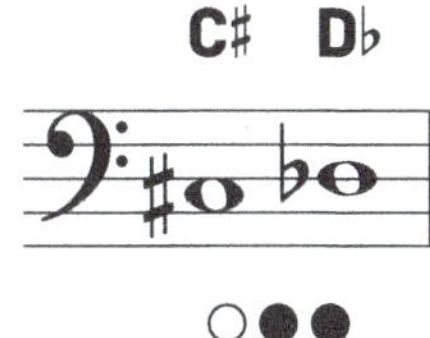

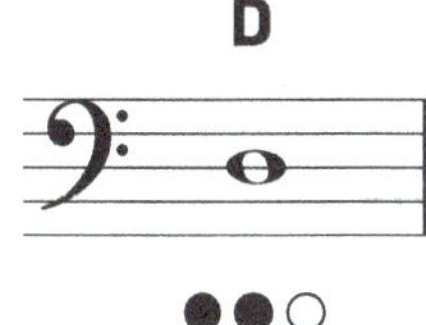

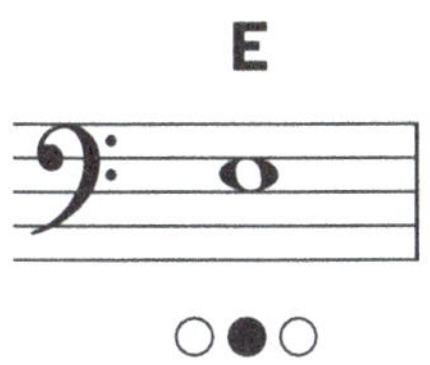

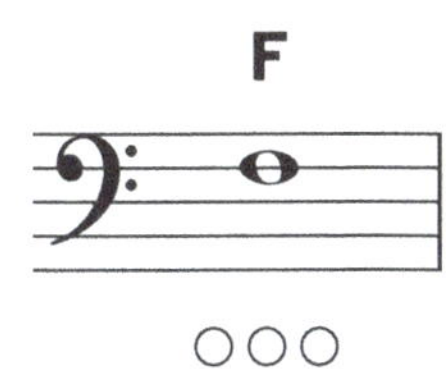

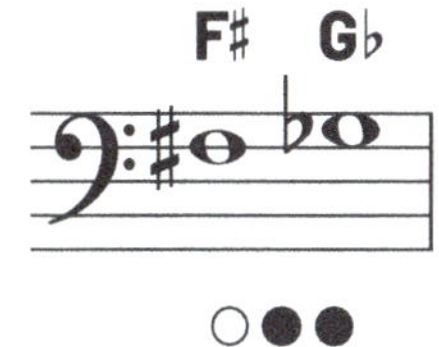

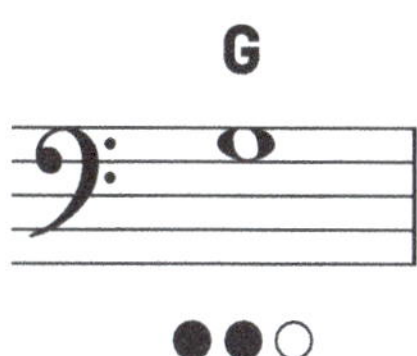

G♯ A♭

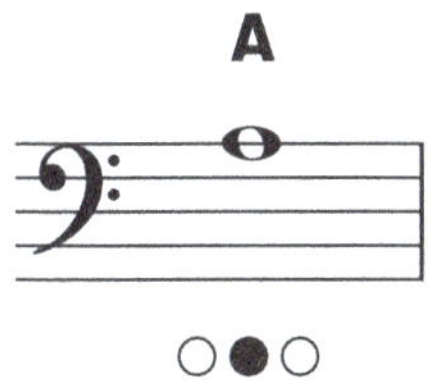

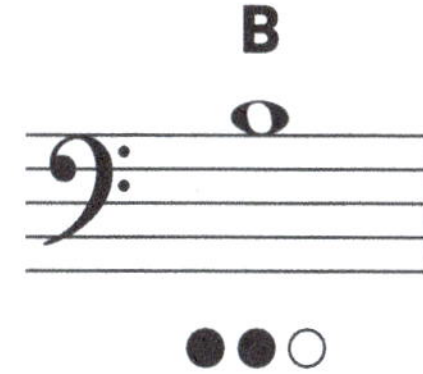

C

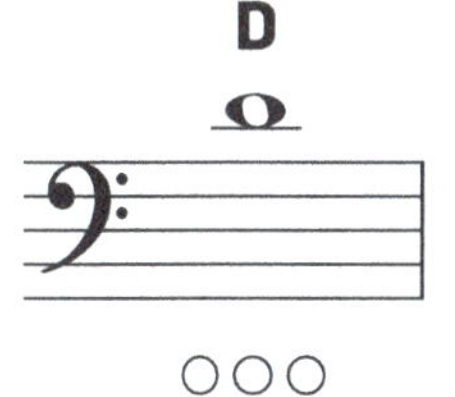

D♯ E♭

E

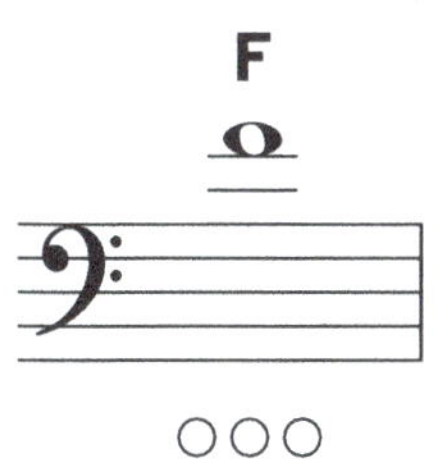

FINGERING CHART

BARITONE T.C.

Instrument Care Reminders

Before putting your instrument back in its case after playing, do the following:

- Use the water key to empty water from the instrument. Blow air through it.
- Remove the mouthpiece. Once a week, wash the mouthpiece with warm tap water. Dry thoroughly.
- Wipe off the instrument with a clean soft cloth. Return the instrument to its case.

Baritone valves occasionally need oiling. To oil your baritone valves:

- Unscrew the valve at the top of the casing.
- Lift the valve half-way out of the casing.
- Apply a few drops of special brass valve oil to the exposed valve.
- Carefully return the valve to its casing. When properly inserted, the top of the valve should easily screw back into place.

Be sure to grease the slides regularly. Your director will recommend special slide grease and valve oil, and will help you apply them when necessary.

CAUTION: If a slide, a valve or your mouthpiece becomes stuck, ask for help from your band director or music dealer. Special tools should be used to prevent damage to your instrument.

3 2 1

○ = Open

● = Pressed down

Instruments and photos courtesy of Yamaha.

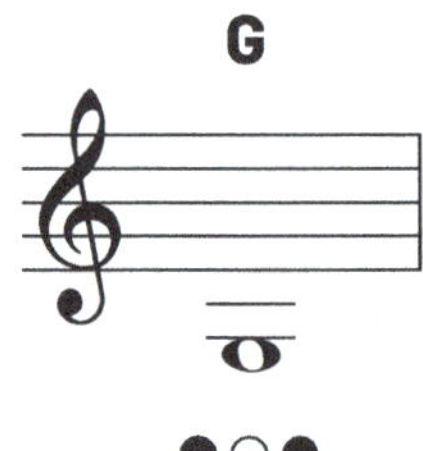

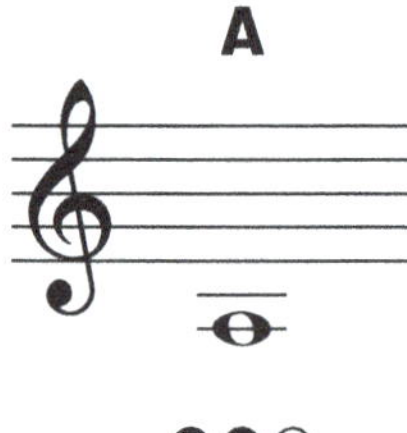

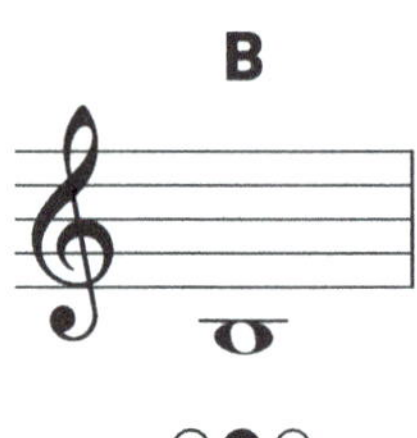

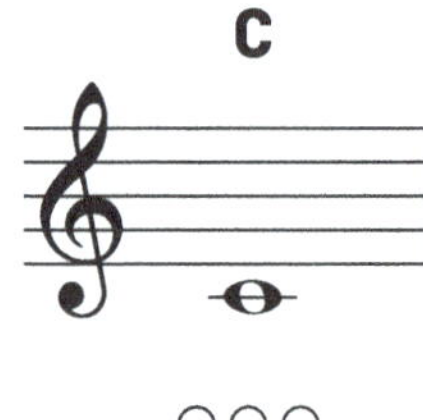

FINGERING CHART

BARITONE T.C.

D

●○●

D♯ E♭

○●●

E

●●○

F

●○○

F♯ G♭

○●○

G

○○○

G♯ A♭

○●●

A

●●○

A♯ B♭

●○○

B

○●○

C

○○○

C♯ D♭

●●○

D

●○○

D♯ E♭

○●○

E

○○○

F

●○○

F♯ G♭

○●○

G

○○○

G♯ A♭

○●●

A

●●○

A♯ B♭

●○○

B

○●○

C

○○○

Student Book Page 46

FINGERING CHART

TUBA

Instrument Care Reminders

Before putting your instrument back in its case after playing, do the following:

- Use the water key to empty water from the instrument. Blow air through it.
- Remove the mouthpiece. Once a week, wash the mouthpiece with warm tap water. Dry thoroughly.
- Wipe off the instrument with a clean soft cloth. Return the instrument to its case.

Tuba valves occasionally need oiling. To oil your tuba valves:

- Unscrew the valve at the top of the casing.
- Lift the valve half-way out of the casing.
- Apply a few drops of special brass valve oil to the exposed valve.
- Carefully return the valve to its casing. When properly inserted, the top of the valve should easily screw back into place.

Be sure to grease the slides regularly. Your director will recommend special slide grease and valve oil, and will help you apply them when necessary.

CAUTION: If a slide, a valve or your mouthpiece becomes stuck, ask for help from your band director or music dealer. Special tools should be used to prevent damage to your instrument.

3 2 1

○ = Open

● = Pressed down

Instruments and photos courtesy of Yamaha.

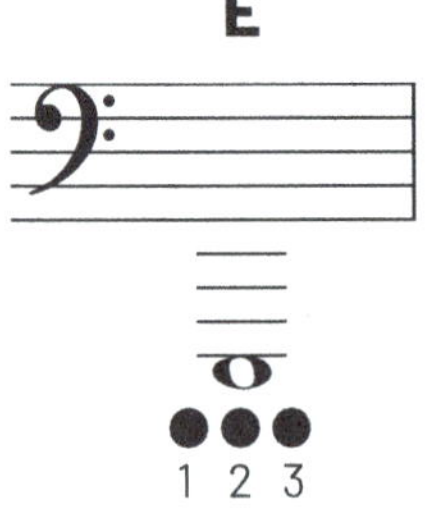

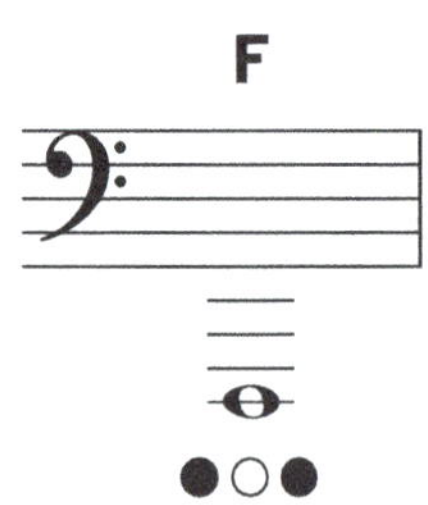

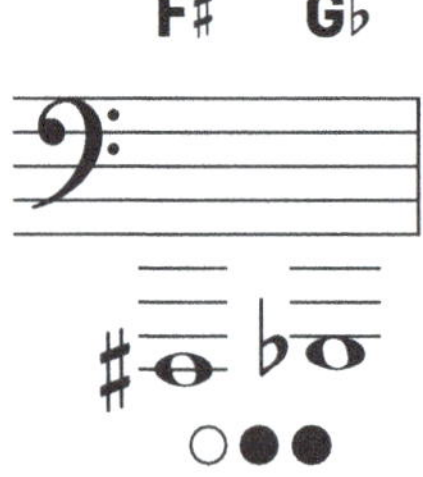

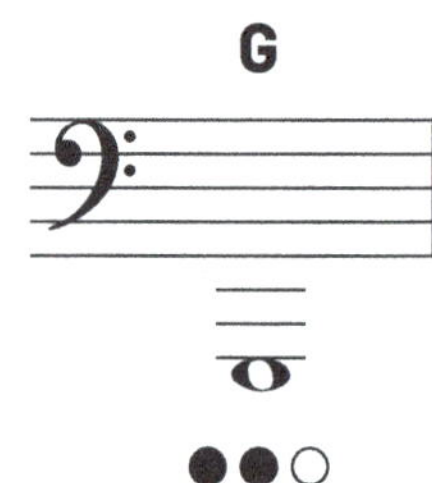

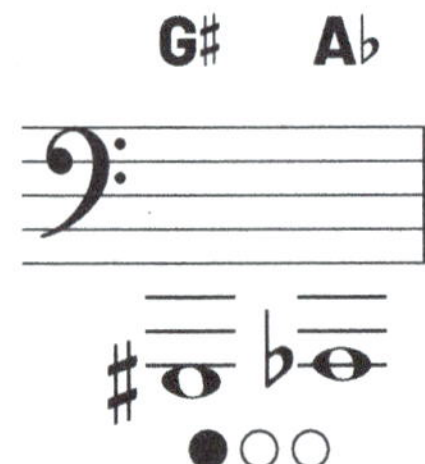

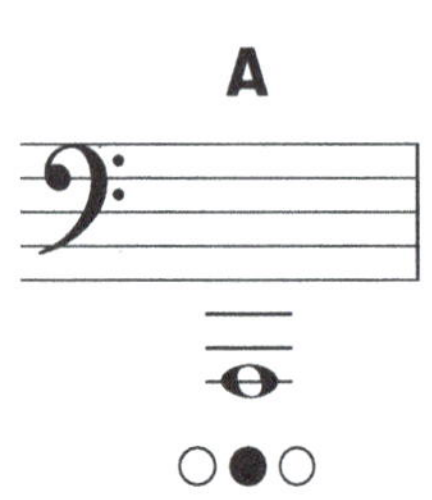

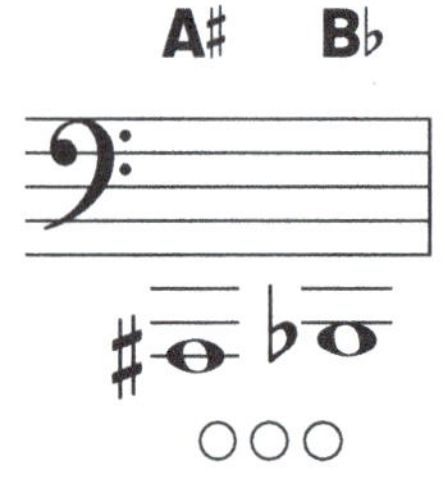

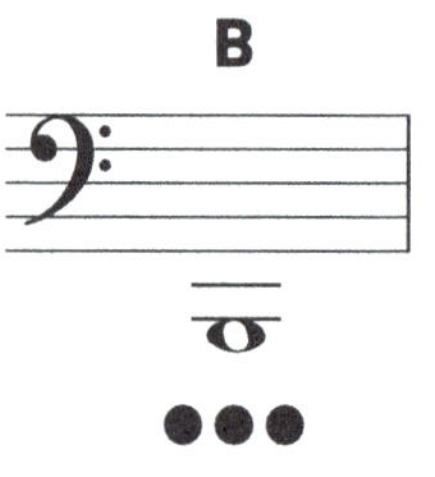

FINGERING CHART

TUBA

C

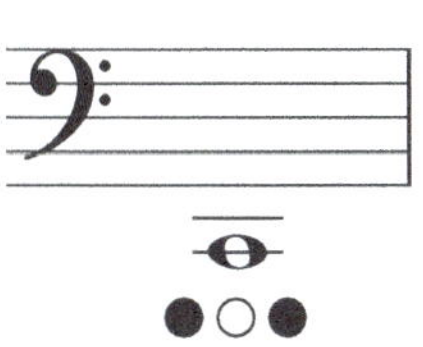

C♯ D♭

D

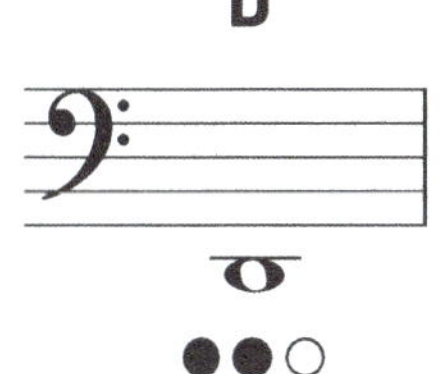

D♯ E♭

E

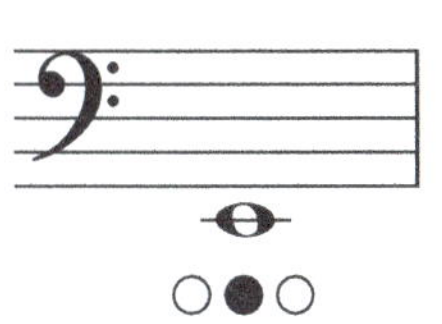

F

F♯ G♭

G

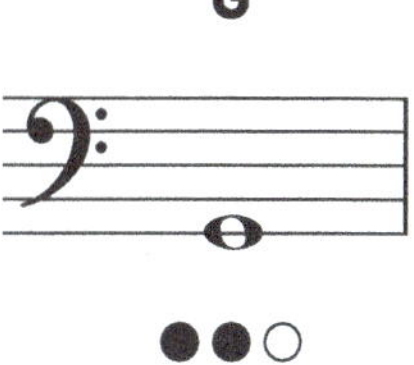

G♯ A♭

A

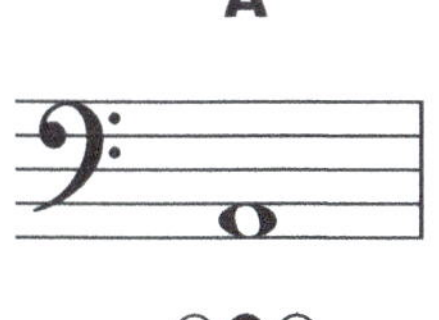

A♯ B♭

B

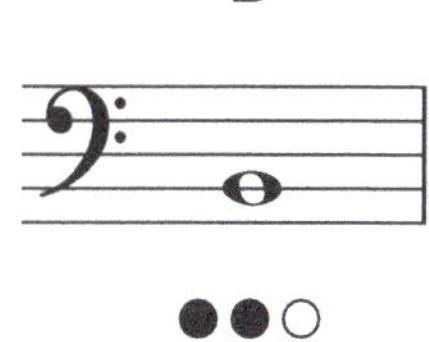

C

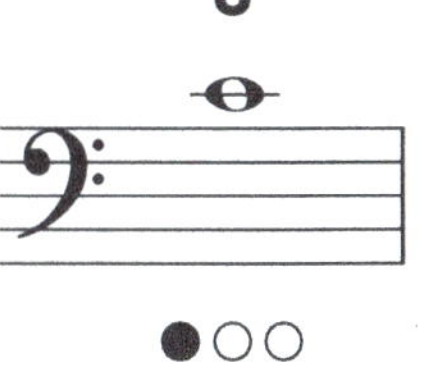

C♯ D♭

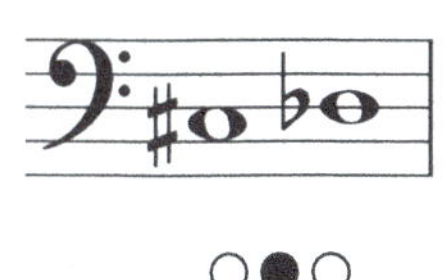

D

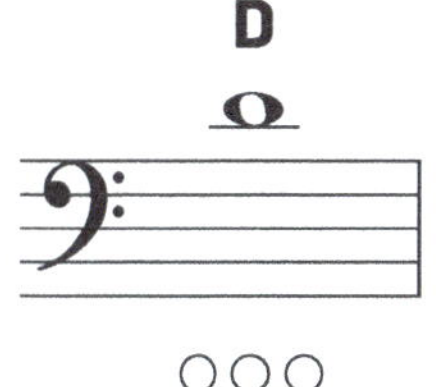

D♯ E♭

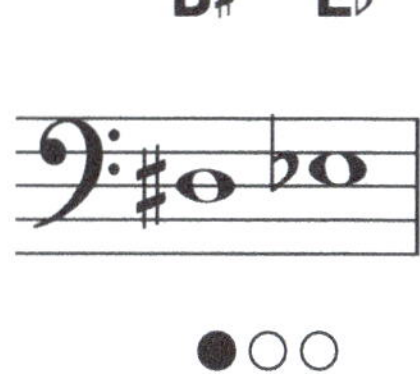

E

F

F♯ G♭

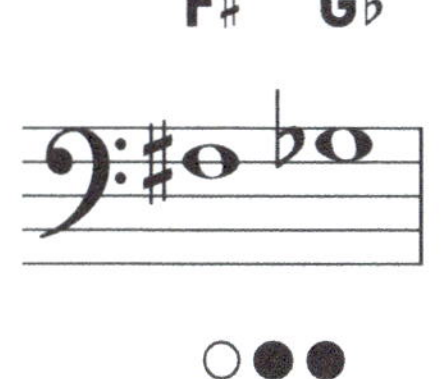

G

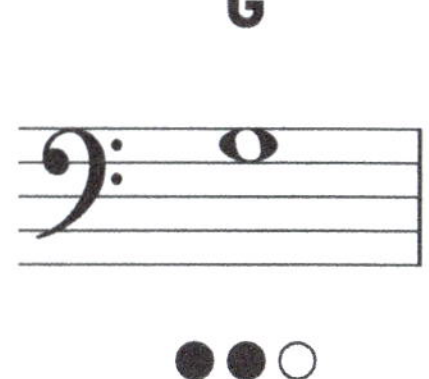

G♯ A♭

A

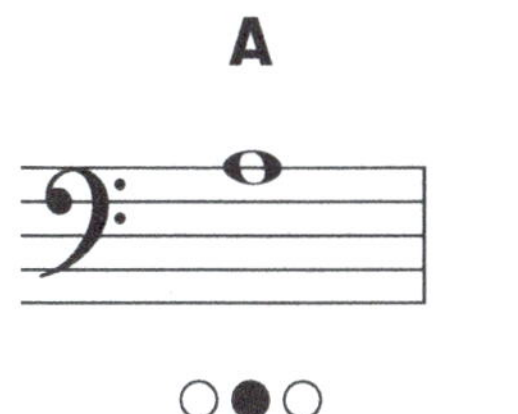

A♯ B♭

FINGERING CHART

ELECTRIC BASS

Instrument Care Reminders

- Be sure your amplifier is turned off before plugging-in or unplugging the audio cable connecting it to your instrument.
- When unplugging a cable, hold it by the plug (not by the wire).
- After playing, wipe off the instrument and strings with a clean soft cloth. Return the instrument to its case.
- Close all the latches on your case when the instrument is inside.
- Keep all 4 strings in tune (at normal tension) to prevent warping of the neck.
- Your case is designed to hold only specific objects. If you force anything else into the case, it may damage your instrument.

strings

4th 3rd 2nd 1st

frets

1st

2nd

3rd

4th

5th

Fingerboard diagrams show where to play the notes. Circles are drawn on the diagram to indicate the fingers to be used to play the notes.

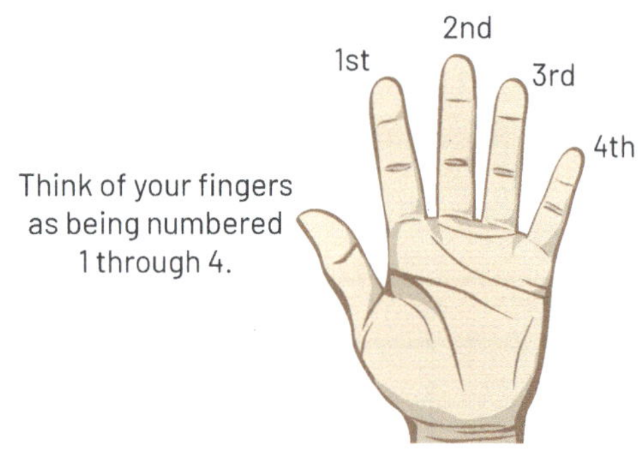

Think of your fingers as being numbered 1 through 4.

Instruments and photos courtesy of Yamaha.

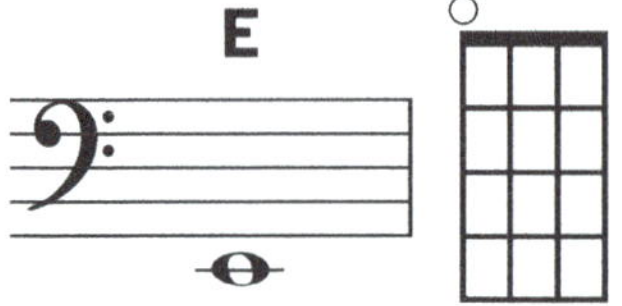

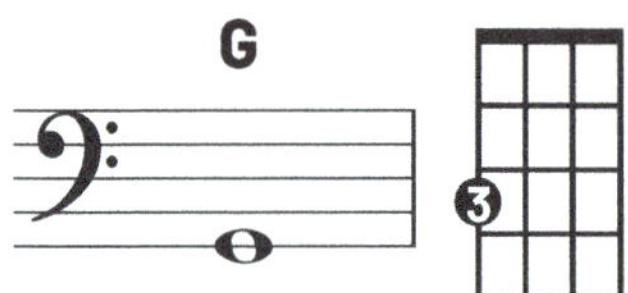

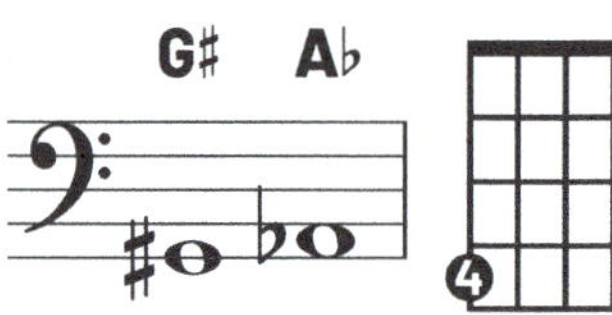

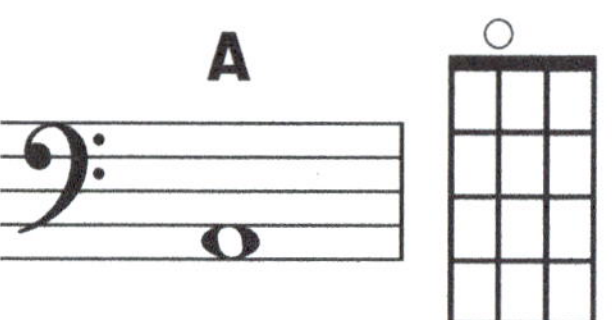

FINGERING CHART

ELECTRIC BASS

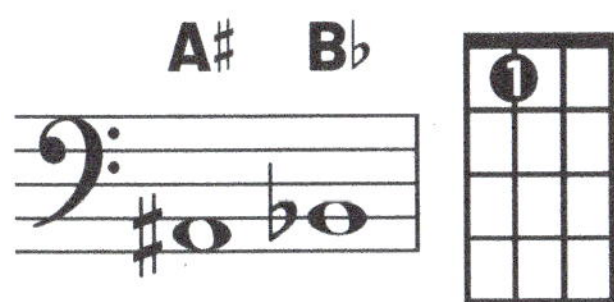

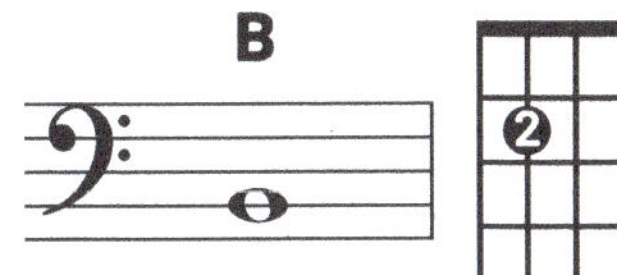

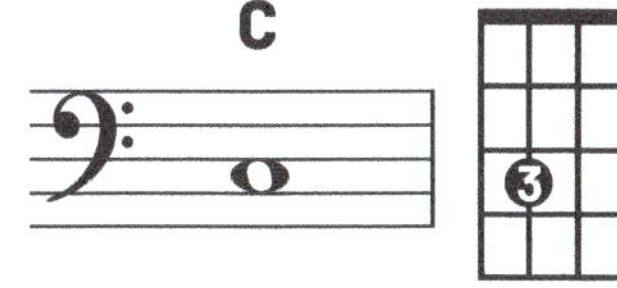

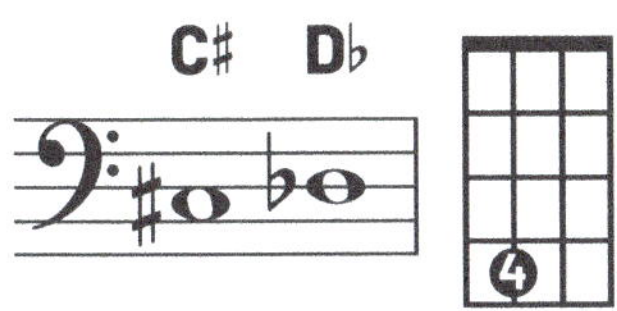

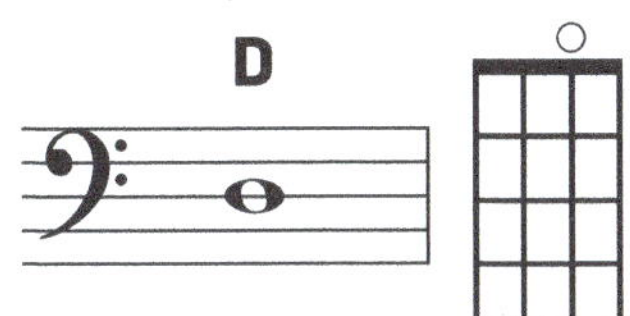

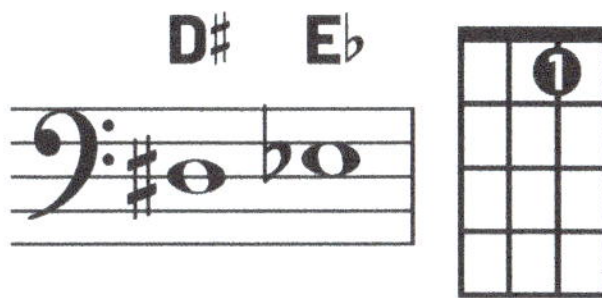

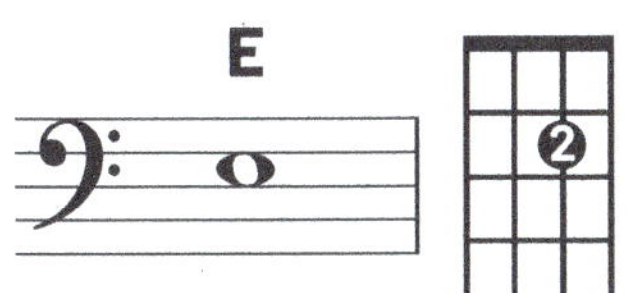

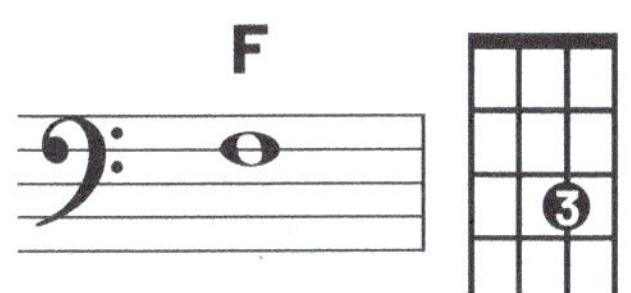

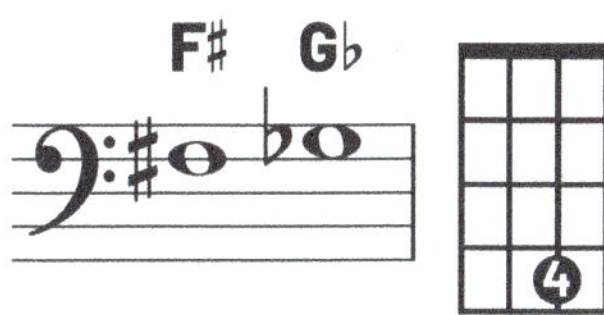

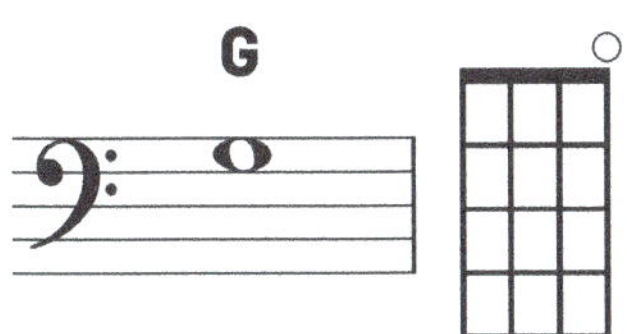

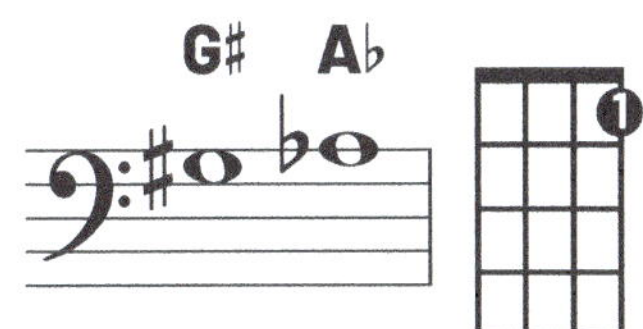

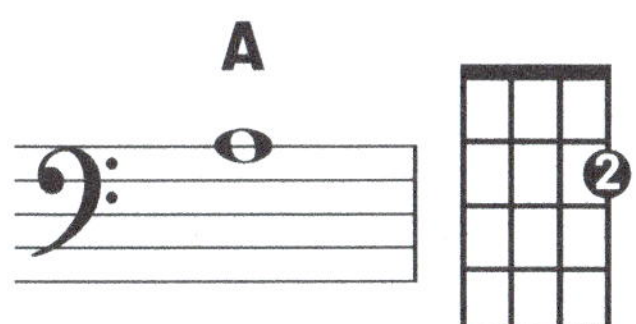

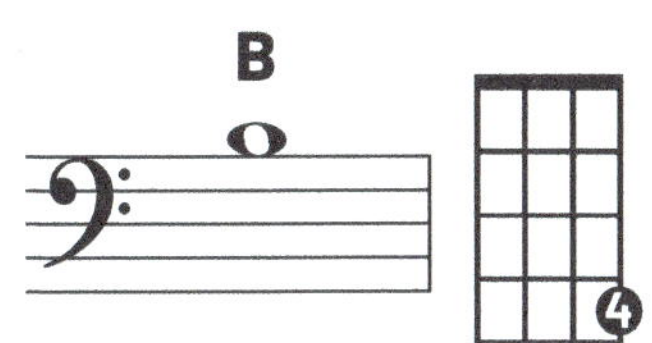

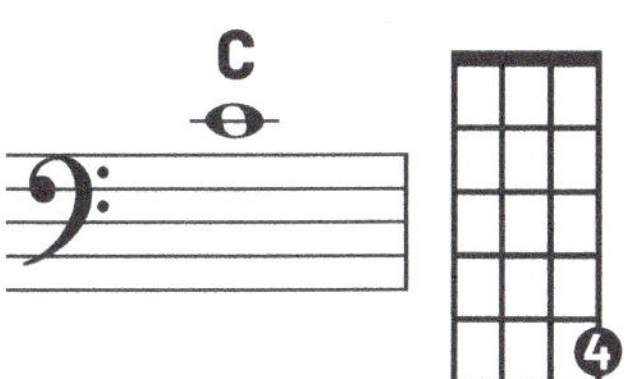

SNARE DRUM INTERNATIONAL DRUM RUDIMENTS

All rudiments should be practiced: open (slow) or close (fast) and/or at an even moderate march tempo.

Instrument Care Reminders

Snare drums occasionally need tuning. Ask your teacher to help you tighten each tension rod equally using a drum key.

- Be careful not to over-tighten the head. It will break if the tension is too tight.
- Loosen the snare strainer at the end of each rehearsal.
- Cover all percussion instruments when not in use.
- Put sticks away in a storage area. Keep the percussion section neat!
- Sticks are the only things which should be placed on the snare drum. NEVER put or allow others to put objects on any percussion instrument.

Instruments and photos courtesy of Yamaha.

I. ROLL RUDIMENTS

A. SINGLE STROKE RUDIMENTS

1. Single Stroke Roll

2. Single Stroke Four

3. Single Stroke Seven

B. MULTIPLE BOUNCE ROLL RUDIMENTS

4. Multiple Bounce Roll

5. Triple Stroke Roll

International Drum Rudiments courtesy of Percussion Arts Society

SNARE DRUM INTERNATIONAL DRUM RUDIMENTS

C. DOUBLE STROKE OPEN ROLL RUDIMENTS

6. Double Stroke Open Roll

7. Five Stroke Roll

8. Six Stroke Roll

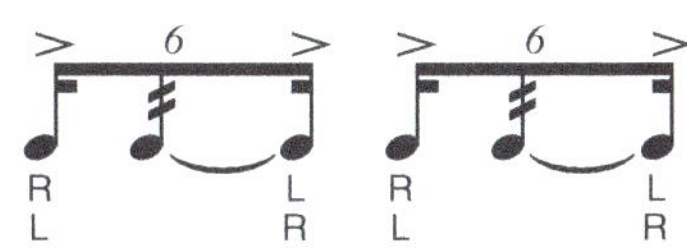

9. Seven Stroke Roll

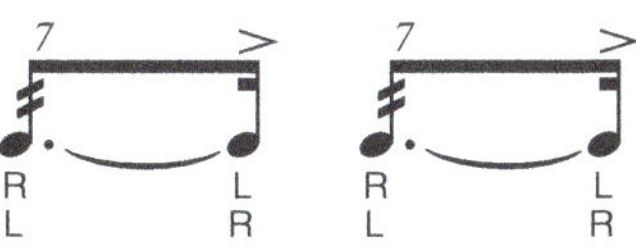

10. Nine Stroke Roll

11. Ten Stroke Roll

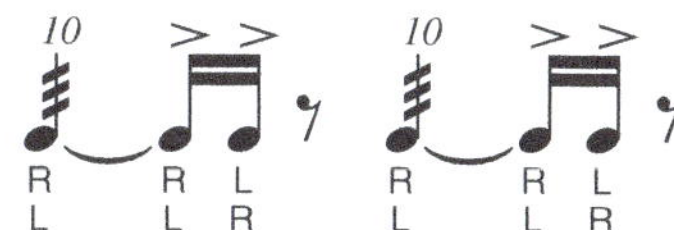

12. Eleven Stroke Roll

13. Thirteen Stroke Roll

14. Fifteen Stroke Roll

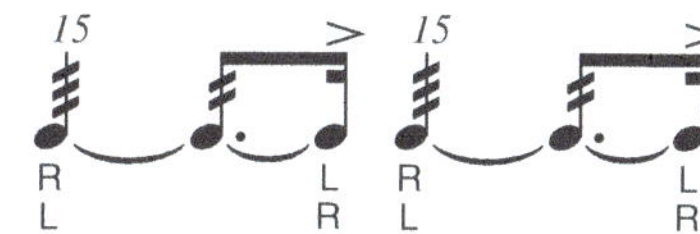

15. Seventeen Stroke Roll

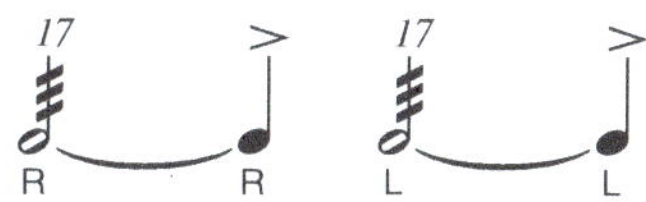

II. DIDDLE RUDIMENTS

16. Single Paradiddle

17. Double Paradiddle

18. Triple Paradiddle

19. Single Paradiddle-Diddle

SNARE DRUM INTERNATIONAL DRUM RUDIMENTS

III. FLAM RUDIMENTS

20. Flam

21. Flam Accent

22. Flam Tap

23. Flamacue

24. Flam Paradiddle

25. Single Flammed Mill

26. Flam Paradiddle-Diddle

27. Pataflafla

28. Swiss Army Triplet

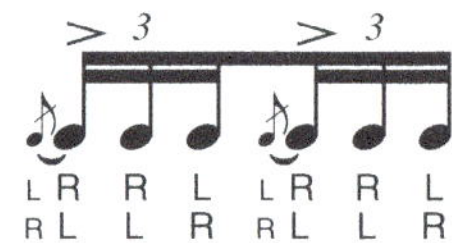

29. Inverted Flam Tap

30. Flam Drag

SNARE DRUM INTERNATIONAL DRUM RUDIMENTS

IV. DRAG RUDIMENTS

31. Drag

36. Drag Paradiddle #1

32. Single Drag Tap

37. Drag Paradiddle #2

33. Double Drag Tap

38. Single Ratamacue

34. Lesson 25

38. Double Ratamacue

35. Single Dragadiddle

40. Triple Ratamacue

Student Book Page 46

KEYBOARD PERCUSSION INSTRUMENTS

Each keyboard percussion instrument has a unique sound because of the materials used to create the instrument. Ranges may differ with some models of instruments.

Instrument Care Reminders

- Cover all percussion instruments when they are not being used.
- Put mallets away in a storage area. Keep the percussion section neat!
- Mallets are the only things which should be placed on your instrument. NEVER put or allow others to put objects on any percussion instrument.

BELLS (Orchestra Bells)

- Bars - metal alloy or steel
- Mallets - lexan (hard plastic), brass or hard rubber
- Range - 2 1/2 octaves
- Sounds 2 octaves higher than written

XYLOPHONE

- Bars - wooden or synthetic
- Mallets - hard rubber
- Range - 3 1/2 octaves
- Sounds 1 octave higher than written

Intruments and photos courtesy of Yamaha.

MARIMBA

- Bars – wooden (wider than xylophone bars)
- Resonating tube located below each bar
- Mallets – soft to medium rubber or yarn covered
- Range – 4 1/3 octaves (reads bass and treble clefs)
- Sounding pitch is the same as written pitch

VIBRAPHONE

- Bars – metal alloy or aluminum
- Resonating tubes located below each bar
- Adjustable electric fans in each resonator create "vibrato" effect
- Mallets – yarn covered
- Range – 3 octaves
- Sounding pitch is the same as written pitch

CHIMES

- Bars – metal tubes
- Mallets – plastic, rawhide or wooden
- Range – 1 1/2 octaves
- Sounding pitch is the same as written pitch

Reference Index

Definitions (pg.)

Composers

World Music

Reference Index for Percussion

Definitions (pg.)*

These page numbers refer to the first section (percussion) of this book.

PERCUSSION TIPS

Additional Teaching Suggestions by Will Rapp

PERCUSSION

1. THE FIRST NOTE
Lift the stick in time with the count-off: "Ready, And, Play", (Lift).

2. COUNT AND PLAY
Begin with right stick in the up position; follow foot-tapping arrows to gauge the speed of the down and up strokes.

3. A NEW NOTE
Remember to lift the stick in time with the count-off.

4. TWO'S A TEAM
Begin with the left stick in the up position.

5. HEADING DOWN
Lift the appropriate stick in time with the count-off.

6. MOVING ON UP
When moving from beat 2 to beat 3 in measure three, remember to prepare the left stick to play by lifting it on the "&" of beat 2.

7. THE LONG HAUL
Lift the appropriate stick in time with the count-off.

8. FOUR BY FOUR
Prepare each stick to play by lifting it on the "&" before each beat.

9. TOUCHDOWN
Remember to lift the appropriate stick in time with the count-off.

10. THE FAB FIVE
Although there are rests in the first and third measures, use the same technique of preparing each stick to play by lifting it on the "&" before the beat.

11. READING THE NOTES
The bass drum should not have any muffling material inside the drum or attached to the heads. Students will eventually learn to control the muffling with their left hand and/or right knee.

12. FIRST FLIGHT
Don't be concerned with the bass drum sound ringing into the rests. Students should focus their attention on the basic technique of pulling the sound out of the drum.

13. ESSENTIAL ELEMENTS QUIZ
Snare drum players should follow the sticking carefully.

14. ROLLING ALONG
Emphasize listening to ensure the quarter notes on both snare drum and bass drum are played exactly together.

KEYBOARD PERCUSSION

1. THE FIRST NOTE
Lift the mallet in time with the count-off: "Ready, And, Play", (Lift).

2. COUNT AND PLAY
Begin with both mallets in the up position; follow foot-tapping arrows to gauge the speed of the legato strokes.

3. A NEW NOTE
Remember to lift the mallet in time with the count-off.

4. TWO'S A TEAM
Begin with both mallets in the up position.

5. HEADING DOWN
Lift the appropriate mallet in time with the count-off.

6. MOVING ON UP
When moving from beat 2 to 3 in measures one and three, remember to prepare the left mallet to play by lifting it on the "&" of beat 2.

7. THE LONG HAUL
Lift the appropriate mallet in time with the count-off.

8. FOUR BY FOUR
Prepare each mallet to play by lifting it on the "&" before each beat.

9. TOUCHDOWN
Remember to lift the appropriate mallet in time with the count-off.

10. THE FAB FIVE
Notice that in measure two, the left mallet will be positioned in front of the right mallet due to the shift from the B-flat note. The left mallet should remain in front of the right mallet for the rest of the exercise.

11. READING THE NOTES
This exercise serves as a review of the previous technique of mallet positioning. On the repeat, the left mallet can still be positioned in front of the right mallet.

12. FIRST FLIGHT
Encourage students to use Alternate Sticking, beginning with the right hand.

13. ESSENTIAL ELEMENTS QUIZ
Due to the placement of the accidentals, it's best to use Alternate Sticking beginning with the left hand.

14. ROLLING ALONG
Begin with the right mallet, keeping it positioned in front of the left throughout the exercise

PERCUSSION TIPS
(continued)

PERCUSSION

15. RHYTHM RAP

16. THE HALF COUNTS
With the basic bass drum technique learned, encourage students to muffle the playing head on the half rests with the right hand.

17. HOT CROSS BUNS
Remind students to continue to count for rhythmic accuracy.

18. GO TELL AUNT RHODIE
Students should begin to pay attention to the placement of bass drum and snare drum notes to ensure a consistent rhythmic feel between the two parts.

19. ESSENTIAL ELEMENTS QUIZ
Students may need to refer to the chart on page 5-A to draw the melody notes on the staff. Make sure snare drums follow the sticking carefully.

20. RHYTHM RAP

21. THE WHOLE THING
At first, the individual multiple bounce sounds may be too short to sound connected to each other. This will improve with practice.

22. SPLIT DECISION
Strive for consistent multiple bounce sounds when moving from hand to hand.

23. MARCH STEPS
Multiple bounces may sound softer than other strokes; if so, relax on the strokes for a more even sound.

24. LISTEN TO OUR SECTIONS
As the title indicates, percussion students should play their own parts, then listen carefully to both the woodwinds and the brass to determine how the entire piece fits together.

25. LIGHTLY ROW
No sticking is printed, allowing students to mark their own appropriate sticking before playing.

26. ESSENTIAL ELEMENTS QUIZ
Listen to the play-along track to hear how the multiple bounce rolls connect together.

27. REACHING HIGHER
Carefully follow the stick position guidelines in the yellow box to properly understand how flams are played. Improper stick positioning for flams is one of the greatest challenges in developing percussion technique.

KEYBOARD PERCUSSION

15. RHYTHM RAP

16. THE HALF COUNTS
Combination Sticking provides a valuable technique to help perform certain passages with good musical phrasing.

17. HOT CROSS BUNS
Use legato strokes for the half notes.

18. GO TELL AUNT RHODIE
While primarily a snare drum sticking technique, Right Hand Lead can be applied to certain melodic passages.

19. ESSENTIAL ELEMENTS QUIZ
An Alternate Sticking pattern beginning with the left hand will allow the sticking to flow with the accidentals.

20. RHYTHM RAP

21. THE WHOLE THING
While either form of Alternate Sticking will work, beginning with the left hand may be more comfortable for students.

22. SPLIT DECISION
If you have both bells and xylophone, have students split up; bells play Part A, xylophone plays Part B.

23. MARCH STEPS
Exercises that begin with an ascending melodic pattern that repeats benefit from the use of the Left Hand Lead system.

24. LISTEN TO OUR SECTIONS
As the title indicates, keyboard percussion students should play their own parts, then listen carefully to both the woodwinds and the brass to determine how the entire piece fits together.

25. LIGHTLY ROW
Strive for a consistent sound throughout this exercise.

26. ESSENTIAL ELEMENTS QUIZ
Students will be most comfortable playing this quiz if they use an Alternate Sticking pattern beginning with the left hand.

27. REACHING HIGHER
Begin each measure with the right mallet. Measure five will work best if students use the Right Hand Lead system (**R RL**).

PERCUSSION TIPS
(continued)

PERCUSSION

28. AU CLAIRE DE LA LUNE
After playing the first right hand flam in measures one and five, you must lift the right stick on the "&" of beat 2 to have your hands in proper position for the rest of the phrase.

29. REMIX
With Alternate Sticking, it is possible to apply the stick position guidelines for flams throughout the entire exercise. Continue to lift the low hand to the up position even when playing alternate single strokes.

30. LONDON BRIDGE
If using Alternate Sticking for this exercise, continue to apply the stick position guidelines for flams throughout the entire exercise.

31. A MOZART MELODY
For now, don't worry about the Triangle sound ringing into the rests; focus the students attention on the basic technique.

32. ESSENTIAL ELEMENTS QUIZ
Strive for a consistent sound with flams.

33. DEEP POCKETS
While the Right Hand Lead system works well for this exercise, the right hand should not dominate the sound. Maintain a consistent sound throughout.

34. DOODLE ALL DAY
Mark in either a Right Hand Lead or an Alternate system of sticking for this exercise.

35. JUMP ROPE
Doubling or Double Sticking is not double bouncing. Even though two consecutive notes are played with the same hand, there will be separate hand motions for each stroke.

36. A-TISKET, A-TASKET
Rudiments should serve as a means to an end, not an end in itself. As a result, rudiments are introduced in the context of an appropriate musical application.

37. LOUD AND SOFT
To produce the louder dynamics when clapping; students must bring their hands farther apart. This will have a direct correlation to the height-of-rise, the distance that the stick moves away from the head.

38. JINGLE BELLS
Lift the sticks higher in order to achieve the forte dynamic.

39. MY DREYDL
Bring the sticks closer to the head to achieve the piano dynamic in measures 5-8. In this way, the height-of-rise controls the dynamics, not excessive force.

KEYBOARD PERCUSSION

28. AU CLAIRE DE LA LUNE
Notice the particular sticking system recommended for the various exercises, and how these choices are determined by the shape (direction) of the melodic line as well as the key signature.

29. REMIX
Ask the students which sticking system they would use for this exercise. Left Hand Lead in measures 1-4; Double Sticking in measures 5-7 is recommended.

30. LONDON BRIDGE
If both bells and xylophone are available, have bells play Part A while xylophone plays Part B.

31. A MOZART MELODY
Using Double Sticking gives the melody a musical, less mechanical sound.

32. ESSENTIAL ELEMENTS QUIZ
Students should strive for a consistent sound in their playing.

33. DEEP POCKETS
Although there are eighth notes for snare drum, the keyboard percussion should be reminded to use Legato Strokes for their half notes.

34. DOODLE ALL DAY
The use of Combination Sticking keeps the mallets in correct position for the entire exercise.

35. JUMP ROPE
Ask the students which sticking system they would use for this exercise. Combination Sticking is recommended.

36. A-TISKET, A-TASKET
Remind students to use Legato Strokes on half notes.

37. LOUD AND SOFT
To produce the louder dynamics when clapping; students must bring their hands farther apart. This will have a direct correlation to the height-of-rise, the distance that the mallet moves away from the bar.

38. JINGLE BELLS
Lift the mallets higher in order to achieve the forte dynamic.

39. MY DREYDL
Bring the mallets closer to the bar to achieve the piano dynamic in measures 5-8. In this way, the height-of-rise controls the dynamics, not excessive force.

PERCUSSION TIPS
(continued)

PERCUSSION

40. RHYTHM RAP

41. EIGHTH NOTE JAM
With multiple bounces on eighth notes, it should be easier for students to connect the multiple bounce sounds.

42. SKIP TO MY LOU
Students may use a pair of yarn mallets to play the suspended cymbal with alternate strokes, or with the same hand to achieve a more consistent sound.

43. LONG, LONG AGO
Be aware of how the bass drum and snare drum parts line up, especially when multiple bounce rolls are played.

44. CANDY MOUNTAIN ROCK
To achieve a good sense of ensemble performance, all three percussion parts should listen how they fit together. Listen to the play-along track to hear how the multiple bounce rolls connect together.

45. ESSENTIAL ELEMENTS QUIZ – WILLIAM TELL
For young students, use a pair of 16" (medium or medium thin) crash cymbals while developing the basic stroke.

46. RHYTHM RAP

47. TWO BY TWO
The stick position guidelines change slightly for Flam Taps. Point out that the low hand always follows the flam in a flam tap rudiment.

48. HIGH SCHOOL CADETS
The cymbals and bass drum players need to listen to each other for good ensemble sound.

49. HEY, HO! NOBODY'S HOME
Note how the tambourine relates to the snare drum part, especially in measure 15 when the eighth notes move with the multiple bounce roll.

50. CLAP THE DYNAMICS
To produce the crescendo when clapping; students must bring their hands farther apart. This will have a direct correlation to the height-of-rise, the distance that the stick moves away from the head.

51. PLAY THE DYNAMICS
Think of the height-of-rise when playing the dynamics.

52. PERFORMANCE WARM-UPS
Focus on the consistency of sound on each percussion instrument.

KEYBOARD PERCUSSION

40. RHYTHM RAP

41. EIGHTH NOTE JAM
Now that eighth notes have been introduced, students should begin to incorporate the Legato Stroke in their quarter notes.

42. SKIP TO MY LOU
The shape of this melody makes the use of Alternate sticking a good choice.

43. LONG, LONG AGO
Ask the students which sticking system they would use for this exercise. Right Hand Lead system is recommended.

44. CANDY MOUNTAIN ROCK
Combination Sticking beginning with the Right hand would be a good choice for this exercise.

45. ESSENTIAL ELEMENTS QUIZ – WILLIAM TELL
At this point, students have been introduced to several systems of sticking. This quiz should reveal which sticking system is most comfortable to each student. Remember, there is no one correct method; the choice of a sticking system is largely a matter of personal preference.

46. RHYTHM RAP

47. TWO BY TWO
While several sticking systems will work for this exercise, you may wish to suggest that students begin on the right hand and use Double Sticking on all of the repeated eighth notes.

48. HIGH SCHOOL CADETS
If students are having trouble with sticking or their playing looks awkward, suggest that they begin the piece with the left hand.

49. HEY, HO! NOBODY'S HOME
Alternate Sticking, beginning with the right hand is recommended for this exercise.

50. CLAP THE DYNAMICS
To produce the crescendo when clapping; students must bring their hands farther apart. This will have a direct correlation to the height-of-rise, the distance that the mallet moves away from the bar.

51. PLAY THE DYNAMICS
Think of the height-of-rise when playing the dynamics.

52. PERFORMANCE WARM-UPS
Focus on the consistency of sound on each keyboard percussion instrument.

PERCUSSION TIPS (continued)

PERCUSSION

53. AURA LEE
Students should develop an understanding of how percussion instruments are used in a piece of music. This part serves to color the sound of the full band.

54. FRÈRE JACQUES
The wood block is the real "time-keeper" of this piece. All three percussion instruments must make the dynamic change for greatest effect.

55. WHEN THE SAINTS GO MARCHING IN
This exercise combines the use of height-of-rise for dynamic contrast and stick positioning for proper execution of flams.

56. OLD MACDONALD HAD A BAND
The suspended cymbal part is similar to a ride cymbal on drum set. Encourage students to use one hand to play the part.

57. ODE TO JOY
The triangle should play a stroke that emphasizes the fundamental sound first, then try the stroke that produces the overtones. Ask your students if they can hear the difference.

58. HARD ROCK BLUES
Review the hand placement for tambourine at the forte dynamic (knuckles on head, half-way between the edge and the center) found on page 11-B. The notes marked solo in bass drum should be very prominent.

59. FIT TO BE TIED
Having learned multiple bounces in eighth notes, snare drums should apply eighth note hand motions to the tied notes in this exercise; that is, two eighth note multiple bounce motions tied into a quarter note release.

60. ALOUETTE
Use the same technique of eighth note multiple bounces as in the previous exercise. The tied roll in the last measure will be played with four eighth note multiple bounce motions tied into a quarter note release.

61. ALOUETTE – THE SEQUEL
Compare the bass drum part to the previous exercise as an illustration of how different notations of rhythm sound the same.

62. IT'S RAINING
This exercise is a good example of how the sticking from a rudimental pattern can enhance the musical phrasing. The character of the fourth beat is conditioned by how it is reached, in this case with a double right hand sticking.

63. NEW DIRECTIONS
The teaching concept from the previous exercise applies here as well, this time with a doubling of the left hand.

KEYBOARD PERCUSSION

53. AURA LEE
Students should develop an understanding of how mallet sticking relates to the written music. The concept of Melodic Sticking allows the player the opportunity to combine the previous sticking systems for the best musical result. If possible, use bells for Part A and xylophone for Part B.

54. FRÈRE JACQUES
Additional practice with the Melodic Sticking concept.

55. WHEN THE SAINTS GO MARCHING IN
Remind students to use Legato Strokes on the long notes.

56. OLD MACDONALD HAD A BAND
Attention to height-of-rise will help to achieve good dynamic contrast without overplaying the instrument.

57. ODE TO JOY
Use Legato Strokes for the quarter notes in this piece as well as the longer note values.

58. HARD ROCK BLUES
For this exercise, a non-legato approach would be appropriate.

59. FIT TO BE TIED
The use of Legato Strokes will allow tied notes to have a fuller sound.

60. ALOUETTE
This melody provides a great opportunity to use Legato Strokes.

61. ALOUETTE – THE SEQUEL
The same Legato Stroke technique is used for any long note value, whether it be dotted or tied.

62. IT'S RAINING
Ask the students which sticking system they would use for this exercise. Combination sticking beginning with the right mallet would be a good choice.

63. NEW DIRECTIONS
Because of the direction of the new note, students should position their right mallet in front of the left for this exercise. In measure seven, using the sticking (**R RL R L**) will allow for a smooth ending.

PERCUSSION TIPS
(continued)

PERCUSSION

64. THE NOBLES
Suggest the use of the Right Hand Lead sticking system so that all multiple bounce roll figures begin with the right hand.

65. ESSENTIAL ELEMENTS QUIZ
Listen for consistency of sound as students move from strokes to flams to multiple bounce rolls.

66. RHYTHM RAP

67. THREE BEAT JAM
Triple meter is a perfect opportunity to use the Double Paradiddle sticking. Point out to the students the relationship of the single to the double paradiddle by asking them to find where the single paradiddle is hidden inside the double paradiddle.

68. BARCAROLLE
Students should understand that the dynamics apply to both parts.

69. MORNING
The same stick positioning guidelines used for flams will also work for Flam Accents.

70. ACCENT ON YOUR TALENT
Students should bring their hands farther apart to emphasize the accented notes.

71. MEXICAN CLAPPING SONG
Strive for a short, precise eighth note sound on the maracas. Holding the claves too tightly will muffle the sound.

72. ESSENTIAL CREATIVITY
Students should be encouraged to compose their own melody for this exercise.

73. HOT MUFFINS
Attention to height-of-rise is important to achieve a contrast between the accented and unaccented notes in this exercise.

74. COSSACK DANCE
Pay attention to how the snare drum and tambourine parts fit together in this exercise.

75. BASIC BLUES
The three separate percussion parts should combine to sound as if one person is playing the drum set.

KEYBOARD PERCUSSION

64. THE NOBLES
Positioning the right mallet in front of the left is suggested for this exercise.

65. ESSENTIAL ELEMENTS QUIZ
Note the sticking system that each student uses for this quiz.

66. RHYTHM RAP

67. THREE BEAT JAM
Alternate Sticking, beginning with the right hand is recommended.

68. BARCAROLLE
Use Legato Strokes for this exercise.

69. MORNING
A combination of Legato Strokes and attention to height-of-rise will help to produce good musical results in this piece.

70. ACCENT ON YOUR TALENT
Students should bring their hands farther apart to emphasize the accented notes.

71. MEXICAN CLAPPING SONG
Begin this piece with the left hand and pick up the mallet to produce accented notes with a full sound.

72. ESSENTIAL CREATIVITY
Like the woodwinds and brass, keyboard percussion students should be encouraged to compose their own melody for the last two measures of this exercise and play their composition for each other.

73. HOT MUFFINS
Starting with the right hand and by positioning the right mallet in front of the left for this entire exercise should allow the students to get to the new note without any problems.

74. COSSACK DANCE
Ask the students which sticking system they would use for this exercise. Alternate Sticking beginning on the right hand would be a good choice.

75. BASIC BLUES
Suggest that students begin on the left hand and use Double Sticking on all of the eighth notes.

PERCUSSION TIPS
(continued)

PERCUSSION

76. HIGH FLYING
Triangle and snare drum players need to listen to each other to ensure proper rhythmic alignment.

77. SAKURA, SAKURA
You may choose to have the percussion section (with keyboard percussion) play this piece while the woodwinds and brass listen; the result can lead to a greater appreciation of the role of percussion in music.

78. UP ON A HOUSETOP
Ask the sleigh bells player to think of eighth notes in their mind in order not to rush the quarter note pulse.

79. JOLLY OLD ST. NICK
As a result of using an eighth note subdivision in the previous exercise, the eighth note rhythms in this exercise should be easier to perform.

80. THE BIG AIRSTREAM
Remind students of the importance of height-of-rise in order to achieve a contrast between accented notes and strokes.

81. WALTZ THEME
Remind students that a flam adds length to a note. A waltz has a better feel when the flams are approached this way.

82. AIR TIME
Sixteenth notes are taught to percussionists so they continue to develop technique. While no dynamics are indicated, remind students to play all rhythms at a consistent volume level.

83. DOWN BY THE STATION
The wood block shouldn't anticipate the entrances at measures 3, 5, and 7 as a result of hearing the fast movement of the sixteenth notes in the snare drum part.

84. ESSENTIAL ELEMENTS QUIZ
Review the technique for playing crash cymbals (page 10-B) and give all percussion students the opportunity to play this part.

85. ESSENTIAL CREATIVITY
As students initially work on this improvisation study, you may wish to have the bass drum simply repeat the two measure pattern to firmly anchor the rhythm.

86. TONE BUILDER
Concentrate on accent placement and height-of-rise.

KEYBOARD PERCUSSION

76. HIGH FLYING
Students should consider the key signature as well as shape of the melodic line when choosing an appropriate sticking system for an exercise. In this case, Alternate Sticking leading with the left hand is recommended.

77. SAKURA, SAKURA
Remind students of attention to height-of-rise in order to achieve effective dynamic contrast.

78. UP ON A HOUSETOP
Observe how students approach the sticking for this exercise. If any passages seem awkward, you may wish to suggest an appropriate choice of sticking.

79. JOLLY OLD ST. NICK
Point out to the students that bells and xylophone sound one octave apart when reading the same pitches (information on range and sounding pitches on page 46). In this duet bells should play Part A and xylophone should play Part B.

80. THE BIG AIRSTREAM
Begin this exercise on the left hand in order to more easily reach the new note.

81. WALTZ THEME
Use Legato Strokes for this waltz.

82. AIR TIME
Continue to reinforce the use of Legato Strokes in this exercise.

83. DOWN BY THE STATION
Use a non-legato approach to the strokes to achieve the style of this exercise.

84. ESSENTIAL ELEMENTS QUIZ
Notice if the students are using height-of-rise to effectively pace the crescendo and diminuendo.

85. ESSENTIAL CREATIVITY
As students initially work on this improvisation study, you may wish to have the bass drum simply repeat the two measure pattern to firmly anchor the rhythm. Have the keyboard percussion students listen to this rhythm as they play their improvised part.

86. TONE BUILDER
Concentrate on consistency of sound.

PERCUSSION TIPS
(continued)

PERCUSSION

87. RHYTHM BUILDER
Here again, accent placement and attention to height-of-rise are the important teaching concepts. As a result, the exercise should have good solid accents with the rest of the pattern played at a relaxed dynamic level.

88. TECHNIQUE TRAX
This exercise combines Single Paradiddles, Multiple Bounce Rolls, and Flam Taps. Strive for consistency of sound and accuracy of sticking.

89. CHORALE
The suspended cymbal serves to add color to this Bach chorale.

90. VARIATIONS ON A FAMILIAR THEME
Students playing the crash cymbals now have the experience of changing to another instrument (triangle) while counting the appropriate number of measures of rest. Encourage them to be ready with all the instruments they will need BEFORE the piece begins.

91. BANANA BOAT SONG
There are several possible sticking patterns for the Eighth Note Two Sixteenths pattern, and these will be presented in subsequent exercises. For now, allow the students to play the piece with the sticking pattern that feels most comfortable, concentrating on the correct counting.

92. RAZOR'S EDGE
If students are unsure of sticking for this exercise, suggest Alternate Sticking.

93. THE MUSIC BOX
Remind students to fill in the Multiple Bounce Rolls with eighth note multiple bounces.

94. EZEKIEL SAW THE WHEEL
Snare drum players should pay attention to how their rhythm fits with the bass drum part.

95. SMOOTH OPERATOR
If students are unsure of which sticking to use, the Right Hand Lead system is recommended for this exercise.

96. GLIDING ALONG
This is an excellent exercise to introduce Doubling as a sticking pattern. The benefit of Doubling will be evident later on, as percussionists encounter similar patterns at fast tempos.

97. TROMBONE RAG
Have students strive for a light sound on the rim of the snare drum in order to enhance the ragtime style of this piece. Accents on the wood block are most important.

KEYBOARD PERCUSSION

87. RHYTHM BUILDER
Double Sticking is recommended on the repeated eighth notes.

88. TECHNIQUE TRAX
A strict Alternate Sticking system should be used for this exercise; it may begin either with the left or right hand.

89. CHORALE
Use Legato Strokes to match the style of the woodwinds and brass in this chorale.

90. VARIATIONS ON A FAMILIAR THEME
Have students identify the sticking systems they used for each section of this piece.

91. BANANA BOAT SONG
While several sticking systems will work for this exercise, suggest using Double Sticking on all of the repeated eighth notes figures.

92. RAZOR'S EDGE
Students should be encouraged to begin with the left hand and keep the left mallet positioned in front of the right mallet for the entire exercise.

93. THE MUSIC BOX
Double Sticking may be used for repeated notes that move over a bar line.

94. EZEKIEL SAW THE WHEEL
If students are having trouble achieving a smooth, consistent sound, have them use an Alternate Sticking throughout.

95. SMOOTH OPERATOR
For practice, suggest Alternate Sticking beginning with the right hand.

96. GLIDING ALONG
For practice, suggest Alternate Sticking beginning with the left hand.

97. TROMBONE RAG
Although there are half notes in the piece, remind students that the style of this music would suggest a non-legato approach to sticking.

PERCUSSION TIPS
(continued)

PERCUSSION

98. ESSENTIAL ELEMENTS QUIZ
Note the soft dynamic level of the music in this quiz. Rhythmic consistency at the softer dynamic levels is essential for developing percussionists.

99. TAKE THE LEAD
The use of Right Hand Lead in this exercise will set up all of the Multiple Bounce Rolls to lead off the right hand.

100. THE COLD WIND
Instead of simply concentrating on one measure at a time, students should now begin to focus their attention on seeing and hearing the two measure groups as a short phrase.

101. PHRASEOLOGY
Continue to apply the concept of phrasing to this exercise.

102. SATIN LATIN
The Double Sticking suggested in this piece really helps to generate a nice Latin feel throughout. The placement of the accents is very important; have students remain relaxed on the entire pattern with emphasis on the accented notes.

103. MINUET
Here is a chance to once again work on Flams as an embellishment of length. Students should strive for a consistent sound on all flams.

104. ESSENTIAL CREATIVITY
Point out to students how the position of the bar lines in the music determines the phrasing.

105. NATURALLY
Remind students to play with a consistent sound, especially when using Right Hand Lead.

106. MARCH MILITAIRE
Notice how the use of Doubling enhances the phrasing in this march, giving the rhythm a constant forward momentum.

107. THE FLAT ZONE
Students should strive to produce a smooth connection between the eighth note multiple bounces, especially in the last measure.

KEYBOARD PERCUSSION

98. ESSENTIAL ELEMENTS QUIZ
Note the soft dynamic level of the music in this quiz.

99. TAKE THE LEAD
Suggest to students that they begin this exercise on the left hand and use Alternate Sticking in order to more easily reach the new note.

100. THE COLD WIND
Instead of simply concentrating on one measure at a time, students should now begin to focus their attention on seeing and hearing the two measure groups as a short phrase.

101. PHRASEOLOGY
Continue to apply the concept of phrasing to this exercise.

102. SATIN LATIN
The roll is one of the more challenging techniques for a developing keyboard percussion student. While rolls are now included on most of the exercises, it should be understood that this technique is reserved for playing on the xylophone and marimba. Rolling on the bells will actually make it more difficult for the woodwinds and brass to play in tune.

103. MINUET
If possible, use bells for Part A and xylophone for Part B.

104. ESSENTIAL CREATIVITY
Point out to students how the position of the bar lines in the music determines the phrasing.

105. NATURALLY
Remind students to play with a consistent sound and bring the mallets closer to the bar for the roll.

106. MARCH MILITAIRE
As a result of the increased range in this piece, students will most likely begin with their right mallet positioned in front of their left to reach the low E natural, but will shift over to the left mallet in front of the right when they reach the roll on high F. This type of shifting is quite normal for a keyboard percussionist, and usually occurs when the mallets cross over the center of the body.

107. THE FLAT ZONE
Players should experiment with beginning with the right hand, then beginning with the left hand. Ask which sticking system feels more comfortable to them. Remind them how the shape of the melody often helps to determine the more appropriate choice of sticking.

PERCUSSION TIPS
(continued)

PERCUSSION

108. ON TOP OF OLD SMOKEY
This piece is a good example of how the percussion section is used to accompany the full band.

109. BOTTOM BASS BOOGIE
The snare drum and suspended cymbal players should listen to each other in order that the eighth and sixteenth note rhythms "lock in" together.

110. RHYTHM RAP

111. THE DOT ALWAYS COUNTS
This is a good time to point out to percussion students how the woodwinds and brass hold dotted notes to their full value in order to produce a longer sound.

112. ALL THROUGH THE NIGHT
The bass drum players should use a longer, slower stroke on the dotted quarter notes in order to achieve full value.

113. SEA CHANTY
Bass drummers should continue to develop the long, slow stroke, pulling the sound out of the head on the dotted half notes.

114. SCARBOROUGH FAIR
Remind snare drummers to use two eighth note multiple bounces and work to achieve a connected sound.

115. RHYTHM RAP

116. THE TURNAROUND
Height-of-rise on accents combined with strokes played close to the head will produce the best contrast for this exercise.

117. ESSENTIAL ELEMENTS QUIZ – AULD LANG SYNE
In addition to the rhythmic values and technique needed to perform this quiz, it is important for the students to recognize the crescendo in measure four as the means to achieving the forte dynamic level for the last four measures.

118. HUNGARIAN DANCE NO. 5
This snare drum solo with piano accompaniment incorporates the various techniques as well as rudiments learned thus far in the book. The addition of both stick clicks and a rim shot enhance the colors that the snare drum can produce.

119. GRENADILLA GORILLA JUMP NO. 1
This exercise focuses on the use of Doubling as well as Paradiddles. Follow the sticking carefully and work for a consistent rhythm.

120. JUMPIN' UP AND DOWN
Paradiddles as well as Doubling are featured again, this time incorporating some Left Hand Lead measures as well.

KEYBOARD PERCUSSION

108. ON TOP OF OLD SMOKEY
Bells should allow the tied notes to ring for the full written value. Xylophone, however, should not roll on this piece.

109. BOTTOM BASS BOOGIE
Since the bells sound two octaves above concert pitch and the xylophone only sounds one octave above concert pitch, it will be necessary for the xylophone to play Part B in order to provide the proper bass line support for the melody line (Part A).

110. RHYTHM RAP

111. THE DOT ALWAYS COUNTS
This is a good time to point out to keyboard percussion students how the woodwinds and brass hold dotted notes to their full value in order to produce a longer sound.

112. ALL THROUGH THE NIGHT
Remind the xylophone player that the roll in measure four has a diminuendo.

113. SEA CHANTY
Attention to height-of-rise will help to produce the most effective dynamic contrast.

114. SCARBOROUGH FAIR
Attention to dynamic contrast is also important in this piece.

115. RHYTHM RAP

116. THE TURNAROUND
Suggest that students use Alternate Sticking so they can concentrate on the rhythms in this exercise.

117. ESSENTIAL ELEMENTS QUIZ – AULD LANG SYNE
In addition to the rhythmic values and technique needed to perform this quiz, it is important for the students to recognize the crescendo in measure four as the means to achieving the forte dynamic level for the last four measures.

118. THEME FROM "NEW WORLD SYMPHONY"
The proper mood of this keyboard percussion solo (with piano accompaniment) can be achieved by using Legato Strokes throughout the piece.

119. GRENADILLA GORILLA JUMP NO. 1
This exercise focuses on roll development. Keep the mallets close to the bar for maximum speed.

120. JUMPIN' UP AND DOWN
Use Alternate Sticking for quarter notes to prepare the rolls that follow.

PERCUSSION TIPS
(continued)

PERCUSSION

121. GRENADILLA GORILLA JUMP NO. 2
Right Hand Doublings, Paradiddles, and Flam Taps are the featured rudiments in this exercise.

122. JUMPIN' FOR JOY
Pay strict attention to the sticking in this exercise; it is challenging!

123. GRENADILLA GORILLA JUMP NO. 3
Listen for consistency in both left and right hand passages.

124. JUMPIN' JACKS
This exercise begins with Alternate Sticking, then shifts to the use of Doubling and Paradiddles. Maintain a consistent rhythmic feel throughout.

125. ESSENTIAL ELEMENTS QUIZ
Have all percussion students play this quiz individually, making note of each student's sticking choices.

126. GRENADILLA GORILLA JUMP NO. 4
This exercise allows a good opportunity to work on Alternate Sticking.

127. THREE IS THE COUNT
Remind students to think of Flams as an embellishment of length, especially in 3/4 meter where there is an emphasis on the first beat of each measure.

128. GRENADILLA GORILLA JUMP NO. 5
Here is one final opportunity to use eighth note multiple bounce motions to produce the rolls in this exercise.

129. TECHNIQUE TRAX
Students now begin the process of using two sixteenth note multiple bounce motions each time they see an eighth note multiple bounce roll figure. Begin slowly at first to make sure everyone understands the concept.

130. CROSSING OVER
Note the sticking that students use to play this exercise. It will give you some idea of which systems are more comfortable at this point.

131. KUM BAH YAH
Point out that it is easier to hear the quality of a Flam when the snares are off. Students should take this opportunity to focus on the quality of their overall sound.

132. MICHAEL ROW THE BOAT ASHORE
You may need to review the Flam Accent (page 15-A) before working on this exercise in order to help the students "see" how it is used in this piece.

KEYBOARD PERCUSSION

121. GRENADILLA GORILLA JUMP NO. 2
Practice Legato Strokes in this exercise.

122. JUMPIN' FOR JOY
Suggest that students use Double Sticking for the repeated quarter notes in this piece, beginning on the left hand.

123. GRENADILLA GORILLA JUMP NO. 3
There should be a slight break between each roll in order to maintain the pulse of this exercise.

124. JUMPIN' JACKS
Suggest using Double Sticking for the repeated quarter notes in this piece, beginning on the right hand.

125. ESSENTIAL ELEMENTS QUIZ
Make sure that the mallets continue to move from note to note without any jerky motions. This will lead to a more accurate performance.

126. GRENADILLA GORILLA JUMP NO. 4
Use Alternate Sticking for quarter notes to prepare the rolls that follow.

127. THREE IS THE COUNT
Practice Legato Strokes in this exercise.

128. GRENADILLA GORILLA JUMP NO. 5
Use Alternate Sticking for quarter notes to prepare the rolls that follow.

129. TECHNIQUE TRAX
Double Sticking can be used in the second measure of this exercise.

130. CROSSING OVER
If students are having trouble achieving a smooth, consistent sound, have them use Alternate Sticking throughout.

131. KUM BAH YAH
If three keyboard percussion students are available, you may wish to have bells play parts A & B and vibraphone on Part C. If a vibraphone is not available, the xylophone could be substituted.

132. MICHAEL ROW THE BOAT ASHORE
Double Sticking can be used when a repeated note goes over the bar line as in measures 4-5.

PERCUSSION TIPS
(continued)

PERCUSSION

133. AUSTRIAN WALTZ
Remember, the style of a Waltz dictates long Flams throughout. Wood block needs to listen to the snare drum carefully.

134. BOTANY BAY
After playing this piece, ask the students if they recognize the phrases. As they play again, have them use the dynamic markings to help pinpoint the phrase structure.

135. TECHNIQUE TRAX
It may be difficult at first for snare drummers to play a multiple bounce roll right after an accented note. Point out that one of the challenges to a percussionist is the "recovery" that follows an accent.

136. FINLANDIA
Students should work to achieve a very soft multiple bounce roll sound for an effective interpretation of this piece.

137. ESSENTIAL CREATIVITY
After students have created rhythmic variations, give each one the opportunity to play the newly created part.

138. EASY GORILLA JUMPS
Bass drum and snare drum players need to listen to each other carefully in order for the part to fit together correctly.

139. TECHNIQUE TRAX
As before, note the sticking that students use to play this exercise. It will give you some idea of which systems are more comfortable at this point.

140. MORE TECHNIQUE TRAX
Remind students to keep their hands close to the drum head and use height-of-rise to position the stick to play the accented notes.

141. GERMAN FOLK SONG
Snare drummers should subdivide in eighth notes for the first two measures to ensure that measure three is played in time.

142. THE SAINTS GO MARCHIN' AGAIN
If the tempo is not too fast, snare drum players may be able to use sixteenth note multiple bounce motions to play these multiple bounce rolls.

143. LOWLAND GORILLA WALK
Playing on the rim of the drum is an effect and does not need to be loud. Relax the hands and emphasize the accents.

144. SMOOTH SAILING
Have students strive for a consistent sound. Alternate Sticking is suggested.

KEYBOARD PERCUSSION

133. AUSTRIAN WALTZ
Students may find it easier to begin each phrase with the right hand and alternate, then play **R L L** in the measures with repeated notes.

134. BOTANY BAY
Students may find it easier to begin with the left hand and play **L R R** in the measures with repeated notes.

135. TECHNIQUE TRAX
Alternate Sticking is suggested for this exercise; it should be practiced beginning with the right hand, then practiced beginning with the left hand.

136. FINLANDIA
Use Legato Strokes throughout this piece.

137. ESSENTIAL CREATIVITY
After students have created rhythmic variations, give each one the opportunity to play the newly created part.

138. EASY GORILLA JUMPS
Suggest the use of Double Sticking for the repeated eighth notes in this exercise.

139. TECHNIQUE TRAX
Alternate sticking is suggested for this exercise to better prepare the rolls.

140. MORE TECHNIQUE TRAX
This exercise should also be played with Alternate Sticking.

141. GERMAN FOLK SONG
There should be a short break in the roll right before the bar line on measures that have consecutive rolls written in the part. This allows the pulse to be maintained from measure to measure.

142. THE SAINTS GO MARCHIN' AGAIN
Suggest that students begin this piece on the left hand.

143. LOWLAND GORILLA WALK
There should be a slight break between the rolls in order to maintain the pulse of this exercise.

144. SMOOTH SAILING
This exercise works best if Alternate Sticking is used. It serves to better prepare the hands to play the rolls that follow.

PERCUSSION TIPS (continued)

PERCUSSION

145. MORE GORILLA JUMPS
Both snare drum and bass drum need to listen to each other in order to achieve a good ensemble sound.

146. FULL COVERAGE
Make sure students work to achieve a consistent sound in the two accented notes. Since they are played with opposite hands, they may sound uneven at first.

147. CONCERT B♭ SCALE
The development of the Extended Roll takes considerable practice. Remind students to stay relaxed and to play a little softer in order to achieve a more blended sound.

148. IN HARMONY
This exercise requires 8 multiple bounce hand motions leading directly into the quarter note release on beat three.

149. SCALE AND ARPEGGIO
Again, 8 multiple bounce motions are used on the half note rolls, and 4 multiple bounce motions are used on the quarter note rolls.

150. THEME FROM "SURPRISE SYMPHONY"
For maximum effect, play delicately on the rim. The big contrast should be when the students play on the drum head in measure eight at the forte dynamic level.

151. ESSENTIAL ELEMENTS QUIZ – THE STREETS OF LAREDO
Bass drum and crash cymbal players should listen to each other to match the length of the dotted half note sounds for true ensemble performance.

152. SCHOOL SPIRIT
By now, percussion students should be developing sticking systems (Right Hand Lead, Alternate, Doubling) that provide musical results. This march allows students to use the sticking system most comfortable to them.

153. CARNIVAL OF VENICE
Teach students to look ahead in pieces such as this one, where we find several percussion instruments written on the same staff. While a single staff system is more difficult to read, students will encounter pieces that are published on a single staff, so this is good practice.

154. RANGE AND FLEXIBILITY BUILDER
Up to this point, students have been using Exercises 86-89 (page 18-A) as Daily Warm-Ups. Here are some additional warm-ups to add to daily practice. For added interest, this exercise can be practiced all Right-handed, then repeated all Left-handed.

KEYBOARD PERCUSSION

145. MORE GORILLA JUMPS
You may wish to suggest that students use Double Sticking for the repeated eighth notes in this piece.

146. FULL COVERAGE
Have the students be careful to play consistently and not hammer notes when the pitches repeat.

147. CONCERT B♭ SCALE
Students may begin scales with either hand; Alternate Sticking is suggested.

148. IN HARMONY
Arpeggios are often easier to play if students lead them with the left hand (**L R L R L**, from measure 2-3) when ascending, and lead them with the right hand (**R L R L R**, from measure 5-6) when descending.

149. SCALE AND ARPEGGIO
Have students begin this scale with the left hand so that the arpeggio will descend with a right hand lead. In measure five, the scale should begin with the right hand so that the arpeggio will ascend with a left hand lead.

150. THEME FROM "SURPRISE SYMPHONY"
Ask the students which sticking system they would use for this exercise.

151. ESSENTIAL ELEMENTS QUIZ – THE STREETS OF LAREDO
Make sure students have written in the correct names of the notes; then have them play the quiz.

152. SCHOOL SPIRIT
By now, keyboard percussion students should be developing sticking systems that provide effective musical results. Allow students to use the sticking system that is most comfortable to them.

153. CARNIVAL OF VENICE
Alternate Sticking is suggested for this piece.

154. RANGE AND FLEXIBILITY BUILDER
Up to this point, students have been using Exercises 86-89 (page 18) as Daily Warm-Ups. Here are some additional warm-ups to add to daily practice.

PERCUSSION TIPS
(continued)

PERCUSSION

155. TECHNIQUE TRAX
Students should look for the Single Paradiddle as well as Double Paradiddle that are hidden inside each Triple Paradiddle. Emphasizing the accents will help increase the overall speed of the rudiment.

156. CHORALE
The triangle and suspended cymbal add both color and interest to this beautiful chorale.

157. HATIKVAH
With six separate percussion parts in this three-system score, students have the opportunity to hear how all the parts work together as well as see how the parts visually align themselves. This is an important first step to developing a vertical approach to music reading.

158. RHYTHM RAP

159. EIGHTH NOTE MARCH
This march provides an excellent opportunity to use both Doubling and Paradiddles to enhance the musical phrasing. Remind percussion students that one very important way they can change the musical phrasing is through sticking choices.

160. MINUET
By now, students should remember the importance of playing long Flams in the Minuet style.

161. RHYTHM RAP

162. EIGHTH NOTES OFF THE BEAT
Bass drum needs to listen carefully to the snare drum part, especially when sixteenth notes are involved. Subdividing in eighth notes will help the student playing bass drum to not anticipate the eighth note rhythms.

163. EIGHTH NOTE SCRAMBLE
Snare drum needs to listen to bass drum in order to correctly place the two sixteenth eighth note pattern at the beginning of this exercise.

164. ESSENTIAL ELEMENTS QUIZ
Snare drum should subdivide eighth notes in order to make a correct entrance in the third measure. Have students note where the crescendo takes place in their parts; the snare drum should simply continue the crescendo started by the wood block in measure six.

165. DANCING MELODY
Remind students to play with a consistent sound throughout, especially in measure five where so many sixteenth notes are together.

KEYBOARD PERCUSSION

155. TECHNIQUE TRAX
Begin this exercise on the left hand and use Alternate Sticking for best results.

156. CHORALE
Remind students to use Legato Strokes for this chorale.

157. HATIKVAH
Alternate sticking is suggested for this piece.

158. RHYTHM RAP

159. EIGHTH NOTE MARCH
You may wish to suggest that students use Double Sticking for the repeated eighth notes in this piece.

160. MINUET
There are several sticking systems which will work for this famous Minuet by Bach. Have students experiment to find the one that works best for their level of technical ability. Above all, the choice should be motivated by musical results.

161. RHYTHM RAP

162. EIGHTH NOTES OFF THE BEAT
Alternate Sticking is a good choice when eighth notes are written off the beat.

163. EIGHTH NOTE SCRAMBLE
This exercise allows for continued practice with using Alternating Sticking with eighth notes off the beat.

164. ESSENTIAL ELEMENTS QUIZ
In this quiz, note the sticking system used by students as well as dynamic contrast they achieve.

165. DANCING MELODY
Have students practice Legato Strokes in this exercise.

PERCUSSION TIPS
(continued)

PERCUSSION

166. EL CAPITAN
Snare drummers should be using sixteenth note multiple bounce hand motions to play these multiple bounce rolls.

167. O CANADA
Because the tempo of this piece is marked Maestoso, there will be ample time to use sixteenth note hand motions with these multiple bounce rolls.

168. ESSENTIAL ELEMENTS QUIZ – METER MANIA
Listening to the bass drum part will help to define the meter of each measure, thus allowing for a stronger rhythmic feeling throughout.

169. SNAKE CHARMER
This piece requires that the musical partners listen carefully to each other: snare drum and cowbell; bass drum and tambourine.

170. DARK SHADOWS
Count carefully in order to achieve the correct rhythmic feel in measures one and three; it's not what the players may be expecting.

171. CLOSE ENCOUNTERS
All three percussion instruments need to sound exactly together in the last measure for good ensemble interpretation.

172. MARCH SLAV
There must be a constant pulse established between the bass drum and suspended cymbal part for this accompaniment to work effectively with the band. If timpani are available, this is an excellent time to briefly introduce the instrument and incorporate it into the piece.

173. NOTES IN DISGUISE
The use of a long Flam sound in this 3/4 meter piece will help to define the style of the piece.

174. HALF-STEPPIN'
Note the tie in the clave part; this produces one of the rhythms that is traditionally associated with this instrument. The tambourine player has a choice of performance techniques (see page 11-B).

175. EGYPTIAN DANCE
If students are having difficulty with the shake roll on the tambourine, they can hold the instrument in more of a vertical position at first. Once a basic shake roll sound is produced, students can return the tambourine to a proper angle for effective performance. The success of this piece depends on the snare drum playing everything at a medium level with good solid accents. Students will enjoy playing this timpani part.

176. SILVER MOON BOAT
Nothing is more difficult for percussion than playing slowly. Students need to subdivide carefully so that entrances are in the correct place.

KEYBOARD PERCUSSION

166. EL CAPITAN
Alternate Sticking is recommended for this march.

167. O CANADA
While students may be comfortable playing this entire piece with Alternate Sticking, they may use Double Sticking on repeated notes, even if the rhythm moves from dotted quarter to eighth.

168. ESSENTIAL ELEMENTS QUIZ – METER MANIA
If students first count out loud and clap, they will have a greater level of success when they play the piece.

169. SNAKE CHARMER
Have students practice Legato Strokes on this piece.

170. DARK SHADOWS
If the tempo is slow enough, students can apply Legato Strokes to this exercise.

171. CLOSE ENCOUNTERS
Legato Strokes can be applied to this enharmonic exercise as well.

172. MARCH SLAV
Although the dynamic marking is forte, students should be reminded to keep the mallets close to the bar when playing a roll.

173. NOTES IN DISGUISE
Have students use a light touch to achieve the proper style of this exercise.

174. HALF-STEPPIN'
Students should practice Legato Strokes on this chromatic exercise.

175. EGYPTIAN DANCE
For best effect, a non-legato approach should be used for this piece.

176. SILVER MOON BOAT
Attention to height-of-rise is important to achieve effective dynamic contrast in this folk song. Legato Strokes are recommended.

PERCUSSION TIPS
(continued)

PERCUSSION

177. THEME FROM SYMPHONY NO. 7
More practice with slow playing; remind students to play softly with an even, consistent sound. The technique for the timpani and bass drum involves a long, slow stroke, pulling the sound out of the drum.

178. CAPRICCIO ITALIEN
Although the crash cymbals are marked forte, care should be taken not to play too loud. Review crash cymbal technique (page 10-B) and work for a consistent sound throughout.

179. AMERICAN PATROL
The difficulty with the Flamacue is in the placement of the left-hand accent on the second note. This must be emphasized even more than the Flam that begins the rudiment in order to sound stylistically correct.

180. WAYFARING STRANGER
Students should use sixteenth note multiple bounce motions to play the multiple bounce rolls in this piece.

181. ESSENTIAL ELEMENTS QUIZ – RUDIMENT COUNTING CONQUEST
Flam, Flam Tap, Flam Accent, Flam Paradiddle, Single Paradiddle, Multiple Bounce Roll, and Flamacue are the 7 rudiments in this quiz.

182. AMERICA THE BEAUTIFUL
Remind students to count multi-measure rests carefully in order to avoid entrances that are either too early or too late.

183. LA CUCARACHA
With the snares off, students can concentrate on achieving a relaxed sound with good attention to all accents. The difference between the dynamic levels of the strokes and the accents really makes the style of this piece work. The claves (opt. cowbell) part is very important and must not be rushed.

184. THEME FROM 1812 OVERTURE
This piece is quite long and involves an active percussion part. Snare drummers need to listen carefully to what the rest of the band is playing to determine how their part fits into the music.

185. CAN-CAN
This exciting percussion ensemble piece can provide a real showcase for the percussion section. Students need to understand that each and every part is important to the overall success of the piece.

186. SWING LOW, SWEET CHARIOT
While the Flam Accent is often written as three eighth notes grouped together, the same rhythm may be written somewhat differently within a piece of music (see measures 11 and 15). Both of the groupings are played the same way.

187. LA BAMBA
The rim knock is an effect used in Latin music, and is much lighter than the rim shot. The student playing the suspended cymbal with the stick should listen carefully to the placement of the rim knock for good ensemble interpretation.

KEYBOARD PERCUSSION

177. THEME FROM SYMPHONY NO. 7
For maximum musical effect, have students play softly with a light touch. If available, bells should play Part A and xylophone should play Part B.

178. CAPRICCIO ITALIEN
Remind students to use Legato Strokes for this piece.

179. AMERICAN PATROL
Alternate Sticking is suggested for this exercise.

180. WAYFARING STRANGER
If possible, students should use Legato Strokes for this piece.

181. ESSENTIAL ELEMENTS QUIZ – RUDIMENT COUNTING CONQUEST
Ask students to look for the ascending and descending parts of the scale.

182. AMERICA THE BEAUTIFUL
Attention to height-of-rise will allow for maximum dynamic contrast without forcing the sound at the upper dynamic levels.

183. LA CUCARACHA
Students may wish to use Double Sticking on the repeated eighth note figures, or use Alternate Sticking if they prefer.

184. THEME FROM 1812 OVERTURE
The use of Alternate Sticking will help to produce a consistent sound on the scale passages in this piece.

185. CAN-CAN
Students should choose the sticking system that allows them the best musical results. Remind them to use Legato Strokes on the octaves from measures 14-27, and again at the end.

186. SWING LOW, SWEET CHARIOT
This duet can be performed with two sets of bells or with bells and xylophone. If bells and xylophone are used, bells should play Part A and xylophone should play Part B.

187. LA BAMBA
Remind students to use height-of-rise to achieve good accent quality as well as dynamic contrast. If bells and xylophone are available, bells should play Part A and xylophone should play Part B.

Authors

DR. TIM LAUTZENHEISER
Founder, Attitude Concepts For Today, Bluffton, IN

JOHN HIGGINS
Managing Producer and Editor, Composer and Arranger, Hal Leonard Corp., Milwaukee, WI

CHARLES T. MENGHINI, D.M.A.
Director of Bands and Dean, Undergraduate Division; VanderCook College of Music, Chicago, IL

PAUL LAVENDER
Director of Instrumental Publications, Composer and Arranger, Hal Leonard Corp., Milwaukee, WI

TOM C. RHODES
President, RBC Music Inc., San Antonio, TX

DON BIERSCHENK
Vice President, RBC Music Inc., San Antonio, TX

CREDITS

Managing Editor and Producer	Paul Lavender
Production Editors	Stuart Malavsky Darlene Kaminski Matt Wolf
Full Band Arrangements	John Higgins
Percussion Consultant and Editor	Will Rapp
Design and Art Direction	Richard Slater Tim Bigonia Nicole Julius
Music Engraving and Typesetting	Thomas Schaller
Assistant to Authors	Darcy Davis
Play-Along Tracks Arrangements and Production	Paul Lavender John Higgins
Additional Arrangements	John Moss
Essential Elements Rhythm Section	Steve Millikan - Keyboards Steve Dokken - Bass Sandy Williams - Guitars Steve Hanna - Percussion Larry Sauer - Drums
Recording and Mixing Engineers	Mark Aspinall
Aire Born Studios, Indianapolis, IN	John Bolt David Price Mike Petrow Ben Vawter
Additional Recording Production	Jared Rodin Mark Aspinall
Project Supervision	Nanci Milam
Aire Born Studios, Indianapolis, IN	Mike Wilson Nina Hunt
Announcer	Scott Hoke

FEATURED INSTRUMENTAL ARTISTS

Flute	Robin Peller Indianapolis Symphony Orchestra
Oboe	Roger Roe Indianapolis Symphony Orchestra
Bassoon	Robert Broemel Principal, Indianapolis Symphony Orchestra
Clarinet, Alto Clarinet, Bass Clarinet	Michael Borschel Indianapolis Symphony Orchestra
Alto, Tenor, and Baritone Saxophones	Jim Farrelly Freelance performer and recording artist
Trumpet	Robert L. Wood Indianapolis Symphony Orchestra
F Horn	Gerald Montgomery Indianapolis Symphony Orchestra
Trombone, Baritone	K. Blake Schlabach Indianapolis Symphony Orchestra
Tuba	Anthony Kniffen Principal, Indianapolis Symphony Orchestra
Electric Bass	Steve Dokken Freelance performer and recording artist
Percussion	Steve Hanna Freelance performer and recording artist,
Percussion	Will Rapp, D.M.A. Director of Bands and Applied Percussion, Kutztown University, PA

The authors wish to give special thanks to Herman Knoll, Vice President of Product Development, for his dedication, leadership, and expertise in the creation of the Essential Elements educational program.